John F. Marszalek

SHERMAN

John F. Marszalek is professor of history at Mississippi State University. He is the author of *Sherman's Other War: The General and the Civil War Press*, and several other books of Civil War and African-American history. He lives in Starkville, Mississippi.

SHERMAN

SHERMAN

☆

A SOLDIER'S PASSION FOR ORDER

John F. Marszalek

Vintage Civil War Library
Vintage Books
A Division of Random House, Inc.
New York

FIRST VINTAGE CIVIL WAR LIBRARY EDITION,
JANUARY 1994

Copyright © 1993 by John F. Marszalek

Library of Congress Cataloging-in-Publication Data
Marszalek, John F., 1939–
Sherman: a soldier's passion for order / John F. Marszalek.—
1st Vintage Civil War library ed.
p.   cm.—(Vintage Civil War library)
Originally published: New York: Free Press, c1993
Includes bibliographical references and index.
ISBN 0-679-74989-6 (pbk.)
1. Sherman, William T. (William Tecumseh), 1820–1891.
2. Generals—United States—Biography.
3. United States. Army—Biography.
4. United States—History—Civil War,
1861–1865—Campaigns.
I. Title. II. Series.
E467.1.S55M34   1994
973.7'092—dc20
[B]   93-6255
CIP

For
Jeanne
and
John, Chris, Jamie

CONTENTS

ACKNOWLEDGMENTS

THE LATE T. T. McAVOY, C.S.C., of the University of Notre Dame first suggested Sherman as a research interest to me, and Vincent P. DeSantis directed my doctoral dissertation. Vincent has since become a friend who continues to provide encouragement and support in all my professional activities.

At Mississippi State University, my academic home for nineteen years, Michael B. Ballard, Charles D. Lowery, and William E. Parrish have regularly read and critiqued my Sherman writings, and they have encouraged me in ways they probably do not realize. So too did my former doctoral students: Robert L. Jenkins, Michael B. Ballard, Kenneth H. Williams, Thomas D. Cockrell, Damon Eubank, and Michael S. Downs. I cut up their book reviews, papers, and dissertations, and in return, they good-naturedly gave me the title the "Cheerful Assassin." Lunchtime colleagues Elizabeth Nybbaken and Clifford G. Ryan knew little about Sherman when we first met many years ago, but they have listened to my Sherman stories for so long that they cannot eat a peanut butter sandwich or potato chip without thinking of him.

Numerous historians generously read part or all of drafts of this book and provided important suggestions. In addition to my Mississippi State colleagues, they are: Albert Castel, Western Michigan University; Lowell H. Harrison, Western Kentucky University; Jay Luvaas, U.S. Army War College; William S. McFeely, University of Georgia; James Lee McDonough, Auburn University; Charles Royster, Louisiana State University; Robert M. Senkewicz, S.J., Santa Clara University; Terry Winschel, Vicksburg Military Park, National Park Service.

Librarians around the nation made research easier, sometimes possible, and always enjoyable. Among the many of these generous people were: Gary J. Arnold, Ohio Historical Society; Connie Cartledge, Library of Congress; Janice L. Haas and Nan Card, Hayes Presidential Center; Martha Irby, Mississippi State University; Phyllis Kuhn, Fairfield Heritage Association, Lancaster, Ohio; Peter Michel, Missouri Historical Society; Sigrid P. Perry, Northwestern University; Marcie Rarick, University of Notre Dame; Susan Ravdin, Bowdoin College; Ann Shepherd, Cincinnati Historical Society; Judith A. Sibley, United States Military Academy; Richard J. Sommers, United States Military Institute; Galen R. Wilson, William L. Clements Library, University of Michigan; and Mary Wright, Huntington Library.

Individuals with a mutual interest in Sherman were generous in sharing their information and insights. Robert David Dawson of Waukegan, Illinois, is preparing an index to the vast Sherman correspondence and not only shared his material with me but has also served as an inspiration when my own work seemed never ending. Charles R. Johnson of Kansas City shared his Sherman bibliography on computer disks. Joseph H. Ewing of Maryland, a descendant of Philemon B. Ewing (Sherman's closest childhood friend, foster brother, and brother-in-law) discussed Sherman with me on a 1987 CBS News "Nightwatch" television program, and we have remained in touch ever since. Jim Macak, a newsman in Los Angeles and the author of a Sherman play, shared insights with me. D. Brooks Simpson of Arizona State University alerted me to pertinent Sherman manuscripts. Numerous friends provided sympathetic ears and room and board. Larry and Wendy Held of Herndon, Virginia, provided soft beds and good fun on numerous research trips; Jim and Beverly Sefcik provided bed, board, good times, and research help in Madison, Wisconsin, and New Orleans, Louisiana. Jim was assistant dirctor of the Wisconsin State Historical Society and is director of the Louisiana State Museum. Jim and Joan Kroll of Denver provided accommodations, friendship over the years, and an introduction to the Denver Public Library, where Jim is head of the Humanities Department. John and Jean Serrie, then of Pennsylvania and now of Maine, and John and Kathy Seggerson of Atlanta similarly provided hospitality. Kathy is also my one-person fan club in Georgia. Sister Mary Perpetua, G.N.S.H., drove me and my wife around New York City and gave us fine accommodations in her order's convent.

Extended research such as the kind required in writing this biography would have been impossible without financial aid from a number of sources. Mississipi State University provided research money and two separate semester sabbaticals. I particularly thank

Charles D. Lowery, head of the History Department; Edward McGlone and Lida Barrett, former deans of the College of Arts and Science; and Ralph E. Powe, vice-president for research. I was also fortunate to receive important travel grants from the American Philosophical Society, the Cushwa Center, University of Notre Dame, and the National Endowment for the Humanities.

Over the years I have had the good fortune of having a host of student assistants. Space precludes mentioning them all, but four are representative of the rest: Cathy Goree, now an administrator at Mississippi State University; Charles Morris, now an attorney in Pasadena, California; Amm Saiffudin Khaled, associate professor of history, University of Chittagong, Bangladesh; and my present assistant, Marzett Jordan. Marzett has been indispensable to the completion of this book. His consistent efficiency and productivity make him the model assistant.

Similarly important in the completion of this book have been secretaries in the History Department: Peggy Bonner, Lonna Reinecke, Karen Groce, and Jean Whitehead. All would agree that Peggy Bonner deserves special mention. There is no more talented organizer, administrator, and wizard of the word processor than Peggy. She has kept me and my graduate students out of more bureaucratic messes than even she realizes, allowing me, as a result, more time to work on Sherman. I feel privileged to be able to work with her and consider her a friend.

At the Free Press, Joyce Seltzer has been an insightful editor whose care, devotion, and talent made the editorial process both challenging and enjoyable. Cherie Weitzner and Loretta Denner were similarly helpful and pleasant.

My family, extended and immediate, has lived with Sherman as long as they can remember. My mother, Regina K. Marszalek, and my mother-in-law, Martha Kozmer, have always been encouraging, as have my brother, sisters, and their spouses: Stan and Carol Marszalek, Doug and Trudy Dedman, Sister Rosalie Marszalek, G.N.S.H., Del and Anna Mae Miller, and Joe and Marilyn Sommers. My sons, John, Chris, and Jamie, have grown up watching me working on Sherman or some other research project. When they were young, they had little idea what it all meant. Since they have reached adulthood, they have become my greatest fans. No other father could be more fortunate.

Jeanne Kozmer Marszalek and I were married in 1965. As she

likes to point out, I have known Sherman longer than I have known her, but she knows him now too and has been so taken by him that she named the puppy our family gave her for Christmas in 1989 General William Tecumseh Sherman (Cumpy). Jeanne has been my greatest support and has shared in much of the work. She has made research trips with me all over the country; she has taken notes; she has cataloged; she has edited; she has typed. She has kept me going when I felt overwhelmed. She and the boys have made the whole project worthwhile.

The following manuscript depositories kindly granted the author permission to quote from their collections: American Antiquarian Society; Art Institute of Chicago; Bancroft Library, University of California, Berkeley; The Beinecke Rare Book and Manuscripts Library, Yale University; Trustees of the Boston Public Library; Bowdoin College Library; California Historical Society, San Francisco; Chicago Historical Society; Cincinnati Historical Society; Colorado Historical Society, Denver; Columbia University, Rare Books and Manuscripts Library; Cornell University Library, Department of Rare Books; Detroit Public Library; Duke University, Special Collections Department, William R. Perkins Library; Franklin D. Roosevelt Library, Hyde Park, NY; Georgia Historical Society, Savannah; Historical Society of Pennsylvania, Phildelphia; Historical Society of Quincy and Adams County, Illinois; Houghton Library, Harvard University; Huntington Library, San Marino, CA; Illinois State Historical Library, Springfield; James S. Copley Library, La Jolla, CA; Louisiana State University, Louisiana and Lower Mississippi Collections, LSU Libraries; Mansfield-Richland County (Ohio) Public Library; Michigan State University, Archives and Historical Collections, East Lansing; Minnesota Historical Society, St. Paul; Missouri Historical Society, St. Louis; New York Public Library, Astor, Lenox and Tilden Foundations, Rare Book and Manuscript Division; North Carolina Division of Archives and History, Raleigh; Notre Dame, Archives of the University of; Ohio Historical Society, Columbus; Oregon Historical Society, Portland; Princeton University Library; Rutherford B. Hayes Presidential Center, Fremont, Ohio; Sherman House, Fairfield Heritage Association, Lancaster, Ohio; South Caroliniana Library, University of South Carolina, Columbia; State Historical Society of Iowa, Special Collections, Des Moines; State Historical Society of Wisconsin, Madison; Syracuse University, George Arents Research Library for Special Collections; Tennessee State Library and Archives, Nashville; Texas Tech University, Southwest Collection; United States Military History Institute, Carlisle Barracks, PA; United States Military Academy Library, Special Collections Division; UCLA, Department of Special Collections, University Research Library; Villanova University, Falvey Memorial Library; Virginia Military Institute Archives, Lexington; Western Reserve Historical Society, Cleveland, Ohio; William L. Clements Library, University of Michigan, Ann Arbor; Yale University, Library, Manuscripts and Archives.

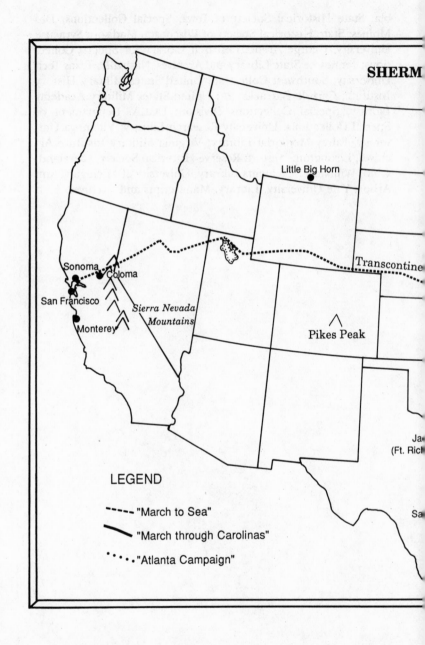

SHERM

Little Big Horn

Sonoma
Coloma
San Francisco

*Sierra Nevada
Mountains*

Monterey

Transcontine

Pikes Peak

Ja
(Ft. Ric

Sa

LEGEND

- - - - - "March to Sea"

—— "March through Carolinas"

• • • • • "Atlanta Campaign"

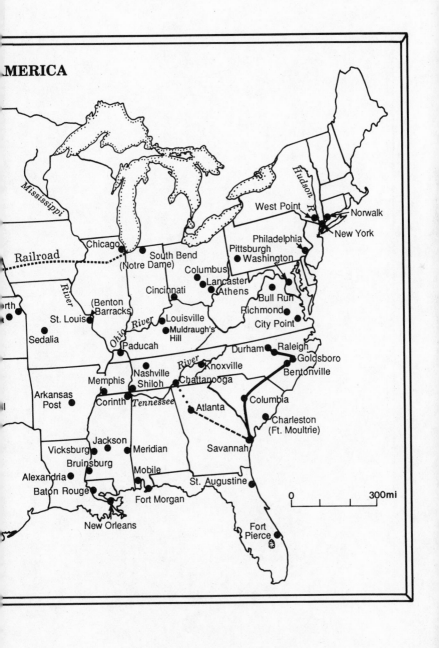

MERICA

Mississippi

Railroad

River

Hudson R.

West Point

Norwalk

New York

Philadelphia

Pittsburgh

Washington

Chicago

South Bend
(Notre Dame)

Columbus

Lancaster

Cincinnati

Athens

Bull Run

Richmond

(Benton
Barracks)

River

Louisville

City Point

rth

St. Louis

Ohio River

Muldraugh's
Hill

Sedalia

Paducah

Durham

Raleigh

Goldsboro

River

Knoxville

Bentonville

Nashville

Chattanooga

Memphis

Shiloh

Columbia

Arkansas
Post

Corinth

Tennessee

Atlanta

Charleston
(Ft. Moultrie)

Jackson

Vicksburg

Meridian

Savannah

Bruinsburg

Mobile

Alexandria

St. Augustine

Baton Rouge

0   300mi

Fort Morgan

New Orleans

Fort
Pierce

PROLOGUE

The historian of the future will note his shortcomings. Not captiously, but in the kind spirit of impartial justice he will set them down to draw the perfect balance of his character. Let him deduct them from the qualities that mark his distinction, and we shall still see WILLIAM TECUMSEH SHERMAN looming up a superb and colossal figure in the generation in which he lived.

—General F. C. Winkler, addressing the Army
of the Cumberland in the year of Sherman's death.

WILLIAM TECUMSEH SHERMAN sat quietly atop his horse that November in 1864. He was a slim six footer with piercing eyes, red hair and beard askew as always, and a face that was a corduroy of wrinkles. Before him his troops trudged forward into the Georgia countryside. Behind him curls of black smoke from abandoned and war-scarred Atlanta rose toward the clouds. His plain, unkempt blue uniform matched the equally unpolished nature of his men. These were veterans of Shiloh and Vicksburg, Chattanooga, Meridian, and the Atlanta campaign. They had seen the worst that war could offer, and they had given as well as they had received. "War is cruelty and you can not refine it," Sherman had told the mayor and city council of Atlanta, and his men had nodded in agreement. They knew it from experience, and they were ready to teach it to the Georgians in their path.

Sherman did not have to give his men elaborate orders. "Forage liberally on the country," he told them, and they understood. After three years of war, commander and soldiers were of one mind. War had to be waged against the entire Confederate society if the Union was to be restored.

Sherman's decision and his willingness to do what was necessary to achieve triumph in this war had deep roots reaching back into his earliest childhood. When he was nine years old, his apparently successful father suddenly went bankrupt and then unexpectedly died, leaving his mother penniless and the family in chaos. He saw then what he would come to see with increasing clarity in later years: order was necessary to success in life. He feared that, like his father, he would not be able to support his family. He saw any personal or public disorder as anarchy and believed it would ruin his chances for success. When the Union split apart, he had to help restore it because it was the clearest symbol of the order he craved. He believed that war was not simply between rival armies but between rival societies and that it had to be fought fiercely so that it could be ended quickly. His genuine affection for Southerners made him determined, toward the end of the war, to avoid further direct and bloody combat. His solution to achieve the order he desired was a war of property destruction, with the ultimate intent to destroy the southern will to keep fighting.

The mid-nineteenth century, the period of Sherman's formative years, was an expanding time, when fortunes could be rapidly made, and people began to believe that success was right at the fingertips of those who reached for it. At the same time, many were afraid that America might be taking the wrong step or that it might be losing its soul as it struggled for riches. Battling the uncertainty that came with rapid social change, most Americans searched for someone or something to shore up the order they thought was crumbling around them. Sometimes they looked to individuals—a president or a charismatic leader. Women were instructed to remain in the home so they might preserve the traditional values that some feared were on shaky ground. Abolitionists saw a slavery conspiracy at the heart of the dislocation they felt, and proslaveryites saw preservation of the institution as a guarantor of civilization. Religious and secular reformers acted to ensure society's salvation through theological and philosophical means. In their quest for stability, the divergent solutions Americans looked to paradoxically produced even more chaotic conditions. This was the society Sherman hoped to bring together.

The destructive methods Sherman employed in the march to the sea were controversial, but he was no villain; he was one of the great military leaders of the Civil War. He knew how to outmaneuver a major Confederate army and how to destroy the Confederate will. He was an appealing individual, whom soldiers, family, and friends idolized. As a major public figure, he was in demand for both the office of the presidency and small social gatherings and public speeches. He impressed his contemporaries, influenced his age, and left a name for posterity.

SHERMAN

CHAPTER 1

---- ☆ ----

UNSTABLE BEGINNINGS

THE HUGE MAN WALKED the one hundred yards down the Main Street hill to the house of his newly widowed neighbor. He would take one of her sons, he said, "the brightest of the lot," promising to "make a man of him." Mary Sherman pointed to Cump, her nine-year-old redhead. She had no choice. She had to give him up as she had given up most of her other children to other sympathetic relatives and friends. Thomas Ewing took the young boy's hand as they went up the hill to his house, and from that point on, he treated him like one of his own. Mary Sherman could only watch it all in helpless yet thankful silence.[1]

Such tragedy seemed impossible for the Charles R. Shermans of Lancaster, Ohio. For hundreds of years before, the family had been leaders, not wards.[2] They had founded towns; they were lawyers and judges; they sat in the legislature and served in the militia. Daniel Sherman, just one example, sat in the Connecticut General Assembly for thirty years and was a driving force in the American Revolution in his community, meeting both George Washington and the marquis de Lafayette in the process. Later generations produced a founding father, Roger Sherman, and nineteenth-century politicians William M. Evarts, George F. Hoar, and Chauncey Depew.[3]

Taylor Sherman, Cump's grandfather, was a lawyer, a judge, and a federal district internal revenue collector. Born in 1758, he later married Elizabeth (Betsey) Stoddard, the daughter of Anthony Stoddard, a Harvard-educated Puritan divine, lawyer, physician, and renowned Indian fighter. Taylor and Betsey's three

1

children all migrated to Ohio—Daniel to become a farmer, Betsey to marry a judge, and Charles to become William Tecumseh's father—as a result of the American Revolution. The British and their Tory allies had burned down the homes of many patriots in Connecticut, prompting the state to set aside land in its "Western Reserve" in Ohio to compensate these war casualties. Taylor Sherman became a commissioner for this so-called Fire-Lands District. He visited the region in 1805 and helped negotiate a treaty to remove the Indians from the area. At that time he purchased the property that later served as the major part of his legacy. This land was the magnet that drew his son, Charles, to Ohio.

Charles R. Sherman was born in Norwalk, Connecticut, in 1788.[4] He learned Latin, Greek, and French in an excellent local school, attended Dartmouth College, and studied law in his father's office. As a youth, he had developed a reputation of being a "wild boy," usually receiving blame for any local prank. In 1810, at the age of twenty-two, he was admitted to the bar, and soon after he married Mary Hoyt, a graduate of a female seminary in Poughkeepsie, New York, and the daughter of a family of successful Norwalk merchants.

Charles and Mary Sherman decided to move West soon after their marriage. Charles went to Ohio alone, hoping to settle on his father's Fire-Lands property, but fierce fighting with Indians caused him to go farther south and settle in Lancaster instead, where he worked hard to establish a law practice. In 1811 he returned East for his wife and first son. The trip took twenty-one days on horseback, with the baby, Charles Taylor Sherman, later an Ohio judge, carried on the front of his parents' saddles.[5]

Lancaster was already impressive enough for one visitor to call it "a handsome little town."[6] Located on the Hocking River in southeastern Ohio, it opened to extensive white settlement only after the 1795 Treaty of Grenville forced the Wyandot Indians north. During 1796–1797, Ebenezer Zane constructed his famous road between Wheeling, Virginia, and Maysville, Kentucky, making the region accessible to white settlers. In payment, Zane received grants of 640 acres at several potential town sites along his route. In 1800 his sons laid out one of these sites, calling it New Lancaster. Zane offered free lots to a blacksmith, a carpenter, and a tanner and donated four lots for public building. Within a month, Fairfield County was organized with New Lancaster as its county seat.

Thanks to Zane's promotion, the town grew steadily. In 1805 its name was shortened to Lancaster, and, by 1818, it had a population of nearly seven hundred people residing in perhaps one hundred houses. The town contained a courthouse and a jail, a post office, a Methodist church, a bank, and two newspapers (one English, the other German). Twelve merchants and numerous skilled workmen plied their trades. Its major attraction continued to be its location on Zane's Trace, the major mail route between Washington and Kentucky. (The great National Road was just twenty-one miles to the north.) At first, people and news reached Lancaster only by foot, horse, or mule, but by the 1820s, four-horse stagecoaches were rumbling in. Usually these vehicles stopped only long enough for the passengers to be fed and the horses changed, but they nevertheless provided Lancaster with an avenue to the outside world, so the little village was never as isolated from the rest of the nation as were some other western towns. For a time, there was even talk of Lancaster's becoming Ohio's capital.

The Sherman family quickly settled into their new home. When the War of 1812 broke out, Charles was already prominent enough to deliver the major address at an April 1812 militia enlistment meeting. The opening line of his speech, which touched themes of home, hearth, and family, was particularly striking: "The crisis has arrived in which your country calls upon you, her constitutional guardians, to rally round her standard and to defend her rights and liberties." A son yet to be born would justify his own actions in 1861 on much the same constitutional grounds.

Neither Sherman nor his unit played much of a role in the War of 1812, and in 1813 President James Madison appointed him to a nonmilitary post, the collector of internal revenue for the Third District of Ohio, a position the young lawyer wanted, as he told a friend, "for the profit of the office." Sherman held his post for four years, supervising deputy collectors throughout his district, and he quickly enhanced his lawyer's reputation for thoroughness, honesty, and joviality.[7]

All went well until the U.S. government responded to a sharp increase in inflationary paper money by decreeing in April 1816 that specie or Bank of the United States notes would be the only acceptable currency for governmental obligations after February 1817. Sherman's deputies had been accepting all manner of paper currency, and this announcement made most of it worthless. Other revenue collectors closed out their accounts before the deadline and avoided the problem, but somehow Sherman did not, and he found himself stuck with stacks of worthless paper. He sold his property and borrowed from friends, but he still crashed, pulling his two bondsmen down with him. Sherman could have declared bankruptcy and walked away from the mess, but instead he took on the debt and spent the rest of his life trying to repay it.[8]

To maintain his growing family and repay his pile of debts, Charles Sherman rode the circuit from 1817 to 1829, first as a lawyer and, after 1823, as a justice on Ohio's Supreme Court. His appointment to the state's highest judicial tribunal demonstrated that his dogged determination to meet his obligations had successfully buttressed his statewide reputation for legal integrity.

Although Sherman was regularly away from Lancaster on the judicial circuit, he was home often enough to father a family of eleven children. Except for the eldest, all were born in the four-room, two-story clapboard house of Connecticut design Sherman had built on Main Street soon after his arrival. Five years later, he added to the front of the original structure to gain a law office and family parlor on the ground floor and two new bedrooms on the second floor. The house was humble, but it served the growing family's needs. Such dignitaries as the duke of Saxe-Weimar, Henry Clay, and the Erie Canal's De Witt Clinton stayed there.[9]

It was in this house on February 8, 1820, that the sixth Sherman child arrived—Tecumseh. Cump, as his brothers and sisters quickly called him, bore the name of the Shawnee Indian leader of the early nineteenth-century Midwest Indian confederation. Charles Sherman had early decided that he would name a son after this Indian whom he had never met but whose courage and military prowess he had come to admire. The neighbors found "Tecumseh" a strange name for a white baby, and one finally summoned the nerve to confront the proud father. Charles answered simply: *"Tecumseh was a great warrior."*[10]

Cump Sherman spent the first years of his life in a comfortable home, in the middle of a vibrant community, with a host of brothers and sisters and two strong female figures, an affectionate mother and a domineering grandmother, Betsey Stoddard Sherman. He resembled his grandmother, whom he credited with providing him with all the common sense he was ever to have. His father was a less significant figure in the household because he was gone so much. Cump's most vivid memories of his father concerned his returns home from the circuit. At those times Charles Sherman gave the first child reaching him the honor of riding his horse Dick back to the stable at the rear of the lot. Although the older children usually beat Cump to the horse, he outran them all on one occasion. He was about six years old at the time, and his achievement had a lasting effect: he was thrown from the horse and received a scar on his right cheek that he was to carry for the rest of his life.[11]

Cump's memories of his father were sparse. He remembered him as "a large florid man of great activity" cultivating asparagus and grapes (which he introduced to Lancaster), or doctoring a sick or injured person when the town physician was not available. Cump recalled his father catching him in the stable crib and ordering him out. Cump obeyed but jumped right back in when Charles Sherman turned his back. He was ordered out again. This time, Cump took umbrage at the tone of his father's voice and decided to run away from home. He packed his clothes and stomped off to live with the family of his closest friend, Bill King. Neither his father nor any other family member tried to stop him, and for the several days he stayed with the friend, his family referred to him as "Cump King." Disappointed at this turn of events, Cump quietly returned home, chagrined at his father's apparent unconcern.[12]

In June 1829, while on the circuit, Charles Sherman developed a high fever. Taken to the local hotel where a physician attended him for several days, he struggled for life. He affirmed his Congregational religious faith but refused the services of a clergyman and asked for a funeral according to the Masonic rite. (He had long been a leader in Ohio's Masonry, this order of more significance to him than any church.) A cousin was there at the end, as was a son, fourteen-year-old Jim, but Charles Sherman died before his wife could reach him.[13]

Cump and the other children were in school when a friend ran up with the news. They rushed home to find their grieving mother, only a month past childbirth, in bed and with a house full of mourners. Grandmother Stoddard warned them to keep quiet and shooed them out of doors, where they sat in the backyard mulling over ways to help their mother survive the tragedy. Charles Sherman had left his wife only the house, its furnishings, and some bank stock worth perhaps $200 a year; most of his earnings had regularly gone into paying off the debts from his disastrous tax collector's career.

As John Sherman later expressed it, their father had "left his family poor in everything but friends." Fortunately, these friends, particularly Masons, passed the hat. Family members stepped forward to take responsibility for the children. The oldest, Charles, had almost completed his studies at Ohio University, so he left to study law with a relative in Mansfield, Ohio. Sixteen-year-old Elizabeth soon married, and fourteen-year-old Jim remained a store clerk in Cincinnati. Thirteen-year-old Amelia went to a relative in Mansfield, and three years later she married. Elizabeth and her new husband took in ten-year-old Julia; seven year-old-Lamp went to live with Cincinnati newspaperman Charles Hammond; five-year-old John later went to live with an uncle in Mt. Vernon, Ohio; three-year-old Susan, one-year-old Hoyt, and the infant Frances stayed with their impoverished mother. Cump was fortunate not to have to go farther than the family of his next-door neighbor, Thomas Ewing.[14]

His father's financial difficulties and his sudden death were pivotal events in Sherman's life. This impressive, important man had died penniless and caused his family's disintegration. More than any factor, his father's failure had a deep impact on Cump. Throughout his life, he worried about remaining solvent, afraid that he would become destitute and that his death would leave his wife and children poor and dependent the way his father had left him.

Cump Sherman entered adolescence carrying the burden of anxiety over the loss of his father whose appearance of success had masked the reality. He experienced the meaning of this loss graphically. His brothers and sisters left him to live with others far away, and he too had to leave home. Sherman's failure to make any substantial comment on his father during his life attests to the intense feelings this death provoked.[15]

The day Cump walked up the hill, his hand gripping that of his burly neighbor, he began a new phase in his life under the influence of Thomas Ewing, one of the leading citizens of early Lancaster.[16] Ewing had been born in 1789 near Wheeling, Virginia, to an impoverished former American Revolutionary soldier, George Ewing. A native of New Jersey, Captain Ewing had decided to go West after the war. Indian problems kept him out of Ohio, so he went to Virginia instead. In 1798, with the Indians suppressed, he settled in Athens County, Ohio. Here his small family lived a hard existence on wild game, eating with the only utensils they had—sharpened sticks.

Life was lonely for young Tom. His closest brother was eleven years his senior, his sisters had their own diversions, and there were no nearby neighbors; his only playmate was a spaniel. Books became his companions. He read everything he could get his hands on, completing the Bible by the time he was eight years old. At the age of twelve, he walked forty miles to acquire a translation of Virgil's *Aeneid;* all his life he could recite from memory this epic's opening lines. When his father, who also read widely, purchased a geography book, Tom memorized it. He participated in the community's library subscription campaign; money was raised so a neighbor traveling to Boston could return home with sixty well-chosen classics, books that formed the basis for Tom's early education.

At nineteen, Tom received his father's permission to go to the Kanawha Salt Works to earn money for his formal education. The process of boiling down the briny water in the huge iron pots to produce the precious salt was hard, tedious labor.[17] Tom did it for three months and then invested his earnings in three months of classes at newly founded Ohio University in Athens. Returning to the salt kettles regularly, he worked his way through school. He received his degree in 1815, becoming the institution's second graduate. A member of the committee awarding him the degree was a young Lancaster lawyer scarcely older than Ewing: Charles R. Sherman.

Ewing returned to the saltworks to finance his law studies, read Blackstone's *Commentaries,* and then moved to Lancaster to study in the law office of Philemon Beecher, a militia general, Ohio legislator, and later congressman. After fourteen months of sixteen-hour study days, he was admitted to the bar in August 1816. Charles Sherman referred one of the first cases he tried.

In 1820 the thirty-one-year-old Ewing married nineteen-year-old Maria, Philemon Beecher's foster daughter. Charles and Mary Sherman and Thomas and Maria Ewing became close friends. In 1823 the Ewings built their house just up the hill from the Shermans, and the two couples and their growing families were in and out of each other's houses continually.

Charles Sherman had begun his career first, but Tom Ewing quickly surpassed him in wealth and influence. He became prosecuting attorney for both Fairfield and Athens counties, and then the Ohio legislature appointed him to help revise the state's law. In 1825 Ohio University awarded him an M.A. degree as a mark of his growing prestige, and he gave the major speech when De Witt Clinton threw the ceremonial shovelful of dirt on the surveyed line of the Ohio Canal. In 1828, while Sherman was on the Ohio Supreme Court, Ewing was admitted to practice before the U.S. Supreme Court. In 1831 he became one of Ohio's U.S. senators and, from this time on, a leading member of the Whig party.

In his law practice Ewing specialized in land title cases, investing his substantial legal earnings in lucrative property purchases, eventually as far west as Kansas. True to his "Salt Boiler" nickname, he bought the Chauncey Salt Works and maintained a lifelong interest in the business that had financed his education and opened the way to a better life.

Tales circulated about Ewing's prodigious strength. It was rumored that in a contest, he had taken an ax by the handle and thrown it over the courthouse steeple. And when he was driving with Daniel Webster in his wagon, he came upon an enormous tree blocking the road. He chopped his way through the obstruction with a speed that left the "Noble Daniel" astounded.

Ewing's intellect was equally impressive. His debating abilities resulted in a second nickname, "Logician of the West." Long years of reading and a retentive mind provided him with an extraordinary supply of facts, which he packed into quotation-filled speeches. He developed a reputation as an effective Senate debater. As a Whig, he opposed Andrew Jackson and spoke out in favor of Henry Clay's American System (National Bank, protective tariff, and internal improvements). He revered the Constitution, viewing it as the great bulwark of the nationalism he considered essential to the nation's progress. Consequently, he supported

Andrew Jackson in the nullification crisis and dined at the White House as a reward. Although a Northerner, he supported Southern slavery, being more critical of abolitionists than he was of slaveholders.[18]

Perhaps because of his humble beginnings, Ewing eagerly sought fine things. His home, an example of the finest architecture of the period, was filled with custom-made furniture, delicate china, a piano, and a library unrivaled in the area. In 1836 he bought some furniture from the widow of a deposed Mexican emperor. Among his guests were Clay, Calhoun, Webster, William Henry Harrison, and other famous Whigs.[19] He attended cultural events and continued to read widely. When it came to religion and churchgoing, however, he personally adhered to no faith and allowed his wife to raise their children in her Catholicism.

Thomas Ewing was a man renowned for his intellect, strength, professional success, and happy family life. In 1829 little Cump Sherman viewed him as the big man who was the father of his friends. Only later did he come to appreciate his foster father's achievements, considering him "an intellectual giant." He was similarly impressed with Ewing's financial success, something he could never admire about his natural father or, as he always feared, about himself.[20]

When Thomas Ewing and his new ward walked up the hill and reached the Ewing house that 1829 day, there were already seven children living there. The Ewings had four children of their own, and they were raising two nieces and a nephew. Philemon B. Ewing (Phil), born less than a year after Cump, was already a close friend. Ellen, four years Cump's junior, three-year-old Hugh Boyle (Bub), and infant Thomas, Jr., became his brothers and his sister. (Charles and Teresa—"Sissy"—were not born until 1835 and 1837, respectively.) Ellen particularly remembered pondering the significance of the redheaded boy she knew as a friend suddenly becoming her brother. "I peeped at him with great interest," she later recalled, never realizing at the time that Cump would one day become her husband.[21]

Thomas Ewing's wife, Maria, was a devout Catholic, and she insisted on Cump's baptism as a condition for his entry into her family. In those days, the Dominican fathers came once a month to offer Mass and administer the sacraments. During one of these visits, Father Dominic Young baptized Cump in the front parlor of the Ewing home. Maria served as godmother, and Phil Ewing was Cump's rather young godfather. Mary Sherman, an Episcopalian turned Presbyterian, gave her permission but did not witness the ceremony. The baptism was unusual. Not only was Cump already nine years old, but he had a name problem: There is no Saint Tecumseh. Father Young insisted that the candidate add a good Christian name to his Indian one. Apparently it was Saint William's Day, June 28, so as he poured water over Cump's head, the priest anointed him "William Tecumseh."[22]

Cump's mother lived less than a hundred yards away in their old house and he still saw her regularly, so his move was probably less disruptive than it might have been. But he must have felt sadness and confusion about living apart from her. His father had died and left him, and perhaps he worried that his mother was abandoning him too. And although he was taken in by friends, Maria Ewing's unshaken belief that an unbaptized person was unclean set Cump apart. Moreover, the matter was important enough to threaten his eviction. To this nine-year-old boy, baptism asserted that he was unclean and that his name was unacceptable, uncomfortable and hurtful judgments to bear.

These conditions of his entry into the Ewing family reinforced young Cump's natural anxiety. And although he had been baptized, he refused to call himself a Catholic or practice that creed. Perhaps he was modeling himself on Ewing, who never considered religion important, but more likely it was the legacy of his strained entry into the Ewing family. Two years after Cump joined the Ewings, his foster father noted that he was still "bashful and not quite at home." Ewing wanted Cump to feel he was "one of the family." In later years he fondly recalled that he "never knew as young a boy who would do an errand so correctly and promptly" as Cump did.[23]

In 1831 Ewing was elected to the U.S. Senate and for most of the years Cump spent in the Ewing household was present only when the Senate was not in session. But unlike Charles Sherman, who had also been regularly absent, Ewing kept up a steady correspondence with his family, keeping them abreast of White House dinners with Andrew Jackson and conversations with John C. Calhoun. He instructed Maria to gather the children around the table at home and have Cump and Phil take turns reading from the nine volumes of S. G. Goodrich's Peter Parley books he sent them—volumes that emphasized geography, history, morality, order, and American superiority, teaching lessons while they entertained. Ewing appreciated this didactic function, while Cump no doubt enjoyed the entertaining window the books gave him on the world. His lifelong interest in geography, his curiosity, and his reverence for the American Union were no doubt stimulated by these books. Peter Parley taught Cump the kind of lessons his foster father considered important for his proper upbringing. If Maria encouraged nightly reading, Ewing insisted, she would "guard the habits of these lads & keep them from falling into vicious practices during my absense."[24]

Ewing regularly sent the children presents, usually articles of clothing or books, and he tried to match the gift to the child. At least once, "Cump felt *very big*" when he received his present. When Congress was in recess, Ewing returned to Lancaster and personally taught his children proper behavior and attitudes. He worked hard at staying close to them. He often worked late into the night in his backyard law office and frequently asked Cump and Phil to stay up and watch the fire for him. They whiled away the time reading adventure books while Ewing tended his affairs.[25]

Most of the time, Cump and the rest of the children were under the direct supervision of Maria Ewing, who occasionally flashed a mother's exasperation at her brood. One time, after they had been in a wagon for three days, returning from a visit to a distant relative, Hugh Boyle Ewing, then under ten years of age, began to misbehave. Maria warned him several times that she would abandon him if he continued. When he ignored her, she stopped the wagon and ordered the driver to put him out and speed off. She stopped the wagon just out of his line of sight and let him catch up. The other children were petrified—even Ellen, who idolized her mother.[26] Cump said nothing as he absorbed the harsh lesson.

Maria gave a great deal of attention to her children's formal education. Thomas Ewing and Charles Sherman had been instrumental in beginning the first school in Lancaster, and the Ewings remained important supporters of local education. When Cump joined them, they made sure he continued attending school regularly. He had begun his education as a very young boy, attending the only available school, one for girls, and suffering the inevitable taunts of his friends. Moving on to a coeducational institution, he apparently enjoyed acting up as much as his natural father once had. He often suffered the schoolmaster's favorite punishment: being placed under a large, upside-down box. On one occasion, he tried to whittle a peephole in the box, but all he received for his efforts was a paddling.[27]

Around 1832 the Howe brothers, Sam and John, took over the local school and provided Lancaster's children with a first-rate education. Cump learned French, Latin, and some Greek. He read avidly: travel, history, novels, Shakespeare, and Sir Walter Scott. He loved to write; one contemporary noted seeing him only "rarely . . . without a pen in his hand." For a time, he and the other Ewing children attended the Howe school during the day and another one in the evening. (Sometimes Cump would even be stopped on the street by a Ewing relative and forced to parse Latin and Greek words.) Cump did well in all his subjects, rising to the first section in each, much to Phil Ewing's chagrin as he remained in the second. Cump spent time helping his foster sister, Ellen, with her arithmetic, and she began to look upon him as her "protector."[28]

Cump did well in school and later praised the Howe brothers as "first rate teachers" and their school as "one of the best in Ohio," but he had a normal youngster's ambivalence toward school. In later life he remembered how the Howes regularly "used to [have to] lick John and me like hell." Cump preferred play—and even work—to school. He and the other Ewings had chores to do around the house, but these tasks—cutting and stacking firewood, tending the fire, taking care of the cow, and getting the mail—were hardly burdensome. Fetching the mail was even fun. When Maria Ewing heard the stagecoach come rumbling into town, she would call out the news, and off Cump and the others would race to see if a letter from Thomas Ewing was aboard. One time, when the storekeeper who handled the post office told them there was no letter from Ewing, Cump got up on his tiptoes, peered over the counter, and announced loudly that he thought he could see one. The storekeeper threatened to vault the counter to discuss the matter further, and the boys gleefully ran away.[29]

In the winter, there was skating, sledding, and throwing snowballs; in the summer, fishing, swimming, and roaming the magnificent Mt. Pleasant near the city. Cump and the others founded the Thespian Society and put on a series of plays. Once before a scheduled eclipse of the sun, they could hardly wait to see if adult stories about chickens roosting during the day were true. For diversion they hung around the local hotel, offering to water visitors' horses at a nearby creek. As long as he was watched, Cump would carefully jog the horse; as soon as he was out of view, he would fly off at a gallop, enjoying the mischief as much as the ride.[30]

Cump and his friends loved to play baseball in a field near their school, next to the garden of a local carpenter named Wolster. All too often, one of the homemade yarn balls landed in Wolster's garden, and one of the braver players had to bolt the fence, run across the freshly spaded garden, and retrieve the ball. Wolster, upset at these incursions, began summarily chopping up any ball that flew onto his land. Not to be outdone, the boys put a rock inside each ball, and the first time Wolster tried to destroy one, he broke his hatchet. Infuriated, he began throwing the balls into his stove. The boys retaliated by stuffing a ball with gunpowder. Wolster threw it into his stove, and there was a fiery explosion, slightly burning the startled carpenter and causing some damage to his house. He chased after the ball players, thrashing the one he caught.[31]

When he was an old man, Cump laughingly remembered how he used to steal a preacher's kindling wood on a Saturday night to try to embarrass the divine on Sunday morning. "Giants among men" like Thomas Ewing surrounded him, he said, but he preferred the company of his friend Bill King, "the worst young rascal in town." He fondly remembered a more adventurous self who, with Bill, hung around the Golden Swan Tavern or rode an old mare out to the hills and talked about the ways of the Indians. Most of his youth, he disliked the color of his red hair, once unsuccessfully trying to dye it another shade because of his foster brother's taunts that he was a "Red-haired Woodpecker." When he became convinced that Indians particularly liked to scalp redheaded boys, however, he came to view his usually detested red hair as a badge of defiance.[32]

Phil, Cump, and sometimes the other children spent many summer days at the farm of an aunt, one of Thomas Ewing's sisters. They grew their own watermelons and many predawn mornings fell asleep in the wagon taking their produce to market. Sunday morning on the farm was the only day Cump and Phil dreaded. Since the farmhouse was far from town and a church, the boys' Protestant aunt locked them in the parlor until they had read a chapter of the Bible. They wasted time searching for the shortest chapter, finally realizing that the searching was taking more time than any reading would. Then they quickly read any chapter and were released from their captivity. Each following Sunday, however, they repeated the same time-consuming process.[33]

Maria Ewing was an even stricter taskmaster. Once a month when the priest came to Lancaster, all the Ewing children had to attend Mass and then endure religious lessons. The lessons were held in a room set aside for visiting priests on the second floor of the Ewing house. Even when the priest was not in town, the family still had a stiff Sunday obligation. Promptly at nine o'clock, Maria Ewing gathered all the children in the dining room and read aloud prayers, Bible verses, segments of Butler's *Lives of the Saints,* and paragraphs from Gobinet's *Instruction of Youth.* She led them in saying the Rosary and asked questions from the catechism. The children knew there was no escape until the entire ceremony was completed.[34]

Most of the children squirmed during the religious observances, but Ellen was different. She came to accept her mother's intense Catholicism and saw religious duty as the primary function of her life. One can imagine her lecturing her recalcitrant brothers with threats of damnation if they did not take the Sunday praying more seriously. No doubt Cump ignored her preaching then, as he was to do later. But Catholicism was and would remain a major factor in his life.

On some predawn non-Mass Sundays in the summer, Maria would pack the children into a wagon and drive off toward the Dominican center in Somerset, some eighteen miles away. The best part of the half-day trip, next to the adventure of the wagon's climbing the many hills along the way, was talking to the old coachman. His constant chatter made the miles slip by, and soon the wagon was unloading in front of the church. After Mass the family visited the priests and the nuns headquartered there, usually not returning home until after dark with the children asleep in the back of the wagon.[35]

There were other enjoyable trips. At least once a year, Cump drove his natural mother the seventy-five miles to visit his grandmother who was now residing with another relative. The trip took three days because Mary Sherman had to stop frequently along the way to exchange gossip and medicines. Cump enjoyed these excursions, no doubt savoring the opportunity to cement the close ties he wanted to maintain with his natural family. And he was always excited when Charles Hammond brought Cump's brother Lamp back to Lancaster for a visit and when brother John came back home after several years in Mansfield, Ohio.[36]

Cump also accompanied Maria Ewing and the rest of the family on their visits to relatives, the Blaines and Gillespies, on the Monongahela River in distant Pennsylvania. He visited Aunt Beecher, General Philemon Beecher's wife, in a nearby house in Lancaster. Maria and Aunt Beecher, the foster mother who had raised her, chattered away in the front room, while the boys gathered in the kitchen with the family retainer, Jupiter, a former slave. They listened for hours to his exciting life story, while watching him skillfully crack hickory nuts and walnuts.[37]

True to his promise, Thomas Ewing had made Cump an equal member of his family. Cump gathered with the Ewings around the dining room table, he visited relatives near and far, and he experienced Thomas Ewing's formidable presence. He still carried the Sherman name, but Cump had become a Ewing. Maria and her five-year-old son, Tom, Jr., went to Philadelphia one year and paid a visit to Cump's sister, Elizabeth Reese. Elizabeth asked Maria how many children she had, and Maria blurted out, "Four." Tom immediately spoke up: "Oh Mother! You forgot Cumpy, our oldest boy."[38]

Despite such acceptance, Cump remained apart. He never called the Ewings "mother" or "father"; they always remained "Mr." and "Mrs." When he wrote to Thomas Ewing, he always mentioned what his natural family was doing, seemingly to remind his foster father of his real roots. He openly admired Ewing, thankful for his charity toward him and the others, but he experienced some ambivalence toward his surrogate father, who grew more and more successful over the years. The contrast to Cump's own father who had died penniless, caused his family to be scattered and his mother to struggle to survive was great. Why could his family not be together as the Ewings were? Feelings of anger and frustration grew in Cump's heart.[39]

Later in life, strained feelings toward his foster father regularly seeped out even as he tried to suppress them. Cump came to accept Ewing's drive for material success, his political ideas of Constitution, Union, and order, his proslavery and antiabolitionist prejudice. At the same time, Cump wanted to stand on his own and be free of his foster father's support. He appreciated Ewing's help but disliked having to receive it, perhaps unconsciously feeling it was not his birthright. His natural father's death in poverty provoked the anxiety that he might suffer a similar fate. The success of his foster father and his kind desire to help keep him from such failure intensified his own insecurity. Cump had to succeed on his own. He could not spend his life walking with his hand steadied by the strong grip of Thomas Ewing. Failure was frightening enough, but success gained only because of his foster father was unthinkable.[40]

It was during these childhood days that Cump began to think about the military. He was a schoolboy in Howe's academy when an Indian uprising caused the Ohio governor to call up the militia. Cump watched in awe as the volunteers congregated in an open field in town. A major general atop an impressive horse "galloping back and forth" organized the milling mob. "The beauty of that charger and the martial bearing of that great leader haunts me even this day. . . . I do not know," he remembered in 1874, "but that I must date my military inspiration back to that moment."[41]

Whether Cump began thinking of West Point at that moment, whether his natural father put the thought in his head, or whether it was all Thomas Ewing's doing is unclear. No matter the idea's origin, it was Ewing, as U.S. senator, who brought it to fruition. In 1833 he wrote to his wife that he wanted Cump to "be ready to go to West Point or to college soon." Aware of Cump's sensitivity to his status, Ewing warned his wife that he did not want their foster son to see West Point as a consolation prize, since Phil would soon be coming to Washington.[42]

Ewing wrote to Secretary of War Lewis Cass to inquire about a West Point appointment in August 1835 when Cump was fifteen years old. In the application, he said that the idea for his foster son's attendance at the military academy had originated with Judge Charles R. Sherman, the boy's dead father. According to Ewing, the judge had wanted his son to "receive an education which would fit him for the public service in the army or navy." Ewing even wondered about any "prior pact" or "promise" of a

West Point appointment for the young Sherman, a good scholar and a fine athlete.[43]

Cass pigeon-holed the application because it had arrived after that year's deadline, but Ewing wrote again in early 1836. Cump received his appointment within a month. Mary Sherman gave her official consent, and Cump sent a brief acceptance. He had taken the first step in his military career, but he expressed little enthusiasm. The thought of four years of "very strict" regimen must have been sobering, and Cump prepared to meet his fate stoically.[44]

Meanwhile, he continued living with the Ewings. In 1834 he worked as a rod-man on a surveying party for the projected Lancaster Lateral Canal. Thomas Ewing was president of the private company building the Lateral between the Ohio Canal and Lancaster, and Cump worked under the local preacher-turned-civil engineer for fifty cents a day. This was his first paying job, and the teenager enjoyed the money, while learning surveying skills that helped prepare him for West Point engineering classes. During 1835–1836 he devoted most of his time to studying French and mathematics, two subjects of particular importance at the military academy.[45]

The day of departure arrived in mid-May 1836.[46] Maria Ewing carefully packed Cump's clothes in a large trunk and no doubt reminded him about proper behavior during the trip and at West Point. She worried about his making such a long trip alone because she was such a homebody herself and preferred the comfort and certainty of home to the adventure of travel. Cump's natural mother must have experienced similar anxiety. The day of his departure they spent a long time alone together inside the Ewing house. When the two came out, they were silent as the lean redhead climbed on board a stagecoach, waved farewell, and began his journey east.

This was Cump's first solo travel experience. He found Zane's Trace in bad repair but arrived in Zanesville unscathed to board one of the coaches that traveled in convoy along the best highway of the day, the National Road. All he saw for three days and nights on the way to Frederick, Maryland, was the inside of the stage's curtain. The weather was that bad.

In Frederick, he could continue on to Washington by railroad car or by another coach. Given his inquisitive nature and the disappointment at having missed seeing the countryside, Cump might well have been expected to ride the rails. But the boy avoided "the novel and dangerous railroad" and took the coach instead. The Baltimore and Ohio Railroad was newly built, the first such in the country, so Cump's reticence is understandable. He arrived at Thomas Ewing's boarding house in Washington on June 1, 1836.[47]

In those days, Washington was alternately a dusty or a muddy village, but it was still a wonderful place for an impressionable sixteen year old. The fabled Andrew Jackson was president, and the newly organized Whig party was vocal in its opposition to what its members, like Ewing, called the tyranny of King Andrew I. Cump spent a week with his foster father, taking in all his eyes could behold. One day, while he was walking past the White House, he peered through the wood railing to see the president of the United States pacing up and down the mansion's gravel walk. Cump shared his natural and foster father's devotion to the Whig party and Henry Clay. He had heard from early childhood that Andrew Jackson was a "tyrant," but it was still a thrill to see that most famous living American, the hero of New Orleans, a figure of mythic proportion. The president, wrapped in his overcoat and cap, did not look as grand as Cump thought he should. Still, the awe-struck young man stood looking through the fence for an hour intently watching Old Hickory "walking with his head down like one thinking about matters of policy." At other times, he saw Vice-President Martin Van Buren, Senators John C. Calhoun, Daniel Webster, and Henry Clay. Thomas Ewing introduced him to S. L. Southard, and Cump received the former secretary of the navy's recipe for success at West Point. "Write in the title page of all your books," Southard advised: " 'Be industrious and obedient and you have nothing to fear.' "[48]

A week later, Cump and two other young men left for West Point. He had now mustered the courage to ride the railroad to Baltimore. Then, by a series of boat and rail rides, he reached Philadelphia, where he visited his sister, Elizabeth, and her family. Another series of boats and rail cars got him to New York and a visit with maternal uncle Charles Hoyt and his family in Brooklyn. A cousin took one look and good-naturedly pronounced Cump "an untamed animal just caught in the far West—'fit food for gunpowder,' and good for nothing else."

For the last leg of the trip, Cump took a steamboat up the Hudson River, enjoying the magnificent scenery as the steamer chugged up the majestic waterway. It was the middle of June 1836. The boat, filled with other would-be cadets just as nervous, excited, and curious as Cump, landed at the West Point wharf. The gangway was quickly let down; he stepped off. Cump's first sight was a soldier in full dress uniform, looking official as he recorded on a slate the names of all the prospective cadets. The soldier instructed them to take the winding road up to the plain.

Cump made the hard climb, reached the plain, passed the barracks, and found the stone building where the adjutant had his office. He knocked, entered, and presented his credentials. He was ordered to the treasurer and was separated from all his money and placed in a room with six other newcomers to wait for the superintendent. Colonel Rene E. DeRussy and several other faculty members entered the room and determined whether the young men could read and do basic arithmetic. Each successful candidate was then issued one lamp, one bucket, one broom, and a pair of blankets, "the sum total of a *Plebe's* estate whereon he was to build his fortune."

All this happened quickly. When Cump finally had a few minutes alone, he sat down in his assigned room and began paging through his copy of the academy regulations. Suddenly he heard a drum; a sharp command rang out: "Turn out *New Cadets.*" Racing out of his room, he ran down the stairs and literally bumped into his fellow plebes, individuals "from Maine to Louisiana and Iowa and Florida." Before they could become acquainted, they were ordered to fall in. They marched clumsily to the parade ground where they witnessed a thrilling sight of the old cadets, that is, the corps of cadets, marching in review, "stepping as one man—all forming a line." It was wondrous to behold; Cump immediately wished he was an old cadet, a participant in this panorama of precision. The order and oneness impressed him. He believed he now knew what West Point was all about, and he liked what he saw.[49]

The cadets' marching ability determined Cump's initial favorable reaction, but there was more to training army officers than parading them around a field, and it was these other elements of officer preparation that regularly stirred national debate. West Point and the Naval Academy at Annapolis were the only institutions of higher learning operated at national expense. Americans during the later Jacksonian years were suspicious of anything that smacked of national control, so West Point always seemed somewhat suspect.

For a time, it looked as though its own deficiencies would doom it. When Sylvanus Thayer became superintendent in 1817, he eliminated abuses of incompetence and political favoritism and instituted most of the academic and disciplinary procedures and practices that were to remain integral parts of the institution. When Cump entered West Point in 1836, Thayer was gone, but the school was still functioning under his system.

The cadet schedule, during the academic year and in the summer encampment, was organized to the minute. In the barracks, cadets rose at 5:30 A.M.; ate breakfast; studied and attended classes until 1:00 P.M.; broke for lunch; studied again until 4:00 P.M.; read and wrote letters until dinner at 6:00 P.M.; and studied until lights were ordered out at 9:30. (Often they studied by concealed candle light long after lights out.) In camp, the schedule was just as full, except that the cadets rose at 5:00 A.M. Even on Sundays, when they were free from most official duties, they still had to sit through a long Episcopal church service. Cump found the chaplain "a great bore."[50]

Cadets studied what was essentially an engineering curriculum with heavy doses of mathematics and French, the language of many of the leading books on war. There were courses in drawing, natural philosophy (physics), topographical drawing, chemistry, engineering (civil and military), mineralogy, rhetoric, and moral and political philosophy. Since more than 70 percent of class time was spent on engineering and allied science courses, West Point was "more of an engineering school than a military academy." When he graduated, Cump was better prepared to be a civil engineer than he was to be a soldier. Except for the summer encampment and a small part of Dennis Hart Mahan's engineering course, cadets received little that might properly be called military science. Mahan presented the distilled ideas of Antoine Henri Jomini, the leading military thinker of the early nineteenth century, but even he spent most of his class time teaching engineering, not strategy.[51]

Perhaps the most valuable of Cump's courses was Chaplain Jasper Adams's on moral philosophy, which assigned James Kent's

Commentaries on American Law. Kent wrote that war dissolved all morality and was fought between all the people of one nation versus all the people of the other. As for civil war, Kent argued that "the central government had to defend the laws of union by force of arms or be disgraced." Although Cump never commented on this course, he later acted according to many of the ideas contained in it.[52]

The faculty during Cump's years at West Point was particularly distinguished. Thayer's system called for a professor in each field of study supported by assistant teachers or section instructors to hear recitations for the mandatory daily grade. West Point was one of the nation's few engineering schools during the mid-nineteenth century, so the professors wrote their own textbooks, which were then used throughout the country. Dennis Hart Mahan wrote several engineering books plus his famous military book, *Outpost.* Claudius Berard penned a French textbook; Albert E. Church wrote four books in mathematics; William H. C. Bartlett wrote books on various topics in physics and was the nation's leading expert on astronomy. Even the drawing teacher, Robert W. Weir, was one of America's leading painters, as well as Cump's favorite instructor.[53]

Cump studied under two superintendents: Major Rene E. DeRussy, who commanded the military academy from 1835 to 1838, and Major Richard Delafield, who took charge until 1845. DeRussy tried to make life more pleasant for the cadets, instituting a ball at the end of the summer encampment and placing greater emphasis on band music. Delafield was stricter, but he authorized the cadets to sleep on iron bedsteads instead of on the floor, as had been the custom, and he substituted oil lamps for candles. His sarcastic ways earned him the title "Dicky the Punster," but Cump liked him anyway.[54]

In addition to the demanding superintendents and faculty, the difficult curriculum, the rigid schedule, and the demerit system (which could result in lowered class rank and extra duty), cadets' living conditions were harsh. They had little furniture in their rooms: a table, chair, lamp, mirror, and washstand. During his first two years at the academy, Cump slept on a mattress on the floor. The only running water was in the barracks' basement. The sole source of heat was an open fireplace in each room, so cadets alternately froze and roasted.[55]

The cadets' clothes were designed for appearance, not comfort. The trousers of the stiff gray and white uniform were buttoned along the side, for reasons of modesty. In 1840 after Cump had graduated, a cadet came back from furlough with the buttons changed to a more anatomically convenient position in the front. The superintendent's wife went into a chaste shock, but the buttons were officially allowed to remain there.[56]

Meals were not a respite from the cadet grind; they were part of it. All of the little food the young men received—meat, potatoes, pudding, bread, and coffee—was boiled. The terrible taste and constant demands on military table etiquette made mealtime stressful. Only the annual Fourth of July celebration provided opportunity for ample eating.[57]

The cadets had few opportunities for recreation. There were no organized physical training courses until horsemanship was introduced in 1839, Cump calling it "a great improvement in cadet life." The only student organization was a society that met to debate issues of common interest. Cadets were allowed little time for anything other than to eat, sleep, study, and drill.[58]

Nevertheless, the young men found ways to spice up their lives. Every chance they had, they would sneak off to Benny Haven's, a tavern located a few miles from the academy, to feast on roast turkey, or buckwheat cakes, or even whiskey. West Point authorities officially decried such practices, but since Benny Havens was a hallowed cadet institution from 1820 until after the Civil War and one of the few bright spots in the cadets' otherwise drab life, it seems clear that the officials winked at the after-hours goings on.[59]

Cump had few problems accommodating himself to the academy's severe environment. In one of his first letters home, he confidently announced, "From what I have seen of my classmates I have no doubt that I might be among the first." His prediction proved correct. He consistently ranked in the first sections of all the subjects, finishing number one in his third-year drawing class and eventually graduating sixth out of a class of 42. (He entered with 119 others.) He would have ranked fourth except for his high demerit total. Cump averaged more than ninety demerits per year for such misdemeanors as speaking in ranks, visiting another cadet's room at an improper time, being late for formation, and improper shoe shine; two hundred demerits meant expulsion. Cump was hardly a model soldier, but he never tried to be. Minor misconduct that earned demerits was unimportant to him. The fact that he never held a cadet office, except membership on an 1837 encampment library committee, did not bother him either.[60]

Cump's fellow students included some of the most famous military figures in American history, all future Civil War colleagues or opponents. When he was a plebe (freshman), Braxton Bragg, Jubal A. Early, Joseph Hooker, John C. Pemberton, and John Sedgwick were in their final year. Other cadets ahead of him included P. G. T. Beauregard, Irvin McDowell, William J. Hardee, Henry W. Halleck, and Edward O. C. Ord. His own classmates included George H. Thomas and Stewart Van Vliet. Coming behind him were Don Carlos Buell, Daniel H. Hill, Nathaniel Lyon, John F. Reynolds, Josiah Gorgas, William S. Rosecrans, James Longstreet, Earl Van Dorn, and John Pope. During his senior year, there was a sad-looking plebe everyone called Sam—U. S. Grant, whom Cump admitted to hardly noticing.[61]

Cump's best friend was William Irwin, a relative from Lancaster who was one year ahead of him. Irwin kept Cump under his care, the two relatives rooming together for several years until Irvin's 1839 graduation. Cump's letters home were full of references to Irwin, their nighttime visits to Benny's, and their sharing of academy frustrations and good times. Cump never mentioned any other cadet, though he shared a room with George Thomas and Stewart Van Vliet for at least one year, and his tent mate during his initial summer encampment was E. O. C. Ord.[62]

During his West Point years, Cump developed the reputation of being "the best hash maker at West Point." ("Hash" was cadet slang for any illicit food prepared in a cadet's room.) He often had a stain mark on his trousers from a secret feast of hot hash on toasted bread. For these clandestine dinners, he regularly smuggled food from the dining hall or from Benny's. Once he carted a half-bushel of oysters from Benny's and prepared an "extraordinary supper." After these secret suppers, storytelling or sneaking off for a nighttime jaunt was not uncommon. Even after Irwin was court-martialed for one such escapade, Cump continued going to Benny's for food and drink and to raise hell. Similarly, he participated with other cadets in an annual New Year's Eve prank in which they towed a cannon to the fourth floor of one of the barracks and simultaneously hoisted the fifes and drums to the top of the flagpole. "Of course," Cump remembered with obvious relish some forty years later, "there was no Reveille *that* morning."[63]

Although he worried about being found unprepared in class, he did not let this concern temper his playful life. Like his father before him and as he had done previously, Cump loved getting into mischief. Dennis Hart Mahan knew that whenever he heard "any slight disturbance denoting fun" behind him, he could be sure it was Cump. When any instructor's question caught him unprepared, Cump would blurt out: "Well, sir, to be frank with you, I haven't studied it." But Cump was such a good student and so good-natured that Mahan and the other instructors usually accepted his admission kindly.[64]

Cump was popular with the other cadets, not least because he received a steady supply of newspapers from his family in Lancaster and subscribed to the *National Gazette*. Since the academy library was heavy on scientific topics and short on contemporary affairs, a newspaper was often the only connection the isolated cadets had with affairs in the outside world. Cump's supply was welcomed.[65]

Cump showed a special interest in Ohio politics. At election time in 1838, he wagered a fatigue jacket on a Whig victory and Thomas Ewing's election. (He lost.) Cump, like his father and surrogate father, was a staunch Whig but did not blindly support that party's every position. He vehemently disagreed with party policy on banks, believing Whigs should stop defending every foible of every bank and instead simply say: "They are necessary and essential to the rapid progress of the country." He similarly believed that the 1840 Whig presidential campaign was ridiculous. He mistakenly thought it a political blunder "to envelope his [Harrison's] name with log cabins, ginger bread, hard cider, and such humbuggery[,] the sole object of which plainly is to deceive or mislead his ignorant and prejudiced though honest fellow citizens—whilst his qualifications, his honesty, his merits, and services are merely alluded to."[66]

Despite all his efforts to hoodwink his superiors and to bend their rules, Cump still looked to them for approval. When the cadets acted quickly to put out a blaze in an academic building, he boasted of the praise the superintendent lavished on them in his official report. In discussing the June examinations one year, he made a similar point. He wrote to his family that he and the other cadets studied hard not only to pass these examinations but also to impress the board of visitors and ensure their "good opinion" of the institution. Approval was especially important to Cump, no doubt because of his childhood experiences. He had lost a father who had paid him little attention, and he had gained a foster father around whom he felt constrained and unsure. He had two families, yet he had none. The corps of cadets helped to fill the space left by parental and familial ambiguity.[67]

That ambiguity is reflected in a letter to his foster sister, Ellen, who had criticized him for complaining about his foster mother's not writing often enough. "I am fully aware how slight are my claims to her regard. . . . Very often I feel my insignificance and inability to repay the many kindnesses and favors received at her hands and those of her family. Time and absence serve to strengthen the claims and to increase the affection and love and gratitude to those who took me early under their care and conferred the same advantages as they did upon their own children. Indeed I often feel that your father and mother have usurped the place which nature has alloted to parents alone." The Ewings had "usurped" their way into his life and psyche. The force of that word indicated Cump's divided loyalties and affections between the family who took him in and the one he worried he might be abandoning. Guilt and resentment filled his being— guilt for taking from the Ewings, resentment at having to do so.[68]

On the surface, Cump knew where he stood: Thomas Ewing was now his father; Maria Boyle Ewing was now his mother. Yet when he ran into some financial difficulties in 1839, he wrote to his natural mother asking her for a five-dollar loan, instead of appealing to the Ewings, explaining: "I do not wish ever to ask Mr. Ewing again for assistance." It was easier for him to take money from his financially struggling mother than from his wealthy foster father.[69]

In the summer of 1837, Cump received a two-week furlough, not long enough to go back to Ohio, so he visited his mother's relative, Charles Hoyt, in Brooklyn instead. Hoyt's house overlooked New York bay and harbor and was "the handsomest place" Cump had ever seen. Every morning before breakfast, Cump used his telescope to take in the sights around him: the sailing ships majestically floating into the harbor, the bustling cities of New York and Brooklyn, and the grand Governor's Island. He toured the city, visiting parks, museums, gardens, colleges, and the old Park Theatre, where he began his lifelong love of the stage. He met an acquaintance from Lancaster "with a great big whore (I expect) on his arm." The painted woman proved less attractive to Cump than did the navy yard. He explored the warship *Ohio* for over two hours "and how sufficient to gratify my curiosity." Breathing freedom after a year's confinement at West Point, and visiting family felt good. "I was perfectly in love with the place when I left," he enthused.[70]

In 1838 when he received an extended furlough, he returned to Ohio for an unfulfilling visit. He returned to West Point via Buffalo and the spectacular Niagara Falls. The chance to leave West Point and enjoy good food proved more significant than seeing the Ewings. He did not express the enthusiasm for visiting them he had displayed the previous summer after staying with the Hoyts.[71]

Other summers he spent in camp. During July and August, "more ladies come [to West Point] than can be well accommodated," even with the "two or three dancing parties each week," he wrote. He worried about the cadets' reputation as "great gallants and ladies men," because "God only knows how I will sustain that reputation." Whether because of shyness, inexperience, or a combination of factors, he seemed to be unwilling to risk encountering the visiting young women by attending a grand ball. When he did extend an invitation to the ball in 1838, it was to his sister Ellen.[72] She could not come.

The all-male stag dance was more to his liking. The last evening of camp, cadets placed lights all over the parade ground and in each tent. Then they did a kind of "country dance only that each one can shuffle and cut up as much as he pleases provided he goes through the figure." The class completing its last encampment sang appropriate songs, and the next morning everyone marched back to the barracks.[73]

The stag dance was a ritual of camaraderie and solidarity—an opportunity for the corps of cadets to let down their military reserve and experience a sense of community. The cadets suffered the rigors of the academy together, yet their fragmented academic sections and separation by classes precluded a sense of solidarity, except when they marched together as a corps and, less formally, in this stag dance. Such unity was important for their psychic survival at West Point, and it extended into their postgraduation military careers. West Point friendships were at the center of military leadership in both the Union and Confederate armies.

To Cump, this ritual may have had another meaning. In this dance, the foster child belonged to the family of cadets perhaps less ambiguously than to his natural or foster families. He enjoyed dancing exuberantly with the other cadets and singing at the top of his lungs. He experienced a togetherness in the military that neither the Shermans nor the Ewings had been able to provide him.

The day he reached his First Class (senior) year was, Cump later recalled, the "happiest day" of his life. He could see the end of West Point and the beginning of a less regimented life among his West Point brothers. The Ewings, however, urged Cump to resign his commission as soon as he graduated, encouraging him to enter a civilian profession, perhaps law. He refused to consider the possibility, going out of his way to disparage the legal profession: "I would rather be a blacksmith," he wrote. He was determined to remain in the army, to stay with his new family, feeling testy because the Ewings seemed to be trying to usurp that too.[74]

His only concern about the army was the location of his first assignment. Would it be in the West, or against the British and Canadians along the disputed Maine–New Brunswick boundary, or against the Indians anywhere? Would he be retained as an instructor at West Point, as the French professor hinted? Would he get a choice assignment and spend his time "dancing, hunting, fishing, and the like," or would he be less lucky and find himself in "some remote corner of the globe to drill drunken first recruits"? He lived in "continual hope and fear of the future" but generally viewed it "in the brightest colors" and was "necessarily contented."[75]

Graduation day in June 1840 finally arrived, and Cump's sixth-place class standing resulted in an artillery commission. (Had his demerits not lowered his fourth-place academic rank, he could have gone into the elitist Corps of Engineers.) Thomas and Phil Ewing on a campaign swing for the Whig presidential ticket of

"Tippecanoe and Tyler Too" visited him during final examination week, but his most faithful correspondent, sixteen-year-old Ellen, did not come, much to Cump's disappointment.[76]

Like many other graduates, Cump later developed a nostalgia for the academy. He visited it every chance he had, regularly addressing graduating classes during the post–Civil War years. Even while still a cadet, he grew lyrical about it in trying to convince Ellen to visit him. "Is not West Point worth visiting?" he asked. "Is not the scenery of the finest order in the world? In the vicinity are there not incidents in its history that render it dear to us all? I might ask a hundred such questions which any individual who has ever been here would be compelled to answer in the affirmative."[77]

Yet when he later came to evaluate his cadet life, Cump expressed no enthusiasm. His discussion of his four years at West Point occupies less than one page in his memoirs. By comparison, his trip to get there receives about the same amount of space. Cump justified his brief account because "to give [even] a mere outline would swell this [book] to an inconvenient size."[78] Considering that his memoirs are over 800 pages and two volumes long, however, it seems that he made a conscious decision not to give a fuller account of these formative years.

Despite the nostalgia of his later years and the familial attachment to his colleagues, Cump did not enjoy the West Point regimen. His accumulation of demerits indicates an inability to accommodate himself to the circumstances there. His high grades and his confession during his last year that he had "very little military duty to attend to and not much study" reveal that he found the work easy. Cump had little outlet for his energy and for his vast curiosity. The tedious memorization did not stimulate his inquisitive mind. At West Point, he acquired the superior attitude of the regular army officer over civilian soldiers and the professional disdain for all volunteer soldiers. Cump came to believe that West Pointers were superior to ordinary mortals, that they were indeed a special group among whom he felt a sense of belonging and approval. But if any of his professors had been asked, they certainly would have "admit[ed] that there was nothing manifested in . . . [his] character [then] . . . that marked him as one destined to play a great part in the greatest war of modern times."[79]

Cump entered adulthood with many unresolved childhood conflicts. He felt rootless, the result of his ambiguous feelings toward his natural and his foster families. Only the army seemed to provide the sense of belonging he yearned for, but West Point life had been frustrating. The new second lieutenant emerged into his new life with his old relationships unsettled and destined to influence his future more than he ever realized at the time.

CHAPTER 2

☆

MAKING SOUTHERN FRIENDS

GRADUATION FROM WEST POINT marked the end of Cump's youth but not of his youthful uncertainty. He was twenty years old, his education complete, eager to begin his military career. Significantly, he was to spend most of his early career in the South, meeting people and having experiences that would influence him for the rest of his days. He continued trying to find himself during these years, groping to chart the right course for his future.

But first he spent the customary postgraduation furlough at home. The Ewing home was full of visitors that summer, so he stayed with his mother down the street. Politicians, including William Henry Harrison, the Whig party's presidential candidate, were in Lancaster planning the upcoming fall campaign. Cump felt too self-important with his fresh commission and monthly salary of sixty-five dollars to pay the Ewing children much attention. Eleven-year-old Jimmy, the later famous politician James G. Blaine, took plenty of notice of Cump, "a tall and very slender young man, straight as an arrow, with a sharp face and a full suit of red hair."

Cump came in for his share of ribbing during the round of social events that summer. One night Ellen Ewing gave "a fancy-dress party," and Cump, though never much on ceremony, appeared in uniform. When a bat suddenly came flying at the dancers, he began flailing away at the pest with his cap. Meanwhile, servants rushed in carrying buckets to battle what they supposed from the noise was a fire. Seeing the bat, they threw the buckets at the flying invader, frightening the onlookers more than the pest. Finally, Cump jumped on a chair and drove the bat toward the open door and out into the night darkness. The crowd broke into relieved laughter, complimenting Cump on successfully winning "General Sherman's first battle."[1]

Cump was anxious to get on with his military life and fight some real battles. He, along with fellow graduates Stewart Van Vliet and George H. Thomas, had volunteered for duty with the Third Artillery Regiment in Florida. Toward the end of the summer, Cump received orders to report to New York's Governor's Island for transportation south. On the way, he decided to pay one final visit on his many friends at West Point. It was against academy regulations to visit cadets during study time, but Cump thought that his lieutenancy gave him special status. It did not. A tactical officer reported his transgression, and the superintendent cited him for "unofficerlike conduct" and confined him to the hotel grounds.

He immediately wrote Superintendent Richard Delafield a round-about apology that Dicky the Punster should have appreciated. "My feelings," he insisted, "prompted me to do a common and friendly act, bid my friends a farewell upon parting with some perhaps forever." Delafield freed Cump from the hotel, but he sent him to his new post with a letter of condemnation. Perhaps fearing Thomas Ewing's wrath, Delafield also informed Secretary of War Joel R. Poinsett, who found the whole thing ridiculous.[2]

Cump left West Point chagrined but unbowed. He accepted temporary command of an infantry recruit company and sailed out of New York harbor in early October 1840, taking with him a recently purchased black pointer dog for companionship. The vessel reached Savannah in mid-October, where the party switched to a smaller ship for the trip to St. Augustine. He deposited the infantry there, bumped into West Point friend Braxton Bragg, and took a small boat toward his station, Fort Pierce, in south Florida.[3]

The young lieutenant had entered a combat zone. The U.S. Army was fighting a frustratingly difficult war against the resourceful Seminole Indians in the swamp-infested wilderness. This Second Seminole War[4] was the result of the general American determination to push the Indians out of the white man's way and prevent them from aiding fugitive slaves. Neighboring slave states were particularly determined to stop what they characterized as the dangerous flow of their chattel to Florida. Andrew Jackson had fought the First Seminole War, hanging two British subjects in the process and convincing the Spanish to sell Florida to the United States or face more incursions. Florida became U.S. territory in 1821 for $5 million. The Seminoles, however, had never accepted Spanish control, so they ignored this transfer and tried to maintain their way of life.

In 1823 the U.S. government negotiated the first of several treaties to try to overcome Seminole intransigence. The Treaty of Moultrie Creek called for the physical separation of the thirteen thousand white settlers and the four thousand Indians, setting aside 4 million acres for the Indians and leaving the rest of Florida for white settlement. Neither side was satisfied: the whites wanted the Indians removed totally; the Indians considered the appropriated land too small. The fugitive slave issue remained too thorny for resolution.

When Andrew Jackson became president in 1829, Florida was caught up in his Indian removal policy. His administration ignored the Moultrie Creek Treaty and convinced a small number of chiefs to agree to migration across the Mississippi River (Treaty of Payne's Landing) by promising them they could see and approve the new land first. In the 1833 Treaty of Fort Gibson, a few chiefs accepted this deal, but most Indians felt betrayed. Pressure from whites intensified, and the capture of alleged runaway slaves living with the Indians increased. In December 1836 the Seminoles retaliated by ambushing two companies of soldiers and killing over one hundred men—some 20 percent of the regulars then in Florida.[5] "Dade's Massacre" became a rallying cry, and battles of the Seminoles versus the settlers and the ever larger military units increased steadily. The Second Seminole War was on.

The settlers and the U.S. Army vastly outnumbered the Indians, who tried to even the odds by adopting guerrilla warfare. In groups of five or ten, they attacked isolated settlements, unsuspecting military units, a wagon, or a house and then slipped away into the maze of swamps and hammocks, safely hidden from army units. One after another the army commanders came in— Winfield Scott, Thomas Jesup, and Zachary Taylor, to name the most famous—and one after another they left, their military reputations tarnished. Every grand new plan, every new negotiation failed; the Indians remained unbowed. Their numbers kept dwindling because of war deaths and forced migrations, but even a single Indian was one too many as far as the whites were concerned.

When Sherman arrived in the fall of 1840, fighting was in its fourth year. The first two stanzas of some contemporary verse captured the nature of this interminable war:

> Ever since the creation
> By the best calculation
> The Florida war has been raging.
> And 'tis our expectation
> That the last conflagration
> Will find us the same contest waging.
> And yet, 'tis not an endless war
> As facts will plainly show
> Having been 'ended' forty times
> In twenty months or so.[6]

Sherman was eager to put his West Point training into practice. He felt himself entering "into a new world" as he made his way to Fort Pierce. He took a steamer from St. Augustine to the bar of the Indian River, where he transferred into a whale boat rowed by four men and a guide. This boat floated him over the sandbar into the mouth of the Indian River outlet, where he climbed into an even smaller vessel. The same crew rowed him through a two-mile channel in the middle of the Mangrove Islands until the party reached a three-mile-wide lagoon in front of Fort Pierce.

As the small boat reached the wharf, Sherman noticed the officers of Company A, Third Artillery Regiment, gathered in welcome (though they seemed more interested in the mail bag he carried than in him). Facing the water were six or seven stilt log houses for the officers, each with a palmetto leaf roof, a bed, deck, chair, and decorations of bird feathers, wild animal skins, and shark teeth. Forming the two other sides of the open rectangle that made up the fort were log houses for the enlisted men. A log stockade protected the intervals between the houses and the flanks. Sherman was sure the fort could not withstand a determined attack, but he was not worried. Like all other army men, he believed the Indians were too cowardly to attack a military post.[7]

Sherman quickly learned that this war against the Seminoles was nothing like the wars of Napoleon that West Pointers thought of when they spoke of combat. A few Indians allegedly representing the many agreed to removal. But when none followed the leaders, the U.S. government ordered the use of force. The troops proved too few to do the job because the Indians picked their targets and then melted away. Good army officers lost their health and reputations and were happy to leave.[8]

The weather governed the pace of the fighting. The army did not campaign during the hot and humid months, so fishing, not fighting, was the order of the day when he arrived. Ashlock, a local guide, proved to be an apt teacher. Sherman learned how to spear shark and catch red fish, sheep's head, and mullet, all of which teemed in the surrounding waters. He helped set up nets to catch green turtles. The captured reptiles were caged and fattened on mangrove leaves for later meals. He consumed oysters, perhaps remembering the bushel he had once smuggled into his West Point room. There were no orange, lemon, or lime trees in that part of Florida, however, and Sherman missed "those splendid Ohio orchards of apples and peaches."[9]

It was a languid life, pleasantly different from the rigidity of West Point. His West Point friend, Stewart Van Vliet, was there to share meals and conversation, so Cump still had the camaraderie of West Point without its suffocating rules and regulations. Others talked of wanting to leave for more civilized duty elsewhere, but he wanted to stay. He was "comfortable" and "in good health." He enjoyed his menagerie of chickens, a fawn, and some crows, laughing that it was hard to tell whether his room "was the abode of man or beast." The veterans conversed about the upcoming summer's torrid heat and the pesky mosquitos, and he soon learned how right they were. Still, perhaps because of the influence of the Peter Parley books Thomas and Maria Ewing had had him read as a child, he determined to use his spare time to study geography, which he insisted was "essential to a true military execution." He believed that battling the Seminoles was the "kind of war which every young officer should be thoroughly acquainted with, as the Indian is most likely to be our chief enemy in times to come." Nothing like the Mexican War or a Civil War was conceivable to the recently uncloistered cadet, but he was predicting his own post–Civil War service accurately.[10]

Sherman experienced no combat but nonetheless saw death. A soldier shot his sergeant in a quarrel over the assailant's wife, one of the unit's cooks. The fishing savant, Ashlock, and most of his whale boat crew were drowned one day while crossing the sandbar. Only that day Ashlock had brought his wife to stay with him, and her presence made his drowning and mutilation by sharks that much more gruesome. Sherman was also personally responsible for a soldier's death. The post doctor wanted ten days' leave to go courting, and Sherman agreed to take his place. The next morning during sick call, he suspected a groaning soldier of faking and ordered the sergeant to run the alleged malingerer around the fort. The running killed the man.[11]

Sherman never shot any Indians. Putting into practice Colonel William J. Worth's strategy of quick strikes against Indian supplies, settlements, and society, the Fort Pierce contingent regularly sent out scouting parties ranging some two hundred miles above the fort and fifty miles below. They saw battle only once, and Sherman was not along that time. Stewart Van Vliet killed an Indian during this engagement, and the sergeant who later fell at the hands of the irate husband allegedly killed three. The sergeant documented his accomplishment by taking scalps and celebrated by going on a drunk. A mortal encounter with the enemy was so rare that when it happened, it caused celebration.

With all the disdain West Pointers could generate for civilians, Sherman disliked the white settlers he met in Florida, calling them "cowardly" for always demanding army help. The militia was the worst "pack of rascals" imaginable. On the other hand, he described some captive Indians as "noble looking" and grudgingly admired how stolidly they accepted their fate; they bore their wounds and their capture without a whimper. "Even an enemy must admire those qualities which have enabled the Seminoles to maintain this country this long," he said, "though those qualities have been chiefly cunning and perfidy."[12]

It was his experience with the Seminole leader Coacoochee that perhaps caused Sherman to develop mixed admiration and disgust for the Indians. At two March 1841 conferences with army leaders, Coacoochee had agreed to lead his followers out of Florida. He then began a tour of army posts, demanding supplies every place he visited. On May 1 he arrived in the vicinity of Fort Pierce. It was a normal quiet day when the sentinel suddenly noticed the approaching Indians. The troops manned their battle stations, but the Indians signaled their friendly intentions. They rode up to the fort's gate and were taken to see Major Thomas Childs, the commanding officer. One of the party, a black man named Joe (no doubt a fugitive slave), spoke English and produced the safe-conduct pass Coacoochee had received from the army high command.[13] Would Childs honor this paper? the black man asked. Childs responded by asking for Coacoochee. Joe replied that he was "close by" and offered to bring him to the fort. Childs turned to Sherman and ordered him to take ten men and bring the chieftain in.

Sherman worried about being led into a trap, but Joe kept saying "only a little way," so Sherman kept going. Some six miles out, the party reached the Indian leader's hammock. Sherman halted his soldiers, instructed them to remain vigilant, and then rode forward with Joe and the other Indians. About a dozen warriors watched Sherman's approach. When he asked for the chief, a handsome, almost delicate individual in his late twenties came forward. The Indian looked up at Sherman, who was still astride his horse, struck his breast, and said: "Me Coacoochee." He tried to engage Sherman in conversation, but Sherman said his only reason for being there was to escort Coacoochee to his "big chief," Major Childs.

Before he would leave, Coacoochee dressed for his meeting with Childs. He bathed in a nearby pool and then donned his finery, including a series of vests, one of which contained a bloodstained bullet mark, and a turban sporting ostrich feathers. Unsuccessful in his attempt to get Sherman to give him a silver dollar for a paper bank note, Coacoochee mounted the horse Sherman had provided and rode into Fort Pierce. He told Childs he was ready to lead his people out of Florida but needed another month and more rations to gather them. Childs agreed to provide the supplies if the Indian leader agreed to have all 150 of his followers ready to migrate by the end of the month. Coacoochee agreed, and then he and his Indian escort got drunk on commissary whiskey supplied by their obliging hosts.

For the next month, Indians regularly came into Fort Pierce for food and drink, but at the end of that time, only Coacoochee and twenty of his warriors appeared. An exasperated Childs arrested the Indian leader and sent Sherman and some troopers on a fifty-mile chase to track down the rest. They found none. Coacoochee and the twenty men captured with him were sent off to New Orleans for migration but then brought back to help round up the rest of his followers. Thus, Sherman had participated in one of the army's rare successes, but he had hardly gathered any combat glory or military experience in the process.[14]

After this brief adventure, Sherman returned to his fishing and savoring green turtle steaks. Despite Fort Pierce's isolation, he kept up with news of the outside world and offered his correspondents strong opinions on contemporary events. Despite his avowed admiration for Henry Clay, the Whig party, and his foster father, he wrote impassioned letters attacking the Whig national bank bill that Thomas Ewing was sponsoring in the Senate. Ewing supported Whig calls for a reestablishment of the Bank of the United States Andrew Jackson had destroyed in the 1830s, but Sherman called all bankers selfish "scoundrels." "If one ever assisted an honest poor man without exaction and usury I would like to hear of it." As for politicians, the turmoil over John Tyler's ascension to the presidency after William Henry Harrison's sudden death in April 1841 showed, once again, their baseness. Their squabbling reminded him of "a farce between two greedy pelicans quarreling over a dead fish."[15]

Although too young to vote, Sherman supported the candidacy of William Henry Harrison because he hoped the former soldier would do "something decisive" in Florida. He hoped for "a war of extermination . . . the most certain and economical method." Harrison's death after only a month in the presidency dashed these hopes and put a cover of gloom over everything.[16]

By July 1841, Sherman had had enough. He became depressed over the slow conduct of the war; he worried about the impact of the murderous summer heat on the soldiers now in combat year round; he felt gloomy whenever left to guard Fort Pierce while others went out into the field; he blamed the Florida mess on military and political inefficiency, a conclusion that made him feel worse. He came to believe that the war would never end and that he would die of old age in Florida. His faithful correspondent, Ellen Ewing, believed Sherman was simply "homesick, but he will not admit it."[17]

In November Sherman was promoted to first lieutenant (luck or perhaps Thomas Ewing's influence allowing him to reach that grade in seventeen months instead of the usual five to eight years). With the promotion came his transfer from Company A at Fort Pierce to Company G in St. Augustine. He had mixed feelings about the move. He knew his unit was accomplishing nothing useful in its sweeps through the countryside, but the exercises had "a peculiar charm" about them: "The fragrance of the air, the abundance of game and fish, and just enough adventure, gave to life a relish." In the end, however, Sherman left with little regret. Life at Fort Pierce had grown stale; St. Augustine meant new vistas.[18]

Just before his departure, Sherman met a supply boat carrying E. D. Keyes, one of Winfield Scott's former aides, whom Sherman greeted with two fat turtles, some oysters, and an abundance of war news. Keyes was impressed with the young lieutenant, describing him enthusiastically as "thin and spare, but healthy, loquacious, active, and communicative to an extraordinary degree." No doubt Sherman must have rhapsodized to Keyes, as he was to do later in his life, about "threading though the intricate mazes of the Everglades in canvas, wading through the endless swamps carrying our 'five days rations, to last ten,' piling up the bushes to make a bed above the water—[and] testing the comparative merits of Alligator & crow stands."[19]

When he reached St. Augustine around Christmas 1841, Sherman left such adventures behind. He received command of a twenty-man detachment at Picolata, a settlement about eighteen miles away. Before the war, an invalid hospital had been built there, but when Sherman arrived, his detachment and a single white family comprised the entire population. He had little to do but keep guard over the road to St. Augustine. The solitude of Picolata and its nearness to St. Augustine and its three thousand people was appealing, and he was pleased to be able to receive mail on a monthly schedule.[20]

He found the many Spanish young women "with some few exceptions . . . ignorant but very pretty with beautiful hair and eyes." They danced with special grace, and he was determined to learn their dances before he left. He noted that these women had "already played havoc with officers of the army," but since the most beautiful ones were already spoken for, only a few more officers would be entranced into marriage. Clearly he was determined not to be one of them. His closest relationship with a woman remained his regular correspondence with his foster sister, Ellen, then sixteen years old. He expressed pride in her prize-winning school artwork and told her that he looked forward to seeing her ride the "wildest horse" around. Next to drawing, vigorous riding was "the most lady-like accomplishment" attainable. Their steady correspondence kept them in as close touch as distance would allow.[21]

In March 1842 military officials declared the costly Seminole War over because it was not worth battling the few remaining Indians. In 1837 there had been nine thousand soldiers in Florida; in 1841 thirty-eight hundred were still there. Nearly fifteen hundred soldiers had lost their lives from battle and disease; the army had spent about $20 million for combat, and it had disbursed an equal amount for other expenses and damages. It had been an aggravating war, but most of the Seminoles in Florida were now in the West.[22]

Sherman considered the war a gigantic waste of time, but he learned an important lesson. He saw concretely what he had heard about in his West Point ethics class: sometimes in war, a military leader had to forgo accepted rules of combat and take unorthodox action. The Seminole War demonstrated the limitations of conventional nineteenth-century military tactics. It was not a battle between two rival professional armies as envisioned by Antoine Henri Jomini and by West Point professor Dennis Hart Mahan. The Seminoles fought with their entire society, and they attacked not merely their blue-coated adversaries but civilians as well. At the same time, the Indians were dependent for military success on their food supply and strength of will. Sherman had learned valuable lessons for the future about the psychological and total dimensions of warfare. It was a kind of justice that a man named Tecumseh should learn such a valuable lesson from Indians.

Sherman and his unit, no longer needed in Florida, were ordered to Fort Morgan, Alabama, to man a long-unoccupied fortress forty miles from Mobile. They made the trip in thick ocean fog, their ship nearly running aground several times. They reached Pensacola, "a pretty place," Sherman thought, but, as in "most southern towns, all the young men of enterprise" had

departed for fame and fortune in the North. The town's population was heavily female and anxious for male companionship.
"God grant that the Bachelor . . . shall escape," Sherman
prayed.[23]

He did. On March 8, 1842, Sherman's company reached Fort
Morgan, located on a long, narrow peninsula guarding the
entrance into Mobile Bay. Sherman was disappointed to find it a
"dreary, desolate" place, filthy and empty. Because he was unit
quartermaster, he had to take a pilot boat the forty miles to
Mobile for necessary supplies.[24]

Sherman liked the city immediately and found its refined
beauty impressive. He saw roses, shrubs, and long, shaded carriage roads leading up to white painted houses situated far back
from tree-lined streets. The hectic activity at the wharves reminded him favorably of New York, but he found the city's
unstable currency and resulting inflation shocking. Buggy rental
was an astonishing six dollars a day; a hotel room cost from three
to ten dollars. He quickly concluded that "none but millionaires
can flourish in Mobile," and his monthly salary of seventy dollars
hardly placed him in that category. He felt happy to be living some
distance from such an expensive place.[25]

Yet Sherman was drawn to Mobile regularly during his three-
month tour at Fort Morgan and for the first time in his life became
deeply involved in society. "The bright button was a passport at all
times to the houses of the best," he quickly found, and the
genuine friendliness of the Mobileans impressed him. One day, a
hundred young people chartered a boat and "marched bodily into
the very heart of the citadel and carried the fort by storm." The
startled Fort Morgan contingent recovered their shaken compo-
sures and conducted a tour of their still-bedraggled fortress. Then
the officers joined their invaders on board the boat for wine, food,
and music (the last provided by a band hired for the occasion).
Sherman and several others took the ship back to Mobile, and
Sherman spent six days enjoying theater performances, art exhib-
its, parties, balls, and even a hot-air balloon ascension.[26]

Sherman's visits to Mobile were rendered especially pleasant
because of Cornelia Bull, the wife of a wealthy cotton merchant
and a cousin on his mother's side. She gave him a warm welcome
and insisted that he visit often. He frequently returned to the
house which had *"Home* spread over all . . . a perfect paradise."[27]

He was happy to be with family, and the peace and quiet, the gardens, the comfortable house, and the good food were a welcome change from uncivilized Forts Pierce and Morgan.

He spent most of his time at the distant Fort Morgan, however, where he found cleaning and fortifying the five-pointed-star fort monotonous and felt isolated. The magnificent fishing in the bay provided some excitement, and the visit of Commodore Alexander J. Dallas and other naval personnel allowed him to discuss what he thought was the slim possibility of war with Mexico.[28] The beauty of Mobile, the welcome of the city's elite, and the warmth of his cousin's family could not completely alleviate the tedium of his military world. Sherman was bored at Fort Morgan and saw no hope for any future excitement.

Increasing pressure from home to resign his commission added to his burden. Ellen Ewing bluntly wondered why he remained in the army rather than beginning a civilian profession. "Every reason exists why I should remain," he answered. "I am content and happy, and it would be foolish to spring into the world barehanded and unprepared to meet its coldness and trials." He knew far too many former officers who had resigned their commissions, only to regret it later. But he wanted his foster father's advice, he told Phil Ewing, being "exceedingly anxious to comply with his [Thomas Ewing's] minutest wishes."[29] Sherman felt torn. He was determined to stay in the army because of the security and camaraderie he felt, but he worried about his foster family's desire. Thomas Ewing wanted his foster son to enter a civilian profession, so Sherman's determination to stay in the army, in a life that he found fulfilling yet boring, pulled him in several directions.

Ellen probed Sherman about another delicate topic—his religious beliefs. Although the Ewings had included him in their religious observances, he had cooperated only reluctantly. He now told Ellen that he had "practiced or professed no particular creed" since his departure for West Point six years previously, though he accepted "the main doctrines of the Christian religion." Like Catholics, he believed "in good works rather than faith," but he could not bring himself to practice that creed.[30]

In June 1842 he and his unit received orders for Fort Moultrie in Charleston harbor. Sherman rejoiced at leaving Fort Morgan, its sand, and its seemingly ever-increasing heat. "Hurrah for Old

Fort Moultrie" rang out as the unit boarded a ship for the trip to South Carolina. The manpower needs of the Seminole War had kept Moultrie uninhabited since the nullification crisis of the early 1830s, but its proximity to Charleston made it a choice military assignment. Sherman was sorry to be leaving his cousin, but everything else about the move made him happy.[31]

He traveled with Companies D and G of the Third Artillery Regiment, and Company K and Braxton Bragg's and George H. Thomas's Company B joined them. Eventually over 250 men were stationed in the Sullivan Island fort, along with the regimental band and "all the other paraphernalia usually attached to Headquarters." Fort Moultrie had originally been constructed of palmetto logs in 1776, but stone and brick walls twelve feet high and a parapet capable of mounting fifty cannon had been added later. Inside there were three two-story barracks. At the foot of the walls was Moultrieville, a collection of "temporary or rather frail houses built by the wealthy to spend their summers." Sherman liked what he saw.[32]

He marveled at Charleston, a city of nearly thirty thousand people, and at the "mountains of cotton" and "tiers of rice" that made the wharves almost impassable. "The yells of the negro stevedores and their songs almost deafen people," he noted. Police and soldier patrols maintained excellent law and order, he found, and the slaves were "all well dressed and behaved, never impudent." In fact, he thought, they felt "very lightly indeed the chains of bondage." There were good hotels available, a well-supplied market, and "magnificent churches and public edifices."[33]

Sherman's limited military duties still did not exercise his boundless energy. Every morning, officers and men rose at reveille, conducted drill at sunrise, had breakfast at 7:00 A.M., held a dress parade at 8:00, and changed the guard at 8:30. On Sunday, there was some extra music and an inspection. The last day of each month, "a thorough inspection of arms, clothing, quarters and everything" took place. Once in a while, Sherman pulled a night of guard duty supervision. Usually, however, he and the rest of the garrison had nothing to do after 9:00 A.M. "Each one kills time to suit himself till reveille of next morning commences the new routine."[34]

Most of the time, the officers had to depend on themselves for recreation. They were a lively group that included some of the later Civil War's luminaries: Union officers Robert Anderson, George H. Thomas, E. D. Keyes, John F. Reynolds, T. W. Sherman, and Stewart Van Vliet and Confederate officers Braxton Bragg and A. C. Myers. These young lieutenants and captains, most just beginning their military careers, talked about "Tactics & History—discussing the relative merits of the old Flint lock [musket] and [the] modern innovation of the percussion cap—lamenting that our fate was cast in so peaceful an era and growling at the slowness of promotion." To Sherman's amusement, one of the captains "contended that there could be no better weapon than the old revolutionary firelock with flint and steel, and in spite of regulations," this same individual "clung to his old Steuben's Tactics."[35]

During the summer months many wealthy Charlestonians left the city to escape the heat and yellow fever and lived in their Moultrie houses, so Sherman had regular company. As soon as the sun set, all of Moultrieville's residents came pouring out of their beach houses to promenade or take carriage rides along the sand—activity that made for a "splendid review before this Fort." Sherman watched with particular interest the young ladies "with flowing robes (called bathing dresses)" tentatively putting their toes into the water "with a scream" and shouting how "glorious" it all was. When most of Moultrieville's residents returned to Charleston in mid-September, life resumed its humdrum routine.[36]

Sherman and his colleagues began to make regular trips into the city for the nightly parties during the social season, when officers were "expected in full uniforms," to add glitter to the scene. At first the round of parties was enjoyable, but soon they became a chore. "They dance only the same old set of French quadrilles, devoid of variety and grace," he complained. It was "painful" for him to watch the clumsy Charlestonians after seeing the "graceful forms and motions" of the beautiful Spanish women of St. Augustine. The conversations were similarly stilted. "Smirks, smiles, pride and vanity, hypocrisy and flippance reign triumphant," he said. His mind became "satiated with the sameness and [the] want of sincerity and feeling." Sherman found the Charlestonians' "preference for rounded edges and gentlemanly amateurism" to be exasperating.[37] Yet he continued to attend the festivities because he saw it as military duty to cultivate the Charlestonians and ensure good military and civilian relationships. As a compromise, the bored officers set up a social duty roster, so only two or three had to attend each evening's party, while the rest excused themselves on account of other obligations, real or pretended.[38]

Even a limited social calendar proved oppressive: "mingling with people in whom you feel no permanent interest, smirks and smiles when you feel savage, tight boots when your fancy would prefer slippers." He longed for relief—"another Indian war in Florida or a long furlough in Ohio"—as his restlessness manifested itself. Moultrie bored him. He craved new adventures, new sights, and new people, an impatient approach to life that was to grow increasingly characteristic in later years.[39]

Sherman tried to keep himself entertained. He often visited the residence of the future hero of Fort Sumter, Robert Anderson, and his invalid wife and spent hours viewing their large collection of paintings and engravings. He wrote numerous letters to relatives and friends (all the while complaining that he hated writing and did so only to receive mail in return). He went fishing in a boat he had refurbished, bobbing on the water while enjoying the cool breezes. He visited plantations as far as fifty miles away to hunt, socialize, and study their operation. When several soldiers deserted, he enthusiastically pursued them. On other occasions he had to serve on inspection and court-martial boards in neighboring states, and he traveled to North Carolina to be a groomsman in an army friend's wedding. The arrival of two Mexican warships with their "mustachioed and whiskered Captains covered with Scars," which Sherman condescendingly believed had been gained "in brawls instead of Battle," was a particularly welcome break from the routine, as was watching the construction of Fort Sumter in the middle of Charleston harbor.[40]

Of all his pastimes, Sherman particularly relished painting. At West Point, he had finished first in his drawing course, completing magnificent representations of male and female figures. When he became oppressively bored at Moultrie during the fall of 1842, he purchased some painting equipment, turning out landscapes and portraits and often becoming so engrossed that he found it "pain[ful] to lay down the brush." Such compulsion bothered him, and he wondered if he should quit painting altogether before it forced him to neglect his official duties. But he kept at it while at Moultrie. Later in life, he might do a sketch here or there, but he never painted with the same intensity. The artist in him apparently could not flourish in the military.[41]

Politics was a constant interest at Moultrie. Sherman refused to admit to any party affiliation because he thought such loyalty was "the veriest tyrant known to man." Still, his loyalty to Thomas Ewing and his admiration for perennial Whig presidential candidate Henry Clay kept him a Whig. During the presidential election of 1844, he finally admitted: "I call myself a Whig." He still insisted, however, that, as a soldier, he was prohibited from any political participation. Besides, politics was too uncertain; it was a "pitch and toss" game.[42]

Sherman had special disdain for the politics he heard preached in South Carolina: the states' rights position that had surfaced in the early 1830s as nullification, the alleged right of a state to nullify a federal law. He was a fervent nationalist and found John C. Calhoun's arguments distressing. South Carolina "aint worth a d-n," he disgustedly argued, because it believed John C. Calhoun's ideas "alone" were "right." He believed that nullification according to Calhoun was keeping South Carolina isolated from the mainstream of American politics.[43]

The talk of conflict against England to secure Oregon and against Mexico and England because of Texas was more welcome. Sherman believed that the United States had to take a stand on these lands to maintain its self-respect. Besides, he wanted "to practice what in peace we [soldiers] can only profess." He said he would "give anything in the world" to fight in Mexico, but by 1846 he saw little prospect for war. Even when Braxton Bragg, George H. Thomas, and Company E departed for Corpus Christi, Texas, in the summer of 1845, he did not see much hope. "Our government talks and bullies a great deal, but when they talk of money they are frightened" and fail to act. Still, as Company E boarded ship, Sherman "could not restrain the impulse to give three hearty cheers," much to his commanding officer's annoyance at "such unmilitary noise."[44]

Sherman had adopted the southern attitude toward slavery: it was part of the natural order. He had a slave in both Mobile and Charleston, and he strongly defended the institution in letters home, on one occasion using Fort Moultrie's sorrow over the death of Braxton Bragg's retainer to demonstrate "the strong attachment between master and slave." He insisted he was "no advocate of slavery" but then said that it was a "delirium" to believe that "oppression and tyranny" were its "necessary accompaniment." He had "never seen the least sign of disaffection on the part of the negroes" anywhere in South Carolina, he argued, and he had "seen them in the cotton fields and rice ditches, met them hunting at all hours of day and on the road at night, without anything but 'How d'ye Massa? Please give me some bac' [tobacco]."[45]

Like the slave owners, Sherman disdained British and New England abolitionists and termed the latter "the ignorant fanatical part" of that region's population. Abolitionism threatened the public order, he believed, because its adherents kept things unnecessarily stirred up. For example, they falsely insisted that Texas annexation would benefit slavery. Actually Texas would eventually serve "as a good receptacle" for the slaves of the older slave states and dilute the problem. Southerners should simply be left alone to solve the slavery problem in their own good time. Sherman, the Ohio Whig, had accepted the proslavery ideas of the Cotton Whigs of the South and was not hesitant to instruct his Whig family and friends in the North about the doctrine.[46]

The same insistence on the status quo determined Sherman's attitude toward the federal government's treatment of the army. He complained profusely about having nothing to do at Moultrie, but he also vigorously opposed any military cutbacks. On August 23, 1842, Congress passed a law reducing the size of the army and cutting officers' salaries because the Seminole War was over. (Sherman lost forty dollars a year.) "Our Congress is getting so Democratic," he shouted, "that every year we are threatened with either disbandment or such a reduction of pay as would drive every reasonable and good officer out."[47]

During the summer of 1843, Sherman visited home for the first time in three years. He saw family and friends in Lancaster and in nearby Mansfield and Columbus. On his long return journey to Charleston by way of the Mississippi River, he kept detailed diary notes. Everything he saw on the river intrigued him: the boats with their varied passengers, sights, and sounds; Cincinnati, Louisville, St. Louis, and New Orleans; an art gallery and a cathedral in St.

Louis; a theater and masquerade ball in New Orleans; and the countryside along the river. He reached Charleston and Fort Moultrie on December 27, 1843, to a "welcome . . . warmer than I had reason to expect or hope from citizens as well as comrades."[48]

This long trip, the end of a five-month furlough, had a profound impact on the young officer. He saw the Mississippi River and the cities along its banks for the first time in his life, carefully jotting down notes about everything within eyesight, including places like Memphis and Vicksburg where he would later conduct military operations. His lifelong love affair with St. Louis developed when he first saw the city on this trip. The farther south he floated on the river, the more beautiful the countryside appeared to him. While on the snowy Ohio River, he had been shivering in winter clothes. Within a day on the Mississippi, he saw "green corn and grass."[49] Over and over in his life, Sherman would return to the Mississippi to try to gain nourishment on its banks.

On February 4, 1844, he was detailed to Colonel Sylvester Churchill, the army's inspector general, to investigate the claims of former volunteer soldiers for alleged government-caused equipment and horse losses during the Seminole wars. He suspected he owed the assignment to Thomas Ewing's influence. He reported to Churchill in Marietta, Georgia, north of Atlanta, on February 12 and began "cross question[ing] and pump[ing] the claimants to see whether the old horse (killed in Florida) is not still [actually] at work in his corn field at home." He experienced "many a rich scene and . . . unfolded some pretty pieces of rascality for an honest and religious people."[50]

Sherman took every opportunity to explore the area, investigating nearby Kennesaw Mountain and its environs. When Churchill moved the inquiry to Bellefonte, Alabama, Sherman carefully explored the western Georgia countryside on the way, making what he called "a topographical sketch of the ground." Then he spent four weeks at the federal arsenal in Augusta. He came to know the geography of the region intimately as he rode back and forth across it. This experience, he later said, "was of infinite use to me and consequently to the Government" during the Civil War. It was over this same ground that he marched on Atlanta and to the sea. He always insisted that "the knowledge of the country I had gained there as a young fellow helped me to win a dozen victories."[51]

When he returned to Moultrie in the late spring of 1844, Sherman found himself at a major turning point in his life. During his 1843 furlough to Ohio, he had discovered that his faithful correspondent and foster sister, Ellen Ewing, had become a grown woman of nineteen. Sherman had repeatedly insisted that he was a confirmed bachelor. On first arriving in Charleston, for example, he had taken a buggy ride with a young woman only to learn later that local custom considered such intimacy tantamount to an engagement announcement. "As an officer of the Army I will never *marry*," he insisted. The army was "a first rate place for a single man but no place at all for one that is married unless the wife is willing to forsake home and often even the comforts of civilized life." When Ellen had playfully suggested that he bring home a young woman he was allegedly seeing regularly, he protested: "I thank the Lord I'm not so far gone as to commit so foolish an act as that."[52]

All this changed during his furlough. Sherman decided to give up his bachelorhood to marry his foster sister. He regularly used the mails as a way to formulate his thoughts, vent his frustrations, and work out his options, but he said nothing about this marriage decision. Neither Sherman nor Ellen ever discussed the reasons for their decision. Sherman wrote Thomas Ewing asking for Ellen's hand, and, despite some momentary hesitation at the thought of his daughter and foster son marrying, Ewing consented. No one else ever commented on the unusual nature of the proposed union.[53]

Sherman had always appreciated Thomas Ewing's help while simultaneously begrudging it. By marrying Ellen, he was more legitimately tying himself to Thomas Ewing. If Ewing became his father-in-law, he need no longer be the usurper of his dead father's place. By marrying Ellen, Sherman was legally joining the family and putting himself on stronger footing with the powerful foster father. He loved Ellen, and, besides, marrying her would solve his ambivalent feelings about his familial status.

Despite their many differences over the years, Ellen was the one woman he felt a steady affection for. She was unwaveringly devoted to him, a certainty in his otherwise changing world. She allowed him to go away for extended periods of time and was always waiting for him on his return. His relationship to her, often through the mail, steadied him as he groped for order in his life. Theirs would never be the perfect marriage, but it suited them both.

In her letter to Sherman accepting his proposal, Ellen expressed a firm resolve that he become a Catholic and a civilian. He remained equally insistent that he would not, although he promised to "examine with an honest heart, and . . . to believe, if possible, the doctrines" of Catholicism. But he found "the doctrinal differences between the several creeds" incomprehensible and labeled each of the religious writers he read a "better Rhetorician and Special pleader than a Christian." He especially disliked Orestes Brownson, the learned convert to Catholicism and Ellen's favorite, calling him a flighty eccentric taken up with whatever cause or idea was in vogue. Sherman refused to embrace Ellen's religion, hoping a face-to-face discussion and "a just liberality" would later solve the problem.[54]

Sherman also refused to resign his military commission. He expected Ellen, as his wife, to follow him wherever duty called. He had wrestled with this issue throughout his military career, but he had always come back to the same conclusion: He could not make a living outside the army. He remained ambivalent, however. When his foster brother, Hugh Boyle Ewing, became interested in West Point, Sherman encouraged him, to the point of angering his foster father. Yet he also told Boyle that he "often regretted" that Thomas Ewing had not provided him with "some useful trade or business" instead of sending him to the military academy. Once too he told his brother John that the main advantage of remaining in the army was security. He felt financially and psychologically secure in the army despite its many other shortcomings.[55]

Sherman beseeched Ellen to keep an open mind, suggesting she spend a year at Moultrie to see garrison life at first hand. At the same time, he demonstrated his own willingness to compromise and began studying the law. He had no problem understanding legal principles but considered himself too poor a public speaker to become a lawyer, having "almost a contempt for the bombast and stuff that form the chief constituents of modern oratory." He confided in Phil Ewing that he had "no idea of making the Law a profession" but could not bring himself to tell Ellen. In writing her, he would talk of the law and then almost in mid-sentence wish she would "see something of the army before it is rejected." He also wanted to respect her father's wishes, several times justifying himself to Thomas Ewing. Sherman did not want to leave the army, but he did not want to alienate his fiancée or his foster father either.[56]

Sherman remained convinced that he and Ellen could settle everything if they could talk things out in person. But he was in South Carolina, and she was in Ohio—their physical distance symbolic of their differences on key aspects of their future. He became so upset over the impasse that he developed a boil on his neck, mimicking Ellen's habitual affliction. Yet the fates intervened to bring the young couple together. On January 14, 1845, while hunting on a plantation near Fort Moultrie, Sherman was thrown from his horse and dislocated his shoulder, providing him with an excuse to return home.[57]

His visit to Lancaster unfortunately made matters worse. Ellen remained determined about religion and the military and now added another condition: She refused to live anywhere but near her family in Lancaster. She coldly rejected his offer to leave the army and find "a residence far south of Ohio." Her attitude "checked the fluency of . . . [his] pen." Each time he tried to write, he ended up destroying the letter. It took him five months to express the agony he felt over the impasse.

He was still willing to compromise. He proposed taking a long leave the following spring, go into northern Alabama, and see if he could make a living there as a surveyor. If he was successful, he would complete his law studies and then resign his commission. It was all very hazardous, of course, but he was "willing to take a risk for her sake." But he still wished she would join him in the army.

As he penned page after page of the letter, his torment grew increasingly evident. He wanted to please her yet could not accept her uncompromising demands. He remained convinced he was "perfect[ly] dependent" on the army "for a living." Even if he could do anything else, he would have to start at the bottom, losing ten years' seniority and experience in the process. He needed a steady income and was determined to earn one on his own: "I shall never depend upon any body, nay not even my brother. I would rather earn my living by the labor of my own hands." The foster child would stand on his own two feet, no matter what it took, and he was convinced this meant the army. Any return to Ohio, as Ellen insisted, would mean a return to the care of his foster father, a prospect he could never accept and a fear Ellen could never understand.[58]

The anguish of the letter shocked Ellen, and she now proposed a compromise—of sorts. She suggested that Sherman consider East Tennessee because one of her favorite clerics, Bishop Richard Pius Miles, lived there. Sherman gently refused to plan his future around a bishop but also apologized for using "stronger language than necessary" in his previous letter. When Ellen offered to let him remain in the army until their marriage, he let the matter drop. Like the question of his religious faith, his disagreement with Ellen over his career and geographical location was temporarily put aside.[59]

Sherman continued to want to marry Ellen, but he was determined to live with her far away from Lancaster. He refused to consider any job in Ohio or any further help from Thomas Ewing. He would show his foster father he could be a success and independently support Ewing's beloved daughter. The foster son was declaring his independence, yet at the same time he was marrying a member of that family in order to cement his relationship with it.

Sherman's years in the South were critically formative for his future. The lesson he learned in the Seminole War, his first trip on the Mississippi River, his exploration of Georgia, his social ties to white Southerners, the intensification of his proslavery attitudes, his support for the Whig party, his opposition to nullification, his suspicion of Congress, and his religious and career difficulties within the context of his contemplated marriage: all would become major issues in the years ahead. For the time being, Sherman could put such thoughts aside. He was engaged, but there were no immediate matrimonial plans. His major concern during his fourth year at Fort Moultrie remained coping with his boredom. The impending Mexican War might provide the excitement and the professional experience that he felt he needed, but for the present there were only more parties to attend, more fish to catch, and more pictures to paint. Meanwhile, across the channel from Moultrie, work on Fort Sumter continued.

CHAPTER 3

——— ☆ ———

GOLD RUSH SOLDIER

WHEN SPRING CAME to South Carolina in 1846, "so little was stirring that a page a year would suffice for history," Sherman disgustedly wrote his brother. News of the progress of the American war against Mexico continued to drift in to Fort Moultrie, and Sherman itched to become part of it. It was bad enough to be bored in peacetime, but to suffer the same fate during a war was intolerable. He wrote the adjutant general in Washington asking for reassignment, the second time insisting that he was not after "more rank" but "a more active kind of life." He did not get combat duty, however; he was ordered to report to the recruiting service at Fort Columbus, Governor's Island, New York Harbor. He arrived there on May, 1, 1846, and Colonel Richard B. Mason, the superintendent, assigned him to Pittsburgh to forward recruits to Cincinnati for transport to the war. He was disappointed but still hoped he might somehow still see combat.[1]

The work in Pittsburgh was easy and hardly time-consuming. The recruiting station already had a sergeant, a corporal, several privates, and a civilian physician who did most of the work. Settled into the St. Charles Hotel, Sherman mostly read and socialized.[2]

One day a group of "one armed men with certificates of pensions in their pockets" came into the station to reenlist. As he completed their paperwork, he conversed with the only "sound one of the party" and learned that they were returning to the army because they had failed as civilians.[3] The encounter clearly upset him. Sound as he was, he was being kept out of the war while such cripples were going. This lack of combat experience might hurt his future military career and force him to become a civilian. Perhaps like these men, he too could not make it on the outside.

Other concerns underscored his anxiety. His mother's financial security continued to be worrisome. His sister Elizabeth, whose alcoholic husband was apparently suffering more business reverses, was another problem. Thomas Ewing's willingness to assist his mother did not help his disposition. He protested to a brother: "If we expect to hold our heads up at all, this should not be permitted. Mr. Ewing has done enough already, and I shall never feel easy so long as he is rendering a favor, though I know he does it with good will and pleasure."[4]

Sherman, as often happened when he was anxious, complained of "a little bilious feeling." He grew even more "intensely excited" when he learned of the Mexican War battles of Palo Alto and Resaca de la Palma. Here he was on recruiting service, "when my comrades were actually fighting." The feeling was "intolerable" and grew worse when he received a letter from an old West Point friend, E. O. C. Ord, urging him to apply for a position with Ord's Company F, Third Artillery, already under orders to go to California and the war. Sherman hesitated. He wanted to go to Mexico, not to California, but he had to do something. He wrote to the adjutant general of the army asking "for any active service."[5]

He did not wait for an answer. Instead he went to Cincinnati immediately to force his way into the war. He escorted a group of recruits, reporting to Colonel Alexander C. W. Fanning, the superintendent of western recruiting. The one-armed grizzled veteran officer demanded to know what Sherman was doing there. The army needed all the recruits it could get, Sherman replied, so he was ready to go on to the combat zone. Fanning became furious; "he cursed and swore," Sherman later remembered, and ordered him back to his post. Sherman admitted he had made the trip "without authority and I suppose wrongfully," but Fanning's tongue lashing crushed him anyway. He wrote his brother: "I feel that my efforts to get to Mexico must prove a failure for some time to come."[6]

When Sherman returned to Pittsburgh on June 29, 1846, after a brief stop in Lancaster, he found orders assigning him to Company F and California. He learned in a private letter from Ord that the unit was already in New York awaiting sea voyage around the horn to the Pacific Coast. Sherman panicked over the possibility of missing this one chance to get to the fighting. He worked far into the night to complete all his paperwork so he could leave the next morning.[7]

At dawn the next day he wrote a hasty letter to Ellen. "Ordered to California by Sea around Cape Horn, is not this enough to rouse the most placid?" He had not been able to pack properly and was upset about leaving without seeing his mother in Mansfield. "What will she think of me?" And what of Ellen herself? He was leaving her and going "upon a wild and long expedition without any token, any memento save a small lock of hair." They were going to be totally cut off from each other. "I'm glad I didn't know of this when in Lancaster," he concluded, "for I should have made a fool of myself. Even here the tears start at the thought of the trouble my wayward life has already given you. . . . You will think of me will you not? but you can not answer, farewell Ellen."[8]

Sherman reached New York City on July 2, 1846, and discovered to his relief that his ship was not scheduled to sail for another two weeks. Army authorities gave him permission to stay with his relatives in Brooklyn, so he had time to prepare for what he hoped would be "an expedition of a novel & grand nature." Shrewdly he wrote his congressman for maps and documents on California, hoping he would "not be lost sight of and be permitted to wear out a life in such subordinate capacity" in "a distant country far from communication with Government or friends."[9]

On Monday evening July 13, a steamboat ferried Sherman's party to the U.S. naval vessel, *Lexington*. There were 113 men and 5 officers in Company F of the Third Artillery. The officers, like Sherman, were all West Pointers: Lucien Loeser, Colville J. Minor, E. O. C. Ord, and Christopher Q. Tompkins. Henry W. Halleck of the Engineers and a civilian physician, Dr. James L. Ord, were also along. Most of the enlisted men were of Irish and German stock, recently recruited in Pennsylvania and Maryland for five years' service.[10]

Winfield Scott, the army's general in chief, had given Captain Tompkins, the expedition's commanding officer, an oral and a written briefing ordering him to cooperate with the navy against Mexican possessions on the Pacific Coast, at either Monterey or San Francisco Bay.[11] Company F was going to California because of the war with Mexico, but its precise destination and its duties upon arrival were left undefined. Sherman craved purpose and certitude, and this expedition contained little of that.

His last letter to Ellen just before sailing revealed his personal life to be as uncertain as his military one. By the time he returned from California, he argued, he would be too old to begin a new career. He would have no choice but to remain in the military. He wanted her to share in the excitement he felt and in his belief that the army was his true place. It was exhilarating to "precede the flow of population" to California "and become one of the pillars of the land," he said. He also planned to go to the Sandwich Islands (Hawaii), to Mexico, and to Europe. He would "see strange countries and peoples, live a strange life." The future would just have to "take care of itself." This was as he wanted it and he only wished she would give his California adventure, and his career, her approval.[12]

As Sherman's personal and professional obligations continued to battle within him, the *Lexington* raised its sails and entered the Atlantic Ocean, each puff of wind taking him further away from civilian life and from Ellen. He was in an all-military world, familiar and reassuring despite the unresolved issues of his future.

His home for the next six months was the *Lexington,* a sloop of war originally constructed in 1826 to carry twenty guns. She had proved too slow (11.5 knots) for battle and had been converted into a store ship in 1843 but still carried six guns for defense. She was 127 feet long with a beam (width) of approximately 38 feet. There were three levels: the spar or upper deck, the berth deck, and the cargo hold below. The berth deck was Sherman's home. The front half provided sleeping areas for the 113 soldiers and 35 sailors. Sherman lived with the other officers in the wardroom, which he described as "a kind of passage way 15 feet broad" with four staterooms on each side. He shared a room with Edward Ord but entered it only to sleep. He spent most of his time on the upper deck or sitting around the mess table in the wardroom.[13]

The *Lexington* was understaffed, so the soldiers were divided into four watches and took turns helping the sailors. The soldiers labored on the deck, while the sailors worked the rigging. Sherman commanded one of the watches. He never became seasick but did worry about consumption, experiencing "a heavy feeling" in his chest, no doubt caused by his heavy cigar smoking and a chronic asthma that would plague him for the rest of his life.[14]

Sherman kept himself occupied writing letter after long letter to Ellen, relatives, and friends. Then he spent hours searching the horizon for a ship to take the mail back to the United States. When not writing letters, he devoured every book on board. Because of his haste in leaving Pittsburgh, the only volume he had with him was Vattel's *Law of Nations,* not a bad choice for a voyage through international waters on the way to a war. The other officers had brought along more extensive libraries, so he read Shakespeare, Dickens, Washington Irving, and travel books like Charles Wilkes's *Narrative of the United States Exploring Expedition* and Richard Henry Dana's *Two Years Before the Mast.* He read and reread every available book about California, to prepare for his entry into that new land.[15]

The use Henry W. Halleck made of his time particularly impressed Sherman. Halleck had recently published his *Elements of Military Art and Science* and earned his "Old Brains" nickname as a result. On board ship, Halleck used every spare moment to read. "When others were struggling to kill time," Sherman remembered, "he was using it in hard study. When the sea was high & ship rolling, the sky darkened so that daylight did not reach his state room, he stood on a stool, his book and candle on the upper berth and a bed strap round his middle secured to the frame to support him in the wild tossing of the ship." His shipmates marveled at his persistence.[16]

Every day at 8 A.M. Sherman and the other officers ate breakfast, and every afternoon at 4 P.M. they had dinner. There was little variety. Breakfast consisted of tea or coffee, hardtack biscuit and butter, cold ham or tongue, and occasionally boiled rice or hominy. Dinner was hot or cold ham, boiled rice, boiled corn beef, chicken or pea soup, dried apple pie, or a boiled dough raisin pudding. (Live pigs and chickens were kept on board to supply these meals.) The daily water ration was one gallon per person.[17]

In his berth at night, Sherman listened "to the creaking of the timbers," wondering how it was possible for anyone to build a ship strong enough to withstand the ocean's constant pounding. Sometimes, scratching and pulling on his closely cropped beard, he debated with himself about proper behavior in case of a wreck. Would it be better "to run on deck and try the chance of a floating spar, or like the monkey clasp my head and go down without a struggle?" No one on board dared show any fear, he confided to Ellen, and if anyone said a prayer, he was ridiculed. So Sherman remained outwardly calm; he tried to deal with his fears alone in his berth away from the eyes of his equally fearful colleagues.[18]

Death was an ever-present danger throughout the long voyage. Shipwrecks were a regular fact of ocean life, and the *Lexington* had the bad fortune to encounter several ship-threatening storms. Sailing around Cape Horn took twenty-six days due to the worst gales and ice storms that the ship's most grizzled sailors had ever seen. Icicles formed on the spar deck. Sherman caught a bad cold, and his fingers grew so stiff he could scarcely hold a pen. Yet he went on deck, curious to see how the ship withstood these uncompromising elements. He learned enough to believe he could bring a ship safely into port if he had to, but his experience at Cape Horn "convinced him that the army is better than the navy, and land a better element to operate on than water."[19]

Always an avid hunter, Sherman discovered a new way to enjoy his favorite sport. Near Cape Horn, albatross and sea pigeons were numerous and pounced down on the deck to scavenge loose pieces of food. Much to the superstitious sailors' disgust, some of the army officers baited fishing line with pork, dropped it on the deck, and then reeled in unsuspecting fowl. The sailors blamed such albatross hookings for the terrible storms around the horn, expressing the theme of Coleridge's mariner. Sherman enjoyed bird fishing too much to worry about any ocean curse. "I don't know when I have had a more hearty laugh than at the simple idea of fishing for birds," he chortled.[20]

When the *Lexington* crossed the equator, her wartime status prevented the usual initiation rite for those crossing the line for the first time. The captain still had Sherman place his hand on a "holy stone" (a hard stone used for scraping the deck), anointed him with sea water, and made him take a humorous oath to behave always "like a true son of Neptune." Sherman eagerly repeated the ritual on the other officers, "taking good care . . . to baptize them well in salt water." It was all done in humor, but it was a ceremony of togetherness, like the stag dance at West Point, a ceremony of the oneness he felt with his fellow army officers. He could not accept Ellen's religion, the one he had been baptized into as a child, or the civilian life he associated with it, but he readily participated in a baptism that tied him closer to his military mates.[21]

Military discipline on board ship was critical and its violation punished. One of the crew, a black steward, was caught with some brandy from the wardroom. Everyone was called on deck; the ship's lieutenant read the captain's punishment; and the steward was stripped and his hands tied to the gangway. The boatswain mate whipped him severely with a cat-o'-nine-tails. Sherman watched impassively, accepting this aspect of his military life as much as all the others.[22]

Sherman's excitement on reaching land found its way into his description of the ship's entry into Rio in September 1846: "Words will not describe the beauty of this perfect harbor, nor the delightful feeling after so long a voyage of its fragrant airs." As they passed the forts guarding the harbor's entrance, Sherman noted what he called "the entire contrast between all things there and what he had left in New York." The ship was greeted in Portuguese, and the *Lexington*'s officer of the deck "answered back in gibberish, according to a well understood custom of the place."[23]

Many other U.S. warships were already in the harbor, and the *Lexington*'s passengers were soon commiserating with other Americans about being "in a land of plenty and sunshine whilst others engaged in war." Sherman, Halleck, Minor, the Ord brothers, and one of the naval officers eagerly went into the city to see the sights. For the next week when he was not on duty, Sherman explored the port city, tasting its food, visiting its churches, going to its opera and theater, gaping at its people, and trying to evaluate what it all meant. His curiosity about other milieus was insatiable.[24] He had exhibited such feelings since his childhood, an indication of his search for a sure family and home. He would travel constantly all his life, trying to find the certitude that kept evading him. If he kept traveling and kept searching, perhaps he would find what he so needed—a sense of belonging to something permanent.

After being cooped up on ship for several months, Sherman showed a special interest in the city's women and its food. The first day he toured the city's main street, "as much to see the pretty girls as the flowers which they so skillfully made" out of the shells, silks and feathers. He ate dinner at the famous Hotel Pharoux and gorged on steak, potatoes, omelet, oranges, bananas, ice cream, ice liquor, coffee, and "fruits of every variety and excellence, such as we had never seen before or even knew the names of." As far as the women of the city were concerned, Sherman wrote home, he never went beyond looking. He exhibited a strong streak of prudishness that made it difficult for him to consider sampling any of the city's pleasures except the food.[25]

Sherman visited churches, more for Ellen's sake than for his own. He was impressed with their architecture, paintings, and statuary rather than with any spirituality they might provide. He discovered a small church and found two black priests leading a small black and Indian congregation, mostly women, sitting on the floor in front of the altar, "more like squaws than good Christians." Later he visited the monastery of Santo Bento, and he again noted the beautiful gilded altars and the many paintings. He did not use these occasions to say prayers, as Ellen in her letters had urged.[26]

Much more interesting to him was a tour he made with Halleck to the top of the highest mountain overlooking the city. He found the view beautiful, but he was even more taken with the workings of the aqueduct, which guided water down the mountain to the people below. He and Halleck, both with engineering backgrounds, minutely examined this waterway, walking along most of its length and marveling at its efficiency. Sherman tried to learn everything, examine it, experience it.[27]

The only aspect of Rio Sherman disliked was the status of blacks. They seemed to be able "to attain all ranks in society, though slavery in its worst form" was "practiced openly." He saw large numbers of slaves carrying bundles on their heads while singing African chants. But he also saw black priests, black lawyers, and black theatergoers. He viewed such black status with stunned disbelief and displeasure. He believed blacks should be slaves; their inferiority precluded them from equality with whites. He might have been born in free Ohio, but he held the proslavery views of his foster father.[28]

In Rio, Sherman learned that the United States was determined to take northern Mexico "regardless of the principles involved." He surmised that such was "pretty much the truth" as he understood it. After the harrying trip around Cape Horn, they met a ship with news that all the fighting in California was over; The navy had already captured all the towns. On arrival he and his army unit would have nothing to do there but fortify some selected spot like Monterey or San Francisco. "No fighting," he worried. "That's too bad after coming so far."[29] The voyage seemed to symbolize his life. He was traveling south to reach the northwest, and when he arrived there, his reason for traveling had vanished. Similarly, he believed, he was getting nowhere just as slowly in his life and career.

At Valparaiso, Chile, Sherman again disembarked. He was disappointed to see that the Chilean city was not as naturally beautiful as Rio but explored it thoroughly anyway. He was "impressed with the character" of the people, noting that, unlike Rio, there were no blacks doing the heavy labor; instead he found "a swarthy set of active fellows" who reminded him of the Seminoles he had seen in Florida. He noted too that there were no slums here because "free labor" did all the work. He did not like Indians, but he looked down on blacks even more, so he found the Indian quality of Chile preferable to the blackness of Brazil.[30]

The British influence in the city was strong. When he attended a hurdles race one day, most of the riders were British naval officers from some of the ships that stopped there regularly. He marveled at the British freedom to participate in athletics, contrasting it with the American military's disdain for such activities. The British encouraged sports and took part in them wherever they went. Sherman liked this side of their national psyche.[31]

Sherman did not know what to make of the "whores and whore dances" he encountered. He was amazed at how easy it was to procure a woman in Force and Main Tops, mountain suburbs just outside Valparaiso. When five soldiers deserted, he spent two days searching for them in the grog houses and sailors' boarding houses there. "Never did I see the exhibition of so much vice and iniquity," he told Ellen. If missionaries would only go there "instead of sowing dissension amongst so-called heathens, they would have stronger claims upon the Charity of the World." Despite the existence of all this sexual activity, Sherman judged the women uniformly unattractive and apparently availed himself of no female companionship—or so he wrote home.[32]

Sherman judged Valparaiso much more severely than he had

Rio. He was cranky all the time, the obvious result of being the only officer to receive no mail from home. He told Ellen he "consoled" himself by realizing that she and his other correspondents lived in the West and did not know sailing schedules. His brief encounter with an American midshipman from Lancaster who knew Ellen increased the homesickness. Sherman seemed to blame Valparaiso for his bad luck and left the city with little regret. Sherman continued to wrestle with his ambivalence about home: desiring to hold on to it, refusing to remain there.[33]

On January 25, 1847, someone finally sighted land, only to discover that a miscalculation had sent the ship forty miles past Monterey. Reversing course, the ship encountered more bad weather, much to Sherman's disgust. On January 26 the *Lexington* approached the harbor at Monterey. The night was pleasantly cool, softly moon lit, and misty. The eager passengers could barely discern the shore for the night fog, but they were able to make out rocky, forested hills in a half-circular land sweep around the port. Ominously, Monterey looked like Valparaiso. Sherman hoped that, upon landing, they would find orders for San Francisco and would soon be on their way again. Still, he immediately studied his surroundings and compared them to several of his maps. "Thank God," he exclaimed, "after 198 days at Sea we have got here." "I am in good health and spirits—ready for a fight."[34]

As the *Lexington* eased into Monterey Bay, a small boat approached to lead the ship into anchorage. Lieutenant Henry A. Wise, the master of the U.S. frigate *Independence,* climbed on board the *Lexington* and proved a storehouse of information. "He told us more news than we could have learned on shore in a week," Sherman marveled. Sherman and his colleagues had been correct in assuming that there were no organized Mexican forces to battle, but they had not known about some intramural American conflict.[35]

Events in California were more complicated than Americans warring against Mexicans. In 1846 American settlers had repudiated Mexican control and established the so-called Bear Flag republic. With the arrival of American naval vessels, however, the stars and stripes had replaced the Mexican eagle and the California grizzly bear. Army general Stephen W. Kearny battled with naval admiral Robert E. Stockton and army explorer John C. Frémont for overall command. Both Kearny and Stockton-

Frémont insisted that their orders gave each supremacy; they demanded that the other step aside. Stockton's sailors and marines and Frémont's California Battalion easily outnumbered Kearny and his company of dragoons, so he stalked off to San Diego to bide his time. The situation remained volatile.[36]

Lieutenant Wise's detailed account, no doubt embellished with gossip and rumors, excited the *Lexington*'s water-logged artillery soldiers. Captain Tompkins ordered full battle gear, and Company F, Third Artillery Regiment, landed and smartly marched through Monterey to its bivouac area on the hill beyond.[37]

The soldiers spent most of their first days inspecting their new home. There were about one thousand inhabitants, but the town hardly looked grand enough to be the capital of California or anywhere else. The few substantial houses were surrounded by numerous adobes of the poor. There was a church, but the most imposing structure in town was the two-story customs house, where Sherman, as unit quartermaster, established himself and the company supplies. The rest of the unit was quartered at the ramshackle fort, which was soon strengthened under Halleck's direction.[38]

The major topic of discussion in Sherman's circle was the army-navy disagreement. "Who the devil is Governor of California?" the officers asked each other. On February 8, 1847, Kearny came to Monterey to see Commodore W. Branford Shubrick, Stockton's recent replacement as navy commander, to try to solve the imbroglio. Despite the controversy between Kearny and Stockton-Frémont, army and navy officers remained friendly, with most blaming Frémont for the problems and considering him an interloper. The day of Kearny's arrival, Sherman was eating dinner with some navy friends on the *Independence*. He watched as a small boat brought the old general on board. Kearny sat grimly in the dingy, wearing his old dragoon's coat and an army cap to which he "had added the broad visor cut from a full dress hat," an alteration he had made to protect himself from the desert sun during his overland trek to California. One of the naval officers, seeing Kearny's attire, wisecracked: "Fellows, the problem is solved: there is the Grand Vizier (visor) by G-d. *He* is the Governor of California."[39]

The facetious naval officer proved correct. After Kearny and Shubrick closeted themselves, Frémont's days were numbered.

Kearny sailed off to San Francisco to meet the recently arrived Colonel Richard B. Mason, carrying orders from Winfield Scott. These orders, dated November 6, 1846, gave Kearny command in California. Later-arriving naval orders agreed, and army reinforcements strengthened Kearny's hand. A Mormon battalion arrived in San Diego, and J. D. Stevenson's New York Volunteer Regiment landed in San Francisco. These troops plus Kearny's company of First Dragoons and Sherman's Company F far outnumbered Fremont's California Battalion. Kearny assigned troops to key locations around the territory and then ordered Frémont to disband his force and report to Monterey. Frémont refused, much to Sherman's disgust and the chagrin of other military officers. In all fairness, Kearny never told Frémont of the new orders, not even when he sent one of his aides, Henry S. Turner, to see him. Frémont continued to believe that Kearny was bluffing. When he came to Monterey and learned about the new orders, he immediately offered to resign. Kearny demanded his obedience. Frémont capitulated, and Kearny indeed became the "vizier" of California.[40]

Sherman had heard much about Frémont and had even consulted his maps, so he was anxious to meet this famous man when Frémont came to Monterey. Sherman rode out to the conical tent just outside town where Frémont was staying. He spent an hour at tea and "left without being much impressed." He never mentioned the visit anywhere except in his memoirs.[41]

Kearny, unlike Frémont, was the epitome of army professionalism, and he made a deeper impression on Sherman. Despite his "reputation of being a stern, exacting Commander," Sherman always remembered him as "almost paternal," a significant characteristic for the foster child to describe in his commander. He particularly recalled that Kearny caused him to shave his beard for the only time in his life. The veteran officer told Cump softly one day: "Lieut. Sherman I have lent my razors to Capt. Turner— when he is done with them he will give them to you." Until Kearny returned east, Sherman took the hint, and he shaved regularly, "though with my tender skin and wiry beard," he said, "it was a painful operation." Army discipline had something to do with it, of course, but filial obedience played a role too. Sherman wanted Kearny to accept him, so he did what he was told, even though it hurt.[42]

Soon after, Kearny left military and civilian control over the Tenth Military District, as the area was now designated, to Richard B. Mason and returned east to deliver Frémont for eventual court-martial. Mason had a reputation for being "harsh and severe," Sherman remembering him as the recruiting commander who had ordered him to Pittsburgh. At first, Sherman worried about Mason's unsmiling bluntness, especially when Mason named him his adjutant. Soon, however, he found the colonel to be "kind and agreeable," another paternal figure. He particularly enjoyed hearing Mason's hunting stories and tales about prominent people like Winfield Scott and Zachary Taylor. His natural father had always been too busy to do that. Sherman was soon happy at his adjutant post, hoping it put him in "a good and conspicuous position" should any fighting break out.[43]

"Fighting seems no longer to be thought of" in California, despite the continued hostilities in Mexico, Sherman soon discovered, and the U.S. Army had little to do. Some native Californians wanted to revolt, but they had no one to follow nor were there any obvious pretenders on the horizon. In April 1847 Sherman discovered that several of his soldiers had tapped unguarded barrels of rum illegally placed on the wharf, so he had the illicit liquor dumped into the bay. When the purchaser complained to Kearny about the loss of his property, Kearny only laughed about Sherman's "making a 'Punch bowl' of the harbor." After that, the bay was routinely referred to as "Sherman's Punch Bowl."[44]

Sherman lived with Doña Augustias de la Guerra Jimeno Casarin and her family, and he became friends with many Monterey residents. He happily explored his surroundings and studied the populace, noting the combination of Americans, Mexicans, and Indians among Monterey's population, with poor Christianized Indians in the majority. A dozen or so men used the title "Don," dressed in colorful clothes, and lived in splendid two-story adobes, but most people were poor. The women were all generally unattractive, he wrote home; the few with any beauty "scorned the vulgar accomplishments of reading and writing" in favor of dancing. During the carnival season, Sherman attended many fandangos, and the Mexican custom of breaking eggshells filled with perfume and gold leaf spangles over the heads of favored members of the opposite sex intrigued him. Several times he arrived home at dawn doused with cologne. He continued to insist, however, that he had no interest in any woman but Ellen.[45]

When a nine-year-old girl died and her body was borne through the city to the accompaniment of a raucous crowd of mourners, a gaily performing band, and gunfire from surrounding houses, Sherman and the other soldiers joined in, firing "a perfect salvo of rejoicing that the child had gone to heaven." The ceremony seemed "peculiar and strange" to him but much more reasonable than the American custom of mourning for a year. When he died, he wrote to Ellen, he did not want his friends "to weep my exit or let it detain them one minute from any occupation or pleasure."[46]

For Ellen's sake, he investigated the local Catholic church, noting that although the town's people were pleased to see so many of Company F's soldiers attending Mass, most of the local congregation were women. The men belonged until they married because the law required it but afterward stayed away. It made sense to Sherman, the baptized but nonpracticing Catholic.[47]

Sherman and Ord spent part of that first month in California exploring the countryside some distance out of Monterey. They visited the outlying ranch of one of the city's dons, and while enjoying a cooked rabbit dish, Sherman bit down on a red pepper and thought his mouth was filled with "liquid fire." They visited the Mission of San Juan Bautista, some thirty-five miles out, where Ord attended Mass, and Sherman, "being somewhat infidel and suspicious, stood at the door, carbine in hand." That night the two men saw firsthand the poverty of the region when they stayed in a rude mud hut and shared the people's slim repast. The experience only convinced Sherman that Americans were correct in waging war against the Mexicans. The Californians "had not done justice to the Country and by Law of nature it has passed into hands more enterprising if not more honest and happy."[48]

Sherman traveled a good deal with Mason as the military governor regularly toured California to monitor what was technically still a war zone. Sometimes this meant camping out and eating whatever food was in their saddle bags; other times Sherman "came in for a share of the pomp and feasting" his commander received. California remained at peace, and Mason's tours were for the sake of intelligence and public relations rather than to direct any troop movements. Rumors of uprisings cropped up regularly, but they always proved to be the figments of fertile American and Californian imaginations. Life developed a tranquil sameness.[49]

Sherman participated in only one incident that vaguely resembled a military operation, and although there was a comic-opera nature to the incident, it showed clearly how eager Sherman was to enforce law and order. In Sonoma, there was an alcalde (chief governmental officer) whom Kearny had ordered deposed because of his election under the old Stockton-Frémont government. Alcalde John H. Nash refused to give up his office, however, insisting that he had been properly elected. Sherman believed that California was under military law and the democratically elected Nash should make way for his military appointed replacement.

Nash unobtrusively held out for about three months, until early July 1847 when Mason decided to evict him. When the army officer on the spot, soon to resign his commission and settle in the community, politely refused to carry out Mason's order, Sherman jumped into the breach. He coordinated his operation with the navy and with eight sailors and a naval officer sneaked into Sonoma to capture Nash. He posted an armed sailor at each corner of the house where Nash was having dinner, banged on the door, and burst in. He and a naval officer, brandishing pistols, arrested Nash and frightened the protesting dinner host into silence. Sherman sailed Nash to Monterey where the old man, whom Sherman admitted he handled "pretty vigorously," arrived "half dead with sea sickness and fear." Nash gladly promised Mason he would make way for the newly appointed alcalde and was never heard from again. Sherman saw the incident as a victory for the preservation of law and order in California.[50]

The activity kept Sherman busy and generally contented, but there were problems. Mail was irregular; even when it did arrive, it was a half to a full year old. California's terrain was too "dry and barren," Sherman insisted, and most of it was unattractive. When some fellow officers offered him the chance to buy property in San Francisco, he thought they were insulting his intelligence: "I wouldn't give two countries of Ohio, Kentucky, or Tennessee for the whole of California." "California is a humbug," he wrote home; "you must not fear I'll take a fancy to it."[51]

By the fall of 1847, Sherman's disposition darkened. Lieutenant Colville J. Minor, one of his shipmates on the *Lexington,* died from what Sherman believed was the "filthiness," dirt, and flies of Monterey. He grew angry at civilians who, unlike the military, refused to act decisively against what they called thieving Indians and looked to the army instead. When the alcalde of San José made such a request, Sherman responded with a curt lecture on self-help. In a sentence that prophesied his later reputation, he wrote: "You tell the people of your District that if they catch indians [sic] in the act of stealing, or of attempting to steal their horse, they should shoot them."[52]

For the next half-year or so, Sherman sank into a more serious depressed state. In early November 1847, he lamented to Ellen: "I am so completely banished that I feel I am losing all hope, all elasticity of Spirits. I feel ten years older than I did when I sailed and, though my health is good, I do not feel that desire for the exercise that I formerly did." The work load as Mason's adjutant had grown staggering. Sherman spent all his time "bending over a table" until, he said, "my head aches almost to the busting." At the end of the day, he fell into bed. His life was in a distressing rut.[53]

Sherman's work load was not at the root of his depression; it was despair at ever getting into the war. He expressed his frustration repeatedly: "To hear of the war in Mexico and the brilliant deeds of the army," he rambled, "of my own regiment, and my own old associates, everyone of whom has honors gained and I out in California—banished from fame, from everything that is dear and no more prospect of ever getting back than one of the old adobe houses that mark a California ranch." Another time he made the same point in clipped tones: "There is nothing new here. No strange events, no hair breath escapes, no battles, no stirring parties, no nothing and this war will pass and I will have to blush and say I have not heard a hostile shot." Everywhere he turned, Sherman received reinforcement for his despair. Fellow officers at other California posts mirrored his frustration. Letters from friends in the Mexican combat zone did not help either, one even saying that Sherman was the only officer from the Third Artillery "to be deprived of the fighting."[54]

Although Sherman was concerned when Ellen wrote about her recurring health problems, he never felt that his appropriate place was at her side. If he had only gone to Mexico instead of California, he wrote, then he would have been closer, and at least they would have been able to correspond regularly. In Mexico he would have been winning the glory he needed to become a successful army officer, and he would have been in regular contact with Ellen and all his loved ones. He felt "perfectly banished" in California. As long as he stayed where he was, he saw no hope of getting into the war, and he knew he could not help her. He expressed more concern about the war than about Ellen.[55]

Even the arrival of the fabled Kit Carson did not help his outlook. Sherman expected to see an imposing figure but found instead "a small shouldered man, with reddish hair, freckled face and soft blue eyes, and nothing to indicate extraordinary courage and daring." Carson's generally withdrawn nature also proved disappointing.[56]

In late spring 1848, messengers arrived from Johann Augustus Sutter, a large California landowner. As territorial military governor, Mason routinely saw many civilians, so it was nothing special for Sherman to usher men into his commander's office. A short time later, Mason summoned him in. The colonel pointed to some ore on top of the papers strewn on his desk and asked: "What is that?" Sherman looked the ore over and asked, "Is it gold?" Had Sherman ever seen gold before? Mason inquired. Yes he had, Sherman answered; he had seen some in north Georgia in 1843.

Sherman called out to his clerk to bring him an ax and a hatchet, meanwhile testing a piece of the stone with his teeth and trying to recall what he had learned in his mineralogy course at West Point. Using the tools the clerk brought in, Sherman beat a piece of the metal flat. There was no doubt about it; it was gold. Yet no one became particularly excited. At the time, Sherman later remembered, "far more importance was attached to quick silver than to gold."

Mason showed Sherman a letter from Sutter telling how James W. Marshall, a former member of Frémont's California battalion, had discovered gold while building a sawmill for Sutter on the American Fork River, some forty miles above Sutter's New Helvetia fort. Sutter wanted preemption to this land, based on some Indian claims he had previously acquired. Mason told Sherman to write Sutter that the United States did not recognize Indian land rights, but until the Mexican War was over, nothing could be done anyway. Besides, Mason counseled (in what was to be an egregious error), no one would trespass on this land.

Sherman wrote the letter; Mason signed it; the two messengers took it back to Sutter; and Sherman went back to his work. It was not until later that he realized that "that gold was the *first* discovered in the Sierra Nevada" and "soon revolutionized the whole country and actually moved the civilized world."[57]

When news reached Monterey "of fabulous discoveries" of gold, the countryside reverberated with excitement. Civilians began flocking to the site of the sawmill, and soldiers deserted to join them. As it published its last issue (for want of help), *The Californian* of San Francisco editorialized: "The whole country from San Francisco to Los Angeles, and from the sea shore to the base of the Sierra Nevada, resounds with the sordid cry of gold! GOLD!! *GOLD!!!*—while the field is left half planted, the house half built, and every thing neglected, but the manufacture of shovels and pickaxes, and the means of transportation to the spot." "The town is deserted," fellow army officer Joseph A. Folsom wrote from San Francisco. "Nothing like useful occupation is known. Mechanics and others have flown to the regions of the blest in one unmingled mass."[58]

Sherman did "not escape the infection" himself. The prospect of wealth excited him, and he jumped at the chance for some adventure. "At last," he wrote in his memoirs, "I convinced Col. Mason that it was our duty to go up and see with our own eyes that we might report the truth to our Government." Sherman had to learn firsthand just what it was that was stirring people this much.[59]

On Mason's orders, Sherman prepared an expedition: Mason, four trusted soldiers, and Mason's black servant, Aaron. They departed from Monterey on June 17, 1848, and when they arrived in San Francisco three days later, they "found that all or nearly all the male inhabitants had gone to the mines." Pushing on, they arrived in Johann Sutter's New Helvetia, which stood three miles from the Sacramento River and a mile from the American Fork. Unlike the rest of the countryside, where "mills were lying idle, fields of wheat were open to cattle and horses, houses vacant, and farms going to waste," New Helvetia was teeming with life.

Sherman, Mason, and party arrived in time for the first Fourth of July celebration ever held in Sutter's empire. The Swiss entrepreneur had arrived in California in 1838 with nothing but his considerable talents and had built up his inland empire through Mexican land grants and by supplying food and other necessities to American migrants crossing the Sierra Nevada into California. He had a reputation for fairness and generosity among the migrants and the Indians with whom he traded. Sherman liked him immediately and thoroughly enjoyed the big bash Sutter threw to celebrate American Independence Day (and to ingratiate himself with his new masters). The food was plentiful, and the champagne, sherry, brandy, sauterne, and madeira flowed liberally. Sherman estimated that the banquet must have cost two thousand dollars.

The expedition left Sutter on July 5, 1848, and traveled twenty-five miles up the American Fork to the so-called Mormon diggings. The hills on both sides were covered with canvas tents and shanties, and more than two hundred men stood in the icy cold water "washing for gold," some with tin pans, others with closely woven blankets. It took four men to operate a rude machine, actually a sifter, known as "the cradle." As soon as word spread of the military governor's arrival, men flocked around him to tell their stories, illustrating their words with profuse samples of the golden metal.

After several days, the party moved another twenty-five miles up the American Fork to the unfinished sawmill. Sutter and Marshall had staked their claims, and only a few miners dared to venture there. Next, the expedition traveled to inspect the so-called dry diggings in the mountains to the left and right of the American Fork where mining activity was heavy. (In all, Sherman estimated that the party saw four thousand men extracting about fifty thousand dollars' worth of gold a day.)

Miners and gold seemed everywhere. Tents dotted the countryside; the sound of men shaking gravel and splashing cold water filled the hills and valleys. Sherman found this phenomenal sight exhilarating. His depression disappeared as his senses filled with new scenes and excited people. Gold improved Sherman's depressed outlook as it would soon excite the entire world.

The party made its way back to Monterey, "all the way giving official sanction to the news from the gold mines and adding new force to the fever." All over California, the frenzy grew; soldiers deserted not only one by one but also in groups; so many sailors left their ships that many vessels were unable to sail. Even more farmers abandoned their crop. Inflation became a problem and fed the frenzy. Sherman's salary began to look smaller and smaller.[60]

The gold rush posed enormous problems for Mason and his adjutant. And when they reached Monterey, they learned the Mexican War was over; California now officially belonged to the United States. The war's end meant that the volunteer troops had to be discharged, and this left only two regular companies, themselves hard hit with gold field desertions. Military power in California was disappearing just when its presence was needed to maintain order. "All the women of the lower country may be ravished & killed," Sherman lamented, "horses stolen & houses burnt & you couldn't get a dozen men to leave the Gold district to go to their aid."[61]

With peace, Mason no longer had any legal basis for military government, yet Sherman saw no other way to maintain order. He agreed with Mason that "the democracy" was too obsessed with gold to object but worried that, once they had filled their pockets, they would "join in the hue and cry of military usurpation." "Colonel Mason will be black guarded in Congress for a Military Despot and Usurper, and those damned curs in Washington will not step in to shield him."[62]

The uncertainty and lack of rule upset Sherman. Mason was doing the right thing, but he might very well be ruining his military career (and Sherman's too) by his actions. Sherman feared the emerging anarchy. It threatened the public order and his career as well. Once more, he found himself at the mercy of larger, uncontrollable forces that would shape his future. California needed order if it was to prosper, and it was up to the army to provide it; civilians certainly could not. Similarly his own life, so full of turmoil since his father's death, needed that same order, and once again the army was his only hope. Order and the military: they were the anchors of his life.

Sherman opposed the peace treaty ending the Mexican War because it did "not impress the Mexican with respect for us" and thus did not guarantee continued future order. Instead of letting them off so easily, Sherman insisted, the United States should have "burned their capital, blown up San Juan d' Alloa, [and] knocked down Mazatlan" as a way of indicting "the obstinate pride, egotism, and nonsense that characterized them as a people." In short, Sherman called for psychological and total war against the

Mexicans. He expressed concepts he had learned in Florida and would later put into practice in the Civil War. He had little tolerance for those who did not acknowledge the rightful bearers of law and order. Such people needed severe lessons to teach them respect and obedience. Military force was the only agent of order, and the nation should not shrink from using it.

Anxious and angry over the inadequacy of the peace treaty, Sherman grew increasingly upset over the impact of inflation on his salary. "The dirtyest [sic] run away nigger can get three times my salary," he complained. Ordinary soldiers could themselves run away, but as an officer, he was honor bound to stay, though "honor and poverty" were becoming "well mixed." His own clerk deserted him and left him bound to his desk, knowing his salary was losing its value while others found wealth and adventure.[63]

Sherman composed the letter and map Mason sent with gold specimens to Washington announcing the discovery of gold. Sherman's words were read, reprinted, mulled over, and acted upon. What particularly stirred the national imagination was the assertion that "the only apprehension [in the gold fields] seemed to be that the metal would be found in such abundance as seriously to depreciate in value." Approximately eighty thousand Forty Niners crowded into California to share the riches. Unfortunately Sherman's personal letters to his brother John encouraging the shipment of salable merchandise from Ohio to California did not have the same effect. Every day, it seemed, Sherman's economic situation worsened. He thought he might have to leave the army, but he knew he had to stay in. "Was I free at this minute, I could improve my condition and prospect in life much," he said, but at the same time he wondered what would become of him if he was caught in a postwar army cutback. He felt powerless.[64]

A second trip to the gold area in September 1848 lifted Sherman's spirits once again. He, Mason, and Lieutenant William H. Warner each invested $500 to start a store in the gold district at Coloma, with Warner's clerk, Norman S. Bestor, the proprietor. They tried to make it appear that Bestor was the sole owner because rumors were afloat that Mason was illegally providing government rations and equipment for the store. Apparently the business existed only from the fall of 1848 to the spring of 1849, but it proved profitable to the investors. Warner records a payment of $496.60 to Sherman but does not say whether this was part of Sherman's share of the profits. In his memoirs, Sherman said each of the partners made a profit of $1,500 on their $500 investment, but he provided no detailed financial data.

Government rations were the source of the store's merchandise, but this was legal. Mason had substituted rations for currency as pay for all the soldiers and had authorized the sale of anything that was not personally consumed. Still, the store's partners tried to camouflage what they were selling. Perhaps rations over and above the allotted number were being sold in the store. At the least, the partners' reticence indicates their concern about appearances, even if no illegality was involved.[65]

The spring of 1849 saw several important changes in Sherman's life. A monthly mail service by steamer ship was inaugurated, so Sherman now felt less isolated. It was typical of Sherman's energy when motivated that he rowed to meet the ship's arrival a mile out in Monterey Bay. On the negative side, General Persifer F. Smith arrived to replace Mason, but Sherman's attempt to return to the East failed. Sherman was disappointed but agreed to move to San Francisco with his new boss. He was sorry to see "Old Richard the 1st," as he jokingly called Mason, leave. He was also sorry to leave behind Doña Augustias de la Guerra Jimeno Casarin and her family, having enjoyed boarding with them. (He had even gained a Spanish nickname: "Castanares.")[66]

Sherman set up his new adjutant's office in the San Francisco Customs House, while living in the old Hudson Bay Company building on Montgomery Street. He hated the city—both the high prices and the living conditions. That first winter, the mud was so deep that mules that stumbled in it sometimes drowned. (A jokester put up a sign on one street: "This street is impassable, not even jackassable.") Flimsy houses were thrown up at outrageous prices, and even the cheapest whisky sold at "two bits a drink." Smith became so financially discouraged that he sent his wife home and told Sherman to move division headquarters into the field at Sonoma. Sherman's store profits were the only thing keeping his personal finances afloat.[67]

He was once again in turmoil: He felt his "hopes in life are all destroyed." Letters from home, now more frequent, added to his burden. Ellen repeatedly wrote of her health problems, particularly boils on the neck, including one, she said, that extended from neck to ear to part of a cheek. In two separate letters, she even told Sherman to marry someone else because her own health was too weak for marriage. Find a young girl, the twenty-five-year-old Ellen advised. Sherman, who was beginning to have problems with asthma, would hear none of it. He told her: "My love for you has never abated, never wavered in the least and upon it you may constantly rely." The army was Sherman's family, but Ellen's constancy was the ballast in his life, even if it was experienced only at a distance.[68]

Once again a military sortie invigorated his spirit. Twenty-eight men from the newly arrived Second Infantry Regiment deserted for the gold mines, and Sherman, visiting Monterey on business, led the pursuers. Six men were captured almost immediately, and by dawn Sherman was leading the pursuit across the Salinas River onto the plain. Ahead was an old adobe ranch house next to a pond. Sherman broke into a gallop as soon as he saw several deserters standing near the water. Familiar with the terrain because it was a favorite hunting spot, Sherman dashed toward the pond and ordered the two men into the house. Dismounting, he walked in on the rest and had them all lined up in ranks by the time the rest of the search party arrived.[69]

The battle of the deserters was over. Along with the capture of Alcalde Nash, this was Sherman's only "military" activity in California. Once again, Sherman demonstrated he had courage, aggressiveness, and boldness in time of stress. He felt proud of himself, happy with the opportunity to test his mettle, even if it was not a real combat.

Once he had established the new headquarters in Sonoma, Sherman received a two-month furlough. Beginning on May 15, 1849, he took several surveying jobs, sounding the bay for General Smith and later marking the boundary between the city of Benicia and Smith's headquarters. The former commander of the disbanded New York Volunteers, J. D. Stevenson, hired Sherman to mark off a projected "New York of the Pacific," paying surveyors $500 plus ten to fifteen lots in the projected city. Sherman sold some of his lots but was stuck with the rest when the speculative venture collapsed. He concocted a land scheme of his own for the Coloma area, but nothing came of it, so he took a job from Johann Sutter, surveying the area between the San Joaquin River and the Sierra Nevada. He also bought and sold lots in Sacramento. In all, he was $6,000 richer for his two-month effort.[70]

He was shocked and frustrated to read in a newspaper that Mason, now back in Washington, had been promoted to brigadier general. He was happy for his old commander but felt disgraced that he had not received a promotion at the same time. After all, he had been Mason's adjutant for two years and should have shared in Mason's good fortune. "Self respect compels me therefore to quit the Profession which in time of war and trouble I have failed to merit." The fear that had followed him throughout the war became a reality. His time in California away from the battlefields had prevented his promotion, he was convinced, and his place in the army was threatened. He told General Smith of his despair, and the veteran officer promised him a trip east to deliver dispatches if only he stayed in the service. Sherman reluctantly agreed.[71]

While he waited for the necessary dispatches to be gathered from the far-flung district, Sherman attended the California constitutional convention as Smith's observer. He characterized the proceedings' politics negatively. There was too much "scheming for office," he said. The only interesting part was the mild debate over slavery. There were so few slaves in the territory, however, that the issue was not a major one.[72]

Sherman also helped organize a survey of the Sierra Nevada for a possible railroad route and was later horrified to learn that hostile Indians had killed his friend Warner as he was carrying out the survey. Sherman immediately wanted revenge against the guilty parties, but the onset of winter prevented any action.[73]

For the remainder of the year, Sherman stayed in the Sacramento area helping friends, including his foster brother, Hugh Boyle Ewing, among the ever-larger group of eastern migrants. Family and friends had long considered Sherman the resident gold expert, and he regularly received letters asking for advice. A Rochester, New York, newspaper and probably others published a bogus advertisement listing his endorsement of a so-called magnetic goldmeter. For his part, Sherman was impressed with the men, women, and children who made the difficult trek to California. Later he cited them as one of the inspirations for his Civil War marches. If they could make it across several thousand miles of wild country, he said, his better-equipped army could make it through several hundred miles of Georgia and Carolina farms and cities.[74]

In December 1849 the dispatches Sherman was to take to Commanding General Winfield Scott in New York City finally arrived. Joe Hooker and Irvin McDowell signed his orders, and he excitedly hurried back to Monterey to say goodby to his friends. On January 1, 1850, he enjoyed a final dinner at Doña Augustia's house, complete with wine, cigars, and cigarettes, both men and women indulging. The next day, with two of the doña's sons in tow for delivery to Georgetown College in Washington, and with E. O. C. Ord, and California's two new senators, William M. Gwin and the irrepressible John C. Frémont, along, Sherman left California aboard the steamship *Oregon.* The *Oregon,* like the *Lexington* three years previously, carried Sherman on a voyage to an uncertain future. In California he had increasingly come to view the army as his family, yet he was returning to firm his ties with the Ewings by marrying Ellen. He hoped he could merge the two by convincing her that he should remain in his military family and not become the civilian she wished he would.[75]

CHAPTER 4

———— ☆ ————

SETTING DOWN ROOTS

SHERMAN'S TRIP BACK EAST in a steamship by way of Panama took only 30 days, in marked contrast to the 198 days going around the horn on the wind-blown *Lexington*. There were no terrible storms nor fishing for birds this time, just the regular rhythm of the steam engine on the calm seas. Only Sherman's emotions were unchanged; both going to and returning from California were times of uncertainty for him. In 1846 he had not known what to expect when he arrived in the strange land; now he wondered if his forthcoming marriage to Ellen would provide the tranquility he hoped for. It would not take him long to find out. The early years of matrimony were to set a tone that would resonate for the rest of their marriage: a devotion to one another within the context of an unending battle of wills over army, religion, finances, and family.

When Sherman arrived in New York in late January 1850, he immediately hailed a carriage to the Ninth Street office of Winfield Scott, general in chief of the army and hero of the recently completed Mexican War. That evening he had dinner with "Old Fuss and Feathers," an overwhelming experience for a young officer. Scott had secured his fame long ago in the War of 1812, and he had emerged from the recently completed Mexican War as a world-renowned military genius. He was the greatest living exemplar of the gentlemenly warfare that his young table mate would demolish as he marched to the sea fourteen years later. Scott loved good food, shiny uniforms, and fine literature,

77

and he excoriated any army officer who was not the cultivated gentleman he was. His nickname characterized him well.[1]

He grilled Sherman closely and then freely expressed his own opinions of California and the recently completed war with Mexico. Sherman gasped when Scott said he thought the nation "was on the eve of a terrible Civil War." He worried about his own lack of combat experience as he heard about the exploits of fellow officers. His friends had actively participated in the war; he "had not heard a hostile shot." He became convinced again that his military career was over.[2]

Scott had no such worries; the nervous lieutenant had made a favorable impression on the fastidious old general. Certainly Sherman's ties to Thomas Ewing and Scott's desire for the 1852 Whig presidential nomination helped influence Scott's good opinion. He endorsed Sherman as "an officer of intelligence" who could "give many explanations of interest" and sent him to see the secretary of war.[3]

Sherman was happy to be going to Washington because he would see Ellen there. The Ewing family had moved into the Blair House upon Thomas Ewing's appointment as the first secretary of the interior. Sherman arrived unannounced to surprise Ellen, who was giving her canary a bath.[4] This was the first time they had seen each other in four years. And except for brief occasions, they had not really seen each other since Sherman's departure for West Point fourteen years previously. They had an enormous amount of catching up to do, and now there would be time for quiet walks and long carriage rides, discussing their past, their differences, and their future. At thirty and twenty-six years of age, respectively, they were no longer youngsters. Sherman tried to convince Ellen of his need to stay in the army; Ellen wanted him to become a Catholic civilian and settle in Lancaster, Ohio. This old impasse, never resolved during their separation, continued even as they prepared to marry.

After finding that Georgian George W. Crawford, the secretary of war, had no interest in California "except as it related to Slavery and the [possible railroad] routes through Texas," Sherman called on President Zachary Taylor. Shortly after, Sherman received a six-month's leave of absence and spent most of the spring in Washington trying to promote his career. He complained to the adjutant general that he had been adjutant for both Mason and Smith, yet his pay had never risen above that of an ordinary artillery lieutenant, and he had not even benefited from Mason's promotion. "I stand alone," he complained, "as the only Chief of Staff who has not been honored by some mark of favor at the same time with his commander. The sting is now too deep ever to be effaced." At the least, he argued, he ought to receive back pay to assuage the pain.[5]

The adjutant general was not impressed, but Sherman kept trying. Since Congress was then debating a bill to establish four new commissary service captaincies, Sherman wrote right back to that official, citing his long tour of duty in California as justification for bluntly asking for one of the posts: "My peculiarly bad luck during the past four years serving in a distant land to the sacrifice of private interest and professional hope must serve as my apology for this request."[6]

While awaiting congressional action, Sherman had a month-long reunion in Ohio with his mother, whom he had not seen since the mid-1840s. Brother John had done well financially and had laid the foundation for his later successful political career. Cump approved of John's financial success but wished his brother would stay out of politics, a chancy profession at best.

Sherman seemed to be focusing on everything but his wedding, and there is no evidence that he and Ellen had settled any of their differences. His letters to her were hardly tender; he remained businesslike about his expressions of affection, and even his warmest words were lacking in passion. He told Ellen that he was prepared "to assume the high trust of your Guardian and Master. I will not promise to be the kindest hearted loving man in the world nor will I profess myself a Bluebeard. . . . All I believe is that, if health be given us and that love and mutual confidence which I trust we both deeply feel continue, we stand as fair a chance for a slight share of worldly contentment and happiness . . . [as any other couple]. You shall be my Adjutant and Chief Counselor and I'll show you how to steer clear of the real and imaginary troubles of this world. Only be contented[,] happy[,] and repose proper trust in me, and I think when the time comes for us to part, which I hope will be many a year hence, you will look back upon a fair and goodly prospect. At all events let us live in that hope." Ellen would be his comrade in life as his fellow officers were his comrades in arms, and he would expect her to accept him as they did.[7]

It was only when he suggested the day for their marriage that Sherman grew lyric: "Let us be married the First of May. I have always rejoiced to see the flowers bloom and nature rub off her gray morose garment for the brighter one of Spring. The day is peculiarly appropriate for we can unite our day of joy with all nature and will have her beauties to cheer us."[8]

Sherman obviously was ready to marry Ellen, and she him. Both accepted the wedding as a settled fact, but he continued to worry about the future, particularly about her wish that he resign from the army. He asked her "freely in your heart [to] consent to let me hold on till the time arrive when I am compelled to act." He promised to decide when his leave of absence was over in August, delaying the problem yet again. "The future is ours. Let us make the most of it."[9]

Ellen wanted him to take over the Ewing saltworks in Chauncey, Ohio, close by Lancaster. The business would provide a substantial standard of living and a domestic stability that the military life, with its constant transfers to far-away places, precluded. Sherman briefly considered the possibility out of love for her, but he did not want to work for his foster father in Ohio, and he did not wish to cut his ties to the army.[10] Particularly now that he was about to marry Ewing's daughter, he needed his independence. The issue was repeatedly put off and for the next ten years festered like an untreated wound, causing continued pain for husband and wife.

Other familial problems weighed heavily on Sherman too. He had recently sent his beloved sister Elizabeth Sherman Reese fifteen hundred dollars, but her alcoholic husband had squandered it in yet another bad business investment. In late April he came away from a visit to her family in Philadelphia more discouraged than ever. Elizabeth and her children were close to starvation. He called his sister a "martyr," but he did not know how to help her. It was all distressing. "I . . . deeply grieve that, when my mind should be free to feelings of advancing happiness, I should be burdened with the weight of Elizabeth's distresses and Reese's extravagances."[11]

Weighed down with anxieties about the future, Sherman developed a severe case of what he called "Mexican Diarrhea." He had never suffered from any intestinal problems during his four years in California, but he thought he must have brought "the poison" back with him. The stress of his return, his worries about his own and his sister's futures, and the excitement of his upcoming wedding worsened the physical problem. He felt so ill that he began to worry about his fitness for marriage, expressing a bridegroom's common reticence or experiencing deeper doubts. Several doctors told him that his chronic asthma was responsible for his illness, and medicines would do more harm than good. An old army physician recommended proper diet and regular exercise. The wedding, he said, could go on as scheduled.[12]

Sherman felt fine on May 1. Much to Ellen and her mother's unhappiness, however, the evening ceremony took place in the Blair House rather than in a Catholic church. Sherman's lack of faith prevented a church wedding, highlighting that problem between bride and groom. Ellen and her mother attended Mass earlier in the day, and the president of Georgetown College, a Jesuit priest, officiated at the late evening exchange of vows, but it was not a complete Catholic ceremony. Sherman appeared in full military uniform "out of respect to the service," though he said he would have preferred civilian dress. Whatever the truth, Ellen saw as clearly as was possible that she was marrying an army officer, not the Catholic civilian she wished Sherman could be.

The wedding was one of the major social events of the season. Some "300 Gentlemen and ladies of historical fame," as Sherman described them, attended the ceremony and dinner, including the president of the United States, his cabinet, Supreme Court justices, congressmen including Daniel Webster, and diplomats. Henry Clay presented Ellen with a silver bouquet holder, which she carried during the ceremony. There was also a full representation of army and navy officers in dress uniform; the popping of champagne bottles reminded one reporter of artillery fire. Ellen became so excited during the formal receiving line that she inadvertently broke protocol and kissed the president.[13]

Immediately after the ceremony, Sherman complained to his old friend E. O. C. Ord in California of having to begin his marriage "with the old song of economy," but he and Ellen left on a honeymoon anyway, accompanied by Ellen's younger brother, Tom. It was not unusual for a sibling to join newlyweds on their honeymoon in the nineteenth century, so no one commented on the trio. They traveled to Philadelphia to see Sherman's sister, attend the Tom Thumb show, and invest in a soap and candle business on Elizabeth Reese's account. Then they moved on to New York, where they had dinner with General and Mrs. Winfield Scott and met Bishop John Hughes, and to West Point, where Cump excitedly showed off his old school to his new bride. Next the threesome traveled across the state to Niagara Falls and Buffalo. They spent June in Lancaster, visiting relatives and friends, with Sherman signing an agreement with his brother to support their mother. Cump and Phil Ewing also inspected the Chauncey saltworks at Thomas Ewing's request, no doubt in the forlorn hope that Cump would like what he saw and decide to stay.[14]

During the honeymoon, Ellen received several letters from her parents expressing sadness at her absence and stating the wish that she and Sherman would settle in Washington close to them. Ellen felt both the inclination and obligation to do so despite her husband's desire for autonomy. These pressures were the beginning of the Ewings' lifelong efforts to keep Ellen nearby. Ellen always felt pulled in two directions: She loved her husband, yet she felt a powerful attachment to home and parents. As a result, the ever-moving Sherman would be often separated from his wife.[15]

The newlyweds returned to Washington in time for the huge Fourth of July celebration at the foot of the Washington Monument. It was here that President Zachary Taylor became overheated and was taken violently ill. Thomas Ewing urged him to see a doctor, but the old soldier balked. By the time he changed his mind, it was too late. He died four days later.[16]

The nation shuddered. Sherman was in the Senate gallery when Vice-President Millard Fillmore took his presidential oath of office. The "simple almost silent ceremony" impressed him, but the concerned look on the senators' faces worried him. He participated in the ceremonial burial of Zachary Taylor, serving as a mounted aide to the adjutant general. "As soon as the vault was closed and the firing done," Sherman remembered, "the crowd dispersed and people began to speculate on the coming changes." To Sherman, the essential uncertainty of politics shone through all the events. As he lectured his brother: "I hope the Political History of the past year will make a strong impression on your mind not to seek honor or distribution through this channel."[17]

Taylor's death and the resulting cabinet shuffle moved Thomas

Ewing from the Interior Department to the U.S. Senate, where he became involved in the congressional struggle over the issue of slavery in the territories gained in the Mexican War. California wanted to enter the Union as a free state, but the South balked at this destabilization of the sectional balance. There were other problems, too: a boundary dispute between Texas and New Mexico, the long-simmering issue of fugitive slaves, and the buying and selling of human beings in the capital of the American democracy. Congress had been debating Henry Clay's compromise package since January, with antislavery Northerners insisting that slavery should not be allowed to spread into the new territories, while proslavery Southerners insisted it should. Both sides warned of a civil war.

Sherman was caught up in the political passions and attended as many of the congressional debates as he could—usually every morning. Ellen teased him that he had "a secret desire to quit the service & enter politics." He particularly enjoyed listening to the oratory of Henry Clay, his long-time Whig favorite. He joined in the conversations going on all over the city, and like everyone else he worried about whether the Union would survive these tensions.[18]

Zachary Taylor's death, the ascendancy of Fillmore, and the cabinet reorganization added to the tense situation. When Daniel Webster, soon to be the new secretary of state, announced plans for his final senatorial speech, the city grew anxious in anticipation. Sherman arrived earlier than usual at the Senate Chambers' visitors' gallery but found it already jammed. Through a combination of impudence and will, he provoked Ohio senator Thomas Corwin to get him admitted to the Senate floor. He sensed the critical importance of this moment in the nation's history.

Sherman took a seat beneath the gallery immediately behind Webster's desk and was soon joined by Winfield Scott. Although Webster proposed the idea of voting separately on the elements of Clay's omnibus bill, thus opening the way to compromise, and though some of his severest critics praised his rhetoric, Sherman was not impressed. He thought the speech "had none of the fire of oratory, or intensity of feeling that marked all of Mr. Clay's efforts," especially an August blast against secession. Then, as a newspaper had paraphrased it, Clay had dramatically shouted: "I love Kaintucky [*sic*] with all my heart and all my soul, but if

Kaintucky were to secede I would shoulder my old musket and be among the first to put her down, down, down." Sherman and the rest of the gallery, jolted by what he later called "a thrill like electricity," jumped to their feet in applause at this oratorical pledge to the union. Webster's speech had elicited no such fire, and Sherman was disappointed.[19]

What came to be known as the Compromise of 1850 eventually passed on five separate votes in September. As far as Sherman was concerned, the most important new law was the admission of California into the Union. He was proud to recall later that he "had witnessed nearly all the steps which attended the acquisition of California from Mexico and its admission as a state into the Federal Union." He had been one of the first Americans into the territory; he had been present at the California constitutional convention; and he had watched Congress pass the statehood bill.[20]

With the Compromise of 1850 enacted, the slavery controversy momentarily quieted, and Congress settled into more mundane work. Sherman continued watching its deliberations, hoping for passage of the bill creating the four new captaincies. In June the bill was still pending, and he had already received orders to join his artillery company in Missouri. A friend urged him to go, advising him not to resign from the army despite his past bad fortune. Others counseled just the opposite. A cousin in California encouraged him to bring Ellen and make his fortune there as a civilian. "California's wealth is exhaustless," Charlie Hoyt insisted, "here in her golden field she holds up to industry and enterprize a brilliant reward." His old friend Ord disagreed. He considered himself "a sadder if not better man and sorry enough that I didn't get married and stay at home like you."[21]

Thomas Ewing learned from Winfield Scott that once the army bill passed, Sherman would receive a captaincy. The news was reassuring to Sherman and decisive. Despite Ewing's insistence that he and Ellen remain in Washington to await developments, Sherman reported to Jefferson Barracks, Missouri, to join Company C, Third Artillery. Ellen did not accompany him. She was pregnant, and the Ewings insisted she remain at home, so Cump unhappily went to St. Louis alone. As he steamed up the Ohio-Mississippi River toward St. Louis, he wished Ellen were with him to observe the passengers and the passing scene. There was a daguerrotypist who claimed to know everyone in Lancaster; an "expert deaf beggar"; professional gamblers occupied with all-night games; and all kinds of musicians, including a no-talent fiddler who sawed away "with a pertinacity that would honor a bull terrier."[22]

Sherman arrived in St. Louis around September 22, but his sense of propriety precluded telling his friends the real reason for Ellen's absence. Instead he said that he always preceded her to investigate a place first. His friends found this explanation odd. He wrote her: "Indeed, were it not for your situation, I would forthwith prepare and insist upon you joining me." "Should you at any time regret having remained at Lancaster," he suggested hopefully, "do not fail to tell me and I will make you a home here that will have all the comforts of one, save the presence of your mother."[23]

In the same letter, Sherman extolled St. Louis's charms. He wondered how Thomas Ewing could remain in "that insignificant town of Lancaster," when St. Louis offered so much promise. "Beyond doubt in time it will be one of the greatest places on the Continent." He hoped Ellen would not allow her mother to continue prejudicing her father against it (and, by extension, continue to keep her away from him.) "Would that you were with me that we could take a buggy ride about this wonderful city," he said.[24]

When he arrived at his post, nearby Jefferson Barracks, he met old acquaintances. Long-time friend Braxton Bragg, now a Mexican War hero, was the company commander. Everyone asked about Ellen. James A. Hardie had even rented a piano for her use and had been looking forward to long discussions on Catholicism. There was much talk of the war in Mexico, Bragg no doubt regaling Sherman with combat stories. Sherman grew increasingly upset, and one night he woke with an asthma attack followed by depression. He missed Ellen, and he worried about his lack of combat experience.[25]

Shortly after, he received an encouraging letter from his old commander, P. F. Smith, prophesying that the "leadership in the next war" would come from the ranks of people like him—lieutenants and captains. This reassurance was strengthened when he discovered the announcement of his appointment as one of the new commissary captains in a newspaper. This promotion set their "fate for better or for worse" in the army, he wrote Ellen, thereby resolving, at least for him, one of their main points of contention.[26]

Sherman's promotion meant he had to leave Jefferson Barracks for St. Louis, where he would be close to the businesses that provided the army supplies in that section of the country. He established himself first at the Planters Hotel and then in a boarding house, some four blocks from his office. He brought furniture for Ellen to use when she arrived later. "But all these but remind me hourly that you should be with me," he pined. "Alone," he said in what seemed to be a warning, "I shall be forced for mere occupation's sake to go and seek company at the hotels, at Theatres and concerts."[27]

Sherman's assignment to St. Louis was temporary; he might soon be sent to Oregon. Such "roving about the world in nothing but changeability," his love of new adventure, and Ellen's obsession about remaining close to home caused strains. He tried to calm her apprehensions, but he told her bluntly that he would not resign his profession, and he would not go West alone. "Doing a duty to me," he said, she should "cast off all fear and prejudice" and go. She should be a good soldier and follow orders.[28]

Sherman traveled to Lancaster to spend Christmas with Ellen, arriving, his mother-in-law thought, "in fine health and spirits." Ellen refused to go to Oregon should he receive orders there, bringing to the fore the unresolved issue. Should transfer orders arrive, he would have to choose between the army and his wife. His spirits quickly dropped. On his way back to St. Louis, he tried to relax by reading Dickens, his choice of authors perhaps a barometer of his dark mood.[29]

His life returned to its pre-Christmas rhythm, but the work and the social life did not ease his loneliness or his uncertainty. He marked the days until the birth of their first child so Ellen and the baby could be with him. On January 28, 1851, Ellen delivered a girl, baptized Maria after Ellen's mother but quickly called Minnie. Sherman responded with a cold letter demonstrating his anger at Ellen and the baby for being in Ohio rather than with him in St. Louis. He hoped that as Ellen grew stronger, she would also gain in the "desire and determination" to leave home. He wanted her to come to St. Louis quickly and without the Ewings. Ellen, however, had hoped to remain with her parents through the winter, sometimes even imagining that she would never have to leave Lancaster again. "I fear I shall be terribly homesick," she worried. Ellen loved her husband, but her marriage had not loosened her close ties to her family. Emotionally she was still unable to leave her father's home, even to be with her husband. Thomas Ewing was a powerful personality whose hold on both Sherman and Ellen was so great that it overwhelmed their love for one another.[30]

Sherman was determined to have his wife and child with him, despite the Ewings' desire to keep them in Lancaster. At the beginning of March, he traveled to Ohio, careful, however, to explain to Thomas Ewing in Washington what he was doing. He became so upset that he suffered from asthma on the boat ride. But his family finally returned with him. Ellen had been reluctant, but Sherman would not have it any other way.[31]

They lived in the Planters Hotel, St. Louis's finest, but Ellen found it too confining after her father's home in Lancaster, so they purchased a small house only ten minutes by carriage or omnibus ride from the center of the city. Although she immediately wanted to furnish her new home completely, Sherman said their finances could not stand such extravagance. No matter, Ellen liked her new house, primarily because of its large guest room. "Come all that can and stay as long as you can," she told her mother and father.[32]

For the next year, Ellen, Sherman, Minnie, and the three live-in servants resided in the home. Then one of Sherman's West Point and Florida friends, Stewart Van Vliet and his wife, moved in to share expenses. Ellen enjoyed dividing household responsibilities with Mrs. Van Vliet, whom she found to be a pleasant companion, despite her Protestant faith. Minnie was a happy child, and everyone enjoyed her immensely. Unlike most bragging parents, however, Sherman insisted on constantly feigning "indifference" toward the baby. He told his brother-in-law on one occasion that Minnie was "like a thousand other babies," though her relatives insisted she was really "an infant Phenomenon."[33] Sherman seemed to struggle to keep some distance from Minnie, perhaps anticipating that mother and child might leave him for Lancaster.

Ellen was content: She received many family visitors; there was a church nearby; most of her acquaintances were Catholics; and many of Sherman's friends were converts (which was encouraging to Ellen's plans for him). Cump regularly accompanied her to church and even attended a lecture by the noted Catholic convert, Orestes Brownson, the individual he had some years previously called a charlatan. Only the specter of his possible transfer to the wilds of Oregon bothered Ellen.[34]

During the spring and summer of 1851, Thomas Ewing and Sherman's cousin, Henry Stoddard, won a litigation, allegedly one of the largest land decisions in American history, over the St. Louis lands acquired by Amos Stoddard, an early nineteenth-century army officer. Thomas Ewing was handsomely compensated for his efforts, and he, his sons, and Sherman purchased a great deal of property in the newly open areas, which Sherman then managed. Ewing authorized him to purchase two thousand dollars worth of city land for Ellen, and Sherman himself invested in prairie land east of town. He traveled to Illinois to acquire land near Edwardsville. But this investment, heavy household expenses, and his inability to collect on some loans he had made in California strapped his finances. Still, he talked about building a house. Present sacrifices might bring future security.[35]

In the spring of 1852, Ellen decided to spend the summer with her parents in Lancaster. She continued to fret about Oregon and, urged on by her family, continued pressuring Sherman to quit the army and take on some civilian occupation. Catholicism also remained a problem, Ellen demonstrating her strong faith by having Minnie dedicated to the care of the Blessed Virgin and saying that she would prefer to see the baby die than have her ever turn away from her religious faith.[36]

Sherman felt uneasy about these developments, especially since he began to find his work tedious and hoped for a transfer to more active duty. Oregon had appeal, and he heard rumors he might be sent to Fort Leavenworth, Kansas. If stories of proslavery filibusterers' successfully annexing Cuba to the United States were true, he might be able to command a commissary office in Havana. Even California began to look good again. "That wild roving life on muleback, sleeping on the ground," and being around "wild gold seekers is enough to strip quiet life here of all interest & charm." His "fancy" kept returning to Monterey and his former haunts, though reason told him that St. Louis was a better place for a family man. Sherman wanted to get away from ledger books, property deeds, and requisitions. Ellen kept looking in the direction of Lancaster toward her parents, while he yearned for more adventure as far away from Ohio as possible. He stayed wedded to the army; she wanted him a civilian. In December, his asthma flared up again.[37]

Both Ellen and Cump received their wishes in May 1852. Ellen and Minnie went to Lancaster for the summer, while Sherman went to Fort Leavenworth on a temporary duty assignment. His family's departure and the resultant decision to sell their house upset him. He suffered a severe asthmatic attack.[38]

Sherman was still ill when he arrived at Leavenworth, blaming his sickness on an all-night card game and an oyster party on board the steamboat. Hard horseback riding cured him, however, suggesting that frustration-induced asthma was the cause of his queasy stomach. He enjoyed his stay in sparsely settled Kansas, as always studying the geography of the area carefully as he rode around. Seeing the wagon trains in Independence, Missouri, beginning their movement toward California triggered his yearning for the Pacific Coast. He wrote Ellen in high spirits, unconsciously expressing his desire for military adventure over married life: "If you should hear of my joining some expedition or other, you must not be surprised for had I authority or permission I would most certainly make some Summer trip of the kind."[39]

Instead, Sherman had to return to St. Louis, once more living alone because his wife and family were in Lancaster. He was lonely, frustrated, and confused. He wanted the best for Ellen and Minnie, but he felt angry about being alone and having his wife supported by Thomas Ewing. As the summer wore on, Sherman grew increasingly upset. "She has been at Lancaster too much since our marriage," he lamented, "and it is full time for her to be weaned." A letter from Thomas Ewing asking him to let Ellen stay longer added to his resentment. He unhappily agreed, but he could not express his bitterness toward his foster father, believing it was his "duty to be governed in a measure by their [Ewings'] wishes." He blamed a safe target, Lancaster: "I have good reasons to be jealous of a place that virtually robs me of my family and I cannot help feeling sometimes a degree of dislike for that very reason to the name of Lancaster."[40]

Upset already, he suffered another more personal loss. His beloved mother, who had been living in Mansfield since 1844 with his brother John, quietly died. His wife was temporarily absent, and now his mother was gone forever. Once again he seemed, to have no family, no home, and to be no better off than he had been as a young orphan. The main difference now was that the huge man who had then come to his rescue was now responsible for much of his misery. The only anchor seemed to be the army.[41]

Sherman received welcome relief from the mounting frustration and personal troubles when he was ordered to New Orleans to clean up corruption in the commissary service there. The two previous commissary officers had ignored competitive bidding, doing business with only one company. One of these officers was related to the owner of the company; the other had his brother hired there and then made a partner. When the army high command learned of this cozy arrangement, they sent Sherman.

He arrived in late October 1852 and established his office in a bank building fronting on Lafayette Square. He quickly came face to face with the problem. The owner of the favored company offered to continue the arrangement. Sherman refused. From then on, he said, the army would buy on the open market at the best available price. There was no more corruption in the New Orleans commissary office. Sherman also completely reorganized the department. He rented a warehouse to avoid having to deal with commission agents. He was saving the government substantial money. As a fellow officer said about him, "If Sherman does not find the error of three cents, necessary to balance his accounts, he will resign his commission and commit suicide."[42]

If only his own finances were doing as well. His "pay which would be ample in an ordinary town" was "utterly inadequate here" and was the reason, he said, that earlier commissary officers had accepted improper favors from merchants. He rented a house about six to eight blocks from his office, for what he considered an exorbitant six hundred dollars per year. He was shocked to learn that natives considered this price "cheap." Still, the house was much nicer than their St. Louis residence, he told Ellen. If she were only there to make it a home. But Ellen was still in Lancaster and set to stay there for several more months. She was expecting their second child in November.[43]

Sherman plunged into the social life of the city and was soon a regular with the other officers at the opera, theater, suppers, and balls. He toured Forts Jackson and St. Philip, visited a sugar plantation, and traveled to Baton Rouge. When he toured Andrew

Jackson's famous War of 1812 victory site, he was appalled to find the battlefield planted in sugar cane and the only marker capsized in a ditch.[44]

But neither social life with fellow officers nor the challenges of his job proved sufficient to overcome the loneliness he felt at being separated from Ellen and Minnie. Thus, Ellen's delivery of a baby girl on November 17, 1852, was a doubly joyful event. He was a father for the second time, and Ellen and the two girls would soon be living with him. The baby received the name Mary Elizabeth, after his recently deceased mother and his sister, but she soon became known as Lizzie. In late December, Ellen, the two girls, a nursemaid, and Sherman's sister, Fanny, arrived. (Cump had invited Fanny to take her mind off their mother's death.) Minnie soon had the run of the house and was inspecting every closet, drawer, and box within reach. Sherman loved it all.[45]

Senior officers invited the Shermans to dinner often and eased their way into New Orleans society. At social gatherings, Sherman expressed his hope that the United States would take Cuba, seemingly not understanding that territory's explosive connection with slavery. Though still a Whig, he criticized Winfield Scott's bitter reaction to his crushing defeat to Franklin Pierce in the 1852 presidential election. He thought the Democrats deserved the election because they had done a better job of supporting their candidate.[46]

Sherman seemed happy once again. His family was with him, and they were living in a pleasant house. He enjoyed his army associates and, despite his blunt reform of the commissary business, was widely liked in the city. But problems remained. Ellen demanded much in the way of material comforts, and New Orleans was too expensive for his army pay. Ellen argued for a move to the civilian sector, but Sherman resisted. He continued to have no confidence that he would survive there. Despite his meager military salary, the army was still the place for him.

All this changed suddenly in early December 1852. St. Louis banker and friend, Henry S. Turner, told Sherman that his quartermaster experience in California, his commissary tours in St. Louis and New Orleans, and his management of his father-in-law's St. Louis property had provided him with an expertise that could prove profitable in the world of finance. Turner's St. Louis bank was planning to open a branch in California, and Turner wanted Sherman to head the operation. The partnership offer intrigued Sherman, but he was not sure about California. How about New Orleans? he asked the St. Louis bankers. No, they answered; they needed him in California.[47]

He hesitated, wary of throwing over his certain commission and his army family for an uncertain business venture in civilian life. A St. Louis friend advised him to demand a larger share of the profits before agreeing to the partnership. Turner tried to resolve Sherman's concern by going to Washington to obtain a transfer to the San Francisco commissary. Instead, Sherman received a six-month leave of absence. He could go to California; if he changed his mind, he would still have his commission. The bank advanced him one thousand dollars, and late in February 1853 he sold all his furniture and sent Ellen and family back to Ohio, much to the Ewings' delight. In March, he boarded a ship steaming toward a possible new career on the familiar streets of San Francisco. He was apprehensive rather than excited. In Lancaster, Ellen settled comfortably into her father's house.[48]

CHAPTER 5

THE DISORDER OF FINANCIAL LIFE

SHERMAN'S MARRIAGE had not provided him with the personal stability he sought. Unfulfilled, he decided to risk his one real home—the army—to see if he could find success and contentment elsewhere. He hesitated because he feared he was taking the ultimate risk of losing both the army and his family. Yet he saw no other choice. He was not gaining economic success in the military, and he was constantly on the move, and these factors were undermining his position with Ellen and Thomas Ewing. He had to do something else; not trying anything new meant a continuation of a life of dependency within the Ewing fold. Moving to California, the site of gold rush chaos, demonstrated the depth of his yearning to better his life. The result was further conflict with Ellen over Thomas Ewing's influence and increased disorientation in general. Successful resolution of Sherman's need for personal stability remained as elusive as ever.

The trip by wooden steamship was uneventful until April 9, 1853, when the vessel was only a night away from docking in San Francisco. Sherman was asleep on a deck chair when he felt a sudden jolt and heard the sounds of shattering dishes and crashing furniture. The ship was stopped dead on a rock, rising and falling with the ocean's swell. Sherman jumped up and helped maintain calm among the frightened passengers, who came pouring out of their rooms. The dark night hindered visibility, so it was an anxious three hours until a foggy dawn finally permitted the lowering of an exploratory lifeboat. Sherman and the ship's captain pored over charts and compass and discovered that the ship was aground a mile offshore near Bolinas Bay, north of San

93

Francisco. The passengers were ferried to land, and, as fit his many years of commissary duty, Sherman did not disembark until he had first fished out a can of crackers and some sardines from the submerged pantry.

When he reached shore, he and a young companion walked two miles until they stumbled upon a small lumber boat about to leave for San Francisco. Sherman sent a note back to the crew of the injured vessel and then climbed on board the small boat. Just inside San Francisco Bay, a swell capsized the vessel, and a passing ship had to rescue the party. Sherman wondered what his two failed attempts to reach the city signified about his future banking career there. Throughout his early life, he had often fallen short of reaching financial security and career satisfaction just when he seemed within sight of it. Some unforeseen event capsized his hopes, requiring numerous rescue efforts to keep his head above water. His shipwrecked arrival in California could not have been more ominous, or, as it turned out, more prophetic.[1]

Sherman found his colleague Henry S. Turner, and rented a small sleeping room. When he looked around the city, he was impressed with "this most extraordinary place on earth." San Francisco had grown to a population of nearly fifty thousand, a phenomenal sixty times as many people as had lived there just five years previously. Wharves extended a mile into the bay and were crowded with ships of all sizes and kinds; new buildings, substantial and ramshackle, had been thrown up everywhere; streets were being extended, sewered, and planked. Gambling halls boasted elaborate lighted mirrors and French table girls, but churches were also becoming more numerous. "San Francisco is quite a large city now and is much better regulated than formerly," Sherman noted, "but it wears the appearance of a mushroom of rapid growth and rapid decay." The cost of living was high, "everybody seemed to be making money fast," he noticed. Since that was his purpose in returning, he felt encouraged.[2]

He studied the city's financial establishment. California had no bank regulatory laws, so anyone could open a financial institution without state interference. Page and Bacon of St. Louis was San Francisco's leading bank, its success having provided the impetus for Lucas and Turner's new institution. Turner had already established the branch bank in rented quarters, assisted by a teller and a former Page and Bacon employee. The bank was receiving deposits, selling bills of exchange, and making loans at the prevailing rate of 3 percent per month. Turner was ready to return to St. Louis and turn the operation over to Sherman.[3]

Sherman was not happy with what he saw. Turner was "too cautious & timid," he thought, and the bank was undercapitalized. He believed the institution needed at least $300,000; the $100,000 originally agreed upon was insufficient for him "to *experience* absolute success." He also wanted to establish a branch in Sacramento or Marysville, but Turner said no. Worries about his wisdom in leaving the army and undertaking this new career resurfaced; he should have demanded more capital before agreeing to come to California. "I sometimes think I am an out & out fool," he moaned. Perhaps he should forget about becoming a banker and return to New Orleans. His asthma flared up as he debated within himself. He finally decided to remain only if James H. Lucas, the bank's senior partner in St. Louis, agreed to provide more captial.[4]

Ellen took advantage of Cump's frustration to press for his return. She said she was worried about his health, but actually she was more concerned about future separation from her parents. Sherman was not moved, and even when Lucas proposed maintaining the capital at its present level, he did not begin packing for home. Instead, he decided to confront Lucas personally in St. Louis. He also told Ellen she had to realize that it was either the army or San Francisco. He would never return to Ohio.[5]

By mid-July 1853, Sherman was back in Missouri. He and Lucas compromised at $200,000 cash capital with additional credit in New York. Reimbursement of all entertainment and travel expenses now augmented Sherman's one-eighth partnership and his $5,000 per year salary. Lucas also gave Sherman permission to erect a new bank building at a cost of $50,000. He was satisfied with these conditions and told Ellen to be prepared to leave Lancaster for California on September 15. He was returning to San Francisco, and she was to join him. He resigned his army commission. There was no turning back. He had to make it as a civilian and replace the familial feelings he was giving up by leaving the army.[6]

Thomas and Maria Ewing resisted Ellen's departure with Cump for the faraway Pacific coast; they had always supposed she would stay with them when Sherman went to California. They appealed to him, once again, to work for the family interests in Ohio. Failing, they made the astonishing suggestion that baby Minnie be left behind. Ellen, who hoped to settle in Lancaster permanently, agreed and then convinced Cump. Minnie was left with her grandparents, a hostage to their determination to bring Cump and Ellen back to Ohio. Sherman might have his wife with him in California, but Thomas Ewing had his daughter and his wife's thoughts. Ellen felt that Minnie's remaining in Lancaster made her "feel in fact as if she had [not] altogether left home." It was not an auspicious start for the fulfillment of Sherman's family needs and his independence.[7]

Sherman too remained securely tied to his foster father. That fact was concretely expressed in a remarkable letter he wrote to Ewing from St. Louis after completion of negotiations with Lucas. This August 22, 1853, letter was his justification for returning to California and taking his family with him. He explained the financial arrangements in glowing terms, expressing complete optimism for his future. Most significant, he began the letter: "I think I have ever shown a disposition in all things to conform to your wishes and now assert my continued wish to do so." And he ended the letter: "I ask your free and hearty consent to ease the shock of Ellen's leaving home." Cump was declaring his independence and simultaneously pacifying his foster father. As much as he wanted his immediate family, he did not want to alienate his adoptive father or lose Ewing's love or his influence.[8]

The trip to the Pacific coast with Ellen and Lizzie in tow contained omens: Ellen and her nurse became severely seasick; one of the native guides inadvertently frightened baby Lizzie during the Nicaraguan crossing, and her nurse became hysterical while being carried to the ship through waist-high surf on the Pacific side. The fates seemed to be protesting Sherman's decision to go to California as much as Ellen opposed it in her heart and the Ewings resisted it by retaining Minnie.[9]

Ellen's prejudice against her new home was confirmed upon arrival. First she noted the exorbitant cost of living. She and Cump signed a six-month lease on a small house on Stockton Street but in early 1854 purchased half of a double brick house on Green Street. Ellen complained about the lack of a yard, the sandy, narrow, crowded streets, the constant wind, and the "absolute plague" of swarming flies and fleas. Army officers who came to call filled her head with further negative opinions. While she walked one day, rain turned the sandy road into mud, spattering her shoes and the bottom of her dress. She openly talked of returning to Ohio. When she became pregnant, her homesickness for her parents and for Minnie increased. She cried often, felt ill all the time, and worried that some disease would kill her daughter in Ohio. Sherman's frequent asthma attacks were also depressing. "This is El Dorado—the promised land—" she pined. "I would rather live in Granny Walters cabin [in Lancaster] than live here in any kind of style."[10]

Thomas Ewing continued trying to entice his son-in-law to come home. Despite his own lifetime of hard labor, he told Sherman that a person's health was not worth financial success. He could ensure a "handsome competence" for him in Ohio, "where fortunes are moderate & comforts cheap & abundant"; that is, the Chauncey saltworks offer was still open. Sherman stood firm. "I would rather be at the head of the bank in San Francisco, a position I obtained by my own efforts, than to occupy any place open to me in Ohio," he countered.[11]

He was supervising the bank's operations and closely superintending the construction of its new building on the corner of Jackson and Montgomery streets. Business was growing, but he worried that the city's banks were not earning enough profit on the 3 percent interest they were charging for bills of exchange. Rather than worry about future solvency, however, he threw himself into supervising the building construction, taking pride in the fact that, by July 1854, his bank would have the most impressive building in town.[12]

At home, matters remained unsettled. Ellen maintained her stubborn desire to return to Lancaster. The acquisition of the four-bedroom house improved her disposition somewhat, and Cump's purchase of a piano provided a welcome outlet. On many evenings, Ellen sat at the piano playing and singing favorite melodies. Cump listened with Lizzie on his knee, the baby keeping time with her head, or he exuberantly danced with the child in tempo to the music. General Ethan Allen Hitchcock regularly came by with his flute to join the Shermans in their music-making. Sometimes the Shermans had as dinner guests clerks from the bank, businessmen, old army friends like George H. Thomas, and the future Russian minister to the United States, Baron deStoeckl.

Most of the time, the family was less happy. Ellen lived mainly for the long letters she wrote to her mother and the return correspondence. She became obsessed with forebodings that Minnie would die before she saw her again or, worse, that the Protestantism of Sherman relatives would influence her. The stress caused the return of her old problem with boils and headaches. Sherman grew increasingly discouraged at his wife's inability to adjust. She repeatedly insisted that they were "making a poor exchange of friends for money" and told him often that she "would rather live near my home poor than to be a millionaire away from it." Sherman, who was working hard to become financially independent, felt hurt; his asthma regularly flared up, often forcing him to go several nights without sleep. During particularly severe attacks, he sat up and breathed the vapors of burning niter paper; its smoke only worsened Ellen's headaches.[13]

In early June 1854, Ellen gave birth to their first boy, William Ewing Sherman, a large baby and another redhead. The bishop of San Francisco performed the christening. Sherman expressed little excitement. "Since baptism," he morosely wrote his brother-in-law, "nothing has transpired to distinguish him from the thousands of babies that crowd us forward to our doom." Sherman saw the new child not as a joyous addition to his family but as an additional check on his economic freedom. "I have a family growing at an awful rate," he told Turner, "that I know will need a great deal to maintain and provide for." He would have to give up his "dream" of "living in St. Louis with a small & certain income, with a farm in Illinois to waste that little on."[14]

His brother, John Sherman, in the meantime had been elected to the U.S. House of Representatives and was steadily making a name in the political arena Sherman insisted he so despised. Philemon Ewing, his foster brother and close childhood friend, was a lawyer in Lancaster with connections through his father to all the leading Whig politicians. Sherman regularly wrote to both men, lecturing them on contemporary events. He maintained his indifferent attitude toward slavery, believing its introduction into Kansas-Nebraska would be impractical. Mexico was "the only proper outlet" for the institution, he said, though he thought the cost of the Gadsden Treaty's acquisition of more Mexican land was exorbitant for the value received. Since slavery would not economically spread much beyond its present boundaries, the best solution to the slavery controversy was for the Northern states to remain calm and show their superiority through dignified action, not harsh words. He warned John not to imitate the antislaveryites but to "avoid the subject as a dirty black one." Instead, John should support legislation favorable to the Pacific Coast, such as the construction of a good wagon road west from Kansas. He thought it was too early to speak of a transcontinental railroad.[15]

Normally Sherman was too busy to give advice on slavery or Kansas. He was pleased with his move to the new bank building during the summer of 1854, but he continued to fret over the uncertain nature of the banking profession. He sent regular reports to Turner at the home office in St. Louis, and, despite the incessant pessimism for which he frequently apologized, the letters indicated that the bank was holding its own in the competitive financial world in which it operated. Still, there were ominous signs. One of San Francisco's city officials absconded with government money and bank notes; then there was no break in the slowest business climate since the discovery of gold; there were constant rumors of bank failure, and Sherman felt "deeply anxious about the sums of money entrusted me by [army] officers." He climbed on his horse one day and rode eighty miles south to hunt geese on his old hunting grounds near Monterey. Even this usually rejuvenating recreation had minimal effect. He suffered an asthma attack and paced all night long to seek relief. Still, he promised Turner he would "try & hold on."[16]

On February 17, 1855, the mail steamer *Oregon* arrived in San Francisco and brought matters to a head. A passenger on board yelled out the news that Page and Bacon of St. Louis had gone under. Its San Francisco branch was the largest bank in the city, so a general bank run was a real possibility. Because of his careful management, Sherman's bank was in excellent condition, having deposits of over $600,000, with over $500,000 of this sum stored in coin and bullion in the vault.[17]

On February 20, an officer of Page and Bacon asked Sherman for help. When Sherman hurried to the competitor's office to survey the situation, he found the bank's officers and major investors gathered. Henry Haight, a bank officer, was noticeably inebriated and muttering that no bank could meet its obligations. Sherman disagreed; his bank was solid, he said. He had come to help, but he wanted nothing to do with a hopeless situation. The bank's supporters showed Sherman a piece of paper they wished to publish stating that they had personally examined Page and Bacon's books and attested to its ability to meet its obligations. Joseph L. Folsom, an old army friend and now one of the city's largest landholders, asked Sherman what he thought. Sherman said such a note was a good idea but inquired whether anyone had actually looked at the books. No, Folsom answered. Then, Sherman said, he advised against signing the statement. This advice enraged Haight, who demanded to know how Sherman could believe that such an inspection was possible so quickly. Twelve hours remained before the newspapers came out in the morning, Sherman responded—more than enough time. No statement was ever published, and the run on Page and Bacon continued. No bank dared declare the usual holiday on George Washington's birthday the next day. In the middle of the holiday parade, however, Page and Bacon announced its closing "for a short time" only. Sherman and all the other bankers in town braced for the inevitable whirlwind.

As he arrived for work on February 23, Sherman found Montgomery Street jammed with anxious depositors. He opened his bank promptly, the night before having carefully counted assets and liabilities and having obtained promises of support from key depositors. If panic developed, he would need to raise only about sixty-five thousand dollars to meet obligations, and he felt confident of his ability to do that. Directing the operation from behind the cages, he told his tellers to pay everyone with proper credentials. A steady stream of depositors withdrew their money, but Sherman made sure the tellers' trays were kept full from funds in the vault.

Sherman and his tellers received an important lift when a group of friendly depositors pushed their way in and conspicuously asked what was going on. Sherman explained for all to hear that despite the rumors of banks' failing all over the city, Lucas and Turner could pay all who demanded their money. Some people then left, but by noon, the bank had paid out $337,000 in cash.

After the lunch hour, Sherman felt confident enough to leave the building and reassure as many depositors as he could find. The run continued anyway, and by 3 P.M. things looked desperate; there was only about $40,000 left in the vault. But Sherman remained steadfast; he trusted that his army friends, individuals like Joseph L. Folsom, Don Carlos Buell, James A. Hardie, Braxton Bragg, John Bell Hood, George H. Thomas, Ethan Allan Hitchcock, Henry W. Halleck, and Joe Hooker, who had deposited $130,000, would back him in this crisis.[18] Those who were there did. Closing time of 4 P.M. seemed agonizingly slow in coming, but when it arrived, the bank was still standing.

Sherman went home for dinner and spent the evening visiting friends to ask them to make payments on their loans. They promised to do what they could. One friend provided a $40,000 check for emergency use, which Sherman promptly cashed at the U.S. Mint. He went to bed that night confident his bank was safe. The next day more deposits came in, and at 4 P.M. there was a cash balance of $117,000, not counting the $40,000 loan. Cump was ecstatic: "So the Battle is over and we are not dead by a d—d Sight," he reported to Turner. Lucas and Turner's reputation had risen enormously, and congratulations for Sherman's handling of the crisis poured in. His bank had "a magnificent future" ahead of it, he boasted. "We weathered it [the run] by excessive caution, by scattering risks, and by not having too many sinking friends to bolster up."[19]

Yet Sherman knew that the future remained uncertain. Only the "true" banking institutions remained standing; the "false & unsound" had fallen. (Seven of nineteen banks had failed.) The whole experience taught him several lessons that he would not forget. All his days he worried about "the invidious dangers of credit."[20] He was convinced that his army experiences had been crucial in getting him through the crisis and that the loyalty of his army friends had been even more important. Conversely, he lost all confidence in merchants and businessmen in general. Too many of them had remained cowering in their offices when they should have been out providing support for the banks. He would repay their disloyalty mercilessly in the future, he promised. As for the press, too many of the city's newspapers had made a bad situation worse by their untrue and unfair reports. He would never forgive them.

Ellen bragged about Cump's achievements to her family in Lancaster, but to his face she admitted that she was disappointed that his bank had survived. Had it failed, she said, they would be going home. Sherman felt deeply betrayed and hurt. "I'd blow this house [bank] into atoms and squeeze dollars out of brickbats rather than let our affairs pass into the hands of a rascally receiver, or more rascally Sheriff."[21] Ellen's desire to live near her family bespoke Thomas Ewing's continued influence over her and the corresponding weakness of Sherman's hope to live independently. Despite his attempts, the magnet of the Ewings pulled her. The loyalty of his army friends was more dependable and drew him closer to them. Their staunch support contrasted starkly with his wife's disloyalty. As he had learned at West Point, the army was his true family.

Sherman's actions during the banking crisis revealed some significant personal traits. He might have chronic doubts about his own abilities and might worry and become depressed, but neither anxiety nor depression affected his performance during the run on the bank; he had grown more secure as conditions worsened, acting swiftly, confidently, and efficiently. But when business as normal resumed, he suffered one of the worst asthma attacks of his life on March 18 and was confined to bed for several days; only the physician's prescription of back-cupping provided relief. The ongoing tensions of his daily life had resumed their ill effects.[22]

Despite their move into a new house on fashionable Rincon Hill one week earlier, Ellen boarded a ship for Ohio, leaving Cump, Lizzie, and Willy behind. Her compulsion for home, parents, and daughter overcame any hesitation about leaving her family and their new home so precipitously. Sherman hoped Ellen's visit home and his willingness to allow her to stay as long as she wished would cure her of homesickness once and for all. He did not like San Francisco himself, he admitted, but "let us submit with some grace and patience." He simply would never go back to Ohio; he would never be anything but "a common loafer" there. In California he held "a high & responsible position." "Really and truly do I wish you to stay at home and make such a visit as will satisfy you so that when you return it will be cheerfully and with contentment that in addition to the cares of my position I will not feel each moment that you are pining for home."[23]

As soon as Ellen reached New York, she wrote Cump a letter expressing her joy at being able to visit her father. She already missed Lizzie and Willie, she confessed, but she was happy that Sherman had insisted they not make the trip. Then she told Cump that they could probably never have Minnie back; her father could not live without the little girl. "The probability is that we will have a large family," she wrote, "and it would seem the most selfish thing to refuse one [child] to Father. Do not ask me to take her away from him. I know you are to [sic] kind to insist upon it." With obvious dejection, Sherman responded: "It is a pity to have children strangers to parents but in some instances such as this it cannot be avoided." Thomas Ewing could not be denied, even if it meant the sacrifice of his own daughter.[24]

Ellen stayed away for seven months. She and Cump corresponded regularly, but the separation was a serious strain. She wrote him long letters expressing how much she missed him and the two children. In California, she had worried about something happening to Minnie and her parents in Ohio. Now she fretted that Lizzie and Willie would meet some untoward fate and Cump would suffer unbearably from asthma. She expressed a renewed affection for Cump, telling him she yearned to be with him and at times could hardly stand the separation. In the future she promised "to give more evidence of love," which, she said, "infirmities of body and temper have trifled & concealed." She worried that her absence might cause him "to seek pleasure" that he "would not otherwise think of." Despite the sexual yearnings, she admitted, in obviously significant words, that the "gratification & pleasure" her visit was providing her father was reason enough for her to remain separated from her husband. Thomas Ewing still came first.[25]

Sherman resigned himself to her absence and became busier than he had ever been. His chief clerk took vacation in October so he had to manage the bank's paperwork by himself, regularly working through the night whenever a steamer was leaving the next morning for the East Coast. Business remained uncertain, but he was pleased with a pay raise and a hint from his friend Turner that he was doing such a good job in California that he ought to become head of the home bank in St. Louis. He was similarly complimented but declined the offer when leading city Democrats wanted him to run for city treasurer. When the California Pioneers scheduled the celebration of the state's admission into the Union, they named Sherman, already on the board of directors, to be the parade's grand marshal. As an official of the company, he went to Sacramento to ride on the first railroad in the state. His public persona was solidifying as his marital one was diminishing.[26]

Sherman hardly cut an imposing figure during these years. He was thin and sickly looking. One of his clerks said of him, "You would have thought he was an invalid to look at his build and peculiarly pinched look about the mouth." Still, his quick movements and rapidity of speech demonstrated his high energy level. He may have been fiscally careful to the point of slow action, but he was never subdued in his behavior. Another clerk said that he never had a "fifteen minute conversation with him. "He has always something to do, either at his house or in the bank."[27]

Sherman, now a single parent, spent a good deal of time with his children. His letters to Ellen were filled with tales of their escapades. He was particularly taken with Willy, whom he called "as fine a looking child as ever was." "After each meal if I don't take him & carry him into the yard, stable, &c[,] he kicks up a row and his weight is no trifle," he reported. He also enjoyed watching the boy make a shambles of his sister's play dinner parties. "She is in perfect awe of him," he chuckled, "and runs in perfect dread when he approaches." For the first time, Cump sounded like the proud parent.[28]

Ellen finally returned to San Francisco in early December 1855, once again leaving Minnie behind with her parents. On arriving, she excitedly ran up the stairs to find Lizzie just out of her bath and Willy playing by the window. Both children were startled to be swept up by this strange woman, and Willy quickly tore himself away to the safety of his nurse's arms. Ellen was pleased that Lizzie seemed to remember her and was particularly touched to hear the child's evening prayers when she said in her lisping voice: "Holy Mary pray for Mama and bring her safe home to me."[29]

Ellen now seemed free of homesickness, but Sherman, though happy to see her, felt anger at her long absence. He tried to suppress his frustration, but a flare-up of his asthma gave him away. Winter's dampness and the constant worry of his business, exacerbated by a general commercial malaise and his decision not to allow businessmen to write overdrafts any longer, added to the stress. In the throes of one particularly bad asthmatic attack, he wrote Turner to have a replacement ready because he might "die at any moment."[30]

When spring came in 1856, his disposition improved and his

attacks grew less severe. He served as chairman of an executive committee memorializing Congress for a wagon road from Missouri to California. He accepted a commission as major general of the California militia and gave a speech at the celebration officially opening a twenty-two-mile railroad. He told his congressman brother John "to avoid localism and to act as a representative of a great developing nation rather than a mere emblem of the freaks and prejudices of a small constituency." In other words, Sherman advised John not to focus on the slavery issue at the expense of the nation. He continued to think it should be left alone. Sherman urged John, once again, to support legislation friendly to California.[31]

Ellen seemed happy directing her house with its staff of handyman, cook, house girl, and nurse. She put less pressure on Sherman to change, and he was happier. But in her heart, she still yearned for Ohio. Pictures of the Ewings were all over the house, and she had Lizzie and Willy talk to the likenesses as though they were alive. On numerous occasions, she tried to deal with her longing for Minnie by dressing Willy in a girl's bonnet or night cap "to make him look like Minnie."[32]

In May Sherman found himself in yet another San Francisco crisis. As the city grew from a sleepy hamlet to a busy commercial and financial center in the space of a few years, San Francisco suffered from the inherent dislocation associated with such change. The so-called better sort—the city's businessmen—never seemed to be able to win when they ran for office against opponents whom they considered unscrupulous, corrupt, and violent. The business class prided itself on having cleaned up the city in 1851 through a vigilante organization, and they were ready to do it again if the occasion arose.[33]

A sensational shooting galvanized the elite into action.[34] James Casey, a member of the Board of Supervisors and editor of the *Sunday Times,* shot a man with the improbable name of James King of William, former banker and editor of the *Daily Evening Bulletin.* Casey was angry over King's documented accusation that Casey had once served time in New York's Sing Sing prison. On May 14, 1856, as King was on his way home, Casey shot him in the chest and then turned himself over to the sheriff, a political associate and one of those widely believed to be responsible for the city's alleged corruption.

When news of the popular King's shooting spread, a near riot ensued. Sherman, who during recovery from the earlier financial panic had threatened to throw Casey and his press out of his building's third-story window if Casey did not stop publishing antibank commentaries, wished a mob had immediately lynched the newsman. He would have approved of that. Once Casey was under legal protection, however, Sherman believed that the law should take its course.

Sherman had recently accepted command of the California militia, so he felt a sense of responsibility for maintaining law and order. He reluctantly decided to investigate. He found the sheriff and a few supporters in a completely indefensible position at the jail. Sherman told the mayor that his militia could do nothing because the situation was militarily hopeless. Meanwhile, the vigilantes kept organizing, supported by the city's leading citizens and almost all its newspapers to become "the largest such extralegal movement in American history," some six to eight thousand strong.[35]

The events that followed show a complicated story of the failure of constituted authority. The mayor asked the governor for help to maintain order. J. Neely Johnson, recently elected to the state house under the Know Nothing banner, was sure he could settle matters because he knew the president of the vigilantes well. Sherman was skeptical, and he was correct. A hastily arranged deal fell through.

On May 20, some six days after the shooting, King died. Casey's fate and that of Charles Cora, another prisoner in jail on shaky murder charges, was sealed. Some twenty-five hundred men, armed with rifles, muskets, and even a field piece, moved against the jail. Another five thousand followed in reserve. From the safety of the International Hotel roof, Sherman, the governor, and the mayor watched, powerless to intervene. A man on a white horse, with a carriage following behind, rode through the crowd. Casey and Cora were taken without opposition to the vigilante head-quarters on the other side of town. Several days later, as King's funeral cortege passed by, Casey and Cora were publicly hanged.

Sherman tried to maintain a low profile, but Ellen spoke out vociferously against what she called the "mob" of *most respectable merchants* " but actually "traitors and pharisees." Friends warned her to keep quiet, but she refused, believing that Casey and Cora had been hanged because they were Catholics. Actually, lingering Know Nothing anti-Catholic prejudice had nothing to do with the executions; it was, after all, a Know Nothing governor who was most active in trying to save the condemned men.[36]

Sherman was disturbed at seeing the city "at the mercy of irresponsible masses," but he continued to try to distance himself from the events and "endeavor not to provoke the special enmity of our New Rulers." Throughout the affair, his antivigilantism made him unpopular and no doubt hurt his business. There were vigilante plans afoot to kidnap him and do violence against his bank.[37]

After about a week, as the vigilantes continued an extensive campaign of political arrests and trials, Sherman was drawn into the fray. The governor decided to put the vigilantes in their place.[38] He called a meeting with General John E. Wool, the commander of the area's U.S. Army unit, to secure the necessary weapons to arm the militia. Sherman agreed that if Wool provided weapons and if David Farragut, the area navy commander, provided a ship, he would call out the troops against the vigilantes.

Farragut forthrightly told Sherman that the law prevented him from providing a ship, but he promised to place one near enough to the city to make the necessary impression. Wool promised full support, even showing Sherman his armory, where Sherman recognized the weapon storage boxes he had brought with him on his first trip to California on the *Lexington*. Johnson then issued a proclamation declaring a state of insurrection and announcing his determination to put it down. Sherman called out the militia.

The city's press remained in an uproar. A group of citizens worked to prevent total war between the militia and the vigilantes, and Sherman was willing to cooperate with them. Then he learned shocking news from a customer in the bank: General Wool had changed his mind and would not supply the weapons he had earlier promised. Sherman immediately demanded a meeting with the general and members of the newly formed Conciliation party. Wool insisted he had never promised any arms. Sherman had been betrayed. Governor Johnson was so angry he refused even to meet with the general.[39]

Throughout, Sherman was torn in several directions. He felt duty bound to defend established authority or else accept a personal responsibility for the anarchy that resulted. At the same time, he agreed with the vigilantes that Casey and individuals like him were despicable characters who deserved what they got for their disorderly conduct. It bothered Sherman to be defending law and order in league with "rowdies, shoulder strikers, and ballot box stuffers." He worried how his stance was affecting his reputation and his business. Most of San Francisco's leading businessmen either were vigilantes or supported the movement. His only argument with them was that "instead of violent remedies the true course was to devise some legal mode of redress," because "a forcible resistance of the law does not end with the case in point, but may rise up against ourselves in some other and less pleasing form." In short, Sherman believed that the vigilante perception of San Francisco's alleged political evils was generally accurate; it was the methods they used that bothered him. As long as he thought there was a chance he might be able to help restore rightful legal authority, he reluctantly tried to do it. Wool's denial of weapons and the growth of a group committed to opposing both vigilantes and the so-called law and order faction caused him to lose all hope. He resigned his militia commission rather than continue in an unwinnable situation. He published an explanation in the local press, and he was pleased to find that most of his friends and business associates applauded his decision.[40]

Concern for his bank and worry about keeping his family with him were the major factors in Sherman's decision to pull out of the battle with the vigilantes. He felt sorry for the governor, and duty still tugged at his sleeve, but, in the end, his determination to become a business success convinced him to resign. Defending what so many important people considered to be unsavory politicians and newspaper accusations that he was planning to use the militia "to lay the city in ashes" were hardly good advertisement for his bank. In the end, business success became more important than antivigilantism; personal achievement was more crucial than support for principles of law and order. Later in his life, Sherman was willing to forgo success to defend established national governmental authority but not now. It was this experience with the vigilantes in California that helped persuade him in 1860–1861 to take a stand against Southern secessionists in order to avoid anarchy of a far greater magnitude than that which occurred in San Francisco.[41]

Sherman followed developments from the sidelines. The vigilantes easily dispersed the militia by capturing their weapons. Sherman was so worried at this collapse of legal authority that he locked all his bank's money into the vault and deployed his clerks to defend the building. At the same time, he worked behind the scenes to bring the governor and the vigilantes together. After six weeks, the emergency was over, and law and order had been restored. The vigilantes celebrated with a giant victory parade, and later, to Sherman's disgust, "as they controlled the press, they wrote their own history" and convinced everyone they had been right.[42]

During the imbroglio, Sherman received some surprising advice from his foster father. The great constitutionalist Thomas Ewing called for "an absolute monarch" to restore necessary order. In a later letter to a local minister and to his brother John, Sherman forcibly stated his own support of constitutional government but admitted that he prefered a dictator to a continuation of vigilante rule. The American governmental system was indeed "too dependent on the popular clamor to be firm and independent." He had little faith in democracy, though he believed it could be more orderly than arbitrary rule by self-appointed saviors.[43]

Sherman responded patiently to brother John's equation of vigilantism with "Bloody Kansas." There were vast differences between Kansas and California, he explained; it was a matter of established government in California and an establishing government in Kansas. Then, of course, there was slavery. "Every question," he surmised, was being "determined not on its merits, but on the nigger question." Unless this stopped, there would be a civil war. He supported Buchanan's bid for the presidency but supposed John's party loyalty would force him to support the Republican candidate, John C. Frémont. Sherman's attitude toward Frémont had not changed: "if he is fit for the office of President[,] then anybody may aspire to that office." Actually, "our Government ought to be strong enough to endure the Devil himself for President." Rather than worrying about elections, Bleeding Kansas, and all the other slavery issues, Sherman once again directed John to get a good wagon road for California.[44]

Sherman's home life seemed to improve. He now ignored Ellen's and her father's calls for a return to Ohio, and though he missed Minnie, he realized that as long as her "Grandma and Grandpa seem to think" her "very necessary to their happiness," she would not be with him. He had Lizzie and Willy and, in early October, another son, named immediately Thomas Ewing after his grandfather. Christmas that year was a happy one. The nursery was "knee deep in toys and doll baby clothing." On New Year's Day, Cump and Ellen conducted their customary open house and received some one hundred callers, including, to Ellen's delight, the city's Catholic archbishop.[45]

As the California economy continued unsettled, Lucas and Turner in St. Louis decided to close their San Francisco branch and open a new one under Sherman's direction in New York. No doubt, Sherman's earlier pessimistic letters influenced their decision, but he was shocked at the news, disappointed that his partners had not come to California first before making their decision. It was true, he admitted, that the promise of 1853 had proved false, and they had never made the kind of profit they had always envisioned. Still, he wrote to St. Louis, "the real cause of the suddenness of your determination" was not lack of sufficient profit but fear that his "life was too precarious to trust." Despite his asthma, he wished he could stay in California forever. It was Ellen who wanted to leave.[46] Sherman attributed much blame for the bank's closing to Ellen. Her constant desire to go home and her exorbitant spending habits prevented him from becoming a financial success. It was not his fault and certainly not the bank's officers; it was hers and the Ewings'. The resentment of the past years surfaced; his uphill struggle to make a life for himself and keep his family together had failed because he had struggled alone.

It took another six months to settle the bank's business in an orderly fashion. Ellen debated whether to stay with Cump to the end or leave for Ohio immediately. Her heart ached for Lancaster, "the only home I love," but "to go home seems a desertion of my husband and my duty to him." Thomas and Maria Ewing had no such qualms. They urged Ellen to come as soon as she could. In mid-April 1857, the bank's May 1 closing was announced. Ellen offered her husband little sympathy because staying there would have required "too great a sacrifice" on her part.[47]

Sherman suffered another asthma attack, continuing to suspect "undue influence" on the part of Ellen and the Ewings behind the bank's closing. Ellen would rather see him "driving a cart of coal in Ohio than be Governor of California," he lamented. But it was Cump's fear of further failure, his uncertainty about what New York might bring, that bothered him the most. He told Turner to be prepared to make all the necessary decisions in New York for at least a year. "I feel some doubt of my powers to cope with the acute operations in New York." In San Francisco, he was "somebody"; in New York he feared being "swallowed up in that vast gulf of mankind." He was going back East again, closer to the Ewings and their powerful influence on his family and future, and he could not depend on Ellen to stand by his side.[48]

By early July 1857, Sherman was in New York, meeting with his St. Louis partners and completing plans for establishing the branch bank on Wall Street. He was pleased that his banking partners retained enough confidence in his abilities to put him in charge of the new branch.

He knew Ellen was happy at leaving San Francisco, a place she despised and a city where he could not maintain her and the children according to her "Ohio notions of nurses, servants, coal, & butter." He knew, too, that Thomas Ewing was relieved that "the family circle" would now "hardly be broken by distance." When Sherman left his family in Lancaster, his son, Willy, unknowingly joined ranks with his mother's family. Willy looked at his father's departure and described it in army terms as a "desertion."[49]

Sherman announced the bank's opening in the New York press near the end of July and mailed out some five hundred circulars to midwestern companies. The firm hoped to specialize in collections payable in the Midwest and provide services for James H. Lucas's many business interests there and in New York. Sherman found lodging, where he often talked far into the night with two fellow boarders, Major J. G. Barnard and Lieutenant James G. McPherson, the latter one of his closest friends during the Civil War.[50]

Business improved "slow but sure" during the first several weeks, but Sherman ignored this steady improvement. He continued to grieve over leaving California, upset that he had no money to show for the years of hard work and suffering there. He remained angry at Ellen and the support she had withheld from him since their marriage. He coldly departed from her, displaying no concern over their separation, and expressing unwillingness to write more often than once a week. His hurt was deep.[51]

Sherman had convinced himself that his St. Louis partners had closed the San Francisco bank solely because of his health problems; consequently, he felt responsible for all their business losses. He decided he was now "utterly disqualified . . . for business." "I am afraid of my own shadow, and if I was only fit for anything I would wipe my hands of this nightmare." He called himself a "madman or [a] fool" for having left California. He should have salvaged more of the bank's money first, but Ellen's homesickness had forced him to leave. He should have never built that "cursed house." He had built it for Ellen, only to have her complain about the resulting financial sacrifice. If only she would now become more understanding, he could still work things out. Ellen was responsible for the California mess.[52]

But there was more. Old army friends had sent him money that he had invested without compensation. Instead of handling these funds (some $130,000) like any other deposits, he had established a trust fund, placed the money into promising investments, and kept separate detailed records of dividends, profits, and interest. During the bank's hard times, this trust fund and the support of these military men had helped keep his institution afloat. When the bank closed, however, some of these investments were lost. Sherman had no more legal responsibility for these losses than he had for any others, but he took personal responsibility for them. His natural father had bankrupted his family by trying to repay self-imposed obligations long ago, and Sherman had become a dependent foster child as a result. Now he was in the same predicament and faced the fear of similar personal failure, the situation even more frightening because it involved his army family. If this bank failure lost him the affection of army friends, what would he have left?[53]

Sherman anxiously grappled with the problem. Exactly how much of the officers' $130,000 was lost is uncertain, though the figure must have been at least $20,000, the value of property he sold to help meet the debt. In 1858 he sold 2,680 acres of California land for $8,000, and he gave up 640 acres in Illinois. At another time, Sherman repaid a friend's $2,000 investment plus proper interest by selling a piece of his property in the St. Louis Stoddard addition. In September 1858 he reimbursed an army comrade by selling 40 acres in Illinois. Letters from these old friends praising his "integrity" and expressing continued trust in his financial judgment were important, but the kind words did not erase the debt or alleviate his fear of financial collapse.[54]

As he discovered that his new banking venture was proving to be as disastrous as his previous one, Sherman grew more anxious. The Panic of 1857 hit in August, and Sherman kept his bank secure, but the times so mirrored the San Francisco crisis that he felt increasingly apprehensive. In early October the feared disaster hit: His home bank suspended payment, thus closing his still-solvent New York branch. Sherman had done his job well and could not be blamed for his bank's collapse, but once again, conditions beyond his control had doomed him, and at the worst possible time. It would be difficult to repay his army friends even while employed. How could he ever do it without a job?[55]

He began calling himself the "Jonah of banking" and accused Ellen of "no doubt be[ing] glad at last to have attained your wish to see me out of the army and out of employment." He remained determined to repay his friends, either by becoming a surveyor for a St. Louis land agent or by selling more property. He wished he had never given up his army commission to become a banker. "Banking & Gambling are synonymous terms," he said.[56]

Near the end of October, a depressed Sherman returned to St. Louis. Although remaining angry with Ellen, he needed her help to decide what to do next. She remained his ballast, despite their differences. James Lucas released all his partners, Sherman included, from any debts incurred in the bank's crash, and this was encouraging. But everything else looked bleak. "I do not see any chance of an income to support my family, and I don't like to have them so dependent," he lamented to Thomas Ewing, the person he and his family remained dependent on.[57]

Sherman tried to salvage his future by returning to the past. He twice wrote his brother, John, asking the congressman to find him a place in the army. He similarly wrote to the adjutant general. There were no army openings, however, so he reluctantly agreed to return to California to settle the bank's outstanding obligations there. By successfully recouping some of the bank's losses, he hoped to assuage the terrible guilt he continued feeling about leaving California.[58]

During his stay in St. Louis, he ran into another down-on-his-luck West Pointer, U. S. Grant, and chatted briefly. All Sherman could later remember was that after hearing of Grant's farming failure and considering his own situation, he "concluded that West Point and the regular army were not good schools for farmers [and] bankers."[59]

Arriving in San Francisco in late January 1858, Sherman found that the closed bank's assets were a confused mess. The bank held real estate once worth $100,000 plus almost $200,000 in notes, bonds, and mortgages, but because land values had so plummeted, no one knew the real value of these holdings. Since he was receiving only expense reimbursement on this trip, he felt "justly punished" for becoming involved in a business as unsteady as banking. He wrote countless collection letters asking debtors to pay whatever they could, promising to "make any discount" the debtor "would have the heart to ask." He half-jokingly wished he had drowned on his first arrival, but then, in a pathetic collection letter, he asked a debtor to save him "from disgrace," and a "punishment . . . more than I deserve." Even James Lucas's letter reporting that the home bank's improved economic situation meant that Sherman could leave California did not help his disposition.[60]

Thomas Ewing chose this precise moment to renew his salt well offer, and in his despair, Sherman reluctantly accepted the long-dreaded proposal, giving up his desired return to the army or any civilian job independent of his foster father. "I am utterly disqualified for business," he wrote his friend Turner, "my experience here has completely destroyed all confidence in myself, and everybody else." "When I leave here, I shall accept some post at the Salt Wells or Coal Mines of Mr. Ewing, where at least I can do no harm if I can't do good."[61]

He poured his heart out to Thomas Ewing, once more seeking his foster father's understanding. He wished he did not have to come back to Ohio, but Ellen's extravagance forced him. "She professes great willingness to live in a log house, feed chickens, or milk cows [but] I know better. She can't come down to that. She requires and must have certain comforts which to another would be superfluities." But he refused to live in Lancaster. "You can understand what Ellen does not—that a man needs a conscious-ness of position and influence among his peers. In the army I know my place, and out here [in California] am one of the pioneers and big chiefs. At Lancaster I can only be Cump Sherman."[62]

His trip to California did not rid him of his guilt feelings over the closing of the San Francisco bank. He told James Lucas that he still felt himself "bound by every principal of honor or honesty to devote any portion of my remaining life to this California business." Whenever the banking firm required it, he would go back to the Pacific coast. Even assurances from St. Louis that he was "justly entitled to an honorable discharge from further care & trouble so far as Mr. Lucas' affairs are concerned" did not seem to help.[63]

He arrived in Lancaster near the end of July 1858 and remained with Ellen and the children all August, committed to begin managing Thomas Ewing's nearby Chauncey coal and salt holdings in the fall. He remained upset at being "as poor as a church mouse" and having to "start where I began 22 years ago." He was convinced that his foster father had made the management offer only to keep Ellen close by. Worse, Ellen and his sister, Elizabeth, argued bitterly over whether Ellen had forced Cump to come home from California. Ellen became enraged at what she perceived to be Elizabeth's slighting attitude toward Catholicism. The bickering was more than Sherman could stand; he had to get away. He asked Boyle and Tom Ewing if he could join their recently established law and property business in Leavenworth, Kansas. He insisted that the family quarrel between Ellen and Elizabeth had convinced him he could not settle in Ohio. Actually Sherman's fears of remaining beholden to Thomas Ewing's charity was at the heart of his desire to leave; the family argument had provided a face-saving excuse.[64]

Thomas Ewing had established his two sons in the Kansas enterprise, so he agreed to let Cump join in. If his foster son would not manage the nearby family business, association with family in Kansas was the next best thing. Ewing made Sherman the manager of his vast landholdings in and around Leavenworth, while Tom and Boyle offered him an equal partnership in their newly established law firm. Sherman accepted both offers, happy at his good fortune in securing a last-minute reprieve from the saltworks, though he had to leave Ellen and the children in Lancaster.

Around September 1, 1858, he traveled to St. Louis to consult with his former banking partners. Kansas was better than Chauncey, but Missouri was best of all. St. Louis meant independence; Chauncey and Kansas meant remaining Thomas Ewing's ward. At first, his job prospects in St. Louis looked good, but nothing developed, and he had to continue on to Leavenworth. On arrival, he noted that although the economic situation in Kansas reminded him of California, he had no choice but to stay.[65]

Leavenworth was a town of about four thousand people, many of them originally from Lancaster. Sherman could do little until Thomas Ewing, Jr., returned to the city from a political trip. As a moderate free soiler, Tom was deeply involved in the territory's chaotic politics, rising in 1861 to become the state's first chief justice and its leading Civil War general. Sherman took advantage of the free time to visit his old friend Stewart Van Vliet, the quartermaster at nearby Fort Leavenworth. Van Vliet offered Sherman a position superintending repairs on the 140-mile military road connecting Fort Leavenworth and Fort Riley. Sherman happily accepted this ten-day job. He particularly reveled in the time he spent with army friends; he felt "perfectly at home with sound of bugle and drum." His attraction for his military family remained unabated. "It makes me regret my being out of the service thus to meet my old comrades, in the open field, just where I most [would] like to be."[66]

The law firm had little work. Sherman handled the banking and real estate side of the partnership, but he quickly decided he had better become a lawyer too. When a local judge came to the office on business, Sherman asked him about admission to the bar. The judge sent him to the courthouse, promising that his clerk would give him the necessary license. Sherman asked about any required test, but the jurist waved him off. Sherman could become a lawyer "on the ground of general intelligence." No test was necessary. The firm's business card proudly announced that "Sherman & Ewing" "will practice in all the Courts of the Territory, and in the North Western Counties of Missouri."

The card was grander than the law office. It was located on Main Street, situated on the second floor of a ramshackle building with an outside staircase that frightened anyone who ventured to climb it. Even the shingle announcing the firm's name, said one observer, was "dingy." Sherman's appearance was only slightly more impressive. A contemporary remembered him then as being of a "middle stature, nervous muscular frame," "bluish-gray" eyes which were "introverted but full of smoldering fire," a "sharp and well cut" mouth, and "a sandy red, straight, short" beard.[67]

Sherman never did much lawyering, apparently appearing before the bench only twice, once in probate and another time in justice court. Both times he lost, and in both instances he left the courtroom disgusted. The details of only one case have been preserved. A client was sued over the value of a farm animal, and when Sherman arrived in Squire Whitney's courtroom to represent this man, the opposing lawyer, Colonel Lewis Burns, was more than ready. Sherman simply presented the facts; Burns rebutted by "hurling, in thunder tones, page after page and volume after volume" from the huge pile of law books on the table before him. None of the precedents had anything to do with the case at issue, but the overwhelmed justice ruled in Burns's favor anyway. Burns sounded as if he knew what he was talking about, the justice said. The episode only reinforced Sherman's low opinion of the legal profession. He stayed out of the courtroom after that. Later he liked to joke about being defeated by an antagonist who was short in stature but long on legal ability. "That little bow-legged gnat beat me slick and clean and came near taking my boots," he laughed.[68]

Without much legal business, Sherman took every opportunity to make money any other way he could. (During this time, Thomas Ewing was buying fifty city lots and some ten acres of other property for Ellen, but these purchases were investments, not a way to meet day-to-day expenses.) When not doing paperwork for the law office, Sherman sold potatoes and corn; participated in horse and mule auctions at the fort; and became a notary public. He desperately tried to earn enough money to bring his family to Kansas and take care of them without Thomas Ewing's help. The more he tried, the worse things became. He grew increasingly exasperated at Thomas Ewing, Jr., who was practicing antislavery politics rather than the law. When Tom decided to remain away that winter, his absence opened the way for Ellen and the children to travel to Leavenworth. Tom offered Sherman the use of his house, and Sherman jumped at the chance.[69]

An excited Ellen and children arrived on November 11, 1858, but Minnie once more remained behind with the Ewings. In her childish hand, she wrote Sherman a brief note hoping he was not "displeased" at her, but she "could not feel willing to leave Grandma," and Maria Ewing "could not feel willing to spare me." Sherman was disappointed but told her she could stay in Lancaster as long as she was a "comfort" to her grandparents. Within the week, Sherman became so ill that he missed two days of work. Although Ellen bragged that homesickness no longer bothered her, she became depressed when her sister did not write her often enough. She suffered from a gynecological problem and had to endure repeated painful treatment. In February 1859, she became pregnant and again began pining for Lancaster. Thomas Ewing encouraged her to come back. To Sherman it all sounded very familiar—and very discouraging.[70]

The winter was difficult for the Shermans. Tom and Boyle were absent, and there was little business. Cump wiled away his time in Tom's house dreaming about building his own home. It was a pipedream. A $100 gift from the Ewings and a $459.08 payment from Lucas for the sale of Sherman's California furniture came at crucial times and helped pull the beleaguered family through the winter. When spring came, Sherman had to send them back to Lancaster, and Thomas Ewing's care, again. He tried to console himself by telling Ellen to keep a strict record of her father's help. She should keep any aid to a minimum; Thomas Ewing had "already been more than generous." He similarly told Ewing: "If I can see fair prospects for making a living here[,] I shall not look elsewhere but I am not content to stay here or anywhere, unless I can be independent of assistance from any quarter."[71]

Once again, Sherman turned to his foster father, ignoring the irony of trying to gain freedom from Thomas Ewing by going to him. He hired himself out to Ewing to open a farm on a large tract of land in Shawnee County on the north bank of Indian Creek, forty miles from Leavenworth and eight from Topeka. His job was to complete the construction of farm buildings and then turn the property over to a nephew Ewing planned to settle there.[72]

Using Ewing's money, Sherman tried several schemes. There was a gold rush at Pike's Peak in the Rockies, and the expected spring and summer torrent of prospectors would have to pass the farm to get there. Sherman considered buying horses and cattle "for a song" from discouraged returning prospectors, but the plan never materialized. He did begin acquiring corn for the travelers to buy for their animals. He and some hired hands put up storage buildings to hold the six thousand to ten thousand bushels of corn Ewing had authorized him to purchase. They worked hard but could barely keep ahead of the delivery wagons. The weather delayed the carpentry work, the wind blowing as cold and hard as Sherman remembered it at Cape Horn in 1846. Fresh snow covered the ground, slowing him down but encouraging him to believe that the corn he was so carefully storing would find buyers. His hands filled with splinters as he worked, but it all seemed worthwhile. Still, he doubted whether there was any hope of "permanent prosperity" in Kansas, his mind recalling San Francisco. "I am doomed to be a vagabond," he worried. "I look upon myself as a dead cock in the pit, not worthy of further notice."[73]

To occupy his mind, Sherman continued writing detailed letters to his brother about slavery, abolitionists, the new Republican party, and other contemporary issues. He was blunt and conservative. He was staying out of the slavery debate in Kansas, he said, although he believed "the Negroes of our Country should remain slaves." He offered to research what he considered was the impossible suggestion that blacks be colonized in Mexico or Latin America. At John's request, he wrote a long report about the possibility of a transcontinental railroad. It would take ten years to complete such a road, he insisted, and he doubted that it would have adequate traffic once it was completed. But he accurately predicted the best route, that it would unify the nation, and that only the federal government was big enough to build it. John had the letter published in a Washington newspaper, and it drew rave reviews, bringing a little excitement into Sherman's otherwise drab life.[74]

Sitting in the rough cabin he had helped build on the wind-swept Kansas farm, Cump dreamed of more cosmopolitan surroundings. He envied John's projected trip to Europe writing a succinct disquisition on the Italian war between France and Austria and sighing, "I wish I were there to watch the operations and changes, but alas! I am in Kansas scratching for a living." He asked John to send him any available exploration reports. As a child, he had read about faraway places in Peter Parley's books. Here again, as an adult, he could imagine even if he could not travel.[75]

His corn speculation proved a complete bust. Defeated again, he complained, "I feel in danger, ready to run to any quarter of the world where I can do anything." Some good news came his way. James H. Lucas cancelled the seven thousand dollar debt on his San Francisco house, and Sherman responded with even greater determination to pull himself out of his financial mess. Ellen wrote of bad health, worrisome pregnancy, fear of death, and continued family feuding. She wanted him back in Ohio on her father's farm. Once again as he battled disappointment, his wife could suggest only what he feared the most: a return to Lancaster as a ward of Thomas Ewing.[76]

There followed a dizzying round of suggestions and countersuggestions from St. Louis friends: superintendent on a hotel building project, a wholesale grocery business, and general superintendency of an iron company. But James H. Lucas wanted Sherman to return to California again, and he agreed to go if Thomas Ewing gave him permission. His foster father was coming to Kansas for five days to inspect some of his property there, and Sherman knew he would pressure him to return to Lancaster. "But I have a strong repugnance to returning to my native place worse off than I left it and prefer to try my fortune elsewhere." He needed Ewing's blessing anyway.[77]

Sherman began seriously pursuing a return to the army, with the security and family feeling it provided. In early June 1859 he wrote to an old army friend in the adjutant general's office. Sherman had invested money in California for later Civil War general Don Carlos Buell, the bridegroom of Richard B. Mason's recent widow. Sherman asked Buell to recommend him for any available vacancy in the Pay Department. "Was I ten years younger & had I not four children I would be too proud to ask any favor of anybody." But he had no choice. Even if any openings developed in the Pay Department, Buell responded, they would all be politically filled. But he had just learned of the new Louisiana Military Seminary looking for a superintendent. If Sherman was interested in that post, Buell would be happy to recommend him.[78]

Sherman and Thomas Ewing spent their allotted time together, and shortly after Ewing's departure, Sherman applied for the job in Louisiana, mentioning his acquaintance with Ewing, Winfield Scott, Braxton Bragg, and a number of Louisiana politicians and soldiers. According to legend, Sherman's letter so impressed one of the institution's board of directors that he refused to consider any other applicants. Actually a board member thought "all from Ohio were real Abolitionists," so he was unhappy over Sherman's election, and there was indeed some "very *violent* opposition" to him. Still, he was elected by a wide margin. Within a few days, board member G. Mason Graham, Richard B. Mason's half-brother, unofficially informed Sherman of his election as the superintendent and professor of engineering, architecture, and drawing at the Louisiana Military Seminary in Alexandria. The job was his if he wanted it.[79]

This quasi-military position appealed to Sherman, but he preferred a return to the army, so he mounted one last-ditch attempt to land a position in the Pay Department. He made formal application; he wrote his senator and his congressman; and he asked army friends, most likely those indebted to him from California investment days, to write letters and make contacts for him. He asked Hugh Boyle Ewing to use his influence with Democratic president James Buchanan. Then a job in Utah and a banking position in London opened up, but he continued to covet the paymastership. He traveled to Washington and tried to pull all the strings he could, no doubt handicapped by Thomas Ewing's long-time opposition to the Democratic party. He failed. Someone else had pulled the strings better and landed the job.[80]

In early August 1859 official word arrived of his selection as military seminary superintendent. The Ewings urged him instead to accept an offer to manage an American bank in London. He was torn. Had he no family, he thought, he would go to England; but in Louisiana he would be doing military work, and he would not have to be separated from his family. The Louisiana offer was a firm one, while the London bank proposal was only a possibility, presented unofficially by his brother-in-law, Boyle, one of the bank's partners. All the incorporators of the proposed bank were, like Boyle, young and inexperienced; were they capable of launching such a major project? He did not want to repeat his California and New York failures. The military seminary, by contrast, was "more certain & reliable."[81]

The seminary's reliability carried the day, but in late August Thomas Ewing made one more try. He took Cump on a four-day tour of the salt wells, coal mines, and farm. Sherman remained unimpressed. He determined to go South, this time not as a

soldier but to make his fortune as a state military school superintendent.[82]

In answer to a West Point request for biographical information,
he facetiously summarized his life since graduation: "I have been
shipwrecked twice, had an arm dislocated from a horse, had some
rather hard admonitions generally not sounding well in history—
have heard a few Indian shots, where powder was decidedly
scarce, so that on the whole my career has been more civil than
military." The army remained his first love, but it had no openings
for him, so he had to remain a civilian. He had to make it in
Louisiana, or else he would have to return to Thomas Ewing's
control, in either Ohio or London. It was all very unsettling.[83]

CHAPTER 6

——— ☆ ———

CONTENTED SOUTHERN SCHOOLMASTER

As SHERMAN ENTERED still another new beginning, he felt less optimistic than he would have wished. He yearned for a return to the army; a Louisiana quasi-military position was a weak substitute. Louisiana was far from Ohio, so he knew that Ellen and the Ewings would always reject it for that reason alone. Looming over all was the slavery controversy, threatening to tear the nation apart and force him to make a fateful choice. Sherman believed that slavery was necessary for societal order, but he also believed the Union served the same function. Family, army, slavery, and Union tore at him from all sides. His task in Louisiana was to discover how he might reconcile these seemingly irreconcilable matters and find personal order.

Now that he had made up his mind to accept the superintendency of the new Louisiana military school, Sherman began looking for advice on how best to organize it. His former West Point superintendent, Richard Delafield, sent him books and papers. Don Carlos Buell penned a long letter of suggestion, as did railroad executive George B. McClellan. Sherman visited a military school in Frankfort, Kentucky, and he wrote the head of the Virginia Military Institute. He tried to prevent an unfriendly reception in Louisiana by asking his brother, John, a rising star in the recently formed Republican party, to be careful what he said about slavery. His new job in the South would be tough enough without the added burden of being identified with an outspoken "black Republican" brother.[1]

Deep down, Cump knew John would do the right thing, but he was not so sure about his wife and her family. When he left

Ellen in mid-October 1859, her letters urged him to return for fear of yellow fever. Ellen and the Ewings no longer insisted that he manage the salt wells and coal mines; they now wanted him to go into banking in England. Leave Louisiana and go to England was to be their constant refrain for the next four months.[2]

Sherman again ignored their appeals. He told Ellen that if his health held and if abolitionists did not cause him to be driven from the South, he would make his career in Louisiana. He had heard that southern military schools were anti-Union, but he was willing to see for himself. "If they [Southerners] deign to protect themselves against negroes, or abolitionists, I will help; if they propose to leave the Union on account of a supposed fact that the northern people are all abolitionists like [Joshua] Giddings and [John] Brown, then I will stand by Ohio and the North West."[3]

Arriving in Louisiana, Sherman boarded a stagecoach in Baton Rouge and rode through a moonlit night toward Rapides Parish, where Alexandria, with its sixteen hundred people, was the parish seat. The heavily pined area was in the approximate center of the state, some three hundred miles by the Red and Mississippi rivers from New Orleans. Large plantations surrounded the town. Thomas O. Moore, the newly elected governor, lived nearby, as did G. Mason Graham, the half-brother of Sherman's former commander Richard Mason and chairman of the military seminary's board of supervisors. Sherman was impressed with Graham, but he was not equally pleased with Alexandria, which he found to be not "much of a town." The seminary was even more isolated, located in the thick woods near Pineville, some three miles away.[4]

The seminary building, three years in construction, was an imposing structure. Sherman called it "a gorgeous palace, altogether too good for its purposes." It was three stories high and had five four-story towers in the gothic revival style of the day. It was located on top of a hill on a four hundred acre site with enormous pine trees surrounding it. The building contained seventy-two large rooms but no furniture of any kind. Sherman playfully wrote his daughter, Lizzie, about his "great Big Castle like those in which the Knights used to live" but where he would soon become an "old and cross" schoolmaster. He saw a challenge and seemed ready to get about meeting it. He planned to turn his "attention to [the] success of the [institution] before

I . . . [turn] my thoughts to personal advantage," he told Thomas Ewing.[5]

On his first several days on the Graham plantation, he, Graham, and three other officials established rules and regulations for the school, modeling them after those of the Virginia Military Institute. Then Sherman moved into the seminary building. He took his meals with the five carpenters whose work he superintended. He soon had these workers making plain furniture, while slaves did general clean-up work. These laborers did not work as fast as he would have wished, but "people don't work hard down here," he surmised. He was pleased to receive a warm letter of welcome from old friend Braxton Bragg. John Sherman joked that he hoped that John Brown's attack on Harper's Ferry would not make life more difficult for him.[6]

Sherman traveled to New Orleans to purchase books and equipment, growing excited over seeing old sights and former friends. He found his old house and walked past the shops where he and Minnie had bought toys and sweets. Visiting his old commissary office made him nostalgic for the army, but a new-found optimism quickly allowed him to put such thoughts aside. "That is now past," he decided. "[I] must do the best in the new sphere in which events have cast me."[7]

But events again seemed to conspire against him. In Washington, his brother John made a major blunder: He joined a number of other Republicans in recommending the 1857 antislavery book, *The Impending Crisis of the South,* written by a Southerner, Hinton Rowan Helper. Southern congressmen were so upset at this endorsement that they successfully blocked John's candidacy to be Speaker of the House. Sherman knew that any Southerner who was acquainted with him realized he was no abolitionist, but others might believe his views paralleled his brother's and hold it against the school. Despite the personal sacrifice, he decided he would resign his post if his association with the institution undermined it. He also felt duty bound to defend his brother against any unfair criticism.[8]

He was pleased to learn that John had never even read Helper's book, and it had been a "thoughtless, foolish, and unfortunate act" to allow his name to be used. "Everybody knows," John insisted, "that the ultra sentiments in the book are as obnoxious to me as they can be to any one." Sherman felt relieved but still wary.

A member of the board of superintendents told him that during such troubled times, all Southern institutions should be in the hands of loyal friends. Sherman responded that his only job was to run the seminary, though he remained loyal to United States. If the nation was torn apart, he could not predict his response.[9]

Sherman tried to protect himself by sending his chief supporter, G. Mason Graham, copies of his brother's latest letters. The moderate Graham was so impressed that he had this correspondence circulated among politicians in the state capital. Bragg also promised Sherman his backing, as did P. G. T. Beauregard, whose son attended the seminary. Sherman was pleased. In February 1860, when he had to go to Baton Rouge on business, he was delighted at his reception. "I cannot but laugh in my sleeve at the seeming influence I possess, dining with the governor, hobnobbing with the leading men in Louisiana, whilst John is universally blackguarded as an awful abolitionist."[10]

Sherman's views on slavery were truly not like John's (who was a moderate on the issue). In fact, they were much closer to those of his Southern friends. While dining with the governor during his visit to Baton Rouge, he told the officials gathered around the table that "the people of Louisiana were hardly responsible for slavery, as they had inherited it." Were he a member of the state legislature, however, he "would deem it wise to bring the legal condition of the slaves more near the status of human beings under all Christian and civilized governments." He would forbid the separation of families through sale and would repeal any law that prevented slaves from learning how to read and write. Such legislation only kept their value down, anyway. The dinner guests listened quietly, and when Sherman finished, one banged his fist on the table and exclaimed: "By God, he is right!" Another time Sherman expressed his belief in black inferiority, his opposition to emancipation, and his plans to purchase house slaves when Ellen and the family joined him. He put out a clear message: he was a supporter of slavery, not because it was politic to hold that position in Louisiana but because he firmly believed that freedom for slaves meant disorder for society.[11]

Sherman's hard work at the school, like his politics, impressed Louisianans. All the effort paid off; the school opened on time, on a cold January 2, 1860, morning. Nineteen prospective students showed up that first day, and others drifted in a few at a time for the rest of the month, eventually reaching sixty-two by May. They were as young as fifteen years of age and were accompanied by worried mothers, who insisted that they had "all the virtues of saints." "Of course," Sherman reported to Ellen, "I promise to be a father to them" all, and this pleased the mothers. When P. G. T. Beauregard sent his son to the school, he asked Sherman to find him "a proper roommate, one of studious and steady habits, who has not seen much of city life and habits."[12]

By January 5 Sherman had the school on a schedule, imposing his own "habits of order, precision, promptness, and punctuality." Breakfast was served at 7:00 A.M.; mathematics from 8:00 to 11:00 A.M.; French from 11:00 to 1:00; Lunch from 1:00 to 2:00; Latin from 2:00 to 4:00; an hour of drill at 4:30; dinner at dusk; and lights out at 10:00 P.M. Three to four cadets shared a room, sleeping on a simple floor bed and enduring spartan sleeping arrangements similar to those Sherman had experienced at West Point.[13]

The faculty was solid. The senior professor was a Hungarian refugee from the Revolutions of 1848, a reputed expert in mathematics, and an Episcopal priest. Anthony Vallas had lived and taught in New Orleans for eight years before coming to Alexandria. Francis W. Smith, the professor of chemistry and commandant of cadets, was a graduate of the Virginia Military Institute and the University of Virginia. E. Berte St. Ange, professor of modern languages, had received his education in Paris and had been a marine in the French navy. Previously he had worked briefly as a private teacher in Alexandria. Finally, there was David French Boyd, Sherman's closest faculty friend and lifelong booster. Boyd would later become president of the school that grew out of the seminary, Louisiana State University.[14]

Day-to-day activities went well, but the debate over the nature of the seminary continued. Graham, Governor Moore, and influential individuals like Braxton Bragg believed that the state needed a military academy. Some other members of the board of supervisors and several faculty members, led by Anthony Vallas, believed the school ought to be oriented toward the liberal arts. Sherman tried to maintain a middle ground, insisting only on his need to have control over the institution. To this end, he espoused a military system of discipline as the only way to govern young men efficiently. When the board went against his wishes and established a faculty board to share control, he thought they had made a mistake; however, he decided he would "submit as tamely as I can because I feel the sting of necessity."[15]

Sherman's calmer disposition was marked. No matter what the problem, the inconvenience, or how lonely he felt, Sherman seemed to be at ease. In California, New York, and Kansas, he had often been depressed, angry, and frustrated at someone or something. Now he ignored petty grievances and was more confident that problems would work themselves out. His job was hardly without conflicts, but he was doing productive work and seeing positive, concrete results. For the first time in a long time, Sherman believed he was building stability in his life. Once more he was in an all male military-style environment, and it seemed to give him both contentment and pride.

The cadets were "a heterogeneous crowd," "the sons of wealthy planters from the rivers, and aristocratic Creoles from the south, the nimble pony-riding Cajeans from the prairies, and the diligent, quiet fellows from the pine woods." Many were away from home for the first time and were intent on stretching the limits of their freedom. Sherman dealt with them fairly and squarely. One weekend when several cadets spent time at a grog shop in Alexandria, the local populace accused them of wrongdoing. Sherman took the cadets' side and told the accuser he wanted specific facts, not "mere general assertion[s]," because the cadets he knew were "well behaved" and showed "no signs of insubordination." However, when one of his "well behaved" cadets drew a knife on another over being called a liar, Sherman convened a court-martial and sent the transgressors packing. When a drawing of a "man naked & urinating" appeared on a classroom wall, Sherman frightened the prankster into admitting the act by threatening to cancel a dancing party. He caught a cadet smoking once and destroyed the tobacco, much to the young man's anger; he called Sherman's action "a breach of propriety" and left school in a huff. Another cadet shouted out some disparaging remarks at a professor, so Sherman reproved him and refused his request to run to his mother. When yet another cadet disrupted a class by raucously laughing and the professor ordered him to leave the room, the student's father wrote a letter to protest against "the arbitrary commands of dictators."[16]

Sherman remained determined to maintain total control over

his charges, but his firm actions did not deter the cadets from continuing to act up. Several ducked a slave in a nearby stream, and others so thickly covered a professor's chair and blackboard with hair grease that it took two slaves half a day to clean it off. Perhaps remembering his own boyhood pranks in Lancaster and at West Point, he enthusiastically joined into what he called "the struggle for mastery." One day, he and David French Boyd were walking through the woods when they passed a group of seemingly innocent cadets. Sherman became suspicious and soon discovered that the cadets were planning to rob some nearby chicken roosts. His vigilance foiled them.[17]

The cadets overlooked Sherman's sternness and sense of duty and saw him as a kind, good friend. He encouraged them to visit him in his quarters after hours, and his room was often filled with young boys intently listening to stories of his life in the army and in California. Whenever he appeared outdoors during recreation period, "tall, angular, with figure slightly bent, bright hazel eyes and auburn hair, with a tuft of it behind that would, when he was a little excited, stick straight up," the cadets happily surrounded him and listened to more stories. When a cadet became ill, Sherman visited the sick boy's bedside regularly until the boy felt better. He shared the cadets' pleasure over receiving their uniforms in the spring, and he scheduled a ball so they could show off their finery to neighboring young ladies. He enjoyed being the pater familias here.[18]

Sherman was similarly strict with the faculty. Anthony Vallas presented a learned disquisition at the school's opening, but the cadets found it totally mystifying. Sherman, who was "no scholar in the professional sense" himself, became enraged. With an angry look on his face and biting his tongue, he whispered to Boyd: "Every d—d shot went over their heads." He determined not to let that happen again. As Boyd put it: "He soon clipped the wings of our grandiloquently soaring eagle, and made him a plain barnyard fowl—a practical, useful instructor."[19]

But Sherman's satisfaction with his new position was not matched among his own family. Ellen and the Ewings knew how content he was, but they never quit trying to get him to leave Louisiana for England. They claimed to be concerned about secession and yellow fever, but the true concern lay elsewhere. Ellen and her father wanted Cump to go to London so that Ellen and the children could remain in Lancaster. Ewing wanted his daughter near him, and she felt the same way even if this meant being separated from her husband. If Cump settled in at the seminary, sooner or later Ellen and the children would leave Lancaster to join him. Thomas Ewing insisted that the political chaos rising out of the slavery issue would force Sherman to leave the South eventually, so he should go when he had a chance. "It is my opinion & that of all your friends here that you had better accept the [London] proposition."[20]

The banking job was financially tempting, but Sherman's San Francisco and New York experiences and his affection for the military had nudged him toward Louisiana and kept him there. What kept the London offer alive in Sherman's mind was his concern over long-term state support for the military seminary, his pay, and Ellen's and her father's pressure. Fifteen thousand dollars for two years in London was substantially more money than the seven thousand dollar salary for the same period in Louisiana.[21]

Sherman presented his demands to six members of the board of supervisors who were in informal session at his friend Graham's plantation: an increase in the seminary endowment from $8,000 to $25,000 a year for two years, a raise in his salary to $5,000 per year, and a house for his family. Sherman explained the London offer, but did not mention resignation. The rump board understood and immediately passed a resolution promising to do all they could to retain him as superintendent. Sherman was pleased and agreed to wait for ten days until the legislature could meet his demands. If the conditions were met, he would remain in his post.[22]

Sherman expressed a new-found self-confidence. He was not sure what he was going to do, he told Ellen, but "if you hear I have concluded to stay here, just make up your mind to live and die here, because I am going to take the bit in my mouth, and resume my military character, and control my own affairs. Since I left New Orleans, I have felt myself oppressed by circumstances I could not control, but I begin to feel footing and will get saucy." But as much as the military life gave him a sense of strength and order, the realm of business threatened chaos. "I suppose I was the Jonah that blew up San Francisco, and it only took two months' residence in Wall Street to blow up New York, and I think my arrival in London will be the signal of the downfall of that mighty empire." If Louisiana was "fool enough to give me $5,000 a year," he said, "we will drive our tent pins and pick out a magnolia under which to sleep the long sleep. But if she don't, then England must perish, for I predict financial misfortune to the land that receives me."[23]

The pressure from home to go to London remained intense and began to wear him down. "The strong preference of my family is all that turns the scale in my mind," he told Graham. On March 1 he reluctantly submitted his resignation. "I have made desperate efforts to escape but I see it as inevitable, and so might as well surrender." Cump gave up fighting Thomas Ewing and obeyed his command. He would accept the London offer.[24]

The military seminary's supporters refused to accept Sherman's resignation. The governor promised to do all he could, and Beauregard urged him to reconsider. Actually Sherman wavered even in his March 1 letter of resignation. He proposed a visit to Ohio to investigate the London offer more completely and to discuss the matter in person with his family. Perhaps, he told Graham, he might be able to change their minds. School authorities agreed, and Cump wrote Ellen to tell the London bank combine to have thirty-five hundred dollars "cash in hand" on his arrival in Lancaster and an absolute guarantee for the rest of the fifteen thousand dollar salary.[25]

Sherman reached Lancaster on March 11, 1860, and quickly went to Cincinnati to meet with David Gibson, one of the major supporters of the London bank. Gibson refused to provide the financial guarantees, so Sherman rejected the offer. However, he waited for Thomas Ewing's return from a business trip before making his final decision. He heard Ewing's pleas but was not swayed. He returned to the seminary on March 30 with the promise of a five hundred dollar increase in his salary waiting for him. Once more, however, he was alone. The promised house was not ready for his family.[26]

One quiet Sunday about two weeks later, Sherman wrote a long letter to Hugh Boyle Ewing seeking to justify his decision. He might not be making much money in Louisiana, but he was making it on his own; he was independent and in control of his own destiny, doing something he felt qualified to do and surrounded by people who admired him and his work. The school provided him with a certainty that he had not felt for a long time. If he left it to take on a better-paying but riskier job, he might fail again.[27]

Ellen still hoped to live in Ohio, though insisting she would leave for Louisiana as soon as Cump asked her. As always, however, she hedged her promises. She would come "aside from the fear of taking the children into that climate in an unpropitious season." In other words, he still had to convince her there was no danger from yellow fever. The proposed house also needed changes. She would have to bring her own servants because she refused to own slaves; she considered them a bad economic investment. Finally, she worried about getting pregnant again so soon after the birth of their last child. "If you think it will do to risk having another baby so soon I wish you would approve of my going down." Sherman, as usual, did not respond to this sexual allusion or the imputation of guilt for the risks of pregnancy. As far as he was concerned, the only justification for his family's still being in Ohio was the lack of a suitable home. Once the state built the house promised him, he would have his family with him, despite Ellen's machinations.[28]

The academic year stretched into the summer of 1860. On July 30 and 31 Sherman supervised the final examinations and capped them with a grand ball, publicizing the event widely. Then he, the cadets, and all the professors, save Boyd, scattered to their homes, not scheduled to return until November 1. Boyd, a young bachelor, agreed to remain behind to watch the premises. Sherman delegated to him all his powers and then wrote him regular letters of instruction throughout the summer.[29]

Although Sherman seemed able to withstand family pressure to quit Louisiana, political pressures posed an increasing threat. The disruption of the Union seemed inevitable, the fires of secession stoked most recently by John Brown's raid on Harper's Ferry, Virginia, and the fateful split in the Democratic party. The nomination of Stephen A. Douglas as a Northern Democratic presidential candidate and John C. Breckinridge as a Southern Democratic candidate resulted in an advantage for the Republican, Abraham Lincoln. Many Southerners made it clear that they would secede should Lincoln be elected. To try to forestall this calamity, some remnants of the defunct Whig party, including Thomas Ewing, established the Constitutional Union party and nominated John Bell for the presidency. Sherman worried as he watched these unfolding events. He had let it be known from his first day in Alexandria that he opposed secession and felt duty-bound to stay with the Union. He fervently hoped that secession would never occur, but if it did, "of course, I would advocate the policy of force."[30]

He demonstrated this concern in the first letter he wrote his friend Graham after arriving in Lancaster for the 1860 summer break. He expressed his amazement at the contrast between the drought conditions in the piney woods of Louisiana and the harvest of one of the best crops ever in the Northern states east of the Mississippi River. "May it not be providential?" he asked. "May it not be one of the facts stronger than . . . blind prejudice to show the mutual dependence of one part of our magnificent country on the other? The Almighty has visited a vast district with drought, but has showered abundance on another, and he has made a natural avenue [Mississippi River] between them." It was unreasonable, the worst affront to order, to break up such a divine connection.[31]

After a few days home with Ellen and the children, Sherman left for Washington, where, through the good offices of his friend D. C. Buell and the Southern-born secretary of war, John B. Floyd, he acquired enough training weapons and ammunition for two hundred cadets. Next he traveled to New York to purchase books and supplies. He shipped several thousand volumes south, including four hundred books on history and geography, most of them on travel, exploration, and discovery. Significantly included among these volumes was Peter Parley's *Universal History,* Sherman no doubt remembering his happy nights around the Ewing table. Once he completed these tasks, he returned to Lancaster, where his fears about secession were stoked.[32]

In letters to Boyd, Graham, and John Sherman, Sherman tried to convince himself that even if Lincoln was elected, nothing would happen. He supported the Constitutional Union party's (and Thomas Ewing's) candidate, John Bell, because he believed Bell's election would give the nation a four-year "truce" to work out the problems over slavery. What bothered him the most, however, was the apparent irrationality of the controversy. He told his brother that Southerners were "arguing not against what you say or what you do but what they imagine you will do when you get the power." Quarreling over slavery in the territories made even less sense, Sherman thought, because "no sensible man with liberty of choice would [ever] think of taking his slaves" to Utah, Arizona, or New Mexico. Sectional blindness and prejudice were at the heart of the dispute: "Here the prejudice is that planters have nothing else to do but to hang abolitionists and to hold lynch courts. There that all the people of Ohio are engaged in stealing and running off negroes. The truth is each does injustice to the other; if all would forget and mind their own respective interests, it would be found that slavery and all other property in the United States" was "at a most prosperous standard." Everyone was making money, so why argue? Sherman asked. If war came because of slavery, "we deserve a monarch and that would be the final result."[33]

Sherman grew increasingly upset at Thomas Ewing's politics. Ewing had switched to Lincoln, and Sherman was concerned about what his Louisiana friends would think. "It is probable," he worried, that "I will be even more 'suspect' than last year." He became bedridden with what he insisted was not asthma but only a bad cold, but he was still sick as he returned to Louisiana in late October.[34]

This illness presaged an onset of anxiety and depression. He began to talk of returning to the army or finding a job on some Ohio railroad, perhaps through George McClellan. He spoke wistfully of the bounty of the Ohio countryside as compared to the sterility of the Louisiana woods. Fearing that his seminary position was doomed to end, he seriously considered going to the salt wells and coal mines in the Hocking Valley. And to complicate matters, Ellen was pregnant again and unhappy at the prospect of another child, considering their uncertain health, the lack of a permanent home, and his less than "congenial position." Sherman's friend, Graham, was no longer on the board of supervisors, having resigned in protest over some new regulations undercutting Sherman's authority. Only the enthusiastic welcome from Boyd, the good condition of the school grounds and buildings, 130 waiting cadets, and warm letters from Bragg and Beauregard dampened the fears. "People here now talk as though disunion was a fixed thing," Sherman learned on his return, however, and his spirits plummeted. Disunion meant war, he told

Bragg. "A fish worm would resist breaking in the middle, much more so a great nation."[35]

Almost immediately, he had to deal with faculty and student dissension. Berte St. Ange was upset at the way his French students had been classified into ability sections. The cadets, whether reacting to Sherman's lessened authority or the constant talk of disunion, proved to be almost uncontrollable at times. In late November, they rioted over their food, smashing dishes and firing weapons. The academic board expelled five of the culprits, but the rest remained restive. During the practice elocutions for the senior cadets, Sherman noted that all seemed to choose a disunion speech defending slavery and the South. He had let it be known that he believed "secession was treason, was *war*," so he found such sentiment distressing.[36]

Graham urged him to vote in the 1860 election to prevent anyone from "impugn[ing] your *motives* for refraining from voting." Since Douglas, Breckinridge, and Bell were on the ballot in Louisiana and Lincoln was not, Graham's point was clear: Sherman ought not let anyone think he supported Lincoln. Sherman naively argued that he did not want "to be subject to any political conditions." He supported Bell, he said, but since the Constitutional Unionist had no chance, his vote was irrelevant. Once the election was over, perhaps conditions would settle down, rumors of South Carolina's secession threats notwithstanding. If secession happened, Cump believed, the result would be "civil war, anarchy and ruin."[37]

Lincoln won the election, and in mid-December, word arrived in the piney woods that South Carolina had quit the Union and other states were preparing to follow its lead. On the governor's orders, Louisiana troops seized the Mississippi River forts and the U.S. Arsenal at Baton Rouge, and then state officials called a secession convention for early January. Over two thousand of the weapons taken from the arsenal were shipped to Sherman's care at an arsenal recently established at the seminary. In late January 1861 Louisiana issued an ordinance of secession.[38]

Sherman had insisted from the start that he could not, in good conscience, stay in Louisiana if it left the Union. Secession meant war, and he could never abandon the Union. In mid-December he had expressed his feelings publicly: "As long as Louisiana is in the

Union I will serve her honestly and faithfully, but if she quits I will quit too. I will not for a day or even [an] hour occupy a position of apparent hostility to Uncle Sam. That government is weak enough, but [it] is the only thing in America that has even the semblance of a government. These state governments are ridiculous pretenses of a government, liable to explode at the call of any mob. I don't want to be premature [however,] and will hold on to the last moment in hopes of change."[39]

Sherman's patriotism was tied to a continuation of the Union, in whose manifest destiny he expressed a firm belief. "I have great faith . . . that the nation will yet be preserved through the efforts of good men north & south. And I have especially great trust that God has destined the United States for a long and prosperous nation life, & not for destruction in the bloom of its youth." But it was not the nation's continuation as much as the results of any collapse that most bothered him. Secession meant disorder and even anarchy. It meant all those terrible things he had experienced during the 1850s: mob rule and California vigilance committees instead of legislative law and judicial judgment. Banks would fail; business would collapse; order would disintegrate. "The law is or should be our King," he insisted. "We should obey it, not because it meets our approval, but because it is the law and because obedience in some shape is necessary to every system of civilized government." This secession movement was nothing but a culmination of the "tendency to anarchy," which substitutes "local prejudices as the Law of the land." "This is the real trouble," he believed, "it is not slavery, it is the Democratic spirit which substitutes mere popular opinions for law."[40]

Looking back on his life, Sherman was persuaded that disorder, circumstances out of his control, had doomed him from the beginning. His father's death, his mother's inability to support him, the uncontrollable Indians in Florida, the chaotic gold rush, the haphazard financial situation in California, the vigilantes, Ellen's lack of financial discipline and her repeated pregnancies, and a host of similar occurrences had brought him a life of failure and distress. He had done his best, but he had never managed to master or control his personal or professional life. And now, when he had finally been able to establish order in his school, this too was threatened. Slave owners thought their survival depended on secession; his survival was cast in doubt by it. Secession meant more than the breakup of a beloved union; it also meant the breakup of the ordered world of the seminary and another failure in a long series of failures in Sherman's life.

When Sherman received the news of South Carolina's secession in December, he paced up and down in his room, "crying like a child," expressing his dismay at what was happening. He predicted the horror of war and its terrible legacy, especially in the South, which he insisted could never successfully battle the more prosperous North. "There can be no *peaceable secession.* Secession means war." "You are driving me and hundreds of others out of the South, who have cast fortunes here, love your people and want to stay." "Yet I must give up all, and go away; and if war comes, as I fear it surely will, I must fight your people whom I best love."[41]

Sherman tried to hang on in Louisiana because he saw no economic prospect for himself anywhere else and because he still hoped the legislature would provide him with the five hundred dollars it had promised for commanding the arsenal attached to the seminary. He tried to ignore Louisiana's call for a secession convention, but when the state's troops captured the Mississippi River forts in mid-December, he admitted the reality and asked to be relieved. The board of superintendents insisted that no capable replacement was available, so he relented. When Louisiana troops took the U.S. Arsenal at Baton Rouge on January 10, 1861, and placed captured weapons under Sherman's care at the seminary arsenal, he could no longer procrastinate. He wrote Governor Moore two letters of resignation, a formal and an informal one. The crux of both letters was a dejected resignation to events out of his control. He wished he did not have to leave, but he felt he had no choice. The same day he composed his resignation, he wrote to his brother urging that "every allowance should be made to Southern politicians for their nervous anxiety about their political power and the safety of slaves. I think that the constitution should be liberally construed in their behalf."[42]

He felt no ill will toward anyone in Louisiana, and no one there criticized him for his stand. The Seminary Academic Board passed two resolutions in his honor, and he received warm letters from Governor Moore, Graham, Bragg, and Richard Taylor, all wishing he would stay but expressing their understanding of his decision to leave. S. A. Smith, the president of the board of supervisors, wondered why he did not become a citizen of Louisiana and stay and fight: "Every one deplores your determination to leave us." "Wherever you go," Braxton Bragg said, "my fervent prayers attend you for success and happiness." As late as 1864, a Confederate officer found that people in Alexandria "cherish[ed] the memory of General Sherman and mourn[ed] his loss. He had great popularity here."[43]

Although his letter of resignation was written on January 18, Sherman did not leave until February 19. He could not go until he felt sure he had discharged all his obligations and collected all the salary due him. Once more, he was facing an uncertain future. In a letter to Ellen soon after his resignation, he wrote: "I am willing to forego my preferences if I can control myself and settle down, but I must have occupation." To guarantee this "control," he said he was willing to go to the salt wells or to an Ohio farm. "I feel no desire to follow an army necessarily engaged in civil war." Cump might go to the salt wells if he wanted to, Ellen responded, but she and her father thought he ought to rejoin the army and defend the Union. Hugh Boyle Ewing and John Sherman agreed. If she were a man, Ellen said, she would fight the secessionists herself.[44]

Sherman quickly came to his senses about the salt wells, but he remained adamant against rejoining the army. The thought of fighting his friends was unsettling, and the economic needs of his family were too severe. He asked John to get him the post of subtreasurer in St. Louis and was excited when his old friend Henry Turner offered the possibility of employment in Missouri. Ellen, meanwhile, asked John to find Cump an army post. Cump continued to refuse. He believed he had only three choices: a job in St. Louis, the Chauncey salt wells, or a farm near Lancaster. He would talk the whole matter over with Thomas Ewing and abide by his decision. Sherman was so upset at having to leave Louisiana and so unsure of his future that he rejected the army, which had always been his major hope of freedom, and accepted the salt wells, which had always been the clearest symbol of Thomas Ewing's continued control over his life. Perhaps his St. Louis friends would save him again, but Ellen had already begun warning him against their alleged secessionist tendencies.[45]

On February 19, 1861, Sherman ordered the cadets into formation and gave them a short farewell. Then he passed through the tear-filled ranks, shaking everyone's hand. When he approached the professors, he broke down and could only point to his heart and whisper: "You are all here!" Then he hurried away. He was less emotional when he said good-bye to Governor Moore and the board of supervisors. He joked with Moore: "Well, good-bye, Governor. I hope that if I should go into the army I'll not catch you, for I should surely hang you. You know you are a traitor. You seized the arsenal at Baton Rouge when your State had not seceded, and you know that is treason." Then he laughed, shook hands with Moore, and left for New Orleans.[46]

During a stopover in the Crescent City, he wrote an affectionate letter to his friend, Boyd. In it, he said he still "fear[ed] anarchy more than a direct conflict on the slavery issue."[47] Instability and uncertainty had been the spectres of his childhood and adolescence, and as an adult he continued to be haunted by the devastation such conditions wrought. "Direct conflict," something that was clear and defined, was a much less threatening phenomenon. It brought forth swift and sure action and well-defined positions rather than blurry lines. If war came, it would mean the nation was coming to grips with its problems, not continuing to avoid them. A properly fought war could eliminate anarchy and force solutions to long-unsettled questions. War for Union, no matter how horrible, was preferable to the chaos of secession. But Sherman was not yet ready to enter into such a war himself, not until he could be sure that the war would be waged efficiently. Although war should bring about a restoration of Union and order, it might intensify the existing chaos. He would have to wait and see what happened before he risked joining in.

———— ☆ ————

CHAPTER 7

RELUCTANT WARRIOR UNDER ATTACK

SHERMAN BOARDED THE TRAIN in New Orleans on March 1, 1861, leaving behind his Southern friends, the military seminary he had established and nurtured, and the cadets he had come to see as his sons. He had been on the verge of putting his life in order in Louisiana, but once more conditions beyond his control had intervened. Abraham Lincoln's election to the presidency had precipitated South Carolina's secession in December 1860. In January 1861, Mississippi, Florida, Alabama, Georgia, Louisiana, and Texas had followed suit. The Union was splintered, and so was Sherman's life. He felt duty bound to forsake personal security for the larger good of the Union, seeing his departure from Louisiana as his patriotic duty. He still had to look out for his family's financial needs, however, so he hesitated about making any further response to the national crisis.

As the train rumbled through the Southern countryside, Sherman listened to passengers who passionately warned of a violent response to any attempt to coerce the seceding states. When the train reached the other side of the Mason-Dixon line, however, the tone and atmosphere in the cars changed considerably. Northern passengers did not seem similarly excited by the political situation. He noted no unusual military activity or preparation in the Northern countryside. What was wrong with Northerners? he wondered.[1]

Ellen and the children awaited his return in Lancaster, happy to have him within the family fold once more. His uncertainty was written all over his face, however, and he quickly turned from his children to two letters that bore uplifting news. One from his brother John, now a U.S. senator, asked him to come to Washington to discuss the crisis. The other was from his old friend Henry S. Turner, speaking for James Lucas and another major stockholder, offering him the presidency of the Fifth Street Railroad Company in St. Louis. Sherman was inclined to accept the job immediately, but he decided to go to Washington first to see what was happening in the nation's capital.[2]

In early March, when Sherman arrived in Washington, pro-Confederate talk could be heard everywhere, even in the War Department. No one seemed particularly concerned, not even Abraham Lincoln. "Mr. President, this is my brother, Colonel Sherman, who is just up from Louisiana," John said in introducing Cump to Lincoln. "He may give you some information you want." "Ah!" responded the president, looking at the thin redhead, "how are they getting along down there?" "They think they are getting along swimmingly," Sherman blurted; "they are preparing for war." "Oh well!" the president casually responded. "I guess we'll manage to keep house." Sherman was stunned into silence. Lincoln's nonchalance confirmed his fears: The nation did not recognize the seriousness of secession and was not making preparations to deal with it. When he and John were alone, he exploded: "You [politicians] have got things in a hell of a fix, and you may get them out as best you can." He was going to St. Louis to support his family; he refused to link his future to an unprepared national administration.[3]

He went back to Lancaster to talk with Ellen. She showed no enthusiasm for St. Louis, but he let her know that the decision had been made to take the job on the urban railroad line. His new locale was no political oasis.[4] As a border slave state, Missouri yearned to have the sectional crisis compromised. The Republican candidates for governor and for president had each finished a distant last in the recent state canvass, so Missouri was not happy with Lincoln's victory at the polls. The new Democrat governor, Claiborne Jackson, bluntly called Lincoln's ascendance a triumph for the hated abolitionists. And he warned of trouble if the new administration tried to force South Carolina back into the Union. Missouri would remain loyal, he promised, "so long as there is any hope that it [the Union] will maintain the spirit and guarantees of the Constitution." If not, "then *they* have themselves practically abandoned the Union, and will not expect our submission to a government on terms of inequality and subordination." He called for a state convention to determine Missouri's future and proceeded to strengthen the militia. His lieutenant governor, Thomas C. Reynolds, went to Washington in January to consult with Jefferson Davis and other secessionist leaders. Upon his return, he began organizing paramilitary Minute Men in St. Louis.

St. Louis congressman Frank Blair, son of long-time Democratic power broker Francis Preston Blair, and brother to Postmaster General Montgomery Blair, led the opposition to this pro-Southern activity. During the 1850s he had been a leading antislaveryite, organizing German immigrants into Wide Awake Clubs (wide awake, that is, to the threat of the slave conspiracy). He now converted these Republican groups into pro-Union military Home Guards. The pro-Southern militia and the pro-Union Home Guards glared at each other in between conducting military drills all over the city.

The legislature generally favored the Union, but it accepted the governor's call for a state convention. Realizing it had a great deal to lose by acting precipitously, the electorate demonstrated its moderate inclinations by electing all pro-Union candidates to the convention. The delegates ultimately supported a proslavery constitutional amendment, but they urged conciliation. Missouri was not ready to join the other slaveholding states in secession, but its support for the Union was conditional at best.

It was to this political minefield that Sherman, a pregnant Ellen, their five children (this time including Minnie), and two servants arrived in St. Louis on March 20, 1861, and took up residence. Sherman found his situation to be as ambivalent as Missouri's. He was a Union man, but his long-time friends and business associates, Turner and Lucas, had Southern sympathies. Frank Blair, on the other hand, despite his Unionist sentiments, had blocked Sherman's hope of gaining a position in the federal subtreasury. Blair was also vehemently antislavery, while Sherman believed Southern slavery was "the mildest and best regulated system of slavery in the world, now or heretofore," and he opposed its abolition. Sherman had given up his successful career in Louisiana to stand up for the Union, but because he was not a Republican and he was not opposed to slavery, he was not acceptable for a desired government post. His resistance to both sides in the debate isolated him politically. "On the question of secession, . . . I am ultra. I believe in coercion," he said. "On the slavery question," however, "as much forbearance should be made as possible. . . . They are widely different."[5]

Sherman nervously settled in and began working for the railway. He left the house early each morning, came home for a midafternoon meal, and then worked far into the night. His two thousand dollar salary was small in the face of his expenses, especially an annual house rental of seven hundred dollars. As usual, Ellen did not allow for their tight finances and furnished the house with "a carpet of the best Brussels" and the finest furniture available. She complained of loneliness away from her father and of Cump's growing obsession with the political crisis gripping the nation and the state. Her brother Charley and John Hunter, a Lancaster friend, worked in St. Louis and lived with them to help meet expenses, and these boarders made her personal life a bit more tolerable. But politics reared its head and limited her social life. Her Unionist sympathies precluded close relations with many of their friends who had secession leanings. She could not visit and receive guests as she would have liked.[6]

Sherman remained torn. Although he soon had the street railway operating efficiently and at a profit, he became increasingly alarmed at the deteriorating political situation. He bemoaned the anarchical condition of the nation and felt a personal connection with the drift toward disunion. He repeatedly visited the federal arsenal in St. Louis, where an old West Point colleague, Nathaniel Lyon, was stationed and observed the gathering of the pro-Confederate state militia at nearby Camp Jackson. He had no military responsibilities, but he worried whether anyone was doing anything to keep the Union together while he wrestled with his conscience.[7]

On April 6 Montgomery Blair, Frank's brother, invited Sherman to become chief clerk of the War Department with the promise of an assistant secretaryship as soon as Congress convened. Reflecting his inner turmoil and ambivalence, Sherman refused because, he told Blair, he could not leave his job and family though he "wish[ed] the Administration all success in its almost impossible task of governing this distracted and anarchical people." Sherman's blunt refusal in the context of his Southern associations in St. Louis caused some to suspect an impending defection to the Confederacy. Perhaps because of this rumor, as well as a letter he received from Louisiana urging him to return and fight for the Confederacy, Sherman changed his mind and wrote to the secretary of war offering his services. But he refused to join a volunteer unit, considering them dangerously inferior compared to the professional regular army. Cameron could investigate his previous military record and appoint him wherever appropriate but only with the regulars. Untrained volunteers were really civilians, not soldiers, and their military incompetence was more of a threat than an asset to any antisecession activity. In short, Sherman expressed his loyalty, but he continued to hesitate about expressing it militarily. He needed more certitude before he would risk his future again. Until "Professional knowledge will be appreciated," he told John, "I will bide my time."[8]

Throughout this period, John Sherman regularly urged his brother to rejoin the army, and Thomas Ewing, Jr., chief justice of the Kansas Supreme Court and a leading antislavery Republican, cajoled every cabinet member and general he could corner in Washington to find a military position for his brother-in-law. The nation's capital remained in turmoil as it prepared for the start of Lincoln's administration. No one seemed to know just what the new president would do about secession once he took office, and rumors abounded. Insiders were jockeying for position, and the Ewings tried to secure Sherman an army post good enough to convince him to change his mind about rejoining the military. Ellen wanted him to help the nation in time of need, but her desire to live in Lancaster once he reentered the army played a significant role in her thinking too.[9]

The national crisis came to a head in Charleston harbor on April 14, a month after Lincoln's inauguration. Confederates opened fire on the U.S. Army garrison in Fort Sumter, ending months of futile efforts to solve the secession standoff. The problem had increasingly come down to the presence of Federal troops in the heart of one of the South's major ports. The South could hardly claim independence if the Federals controlled so significant a part of its territory. If the national administration pulled the army garrison out of one of its forts, this action would be viewed as acceptance of secession. Neither side could back

William Tecumseh Sherman was born in 1820 in this simple frame house in Lancaster, Ohio, the sixth of eleven children. *(Sherman House, Fairfield Heritage Association)*

Sherman's young world was rocked when, upon the death of his father in 1829, the nine-year-old was taken into the far more substantial home (below) of the neighboring Ewing family. The affluence of Thomas Ewing (at right) stood in marked contrast to the financial failure of Sherman's father, and fueled the boy's desire for success and for a secure family life. *(Archives of the University of Notre Dame)*

Academy Buildings, W.P.

Sherman found a new home at West Point, which he attended from 1836 to 1840. He thrived amid the camaraderie of his fellow cadets.
(Special Collections, United States Military Academy Library)

At West Point, Sherman discovered his aptitude for engineering and organization, and also found that he loved to draw. His drawings, like this one from 1838, demonstrate his energetic spirit and creativity, qualities he later brought to his military leadership.
(Sherman House, Fairfield Heritage Association)

Sherman made lasting friends in the South while he was stationed at several army posts there, including Fort Moultrie in Charleston harbor.
(National Archives)

While in the South and in California with the army, Sherman realized his love for his foster sister, Ellen Ewing, shown here in a later portrait. He married her in 1850.
(Ohio Historical Society)

During the 1850s Sherman was unable to earn a decent enough living in the army to support a family, and consequently he tried his hand as a civilian banker in San Francisco. This view of the city is dated 1852.
(Library of Congress)

His foster parents and in-laws, the Ewings, opposed the move to California. Sherman agreed to leave his firstborn daughter, Minnie, with his mother-in-law, Maria Boyle Ewing, in the first of many painful concessions he would make to maintain domestic order.
(Archives of the University of Notre Dame)

As head of the San Francisco militia, Sherman was unsuccessful in his attempt to impose order on vigilante lawlessness, here illustrated by the hanging of two men deemed murderers by the Vigilance Committee. Moreover, he was battered financially, and his success as a banker in turbulent, Gold Rush–era California was short-lived. *(Library of Congress)*

Dejected after his bad fortune in California, Sherman drifted from job to job, reaching a low point in Kansas, where he inhabited this humble shelter in 1859. *(Archives of the University of Notre Dame)*

Sherman was frequently separated from his family while seeking economic stability. However, he used his artistic talent to communicate with them, as shown in this drawing he sent to his children in 1859.
(Archives of the University of Notre Dame)

While Sherman struggled, his natural brother John Sherman, who had also left home after their father's death, had become a leading member of the House of Representatives. John repeatedly steadied Cump during difficult times and ultimately urged him to return to the U.S. army.
(Archives of the University of Notre Dame)

For Sherman, one of the most satisfying periods of his life was his stay in Louisiana (1859–1861). Unable to find a position in the army, he had taken a post as Superintendent at the Louisiana Military Seminary. There he found once more the military camaraderie he had experienced at West Point. The school appears behind him. *(National Archives)*

CHARLESTON

MERCURY

EXTRA:

Passed unanimously at 1.15 o'clock, P. M. December 20th, 1860.

AN ORDINANCE

To dissolve the Union between the State of South Carolina and other States united with her under the compact entitled " The Constitution of the United States of America."

We, the People of the State of South Carolina, in Convention assembled, do declare and ordain, and it is hereby declared and ordained,

That the Ordinance adopted by us in Convention, on the twenty-third day of May, in the year of our Lord one thousand seven hundred and eighty-eight, whereby the Constitution of the United States of America was ratified, and also, all Acts and parts of Acts of the General Assembly of this State, ratifying amendments of the said Constitution, are hereby repealed; and that the union now subsisting between South Carolina and other States, under the name of " The United States of America," is hereby dissolved.

THE

UNION

IS

DISSOLVED!

In December 1860, South Carolina seceded from the Union. In April 1861, the Confederates fired upon Fort Sumter and war broke out. Sherman left his beloved South despite having finally found economic and emotional satisfaction; maintaining the Union was now his first priority.

(South Caroliniana Library, University of South Carolina)

down, so the Southern attack required a Northern response. Lincoln called out the state militias to quell the insurrection, and his action brought on the secession of more slave states. Full-scale war had begun.

Fort Sumter did not alter Sherman's determination to stay out of what was now a shooting war. He remained unconvinced of the Union's determination to act decisively and continued refusing to join its army. A dramatic event nudged him along a bit. Jefferson Davis sent arms and ammunition from the captured arsenal in Baton Rouge to the pro-Confederate state militia at Camp Jackson in west St. Louis. Fearing an attack upon the arsenal, Nathaniel Lyon, temporarily commanding the Department of the West, surrounded the encampment at Jackson on May 10 and, without firing a shot, forced the militia to surrender.[10]

When the Federal troops, many of them Blair's recently mustered Home Guards, moved against the vastly outnumbered Confederates at Camp Jackson, excitement gripped the city. Sherman came home for his usual midday meal and found his two boarders determined to forgo dinner to watch the expected fireworks. Sherman warned them about the dangers of a firefight, but they insisted. He ate his dinner and then allowed his own curiosity to lure him, along with his seven-year-old son Willy, toward the arsenal.

They encountered a large crowd observing the Federals marching the captured militia into custody. He and Willy watched as the troops proceeded with their prisoners, with a band providing martial cadence. The column stopped near them, and Sherman exchanged pleasantries with Major Rufus Saxton, the ranking officer and an old acquaintance.

When the march began again, a drunk tried to pass through the troops to the crowd on the other side. A sergeant, attempting to stop him, knocked him down an embankment on the side of the road. By the time the drunk had picked up his hat and climbed back up to the road, the regulars had already passed, and a unit of Home Guards was marching by. The drunk fired a pistol and struck an officer in the leg. In their confusion, the volunteer soldiers opened fire. As Sherman heard the bullets crashing and whizzing all around him, he threw Willy down in a ditch and covered him with his body. There were twenty-eight fatalities that day and an undetermined number of wounded.

Civil War had come to St. Louis, and it was, as Sherman had feared, a veritable anarchy. The volunteers had proved just as incompetent as he had always feared they would be. Yet they were Lincoln's main bulwark against secession. The situation looked bleak. "We cannot have two kings," Sherman surmised. "Of the two[,] the United States must prevail." Still, he was not ready to help enforce order, not when the situation was so chaotic. "I shall continue in my first resolve to mind my private interests so as to become independent of any body so that I can not be kicked about as heretofore[;] . . . if the country needs my services, it can call for them." Sherman was just not willing to put himself on the line when the prospects for success were so slim. The last thing he wanted was another failure and yet another return to the care of his foster father. If the government organized itself and promised a better chance for success, it could let him know, and then he would consider joining it.[11]

In early June, his relatives' activities on his behalf resulted in a summons to Washington to become colonel of a newly formed Thirteenth Regular Army Regiment. There were even rumors that he would become a major general or the army's quartermaster general, but he protested, citing his lack of Mexican War combat experience; colonel was about the right rank. Since he was offered a post in the regular army, he felt more confident about his prospects. Still, he would insist on clear government determination before he joined. Union and personal success remained intertwined, and both could be guaranteed only by organization and determined effort.[12]

Sherman arrived in Washington on June 11 and called on Secretary of the Treasury Salmon P. Chase, made an appointment to see the president, and found his name listed as Thirteenth Infantry Regiment colonel on an adjutant general's list. When he visited Winfield Scott, the old soldier promised him a brigadier generalship, considering him as worthy of the rank as Irvin McDowell, Scott's personal choice to lead the Union movement into Virginia. When Sherman conferred with McDowell, his old acquaintance asked him to join his army of invasion. The more people he talked to, the more confident he became of the government's determination to crush the secession. He was still not totally convinced, however, so he kept looking and talking.[13]

He visited the military camps in Washington, Virginia, and

Maryland and pumped officers, high and low, for information. He saw his brother John, soon to take his seat in the Senate, but still an aide-de-camp in General Robert Patterson's force in Maryland. He and John watched as Patterson began moving his troops closer to Washington. They witnessed the spectacular scene of the nine-thousand-man force wading waist deep across the Potomac River. He had a long talk with an old friend George H. Thomas, a Virginian who had decided to stay with the Union. The two bent over a large map on the floor and pointed out cities—Chattanooga and Vicksburg among them—that would be crucial in the war. He grew more optimistic.[14]

On June 21 Scott made Sherman an inspector general and sent him on an official circuit around Washington to evaluate the military situation. Scott kept his own counsel, however, so Sherman could not fathom his plans except that the general was determined to avoid any precipitous forward motion. Sherman enjoyed his job, particularly the insight it provided him on the military situation in the nation's capital. When on June 30 he was transferred to McDowell's army and made commander of the Third Brigade of Daniel Tyler's First Division, he accepted the orders without murmur. His new unit was made up of newly mustered volunteers, but he rated it as good as might be expected. His inspection tours and the results of his conversations convinced him that the Union was taking matters more seriously, and it was worth taking a chance on joining.[15]

He remained suspicious of the volunteers, however, and the first time his troops saw their new commander, they were as unimpressed with him as he was with them. Here was this "tall gaunt form clad in a thread bare blue coat, the sleeves so short as to reveal a long stretch of bony wrist, the trousers at least four inches less than the usual length." He sported "a bushy untrimmed beard"; his cheeks were "hollow"; and below "a shock of dark auburn hair" was "a great bulging forehead" and "a pair of sharp piercing eyes." He looked more like a disheveled farmer than an army officer, and several volunteers thought about demanding a replacement.

But their poorly dressed commander quickly won them over; he "revolutionized the brigade militarily." He trained his troops incessantly but charmed them with his friendliness and ability to tell stories about his adventures in California and Louisiana. John

Sherman paid regular visits, and Sherman proudly introduced the senator. Although the brigade still thought it strange to see Sherman walking around the camp in "a broad brimmed straw hat" and other nonmilitary garb, they came to appreciate him and ignored his eccentricities.[16]

Sherman's command was difficult. His 3,400-member unit, consisting of the Thirteenth, Sixty-seventh, and Sixty-ninth New York regiments, the Second Wisconsin Regiment, and Company E, U.S. Artillery, was willing to learn but except for his old artillery outfit, a regular unit, they lacked experience. He tried to whip them into shape by training them continually, but he soon discovered that they were still civilians. When Lincoln had issued the call, they had volunteered for ninety days' service. By the time they had signed the official muster book in Washington, however, their time was about up, and they were ready to go home. Sherman consulted the adjutant general, who ruled that their ninety-day service did not begin until their official sign-up; they had not yet fulfilled their obligations. Winfield Scott defused the matter by writing the commanding officer of the Irish Sixty-ninth New York Regiment a flattering letter saying that "he knew his Irish friends would not leave him in such a crisis." Sherman's open disdain for volunteer soldiers intensified with their desire to leave so precipitously. His voice became hoarse from shouting at his men, and his disposition grew correspondingly worse. Ellen's insistence that he visit her old Catholic school in Georgetown added to his bad mood. When one of the nuns gave him some relics to take into battle, however, he obligingly promised to carry them in his holsters.[17]

While Sherman trained his unit, the Union grew impatient at the lack of action against the Confederates. "On to Richmond!" rang out in the press, the populace increasingly convinced that Southerners would run at the first whiff of gunpowder. Sherman agreed with Winfield Scott and other experienced soldiers that any hasty offensive against P. G. T. Beauregard's Confederate troops gathered at nearby Manassas Junction would be unwise. With Congress meeting in a special session, however, public pressure intensified. The sooner the Union military moved forward, the public believed, the sooner the South would capitulate and the sooner life could return to its presecession norm.

Sherman knew that this was wishful thinking. He knew that Beauregard, the Creole general who was both a friend and the father of two cadets in Sherman's Louisiana Military Seminary, would not quit easily. G. Mason Graham, Sherman's closest Southern friend and a long-time pro-Unionist, demonstrated the depth of Confederate determination when he wrote to Sherman: "Those of us who were *the last* to give up the Union, will be *the last* to give up the principle of *the right of a people to make their own government*—we will live to maintain it, or we will *die* in defense of it—[even though] our 'cities, towns, yea people' *may* be destroyed." War against such determined people would be difficult, Sherman realized. "War is a terrible thing," he told his daughter in words that he would echo even more strongly in later years. "We must fight and subdue those in arms against us and our government, but we mean them no harm." Deep in his heart, Sherman continued to wish, as he had in Louisiana, that war could be avoided, that somehow the South would see reason and rejoin the Union. Then he would not have to fight against friends. Then he could try once again to bring order to his personal life—after it had been secured in the public arena.[18]

The popular pressure to respond to the Confederacy continued to increase, and the military felt compelled to go on the offensive. On July 15, Irvin McDowell's thirty-thousand-man fighting force (including Cump's Third Brigade, First Division) began a move toward Centreville, some ten miles from Manassas Junction, an important railroad center where Beauregard's twenty-two-thousand Confederates were encamped. Meanwhile, Robert Patterson's eighteen-thousand Unionists were ordered to keep Joseph E. Johnston's eleven-thousand-man Shenandoah Valley force occupied. Johnston slipped away, however, and joined Beauregard before the battle began.

The Union march into the Virginia countryside proved to be an omen of the later battle's outcome. At first, McDowell's army made good progress, but during the second day, it broke down as its untried volunteers fell out of ranks for water and food. Sherman's unit proved particularly eager to forage, and nothing he or his officers could do seemed to restrain them. Sherman personally caught a soldier walking along the road carrying some freshly butchered mutton on his shoulder. It was "rebel mutton," the soldier insisted. Unimpressed, Sherman had the man arrested and stored away another reason to justify his antivolunteer prejudice.[19]

Fighting began in earnest on July 21. Sherman's unit held that part of the battle line in front of the Stone Bridge by which the Warrenton Turnpike spanned a small stream known as Bull Run.[20] Tyler's division was to act as a decoy for a two-division Union force attempting to envelop the Confederate left flank several miles away. The Union advance began around dawn and proceeded steadily. Sherman could hear the firing and see the dust from the Union column. He saw Confederate troops in front of him being shifted to their left, but he waited until his division commander gave him a direct attack order. Then he led his force across Bull Run via a ford he had discovered earlier in the day, the crossing located half a mile above the bridge. Although grazed in the knee and shoulder and with his horse shot out from under him, he pressed his attack. He had never before seen men die in battle or experienced the carnage of war. The sight of dead and mangled humanity was shocking, as were riderless horses "with blood streaming from their nostrils, lying on the ground [still] hitched to guns, gnawing their sides in death."

The brigade kept pressing forward and helped drive the Confederates from Matthews Hill to Henry House Hill. There the appearance of Thomas Jackson's brigade (which stood like a "stonewall") rallied the Confederates; their musket fire became so intense that the Federals were stalled. Fresh troops appeared from the original Confederate right and turned the tide. The increasing casualties and the sight of the dead and wounded began to take their toll. The Union soldiers hesitated before slowly drifting back across Bull Run. The entire Union army was soon in retreat. It was about 3:30 P.M., some twelve hours after the battle's inception.

McDowell, Sherman, and other officers tried to halt the withdrawal, but the soldiers had given their best effort and were not about to return to the battle. The officers had to accept the defeat. Sherman and his unit proceeded back the five miles to Centreville, where McDowell planned to make a stand that night. Sherman deployed his troops and then fell asleep under a tree. His division commander soon awakened him and announced that McDowell had changed his mind (or the men had changed it for him): Union troops were to continue back to Washington.

The Federal retreat, at first hasty and disorganized, turned into panic. Sherman never saw any evidence of Confederate pursuit, but the exhausted and frightened soldiers did not care to learn for themselves. Their determined effort to make their way through terrified civilians who had come to view the battle resulted in tangled confusion. Sherman watched in horror. All his worst suspicions about volunteer troops, inadequate training, and national unpreparedness were being acted out before his eyes. "I had read of retreats before," he told his wife, "have seen the noise and confusion of crowds of men at fires and shipwrecks, but nothing like this. It was as disgraceful as words can portray."[21]

When Sherman reached Washington's Fort Corcoran, the sight was even more discouraging: The army had "degenerated into an armed mob." Many officers had been killed or wounded in the battle. The trauma of the soldiers' first encounter with war was marked. Sherman's own brigade had suffered 609 killed, wounded, and missing. The men were milling around aimlessly, making little effort to find their units, interested only in avoiding further gunfire. The disorder and fear he saw everywhere prompted Sherman to take charge. He ordered the ferry to stop transporting any soldiers across the Potomac if they were not with their units and asked the adjutant general in Washington to post guards on all the bridges leading into the capital. His quick action worked. Order slowly began to return. He had proved himself to be "the star . . . of the whole army that fought on July 21."[22]

The breakdown of army discipline frightened him, and for the next several days he worked around the clock to ready his unit for a possible Confederate attack. Many of the men, exhausted from the battle, wanted to rest and eat, but Sherman ridiculed such "unsoldierly conduct" and "called them a pack of New York loafers and thieves." The soldiers responded with hoots and even unfairly accused him of deserting them during the battle. He was discouraged enough to tell the adjutant general to discharge all "scared" officers and men. They were nothing but "a mere rabble" and would only "complicate any attempt at defense."[23]

Once more, many soldiers decided they had done their duty. They were going home, no matter what some martinet in Washington said about ninety days being numbered from their official sign-in and not their enlistment. The Sixty-ninth New York Regiment in particular was preparing to depart. On July 26 one of their officers tested Sherman's resolve to use artillery against anyone who tried to leave. "Colonel, I am going to New York today. What can I do for you?" he asked. Sherman said he remembered signing no pass. Oh, he needed no permission, the officer responded; he had served his time, so he planned to go back to his law practice. Sherman, noticing a growing crowd of eavesdropping enlisted men, knew he had to take a strong stand. "Captain," he retorted, "if you attempt to leave without orders, it will be mutiny, and I will shoot you like dog!" As he spoke, Sherman kept his hand conspicuously placed beneath his coat. The officer skulked off, and the enlisted men melted away.

That same day, Abraham Lincoln and his secretary of state, William H. Seward, paid the unit a visit in an effort to encourage the troops. Sherman's unsatisfactory interview with the president was still fresh in his mind, and he did not believe Lincoln was a forceful or determined leader. He jumped into the carriage to direct the driver and simultaneously told the president to "discourage all cheering, noise, or any sort of confusion." There had already been too much of that before Bull Run. Battle called for "cool, thoughtful, hard-fighting soldiers—no more hurrahing, no more humbug." Lincoln nodded and smiled. When he spoke to the men in their various camp areas, he discouraged any show of enthusiasm. "Don't cheer, boys. I confess I rather like it myself, but Colonel Sherman here says it is not military; and I guess we better defer to his opinion."[24]

As Lincoln spoke, Sherman listened with increasing attention, gaining a new-found respect for the president. Lincoln told the soldiers that "the days were sad, but brighter ones would come; that the rain was falling, but the clear sky was beyond, and soon would be clear again; they should not be discouraged, but think of the to-morrow that awaited them, having faith in the nation and in the final success, which was as sure to come as there was a God in heaven." "That speech reached every heart, nerved every arm, and made stern patriots out of timid and wavering men," Sherman later remembered. He had heard "Clay in his palmiest days . . . and most of our celebrated orators, and . . . have never heard a man who spoke to the hearts of his hearers, as Mr. Lincoln spoke to our soldiers that day."[25]

At the Sixty-ninth Regiment camp, the officer whom Sherman had recently reprimanded stepped forward. "Mr. President," the officer said, "I have a cause of grievance. This morning I went to speak to Colonel Sherman, and he threatened to shoot me." Lincoln, still in the buggy, responded in disbelief. The officer repeated the accusation, so Lincoln bent his tall frame over and in a mock whisper said: "Well, if I were you, and he threatened to shoot [me], I would not trust him, for I believe he would do it." The enlisted men erupted in laughter, and Sherman viewed the president yet more appreciatively.[26]

This incident did not end Sherman's problems with the volunteers. A few weeks later, some two hundred of them staged a strike, refusing to perform any duties because their enlistments were up. Sherman repeatedly ordered them back to work, but sixty-five die-hards refused to budge. He had these recalcitrants arrested, marched down to a prison ship, and thrown into the brig. Clearly he would not tolerate insubordination.[27]

The frightening results of the battle, the ensuing press censure of what the populace perceived as the incompetence of Union leadership in the fighting, and the near mutiny of the volunteer troops who had failed so miserably in combat had a profound impact on Sherman. When George B. McClellan took command of Union forces in late July, he found Sherman anxious and depressed. Sherman, who had joined the army only after he became convinced that the federal government was becoming serious about the crisis, once more saw the Union effort as being in total disarray and with little hope of success. On August 17 he told Ellen: "I have not undressed of a night since Bull Run, and the volunteers will not allow of sleep by day." Frustrated, he lashed out in all directions. "The proud army characterized as the most extraordinary on earth has turned out the most ordinary." "I never saw such a set of grumblers as our volunteers. . . . I shall make a requisition for two nurses per soldier to nurse them in their helpless, pitiful condition."[28]

Sherman saw the Union's failure stemming from a more fundamental source than untrained volunteers: Democratic practices had prevented order and discipline among the forces. "The want of organization and subordination of our people is a more dangerous enemy than the armies of the South." "Our adversaries have the weakness of slavery in their midst to offset our democracy, and 'tis beyond human wisdom to say which is the greater evil." Unless the North became less democratic in its procedures, the Union cause was hopeless. "We have to go through the experience of other nations and learn that the many at last must be governed by the few." But as long as newspapers fanned the erroneous belief that "vox Populi, vox dei," there was little chance of improvement.[29]

Having concluded that the national anarchy was due to a lack of an imposed order and discipline, Sherman reflected on the impact of this fact on his own life. He had performed in exemplary fashion during the battle and after but nevertheless felt "disgraced." The lack of military discipline among the civilian volunteer soldiers and his own inability to impose it were responsible for the chaos. His distaste for what he saw about him made him want to "sneak into some quiet corner," but he could not do that. "The bluer the times the more closely should one cling to his country. I do not say I love my country[,] . . . [but] I do not know why we should not have a government." He could not understand why civilian leaders did not realize the need for a determined war effort. Success in war was impossible if troops were not sufficiently trained or even available for more than ninety days. Sherman did not use the term, but he was calling for a total effort—a commitment to do everything necessary to wage war efficiently and successfully. The Union represented the order Sherman desired and needed to direct his own life. And yet the nation seemed to lack the purpose and strength essential to impose that order and win the war. He hoped change would follow the Bull Run disaster; if it did not, the fate of the Union, as well as his own, was in jeopardy.[30]

In mid-August, Sherman was unexpectedly promoted to brigadier general of volunteers and soon after received a note from an old Fort Moultrie friend, Robert Anderson, the hero of Fort Sumter and the recently appointed commander of the Department of the Cumberland in Kentucky and Tennessee, asking Sherman to meet him at the Willard Hotel in Washington. There, in the presence of Tennessee senator Andrew Johnson and several other border state luminaries, Anderson told Sherman that he wanted him to go to Kentucky as his deputy. Sherman was happy to leave the chaos of Washington, but when he and Anderson later met with Lincoln, he exacted a promise that he would never be asked to command again. Lincoln jokingly agreed, quipping that he did not have enough command positions anyway. Sherman was deadly serious. As long as the Union chose to depend on inadequately trained volunteers for military service, Sherman would not assume a command position. He could not lead while Union plans and strategies were so ill formed and defined. "Not till I see day light ahead do I want to lead, but when danger threatens and others slink away I am and will be at my post."[31]

As Sherman traveled toward Cincinnati and a September 1, 1861, meeting there with Robert Anderson and George H. Thomas, he mulled over the disappointing past of Bull Run and the uncertain future in Kentucky. As he understood his new job in the Department of the Cumberland, he was to become acquainted with Kentuckians, discover their loyalties, and then help organize the Unionists into military units. Once Kentucky's place in the Union was ensured, then Federal forces were to march into East Tennessee to protect that state's Unionists. With the experiences of the Bull Run disaster and recurring problems with volunteers, he worried how Kentucky and Tennessee (and therefore the Union) could be preserved. "War like a grim monster demands its victims and must have them. How few realize the stern fact I too well know. . . . Our northern states deal in hyperbolic expressions of patriotism, but allow our armies to be in a large minority at every point of attack." He wanted the nation to provide all the troops and supplies the army needed and do it immediately. War required concrete action, not patriotic rhetoric.[32]

Kentucky was a major strategic area.[33] Kentuckians, like Missourians, had attachments to both the North and the South and were ambivalent. The Mississippi River had long been the conduit for Kentucky commerce, but the ever-growing railroad networks were increasingly carrying Kentucky goods in a northerly direction. Kentuckians supported slavery, but their long and proud Union tradition and their spirit of compromise, as personified in Henry Clay and John J. Crittenden, made them unhappy with the prospect of disunion.

Kentucky had early shown its reluctance about secession. In November 1860, despite the fact that Southern Democratic presidential candidate John C. Breckinridge was an important Kentucky politician, he received fewer votes in the state than did the moderate John Bell, whose Constitutional Union party platform called for preservation of the Union. Republican Abraham Lincoln, whose birthplace was in the state, received only a smattering of votes, his identification with antislavery forces frightening the state's slaveholders. Still, when South Carolina and several other slave states seceded because of Lincoln's election, Kentucky refused to follow suit. Governor Beriah Magoffin supported slavery but opposed leaving the Union. When Fort Sumter was attacked in April, the Kentucky legislature voted on May 20 to proclaim the state's "neutrality."

During the period of this so-called neutrality, Union and Confederate sympathizers organized military units. Simon Buckner, the state's inspector general, commanded the pro-Confederate state guards, and Unionists organized their own Home Guards. Both sides seemed determined to continue the existing uneasy peace.

In the June 1861 congressional elections and the August legislative canvass, however, pro-Unionists won overwhelming victories. Camp Dick Robinson was established to recruit Unionist soldiers. As the Unionists grew in strength, they began to question neutrality. Confederate sympathizers continued to support that concept because it was their only option.

If there was any doubt about Unionism's strength in Kentucky, it was resolved in early September. Confederate troops under Gideon Pillow captured the key city of Columbus, and Union troops under U. S. Grant immediately retaliated by taking Paducah. An angry Governor Magoffin condemned both sides for violating the state's neutrality and demanded that both withdraw. The Union-dominated legislature, however, passed a resolution demanding only a Confederate withdrawal and placed the state volunteers under Robert Anderson in Louisville. Simon Buckner's open Confederate stance forced him to flee the state to avoid arrest. George H. Thomas took command of Camp Dick Robinson in central Kentucky, and William "Bull" Nelson, the naval officer turned soldier, established Camp Kenton in the northeastern part of the state. In the West, Grant retained command of the troops ensconced in Paducah. There was little coordination among all these forces, but the Union's growing military presence in the Blue Grass state was obvious.

The Confederates were still in evidence but not in equal strength. Kentucky was part of the enormous Confederate Department No. 2, stretching from the Appalachian Mountains in the East to the trans-Mississippi in the West, and commanded by

Albert Sidney Johnston. When Johnston took control of the department on September 10, he quickly named Simon Buckner a brigadier general and ordered him to fortify Bowling Green, a key part of his long defense line. Meanwhile, Tennessean Felix Zollicoffer operated in the southeastern part of Kentucky, in the area of the Cumberland Gap.

In their determination to assert military control over Kentucky, both Union and Confederate forces planned to recruit Kentuckians and gain additional support from surrounding states. By the best estimates, Kentucky provided 90,000 enlistments to the Union forces (plus about 10,000 to the Home Guards), while Confederate enlistments were between 25,000 and 40,000. As of December 1, 1861, there were 26,872 Kentuckians in the Federal forces and only 7,950 on the Confederate side.[34]

Before Sherman could reach this cauldron of Union and Confederate activity, he went on a lightning tour of Indiana, Illinois, and Missouri in search of men and supplies. In Indianapolis and Springfield, the Indiana and Illinois governors insisted that their men and arms were already committed to McClellan in the East or Frémont in Missouri, so Sherman hurried to St. Louis to see Frémont. The Pathfinder remembered him from their 1847 meeting in California and conversed pleasantly, but he talked only of his own dire needs in Missouri; he had no troops to spare for Kentucky.[35]

Sherman hurried toward Louisville, the headquarters of his new department, disappointed and convinced that the Union cause had little hope when it could not provide the necessary arms and men to fight the war. It was "wrong for Northern Politicians [to be] constantly praising the resources and population of the North when we cannot realize them," he complained. During a stopover in Cincinnati on his way from St. Louis to Louisville, Sherman pessimistically evaluated the situation in a letter to his senator brother. He did not believe the average Kentuckian really wanted to remain in the Union despite the recent election preferences. He insisted that the state's safety required an army of 100,000 men, though he had no idea where so many were to come from. He contrasted the apparent indifference of Unionists everywhere with what he believed was Confederate fervor. "If they are united, and we disunited or indifferent, they will succeed," he concluded.[36]

When he arrived in Louisville in early September 1861, the city was rife with unfounded rumors. Buckner was fortifying Bowling Green and was rumored to be advancing toward Louisville. Zollicoffer was allegedly on the march in the southeastern portion of the state. The recent Confederate capture of Columbus and Grant's occupation of Paducah were major topics of conversation. The former U.S. secretary of the treasury, James Guthrie, now president of the Louisville and Nashville Railroad, told about the burning of a railroad bridge just thirty miles outside Louisville. Rumor put Louisville in imminent danger.[37]

This was startling news. If it was true, a Union disaster seemed certain. Sherman, Anderson, and Unionist leaders did not try to verify the stories before deciding that Sherman would take the Home Guards, augmented by any troops Anderson could forward later, and occupy Muldraugh's Hill, a small range of hills separating the Salt Creek and the Green River, about forty miles from Louisville, near Elizabethtown. It sat astride Guthrie's important railroad, and Buckner had once used it as a training camp. Sherman's task was to prevent the Confederates from using it as a staging area for the feared attack on Louisville.[38]

Sherman left the city with about a thousand men, quickly found the burned bridge, and began repairing it. Then he occupied Muldraugh's Hill. Anderson sent him troops as soon as any arrived from neighboring states, and by October 1 Sherman had between four-thousand and five-thousand inexperienced volunteers. When many of the Home Guards slipped away, Sherman lamented the quality of the troops who remained, his inability to supply them properly, the weakness of his position, and his uncertainty about the exact size and plans of the enemy troops to his front. He told his soldiers "to make up your minds that we will all die right here." They responded by referring to him as "a gruff old cock," though later changing this to "old pills" because they found him such "a bitter pill to swallow." As they got to know him better and recognized his concern for them, they called him "old sugar-coated."[39]

Fortunately for Sherman, Buckner had no offensive design and held similarly inaccurate estimates. On September 27, for example, when Sherman was reporting that he had four-thousand men to hold off what he said was Buckner's fifteen-thousand-man force, Buckner was complaining that he could never hold off

Sherman's thirteen-thousand to fourteen-thousand men with his six-thousand soldiers. The Confederates kept moving and feinting and marching, however, and they convinced Sherman and the other Unionists that there were more than enough of them to crush the minuscule Federal units in Kentucky. Actually, the Confederates posed no significant threat in numbers or design. In October Albert Sidney Johnston complained that he had no gunpowder for any campaign.[40]

But Sherman, swallowing the Confederate ruse, was convinced that his force and the Union cause in general were in mortal danger. For the three weeks on Muldraugh's Hill, he remained apprehensive. He worked day and night issuing orders, writing letters, beefing up his fortifications, inspecting his camps, and pacing, constantly pacing. He gave himself little time to eat, change his clothes, or even get much sleep. His unmilitary attire and his overactive imagination were the talk of his troops. He believed that the young and energetic Kentuckians favored secession, while the older population was pro-Union and reluctant to participate. He had no basis for the assertion, making such claims only out of frustration. His own troops were mainly from Ohio and Indiana, and even his so-called Kentucky regiments were filled with out-of-staters, so this fact made him speak out so unreasonably.[41]

He feared that spies infested his camp, local people feigning friendship but actually passing information and goods to Buckner and Johnston. Secretary of State Seward had complained about the extent of the smuggling going on in Kentucky, and Sherman was not surprised. He was, however, more concerned about newspaper reporters than treacherous locals. Correspondents seemed to be everywhere, and the stories their newspapers published provided more information than Sherman thought ought to be printed. He tried to plug the journalistic leaks by excluding all press people and threatening to hang a New York reporter who tried to remain. But the more he tried, the less successful he was, and the more press animosity he created. He ejected a reporter, only to see him return or have another one take his place. The press had hurt him during his banking and vigilante days in California. Would they do it again here?[42]

His lack of sleep and the chilly weather brought on a cold and made him fear a return of his dreaded asthma. Everything looked dismal: "I don't think I ever felt so much a desire to hide myself in some obscure place, to pass the time allotted to us on earth, but I know full well that we cannot if we would avoid the storm that throttles us, and perforce must drift on to the end. What that [end] will be God only knows."[43]

Despite his pessimism and Lincoln's previous promise, he had the responsibility for all Kentucky placed in his hands. Robert Anderson, worn out from the Fort Sumter siege and the cares of his Kentucky command, resigned his position on October 8. Sherman had to take over. He wrote the adjutant general and expressed his frequently stated belief in the preponderance of Confederate forces. He estimated he would need at least sixty-thousand men to match his opposition. Lorenzo Thomas responded with the hope that Sherman would capture the Cumberland Gap and proceed into East Tennessee, hardly a reassuring comment. Sherman was worried about holding on to Kentucky, and his superiors now were calling on him to capture Tennessee. He believed the view from Washington was unrealistic, and he had to try to open their eyes to the danger he perceived around him.[44]

Since he knew Abraham Lincoln, and his brother and father-in-law had influence with the president, Sherman felt no compunction about writing directly to the White House. He told Lincoln of his inadequate troops and supplies. At the end of the first of these letters, he curtly demanded: "Answer." He wrote to Grant of his fear of being overrun. When he telegraphed Secretary of the Treasury Salmon Chase for assurances that he would be adequately supplied, Chase provided the requested promise but then included a postscript that Sherman was not so happy to hear: "May I add, do not overestimate your enemy's force so much as to delay . . . your aggressive movements." When Ellen said she found his gloomy letters discouraging and asked for a happy one instead, he coldly replied that he did not know "how any body could be cheerful now." Newspaper spies made his small force "liable to be overwhelmed." These worries plus too many cigars (he smoked eight to ten a night), too many drinks, and too much letter writing were giving him headaches, he concluded. Even news of the imminent arrival of the secretary of war and adjutant general did not improve his disposition. In his dark mood, he could not imagine what these officials could do to salvage what he saw as an increasingly hopeless situation.[45]

But he wanted to alert them. He and James Guthrie met Secretary of War Simon Cameron, Adjutant General Lorenzo Thomas, and their party in Jeffersonville, Indiana, on October 17 and escorted them across the river to Sherman's room on the first floor of Louisville's Galt House. Sherman said he preferred to speak to Cameron alone; there were too many strangers in the room. But Cameron responded: "They are all friends, all members of my family, you may speak your mind freely and without restraint." Sherman remained skeptical, and to prevent anyone else from entering the room (and perhaps to make himself feel more secure), he locked the door.[46]

He launched into his overly pessimistic view of affairs. Indiana and Ohio levies were being sent to McClellan or Frémont, while Kentucky received only a few men and defective muskets. Consequently, Union forces in the state could not prevent the Confederate capture of Louisville. Cameron found this hard to believe: "You astonish me! Our informants, the Kentucky Senators and members of Congress, claim that they have in Kentucky plenty of men, and all they want are arms and money." Untrue, Sherman responded, turning to Guthrie for confirmation. The experienced politician eagerly concurred, adding that "no man who owned a slave or a mule in Kentucky could be trusted."

Cameron ordered Thomas to forward all the area's unassigned troops to Kentucky, hoping that these men would be used to capture the Cumberland Gap and move into East Tennessee. Sherman responded by pulling out a large map of the United States. He demonstrated that McClellan and Frémont each had only a hundred miles of front to protect, while he had three hundred. McClellan had a hundred thousand men, and Frémont had sixty-thousand; he had only eighteen-thousand. In order to defend Kentucky adequately, he said, he would need at least sixty-thousand men; in order to go on the offensive, he would need two hundred thousand. "Great God! Where are they to come from?" Cameron exploded. Sherman angrily responded that there were plenty of Northerners who wanted to volunteer, but the War Department kept discouraging them. Cameron asked Thomas to make note of the conversation, promising Sherman to help as much as he could, though insisting that Sherman overestimated his needs. The party proceeded to Lexington, where other Kentuckians told Cameron a similar story: The state needed outside help to prevent a disaster.

Sherman never received enough additional troops and supplies to meet his perceived needs. He told Ellen, inaccurately, that he was outnumbered three to one, and then a week later he told John that it was five to one. (*Louisville Journal* editor George D. Prentice told Lincoln it was seven to one.) Sherman said he knew some people thought he overstated the threat, but they were wrong. Louisville was indeed in imminent danger, and he would gradually have to position all his troops closer to the Ohio River. Confederate forces in Kentucky were strong enough to take southern Indiana and Illinois and capture St. Louis. "I tell you, and warn you of the danger so far as my power goes," he told John. The more he thought about his situation, the more desperate he felt and the worst it seemed. He was actually not outnumbered, but he and many other Unionists thought they were and acted accordingly.[47]

When, on October 30, the *New York Tribune* published Thomas's official report of the Cameron-Sherman meeting, Sherman was stunned. He later learned that some of the loungers that evening had been newsmen, including Cameron's favorite, Samuel Wilkeson, a *Tribune* reporter. This leak reinforced his view of the press as a major threat to his hopes for success in Kentucky. The indignation of other newspapers at the revelations of shortages in Kentucky made less impression on him than the *Tribune*'s ridicule of his troop projections and his antipress activity.[48]

When McClellan replaced Winfield Scott in overall Union army command on November 1, he asked Sherman for regular reports. Sherman responded with one gloomy letter and telegram after another. He wished for a return to his old brigade in Washington; he demanded his transfer from Kentucky. He made similar complaints to Ohio's governor, William Dennison. McClellan became concerned enough to send a personal observer to Kentucky; Colonel Thomas M. Key spent several days with Sherman and decided he was on the verge of nervous exhaustion. The stress of command was getting to him, and this, rather than any real shortages, was the reason for the disturbing correspondence.

Sherman's eccentric behavior, long whispered about, now

became a major topic of open conversation. Sherman stayed up until 3 A.M. most nights at the telegraph office waiting for dispatches, and, when it closed, he paced the corridor leading to his hotel room until dawn. He would tell anyone who would listen his catalog of worries. People thought his behavior was strange and grew alienated at his frequent outbursts of "sternness, abruptness and roughness." Tennessee senator Andrew Johnson thought Sherman was "much of the time incapacitated for command." The assistant secretary of war, Thomas W. Scott, bluntly pronounced what many others had been thinking for some time: "Sherman's gone in the head, he's luny." In fact, he was far from crazy, but he was clearly upset and could not hide it. On November 13 Don Carlos Buell replaced William Tecumseh Sherman in Kentucky. Sherman was sent to Halleck in St. Louis.[49]

Sherman was happy to give up the responsibilities of Kentucky, but his depression deepened with the realization of yet another personal failure: He had been unable to bend Kentucky to his will, to mobilize its force and achieve success. He admitted to Ellen sometime later that he had contemplated taking his own life in Kentucky; only thoughts of his children had stayed his hand. He sank so low that a staff officer urged Ellen to come out to calm him. She first contacted John Sherman, who hurried from Washington to travel with her. Sherman acted withdrawn and frustrated, and his wife and brother were unable to break into the shell of anxiety and depression he had constructed around himself. When John bluntly told him that he was "not only in error but . . . laboring under some strange illusions," Sherman roused himself enough to disagree strongly and warn John of "a simultaneous attack on St. Louis, Louisville, and Cincinnati." He was happy to be leaving Kentucky, he said, but he wished he could "now hide . . . in some obscure corner." "Our Govt is destroyed, and . . . no human power can restore it."[50]

Sherman left Kentucky under a cloud of controversy and arrived in Missouri in late November. Halleck, his 1846 shipmate and later California colleague, greeted him warmly and sent him to inspect troops. Despite the rumors about Sherman's behavior in Kentucky, Halleck gave him the authority "to assume command" of the three divisions at Jefferson City, Tipton, and Sedalia, if he thought it "advisable for the public service." As he made his tour, Sherman carried his Kentucky depression with him, and what he saw in Missouri only added to it. He began worrying about Sterling Price's Confederate army's falling on the scattered Union forces. He feared the effects of the winter wind on the troops camping on the flat prairie. For purposes of defense and health, he recommended a troop consolidation to a more protected area. Halleck was skeptical and sent Dr. J. B. Wright, the department's medical director, to evaluate Sherman's mental state. The physician diagnosed his condition as "one of such nervousness that he was unfit for command." Halleck ordered Sherman back to St. Louis where Ellen waited for his return.[51]

Sherman had left Kentucky under a cloud; now his common-sense advice to consolidate scattered forces (an action that Halleck would later take himself) was seen as another example of panicky overestimation of the Confederate opposition. He was called from the field to headquarters because of his worried wife's arrival and because his commanding officer was apparently upset at the physician's report. He was a forty-one-year-old brigadier general, yet everyone seemed to be patting him on the head and insisting that he go away for a rest. Reluctantly Sherman agreed to a twenty-day leave. He would go home with Ellen—back to Lancaster, back to his foster father's care.

As Sherman left, Halleck wrote to McClellan. Sherman had been "completely 'stampeded,' and was 'stampeding' the entire army," Halleck reported. "I am satisfied that General S[herman]'s physical and mental system is so completely broken by labor and care as to render him for the present entirely unfit for duty. Perhaps a few weeks rest will restore him. I am satisfied that in his present condition it would be dangerous to give him a command here."[52]

Freed from the stress of command, Sherman calmed down and seemed more himself. Thomas Ewing was in Washington, so he did not have to deal with his foster father's disappointment immediately. Then a brief reference appeared in the *New York Times* and in all the Cincinnati papers to "disorders" that had removed General Sherman from command, "perhaps permanently." Sherman became noticeably more morose. On December 11 a headline in the *Cincinnati Commercial* plunged him down even further: GENERAL WILLIAM T. SHERMAN INSANE. The accompanying article accused him of being "stark mad" in Kentucky;

telegraphing the War Department three times in one day for permission to retreat into Indiana; frightening Kentuckians with "the most astounding representations" of Buckner's army; retreating from the Cumberland Gap ("one of his mad freaks"); and issuing orders in Missouri that were so ridiculous that subordinates refused to obey them. It was unfortunate, the article concluded, that Sherman was in such dire straits, but it was better to have him lose his mind than to have the country lose Kentucky.[53]

The issue of Sherman's sanity was soon being discussed all over the nation. In Lancaster, his son Tommy came home one day upset over a schoolmate's accusation that "Papa was crazy!" Sherman was worried that his foster father would be "mortified beyond measure at the disgrace" of seeing him accused of insanity, and he wrote him a long letter of justification. "In these times tis hard to say who are sane and who insane," he hedged. Sherman felt so badly that he needed his foster father's reassurance even more than usual: He needed Thomas Ewing to tell him that he was not crazy, as everyone seemed to be saying. He was, in fact, perfectly sane, but the stress of the disorganized war effort had thrown him off-stride and made him worry inordinately. He exaggerated the Confederate threat, but so did many Kentuckians. But he was the soldier, and they were the civilians; he should have known better.[54]

Sherman looked for reassurance from Halleck. In a letter he justified his apprehensions in Missouri on his familiarity with Southerners and denied that he was crazy. He knew of no one refusing his orders and blamed the whole brouhaha on the indignation of a reporter he had excluded from his camp. "These newspapers have us in their power, and can destroy us as they please, and this one can destroy my usefulness by depriving me of the confidence of officers and men."[55]

The Ewing family organized a response to the newspaper insanity charge, and Philemon Ewing sent Halleck a copy. The letter said that "every material statement in the paragraph" was "false." Sherman never telegraphed the War Department three times in one day and never suggested retreating from Kentucky. He never commanded a brigade in Missouri, and no subordinate ever refused to obey any of his orders. As for Sherman's frightening the people of Louisville, Phil could not see how their fright—or nonfright—had anything to do with his sanity. He correctly insisted that Sherman was simply exhausted from heavy command responsibilities; he had done nothing to warrant being labeled crazy.[56]

Newspaper correspondents used the occasion to repay Sherman for his overt antipress prejudices and activities, and newspapers were filled with reports of his alleged insanity and assertions that reporters had known it all along. *Frank Leslie's Illustrated Newspaper* perhaps expressed general press opinion best: "General Sherman, who lately commanded in Kentucky, is said to be insane. It is charitable to think so." Even some of his troops in the Blue Grass State agreed. Men of the Thirty-fourth Illinois Volunteers reacted to the accusations with a simple, "We knew it."[57]

The press attacks became widespread. It was just like California; newspapers were worsening an already chaotic situation. The Ewings wanted Sherman to institute a lawsuit, but John Sherman and Halleck urged him to ignore it all. John Sherman, who spoke to Lincoln on his brother's behalf, blamed the whole mess on Cump's "serious mistakes." He had overestimated the enemy and underestimated his own troops; he had made "hasty . . . demands . . . [with] inexcusable impertinence"; and he had ejected newspaper reporters who had "the power to create prejudice against him." Press attacks were "transient," and the best response was to ignore them.[58]

Halleck made light of the whole matter. He told Phil Ewing that when Sherman had arrived in Missouri, his exhausting service in Kentucky had already broken his health. Those who did not know him "may have drawn wrong inferences from his broken-down appearance and rather imprudent remarks." Halleck was quick to add: "No one who was personally acquainted with him [obviously people like Halleck] thought that anything was the matter with him except a want of rest." Finally, he reassured Sherman himself that he had countermanded his consolidation order not because he thought it was "unwise" but because it was not timely. He had later sent an inspector who had agreed with Sherman's assessment, and Halleck had then ordered the exact movement. But "in all fairness and kindness," he warned, the remarks Sherman had made about the enemy's invincibility had "led to unfair & harsh comments by those who did not know him. I say this merely to put you on your guard in the future." Halleck left unmentioned the derogatory remark he wrote to his own wife that "certainly" Sherman had "acted insane."[59]

Ellen, Phil, and Thomas Ewing were convinced that Sherman's whole problem was caused by a conspiracy among military men, including Halleck, McClellan, and John Pope, aided and abetted by newsmen. Ellen thought it was particularly suspicious that while the *Commercial* was damning Sherman, it was devoting columns of praise to Pope. At another time, she blamed McClellan; he "absorbed all the resources of the country & *ignored* the west." The Ewings thought a lawsuit was the only way to deal with the slander, though Thomas Ewing also urged John Sherman to institute a formal investigation. But even Ewing recognized that any suit or investigation would be useless if Sherman continued making unguarded statements. He advised his son-in-law to keep quiet.[60]

Sherman returned to Missouri about a week after the appearance of the insanity accusation. On December 23, Halleck gave him a safe command, supervising Benton Barracks, a camp of instruction near St. Louis. He trained troops and sent them forward into the war. He opposed any lawsuit because he feared further publication would only hurt him more. Ellen inundated him with mail, expressing her frequently hysterical reaction to the insanity imbroglio. It all sounded very familiar: She insisted he accept her father's advice and institute a suit; she wished he would become a Catholic and depend on God; she worried about his physical health and about what she said were instances of mental problems in the Sherman family; she wanted to come to see him; she even suggested that he take a long leave from the military and recuperate by running her father's salt well business back in Ohio. She still did not understand.[61]

Sherman worried about disgracing his family; he felt guilt about his inability to support some Tennessee partisans who had died on a bridge-burning expedition he had ordered; and he felt upset over having to fight Southerners, people like the ones he had come to admire during his stays there. Though he maintained his opposition to holding command, he worried that the minor post he held at Benton Barracks was demeaning. Once again he talked about taking a paymaster's job—anything to get a fresh start. He did not know what he wanted, but it was clear he wanted to avoid anything that would focus further attention on him.[62]

In early January 1862, a frustrated Ellen took matters into her own hands. She wrote to Abraham Lincoln, "appeal[ing] in confidence . . . for some intervention in my husband's favor & in vindication of his slandered name." She detailed what she believed to be the conspiracy against him in Kentucky and Missouri and then asked Lincoln to transfer him to the eastern war. When a week brought no response, she traveled to Washington and, in company with her father, she saw Lincoln. The president received her politely, no doubt concerned about maintaining Thomas Ewing's political support, and responded charmingly with words of praise for Sherman. He admitted that Sherman's behavior in Kentucky had been disturbing, but he certainly had not considered him insane. He listened but did not comment on Ellen's insistence that there was an army conspiracy against her husband. Never once did Lincoln promise anything, but Ellen and her father left the meeting satisfied with his attitude. Ellen continued to believe that willful army disregard was responsible for Sherman's problems, but she never included Lincoln in her gallery of villains.[63]

Meanwhile, Sherman, though now suffering from bouts of rheumatism, kept busy with his recruits at Benton Barracks. Regiments of soldiers regularly left his camp for the active war after training under his watchful eye. A Minnesota volunteer corporal described him at this time in a manner reminiscent of earlier statements about his careless manner of dress in Kentucky. He "had so little of the military about him that I concluded he was a preacher." The soldier soon learned his impression was inaccurate. An officer had stupidly marched his troops onto some ice, and Sherman responded with some decidedly unpreacherlike language. Clothes meant little to him, so he continued to pay no attention to criticism of his dress.[64]

Once in a while something happened to make him laugh. He was making his usual rounds of the encampment, ill dressed as always, this time in an old brown coat and stovepipe hat. He came upon a soldier beating a mule and demanded several times that the man stop. The soldier refused. "I tell you again to stop," Sherman insisted. "Do you know who I am? I am General

Sherman." "That's played out!" replied the mule beater. "Every man who comes along here with an old brown coat and stove-pipe hat on, claims to be General Sherman."[65]

Some contemporaries and even some later historians have insisted that Sherman lost his mind in Kentucky and Missouri. They are wrong. He experienced a terrible bout with anxiety and depression that came close to incapacitating him, but he remained whole. His need for Union success caused him to overestimate the enemy and underestimate his own side, resulting in overly pessimistic evaluations of the military situation. The more he craved success, the more he looked for order, and the more desperate he became, the more eccentrically he behaved. He knew that he had miscalculated badly in Kentucky, but he had to continue insisting he was right or risk admitting that the insanity accusations were accurate. He knew there was no army conspiracy; there was only disorganization and an unwillingness to face the reality of the crisis. Sherman saw in Kentucky and Missouri, as he had at Bull Run, an unprepared, disorganized Union effort waiting to be overwhelmed. It depressed him to think that he could do nothing about it.

Sherman's personal military situation underwent a major improvement in mid-February, no doubt partly due to the unrelenting Ewing pressure. Halleck, as he had earlier promised Sherman, the Ewings, and even McClellan, gave his old friend a new command. When he promoted U. S. Grant to command of the Department of West Tennessee, he made Sherman head of the Department of Cairo, headquartered at Paducah in western Kentucky. Careful as ever, Halleck immediately wrote to Thomas Ewing, justifying his handling of Sherman's problems. It was important that Ewing understand Halleck's motives because his political influence could prove troublesome. Halleck acknowledged seeing the accusations against Sherman but insisted that he considered them to be the "grossest injustice" and not "worthy of notice." Ellen was thrilled. "May ecstacy & glory ever attend you!" she wrote Halleck.[66]

The commanding general did not know it at the time, but he had done more than put Sherman back into the war: he had brought Grant and Sherman together for the first time and begun the solution to Sherman's problems with the Union war effort. From Paducah, Sherman forwarded troops to Grant and applauded as the purposeful general added Fort Donelson to his recent victory at Fort Henry. It felt good to be associated with such a "most extraordinary and brilliant" success. Finally Sherman saw the makings of an organized and effective war plan. He believed that his failure in Kentucky had been due to the overwhelming lack of purpose, strategy, and materials on the Union side. Now the war machine was being oiled and streamlined, and he was back in command of a fighting unit. He still harbored enormous doubts about himself and about the nation's ability to put down the seceding states, but he saw a glimmer of light where recently there had been only darkness. He liked the cut of Grant—a well-organized man who acted decisively. Sherman and the Union war effort might just benefit from their association with him.[67]

———— ☆ ————

CHAPTER 8

REBIRTH AT SHILOH

MARCH 1862 ARRIVED in Paducah, Kentucky, with Sherman forwarding troops to Ulysses S. Grant and raising his own division for active service in the field. He seemed to be much calmer, the result of his growing relationship to Grant. The more he watched Grant, the more impressed he was. The unimposing general had experienced failure all his life as Sherman had, yet he was now achieving spectacular success.[1]

Born in 1822, the son of Jesse Grant, a western entrepreneur who never quite became the success he always thought he deserved to be, and Hannah Simpson Grant, a reserved woman no one seemed to know much about, the young Ulysses made little positive impression on his contemporaries. He was the butt of ridicule when, at the age of eight, he mishandled the purchase of a horse. Later a young boy mocked the West Point uniform Grant thought would gain him status. Upon graduation from the military academy, he was disappointed not to get a commission in the cavalry where he could enjoy his love of horses; he had to settle for the less glamorous infantry. His only satisfaction during these years was falling in love with Julia Dent, his military academy roommate's sister.

Before they could marry, however, he served in the Mexican War, once more making no significant impression on his contemporaries. He married Julia in 1848, and for the next four years, they traveled between army posts in Michigan and New York, with Grant remaining in military obscurity. When he was ordered to the Pacific coast, Julia did not travel with him, and he had to spend two lonely years on his own. As he had in his youth, he once more displayed a lack of sound business sense. He allowed himself to be talked into a shaky San Francisco store business arrangement and lost his investment. More significant, loneliness at the separation from wife and family caused severe depression, and he took refuge in the bottle. This depression caused him to resign his army commission, but the inaccurate label of drunk stuck (it still does despite the lack of historical evidence to support it).

Departing the army in 1854 he went to Missouri to farm on the land of his father-in-law. He worked hard for four years, but he could not make a go of it, one winter forced to sell firewood on St. Louis street corners in order to survive. One of the people he encountered during these years was another down-on-his luck West Pointer named William T. Sherman. The two failures spoke briefly and went their separate ways.

In 1858 Grant left the farm, still a failure. He tried his hand at bill collecting in St. Louis, but in December 1859 he had to ask his father for economic help. In the summer of 1860, he and his family traveled to Galena, Illinois, where he went to work selling leather in his father's store. It was a crushing blow in a life that seemed increasingly hopeless. U. S. Grant seemed doomed to failure.

Then the war came, and Grant's fortunes took a dramatic turn. As the nation responded to Lincoln's call for soldiers after the attack on Fort Sumter, the town of Galena turned to Grant, its only West Point graduate. He successfully recruited a company of volunteers and allowed another townsman to assume the captaincy. He expected a colonelcy, a rank commensurate with his regular army experience, but no commission arrived, and once again he had to reach out for help—this time to ask his congressman to get him into the army.

Grant's first military actions in the fall of 1861 demonstrated his ability to organize and to act swiftly and decisively. His successes at Paducah, Kentucky, and Belmont, Missouri, were hardly major victories, but they were successes and demonstrated his willingness to fight—rare in Union generals during those days. And in March 1862, when he captured Forts Henry and Donelson on the Tennessee and Cumberland rivers in Tennessee and demanded unconditional surrender, the nation took notice. U. S. Grant became "Unconditional Surrender" Grant, the nationally known no-nonsense Union officer who got results when other generals seemed paralyzed.

He had turned his life around, finally enjoying the success that had eluded him all his life. Sherman was particularly impressed. Grant's approach to war was paying him rich dividends. His victories at Forts Henry and Donelson demonstrated to Sherman that if the Union put its mind to it, it could achieve success. To Sherman, Grant was proof of the importance of purpose and order, a beacon to lead the Union cause out of the chaos that was hampering its war effort. Grant was showing Sherman that it could be done, and Sherman was encouraged at the sight.

Ellen was thrilled at Cump's improved disposition and his affectionate comment that her support during the insanity crisis made him "love and honor" her "more than ever." She could not, however, resist her usual caveat: "You only want Christianity to make you perfect." This provoked Cump's response: "I see the mistakes I have committed in the most glaring shape and fear that all the world does the same." He felt better, but he suffered from wounded pride. He just wanted to forget it all, if he could, and Ellen's detailed accounting of Ewing machinations to get retractions from the press reopened old hurts. When she continued to insist that he was a victim of a plot carried out by Commanding General George B. McClellan, whom she labeled a Confederate spy, he became sufficiently upset to have an aide tell Thomas Ewing, Jr., that he wanted no further family help in Washington. He wished only "to be left alone." He was perfectly content where he was, associated with Grant and hopeful of better days.[2]

Sherman believed that the only way to redeem his reputation was on the battlefield. For the first time since Louisville, he had his own unit, a volunteer division, and he was anxious to prove himself in combat. He reported to C. F. Smith at Tennessee's Fort Henry in mid-March 1862 and was ordered to cut the Charleston and Memphis Railroad between Corinth and Iuka, Mississippi. Corinth was the junction of the east-west Charleston and Memphis and the north-south Mobile and Ohio railroads, and Union troops were preparing to move against it. Although rain and flooding hampered this so-called Yellow Creek expedition, Sherman was exhilarated. People lined the Tennessee River shore, welcoming him and his soldiers "by the waving of handkerchiefs, clapping of hands, &c." During the expedition, Sherman noted a landing along the west side of the Tennessee River with a road leading to Corinth, only twenty-two miles away. Unlike most other such locations along the river, this one was high enough above the water to preclude any danger of spring flooding. He alerted Smith that this Pittsburg Landing seemed like a good place to disembark troops for movement against the Mississippi city.[3]

After a personal reconnaissance, Grant endorsed Pittsburg Landing. Sherman's division and those of Illinois politician/volunteer generals Stephen A. Hurlbut, John McClernand, Benjamin Prentiss, and W. H. L. Wallace were ordered to establish camp there. Lew Wallace's division was placed at Crump's Landing, Tennessee, six miles down river, and a small force was kept with Grant at Savannah, Tennessee, nine miles away. Sherman suggested placing troops at other locations too, with all forces close enough to move "concentrically" against any desired target.[4]

Pittsburg Landing seemed like a good site. It was a flat surface of land, roughly three miles in both width and depth, bounded on the north by Snake Creek and its tributary, Owl Creek, and on the south by Lick Creek. These streams were swollen and deep, providing protection for the flanks. Any attack on the Union troops could come only through the three-mile opening between the two creek systems. But no one imagined any attack. Union troops believed they were at Pittsburg Landing only to await the arrival of Don Carlos Buell's twenty-thousand-man Army of the Ohio. Once Halleck arrived to take overall command, the combined force would attack Corinth.

Sherman's and Prentiss's divisions established their camps three miles from the landing, near a small Methodist country church called Shiloh (the name ironically meaning "a place of peace"). Sherman's division camped roughly in the center of the opening with Prentiss to his left. Behind Sherman was McClernand's division, then Hurlbut's, and finally Wallace's, closest to the landing. In all, there were about thirty-five-thousand Union soldiers, with another seventy-five hundred under Lew Wallace at nearby Crump's Landing. The location of their camps, the lack of coordination between them, the absence of any entrenchments, and Grant's presence at Savannah indicated that Union troops were there to bivouac, not to fight.

Corinth, the object of this Union activity, was defended by a forty-thousand-man Confederate force recently gathered from distant reaches of the South and commanded by Albert Sidney Johnston and P. G. T. Beauregard. The Confederates were preparing to do the unexpected: attack the Unionists at Pittsburg Landing before Buell could arrive. Johnston outlined a plan to hit the Union left flank especially hard and then drive along the Tennessee River to separate the Unionists from the landing and any hope of linkage with Buell and his Army of the Ohio. The plan was to drive Grant's force into the swampy ground around Owl and Snake creeks. Johnston, however, chose a formation ill suited for this purpose: three lines parallel to the Union front. William Hardee's corps was to form the first line; Braxton Bragg's corps was to take its position in a second line behind Hardee; and Leonidas Polk's corps was to form the third line. John C. Breckinridge was to provide the reserve. The three lines were to attack across a broad front, with no special concentration of forces or effort against the Union left. Confederate leaders would have been hard-pressed to choose a worse formation to drive the Unionists away from the landing.

The forty-thousand Confederates moved out of Corinth on April 3, 1862, some three hours later than planned. The twenty-two-mile march took all that day plus two more. They were not in position to attack until late afternoon of April 5, so their generals decided to wait until the following morning. That night Union and Confederate soldiers slept only a few miles apart. Amazingly, the Union camps did not realize the proximity of the enemy, despite the noise made by the ill-disciplined Confederates. The Union high command, not expecting an attack, simply ignored all information to the contrary. Units carried on normal reconnaissance, but no one investigated the intelligence gained.

Instructions and reports of numerous reconnaissance activities fill Sherman's correspondence at this time. After the Yellow Creek expedition, he conducted an unfruitful joint reconnaissance/railroad wrecking raid toward Corinth. Finding enemy pickets to his immediate front as early as March 20 and, though suffering from diarrhea, he led an extended reconnaissance of Pea Ridge, ten miles beyond his lines toward Corinth. In early April, he once more sent several of his regiments and some cavalry to try to trap enemy pickets; he mounted a river expedition toward Iuka, Mississippi; and he marched a brigade three miles down the road toward Corinth "by way of drill and instruction."[5]

Nothing he saw or heard was worrisome. The weather was "Springlike, apples & peaches in blossom . . . Bluebirds singing and spring written upon the hill sides." "We are constantly in the presence of the enemy's pickets," he realized, "but I am satisfied that they will await our coming at Corinth or some point of the Charleston Road." Yes, there were enemy troops to his immediate front, but they were there only on reconnaissance. He refused to predict the future; that had caused him trouble before, and he would not indulge in it again. When an aide asked him why the Union troops did not just march out after the rebel army, Sherman responded: "Never mind, young man, you will have all the fighting you want before this war is over; it will come fast enough for you after awhile."[6]

On April 4, Sherman received the ultimate reassurance: Grant saw no threat of enemy activity against his forces; an attack against Lew Wallace at Crump's Landing was only a remote possibility. Sherman's respect for Grant gave him no reason to question his commander now, especially since "they'd call me crazy again" if he did.[7]

As he accepted Grant's evaluation, however, he ignored some concrete intelligence. He had sent out the Fifth Ohio Cavalry Regiment and an infantry company to investigate the capture of several of his pickets, and they encountered so much enemy artillery two miles out that they had to be reinforced by two infantry regiments. Sherman estimated that, in addition to some cavalry, the enemy had two infantry regiments and an artillery battery to his front, but he was pleased to report that "all is quiet along my lines now." "The enemy is saucy . . . [but] I do not apprehend anything like an attack on our position." Grant was happy at the news; this was what he believed too. The two, who later would work so harmoniously in leading Union forces to victory, now only reinforced erroneous ideas in one another.[8]

During the night of April 5, when Union and Confederate armies camped within a few miles of each other, Sherman had no inkling of danger. Subordinates' suggestions to the contrary annoyed him. Major E. G. Ricker of the Fifth Ohio Cavalry Regiment interpreted the April 4 encounter to mean that the enemy was nearby in large numbers. Sherman disagreed: "My dear sir, it is impossible that they should think of attacking us here, at the base of our operations—[a] mere skirmish, sir." In a similar vein, he told Colonel Jesse Appler of the Fifty-third Ohio Infantry Regiment that he had better stop issuing warnings about enemy to his front, or he "could take his damn regiment back to Ohio." Sherman grew so angry at Colonel Thomas Worthington of the Forty-sixth Ohio Regiment for his insistent warnings that he court-martialed the man and made an enemy for life.[9]

Colonel Everett Peabody, the commander of Prentiss's First Brigade, was one Union officer who could not ignore his forbodings. Early on Sunday morning, April 6, Peabody ignored Prentiss's derision and sent two infantry companies out to probe the 3 A.M. darkness to his front. At about 5 A.M., these pickets ran into outposts of the first Confederate battle line, just one mile away. The two advance parties began firing on each other. Peabody sent word back, and Prentiss roused his troops just before the Confederates, under William Hardee, came crashing through the woods. The Battle of Shiloh was on.[10]

Sherman's division, located to the right and behind Prentiss's camp, had its own nervous regimental commander. Jesse Appler had sent out skirmishers during the same early morning hours. They returned before dawn with news that they had heard firing to the south—the fighting between Hardee's and Peabody's pickets. Then a wounded soldier came stumbling into the camp screaming for a battle formation because the enemy was on its way. Appler issued the order and sent word up the chain of command. At first, Sherman ignored this warning, considering the source, but then he decided to investigate for himself. Around 7 A.M., he and his staff rode out some four hundred yards in front of his division's camp. Though enemy fire killed Sherman's orderly at his side, he was still not cognizant of a full-scale Confederate attack.[11]

It was not until 8 A.M., that he "saw the glistening bayonets of heavy masses of infantry . . . and became satisfied for the first time that the enemy designed a determined attack on our whole camp." By this time, he had his entire division in line of battle to meet the Confederate advance. Within the hour, many men in Appler's regiment, led by the colonel himself, had broken ranks and were rushing to the rear. Most of these poorly trained Union soldiers had never been in combat before, and the shock of battle was traumatic. Soldiers all over the battlefield panicked, but the majority made a determined defense. Slowly but inexorably, however, the Confederate surge forced the Union troops back.

Minié balls fired from rifle muskets and artillery cannon balls were whizzing and crashing everywhere as Confederates attacked the hastily formed Union line. The Confederate three-parallel-line formation quickly disintegrated into an extended single line, but it kept driving the Federals back. Prentiss retreated until he came to an old road, sufficiently sunken to give him some protection from the attackers, and then took a stand. Wallace, McClernand, and Sherman extended the Union line to Prentiss's right, and Hurlbut to his left. Grant arrived in the middle of the morning and hobbled around the battlefield, his ankle severely bruised from a recent riding accident. About 10 A.M. he appeared at Sherman's position and praised the effort his division was making. He had already ordered Lew Wallace to rush over from Crump's Landing, but Wallace was nowhere to be seen. Buell's forces, though nearby, had not yet arrived either.[12]

The battle scene grew ever more awful. The dead piled up, and along the Tennessee River, large numbers of frightened men congregated in small groups, seeking safety from the carnage. Sherman and Prentiss had absorbed the early brunt of the Confederate attack, and the number of casualties in their divisions was very high. Sherman himself had three horses shot out from under him. "Well, my boy, didn't I promise you all the fighting you could do?" he asked his aide as the soldier gave him a fresh mount. Buckshot hit a bone in his right hand and lodged there. A projectile tore through his hat, and a spent minié ball struck him in his metal shoulder strap, but its lack of velocity prevented any serious damage. (In Lancaster, false rumors spread that a cannon ball had cut his hand in half, and later Ellen and the Ewings were horrified to hear that his entire hand had allegedly been amputated.) Sherman seemed cool and intense, a model of concentration. He rallied his forces, and they gave ground grudgingly.[13]

Noon found Sherman, with his hand bleeding, his arm in a temporary sling, his face smeared with blood and dirt. The battle raged around him, but he calmly ordered an artillery battery into position just in time to stop a charging enemy column. When Confederate infantry tried to overrun the guns, he shifted some of his own infantry and beat back the attempt. He seemed to be everywhere, maneuvering companies, encouraging individuals, and even instructing his green troops on such basic knowledge as "how to cut the fuzes of their [artillery] shells."[14]

Prentiss's sunken road position and his soldiers' personal heroism allowed his troops to hold on, while Sherman and other troops around him were forced back. Again and again, the Confederates mounted frontal attacks on Prentiss's line in the middle of the battlefield. Each time they were repulsed. They began to call the area the Hornet's Nest. Even the massing of sixty-two artillery pieces, the most in American history up to that time, could not budge Prentiss. He held on as Grant had ordered him. Behind him, the rest of the Union army established a final defense line protecting the river landing. Prentiss was finally forced to surrender but only after he had gained valuable time for the rest of the army. The Confederate attack had not driven the Unionists into the Owl/Snake Creek swamps as planned. The Union force established a line of defense around Pittsburg Landing. The Confederates were winning the battle but losing it as well.[15]

In mid-afternoon, the attacking Confederate army suffered a serious setback in the loss of its commanding general, Albert Sidney Johnston. While foolishly trying to provide tactical leadership at the front, Johnston was struck in a leg artery by an enemy minié ball and quickly bled to death. Beauregard, who had been providing actual overall leadership throughout the battle, now formally took on the task. In late afternoon, he looked over the situation and halted the Confederate attack until the next morning. He convinced himself that Buell could not reinforce Grant. Meanwhile Lew Wallace arrived, and the first elements of Buell's army began stepping off transports onto the landing. Beauregard had made a serious miscalculation in a battle that abounded with them.[16]

On the battlefield itself, a pond served as a symbol of the carnage. So many wounded and dying men from both sides came to refresh themselves in this small pool that its waters became red from their blood. It is still known as the Bloody Pond.

That evening and into Monday morning, rain pelted the wounded and dying who lay on the battlefield moaning and screaming in agony. From the river, Union gunboats lobbed shells into the Confederate army encamped where Union soldiers had slept only the previous night. Beauregard and Bragg, lodged in the same tent their old friend Sherman had occupied, plotted their tactics for the following morning while their soldiers plundered the tents of less important Federals. The rain, the anguished cries, and the navy shells kept both Confederate and Union soldiers awake that awful night, but the Unionists had the advantage of seeing Buell's army tramping on line throughout their sleepless vigil. At 5 P.M. Grant told an incredulous Sherman to get ready for the offensive the next day. When Sherman saw Grant again that night around 11 P.M., he was standing under a tree, holding a lantern and chewing on a cigar, his coat collar pulled up and his hat turned down against the rain. Sherman, similarly disheveled, was ready to ask Grant about his retreat plans, but at the last moment decided against it. Instead, he said: "Well, Grant, we've had the devil's own day, haven't we?" "Yes," the soaked commanding general responded, "lick 'em tomorrow, though."[17]

At dawn the next day, Grant launched a full-scale attack and quickly gained the momentum. Now it was the Confederates' turn to fall back, but like the Unionists the previous day, they did so grudgingly. The addition of Wallace's and Buell's forces gave the Union army another twenty-seven-thousand men, providing them the numerical advantage that the Confederates had enjoyed on Sunday. The Federals steadily regained lost ground. By late Monday afternoon, it was all over. The exhausted Confederates began limping back toward Corinth, leaving behind an equally drained Union army.

Grant did not have the heart to order a full-scale pursuit, but he did send Sherman with some cavalry and two brigades of infantry after the retreating Confederates. About six miles from Shiloh, when Sherman ordered one of his colonels to execute a simple tactical maneuver, he discovered, to his horror, that the officer was totally ignorant of tactics. Sherman had to teach him in the midst of the battlefield. Then Sherman's men ran into the Confederate rear guard commanded by his later nemesis, Nathan Bedford Forrest. Forrest charged the Union cavalry and infantry, and, to Sherman's shock, his troops broke and ran. He and his staff found themselves in an exposed position. He quickly formed his rear troops; he rallied the broken units on this line, and they soon drove off the Confederates, wounding many, including Forrest himself. Sherman decided against further pursuit. He buried his dead, cared for his wounded, and, with his "troops fagged out by three days' hard fighting, exposure, and privation," moved toward his original camp near the Shiloh church. The battle was over. The Confederates had suffered 10,700 killed, wounded, and missing. Union troop losses were over 13,000. Of this number, Sherman's division lost over 2,000 men.[18]

As Sherman returned to the still-littered battlefield, his appearance caused a cheer to go "rolling down the line" of the troops. "He rode slowly, his grizzled face beaming with animation, his tall form swaying from side to side, and his arms waving." "Boys," he yelled, "you have won a great victory. The enemy has retreated to Corinth." One member of Buell's army was so taken with his former Kentucky commander that he later said that if Sherman had asked the men to move on Corinth right then, they would have done so enthusiastically.[19]

Sherman had returned to a hellish scene. The dead were being buried; the wounded were being cared for in the first field hospital in U.S. history and then placed on river transports for movement north; the animal and weapon wreckage of war was still being cleaned up. "Wagons hauling in dead men and dumping them on the ground, as cord wood, for burial in long trenches, like sardines in a box. Wounded men with mangled legs and arms, and heads half shot off, horrible to behold, and still more of the wounded appealing for water, and for help in any form." Sherman scrounged among the human, animal, and material debris because the Confederates had stolen his bed and bedding and had killed three of his horses from beneath him. He had to content himself with a small tent, borrowed clothes, and two rather mediocre horses. His wounded right hand remained sore, but otherwise he felt fine.[20]

Buell's army, which had arrived late on the first day, contained troops Sherman had commanded on Muldraugh's Hill in Kentucky. When the soldiers saw him, they broke out in cheers. "Such shouting you have never heard," he happily noted. After the battle, he visited their camps and was even more gratified at his reception. He also came across one of his Louisiana cadets among the captured Confederates and learned that many others had taken part in the battle. He gave this young man, who only a year before had been his student, some socks and other clothing. He donated bandages his foster mother had sent him to the surgeons caring for the wounded.[21]

Looking back on the victory, which he would later term "the

most important which has ever occurred on this continent" and "the turning point . . . which made all our western campaigns possible," Sherman seemed proud of himself and happy that "at last" he was "redeemed from the vile slanders of that Cincinnati paper." The huge numbers of troops involved in the battle began "to approximate my standard," he insisted, demonstrating that his estimates in Kentucky might not have been all that wrong. He was especially pleased that Thomas Ewing could recognize his redemption. With satisfaction, he read a statement of support that Ewing had anonymously sent to the *Louisville Journal.* Ewing's words were "significantly complimentary[,]" Sherman said, "more so than I merit from such a high source." And when Ellen told him how "exceedingly well pleased" her father was and how he was "very proud of you" and could "hear nothing of you without emotion," Sherman's satisfaction crested. Not only had Shiloh wiped away the stigma of Kentucky, but it had also provided the occasion for Thomas Ewing to express the approval that Sherman had always craved.[22]

Sherman also gained a concrete mark of approval from Washington: a promotion from brigadier general to major general of volunteers, the result of Halleck's and Grant's fulsome praise of his Shiloh conduct and the pressure exerted by John Sherman and Thomas Ewing on Abraham Lincoln. Just a few weeks before, Washington had been filled with stories of Sherman's alleged insanity; now Thomas Ewing, Jr., heard an army officer tell a crowd of onlookers in the Willard Hotel that "if Napoleon Bonaparte had commanded at Shiloh, he would have made General Sherman a field marshall on the field of battle."[23]

Shiloh had won Sherman glory, but it had also shown him how horrible war could be. "I still feel the horrid nature of this war[,] and the piles of dead . . . & wounded & maimed make me more anxious than ever for some hope of an end." "But," he concluded unhappily, "I know such a thing cannot be for a long long time. Indeed I never expect it or to survive it." He worried about the size of the Confederate army in Corinth, and, as he used to do in Kentucky, he vastly overestimated it—believing there were 130,000 Confederates, many more than the "inferior numbers" in Halleck's force. (Actually, Halleck had 110,000 men, and Beauregard had 66,000.) Once again, he contemplated the consequences of defeat, worrying that if Halleck's army was defeated in its attempt to take Corinth, nothing stood in the way of Beauregard's reaching the Ohio River.[24]

"I am a subordinate & it is none of my business now," he decided, expressing renewed insecurity about his leadership abilities. "I do not see far enough into the future & am not gifted with that amount of Hope & reliance on Providence which the case calls for in a leader." Shiloh may partially have lifted Sherman's spirits, but in many ways he still carried with him the anxieties that had plagued him in Kentucky.[25]

Sherman's uncertainties were aggravated by the criticism heaped on the Union military for their performance at Shiloh. The boatloads of wounded, the huge number of dead, and the suspicious circumstances surrounding the battle's inception caused the public, stirred by critical reporters and politicians, to cry out in protest. In Kentucky Sherman had been branded as insane for his alleged inadequacies; now U. S. Grant, an individual for whom his admiration had grown because of Shiloh, was being accused of drunken incompetence. Why had Union troops been so badly surprised at Shiloh that Sunday morning, the press asked; their answer was that Grant had not done his job, no doubt because he had been guzzling whisky. "There was no more preparation by Gen. Grant for an attack," said one newspaper, "than if he had been on a Fourth of July frolic."[26]

Halleck's arrival after the battle resulted in Grant's demotion to a secondary post, so Grant decided to quit. Sherman saw in Grant's predicament his own in Kentucky, and he rushed off to see him. He found his friend with all his office and camp chests in a pile outside the tent, prepared for transport. In his tent, Grant was methodically tying correspondence together into small stacks. What was wrong? Sherman inquired. "Sherman, you know. You know that I am in the way here. I have stood it as long as I can, and can endure it no longer." He was going to St. Louis, Grant said, though he had no real prospects there. Sherman protested. He told Grant that Shiloh had removed his stigma, and something would soon change Grant's fortune, too. The small, unimpressive man with the ever-present cigar in his mouth listened. Sherman grieved for Grant, who was "not a brilliant man . . . but . . . a good & brave soldier, . . . sober, very industrious, and as kind as a child. Yet he has been held up as a careless criminal, a drunkard, tyrant, and everything horrible." If a person like Grant, whom

Sherman saw as a beacon of purpose and order to the Union cause, could be driven from the army, what hope was there for anyone else, especially Cump Sherman? In the end, Grant decided to stay, but Sherman remained upset.[27]

As he had done in Kentucky and as far back as his banking days in California, Sherman railed against newspapers to vent his frustration. He blamed the press's inaccurate sensationalist reporting for Grant's predicament and the whole unpreparedness controversy. Sherman insisted in the days after Shiloh, as he was to do for the rest of his life, that Union troops had not been surprised that Sunday morning. Certainly no one had expected the Confederates to make an attack, but when it came, the troops had been in line and fought bravely—except for those cowards who ran and told lies to reporters. If newsmen would take the time to speak to those who knew the true story, they would know how inaccurate their reports were.[28]

Beginning with Whitelaw Reid's dramatic account in the April 14 *Cincinnati Gazette,* newspapers all over the country had published damning accounts of Union generalship at Shiloh. Yet this time newsmen treated Sherman favorably. Agate, as Reid signed himself, described Sherman as "dashing along the line, encouraging them [his troops] everywhere by his presence, and exposing his own life with the same freedom with which he demanded their offer of theirs." Sherman ignored the kind words and rose in righteous anger at the press criticism of Grant, Prentiss, and others. His letters in the months after Shiloh were filled with angry references to the hated newsmen, "the most contemptible race of men that exist, cowardly, cringing, hanging round, gathering their material out of the most polluted sources." He blamed them for causing the war and continuing it. "I have at times felt I would prefer to be governed by Davis, Beauregard, & Bragg [than] to be abused by a set of dirty newspaper scribblers who have the impudence of Satan."[29]

A politician joined in the condemnation of Union forces. Benjamin Stanton, the lieutenant governor of Sherman's home state of Ohio, visited Shiloh soon after the battle and then returned home to publish, in his home town newspaper in Bellefontaine, a scathing attack on Union leadership. Although Stanton did not mention Sherman, Sherman jumped to the defense of his colleagues. He wrote a bitter letter, to which the Ohio politician quickly responded and included Sherman on his list of guilty generals. The controversy raged into the fall, with letters flying back and forth, published in the press and in pamphlet form. Thomas Ewing took up the cudgels and wrote some scathing briefs of his own. No doubt, Stanton had hoped to use the Shiloh debacle as a way to gain some political favor in his home state, never expecting anything like Sherman's and the Ewings' responses. He had not counted on Sherman's determination to protect friends from the kind of unfair treatment he believed he had received in Kentucky and Missouri. Sherman fought it out with Stanton, using the episode as a way to lessen his frustration over his Shiloh success's being marred by press and political attacks.[30]

The controversy surrounding the battle and the sight of the fleeing inexperienced troops did provoke Sherman's anxiety. Once more he worried that an excess of democracy was responsible for the nation's (and his) problems. Newsmen wrote their sensational and false accounts because the people wanted to read that officers, not privates, were at fault. He hoped the war would not end until the entire nation came to realize that "the written Law is our King and a man may look & read his duty without consulting the daily newspapers." That was what this war was all about: to prevent continued movement toward a fatal calamity— the "tendency to anarchy." The nation needed order to survive, and he would give his all to achieve it. Anarchy, this time in the form of journalistic and political sensationalism, was threatening his recently gained success. The press's unprincipled attacks threatened to turn victory into failure.[31]

Once more, the Ewings worked hard on his behalf. They talked of publishing a formal defense, but in mid-April, Thomas Ewing decided that none was necessary. Instead he told Tom Ewing, Jr., to show Abraham Lincoln a copy of Halleck's post-Shiloh endorsement. He should also point out, Ewing said, that if Sherman had been in command at Pittsburg Landing, "the caution & appreciation of danger" that caused him problems in Kentucky and Missouri would have saved the day "and insured an easy victory" at the landing.[32]

John Sherman had consistently opposed any printed defense of Cump's earlier performance, but on May 9, even before he saw his brother's Shiloh report, he took to the Senate floor to defend Sherman and all Ohio troops. Then he wrote a letter to the *Cincinnati Commercial* that praised Sherman's "gallant conduct" at Shiloh and stated that his recent promotion provided "a proper occasion" for discussing the truth of Kentucky. He claimed that his brother's assertions there had actually been "a remarkable evidence of his foresight and sagacity" and hardly evidence of insanity. The *Cincinnati Gazette* disagreed, but, except for Ellen, the insanity charge had indeed been buried on the Shiloh battlefield.[33]

Meanwhile, Sherman anchored the right wing of the Union force, slowly bearing down on Corinth in late April and May. When the city fell on May 25, he expressed no disappointment at taking a month to advance twenty-five miles to find an abandoned town. As he told his soldiers in a statement of thanks: "They boldly and defiantly challenged us to meet them at Corinth. We accepted the challenge and came slowly and without attempt at conceal-ment to the very ground of their selection and they had fled away. . . . It is a victory as brilliant and important as any recorded in history, and any officer or soldier who has lent his aid has just reason to be proud of his part." But, he cautioned, this victory did not mean the war was over; the enemy had still to be shown that "they must obey the laws of their country and not attempt its overthrow by threats, by cruelty and by war. They must be made to feel and acknowledge the power of a just and mighty nation." "I contend we are fighting for the supremacy of *Written Law,* as against the Rule of mere party and popular prejudice."[34]

Shiloh was to remain of crucial importance to Sherman all his life. It was especially tied into his lifelong admiration for Grant. Here he saw firsthand Grant's steady determination and how it snatched victory out of defeat. Shiloh was an important event in his life because he saw that Union forces could, given the right leadership, stand up to the Confederates. The Federal army could overcome chaos and be successful.

Shiloh had a mystical quality about it for all who fought there. A camaraderie of soldiers who had survived the worst of war lived on as long as they did. Perhaps Sherman captured the feeling best during an address to the Society of the Army of the Tennessee in 1881. "Who but a living witness can adequately portray those scenes on Shiloh's field, when our wounded men, mingled with rebels, charred and blackened by the burning tents and under-brush, were crawling about, begging for someone to end their misery? Who can describe the plunging shot shattering the strong oak as with a thunderbolt, and beating down horse and rider to the ground? Who but one who has heard them can describe the peculiar sizzing of the minie ball, or the crash and roar of a volley fire? Who can describe the last look of the stricken soldier as he appeals for help that no man can give or describe the dread scene of the surgeon's work, or the burial trench?"[35]

CHAPTER 9

RESTORING ORDER TO MEMPHIS

HALLECK'S GRAND ARMY stood in possession of Corinth, Mississippi, after a slow campaign—an advance of less than a mile a day
and construction of earthworks at every stop. There was no Shiloh
surprise this time, but there was no dramatic victory either. Union
troops had Beauregard and his Confederates on the run. Albert
Sidney Johnston's original western defense line, first shattered by
Grant at Forts Henry and Donelson, was now totally destroyed. To
the south, New Orleans was on the verge of capture; Vicksburg
and Port Hudson were inviting targets on the Mississippi River;
and even far-away Mobile was vulnerable. Memphis, just to the
northwest, was Halleck's for the taking, its Confederate troops
departing at Corinth's capture. In all directions, Halleck had
military opportunities. He did not take them. One-third of his
soldiers and one-half of the Union generals had a form of
intestinal illness, and Halleck feared further sickness. He divided
his army into smaller units and gave them housekeeping tasks—
and missed a magnificent opportunity.[1]

Sherman agreed with his commander's decision. He believed
the summer heat was dangerous to marching troops, so he
opposed pursuing the fleeing Confederates. He supported the
splitting of Union forces and the repairing of railroads and
communications in Kentucky, Tennessee, and Mississippi. It was
better to organize carefully rather than move precipitously and be
sorry. Once all was in order, however, he believed that Union
troops should take control of the Mississippi, "and then let
matters rest awhile till the people recover from their bitter hates."
Sherman gave little thought to the offensive. Like Halleck and

Winfield Scott, the former commanding general, he took a conservative approach toward the war effort. He still hoped Southerners would come to their senses before more battles were necessary.[2]

This period was to witness an important metamorphosis in Sherman's thinking about war. To this time, he had thought, like most other military men, only of battles. Now he came face to face with the fact that war was more than soldiers, more than set conflict. The idea that war included the entire populace—its determination to fight and its material goods—became evident to him. A new philosophy of war that would govern him for the rest of the conflict was born during the Memphis months.

It was therefore appropriate when Union troops took Memphis on June 6 that Sherman was busy establishing a supply depot at Corinth and securing the Memphis and Charleston Railroad west toward Memphis. He spent most of June and July, in fact, repairing bridges and trestles, refurbishing locomotives and platform cars, securing the town of Holly Springs, Mississippi, and surviving his first ambush by civilians under arms—guerrillas— near Wolf River in Tennessee. He became ill from the oppressive heat, but he maintained his equilibrium. He convinced Ellen that he neither needed to come home nor have her visit him.[3]

On July 21, 1862, Sherman undertook a new responsibility. Halleck appointed him the military governor of Memphis, indicating that any concern about his Kentucky and Missouri reputation was gone. His appointment to pacify such an important section of the Mississippi River dramatized his increasingly important role in the war and provided him with the opportunity to rethink his military attitudes. His years as a banker in San Francisco and New York, his experience as a property manager in St. Louis and Leavenworth, Kansas, and his term as street railway president in St. Louis gave him excellent credentials for administering an urban center like Memphis. He entered upon his new position with a relish.[4]

Unhappily, Halleck was called to Washington to become commanding general, and Sherman felt "heartfelt pain." He believed Old Brains had created "order, system, firmness, and success" out of "Mexican anarchy." This had helped him and the Union survive low points in both their existences and had made success now seem possible. Perhaps Halleck was just the man to bring the same results to the overall Union military effort, but Sherman would miss him in the West.[5]

When he took command in Memphis, Sherman quickly let it be known that his major priority was to ensure order in western Tennessee. The major commercial city, with a peacetime population of twenty-three thousand, was in almost total disarray. Trade was at a standstill. Many businesses were boarded up. The city's leading newspaper, the *Daily Appeal*, had fled the city, printing presses and all, and so had numerous prominent citizens. Hundreds of hungry Northern entrepreneurs had arrived with the Union troops in June and were jockeying for economic position. Black and white prostitutes did a thriving business. Confederate flags defiantly flew from the private homes of some native white Memphians, and these sullen and uncooperative people used every opportunity to smuggle goods to the guerrilla bands infesting the surrounding countryside. Five previous Union generals, including Grant, had already tried unsuccessfully to restore some order to this chaos, so Sherman clearly had a difficult task before him.[6]

A river of regulations flowed from his temporary office in the Gayoso House, the city's leading hotel. He ordered all businesses and public places to reopen. He reiterated all his predecessors' pronouncements, including the regulation requiring men of military age either to take a loyalty oath or leave the city. He pushed work on Fort Pickering, Grant's emplacement for guarding land approaches to the city, and established rules for the slave labor on the project. He required accurate book-keeping on the use of slaves for later payment to loyal slaveholders. He restricted trade to five roads and made it subject to military inspection. When he found that Confederate sympathizers refused anything but gold and silver for their cotton and then forwarded such specie to their military, he violated War and Treasury Department policies and prohibited such trade. He ordered his quartermaster to rent all vacant buildings, holding the revenues for later payment to loyal owners. Publicizing the achievements of any military leader or unit caused problems and was therefore "wrong and criminal," he lectured the press, urging them to support "system, order, government." If they refused, he warned, he would consider them "greater enemies to their country and mankind than the men who, from a mistaken sense of State pride, have taken muskets."[7]

When he attended Episcopal church services one Sunday morning and noticed that the minister omitted a customary prayer for the president of the United States, he stood up in his pew and recited the prayer out loud himself. Still, he understood his delicate position. He told Mayor John Park that because of the war, "the military for the time being must be superior to the civil authority, but [it] does not therefore destroy it." The two had to cooperate. He promised to take care of military matters, and he expected the mayor and city government to maintain civil order. If this meant hiring more policemen and raising taxes, he approved and would even help collect the necessary revenues. He tried to adhere to a policy that "every opportunity should be given to the wavering and disloyal to return to their allegiance, to the Constitution of their birth or adoption."[8]

Within a week Sherman had most of his regime in place. Four hundred persons took the oath of allegiance, and eight hundred slaves, all registered and their time carefully recorded, worked on the fort. He continued debating Treasury and War Department officials over his restriction to trade in gold and silver and extended it to include salt, another commodity he considered to be contraband. His patrols told him there were no Confederate forces in the area, so he faced no military threat. The more he looked around, the more he liked Memphis, calling its suburbs even more beautiful than those of his favorite city, St. Louis. And, importantly, many Memphians were beginning to like him.[9]

But there were irritations, constant minor battles between the commanding general and the unyielding city populace. Civilian requests for the recovery of lost slaves beset him daily. "Every nigger has run off, and of course I am supposed to be in immediate possession," he complained. "Miss Nancy raised in her mistress's bosom and nursed like her own children, has run off, and the whole family must rush to Gen. Sherman. Father, brother and all gone to fight us, but of course I must neglect all business to catch Miss Nancy." Sherman had early told his troops that "the well settled policy of the whole army now is to have nothing to do with the negro," but like most other Union commanders, Sherman found himself spending an inordinate amount of time dealing with fugitive slaves. His military-civil function complicated his task, as did his proslavery attitude within the context of the July 17, 1862, Confiscation Act and Lincoln's September 22 Emancipation Proclamation.[10]

On first arriving in Memphis, Sherman had established a simple fugitive policy. He placed the slaves under his jurisdiction at work on Fort Pickering, and soon had a thousand working there, another two hundred working for the quartermaster on the levee, and three hundred to four hundred as teamsters and cooks in the regiments. He issued each slave one pound of tobacco a month plus shoes and pants, all to be carefully recorded for charge "to the proper party on the final settlement of accounts." Sherman fully expected to pay slaveholders for the use of their chattel; he did not foresee emancipation. "When negroes are liberated," he argued, "either they or masters must perish. They cannot exist together except in their present relation." In short, any kind of slave freedom was counterproductive. The Confiscation Act's emancipation of the slaves used in the Confederate war effort would prove troublesome because Southerners would now believe they had "no alternative [but] destruction or submission."[11]

Sherman promulgated his own interpretation of this new law. He intended to keep working slaves on Fort Pickering, he said, but now he gave them the opportunity to return permanently to their masters at the end of any week. He would "entice" no fugitives, nor would he force any of them to return to their masters. Quartermasters and regimental commanders could use black labor, but "the question of wages must remain open and unsettled" until further orders, and no officer or enlisted man could hire a slave for personal service. It was "neither his duty nor pleasure to disturb the relation of master and slave," he insisted. The courts could decide that later. His own view was that the judiciary would return the slaves of loyal slaveholders and free those of rebels. To make sure his attitude was known at the highest judicial levels, he wrote U.S. Supreme Court justice John Catron that the sticky matter of fugitives needed quick solution and that loyal slave owners should receive some protection.[12]

When his senator brother supported emancipation, Sherman disagreed vehemently. Universal emancipation would indeed hurt the Confederate cause, but it was an "impossible task." "Where are they [freed slaves] to get work? Who is to feed them, clothe them, and house them?" How are they to be kept from becoming "thieves, idlers or worse"? Besides, he concluded confidently, "Not one nigger in ten wants to run off."[13]

When Lincoln issued his dramatic Emancipation Proclamation, Sherman openly opposed it because it undermined an institution he thought worthwhile. Still, when a Memphis judge tried to negate the Confiscation Act, Sherman responded strongly. He opposed emancipation, but he would enforce the law because that was his duty and because the law ensured order.[14]

At least once, Sherman used the slave issue to drive home the futility of secession. He told a slave owner, in answer to the man's request, that he could only claim his fugitives from the U.S. marshal. When the slave owner searched for that official, a Union army officer told him he was out of town. "When do you think he left?" the man asked. "About the time Sumter was fired on, I fancy," replied the officer. The slave owner returned to Sherman and asked for another way to get his slaves; Sherman said there was none. "The law provided a remedy [1850 Fugitive Slave Law] for you slaveholders in cases like this; but you were dissatisfied and smashed the machine. If you don't like your work, you had better set it running again."[15]

As he attempted to fit his proslavery attitude into an increasingly antislavery Union war effort, Sherman also grappled with the problems of keeping Memphis economically viable without simultaneously aiding the enemy. Smuggling was a major problem. Guards on the five trade roads felt squeamish about searching beneath women's crinoline skirts, so a good deal of contraband left Memphis for the Confederate army that way. Among those few apprehended included a woman who had tied twelve pairs of boots containing whiskey and other goods beneath a large girdle. Confederates also used the stomachs of dead animals as hiding places for contraband. At least one funeral procession included a hearse containing medicine for the Confederate army.[16]

Union guards were sometimes bribed, and this too added to the problem. Sherman tried to close this avenue by issuing a regulation against military impropriety, but the smuggling continued anyway. He thought about prohibiting trade altogether, but the Treasury Department said no. Only when Unionist sentiment seemed to be on the increase did he encourage trade as a way of promoting even greater loyalty to the Union among Confederates.[17]

The biggest problem Sherman faced in Memphis and the one that affected him the most was the problem of guerrillas. The countryside around Memphis was filled with irregulars—armed local residents who harassed the Federal military and local Unionists, sniping at patrols, burning bridges, disrupting trade, and firing on Mississippi River boats. Sherman had long argued that all Southerners were united behind the war effort. His experience in Memphis with slaveholders, judges, traders, smugglers, and guerrillas convinced him. He began to feel that he was fighting a war not only against the enemy's soldiers but also against the enemy's entire society. As he told Secretary of the Treasury Salmon P. Chase, "When one nation is at war with another, all the people of one are enemies of the other."[18]

In early July after hit-and-run partisans had fired on one of his supply trains, he ordered the arrest of "25 of the most prominent [men] of the vicinity." "I am satisfied," he told Halleck, that "we have no other remedy for this ambush firing than to hold the neighborhood fully responsible." Later he was even more blunt: "All the people are now guerrillas" and should be made to pay for their activities. His senator brother and his wife supported this view, with Ellen particularly vehement and, one might argue, prophetic in her advice. "I hope this may be not only a war of emancipation but [also] of extermination & that all under the influence of the foul fiend may be driven like the Swine into the Sea. May we carry fire & sword into their states till not one habitation is left standing." Sherman and his family saw everyone south of the Mason-Dixon Line as an implacable enemy.[19]

Sherman was particularly incensed at guerrillas for sniping at river boats, and he warned against the practice. The irregulars backed off for a time, but in late September a packet boat with passengers and private goods was fired on near the town of Randolph, Tennessee. Sherman asked no questions and conducted no detailed investigation. He simply sent a regiment to destroy the town. To make his point even clearer, Sherman threatened the expulsion of ten Memphis families for every boat attacked.[20]

His action shocked the city and caused several Confederate

officers to lecture him on civilized warfare. He was indignant. How could anyone condemn him while condoning the barbarous tactics of guerrillas' shooting at undefended civilians on defenseless boats? Where did true barbarity lie: in firing on steamboats filled with women and children or in saying that "the families of men engaged in such hellish deeds shall not live in peace where the flag of the United States floats"? If Confederate authorities did not disavow continued ambushes, he warned, he could not promise that "in future cases I will be so easy. Misplaced kindness to these guerrillas, their families, and adherents is cruelty to our people." True to his word, Sherman ultimately evicted thirty-two individuals and two families.[21]

Sherman had always been a conservative. He believed war had to be fought according to generally accepted rules of conduct, or the result would be anarchy and defeat. On June 18, 1862, he had issued a stern order outlining rules for foraging, warning that no soldier could take any private property for his own use, no matter if that property belonged to "friend or enemy." Three months later, he no longer lectured his troops on pillaging. He still threatened dire punishment to anyone who stole for his own use, but now he had come to approve official foraging. "I take freely of corn, horses, wood and lumber, brick, everything for the Government, but allow no individual plunder," he said. Sherman saw nothing wrong with collective pillage, condemning only the private kind, a distinction his soldiers could hardly have been expected to understand. His perception of the rules of war had changed.[22]

It was the guerrillas who fostered this transformation. At first, he tried to deal with their depredations through conventional military means, but he found that taking and defending areas only allowed the enemy to lay siege to the places and "make the detachment prisoners." So he tried a more radical measure. He destroyed Randolph and issued a family expulsion order. Controversy swirled around him as his superiors remained supportively silent. Sensitive to the furor, Sherman mulled his position over, as he always did, in his letters. In one, he used an expression that indicated the influence of some lessons he had learned in Florida fighting the Seminoles: to defeat the warriors, it was necessary to defeat the entire supporting tribal structure. "We are not going to chase through the canebreaks and swamps the individuals who did the deeds," he said in Memphis in 1862, "but will visit punishment upon the adherents of that cause which employs such agents." Or as he prophetically told Grant, "They cannot be made to love us, but [they] may be made to fear us."[23]

Sherman came to the conclusion that old-style warfare would not work in this war against the South as it had not worked against the Seminoles in Florida. A more total kind of war was necessary to overcome the Confederates. He began talking about changing the Constitution to allow an even more revolutionary idea: "We must colonize the country *de novo* beginning with Kentucky and Tennessee, and should remove four millions of our people at once south of the Ohio River, taking the farms and plantations of rebels." "I deplore the war as much as ever," he said, "but if a thing has to be done, let the means be adequate." "We must colonize and settle as we go south. . . . Enemies must be killed or transported to some other country."[24]

In Sherman's eyes, the Confederates had already changed the nature of war. Their support for guerrillas, their destruction of property, their smuggling, and their use of spies had already brutalized warfare despite his efforts to keep it in a civilized mode. In Kentucky, he had seen Southern generals confiscate slaves, horses, and farm produce. More recently, John Hunt Morgan, Kirby Smith, and Jeb Stuart had conducted raids against civilians. He and other Union army leaders had no choice; they had to retaliate in kind. When Confederate general John C. Pemberton protested the alleged killing of a civilian by a Union patrol, Sherman characterized whatever happened as "the legitimate and logical sequence of the mode of warfare chosen by the Confederate Government—by means of guerrillas or partisan rangers." "We, too, must imitate and surpass their game," he later wrote, "and [must] compel all men and corporations to at once espouse the cause of their State and National Governments, thereby securing full right to protection, or openly to rebel and forfeit their property and their lives." Anyone living in the Confederacy who accepted rebel rule was fit target for Union arms. After all, the Confederate army was doing the same thing, and it had done it first. Total war was the reality.[25]

Most of the time, Sherman did not have time to ponder the nature of war. He was too busy with the details of superintending Memphis. On a normal day in his camp on the edge of town, he rose before daybreak and composed his official correspondence before anyone else was awake. He had breakfast at 7 A.M. and then faced the barrage of complaining civilians. Daily he inspected the defense lines around the city and visited his five regiments camped along the major trade roads. On Sundays and Wednesdays he held military reviews, many of these open to the public. Despite his usual unconcern about his appearance, he could look militarily striking on these occasions when he wanted to. Sitting astride a horse, his six-foot frame, reddish beard and hair, weathered face, and ramrod posture in Union blue was impressive to his soldiers and the watching civilians. On such occasions he looked very much the dominating commander he was.[26]

Sherman had problems with rowdy soldiers and civilians—some people said because of his refusal to regulate liquor and prostitution. He refused to take action against the thriving bordellos, and he encouraged the reopening of saloons to raise tax revenue. He considered prostitution and liquor private matters and not within his jurisdiction. But though problems of all kinds regularly flared up in the city, most of the time he quickly solved them. Trade flourished as never before, said the *New York Herald,* and Sherman told Grant in late summer that Memphis was "as orderly as St. Louis, Cincinnati, or New York." He donated cord wood, medicines, and money to the poor and successfully urged his soldiers to give their surplus supplies to the less fortunate. His reasoning was both compassion and efficiency. Memphians felt more kindly toward their captors, and the result was the slow growth of Unionism, in the form of Union clubs, in this seat of secession.[27]

For diversion Sherman went to the theater, enjoying drama "sometimes not of the highest order, but enough to rest the Brain overburdened with care & anxiety." He made social calls all over the city, regularly visiting Ellen's favorite cousin and his own childhood friend, Mother Angela, a nun from Notre Dame, the head of the Memphis Union hospital. He avoided attending church services, however, joking with another nun that his old friend, the bishop of San Francisco, had exempted him from praying because Ellen was "pious enough for half a dozen ordinary families."[28]

Sherman was especially pleased with the month-long fall 1862 visit from Ellen and the children. He watched with particular enjoyment as a company of soldiers adopted his six-year-old son, Tommy, and outfitted him with a soldier's blouse complete with corporal's chevrons. With his usual good humor, he also tolerated Ellen's fussing over his wardrobe and living accommodations.[29]

Yet Sherman struggled with strains as well. He worried about dying, as most other soldiers did, but he also worried that Southern children were taught "to curse my name and each night thousands kneel in prayer & beseech the Almighty to consign me to perdition." He regretted having to expel women and children from their houses and watching his soldiers plunder enemy homes. Ellen and Thomas Ewing thought it "a great thing to be a high general," he told his daughter, but it bothered him to be fighting "old friends who would now shoot me . . . and who look on me as a brutal wretch."[30]

Sherman's major agitation in Memphis was the press. Although he controlled the local newspapers that remained in operation, he was unsuccessful in his attempts to exclude all Northern reporters. Generally correspondents wrote favorable articles about his administration, and most of what they printed was hardly sensitive information. Still, he threatened them: "You boys had better be careful what you write or I will be down on you." He went so far as to have several arrested, including, at Grant's request, Warren P. Isham of the *Chicago Times* for fabricating a false story about Confederate gunboats' breaking the blockade at Mobile. Like his policy toward foraging and guerrillas, his attitude toward the press bordered on total suppression. He came to argue that a military commander should be allowed to suppress newsmen not only when they printed military secrets but also when they disagreed with him. "Success is demanded," he said, "and yet the means to attain success are withheld." Newspapers insisted on the victory of Union arms, but they refused to be censored to ensure that victory. Sherman was unable to suppress newsmen completely in Memphis, as he was not yet able to wage total war against the South, but the strategic advantages of doing so had become apparent to him.[31]

Sherman periodically became depressed over what he called the "division and anarchy" of the North. Politicians battled among themselves as though there was no war. He saw "no clear, well-defined [war] issue," no unity on the war's purpose. "We are groping in a mist, and, in spite of the teachings of history, we seem to mistrust our only compass of safety, viz, the written compact of Government—our Constitution." "The Law must be vindicated and all must bow to the majesty of the Law. This is the best way to break the back bone of the Rebellion." Confiscation acts, freedom of the press issues, conscription of troops under political auspices and for political gain, and any other diversion to Sherman's major focus of restoring the Union, he found exasperating. He saw such lack of focus as anarchic and thus potentially fatal to success.[32]

In November the stalled Union military machine began to rouse itself, and Sherman put into practice his perceptions about war. There were no Confederate troops near Memphis, but seventy miles away in Mississippi, along the Tallahatchie River and even farther south along the Yazoo River near Vicksburg, large numbers were digging in under the command of the recently arrived John C. Pemberton. In mid-November Grant told Sherman he wanted to test the Confederates on the Tallahatchie. Sherman agreed and began preparations. He grew exasperated with his quartermaster over his transportation needs, but the browbeaten officer insisted he had no more horses or mules. Colonel Benjamin H. Grierson, later a famous cavalry leader, overheard the conversation and jumped in: "There is no need for any trouble in the matter for I can get you 2,000 mules and horses by tomorrow night and more." "How?" Sherman inquired. "Where in the world can you get them?" "Take them from the rebels wherever they may be found," answered Grierson. "We must have them," Sherman said excitedly. "Do it, Grierson—do it!" Grierson did, filled Sherman's need, and demonstrated concretely that civilians could no longer be shielded from warfare.[33]

On November 26 Sherman left Memphis with about eighteen thousand men: twenty-six regiments of infantry, ten field batteries, one cavalry regiment, and his horses and mules. When this force and Grant's thirty-five thousand men arrived on the Tallahatchie River, they found substantial entrenchments two miles back of the river but discovered that the enemy had fled to Grenada on the Yalobusha River, some sixty miles away. The cavalry pressed the retreating Confederates, but Sherman quickly pulled back. It made no sense to go to Grenada because it had no strategic importance. Vicksburg did. Grant agreed, and on December 8, he ordered Sherman to return to Memphis, take command of the troops gathered there and at Helena, Arkansas, and then cooperate with Admiral David Dixon Porter against Vicksburg.[34]

Sherman's new command meant he no longer retained jurisdiction over Memphis. Ellen, who was visiting the city at the time of his departure for the Tallahatchie, heard all sorts of evaluations of him and his tenure in the city. Some secessionists bragged that Sherman's force "would be worse whipped than any people had ever been yet." Other pro-Confederates kept a public silence, but some of the wealthier ones privately said that they appreciated his fair treatment. Unionists were loud in his praise. Episcopal bishop James H. Otey wrote a prayerful gratitude for Sherman's fine job, and the Washington Union Club passed a resolution of thanks. Cump looked "thin & worn being more wrinkled than most men of sixty," Ellen noted of her forty-two-year-old husband, "but he was so cheerful & well that I soon ceased to lament those marks of time & fear." Even Sherman gave himself high grades: "I am very popular with the people here and [with] officers and indeed with all my men."[35]

When Sherman returned to Memphis to prepare his Vicksburg expedition, the "manifestations of kindness" overwhelmed him. The Union Club cajoled him to make a speech, and he uncharacteristically said that if the progress made in Memphis during the past four months was used as a yardstick, the war would not prove to be as difficult as it had always seemed. Memphis streets were now lively; theaters played to full houses; and the entire city looked "prosperous." The clergyman who four months previously had omitted the prayer for the president now preached a Unionist sermon. Order reigned where, on his arrival, all had been chaotic. "Indeed in Memphis, I feel I have achieved perfect success," he concluded.[36]

This last statement was extraordinary. Consistently—in the army, as a banker in California and New York, as a lawyer/real estate agent in Kansas, as an educator in Louisiana—Sherman had almost pathetically groped for success. Each time, he had failed. During the early years of the Civil War, he had equated the debacle at Bull Run with his personal failure. In Kentucky and Missouri, not only had he failed, but he had also been publicly labeled as an insane failure. When he had performed well at Shiloh, a critical press and an even more critical home state politician had tried to rob him of his victory's joys.

All these failures and indignities had melted away in Memphis. In his role as military governor, he was able to use his skills successfully, and without the influence or advice of his foster father. His wife now begged him to let her leave Lancaster and come to visit him, as she had previously begged him to let her go back to Ohio to see her father. Where previously she had become depressed about not living in her family home, now she refused Thomas Ewing's pleas to live there with her children and insisted on moving to her own house in Lancaster. She even considered moving to Cincinnati to allow herself to live apart from her father.[37]

Sherman had earned Thomas Ewing's respect and that of his home town. A group of friends from his New York banking days sent him a ceremonial sword in honor of his war achievements, and he forwarded the gift to Lancaster for his children. Its arrival resulted in what Ellen called "a proper ceremony" under Thomas Ewing's beaming eye. The sword was put on public display in a window of one of the local banks. "Many of the old people, who knew your Father, take as much pride in you as if you were their son," Ellen reported. Thomas Ewing, as Cump's foster father, received plaudits for successfully raising the redheaded orphan boy. Ellen told Cump how "proud" her father was.[38]

Sherman finally was able to feel "perfect success." He had made it on his own and felt good. He had imposed order on the chaos of Memphis through his own methods. Those attributes of decisiveness, clear priorities, and confident sure action had proved their worth. Now he was ready to expand his area of operation and apply them in a wider sphere.

CHAPTER 10

—— ☆ ——

BATTLING THE BAYOUS TO REACH THE VICKSBURG FORTRESS

SHERMAN'S WORK IN MEMPHIS had been pivotal. His success in producing order out of chaos boosted his self-confidence, and his experience with the guerrillas led him to look at war in a new way. Over the next year he continued to grapple with the nature of war and to refine his thinking about it. The campaign he was to fight with Grant to take control of the Mississippi River taught him valuable lessons, and later he would put these ideas to increasingly effective use.

Sherman had long realized the strategic importance of the Mississippi River. As early as 1843 when he first traveled its length and increasingly in the years after, he believed the nation's greatness would be determined in its valley rather than anywhere else. When he departed Louisiana in 1861, he tried to convince his friends there that for the Mississippi, if for no other reason, the North would battle secession. In December 1862 when Grant put him in command of an expedition to capture Vicksburg, the last barrier to full Union control of the river, he saw the assignment as a great compliment: "My faith can not be shaken that the possession of this great Artery will be the most powerful auxiliary in the final steps that must restore the Sovereign power of our Government."[1]

Vicksburg was a formidable bastion. Located just south of where the river made a horseshoe bend, the city stood on top of an extended ridge of land called the Walnut Hills, some two hundred feet above the water. Ten miles north of the city, the Yazoo River flowed from the hills and emptied into the Mississippi. The hills and the two rivers formed a rough triangle of land heavily overgrown and pockmarked with bayous and swamps. Levees varying in height from four to eighteen feet added to the military impregnability of the area. In a hard rain, only the levees and the bluffs remained dry.[2]

Sherman's orders were to move troops down the Mississippi River on transports and attack the Confederates in the triangle of land north of Vicksburg. Simultaneously Grant, on the Yalobusa River to the north, would prevent other Confederate forces from reinforcing Vicksburg. It was hoped that Nathaniel P. Banks, the commander of Union troops in northern Louisiana, would move up the Mississippi and attack from below.[3] Some part of the Union attack would break through and overwhelm Stephen D. Lee and his Confederates on the Walnut Hills defending Vicksburg. The Confederacy then would be divided in two; the thoroughfare of northern commerce would again be open; Union troops in the upper and lower valley would be linked; and the Northern populace would be distracted from Union failures on the Virginia front, at least temporarily.

National politics and intraservice rivalry complicated the campaign. In November before receiving Grant's attack order, Sherman had learned from Admiral David D. Porter, the brusque old salt with whom he was to develop a close friendship during these months, that another general was planning an expedition against the Mississippi Gibraltar. John A. McClernand was a prominent Illinois politician and a Springfield neighbor of Abraham Lincoln. He had convinced the president that his successful recruitment of midwestern troops gave him the right to lead the campaign for the restoration of the Mississippi River to Union control. McClernand was a politician and a non–West Pointer, two breeds of humanity Sherman could not respect in officer's uniform. He and Sherman had already served together at Shiloh, and Sherman had found him to be more adept at public relations than at military science. He could never accept McClernand as his leader. As Sherman prepared his own expedition against Vicksburg, he worried about McClernand's elevation to command over him. Sherman tried to proceed before McClernand could reach Mississippi, later admitting that "the preparations [and departure] were necessarily hasty in the extreme."[4]

Sherman's relationship with David Dixon Porter was more positive. The two men first met in Memphis prior to the departure of the expedition, and they hit it off immediately. Thinking Sherman would be dressed in full uniform, Porter donned his best, "the splendor of which rivaled that of a drum major," he later remembered. Sherman, hearing that Porter preferred "working clothes," dressed with his usual unconcern. The two laughed when they saw each other. Sherman's rapid-fire speech intrigued Porter. "'Halloo, Porter!'" Sherman intoned. "'I am glad to see you; you got here sooner than I expected, but we'll get off to-night. Devilish cold, isn't it? Sit down and warm up.'" Before Porter could respond, Sherman continued: "'Here captain'—to one of his aides—'tell General Blair to get his men on board at once. Tell the quartermaster to report as soon as he has six hundred thousand rations embarked. Here, Dick'—to his servant—'put me some shirts and underclothes in a bag, and don't bother me with a trunk and straps enough for a regiment. Here captain'—another aide—'tell the steamboat captains to have steam up at six o'clock, and to lay in plenty of fuel, for I am not going to stop every few hours to cut wood. Tell the officer in charge of embarkation to allow no picking and choosing of boats; the generals in command must take what is given them—there, that will do.—Glad to see you, Porter; how's Grant?'"[5]

Porter and Sherman immediately developed a close personal bond, their mutual belief in the importance of the Mississippi River providing the cement. The more Sherman thought about his role in this expedition, the more content he felt, his confidence in Porter and Grant giving him optimism. "My part is exactly what I would have chosen, and I find all enthusiastic & rejoiced that I lead it." If Vicksburg fell, then "I can make that state [Louisiana] admit that 'Union is a necessity.' This is all my ambition," he said, "and I hope I will be permitted to stick to the Mississippi." Opening the river between the North and New Orleans would not only benefit the Union cause; it would mean success in the eyes of others whose approval he wanted—friends in the South. He could not promise to "achieve miracles," but acting with Grant and Porter, he believed he "must produce good results." He had heard rumors of a Confederate plot to retake northern Mississippi, but he had too much confidence in Grant to worry about such an occurrence.[6]

Sherman organized his force into four divisions and forbade all civilians from coming along, particularly warning reporters that they would be arrested as spies if they accompanied the expedition and published anything about it. When the flotilla left Memphis on December 20, however, a number of reporters managed to be on board.[7]

The twenty-thousand-man expedition traveled to Helena, Arkansas, where it added another twelve thousand men, creating a fleet of seventy jammed transports and six to eight gunboats. One transport alone reportedly carried fifteen hundred men, six hundred mules and horses, eighty wagons, and an artillery battery. E. Paul Reichhelm, sergeant major of the Third Missouri Infantry Regiment of Frederick Steele's Fourth Division, viewing the massed ships, thought them "a grand sight." The only worry Union forces had, Reichhelm said, was that the flotilla looked so impressive that the enemy might "skedaddle at our approach."[8]

The expedition departed Helena on December 22. Along the way, it encountered guerrilla fire from shore, and Cump periodically landed troops. "Soon the whole river was lined by burning dwellings and plantations." On Christmas Eve, "songs and speeches, tobacco and some little whiskey punch" kept the officers distracted from their homesickness. At 3 A.M. on Christmas morning, the expedition stopped at Milliken's Bend on the Louisiana side of the river, drove off a few pickets, tore up the Vicksburg, Shreveport, and Texas Railroad, and burned some cotton and corn. On the morning of the twenty-sixth, the boats moved up the Yazoo River and landed on the Johnston and Lake plantations, two of the few inhabited areas in the land surrounded by the Mississippi and Yazoo rivers and the bluffs of the Walnut Hills. That night, the troops were "exposed to the most horrible storm and cold rain" many had ever seen.[9]

The foul weather made the geographical obstacles even worse. In order to reach the Vicksburg road, which was at the foot of the high bluffs, the troops had to cross swamps and bayous, circumvent a Confederate barrier of fallen trees (abatis), and then cross Chickasaw Bayou and its bank, the former a formidable body of water ("20–25 feet wide and of a depth sufficient to drown a man on horseback)." It was a single channel from the Yazoo River to near the foot of the hills where it branched left and right, forming an open Y and serving like a moat before the bluffs. Beyond the bayou was another abatis of even more formidable trees, a dike, and, in front of the steep bluffs, an open plateau, "which was under a direct and enfilading cross fire from batteries and rifle pits, commanding every inch of the ground." The position was, in Sherman's words, "strong by nature and by act." Signal towers on the ridge provided observation of every movement of the Union troops below.[10]

Sherman reconnoitered the battlefield carefully and recognized the obstacles. He issued assault orders anyway. A black man told of Northern troops in nearby Yazoo City, and Sherman erroneously thought it was Grant. He knew that Confederate general Earl Van Dorn had successfully raided Grant's supply base at Holly Springs, but he believed time was at a premium, so he did not bother to investigate the black man's report. His four-division force moved out in four parallel columns on December 27. The soldiers drove the pickets back but quickly stalled under the accurate Confederate fire. "This piece of land is all cut up with the Bayous," Sherman wrote Porter. "We get across one only to find ourselves on the Bank of another." That night "it was mercilessly cold," Sergeant Major Reichhelm recalled, and "no fire was allowed. . . . The ground was wet and swampy, and rest was nearly impossible." Night-long Confederate shot and shell also kept "the sleep from our eyes." With dawn and a little coffee, however, "good spirits soon came back."[11]

The next day more men died in inclusive fighting. On the twenty-ninth, Sherman decided to mount "a prompt and concentrated movement to break the center." He had heard nothing from Grant or Banks, but "time being everything to us," he decided to act. The attack proved to be a disaster. As a later historian described it, "The terrain provided a 'funnel effect,' forcing more and more Federals into . . . [a] smaller area," where they were exposed to the concentrated fire of the Confederates. Amazingly, some Federals overran the first rebel rifle pits and came to within several hundred yards of the main defense line before being driven back. In some places, Confederates fired straight down on their attackers from their elevated positions on the bayou's levee. In another place, the firing pinned down the Union soldiers so completely that they did not notice a Confederate counterattack and were easily overrun. Fresh troops moving up were disheartened by the scene of carnage ahead of them. "Dead and wounded soldiers lay . . . among the trees and bushes and others dragged themselves toward the rear. The crying, groaning and sighing of the wounded was really pitiful." Sherman's thirty-two-thousand-man force suffered nearly eighteen hundred casualties against only two hundred for the fourteen thousand Confederate defenders. The night of the twenty-ninth found Union troops back in their original positions. "I assume all responsibility," Sherman told Grant, "and attach fault to no one." His first independent combat command was a failure.[12]

That evening Sherman boarded Admiral Porter's ship looking "as if he had been grappling with the mud and got the worst of it." The results of the day's fighting devastated him, and he worried that reporters would once again excoriate him. They did. Although Northern newspapers at first were complimentary, by January 12 they were questioning Sherman's sanity for ordering a solo attack against such an impregnable fortress. The *Cincinnati Gazette* reprinted slander from the *Memphis Appeal*, then being published in Jackson, Mississippi, that Sherman was "confined to his stateroom perfectly insane."[13]

Sherman tried to find some way to reverse his setback. While he pondered, his troops spent another night "with nothing on our bodies but the thin blouse and pants . . . exposed to the merciless cold and howling storm." "There we stood," Sergeant Major Reichhelm reported, "leaning against a tree or stump in silent resignation to our fate. Not a word was uttered." Worse than the cold was their commanding officer's uncertainty. Once during the evening of December 29 and again early the next morning, Reichhelm's unit received orders to attack, only to be called back at the last minute. Sherman finally decided that another assault would be suicidal. He put ten thousand troops on Porter's boats to attack Haynes' Bluff farther up the Yazoo. The rest of the troops were to keep the Confederates busy at Chickasaw Bayou. All was in readiness when a heavy fog forced cancellation of the Haynes' Bluff attack. Sherman withdrew all his troops onto the transports, fearing a flood. (He noticed twelve-foot water marks on the trees.) By January 2, 1863, Sherman had all the disgruntled troops safely back on the boats. "Well we have been to Vicksburg and it was too much for us, and we have backed out," he wrote Ellen. That same day, making the defeat even more bitter, John McClernand arrived to take command of the expedition.[14]

The newcomer did not make an impressive appearance, not to a reporter or Sherman's officers. "His beard and hair were black, his countenance swarthy, his form slight, and he appeared to be 'fussy,' irritable and nervous. There was something fidgety about him," an observer commented, "that affected all who came in contact with him." As gunboats fired on the Confederate positions, McClernand, watching along the river bank, tried to impress observing newsmen. He "waved his hat and yelled like a mad man,—'Give 'em hell.' "[15]

Sherman and Porter had already agreed on a face-saving gesture for the Chickasaw Bayou fiasco, an attack on Arkansas Post (Fort Hindman) fifty miles up the Arkansas River, the source for some recent attacks against Union boats on the Mississippi River. When McClernand met Sherman and Porter for the first time on the admiral's flag ship, he announced his own plan for attacking Arkansas Post as a way, he said, of "stirring up our troops which had been 'demoralized by the *late defeat*.' " Sherman became visibly upset at this jibe, but he maintained his composure. McClernand then curtly boasted that if Porter gave him enough gunboats, he would take the fort. Sherman still said nothing, but Porter could keep silent no longer. "I'll tell you what I will do, General McClernand" he said. "If General Sherman goes in command of the troops, I will go myself in command of a proper force and will insure the capture of the post." McClernand was stunned; Sherman quickly called Porter outside the cabin. "Admiral, how could you make such a remark to McClernand? He hates me already and you have made him an enemy for life." "I don't care," Porter replied, "he shall not treat you rudely in my cabin." The two men, their friendship solidified, went back in, and McClernand quietly agreed that Sherman would lead the troops in battle, though he would remain in command. Soon after, McClernand officially renamed the forces the Army of the Mississippi. Sherman became his subordinate, taking command of a corps in the army.[16]

The soldiers were as testy as their leaders, Sergeant Major Reichhelm describing them as "quite unmanageable" and verging on "open mutiny." They whispered that Sherman had been arrested for attacking Vicksburg with an inadequate force, the rumor attesting to their loss of "all confidence" in their general. They were also upset over their uncomfortable conditions. The harvesting of wood to fire the boats' boilers was exhausting work, especially since almost everyone was ill from the cold and rain. The little available food was terrible. The boats themselves were so crowded and so filthy that "the air [was] stinking and unfit to breath." Sherman's soldiers were demoralized; they needed a lift, and the Arkansas Post plan provided that boost. The soldiers considered it "very timely and well conceived." They inhaled a breath of "new life" despite the stench of the boats. They were happy to have the chance "of reestablishing our good reputation, somewhat marred by the late failure at Vicksburg."[17]

The Sherman-McClernand soldiers and the Porter gunboats captured Arkansas Post on January 12, 1863, after two days of fighting and a thousand Union casualties. The navy so silenced the fort that the army units placed in position by an unobserved flanking movement were able to force a surrender of nearly five thousand Confederates. Sherman played an unusually visible role in the battle. The evening before the assault, he crawled near enemy lines and spent the night watching and listening to the Confederates (and appreciating the talent of their reveille bugler). During the battle itself, he remained so much in the forefront that one Confederate rifled cannon repeatedly fired on him. When the fort was captured, he fed the Confederate commander and even invited him into his sleeping quarters. It was as if he want-ed to let both friend and foe know that although Sherman might no longer be overall commander, he was still very much in charge.[18]

Everyone involved in the battle considered Arkansas Post a major victory, but one of Sherman's aides put it in proper perspective. He told Ellen Sherman that "the fighting compared with Shiloh was not a good quail hunt." But at least it was a victory, and, considering the Chickasaw defeat and the debacle at Fredericksburg in Virginia that same month, the North was happy to hear any favorable battlefield news. Sherman seemed equally pleased but still suspicious of McClernand. "As usual my troops had the fighting and did the work," he concluded, "but of course others will claim the merit and Glory. Let them have it. The soldiers know who studied the ground ahead and directed the movement. . . . Success perfect."[19]

The victory at Arkansas Post, elevating though it was for troop and officer morale, could hardly make up for the Chickasaw Bayou repulse. It received only passing mention in newspaper columns, correspondents continuing their critical reports from the Bayou. Sherman might try to convince himself that everything was a "success perfect" in Arkansas, but it was not the case. The Vicksburg failure would not go away easily.

And neither would McClernand. In the days after Arkansas Post, Sherman called McClernand "unfit and . . . consumed by an inordinate personal ambition." He increasingly saw him as the personification of disorder in the military—a leader untrained and unskilled in military command and discipline. He told his brother that he had to accept his Vicksburg defeat and the fact that McClernand would unfairly get the credit for the Arkansas Post victory. He could resign in protest, but "I will not introduce disorder in a country now on the brink of anarchy [because of political actions like McClernand's appointment.]" In short, McClernand and individuals like him were really responsible for disasters like Chickasaw Bayou, yet they unfairly snatched up the glory they could find elsewhere.[20]

As he stewed over McClernand's presence and while the newspapers printed their stories of his alleged insane activities in Mississippi, Sherman composed his own battle report. He grew certain that McClernand was trying to delay its publication so "that he might twist and turn his own to his own honor and glory." Admiral Porter blamed the Chickasaw defeat on the failure of the original plan, on the rain, and on subordinates who had not functioned as well as they should have. He had only praise for Sherman: "Sherman managed his men most beautifully." "He did nobly until the rain drowned his army out of the swamps." Meanwhile, Ellen and her mother let Sherman know of their continued confidence, while Thomas Ewing circulated among Washington political and military leaders to make sure that Sherman's reputation remained unscathed there. Irvin McDowell, who had himself suffered a precipitous fall after Bull Run, expressed continued confidence in Sherman, as did Don Carlos Buell and E. O. C. Ord. Officers from his corps wrote Grant indicating their support and asking that their letter be published. Grant himself later wrote a strong letter of praise for Sherman to Lincoln.[21]

These expressions were welcome but provided little relief from Sherman's sinking feelings. Once again sliding into a depressed state, he wished that he "had been killed long since." "Here we are at Vicksburg," he complained, "on the wrong side of the river." The "perfect success" he had felt at Memphis and the "success perfect" he had expressed after Arkansas Post meant nothing now. He sat in the Louisiana swamps, his recently hard earned reputation in shambles again. Once again, success seemed to have turned to failure.[22]

The press appeared to Sherman as "more alarming than the batteries that shell at us from the opposite shore." Their attacks cut deeply; worse, they represented a great danger to the Union cause. "In writing me down are they not writing the cause and the Country down." In his despair, he sought, and found, a target for his rage at defeat and the disorder of the Union strategy and performance: "I am going to have the correspondent of the New York *Herald* tried by a court-martial as a spy . . . to establish the principle that such people cannot attend our armies, in violation of orders, and defy us, publishing their garbled statements and defaming officers who are doing their best." Reporters were clearly a nuisance to all army officers, but they were hardly a major threat to Union arms. To Sherman, however, the disorder he believed they helped create made them seem more dangerous than they really were.[23]

The *Herald* reporter in question was Thomas W. Knox. Before the war, he had been a school teacher in New England and had traveled widely in the West. He was a large man with a perpetually sarcastic expression on his face. At the beginning of the war, he had joined the *New York Herald,* probably the most widely read newspaper in the nation. When General Lew Wallace had wanted to establish a Union editorial policy for a Memphis newspaper, he had appointed Knox as one of the co-editors. Knox was one of the correspondents who had ignored the exclusionary order, accompanied the expedition to Chickasaw Bayou and Arkansas Post, and then published a report critical of Sherman's leadership and his alleged lack of concern for his wounded men.[24]

Learning of Sherman's anger, Knox wrote him a conciliatory

letter denying any knowledge of the exclusionary order until the expedition had already reached the battle zone. He had gone into the bayou area only twice, he said, remaining on ship the rest of the time. When he had written his article alleging mismanagement and callous disregard of the wounded, he had based it on the best available information. Now, having seen Sherman's and other officers' battle reports, he realized "he had labored under repeated errors, and made in consequence several misstatements." He was now convinced of Sherman's "prompt, efficient, and judicious" actions during the battle. He would be happy to print a retraction.[25]

Sherman ignored the olive branch. Obsessed with the flagrant disobedience of journalists, he had Knox arrested and personally cross-examined him. Knox displayed no contrition now, boldly asserting: "Of course, General Sherman, I had no feeling against you personally, but you are regarded the enemy of our set, and we must in self-defense write you down." As Sherman grew livid, Knox named Frank Blair as his source.[26]

Sherman saw himself as a man with a mission. He asked Admiral Porter for a letter of support ("whether I acted the part of an intelligent officer or that of an insane fool"). Porter forthrightly said he had performed excellently. Sherman sent Frank Blair, one of his division commanders and Knox's friend, twenty-two detailed questions about the Chickasaw Bayou battle and the general's relationship with the reporter. Blair answered completely, saying he had only criticized Sherman's choice of attack site. Finally, Sherman sent all the material he had gathered to his senator brother in Washington and wrote to his commanding general, U. S. Grant, and to his wife and a brother-in-law. Like a good general, Sherman secured his flanks before attacking his enemy.[27]

The court-martial met on February 5, 1863.[28] Sherman accused Knox of being a spy, providing information to the enemy, and accompanying the expedition in violation of orders. He based his case on two regulations: his own General Orders No. 8, which had excluded all nonmilitary personnel, especially reporters, from the expedition transports, and War Department General Orders No. 67, which forbade the printing of any information from any army area without the consent of the commanding officer.

The court remained in session for several weeks. Sherman

appeared as the prosecution's only witness, while Knox, helping in his own defense, called on several character witnesses. Sherman insisted that articles like Knox's ended up in enemy hands and provided valuable intelligence. Knox retorted that Grant, as overall commander of the expedition, had given him permission to go along, so Sherman's General Orders No. 8 was irrelevant. Similarly, the War Department General Orders No. 67 had never been enforced, so it had no relevance. Finally, unless Sherman could specifically prove that the article in question had actually reached the enemy, he had no case.

After final arguments, the court went into closed session and issued its decision four days later. It found Knox guilty of the third charge, disobeying orders. He was sent outside army lines, to be arrested if he ever returned.[29] Sherman had achieved a major victory. Not only had he instigated the only court-martial of a reporter in American history, but he had also gained a guilty verdict against Knox and his expulsion outside the lines. But Sherman had wanted Knox found guilty on all charges and specifications and executed. Since the court had not ruled this way, Sherman rejected its decision as useless. He had frightened the press into silence, but his anger at not winning a total victory precluded recognition of his gain. The disorder provoked on the battlefield by undisciplined journalists who cared more about making news than about winning the war remained a threat. If the court had sentenced Knox to death, journalists would have been taught an unforgettable lesson. The little it actually did was not enough to sooth Sherman's rage at nonbelligerents, whom he saw as getting in the way of the war and bringing anarchy in their wake. When dealing with an enemy, there were no half measures for Sherman.

The military situation added to his frustration. His camp at Young's Point, Louisiana, was across the river from Vicksburg, so near, yet so far away. The rain continued to fall, causing the surrounding swampy land to become so saturated that in the spring the troops had to camp on the sides of the narrow levees or on the transports. Soldiers who died of disease had to be buried on the levees, the only dry land deep enough for graves. It was one of the wettest seasons area residents could remember, making the bayous and swamps protecting Vicksburg that much more impregnable.[30]

Grant arrived in late January to supersede McClernand in overall command, but he had no answer to the military problem. His original attack plan had failed miserably, and he dared not return to Memphis to try again because he feared the effect of such a retrograde movement on Northern public opinion and on his military career. He had to attack Vicksburg from his present position. As long as the water level remained high, however, he could not find enough dry land to launch a substantial assault. So there he was—unable to retreat and unable to advance, stuck in the muddy swamps.

He had to do something or else watch his army and his political support deteriorate, so he devised a series of unconventional plans.[31] First he tried to complete a canal across the Louisiana peninsula formed by the Mississippi River's horseshoe bend. (General Thomas Williams had begun this canal during summer 1862, and Abraham Lincoln particularly liked the idea.) The hope was to get the river to change channels so transports could bypass Vicksburg's guns and deposit troops safely on the dry land south of the city.

Sherman had little confidence in the project, but his corps was given the canal-digging task. From late January, throughout February, and into March 1863, while busy with the Knox court-martial, Sherman was in charge of a project he believed was doomed to failure. No one could "count" on the Mississippi River, he told his brother-in-law: "It may go thru our canal or decline to." Admiral Porter, now his close confidant, was even more forthright. He called the canal "simply ridiculous . . . improperly located, in the first place, and . . . not properly cut, in the second." Sherman and Porter were correct. The scheme failed, as did another one seventy-five miles to the north.[32]

Rather than trying to turn Vicksburg's left flank as he had attempted on the two previous attempts, Grant decided to make an effort against the right. He blasted an opening in a levee on the Mississippi River three hundred miles north of Vicksburg, thus connecting the river with waterways in the area north of Vicksburg. A division of troops, called the Yazoo Pass expedition, steamed through this maze of waterways toward the city's right flank. The expedition progressed to within one hundred miles of Vicksburg, but a hastily constructed Confederate earth and cotton bale "Fort Pemberton" near the juncture of the Yalobusha and Tallahatchie rivers repeatedly beat it back.[33]

Undaunted, Grant made another attempt north of Vicksburg. On March 16 he returned with Porter from an extended reconnaissance. They had discovered that by leaving the Yazoo River at Steele's Bayou, a ship could traverse a bayou/river system and reach Vicksburg's right flank farther north, near Yazoo City. Grant told Sherman to detail a pioneer troop to help cut out the overhanging trees through Steele's Bayou, Black Bayou, and Deer Creek. Sherman immediately undertook the task but found that Grant had been overenthusiastic. The water system was not as navigable as the commanding general thought. But Sherman pushed the work, and Porter commanded a squadron of eleven ships in the breakthrough attempt. Movement was torturously slow, the ironclads pushing aside limbs and trees but the wooden ships suffering severe damage. Sherman reconnoitered the flooded countryside in one of Porter's tugs.[34]

Porter's flotilla, supported at some distance by Sherman's regiment marching along the bank, plowed along, at one stretch in Deer Creek making only four miles in twenty-four hours. The expedition frightened the Confederates enough to cause them to destroy the area's cotton and to topple trees into the waterway to trap the boats, and sharpshooters began firing on the sailors. The ships found themselves in danger of being cut off. Porter sent a black man with a tissue-paper note hidden in some tobacco to Sherman. Sherman immediately ordered a brigade to hurry the twenty-one miles to Porter. Conditions grew increasingly worse for the slow-moving boats, however, and Porter called for more help. On the night of March 21, Sherman led two brigades through the swampy terrain, using candles as the only illumination in the black night. The next day, wet and exhausted, they reached the boats, Sherman arriving first, riding on a recently sequestered horse.

"Halloo, Porter," he yelled. "What did you get into such an ugly scrape for? So much for you navy fellows getting out of your element; better send for the soldiers always. My boys will put you through!" He drove off the Confederates, prevented any further attempts at felling trees, and helped the boats out of their predicament, losing but two men in the process. Another of

Grant's schemes had failed, however, and Sherman had seen the failure firsthand.[35]

Sherman took the abortive expedition in stride. On April 6 he remembered that it was the anniversary of Shiloh and bragged that Grant's army had made as much progress as anyone could possibly have expected in a year. "We have isolated the Trans Mississippi from the East," he boasted. "Let the other Grand Armies do as much." Vicksburg would not fall "on this move," he realized, but "eventually" a great force would successfully assault it from the east. Sherman continued to believe implementation of the original plan was the only way to capture the Mississippi Gibraltar. And he seemed confident it could be done despite the press, a gullible public, and "dirty dog[s]" like McClernand.[36]

Sherman's confidence did not last. In mid-March a delegation of Thomas W. Knox's friends visited Abraham Lincoln in the White House with a petition asking for a presidential pardon. After bantering with the group, Lincoln avoided a potential problem by agreeing to Knox's return to the Vicksburg area but only if Grant agreed. He had satisfied the delegation without alienating his general. When Knox appeared in Grant's headquarters with Lincoln's letter, Grant angrily told him that he could not stay unless Sherman agreed. Knox blithely wrote Sherman, but the stunned general refused vociferously. If Knox came as a soldier, he would welcome him, but if he came "as the representative of the press, which you yourself say makes so slight a difference between truth and falsehood, [then] my answer is, Never." Knox got the message; he left for good. "If the press be allowed to run riot, and write up and write down at their pleasure," Sherman told Grant, "there is an end to a constitutional government in America, and anarchy must result."[37]

Meanwhile, Vicksburg stood as impregnable as ever, its natural defenses having thwarted every plan Grant had concocted. The Yazoo Pass and Steele's Bayou failures were particularly depressing because Grant was now out of ideas. He told Sherman: "I had made so much calculation upon the expedition down Yazoo Pass, and now again by the route proposed by Admiral Porter, that I have really made but little calculation upon reaching Vicksburg by any other than Haynes' Bluff." Was Sherman's long-held confidence in Grant misplaced? Had Sherman lost his career in the mud of Chickasaw Bayou and the clinging vegetation of the Mississippi countryside?[38]

In later years, Porter analyzed the situation well in a book on the Civil War navy: "These persistent attempts of the Army and Navy . . . kept the enemy continually on the alert, and obliged them to be moving through a country filled with all kinds of obstacles and made them doubtful where the blow would fall. . . . The Confederate soldiers were worn out and dispirited. . . . They were compelled to live upon the country when they were to expel the invaders, and this soon exhausted the stores in the invaded district on which the people in Vicksburg depended when the hardest time should come."[39] So Sherman might feel bad, but the Confederates should have felt worse. Vicksburg's days were numbered.

Sherman maintained his faith in Grant, but he worried that his friend did not understand politics. Grant had been bogged down for months, and Northern politicians and newspapermen were growing increasingly impatient, one reporter calling him "the foolish, drunken, stupid Grant, . . . an ass." Lincoln continued to support him, but how long could the president withstand the pressure? And there was McClernand. Sherman was convinced that the Illinois general would leapfrog over Grant the first chance he had. Grant better be careful, Sherman worried, or he would lose his command.[40]

Sherman saw only one solution to the dilemma: use the old December plan. He urged Grant to move back to Memphis with most of his troops and then strike against the Mississippi stronghold by way of Grenada. Meanwhile, a simultaneous attack should be made at Haynes' Bluff. A joint attack, even without Nathaniel Banks, would result in Vicksburg's capture. He made these arguments personally to Grant, and on April 8 he wrote him a letter expressing the same sentiments. He hoped his letter would force McClernand to take a position, too, and thus nullify his potential for "I told you so" later.[41]

Grant disliked McClernand almost as much as Sherman did, but he did not fear him enough to put him on the spot just then. Similarly he never seriously considered moving his army back to Memphis, as militarily valid as that option might be. He correctly understood the politics of the matter better than Sherman did. Northern public opinion would view any movement away from Vicksburg, for whatever valid reason, as a retreat and an admission of failure. Grant stuffed Sherman's letter in his pocket, took another drag on his cigar, and tried yet another new approach. He would have the fleet run the batteries in front of Vicksburg while the army marched down the west side of the river. At some point south, he would have the navy ferry his army across the river, and then he would make his attack on the city from the dry land below.[42]

Grant put the army/navy force in motion on the night of April 16. A Union fleet under Admiral David D. Porter, consisting of seven ironclads, three transports, and ten barges, formed in single file on the Mississippi River at the mouth of the Yazoo. Cotton and hay stacked on the ships' decks offered some protection from Confederate weaponry. The flagship *Benton*, with Admiral Porter in command, went first. When it reached the first Vicksburg batteries about 11 P.M., the Confederates torched old buildings and tar barrels to brighten a clear, starry but moonless night. Their batteries opened fire. With all pretext of secrecy gone, the ships answered the Confederate guns by pouring broadsides of their own into the city. For two hours the firing continued; Union vessels took numerous hits, but only one boat was lost. On April 22 six more steamers with twelve barges in tow duplicated the dangerous feat.[43]

Sherman participated actively in this dramatic offensive. He and selected soldiers went out on the river below Vicksburg in eight small boats to help disabled boats as they floated by. During the first sail-by, the *Henry Clay*, a transport, was a floating inferno by the time it reached him. There was nothing Sherman could do for the boat, but he was able to pick up its pilot floating by on a piece of debris.[44]

Admiral Porter well remembered Sherman's activities that night. "Are you all right, old fellow," Sherman yelled out as he climbed aboard Porter's flagship. After learning of the few injuries aboard, Sherman joked: "You are more at home here than you were in the ditches grounding on willow-trees. Stick to this, old fellow; it suits Jack better. There are a lot of my boys on the point ready to help if you want anything. They hauled this boat over for me. Good night! I must go and find out how the other fellows fared." Sherman received a warm welcome as he clambered aboard each ship to congratulate its captain for successfully reaching safety.[45]

The reputation Sherman had with his soldiers now spread to the navy. His men viewed him "as one of the best men in the army—if not the very best." What they particularly liked about him, as he demonstrated on the river to the fleet, was his willingness to be among them. He personally chose every tactical and camp site for his army and, no matter the weather, he was out "looking over the ground." When not reconnoitering, Sherman frequented the camps, making sure his men were safe and content. He was clearly an enlisted man's general, and they appreciated his interest.[46]

Meanwhile, army units, with McClernand's Thirteenth Corps in the lead, marched down the west side of the Mississippi, purposefully moving to meet the fleet and providing transport across still flooded areas. Another obstacle stood in the way. The Confederates had fortified Grand Gulf, twenty-five miles below Vicksburg at the mouth of the Big Black River, and its subjugation seemed necessary for a successful Union landing on the east bank. Porter and the fleet peppered the fort on April 29, but Grant never ordered an assault because the Confederate positions seemed oblivious to the naval gunfire and he feared a Union slaughter if he tried to land. Instead, he ran the Grand Gulf batteries at night and took his troops some ten miles farther south. He landed them at Bruinsburg the next day, thereby outflanking the fort and causing its evacuation. The way to Vicksburg seemed open.[47]

Sherman was concerned about the adequacy of Grant's supply line. Grant had told Sherman to move his Fifteenth Corps south to join with the rest of the army and simultaneously gave him responsibility for the supply base at Milliken's Bend. Sherman ordered his soldiers forward on April 25 but immediately countermanded his march order so he could concentrate on improving the flow of provisions. He organized the Milliken's Bend supply depot and worked on the supply road, warning Grant of the logistics problems posed. He continued to oppose Grant's plan and worried about being blamed for any resulting disaster.[48]

Grant gave him yet another task. In an order striking in its tentativeness and its concern for a subordinate's sensibilities, Grant asked Sherman to take pressure off the Grand Gulf offensive by making an elaborate feint at Snyder's Bluff, near Chickasaw Bayou, thereby returning to the site of his December debacle. "I am loath to order it," Grant said, "because it would be so hard to make our own troops understand that only a demonstration was intended, and our people at home would characterize it as a repulse." Sherman immediately promised to "make as strong a demonstration as possible" at Haynes' Bluff. His troops would be made to understand what was going on, and it was "none of the business" of the public or anyone else. "You are engaged in a hazardous enterprise," he concluded, "and, for good reasons, wish to divert attention; that is sufficient to me, and it shall be done." Grant could depend on Sherman's loyal cooperation, even if it resulted in new attacks on his competence from "sneaking, croaking [newspaper] scoundrels."[49]

On April 29 a navy squadron, with ten of Sherman's regiments aboard, steamed up the Yazoo River to carry out the feint against Confederate emplacements. The following morning, the fleet opened fire on Drumgould's Bluff, one mile below Snyder's Bluff. The transports made elaborate appearances of landing and caused the Confederates to man the opposing fortifications. For the next four hours, the gunboats and the emplacement batteries dueled one another while the army casually landed a foraging party to try to capture some cattle the soldiers had noticed on the plantation opposite their boats. At 3 P.M. the soldiers landed in force, making a loud demonstration, though flooded conditions made it possible for only two soldiers abreast to move across a levee. Other troops stepped on shore the morning of May 1, and they too tried to give the impression of a full-scale assault. A message from Grant dated the twenty-ninth cut short all the theatrics. Grant informed Sherman of his passage past Grand Gulf and ordered him to come quickly in support. That evening, the flotilla departed from the Yazoo swamps for Sherman's camps at Milliken's Bend and Young's Point, from where he marched his men to a rendezvous with Grant below Vicksburg.[50]

Sherman always insisted on the importance of his demonstration, arguing that the Confederates had been sufficiently diverted to allow Grant to land unopposed at Bruinsburg. In fact, there is little evidence that Grant needed Sherman's feint; he would have landed successfully without it. But it is fair to conclude that Grant's unorthodox move south, coupled with Sherman's demonstration, Benjamin Grierson's simultaneous cavalry raid down the length of east Mississippi, and the earlier bayou expeditions, confused the Confederates and their already disorganized command structure.[51]

As soon as Sherman began moving south, his quartermaster's mind returned to the problem of provisions. He loaded his troops with all they could carry, making sure they understood the precarious supply situation. When Grant told him to send 120 full supply wagons to the captured Grand Gulf, Sherman worked to comply. He opened another road and told a subordinate to investigate further river traffic past enemy batteries. "Keep everywhere hauling stores forward," he ordered. "I will push ahead, and arrange to cross [at] Grand Gulf and follow Grant wherever he may be." He was so worried, however, that when three brigadier generals arrived at his headquarters, he tried to send them away. "What I want is mules. If they will send me the mules, they can keep the brigadiers."[52]

Sherman reached Grand Gulf on May 7, having marched eighty-three miles down the west side of the Mississippi River. By that time, Grant had already made a profound decision. He thought of linking up with Nathaniel Banks to subdue Port Hudson, and then move against Vicksburg. But Banks would be a month in coming, and Grant did not want to give the Confederates that much time to react. He decided to move against Vicksburg on his own, living off the countryside and the supplies coming from Milliken's Bend.[53]

Fortunately for Grant, he faced an enemy with conflicting strategic views. John C. Pemberton, the commander of the Vicksburg defenses, had been ordered by Jefferson Davis to hold the city. Joseph E. Johnston, commander of Confederate forces in the West, believed that Pemberton should worry less about Vicksburg and cooperate in concentrating the scattered fifty thousand Confederates to defeat Grant before he reached the city. The two men were never able to resolve this disagreement, and Grant was the beneficiary of their indecision.

While the Confederates debated, Grant moved. He sent his troops from their Bruinsburg landing into nearby Port Gibson. Fighting a day-long battle there on May 1, Grant swept aside the Confederate opposition and took control of the city and its roads leading to Grand Gulf, Vicksburg, and Jackson. Pemberton had no choice but to withdraw his detachment from Grand Gulf and allow Grant to establish his southern base there. With the addition of Sherman's corps, Grant now had about forty-five thousand men. He moved north on a broad front, using the Big Black River to anchor his left. Pemberton, concerned that Grant meant to attack the railroad near Edwards Station, left a large reserve at Vicksburg and moved out to try to block him. A Confederate brigade had no success with Grant at Raymond on May 12, but after this skirmish, Grant decided he would neutralize Jackson first before proceeding against Vicksburg.

Grant sent McPherson's Seventeenth Corps toward Jackson by way of the Clinton Road; Sherman's Fifteenth Corps took the lower road through Mississippi Springs; McClernand's Thirteenth Corps remained at Raymond to block any Confederate threat from Vicksburg. Grant traveled with Sherman. The two units reached Jackson in a driving rain on May 14. Johnston hoped only to delay long enough to remove supplies to Canton north of the city where he hoped to concentrate with Pemberton. The rain helped his cause, but when it let up, Union forces went on the attack and drove the Confederates out of the city.

Through a spy, Grant learned of the Confederate plans, so he immediately had McPherson's corps and one of Sherman's divisions link up with McClernand's corps and march west to prevent any juncture. Sherman was left behind in Jackson to destroy railroads, a foundry, a cotton factory, and anything else of military value. He and Grant personally stopped work at a tent factory and ordered it burned.

Sherman planned to destroy only military targets in Jackson. A businessman approached him and professed his Unionist sentiments, causing Sherman to remark that his loyalty was obvious from his establishment's name. The former United States Hotel was now the Confederate Hotel. Still, he told the man, he had no plans to burn his property. As he was leaving town, however, he noticed the building in flames. He surmised that some of his soldiers, former prisoners of war, had torched it to repay the owner for his refusal to serve them when they had earlier passed through the city as prisoners. He was not pleased with such revenge, but he shrugged it off.[54]

Throughout this long Vicksburg campaign, Sherman had ruminated over the role of pillage and destruction in the war effort. In early December 1862 he had spoken out against "indiscriminate and extensive plunder," insisting that "our mission is to maintain, not to violate all laws, human and divine." He tried to deal with the problem then by ordering his subordinate commanders to permit necessary foraging only under strict officer control. In early January, he had spoken out once again against pillage, threatening severe punishment to any soldier who took anything for his private use. But, he insisted, pillagers were a definite minority in his army; they were the "cursed stragglers." He asked "the good officers and soldiers of whom he is proud to know his corps is mostly composed, to aid him in bringing to condign punishment the cowardly rascals who hang back when danger threatens, but are foremost in stealing, robbing, and plundering."[55]

Yet he continued to draw questionable distinctions and to blame the other side for inciting the destructive activities. In late March and early April 1863, just before Grant began moving south, Sherman sent one of his divisions to punish a locale near Deer Creek for allowing guerrillas to fire on Union river boats. "Let all the people understand," he boomed, "that we claim the unmolested navigation of the Mississippi River, and will have it, if all the country within reach has to be laid waste." If Union boats were left alone, however, then "we will spare them [Confederate civilians] the ravages of war as much as we can[,] consistent with our own interests." As long as Confederates fired on boats, he would make them pay by destroying their property.[56]

Sherman also claimed the right to forage for his troops' needs, insisting on a similar right to destroy goods. "The destruction of corn or forage and provision in the enemy's country is a well-established law of war, and [as] justifiable as the destruction of private cotton by the Southern Confederacy." Sherman had come to view war as barbarism and not a conflict between gentlemen. In order to destroy the anarchy that the Confederacy had loosed, he believed counterwar was inevitable. He would impose his own brand of barbarism to destroy that of the Confederate war effort. "We are forced to invade; we must keep the war South until they are not only ruined [and] exhausted, but [also] humbled in pride and spirit."[57]

Meanwhile, Sherman rushed to rejoin the rest of Grant's army. He did not participate in the Union victory at Champion Hill on

May 16, but he rapidly marched for Vicksburg by a northernmost road. Just past Bolton, Sherman rode into a yard to get a drink of water. As he sat on his horse refreshing himself, he noticed a book on the ground. He asked a soldier to hand it to him and discovered that the volume was a copy of the Constitution of the United States. On the title page he found the scrawled words: "Jefferson Davis." A slave told him the land indeed belonged to the Confederate president, a place he had purchased for emergency use. Jefferson Davis's copy of the Constitution of the United States was now the war prize of a Union general.[58]

Sherman rushed his troops toward Vicksburg, making the twenty-seven miles to the Big Black River on May 17 in what Grant later called "an almost unequalled march." At Bridgeport, several miles upstream from where the main body of Confederate troops had already retreated and burned all the bridges, Sherman's men encountered only a small rebel force on the west bank of the river. Sherman crawled behind an available corn crib to evaluate the situation. He ordered some guns forward, and their shells quickly convinced the eleven Confederate soldiers to surrender. He had his men float a pontoon bridge across the river, but it was nightfall before the crossing could begin. Grant appeared and sat down with him to watch the activity. The bridge swayed under the tramping feet, the way illuminated by pitch-pine fires. The two Union generals quietly watched their marching men in the barely lighted darkness of a Mississippi night, deep in the heart of the Confederacy.[59]

Grant's army continued racing Pemberton for Vicksburg, with Sherman's corps attempting to outflank the Confederates to the north. When he and Grant approached Haynes' Bluff, they galloped past their skirmishers to get there first. They found the fortress abandoned. As he eagerly surveyed the scene of his December debacle, Sherman profusely showered Grant with praise, telling him that up to now, "he had felt no positive assurance of success." But he knew now they had just completed "one of the greatest campaigns in history." No matter what still lay ahead, "this was a complete and successful campaign."[60]

But it was hardly over. Pemberton beat Union forces to the Vicksburg emplacements. By the evening of May 18, he and his thirty-one thousand soldiers sat safely in Vicksburg, while Grant's fifty thousand troops began to form a semicircle around the city.

Sherman's corps held the northernmost position, McPherson held the center, and McClernand arched around toward the southwest. Admiral Porter's gunboats controlled the Mississippi River. The city was surrounded, and Sherman felt particularly relieved that the Union supply line was again restored.[61]

Pemberton had prepared well, having used his seven-month tenure as Vicksburg commander to construct a fortress of formidable proportions. The defense line used a series of natural ridges and deep fronting ravines and arched from a point one and a half miles above Vicksburg on the river around to a point some two miles below the city, and it was eight to nine miles long. At roads and a railroad crossing, Pemberton had established nine forts whose earthen walls were as much as twenty-feet thick and fronted by deep ditches up to eight feet deep. He had 172 artillery pieces. The rain-worn gullies provided natural impediments, and fallen trees provided further protection and a clear field of fire. Sherman described it well: "The deep washes and ravines with trees felled make a network of entangled abatis all round the city, and if we had a million men we would be compelled to approach it by the narrow heads of columns which approach the concealed trenches and casements of a concealed and brave and desperate enemy."[62]

Grant had to attack this fortress. His men would have it no other way, and he believed the Confederates were so dispirited from having been routed in the recent campaign that they would crumble. If he attacked them before they could adequately set their defenses, he was confident he could win. Sherman agreed.[63]

Grant ordered an assault for 2 P.M. on May 19. Sherman's troops, the first to arrive on the scene, made the strongest attack, but though they reached the walls of Stockade Redan, one of the city's forts, they were driven back with heavy losses. McPherson and McClernand were able to accomplish even less. Casualties were high, Grant losing about a thousand men while the entrenched Confederates lost much fewer. Sherman was particularly grieved because his regular army regiment suffered heavy losses.[64]

The bloody repulse did not deter Grant. He called his officers into conference and told them to prepare for a 10 A.M. simultaneous attack on May 22 along a three-mile front in the middle of the crescent defense line. Sherman personally reconnoitered the area to his front and chose to aim his attack at the right side of

Stockade Redan, with a diversionary thrust about a mile to the west. He carefully positioned his artillery and at precisely 10 A.M. (all Union watches having been synchronized) he joined the rest of Grant's troops in launching the attack. From a concealed point within two hundred yards of the Confederate post, Sherman watched as 150 volunteers, labeled the "forlorn hope," charged up Graveyard Road to the ditch in front of the redan, placed a plank across the ditch, and tried to open the way for the infantry following behind in line of battle. As the infantry came into range, the Confederate defenders unleashed a torrent of shot and shell, inflicting severe loss on the attackers. For two hours, the Union troops doggedly pressed forward, twice actually placing flags on the exterior slope of the fort. But they failed. In Sherman's words, the Union attack was "swept away as chaff thrown from the hand in a windy day."[65]

Despite the carnage, Sherman's troops kept fighting, their determination on both days exemplified by the May 19 actions of a musician named Orion P. Howe. During the worst part of the battle, the teenager came running up to Sherman demanding ammunition for a hard-pressed regiment. "All right, my boy," Sherman answered, seeing that Howe was bleeding from a wound on his leg. "I'll send them all they need, but . . . you had better go and find a surgeon and let him fix you up." The boy saluted and began moving to the rear, only to come rushing back to tell Sherman the proper calibre of the needed ammunition, worrying more about the regiment than about his wound. Tears came to Grant's eyes as he witnessed the scene. Sherman later helped the courageous musician obtain a Naval Academy appointment.[66]

Despite similar bravery all along the line, the Union assault was a failure. A messenger arrived from McClernand insisting that the Illinois general was on the verge of a breakthrough and needed only diversionary help from Sherman and McPherson to succeed. Grant was skeptical, but Sherman told him he had to provide the requested support. He and McPherson renewed their attacks. The results were calamitous again. Sherman later learned that McClernand had exaggerated his success and as a result caused the needless slaughter of additional Union troops. His outrage against McClernand intensified. He otherwise took the two repulses in uncharacteristic stride, however, maintaining his trust in Grant.[67]

The Union army now began siege operations, extending trenches forward toward the Confederate positions while regularly firing artillery shells at the enemy fortifications. Sherman supervised this activity on his side of the line and several times so narrowly escaped sharpshooters' bullets that even Abraham Lincoln received reports of his serious injury. Actually he felt fine, living in "a good tent [with] plenty to eat and drink" and five horses to suit his needs. Ellen hoped he would take advantage of the recent arrival of a chaplain from Notre Dame to become a Catholic. Sherman ignored her religious advice and the warning that he keep his head down.[68]

A later assault was made on the Vicksburg defenses, but it proved secondary to the siege operations. After the drama of Grant's magnificent movement through the Mississippi countryside to reach Vicksburg and after the horror of the failed assaults, Vicksburg's future would be decided by the mundane duo of shovels and starvation.

Sherman and Grant knew they could eventually starve Pemberton into submission, but they worried about Johnston's relieving the siege by consolidating the troops from Jackson with reinforcements from other parts of the Confederacy. Rumors circulated regularly that Johnston already had thirty thousand to forty thousand men and was on his way. Grant ordered Sherman to meet this supposed threat by establishing a defense line to the east from the railroad bridge on the Big Black River to Haynes' Bluff. On June 22 Grant gave him one division from each of the three corps in the siege trenches plus a newly arrived corps from Tennessee (thirty-four thousand men in all) to block Johnston.[69]

Sherman assumed his new responsibility with a relish. He regularly reconnoitered the entire length of his line, keeping an eye on the Confederates doing the same on the east bank of the Big Black. He established entrenchments and felt confident that he could prevent Johnston from attacking Grant's rear. His spirits and optimism soared with Grant's mid-June firing of McClernand for unauthorized publication of a report on the Vicksburg assaults. The report congratulated McClernand's own troops and made insinuations against Sherman's and McPherson's. Sherman argued that the report "perverts the truth to the ends of flattery and self-glorification." When Grant sacked McClernand, Sherman was ecstatic. McClernand's "riddance," he said, "was a relief to the whole Army." A major impediment to the Union war effort was gone.[70]

After the hectic nature of the earlier campaign, Sherman now had to be vigilant only for Johnston's possible approach. He daily criss-crossed his area and strengthened his defenses. He was pleased to discover a distant rebel relative and regularly took meals with the family. He discovered that the mother of one of his Louisiana Military Seminary cadets was a refugee in the Vicksburg area and made a special effort to see her, viewing the woman as an old friend and not the enemy. He found her sitting on a veranda visiting with a dozen other women. During their conversation, Sherman discovered that she had a son inside Vicksburg. She lamented: "Do, oh do General Sherman spare my son." In the same breath, however, she called Lincoln "a tyrant" and the Union army "murderers, robbers, plunderers, and defilers of the houses and altars of an innocent & outraged People." When Sherman inquired about the woman's husband, she tearfully responded that he had been killed at Bull Run. Suddenly the dozen women burst into tears, a development Sherman found "most uncomfortable," so he quickly rode away, saddened that the war had made friends into stubborn enemies.[71]

Sherman's careful troop placement kept Johnston away; the siege continued. Conditions for the soldiers and civilians inside Vicksburg plummeted as supplies and ammunition began to run out. To escape the constant Union bombardment, Vicksburg's inhabitants dug caves, sometimes of the most elaborate kind, where they spent most of their time. Disease in the city became a serious problem, and the Union trenches drew ominously closer every day. The Pennsylvania-born Pemberton was determined to hold on, but the longer the siege lasted, the less faith his fellow Confederates had in him. He kept hoping for Johnston, but Johnston never came. On July 4 Pemberton surrendered his garrison. At the same time in the East, Lee was retreating from Gettysburg. U.S. troops could savor two major victories on the same symbolic day.

Sherman considered Vicksburg's fall "the first gleam of daylight in this war." He felt confident enough to compare himself to Grant, the victor of Vicksburg: "I have a quicker perception of things than he; but he balances the present and remote so evenly that results follow in natural course."[72]

When Union troops marched into the city, Sherman was not among them. He was crossing the Big Black River in pursuit of Johnston in Jackson. "I did hope Grant would have given me Vicksburg," he said, "and let some one else follow up the enemy inland, but I never suggest anything to myself personal, and [do] only what I deem necessary to fulfill the purposes of war." He sent Grant an effusive letter of praise for the campaign and for his mild surrender terms. But he also reminded Grant and Porter of his own role in the success. "Though in the background as I ever wish to be in civil war, I feel that I have labored some to secure this glorious result," what in later years he called "the most *decisive* event of the whole war."[73]

Sherman told his troops "to give one big huzza and [then] sling the knapsack for new fields." The Union force moved rapidly east, meeting little resistance and receiving reinforcement from Sherman's old friend E. O. C. Ord, McClernand's replacement as Thirteenth Corps commander. By July 8 the army was at Clinton, battling thirst in the stifling heat. The retreating Confederates had slaughtered cattle and let them decay in all the available ponds. On July 10, Sherman was at Jackson, holding the center of the Union assault line. He established a siege on July 11 and soon ordered intermittent harassing artillery fire into the city. By July 17 Johnston had evacuated the battered capital. Sherman chased the fleeing Confederates, but they remained out of reach, and the scorching sun and the paucity of water halted any further pursuit. He had driven Johnston off and together with the Confederates had devastated the country in a thirty-mile radius of Jackson. The railroad forty miles north and sixty miles south was destroyed. The city suffered both from Confederate and Union looting and torching. "Jackson, once the pride and boast of Mississippi," Sherman noted, "is a ruined town." Its "inhabitants," he said, were "subjugated" and calling "aloud for mercy."[74]

Once the fighting was over and Jackson officials "admit[ed] themselves beaten [and] subdued, and charge[d] their rulers and agitators with bringing ruin and misery on the State," Sherman became the great conciliator. He urged Grant to allow him to provide Jacksonians with food and provisions and to establish a trading depot in return for a Confederate promise to stay out of western Mississippi. Grant was not so sure about the depot, so Sherman did not push the idea, satisfying himself with supplying

Jackson's inhabitants with the necessities of life. He thought the Union army should do all it could to convince these Mississippians that their war effort was a mistake and that they ought to return to the Union. "War was not a remedy," he said, "for grievances or supposed grievances, for which our fore-fathers provided the Supreme Court of the United States to arbitrate and remove."[75]

In Memphis, Sherman had first used violence against Confederate civilians as punishment for guerrilla activities. But he had also recognized the importance of encouraging and rewarding pro-Union activities. He followed this same policy in Jackson: punish the Confederate populace for any recalcitrance; help them when they are defeated, especially when they admit the error of their ways. His purpose was to convince Southerners to admit their mistake, stop fighting, and return to the Union.

Sherman was an early psychological warrior, using both the stick and the carrot to win over defeated populations. When the war was in progress, he was unforgiving, justifying "whole sale destruction" to the scourge of war. Once the fighting was over, he was concerned about noncombatants and their loyalties. When he caught a soldier burning down a cotton gin during the march back to Vicksburg at a time when the torching "in no way aided our military plans," he had the soldier and his accomplice court-martialed. He could tolerate pillage in battle but not in its absence.[76]

He was terribly fatigued and was ready on July 27 to go into camp on the Big Black River to rest and reorganize. He felt excited about the outcome of the campaign. "The fall of Vicksburg & [the] consequent capitulation of Port Hudson, the opening [of] the navigation of the Mississippi and now the driving out of this Great Valley [of] the only strong army that threatened us completes as pretty a page in the history of war & of our country as ever you could ask my name to be identified with." When Grant effusively recommended him for promotion to the regular army rank of brigadier general and Halleck quickly sent word of its acceptance, his personal success seemed guaranteed. He immediately informed Thomas Ewing. He had shared in one of the major achievements of the war, and Grant, its major architect and a man he held in the highest respect, was willing to share the praise with him. Charles A. Dana, the secretary of war's personal emissary to Grant's army, enthused, "What a splendid soldier he is." Even the press was favorable. According to John Sherman, his "popularity" was "second only to that of Grant."[77]

Sherman was so content that he even granted Ellen's long-expressed request to come for a visit. He refused to go on furlough himself; he had to remain with his men. The United States was standing up to secession, and the Vicksburg victory "had a [particularly] powerful effect. They [the Confederates] are subjugated. I even was amazed at the effect." Sherman was becoming convinced that, despite all its deficiencies, the United States, through the agency of the army, was going to remain whole and overcome anarchy. Since he was now an important part of that military, its success and that of the nation would be his success too, an exhilarating realization. "The secessionist of the South, the autocrat of the North, and the anarchist everywhere" were all on the run.[78]

The victory was won; McClernand was gone; Grant had proved himself to be the military genius Sherman had long believed him to be; the nation seemed on the verge of survival; and Sherman was sharing in these triumphs. He exultantly praised his troops for their role in these victories. His peroration seemed aimed at himself more than at his soldiers. "Let the magnificent result give to all new hope and assurance that, by discipline, by patient industry, by courage and confidence in our country and cause, the United States of America will instead of sinking into Mexican anarchy, arise with proud honor and glory, and become what Washington designed it—'The freest and best regulated Government on earth.'"[79]

In the middle of August, the Sherman family left Thomas Ewing's house in Lancaster and traveled to Vicksburg to share their husband and father's success. The disappointments of the past seemed far behind. The present provided a rarely felt contentment, and the future was promising. Sherman saw a smiling wife and excited children, particularly his favorite, nine-year-old Willy. At last, he was able to enjoy a long-sought success. Order and stability had finally been achieved and reigned in his family as it did in the war itself.

CHAPTER 11

—— ☆ ——

PRACTICING DESTRUCTIVE WAR IN MISSISSIPPI

THE DUAL VICTORIES on July 4 at Vicksburg in the West and Gettysburg in the East resulted in an optimism in Union army ranks not experienced since early in the war. Union soldiers felt pleased with their spectacular successes, though they realized that the Confederates were not yet ready to stop fighting. Lee's army still stood before Richmond, and Braxton Bragg's Army of the Tennessee remained a formidable foe in the heartland. The Southern populace was defiant as ever, confident that its armies would rebound from the defeats. Union soldiers had many more battles to fight, but, for now, they just wanted to rest and recuperate.

Sherman's Fifteenth Army Corps settled comfortably into camp at Parson Fox's, an area along the Big Black River, about twenty miles east of Vicksburg. Conditions were so tranquil that many officers and men, exhausted from the hard campaign, went on leave. Sherman, however, refused to take a furlough himself, believing that his place was with his army, not his family.[1]

Sherman's camp was nestled among some large oak trees. The officers' tents were pitched in a long row with the mess hall, made of native cane, at one end. The headquarters detachment, a battalion from the Thirteenth Infantry Regiment, had its camp directly behind and mounted its guard and held parades in the open field in view of the officers' tents. "I have a healthy camp," Sherman said, "and have no fear of yellow or other fevers." Ellen and four of the children, twelve-year-old Minnie, eleven-year-old Lizzie, nine-year-old Willy, and six-year-old Tommy, came to spend six weeks with him. (Four-year-old Elly and two-year-old

232

Rachel remained behind in Lancaster.) Officers' wives regularly visited their husbands throughout the war, though until this time Sherman had opposed the idea for reasons of discipline.[2]

Since Sherman would not leave his men, he was happy to be reunited with his family on his home turf, amazed that Minnie was now a "beautiful woman," but particularly pleased to have his nine-year-old namesake, Willy, at his side. Willy had been born in California during Sherman's banking days. Not only did he resemble his father, but he also had inherited his love for the military. Sherman watched with pride as soldiers of the first battalion of the Thirteenth Regiment made Willy a sergeant, taught him the manual of arms, and included him in their guard mounting and parade ceremonies. Sherman enjoyed having Willy ride with him on inspection tours, pleased at his obvious interest in everything martial. As early as his West Point days, Ellen and the Ewings had frequently urged Sherman to leave the military and work in the civilian sector, so it felt good to have at least one family member sharing pride in his profession.

Sherman had special feelings for Willy. Years earlier in California, he remembered, Willy often rose early (as Sherman habitually did) and gathered wild food for the family goat. The small boy would stand in front of the stable, with the usually fierce goat's front paws affectionately resting on his shoulders. Sherman cherished tales of Willy's fearlessness such as the time when Willy, about five or six years old, sat with other relatives in the Ewing parlor in Lancaster and listened to ghost stories. Outside, a raging storm added a frightening realism to the tales of horror. Jokingly someone said: "Willy, what would you think of going up stairs and finding out if there are any ghosts there? They always come in the dark." Fine, the young boy responded, eagerly climbing the stairs and carefully inspecting all the darkened rooms on the second floor. "No ghosts there," he nonchalantly reported on returning, his calm expression indicating no fright.[3]

Sherman felt pride in his other children, too. He later joked about one camp incident involving Tommy. A Confederate, visiting under a flag of truce, struck up a conversation with Tom. Expressing his pride, Tommy blurted out: "Why[,] father can whip you fellows everytime." The Confederate asked how Tom could be so sure, and the boy proceeded to give details about the numbers and locations of Union troops. "Why, you young traitor," Sherman said on his return, "you must be court-martialed and you will probably be shot."[4]

During their visit, the Sherman family went to Vicksburg frequently and socialized with Grant's family and with General McPherson. After dinner, they often enjoyed the singing of former slaves, like the man known simply as "Old Shady." Sherman gave them a tour of the siege lines and allowed the children to gather battlefield souvenirs. A military band regularly provided festive music. Even the usually dissatisfied Ellen was at ease. She enjoyed her living quarters: two large hospital tents pitched together to form a bedroom and a "parlor." Minnie, Lizzie, and a servant from Ohio slept in a small tent next door, and Willy and Tommy bunked in their Uncle Charley Ewing's army tent a little farther away. Ellen also appreciated the added services of Sherman's three servants. In addition, her brother Boyle was an officer in Sherman's corps, and she was able to attend Mass regularly because a Notre Dame priest, Father J. C. Carrier, was a chaplain with the army. It was a rare period of family togetherness, both physically and spiritually.[5]

Sherman remained euphoric over the Vicksburg victory. He took pride in his accomplishment and welcomed letters from his brother, from the head of the Western Sanitary Commission, from a vacationing Frank Blair, from his old West Point professor Dennis Hart Mahan, and, most important, from Thomas Ewing, all praising his part in the Vicksburg triumph. Even newspaper reporters treated him kindly, and people in Ohio cheered the mere mention of his name. His effusive letters of thanks to Grant and Halleck for his promotion to regular army brigadier general clearly expressed his satisfaction at all his recent good fortune. Sherman proudly informed his foster father that his promotion was based on merit, and "no newspaper clamor, no side influence, no management." He pointedly told Ellen: "I beg that my friends allow me to play my own game of Life."[6]

Despite the presence of his family, Sherman was anxious to get on with the war. On Grant's order, he sent a cavalry force to repair the railroad back to Memphis. His instructions to the expedition's leader revealed his approach to military action: hard war but soft peace. He told the cavalry commander that it was *"now* [italics added] to the interest of our Government that all plundering and pillaging should cease." Yet, he said, continued opposition to U.S. authority should be summarily punished. If an allegation about guerrillas' murdering a slave was true, he told a subordinate, "send a couple of regiments . . . with orders to burn the house of some known secesh, and give notice it will be repeated as often as they please."[7]

When the chairman of a Vicksburg citizens' committee complained about insufficient Union provisions for the area's people, Sherman took the opportunity to express his ever more harsh war philosophy publicly. "I contend," he lectured, "that after the firing on our steam-boats navigating our own rivers, after the long and desperate resistance to our armies at Vicksburg, on the Yazoo, and in Mississippi generally, we are justified in treating all inhabitants as combatants and would be perfectly justifiable in transporting you all beyond the seas if the United States deemed it to her interests; but our purpose is not to change the population of this country, but to compel all the inhabitants to acknowledge and submit to the common law of the land. When all or a part of the inhabitants acknowledge the just rights of the United States, the war as to them ceases."[8]

Sherman had no patience with forces undermining the Union's efforts to restore order and stability in the nation. He was angered at the activities of Northern peace advocates, the followers of Clement L. Vallandigham, the so-called copperhead from Ohio, "cowards" who tried "to cover up their cowardice by a plea of Peace." "Today I declare I have no more sympathy with the misled but brave man who shoots at my heart . . . than of the Miscreant who tried to deceive a People by calling his cowardice patriotism. Take the bold ground," Sherman advised an Ohio politician. "Disfranchise all who will not help this Country."[9]

Sherman believed deeply that men would not continue fighting if they knew their women and families were suffering in the war. He intended to demoralize his opposition, he said, by burning, destroying, and laying waste. "This may seem cruel, but it is sharp and short. Procrastination in war is a greater evil than cruelty. We fight for success. Everything that tends to that is legitimate." At the same time, Sherman worried that his "soldiers were fast degenerating into robbers. I have checked it," he told his brother, "not on account of the poor people as for our own sake. On the discipline of our armies must be built the future Government of this country." Promotion of Union success and prevention of Confederate anarchy continued to be the bedrock of Sherman's philosophy of war.[10]

Halleck asked Sherman what advice he might give Lincoln on the matter of reconstructing Louisiana, Mississippi, and Arkansas. Sherman responded with a lengthy letter. He opposed any civilian government until after "*all* the organized armies of the South are dispersed, conquered, and subjugated." He would plainly "assert the broad doctrine that . . . the United States has the right, and also the physical power, to penetrate to every part of our national domain, . . . that we will do it in our own time and in our own way; . . . that we will remove and destroy every obstacle, if need be, take every life, every acre of land, every particle of property, every thing that to us seems proper; that we will not cease till the end is attained; that all who do not aid us are enemies, and that we will not account to them for our acts. If the people of the South oppose, they do so at their peril; and if they stand by, mere lookers-on in this domestic tragedy, they have no right to immunity, protection, or share in the final results." "All therefore I can now venture to advise is to raise the draft to its maximum, fill the present regiments to as large a standard as possible, and push the war, pure and simple."[11]

Sherman saw himself as a man of action who should not have to stop and justify his Union-saving activity at every turn. War was to be waged totally if it was to be waged at all. It made no sense to fight the South and talk about reconstruction at the same time. If Southerners did not want to suffer the inevitable ravages of war, their salvation lay in stopping the war, not in expecting the other side to be gentle. When victory was achieved, however, stop the bloodshed and destruction immediately and help those in need irregardless of any oaths of allegiance. Provisions should be "issued as a pure charity to prevent suffering, just as we would to the Indians on the frontier or to shipwrecked people." By the same token, however, "we are in no measure called on to accommodate the people till they positively submit openly and frankly to our just authority."[12]

Sherman was convinced that the war would eventually result in complete reunion. Once a truce team came into his camp with a letter for Grant. Sherman was a gracious host to the messenger, providing a dinner complete with wine and cigars. During the jovial conversation, a Confederate officer said the Federals should stop fighting because they could never conquer 8 million people, and, even if they could, hatred made "reconciliation impossible." Sherman disagreed, pointing out that Union and Confederate officers were being friendly enough just then. That was different, the Confederate insisted; officers were gentlemen; the common soldier was not. Sherman took the Confederate to some nearby enlisted men's campfires where they found Sherman's guard and the Confederate's escort companionably drinking coffee together. The Confederate grudgingly admitted that Sherman was right.[13]

While Sherman remained in camp and conditions remained relatively quiet in the West during that summer of 1863, William S. Rosecrans's Army of the Cumberland was making good progress against Braxton Bragg's Confederate Army of Tennessee. On September 8, 1863, Rosecrans maneuvered Bragg out of Chattanooga, but then disaster struck. At Chickamauga Creek, just across the Georgia boundary from the Tennessee city, the Confederates took advantage of a gap in the Union line to devastate a portion of Rosecrans's force. Despite George H. Thomas's determined stand, which earned him the title "Rock of Chickamauga," the shocked Union army staggered back into Chattanooga, where it found itself under siege in what threatened to become a Union Vicksburg.

Sherman, ordered to relieve Rosecrans, moved his headquarters on September 27 to a riverboat heading for Memphis on the first leg of a long march across Tennessee. As he and Ellen boarded the boat, they were still concerned about Minnie's recent bout with fever. Sherman sent an officer to fetch Willy from General James B. McPherson's house. Looking proud of himself and carrying a double-barreled shotgun, Willy came aboard the ship. When he complained of diarrhea, Ellen put him to bed and called a regimental surgeon. The physician diagnosed the problem as dysentery and malaria.

Willy's condition grew critical rapidly, and the doctor urged the utmost speed in reaching Memphis. On arrival, the boy was moved to the Gayoso Hotel and given every available medical treatment. Nothing helped, and Father Carrier was called in to administer spiritual comfort. Willy, so fearless in life, displayed the same courage in the face of death. He told the priest that if it was God's will, he would accept death, though he did not want to leave his father and mother. Carrier told him that he would see them again in heaven, so Willy became more resigned. Ellen began crying, and Willy reached out and caressed her face. He died peacefully with his family around him.[14]

Sherman was devastated. "His loss to me is more than words can express," he told Halleck. He wrote an emotional letter to the commander of the unit that had made Willy its sergeant. He promised the soldiers in that battalion that they all had "a key to the affection of my family . . . [and] that we will share with them our last blanket, our last crust." To six-year-old Tommy, he wrote: "You are now our only boy, and must take poor Willy's place, to take care of your sisters, and to fill my place when I too am gone." "Sleeping—waking—everywhere I see poor little Willy," Cump wrote Ellen. "Why should I ever have taken them [the family] to that dread climate," he tormented himself.[15]

A distraught Ellen took the boy's body back to Lancaster for burial. "My heart is now in heaven," she moaned, "and the world is dark and dreary." She worried that, in her concern for Minnie and her own health, she had somehow neglected Willy and wanted reassurance from Cump. Become a Catholic, she pleaded, so "that you will die in the faith that sanctified our holy one whom we have just given up to God." Ellen was filled with anxieties. "Since we lost dear Willy," she told Cump, "I feel that evils of all sorts are likely to come upon us."[16]

Sherman had to move his troops toward Chattanooga; he had no time for misery. In his grief, though, he displayed little enthusiasm for the task, believing there was a better way to relieve Rosecrans. He suggested that New Orleans troops destined for combat in Louisiana and Texas be sent east instead along the Gulf Coast, while his troops be sent through Meridian, Mississippi, and Selma, Alabama to the same area. The two forces could combine at Pascagoula, Mississippi, and launch a devastating attack against Mobile, forcing the Confederates around Chattanooga to abandon the siege. Since he had "abundant faith in Halleck," however, he would "play his game" and move to relieve Rosecrans.[17]

The "game" proved to be tedious. The distance from Memphis to Chattanooga is over three hundred miles of steep, rolling hills, the Tennessee River, and unfordable streams. Supply was a major problem. Halleck's order told Sherman to move with all dispatch toward Rosecrans but to repair and guard the Charleston and

Memphis Railroad. Sherman had no confidence in this railroad's security, so he shipped supplies on the Tennessee River as much as he could, and he even marched artillery, horses, and his entire fourth division over land.

On October 11, just twenty-four miles out of Memphis, Sherman ran into trouble. He, his staff, and the headquarters detachment, some 260 men, were riding in a special train when they came upon a skirmish between several thousand Confederate cavalry and the 240-man Union garrison near the Collierville depot. Sherman ordered the train stopped, his troops went into battle formation, and the train backed into the depot. General J. R. Chalmers, commander of the attacking Confederates, sent a surrender demand, but Sherman ordered Colonel D. C. Anthony, commander of the town's garrison, to refuse it.

The Confederates opened with artillery fire that damaged the rear of the train, and rebel infantry captured several Union horses, including one of Sherman's favorites. Sherman remained "as calm and unconcerned as though he was standing on parade, instead of in the most exposed position in the works," an inspiration to those around him. "I was somewhat frightened at first," remembered the train conductor, "but when I saw such a great man as he so unconcerned amid all the balls flying around him, I did not think it worthwhile for me to be scared." "General, . . . you will surely be hit if you don't keep under cover," warned a noncommissioned officer. "Sergeant," replied Sherman, "attend to your business, sir; attend to your business, I will take care of myself, sir."[18] The Federals, under Sherman's leadership, held their ground, and, after several hours of fighting, the Confederates withdrew.

Sherman had seen firsthand the precariousness of his hold on the Charleston and Memphis. He could not protect it all the way from Memphis to Chattanooga. "I don't like this railroad," Sherman bluntly told Grant, "it lies parallel to an enemy's country, and they can break it when they please." His troops were insufficient to guard the tracks and move quickly to Rosecrans's rescue too. "To depend on a road so precarious as this would tie us down to localities that can have no material influence on events." Instead, he "would prefer to move about and learn to live on the corn and meal of the country." Grant was not in charge, however; Halleck was, and "Old Brains" wanted the railroad secured.[19]

Within a week, Sherman's complaints were fortuitously relieved. On October 16 Halleck made Grant overall commander of the Departments of the Ohio, Cumberland, and Tennessee; he thus became commander of the West. Soon after, Grant gave Sherman his old command over the Department and Army of the Tennessee and replaced Rosecrans with George H. Thomas as commander of the Department and Army of the Cumberland. Grant immediately told Sherman to forget about repairing the railroad and concentrate instead on reaching Chattanooga as quickly as possible.[20]

Sherman undertook his increased responsibilities with energy and confidence. "With Grant, I will undertake anything in reason," he said. Letters flew from his desk to subordinates throughout his department. He was in control, and he made sure everybody knew it. He told his subordinates to inform civilians that "they must organize and put down robbers and guerrillas. If they cannot, then they will be liable to be overrun and plundered by both sides. They must manifest not only a Union sentiment, but must unite in self-defense and in such a way as to assist the National Government." When people in Paducah, Kentucky, resisted Union occupation there, he threatened to "have the chief men banished and their property destroyed." He would tolerate no nonsense. He repeated these convictions in his first general order: "The people who occupy this department had better make a note of this and conduct themselves accordingly." The "or else" was left unsaid, but it was patently clear.[21]

The threat was real. Guerrillas captured the son of his chief of artillery in a farmhouse near the line of march. The captors tied the young officer to the railboard of a wagon and drove him away. Since Sherman could spare no cavalry to chase the guerrillas, he called in four of the leading men of nearby Florence, Alabama. They protested ignorance of the marauders, but Sherman said either the guerrillas returned the soldier or he would tie the four of them to wagon railboards of their own. The young man was freed the next day.[22]

Sherman also took the opportunity to lecture his old nemesis, the press. He told a subordinate in Memphis of his anger over garbled accounts of the Collierville skirmish. Tell the editors, he said, that he would tolerate "no anonymous letters, no praise or censure of officers, no discussion of the policy and measures of Government without the article is reviewed by the commanding officer . . . and editor responsible for the general tenor of extracts of other papers." He wrote directly to a Memphis editor the next day. "Now I am again in authority over you, and you must heed my advice," he said with obvious gloating. "Freedom of speech and freedom of the press, precious relics of former history, must not be construed too largely." "I wish you success, but my first duty is to maintain 'order and harmony,'" and he could not accomplish this unless he kept the press muzzled.[23]

J. B. Bingham, the Memphis editor and a friend of Tennessee military governor Andrew Johnson, had the temerity to ask for a clarification, and Sherman obliged with his philosophy of war. As a general, he said, he had the "right to use every man, every influence, every moral, intellectual, and physical power within my limits to restore quiet, order, [and] peace." "If a man disturbs the peace, I will kill him or remove him; if he does anything wrong and there is no civil power in existence, the military power does exist and must act, for we must have some law. Nature abhors anarchy. As of a man, so of a combination, or the press, or anything; all must act in concert to stop war, strife, and anarchy. When these are done, peace restored, civil courts and law respected, then you and all are free again." In short, total war was the only way to end this conflict.[24]

Meanwhile, Sherman pushed his four divisions toward Chattanooga, normally moving at the head of his column. Brief skirmishes took place here and there, but his force encountered no major opposition. By November 8 he was in Fayetteville, Tennessee, still over a hundred miles from his destination. Directly ahead were "old stomping grounds" where as a young lieutenant in the 1840s, he had assisted Inspector General Sylvester Churchill. On November 13 Sherman and the first columns of the Fifteenth Army Corps reached Bridgeport, Alabama, astride the Memphis and Charleston Railroad and near the connecting Nashville and Chattanooga Railroad, some thirty miles downstream from Chattanooga. They had traveled over six hundred miles from their Vicksburg camps, accomplishing what the *London Spectator* called an "extraordinary march." Bridgeport was a good logistics center for Union troops, but from there to Chattanooga the treacherous terrain and Confederate sharpshooters made supply difficult.[25]

Sherman took a steamboat into Chattanooga, arriving there on November 15. Grant was pleased to see him. The two men had grown close during this conflict because of their shared difficulties and triumphs, and they greeted each other cordially. Grant, who welcomed other officers almost coldly, offered Sherman a cigar and, pointing to a rocker, said good-naturedly: "Take the chair of honor, Sherman." "Oh no! that belongs to you, general," Sherman replied. "I don't forget, Sherman, to give proper respect to age," Grant insisted jokingly. "Well, then, if you put it on that ground, I *must* accept," Sherman answered in equally good humor.[26]

General O. O. Howard, Sherman's later subordinate and the postwar head of the Freedmen's Bureau, met Sherman for the first time during this meeting. He was impressed with Sherman's "memory for detail," particularly "his ability to carry with him the knowledge of places and localities long since seen." While Grant spent most of his time in solitary silence, Sherman carried on a lively conversation with everyone around him. Howard was pleased to see how well Grant and Sherman worked together. Sherman, he said, "would draw up five plans of campaign . . . , while General Grant would weigh the matter and select the best." As W. B. Hazen, another general put it, Grant and Sherman "were new, and different from the commanders we had known before. They wore vests and coats unbuttoned. . . . A sort of outspoken frankness upon military matters" was the new order of the day.[27]

The morning after the initial meeting, Sherman and Grant, Howard, Thomas, and Baldy Smith walked out to a point on the Union defenses where they could view their own and the enemy's positions. Not a thousand yards off, Braxton Bragg's Confederate pickets patrolled the outer fringes of the encircling emplacements. Sherman saw for the first time how desperate the situation was. He blurted out: "Why, General Grant, you are besieged." Grant laconically replied: "It is too true." The Confederates had the Union troops trapped in Chattanooga. The Tennessee River blocked the Federals on the north; Lookout Mountain was a barrier on the west; entrenched Confederate soldiers held Missionary Ridge on the east and south. Sherman, Thomas, Smith, and several others inspected further, Sherman and Smith crawling behind some trees along the riverbank to get as close to the enemy as they could safely go. "I can do it," Sherman concluded after his reconnaissance.[28]

He hurried back to Bridgeport, taking his turn at the oars of the boat he and four soldiers commandeered to row back. Sherman rushed because Grant could not spring into action until all his troops were in position. His plan called for Sherman's force to attack on the left against Bragg's right flank. Thomas's Army of the Cumberland was to hold down the middle, and three divisions under Joe Hooker were to invest the enemy left. More specifically, Sherman took his three divisions, Howard's corps, and Jeff Davis's division from the Army of the Cumberland under cover to a position across from the mouth of the South Chickamauga Creek, trying to persuade the Confederates that they were reinforcements for Ambrose Burnside, then besieged at Knoxville. Actually Sherman was to cross the Tennessee River on a specially made bridge just below the creek and strike Tunnel Hill at the north end of Missionary Ridge. Once he secured the ridge, he was to extend to his right to a position blocking any Confederate retreat. Meanwhile, Thomas was to hold the Union middle and right flank and attack when Sherman had established himself on the ridge. He was to move toward the left to link up with Sherman and drive the Confederates off the entire ridge. Hooker's task was to threaten Lookout Mountain on the Union right and keep Bragg confused as to Sherman's attack on the left. (Hooker would find the opposition so light that he actually scaled and captured the mountain.)[29]

Sherman's force successfully crossed the river on pontoon boats during the night of the twenty-fourth, Sherman at the water's edge quietly directing his soldiers into the boats. They met only token opposition and after establishing a foothold on the opposite shore put in place a previously prepared 1,350-foot pontoon bridge for the rest of the troops. Sherman later bragged that he "doubt[ed] if the history of war can show a bridge of that extent . . . laid down so noiselessly and well in so short a time."[30]

At 1:00 P.M., with Hooker already engaged at Lookout Mountain, Sherman began his attack, advancing in three parallel columns, the low-hanging clouds shielding his movements from the enemy. By 3:30 P.M., he had taken what he thought was his objective, the north end of Missionary Ridge. To his shock, he found that Missionary Ridge was not a continuous elevation; there was a deep depression or ravine between his position and his objective, Tunnel Hill. Sherman was so flabbergasted that instead of pushing his advantage, he fortified the first hill and forfeited his momentum. That night "the sky cleared away bright and a cold front filled the air, and our camp fires revealed to the enemy and to our friends in Chattanooga our position on Missionary Ridge."[31]

Early the next morning, Sherman and his staff made a lightning inspection of his entire line, trying to understand as best they could the military situation. At daybreak, he ordered his troops forward, the two brigades of his brother-in-law's division leading the way. Pushing Brigadier General Hugh Boyle Ewing back toward his unit as he explained his orders, Sherman concluded: "I say, Ewing, don't call for help until you actually need it." Men of General John M. Corse's brigade made a lodgement beyond the depression, but they were stopped there. Corse was severely wounded, and the Confederates counterattacked and stymied the Union efforts. The two sides were so close to one another at one point that Confederates threw rocks down on some of Sherman's troops.[32]

Waiting on the first elevation to reinforce their hard-pressed colleagues, soldiers hugged the ground to seek protection from the Confederate artillery and small arms fire. Suddenly they saw their commander ride up behind them. Sherman reined his horse and sat nervously twisting his red whiskers while he peered anxiously toward the rebel works on the hill. A soldier jumped up and yelled: "This is no place for you, General, the enemy's batteries sweep this ground with canister." Sherman nodded his head sharply, continuing to watch the fighting to his front. Then just as suddenly as he had come, he wheeled his horse around and dashed to another part of the battlefield.[33]

At that time and later, Sherman remained convinced that his attack had drawn "vast masses of the enemy to our flank," thereby taking pressure off Thomas and allowing his troops to achieve one of the most dramatic events of the entire war. Thomas's men attacked the middle of the Confederate line and made the headlong dash up the mountain to rout the enemy. Sherman insisted that "we attacked and forced Bragg to detach from his Centre to such an extent that when the Army of the Cumberland advanced in the afternoon the Centre was pierced and broken back, and the Battle won." He also insisted that Grant's plan had always envisioned Sherman and Hooker's putting pressure on the flanks to allow Thomas to break through in the middle. "The whole plan succeeded admirably," Sherman wrote in his *Memoirs*.[34]

Sherman simply did not remember it correctly, or he had talked himself into rationalizing what actually happened. Grant's plan had consistently called for Thomas's role to be secondary to Sherman's. Sherman's attack was the major one, with everyone else in support of him. In fact, he failed to break through on the flank as he was supposed to, and there is no evidence that he drew any troops from the Confederate positions in front of Thomas. He and his troops fought valiantly, but they did not accomplish their mission.[35] It was only the common sense of the common soldier in Thomas's Army of the Cumberland that carried the day. The Union attackers realized that they could not simply capture the rifle pits at the foot of the ridge and stop there, as orders seemed to indicate, because then they would be in an exposed position. They had to keep moving or be decimated. None of the generals at Chattanooga, Union or Confederate, deserved much credit. Grant's orders were never as clear as they could have been; subordinates were confused, and attacks did not take place with the coordination they should have. On the Confederate side, the defensive positions were defective, and Bragg's leadership was poor. Even Jefferson Davis shared in the blame. He sent James Longstreet to Knoxville despite Grant's concentration at Chattanooga, and thus he weakened Bragg's army. To his discredit, Bragg was only too glad to get rid of Longstreet, so he readily acquiesced in Davis's order. The real heroes of that battle were not the generals but the charging privates and the lower-level officers who encouraged them on.

Thomas's charge broke the siege of Chattanooga, and Grant had another success to add lustre to his ever-growing reputation. Unfortunately for the Federals, Bragg and his Confederates were able to get away from Sherman's and Thomas's pursuit. The decisive victory was not a rout. It did not matter to the exhausted Union soldiers; they had accomplished what they had set out to do: freeing themselves from Confederate encirclement.

Sherman and his soldiers looked forward only to rest after the months of hard marching from Memphis and the hard fighting at Tunnel Hill. They had not seen their Bridgeport camps for seven days, existing on only two days' rations, no change of clothes, and one coat or blanket per man. But Grant had other plans. He ordered Sherman to relieve Burnside at Knoxville, some eighty miles distant. Burnside's troops were on the verge of starvation, Grant said.

Sherman was displeased with the order and worried that his troops were too tired and ill equipped to navigate in cold, mountainous East Tennessee. Bad memories of the region from his 1861 Kentucky stay affected him even more. "Recollect," he told Grant, "that East Tennessee is my horror." He would go there as ordered, but he wanted to get out as soon as he had accomplished his mission.[36]

On December 5, after six days of hard marching, Sherman met a member of Burnside's staff just outside Knoxville; Longstreet had retreated back to Virginia the previous night. When Sherman rode into the city, he immediately saw a pen containing fattened cattle. He found the general and his officers in a comfortable mansion and had a turkey dinner with them, complete with full linen and silverware. He could not resist telling Burnside that this repast hardly looked like starvation to him, and Burnside sheepishly admitted that his situation had never been as bad as it had seemed. His army could have survived a much longer siege, but he was still happy that Longstreet had departed at Sherman's approach. Sherman wished he had not pushed his troops so hard.[37]

Sherman and his men were now truly exhausted, many of his troops suffering from "bleeding feet [which they] wrapped in old clothes or portions of blankets that could ill be spared from shivering shoulders." Sherman wanted to go home for Christmas "to comfort my family, almost heart-broken at the death of our oldest boy and at the declining health of Mr. and Mrs. Ewing." But he also wanted to get back to the Mississippi as soon as he could to safeguard Union control over it, and this meant clearing the area of the hated guerrillas once and for all. "To secure the safety of the navigation of the Mississippi River, I would slay

millions," he said. On that point I am not only insane but mad."
He was convinced that the only way to stop the marauders behind
Union lines was to punish the entire populace and convince them
that they could not support such raiders with impunity.[38]

Before he could go to Lancaster, he met with Grant and the
high command in Nashville. He recommended his long-desired
raid on Meridian, Mississippi, as the best way to clear the
Mississippi Valley of guerrillas, and he gained Grant's approval.
Then Grant took Sherman, Philip Sheridan, Grenville Dodge, and
several of the other generals to military governor Andrew Johnson's beautiful home. Johnson looked at the battle-weary crew
"with a very quizzical eye" but then forgot about their unkempt
appearances as he launched into a fist-slamming tirade against the
Confederates. The officers left "rather disgusted" at Johnson's
performance. Sherman suggested that they take some recreation
and go to the local theater to watch a performance of *Hamlet*. He
loved the theater and took every chance he could to attend any
performance, especially a Shakespeare play. He always found the
Bard relaxing. To the delight of the soldiers in attendance and
Sherman's frustration, the actors were awful. The audience
boisterously ridiculed them, and Sherman expressed his outrage
increasingly more loudly. Grant finally suggested that they better
leave before the audience recognized them and rioted. Sherman
then expressed a craving for oysters. The group found a restau-
rant that served seafood, but the female proprietor, not knowing
who they were, cut short their meal because of the military
curfew. The most powerful Union military men in the region
good-naturedly left.

The following evening, General Gordon Granger had the
generals over to dinner, and his Southern mother-in-law launched
into a rampage against Sherman's foraging. At first he said
nothing, but then, losing his patience, he responded hotly:
"Madame, my soldiers have to subsist even if the whole country
must be ruined to maintain them." Of the two armies, if one had
to starve, he said, it would not be "the army that is loyal."[39]

Although Sherman continued to believe that Halleck was
superior in the qualities needed to command the entire army, he
felt Grant had the capacity for doing more military good than any
other man in America. He was on good terms with both men,
pleased with the way the war was progressing, and confident that

he had the right to share in the military glory. He could legitimately feel secure about himself and his choices.[40]

Yet he continued to manifest insecurities. When approached for autographs, photographs, and offers of biographies, he refused because, he said, "I don't want to rise or be notorious, for the reason that a mere slip or accident may let me fall." Even the warm reception he received when he arrived in Lancaster and felt Thomas Ewing's pride was not enough to quiet his fears that his success was only temporary. Willy's death reinforced his gloomy outlook. Ellen continued to grieve over the tragedy, and much of Sherman's Christmas visit was no doubt spent in mutual recrimination and consolation. Thomas and Maria Ewing's severe illnesses only sharpened his perception of life and fame as fleeting and uncertain.[41]

The furlough was all too brief. The train from Lancaster arrived late into Columbus, Ohio, so he had to while away the time waiting for the next train to Cincinnati. He played cards at a tavern. His slender form and dark red hair had changed little during the war years, but wrinkles on his face and crow's feet at the corners of his eyes marked the wear and tear of the campaigns. He still did not look like a military leader, observers continuing to think he resembled "a minister more than the war dog" he was. On a nearby sofa covered with shawls and coats slept thirteen-year-old Minnie, returning to a convent school in Cincinnati. Father and daughter finally reached the river city at 4 A.M. and checked into a hotel room that was so cold they had to bundle together to stay warm. The next morning Sherman welcomed a constant stream of admiring visitors and then reluctantly took Minnie to the Mount Notre Dame Seminary, consoling himself when he left her that "all of life is a sacrifice." He had to leave the circle of family to go back to the tasks of war.[42]

In these early days of 1864, Sherman seemed to be in constant motion. He boarded a steamboat in Cincinnati and fought the icy Ohio and Mississippi rivers to visit his commands in Cairo, Paducah, Memphis, and Vicksburg. He was anxious to implement his raid across central Mississippi. He wanted to destroy Confederate supply and transportation facilities at Meridian in order to prevent Confederate "mounted devils" from continuing to threaten the Mississippi River and west Tennessee. He told Hurlbut at Memphis and McPherson at Vicksburg to prepare two divisions apiece for the operation. At Memphis, he told William Sooy Smith, the cavalry officer Grant had sent him, that he wanted to destroy Nathan Bedford Forrest, the Confederate cavalry officer who had been causing havoc in north Mississippi and western Tennessee. He also talked about cooperation with Nathaniel Banks in a proposed Red River expedition against Shreveport, Louisiana, but worried that the shallowness of the river would prevent any navy participation. He traveled and he planned, scarcely stopping in one place long enough for the inhabitants to know he was there. Newspaper rumors placed him at widely separated places, and he enjoyed the confusion he was causing among the press. If reporters were confused, so was the enemy.[43]

One fact that he wished to broadcast to the South, however, was that punishment awaited those who continued to oppose him. He ordered General A. J. Smith to move his forces from Columbus, Kentucky, into western Tennessee in conjunction with the forth-coming Meridian expedition. He told Smith to "punish the country well for permitting the guerrillas among them." "Take freely the horses, mules, cattle, &c. of the hostile or indifferent inhabitants," he said, "and let them all understand that if from design or weakness they permit their country to be used by the public enemy[,] they must bear the expense of the troops sent to expel them." Warn them, too, he told Smith, that he planned to institute banishment of "all people who are deemed opposed to the reestablishment of civil order." "But in counties where the people have acted properly," he concluded, "a broad distinction should be made. I attach no importance to oaths or opinions, but the people must be construed friends or enemies according to their general behavior."[44]

He lamented to Minnie that in every one of his battles now, he was fighting "some of the very families in whose homes I used to spend some happy days" in South Carolina and Louisiana. "Of course I must fight them when the time comes," he said with clear sadness, "but wherever a result can be accomplished without battle I prefer it." Destruction of property, he believed, was better than taking lives, especially when those lives belonged to friends. A raid from Vicksburg through Jackson to Meridian was more appealing to him than any pitched battle, such as Shiloh or Chattanooga. If he could tear up railroads, destroy crops and supplies, and punish the area's inhabitants for harboring guerrillas, he would achieve an important victory. If the Meridian raid proved successful, it would show once and for all that crippling the enemy's ability and will to fight was the most efficient, and least fatal, way to wage war.[45]

He already had Grant's blessing, so he wrote Halleck asking for diversionary support from Union troops in Chattanooga. He promised to help Nathaniel Banks at New Orleans with his Red River expedition but wanted Banks first to support his Meridian raid by feigning movement against Mobile, Alabama. He organized another diversionary movement, this one a joint army-navy operation up the Yazoo River. He planned his Meridian raid in conjunction with other operations throughout the region in order to prevent the enemy from reacting in force against him.[46]

By the end of January, his plan was in place. It was a carefully organized operation, utilizing the vast array of Union military power in the region. On February 1, 1864, Sherman was to lead twenty-thousand men from Vicksburg and move quickly through Jackson, then 130 miles to Meridian. "Not a tent will be carried, from the commander-in-chief down," he ordered, determined that the army would travel as unencumbered as possible. At the same time, William Sooy Smith's seven-thousand-man cavalry was to leave Collierville, Tennessee, and ride south through Pontotoc, Okolona, and Artesia, Mississippi, to Meridian. The Yazoo expedition would start at the same time. Although Sherman had no control over troops in Chattanooga and Louisiana, he hoped they too would keep Confederate troops bogged down.[47]

On the eve of his departure for Meridian, Sherman was preoccupied with thoughts of the hostile civilians whom he would encounter on his march. He sought historical precedents for the treatment of such civilians, bothered by the swelling charges of Southern protest against his war tactics. He wanted Southerners to know that his kind of war—total war—fell within the framework of earlier conflict. He wanted them to realize that they were responsible for their own suffering. They had brought on the war, and he refused to be blamed for the legitimate suffering they experienced because of it. In Europe, he said, "whence we derive our principles of war," warfare was conducted between competing monarchs and their hired armies; civilians were not supposed to be bothered. Yet when British monarchs William and Mary sent armies to put down a revolt in Ireland, the civilians were not only warred against, but they were also driven off their lands and replaced with other settlers. Clearly the English had waged war against people, and so could he.

"When the provisions, forage, horses, mules, wagons, &c. are used by our enemy it is clearly our duty and right to take them, because otherwise they might be used against us." Houses and other buildings left vacant by departing rebels were also fair game. As for women and children, "so long as non-combatants remain in their houses and keep to their accustomed business[,] their opinions and prejudices can in no wise influence the war, and therefore should not be noticed; but if any one comes out into the public streets and creates disorder, he or she should be punished, restrained, or banished."

"The Government of the United States has . . . any and all rights which they choose to enforce the war—to take their lives, their homes, their lands, their everything." "War is simply power unrestrained by constitution or compact." It did not have to be that way, however. Southerners did not have to keep up "the war, anarchy, bloodshed, and the foulest crimes that have disgraced any time or any people." "To those who submit to the rightful law and authority[,] all gentleness and forbearance; but to the petulant and persistent secessionists, why, death is mercy, and the quicker he or she is disposed of the better. Satan and the rebellious saints of Heaven were allowed a continuous existence in hell merely to swell their just punishment. To such as would rebel against a Government so mild and just as ours was in peace, a punishment equal would not be unjust."[48]

As Sherman began his march on Meridian to destroy railroads and anything else of value to the enemy in central Mississippi, he expressed great confidence in himself: "I am now so situated that dismissal for any cause not involving absolute wrong would not concern me." "Having done a full share of the real achievements of this war I need not fear accidents." Neither the press nor anyone else could hurt him. "I do believe," he told Ellen, "I can do more on the Mississippi than any Genl officer in the service except Grant."[49]

Such outward confidence did not preclude a sudden outburst upon hearing an unfounded rumor that his Army of the Tennessee would not, like Hooker's and Thomas's armies, receive the thanks of Congress for its part in the Chattanooga fighting. "I am now on the wave of popularity and the next plunge is away down, down. I know it well and would avoid it, but how is the question." Once more, his anxiety provoked thoughts of death or a return to California. Sherman feared something happening to humble him again.[50]

Although he let it be known that no reporter would be welcome on the expedition, he liked the *Herald*'s D. B. R. Keim and let him come along, choosing to label him one of McPherson's aides. Sherman had absolute control over reporters; he could exclude them or allow them in, as he saw fit. Such power meant freedom from press harassment, and this was reassuring.[51]

His continued warm reception in Union-occupied but still Confederate Memphis was also uplifting. At every theater and public gathering, "there was a storm of applause" from people who saw him. During January some of the city's leading citizens held a well-attended dinner in his honor and insisted that he make a speech. Unlike Grant, who shrank from public speaking, Sherman jumped at the opportunity. By going to war, he said, Southerners had violated the code of honor of any gentlemen's club. They had willingly voted in the 1860 election but then chose war when the results had not been to their liking. In Louisiana, whose secession he had witnessed, the capture of the federal arsenal had "insulted the United States, and made us choose between an active war or silent submission to an usurped power." Did they not "respect us the more for our determined and successful efforts to resent these insults than if we had tamely submitted"?

Sherman received warm applause, favorable accounts in newspapers, and an invitation from the local Union Club to speak at one of its meetings. Jokingly he predicted that, after the war, Grant would run for mayor of his home town, and he would run for mayor of Memphis. His audience reacted approvingly, and so did the reporters who heard him. Only Ellen, still depressed over Willy's death and worried about her mother's deteriorating health, commented negatively on his triumph: "How hollow all such pleasure must seem to you."[52]

Sherman and his two major subordinates, James B. McPherson and Stephen Hurlbut, concentrated their four divisions in Vicksburg. Sherman learned from a spy that General Leonidas Polk had his headquarters at Meridian, with two divisions of infantry and two cavalry divisions, including Forrest's troops, scattered over Mississippi. There were perhaps seventeen thousand Confederates at Polk's disposal, but he apparently had no inkling of Sherman's intentions and seemed to be making no attempts at consolidation. The way to Meridian was open.[53]

Sherman's troops left Vicksburg on February 3, 1864, in two columns, the right one, the Seventeenth Corps, under McPherson and the left one, the Sixteenth Corps, under Hurlbut. There was also a small cavalry force of about thirteen hundred men serving a screening function. In all, Sherman had about twenty-thousand men. Crossing the Big Black River, the columns cut themselves loose from their supply base and lived off their wagons and the countryside. They met little opposition until the fifth day's march (February 8), which Sherman later described "as one continued skirmish for eighteen miles." The Union soldiers pushed the few Confederate cavalry defenders through and out of Jackson, adding further affliction to an already "afflicted town."[54] The next day, they crossed the Pearl River with no opposition.

Progress was steady despite the terrible roads. On February 12, they ran into trouble. Sherman had decided to spend the night in Decatur and personally ordered one of Hurlbut's regiments to guard the town's crossroads until the head of McPherson's column, some four miles behind, came into view. Sherman found a log house, unsaddled his horse, and was soon asleep. Shouts and gunfire roused him. His aide rushed in with news that a Confederate cavalry unit was launching an attack. Where was the infantry regiment he had posted? Sherman asked. They had marched away, he later learned, on the mistaken assumption that the cloud of dust behind them was caused by the head of McPherson's column. Sherman ordered his aide to chase down the departing regiment, meanwhile hastily organizing the few staff officers and clerks around him to make a stand at a nearby corn crib. The aide quickly appeared with the errant regiment, and the enemy cavalry was easily driven away.

He reached Meridian in a heavy rain on February 14 to find that Polk had abandoned the city and moved east. Sherman thought about pursuing him into Alabama but decided against it because Sooy Smith and his cavalry were nowhere to be seen.

Sherman had central Mississippi to himself, having chased the enemy army away and cut a wide path of destruction along his route. Barns and houses were invaded and sometimes damaged or destroyed; farm produce and animals were taken and consumed; slaves were freed; and anything with war-making potential burned. After a day of rest, he put his men to work in Meridian on April 16 "with axes, crowbars, sledges, clawbars, and with fire." For five days the soldiers destroyed the city's supply potential and tore up over a hundred miles of railroads and innumerable trestles and bridges in all directions from the city. "Meridian, with its depots, store-houses, arsenals, hospitals, offices, hotels, and cantonments no longer exists," Sherman reported. "I have no hesitation in pronouncing the work as well done."

The absence of Smith and the cavalry was the only worry. When he had instructed Smith on the raid, Sherman had emphasized the necessity of meeting Forrest head-on and not worrying about being outnumbered because Forrest had only four thousand riders to Smith's seven thousand. Sherman sent his cavalry as far north as Louisville, Mississippi, to see if Smith could be located, but it was only after he had returned to Vicksburg that he learned what had happened. Smith had not embarked from Tennessee until February 11, a day after he was to have been in Meridian. On February 21 he skirmished with Forrest at West Point and became so frightened that he had immediately retreated. On February 22 Forrest caught up with him at Okolona and sent him into panicked flight. Sherman was enraged and said so in his report.

Sherman decided against any further delay and ordered his troops to march back toward Vicksburg, with long lines of fugitive slaves, estimated at from five thousand to eight thousand in all, steadily augmenting the columns. "They form a mournful curiosity," an observer noted, "with their lacerated backs, branded faces, and ragged garments. They are of both sexes, and of every shade of complexion. They vary in age from one month to one hundred years. . . . Some were on foot, some on horseback, some in ox-carts." They had no idea where they were going, but the road led away from slavery, and that seemed good enough for them. In some cases it led to starvation, disease, or mistreatment at the hands of the army, but it was freedom still, and on they came. Sherman was no emancipator and tolerated the fugitives only reluctantly. He saw them not as a people eagerly seeking freedom but as a disorderly encumbrance on his war activities. He was not consciously cruel to them, but he made little effort to make their lives easier.[55]

Sherman left his troops at Canton with orders to follow him to Vicksburg at a more leisurely pace. He turned his attention to his projected cooperation with Banks on the Red River. He believed they could achieve on the west side of the river what he had just accomplished on the east: enough quick destruction to prevent any further threats on the Mississippi River and the consequent release of Union troops for offensive activity elsewhere. The Meridian raid was a complete success. The enemy was stymied for the indefinite future, he thought. He had "baffled the sharp ones of the press and stampeded all Alabama." "However extravagant my early assertions may have seemed," he said in reference to his 1861 warnings against newspapers in Kentucky, "now they are verified by time." Total secrecy was the formula for success.[56]

Although the damaged and destroyed Confederate railroads were back in working order within a month, the Meridian expedition had demonstrated something far more important: a paucity of Confederate troops; much of the Confederacy was a hollow shell. When Sherman later contemplated a march to the sea, the important lessons of Meridian were instrumental in his thinking. He could march an army through Confederate territory with impunity and feed it at the expense of the inhabitants. He could wage successful war without having to slaughter thousands of soldiers in the process.[57]

Sherman hurried to New Orleans to consult personally with Banks, stopping first at Natchez in response to a letter from his closest Louisiana Military Seminary friend, David F. Boyd, now a Confederate officer. The classics professor and later president of Louisiana State University had been Sherman's right-hand man during one of the most successful times in Sherman's life, but he was now a prisoner of war. He wrote Sherman to ask for transfer to another POW camp to improve his chances of parole. Sherman had an emotional reunion with his cherished friend and took Boyd with him down the Mississippi to New Orleans. Boyd told him that old friends spoke of Sherman "a great deal, some with marked respect and others with bitter hatred." Sherman gave Boyd the freedom of the Crescent City, offered him financial help, and arranged a quick exchange. The separation of the two old friends was sad. Boyd asked that he and Sherman remain *"private friends"* though they were *"public enemies."* "May God protect you & carry you thro' this wicked war," Boyd concluded. Sherman responded with assurance of his "strong personal attachment" and told Boyd to use their friendship if he ever needed anything in New Orleans. In the most concrete instance of his war years, Sherman saw that he was fighting friends, as he had always insisted. The war had to be ended as quickly as possible to prevent him from having to kill Boyd and others like him, and the Meridian method was the way to do it.[58]

Sherman found New Orleans changed from only a few years previously. He attended a variety of social gatherings and had a productive meeting with Banks. The Massachusetts Republican politician-turned-general was prepared for the Red River expedition but determined to delay until after the inauguration ceremonies for the state's new Union governor. New Orleans's capture in 1862 had opened the way for Louisiana's pacification, and the inauguration of a Unionist governor was an important step in the restoration of order in the area. Banks tried to entice Sherman to participate in the ceremony, but Sherman insisted that he had to rush back to prepare the ten thousand troops he had promised would rendezvous with Banks in Alexandria on March 17. Actually, as he had told Halleck earlier, he opposed restoration of any state government until the war was won. Political concerns had no place in an all-out effort to end the war.[59]

Sherman returned to Vicksburg on March 6 and placed a division each from McPherson's and Hurlbut's command under the leadership of A. J. Smith. Both Grant and Sherman made it clear to Banks that he could have these troops only for thirty days because Sherman would need them for offensive operations of his own. The expedition began encouragingly enough, with Smith taking Fort De Russy in Louisiana, but the escape of the defending Confederate troops foretold the expedition's problems. General Frederick Steele, commander of the Department of Arkansas at Little Rock, did not cooperate as planned, and Banks did not push operations energetically. The Red River expedition was a failure.[60]

In early March, Grant received news of the Senate's readiness to confirm him in the post of general in chief. Sherman was tremendously flattered when Grant credited him and McPherson for all his success, but he worried what this promotion might mean. He considered Grant "Washington's legitimate successor" and felt he would continue to be successful if he stayed "simple, honest, and unpretending" as he had always been. These qualities and his "simple faith in success" were the keys to his victories. "For God's sake and your country's sake," Sherman told Grant, "come out of Washington." "Take to yourself the whole Mississippi Valley. . . . The Atlantic slopes and Pacific shores will follow its destiny as sure as the limbs of a tree live or die with the main trunk."[61]

Sherman must have realized that if Grant moved to Washington, he would take his friend's place as commander in the West. Yet he sincerely worried about Grant in the political whirlwind of the capital city and did not want him to go. When Sherman went to Nashville in mid-March to assume command over military operations in the West and make plans for the future, his genuine affection for the man he was succeeding was evident. Grant asked Sherman to go with him to a sword presentation. After the mayor of Grant's home town made a polished speech, Grant fumbled around in all his pockets and finally pulled out a crumpled piece of paper and bashfully handed it to the mayor to read in response. "His whole manner was awkward in the extreme, yet perfectly characteristic," Sherman said. "I could not help laughing at a scene so characteristic of the man who then stood prominent before the country, and to whom all had turned as the only one qualified to guide the nation in a war that had become painfully critical." Sherman gained some self-confidence from this incident. If the shy Grant dared assume overall command in Washington, Sherman could do the same in the West. If he could be successful serving with Grant in the same area, he could be successful serving with his friend within the same nation.[62]

Sherman assumed his new post, commander of the Military Division of the Mississippi, with confidence. He traveled with Grant to Cincinnati to complete planning for the future, finding a pregnant Ellen still morose over Willy's death and her mother's recent death and determined to see him become a Catholic as recompense. Then he traveled throughout his military division inspecting troops and defenses, conversing with subordinates, and learning about his new command. He felt clearly in charge, ready to embark on what he and Grant hoped would signal the end of the war. Grant was determined to pressure the enemy on all fronts, allowing no room for maneuver and concentration. Sherman was eager to cooperate. At last, the Union had two talented aggressive generals in place.[63]

Sherman was finally in position to accomplish what he had envisioned in Louisiana in 1861. At that time, he had become convinced that he could become a success only if the war effort preserved the Union. Now the Union could be preserved only if Sherman was successful; and Sherman could be successful only if he helped preserve the Union. The two were no longer intertwined solely in his mind. They were now intertwined in fact.

CHAPTER 12

——— ☆ ———

ATLANTA FALLS

IT SEEMED LIKE A DREAM that spring of 1864. William Tecumseh Sherman was commander of the Union war effort in the entire West, from the Appalachian Mountains to Arkansas. He had become the second most powerful military man in the Federal army. All his life he had strived for acceptance and success—in his family and in the world—and always he had fallen short. During the war he had failed miserably in Kentucky and Missouri, and the Chickasaw Bayou fiasco in December 1862 had resurrected the earlier suspicions that he was crazy. Then after he had placed his faith in Grant, confident that this unassuming man was finally bringing determined purpose to the Union war effort, Grant came close to resigning his commission because of the surprise at Shiloh. But Grant picked himself up, continued pushing forward, and achieved success at Chattanooga and Vicksburg. It could be done, Sherman saw, and he could share in it. Grant gave him the credit he craved and the respect he thought he deserved. During their March 1864 meetings in Louisville and Cincinnati, Grant included him as a valued partner in the planning. They determined to coordinate their offensives. Grant would go after Lee in Virginia, while Sherman would press Joseph E. Johnston in Georgia. They agreed on a logical strategy of going after Confederate armies rather than battling over geographic location. Sherman felt good. The Union war effort was organized; it was proving successful; and he was receiving his just due.[1]

The Confederates, reeling from their Chattanooga repulse and stung by Sherman's Meridian raid, nonetheless remained a formidable foe. Led by Joseph E. Johnston, one of their premier generals, and assisted by such stalwarts as Leonidas Polk, John Bell Hood, Benjamin F. Cheatham, William J. Hardee, and Patrick R. Cleburne (and no longer handicapped by the inept Braxton Bragg), the Army of Tennessee was a powerful opponent. It waited behind strong entrenchments around Dalton, Georgia, some thirty miles from the Union stronghold of Chattanooga. Behind it were Atlanta, a major railroad and manufacturing center of twenty thousand people, and the rich Georgia agricultural food basket. Deep rivers and streams, rough mountains, steep ravines, lush forests, and entangling underbrush provided excellent defensive positions.

Sherman recognized these Confederate advantages. When he visited old friends George H. Thomas, James B. McPherson, and John M. Schofield, the leaders of the Army of the Cumberland at Chattanooga, the Army of the Tennessee at Huntsville, and the Army of the Ohio at Knoxville, he was pleased at the spirit of cooperation he found. He was concerned, however, about the large numbers of soldiers still away on furlough, and he realized that the supply task he faced in any offensive operation against Johnston would be stupendous. No waterway was available for his use, so he had to depend on wagons and an extremely vulnerable railroad.

Sherman had distinct advantages over his rival, Joe Johnston. His friendship with Grant stood in marked contrast to the long-standing feud between Johnston and his superior, Jefferson Davis, dating back to a series of disagreements from the earliest days of the war. Sherman had a hundred thousand confident men under his direct command: Johnston only had fifty thousand (soon to grow to sixty-five thousand), and it was an army that had experienced repeated defeat. Sherman had a plan of action; no one was sure just what Johnston had in mind. Finally, Sherman was to prove himself a logistical genius, whose rear areas of supply and support became so organized that Confederate thrusts had little, if any, impact on them throughout the Atlanta campaign.

The key was the railroad. Sherman worried that Confederate raiders and guerrillas might easily cut the road and shut off his supplies. He told a subordinate that the road had to be defended "if only fifty men have to fight a 1,000." But he had a more fundamental problem. Even without Confederate interference, thirteen hundred tons of goods were required every day to feed and supply his huge force; this meant 130 railroad cars (1,000 in all) daily traveling down the Louisville and Nashville Railroad to Nashville, the Nashville and Chattanooga to Chattanooga, and the Western and Atlantic to Atlanta. There were not enough railroad cars on these roads to do the job, so he decided to commandeer any that came within his jurisdiction. Soon, he exaggeratingly boasted, he could see on his tracks, the " 'Pittsburg & Fort Wayne,' 'Delaware & Lackawanna,' 'Baltimore & Ohio,' and indeed . . . the names of almost every railroad north of the Ohio River."[2]

But even this was not enough. Sherman received permission from Washington to close the roads to anything but military freight. Soldiers marched and horses and cattle were driven, but civilians and their goods were systematically excluded. This included "Sanitary Commissions, Religious orders, and special Charities"—what Sherman called the "pious and curiosity seekers." There was only enough room in the cars for the army's needs; no one else was welcome. Later, he would even prohibit civilian use of army provisions. To drive the urgency across to a Nashville commissary officer, he told him that "if you don't have my army supplied and keep it supplied, we'll eat your mules up, sir—eat your mules up."[3]

Sherman was not totally unreasonable. Mary Ann Bickerdyke, a volunteer charity worker affectionately known to the troops as Mother Bickerdyke, stormed into his headquarters in Chattanooga and demanded he reserve space in his railroad cars for medical supplies from charitable organizations even if he excluded relief workers. Sherman, who had tremendous respect for this hard-driving volunteer (unlike the disdain he held for most such voluntary aides) grumpily tried to ignore her complaints. She pressed home her arguments. "Have some sense about it now, General," she chided, and Sherman burst into laughter. He agreed to allow a regular flow of medical supplies on his strapped railroad, though he continued to refuse to allow any volunteers. The army could take care of its own. He continued to concentrate exclusively on the necessities of the upcoming campaign but was willing to compromise if convinced that his primary focus was not affected.[4]

Sherman worked to get all the furloughed veterans back to their units as quickly as possible. He telegraphed state governors, army officers enjoying their own leaves, and Nathaniel Banks who still had ten thousand of Sherman's men in Louisiana. "By May 1st," he wrote a relative, "I hope to have a host as vast & terrible as Alaric led into Rome's doomed empire." After thorough consultations with all his army commanders, he reorganized the Armies of the Cumberland, Ohio, and Tennessee. He had them strip down to the bare essentials, even to the point of carrying along no tents, commanders and enlisted men alike. At the same time, he shored up defense forces in rear areas to ensure no surprises there from Confederate raiders like Nathan Bedford Forrest. He even asked the judge advocate general for the power to order the death penalty against guerrillas and spies but was unsuccessful. He considered newsmen to be subversives and continued his antipress activities as part of his reorganization efforts.[5]

Sherman worked day and night to get his army organized, dominating the process through the force of his personality and determination. He made it clear that the only matter that counted was preparing completely for the upcoming battles. Everything in the area of his command—and this was, after all, the entire middle of the nation—had to be concentrated on the war effort. He had come to see every Southerner, civilian and soldier, as the enemy; so too he considered every Unionist and every material good to be part of the war effort against the enemy. This ability to see war as total and to organize the vast resources to conduct that war made him the great military commander he showed himself to be that summer. Even before he began maneuvering his huge forces in battle, he had demonstrated military greatness.

While Sherman prepared, the enemy did not lie still. On April 12 Nathan Bedford Forrest's cavalry captured Fort Pillow, above Memphis, and slaughtered its black defenders after they surrendered. An angry Grant fired the Memphis commander and ordered Sherman to conduct a thorough investigation. Meanwhile, Sherman also remained unhappy with Nathaniel Banks's unsuccessful Red River campaign and his failure to return the troops Sherman had lent him for temporary use.[6]

All Sherman's organizing activity, the continued battle to achieve the total effort, was stressful. He ventilated his frustrations, as usual, in the many letters that flowed from the feverish scratchings of his pen. He told his senator brother to be kind to

Grant as he began his campaign in the East, or he would quit "and let you slide into anarchy." He grew increasingly angry at newspaper men, chaplains, nurses, volunteers, and other nonmilitary people who demanded room on his supply trains and vehicles. He resented what he called "the sickly sycophantic meddling of newspaper men, [and] of sanitary & religious humbugs." "Two hundred pounds of powder or oats are worth more to the U.S. than that amount of bottled piety." He continued to insist that the war was not about slaves; it was about the preservation of the Union and order. He maintained that the South would have to be "repeople[d] . . . and the sooner we set about it the better." "To make war," he told the assistant secretary of war, "we must and will harden our hearts." As if to show what he meant, he told steamboat captains in rear areas that anyone caught engaged in anti-Union violence "should be disposed of summarily, viz drowned or killed on the spot." He would let no one or nothing stand in the way of the determined war he planned to wage.[7]

The one consistently and reassuringly satisfying area was his relationship with U. S. Grant. In early April Grant gave Sherman his orders for the upcoming campaign, saying only that Johnston's army was the target and leaving the details to him. Sherman was pleased, exuding confidence in his ability to do the job. He said he would march on Johnston and, given the opportunity, turn on Atlanta. But he promised "ever [to] bear in mind that Johnston is at all times to be kept so busy that he cannot, in any event, send no part of his command against you or Banks."[8]

As the time for the movement drew nearer, Sherman only worked harder to get ready. He expressed feelings of affection for his family, realizing, as always, that his death in combat was a possibility. He wrote to his oldest daughter of the beauty around him: "The leaves are now coming out and the young flowers have begun to bloom. I have gathered a few, which I send in token of my love." He told son Tommy: "Whatever may now happen to me you are old enough to remember me and will take my place. . . . Whatever I do is for you and our country. We must have peace and that can only be had by Battle." He reminisced about Willy with the president of Notre Dame, calling his dead son "a beautiful vision about which clusters and will ever cluster our warmest feelings, binding us all together on this earth in close ties of love and affection." "Believe me always true to you," he told Ellen, "&

mindful of your true affection." As he prepared for what he knew would be one of the greatest events of his life, he reached out to embrace his wife and family.[9]

Annoyingly, reporters and civilian war volunteers continued to insist that his determination to organize everything for the military effort was excessive. They believed that they and their newspapers and supplies deserved a place on army trains and tried to put political pressure on Sherman to get their way. Responding to the outcry, Abraham Lincoln sent a carefully worded inquiry to Sherman wondering if the controversial railroad order might be modified. "I will not change my order," Sherman responded, "and I beg you to be satisfied that the clamor is partly humbug. . . . Every man who is willing to fight and work gets a full ration, and all who won't fight or work should go away, and we offer them free passage in the cars" to leave. Sherman refused to refight an issue that he had settled in his own mind and was no longer debatable. He had to use the railroad exclusively for military use if his army was even to survive, let alone battle Joseph E. Johnston. Anyone who thought otherwise was not worthy of concern.[10]

The Confederate general and his fifty thousand men were entrenched in front of Dalton, Georgia, on an eight-hundred-foot-high ridge known as Rocky Face. The Western and Atlantic Railroad pierced this ridge at Buzzard's Roost, but the Confederates had this opening well covered. They similarly protected Dug Gap, a much narrower cut. A frontal attack on the ridge or either of these openings would be suicidal, so Sherman decided on an approach he was to follow throughout the campaign: a wide flanking movement to sweep around and try to get behind his enemy's fortifications. And as he was to do consistently in the future, he placed Schofield's 13,000-man Army of the Ohio on the left of his line; Thomas's 60,000-man Army of the Cumberland in the center, and McPherson's 24,500-man Army of the Tennessee on the right. Schofield and Thomas were to demonstrate against Johnston's right and center, while McPherson made a wide swing for Snake Creek Gap, another opening in the ridge, south of Dalton.

It was a brilliant plan and caught Johnston completely off guard. McPherson reached Snake Creek Gap on May 8 and pushed through to within a mile of Resaca, a town eighteen miles south of Dalton on the Atlantic and Western Railroad. There he ran into four thousand Confederates and worried that Johnston might send reinforcements and cut him off from the rest of the army. He fell back on Snake Creek Gap and dug in. Johnston quickly realized what had happened and shifted his entire army into strong positions in front of Resaca, blocking the major part of Sherman's army, which had also moved there. In the process, however, Johnston had abandoned Dalton.

The two armies dug in, Sherman riding the line to evaluate the situation. "Take it easy to-day," he told some troops, "for you will have work enough to-morrow. It will be quick done, though." And it was. After several bloody attacks by both sides on May 14 and 15, Johnston once more found himself in danger of being flanked and retreated.[11]

Sherman had flanked his opponent out of his strong defensive position on Rocky Face and had gained a significant amount of Georgia territory. Still, Sherman expressed deep disappointment that McPherson had not pushed through Snake Creek Gap to Resaca, believing that if he had, the Union army would have trapped Johnston and decimated his force. "Well, Mac, you have missed the great opportunity of your life," he told his subordinate. McPherson insisted that such an action would have been foolhardy and might have resulted in a Union disaster. He was wrong. Having gained the momentum, he should have pressed on before Johnston had a chance to recover. He did not, and Sherman was justified in being upset over a missed opportunity.[12]

As Johnston retreated from Resaca the night of May 15, Sherman drove his troops in pursuit and forced constant skirmishing on the Confederates. Johnston moved toward Calhoun but found it an unsuitable place for effective defense and pushed on toward Adairsville, which he also found wanting when he arrived there on May 17. At Kingston, farther south, the railroad turned east toward Cassville. Sherman followed along a broad front, using every road available to him, concentrating when he thought Johnston was preparing to make a stand.

Johnston thought he could take advantage of this situation. He noted that there were two roads between Adairsville and Cassville and was certain Sherman would divide his troops to utilize both. Johnston hoped to attack one force and defeat it before the other could come to its aid. Unfortunately, John Bell Hood, who had been criticizing Johnston for lack of aggressiveness, allowed a small Union force behind him to keep him from attacking. The Confederates could do nothing but keep moving south of the Etowah River, where they prepared to take on the pursuing Federals. It was May 19.

Twice during this time and on numerous other occasions during this campaign, Sherman came close to death. At Adairsville, he was at the head of Thomas's column and attracted artillery fire that killed several horses and wounded a staff member near him. At Cassville, Sherman and Thomas were out with the skirmish line trying to evaluate the terrain and saw small arms fire "cutting the leaves of the trees thickly" all around them. They decided that was no place for generals and hurried back to a nearby battery.[13]

With Johnston dug in at Cassville, Sherman once again maneuvered for advantage. Johnston was shocked when Hood and Polk told him that they were convinced some Union artillery could enfilade a part of the Confederate line. Johnston ordered another retreat, this time some fourteen miles farther southeast to the Allatoona Pass. Confederate troops were now only thirty miles from Atlanta.[14]

Sherman's well-oiled military machine seemed to be functioning without a sputter. While he had been pressuring Johnston's army, Union general Jeff C. Davis had taken the important city of Rome, Georgia. Crews were repairing the railroad line to Resaca, and this city now became the forward supply point. Army morale was higher than ever, and in Washington Abraham Lincoln and his administration were excited, Edwin Stanton telegraphing "the admiration of the President, of the Department and of all loyal people." Thomas Ewing, Jr., thought his brother-in-law was "on the path to glory and stands a first rate chance of being the Hero of the War." Even Sherman remained uncharacteristically optimistic. "I think I have the best army in the country," he boasted to Ellen, "and if I can't take Atlanta and stir up Georgia considerably I am mistaken."[15]

Union soldiers were already making their mark on the countryside, and when Sherman conducted his usual personal reconnaissance in the Cassville area, he showed that his determination to fight a total war did not preclude his genuine affection for the people in his path. He stopped at a small plantation house and had a friendly conversation with an old woman inside. "Well, have the boys taken much from you?" Sherman asked. "Almost all I have," she answered. "Sherman was here; he is a right nice un; the poor man said he was hungry; so I got him something to eat." "Sherman" said his men needed food too, the woman continued, so he took even more, "but he left me something he called a purtection paper." At this she pulled out a rumpled scrap and handed it to Sherman. It read: "Sergeant Take-them-all gives general protection to this poor, lone widow, with her husband in the army, and to her helpless chickens and roosters; that is, what's left of them." All the soldiers who read this "purtection," she said, just "laughed at it; it 'pears like they have drefful little respect for their general." "I am afraid so, madam. If you give me some paper I'll write one they won't laugh at." "And are you an officer?" "Yes, ma'am."[16]

As a young lieutenant, Sherman had explored the area where he was now fighting. While working with the inspector general in the 1840s, he had ridden around the Etowah River region, had climbed Kennesaw Mountain, and had passed through Allatoona Gap. He knew from that experience just how formidable Allatoona was, so he never considered a frontal attack on Johnston there. He decided to give his men a few days rest and then maneuvered them away from the railroad. With twenty days' supplies in his wagons and on his men's backs, he sent his army on a wide flanking movement to his right toward Dallas, fourteen miles beyond the Etowah River and an equal distance from the railroad at Allatoona Gap. By taking Dallas, he would force Johnston to abandon Allatoona in order to block this threat on Atlanta itself. He was confident Johnston would soon be retreating behind the Chattahoochee River.[17]

The movement, which began on May 23, proved to be a nightmare. The terrain was full of dense forest and underbrush, deep ravines and steep hills, a few half-cleared farms, and innumerable streams bordered by quicksand. The rains began on May 25, turning the mediocre roads into slippery bogs. "The soldiers became so bespattered with mud," Sherman later remembered, "that we could scarcely distinguish friend from foe." To make matters worse, Johnston discovered Sherman's strategy and shifted his army to meet his advance. The Federals intercepted a Confederate dispatch, so they were not shocked when they had to fight three days of fierce clashes at New Hope Church near Dallas.

So many soldiers were killed and maimed that the men referred to the area as "Hell-Hole."[18]

At Pickett's Mill, as Sherman tried to turn the Confederate right, sixteen hundred Federals fell during an attack on the Confederate position, inflicting only five hundred casualties in return. Sherman then began shifting McPherson's Army of the Tennessee, which was located on the Union right, to the east (toward the left), in order to fill some gaps and then move his entire force back to the railroad and his supplies. Progress was slow; Johnston kept pressure on McPherson. On June 3, however, all of Sherman's forces had moved east and reached Acworth and the railroad below Allatoona.

Throughout the constant skirmishing that made up this Dallas movement, Sherman was all over the battlefield, sharing the dangers with his men. He and a number of his officers in the Army of the Tennessee came under fire while conversing on May 30. A minié ball tore through John A. Logan's sleeve and hit another officer in the chest, its force fortunately blunted by the diary he always carried.[19] Sherman seemed fearless in the face of such danger. Throughout the war, his family had and would repeatedly warn him to keep his head down, and soldiers on the scene did likewise. He ignored them all and braved shot and shell. Consequently, he had little sympathy for those who were not equally courageous. One day during the Dallas stalemate while seeking shelter from some particularly heavy shelling, Sherman heard a soldier crouching behind a nearby tree crying out every time a shell burst nearby. "O Lord! O Lord! if I get out of this, I'll never be caught again. O, dear! O, dear! . . . I know I'll be killed!" To scare the skulker even more, Sherman began throwing rocks against the tree. "That's hard firing, my man," yelled Sherman. "Hard! O, it's fearful. I think thirty shells struck this tree while I was here." When the firing stopped and the soldier saw it was General Sherman yelling at him, this realization frightened him more than the bombardment. He ran back to his command. Later, Sherman issued a special order condemning all skulkers and deserters, warning of "instant death or the harshest labor and treatment."[20]

Sherman demanded of his men what he asked of himself and the nation as a whole: a no-holds-barred effort. He loved his soldiers, and they loved him, but if they failed to produce what he demanded of them, he had no compunction about disciplining them. Their job was to risk their lives for victory; anything less was unacceptable. For his part of the bargain, he tried not to put their lives in danger unnecessarily.

The longer this campaign of maneuver lasted, the more impatient Sherman became. He complained to Ellen on June 1 that "we are still hammering away but not making as much progress as I could wish." His army had bogged down into constant skirmishing and now seemed to be progressing by the foot instead of the mile. He was particularly upset with Thomas's army, "which is dreadfully slow. A fresh furrow in a plowed field will stop the whole column, and all will begin to entrench," he complained to Halleck. Despite his impatience, Sherman had actually achieved another important victory. Once again he had flanked Johnston out of a formidable defensive position and had moved still closer to Atlanta.[21]

What particularly bothered him, however, was that these victories seemed to be weakening his army, while Johnston appeared to be maintaining his strength. He estimated that he had inflicted 8,700 casualties on Johnston's 65,000-man army while suffering 9,300 to his 100,000 man force, a highly favorable ratio. But as he took more and more territory, he had greater and greater manpower problems. He had to leave garrisons at Dalton, Kingston, Rome, Resaca, and now Allatoona Pass to prevent their recapture. "I am fully aware that these detachments weaken me in the exact proportion our enemy has gained strength by picking up his detachments." And the thin railroad supply line grew longer and ever more susceptible to disruption. Sherman knew he was winning, all right, but how long could he survive such victories? "Johnston has managed to skillfully keep up the spirit of his army and people by representing his retreat as strategy . . . [despite the fact] he has abandoned to us the best wheat-growing region of Georgia and all its most valuable iron-works and foundries."[22]

Guerrillas and raiders in Tennessee, Mississippi, and Kentucky were also troublesome. On June 10 Nathan Bedford Forrest defeated a Union force under Samuel Sturgis at Brice's Cross Roads in Mississippi. Sherman grew so apprehensive about Forrest that he ordered General A. J. Smith, who had been belatedly released by Nathaniel Banks, to cancel orders to cooperate with Henry Slocum in a movement against Mobile, Alabama, and instead go after Forrest. Smith obeyed and on July 13, 14, and 15 defeated the Confederate raider who was under Stephen D. Lee's command at Tupelo, Mississippi.[23] Then he retreated back to Memphis.

The guerrilla situation in Kentucky remained muddled. Sherman wrote General S. G. Burbridge there and told him to take severe action. He said all military officials were to recognize "that guerrillas are not robbers, but wild beasts, unknown to the usages of war." Since civil government could not deal with them, he said, "to prevent anarchy, 'which nature abhors,' the military steps in, and is rightful, constitutional and lawful." Anyone helping a partisan should be arrested and when three or four hundred had been collected, they should be shipped down the Mississippi River and colonized in some distant land. "I do not object to men and women having what they call 'Southern feelings' if confined to love of country and of peace, honor, and security, and even if little family pride; but these become 'crime' when enlarged to mean a love of war, desolation, famine, and all the horrid attendants of anarchy."[24]

Success against another purveyor of anarchy in Sherman's eyes, the press, made up for Sherman's frustration with the Kentucky guerrillas. On May 20, just two weeks into this military campaign, he had issued a harsh antipress circular encouraging soldiers to write home but insisting that reporters had to be kept away because they and the information they printed were "dangerous to the army and to our cause." He stirred up a hornet's nest of protest but stood his ground, believing he was "exactly right." The press had to be kept out to ensure military success; his Kentucky experience and the Thomas Knox court-martial had convinced him of that. "The paucity of news from the army at this time in Northern papers is most satisfactory to me." Still, as he had during the Meridian raid, Sherman allowed the *New York Herald*'s De B. Randolph Keim, James B. McPherson's friend, to travel with his army. When this reporter publicized the Federal success in breaking the Confederate signal code, Sherman became furious and ordered his arrest.[25]

He was increasingly concerned with state agents' recruiting freed slaves for the Union army. Northern states unwilling to fulfill their draft quotas with skilled workmen needed in the booming war industries sent recruiters into the South to gather prospective soldiers from among fugitive slaves. Sherman saw these agents as prejudicial to order and demanded that they stay away. Like the newsmen and civilian volunteers, Northern politicians similarly bombarded Lincoln. The president personally asked Sherman for his cooperation. Sherman acquiesced but in a fit of pique in late July wrote a Massachusetts recruiter a stinging letter of protest. When it was published, Sherman's racist views became public. Blacks should be used as laborers, such as in units he had established for digging entrenchments, but he was convinced they were useless as soldiers. "It is an insult to our Race to count them as part of the [draft] quota," he indicated another time. "A nigger is not a white man, and all the Psalm singing on earth won't make him so." Despite the years of combat against the Confederacy, Sherman, like most of his soldiers, maintained the racial views of a Southern slaveholder.[26]

Raiders, reporters, and recruiters were nuisances, but Johnston's army was still the main problem, and it was still at large. Sherman was confident that since Johnston had abandoned Allatoona Gap, he would immediately fall behind the Chattahoochee River. Instead, Johnston dug in his army on Kennesaw Mountain, Lost Mountain, and Pine Mountain, the three forming what Sherman called "a triangle. Pine Mountain, the apex, Kennesaw Mountain and Lost Mountain the base, covering perfectly the town of Marietta, and the railroad back to the Chattahoochie." The June 8 arrival of Frank Blair and the nine-thousand-man Seventeenth Corps replaced Sherman's losses, so Sherman was able to press forward with renewed strength. On June 10 he moved his army forward to Big Shanty on the Western and Atlantic Railroad close to Kennesaw, delaying long enough for the railroad to be repaired down to his position.[27]

He began to test the Confederate entrenchments, suspecting Johnston's lines were stretched too thin. Sure enough, Johnston gave up Pine Mountain on June 15 and Lost Mountain on June 16. On the twentieth, he shrank his lines again, making Sherman think he was withdrawing to the Chattahoochee. In fact, Johnston was concentrating his lines for better defense. Sherman was disappointed to find his rival now firmly entrenched on Kennesaw Mountain.[28]

As Sherman studied the Confederate positions, he knew from his 1840 explorations that he had a major problem. The seven-hundred-foot-high Kennesaw Mountain commanded the surrounding countryside, providing Johnston with a superb view of Federal activities below. His entrenchments were characteristically formidable. Both sides had, in fact, become experts at throwing up defense works, and the ones on Kennesaw were state-of-the-art examples of the craft. "A line of heavy saplings, set with four rows of sharpened stakes" first greeted any attacker. "Next. An intricate network of young trees that had been a standing thicket but were now hacked on one side, bent forward and held in place by heavy stakes driven crosswise in the ground, while all the limbs were trimmed to sharp points." Behind all these impediments were a series of earth and log embankments, so high that only the defenders' eyes could be seen. Tied into the terrain, these defense works were virtually impregnable.[29]

Sherman repeatedly rode his lines. He studied the terrain, and he pored over his maps looking for some weakness. The driving rain had turned the roads into quagmires, making flanking movements extremely difficult even if he could make one under the watchful eyes of the Confederate sentinels on the mountain. A frontal assault made no sense either. The defenses were too strong, and that was not Sherman's style. As early as June 5, he said: "I will not run head on his fortifications." He made a similar comment on June 9: "I will not run hot-headed against any works prepared for us." On June 13 he insisted: "We cannot risk the heavy losses of an assault at this distance from our base."[30]

By June 16 Sherman was having second thoughts. The more he analyzed the situation, the more he came to believe that a frontal assault might be the best move: "[I] am now inclined to feign on both flanks and assault the center. It may cost us dear but in results would surpass an attempt to pass around." He had to do something, but both a flanking movement and a frontal assault had "difficulties and dangers." What finally convinced him to attack straight ahead was his perception "that the enemy and our own officers had settled down into a conviction that I would not assault fortified lines. . . . I wanted, therefore, for the moral effect to make a successful assault against the enemy behind his breast-works."[31]

Sherman's plan was not an attack along the entire line. His June 24 order was for division-size units to punch two holes through the Confederate defense line, drive some two and a half miles toward the railroad below Marietta, and thus allow his entire force to defeat the three isolated Confederate segments. On June 27 Thomas was to assault a point of his choosing in the center; McPherson was to feign an attack against Johnston's right and actually hit a point south of the mountain; Schofield was to demonstrate on Johnston's left and threaten his rear. Sherman hoped Johnston would be taken in by these ruses and move troops to his flanks so the frontal attacks would work. If they did, Sherman would win a great victory; if he failed, the casualties would be heavy but not devastating.[32]

The attack was a colossal failure. Despite the terrain, the entrenchments, and the hundred-degree heat, the Federals were able to get within several feet of the Confederate line in places, but they could not break through. Officers and men fell in droves—some three thousand Federals and eight hundred Confederates in all. "I never saw so many broken down and exhausted men in my life," a Southern soldier said after the battle. "I was sick as a horse, and as wet with blood and sweat as I could be, and many of our men were vomiting with excessive fatigue, overexhaustion and sunstroke; our tongues were parched and cracked for water and our faces were blackened with powder and smoke, and our dead and wounded were piled indiscriminately in the trenches."[33]

Sherman poured out his distress in a letter to a Southern woman he had known as a little girl on Sullivan's Island outside Charleston. "My heart bleeds when I see the carnage of Battle, the desolation of homes, the bitter anguish of families," he said, but he had to go on so "our common country should not perish in infamy and dishonor." The war "has assumed proportions at which even we in the hurly burly sometimes stand aghast." He told Ellen: "It is enough to make the whole world start at the awful amount of death and destruction that now stalks abroad. Daily for the past two months has the work progressed and I see no signs of a remission till one or both and all the armies are destroyed, when I suppose the balance of the people will tear each other up. . . . I begin to regard the death and mangling of a couple thousand men as a small affair, a kind of morning dash—and it may be well that we become so hardened."[34]

He had to proceed, despite the carnage. He asked Thomas whether his men could attack again, and the weary general sighed:

273

"One or two more such assaults will use up this army." Sherman understood and turned once more to flanking. Schofield's demonstration had been more successful than expected, and he had placed several brigades across Olley Creek and was threatening Johnston's rear. Sherman now ordered McPherson to swing behind Thomas and Schofield and reach for the Chattahoochee. Johnston saw no alternative. He pulled off Kennesaw on July 2. The next morning, Sherman watched through a telescope as a single skirmisher slowly made his way up the mountain until "he stood upon the very crest." "Though he was four miles away," Sherman said, "I could seemingly hear him call to his comrades, 'Come along.' "[35]

Sherman had done it again. He had once more forced Johnston out of a strong position. This time, he had paid a major price, one that would be held to critical scrutiny. Significantly, however, he never questioned himself, insisting as late as 1881: "I then believed and still believe we ought to have broken that line." Unlike Kentucky and Chickasaw Bayou and all the other times in his life when defeat had caused him to fear failure and become depressed, this time he maintained his confidence. "Had the assault been made with one-fourth more vigor," he said, his troops would have broken through. "We lost nothing in morale by the assault," he wrote Grant.[36]

In truth, Sherman had committed a military sin: impatience. He wanted to achieve the climactic victory and end the drawn-out campaign right then. So, like Lee at Gettysburg and most other Civil War generals throughout the war, he opted for a futile frontal attack. The result was disastrous. He could instead have waited for the rain-soaked roads to dry and sent McPherson on another of his successful flanking movements. That was what he did after the failure of the direct assault. The Union attack was hardly "murderous, cruel, and wholly unjustifiable," as one of Sherman's generals later spitefully insisted, but it certainly was unwise. And though he never admitted it, Sherman had to know deep in his heart that he had been wrong. After Kennesaw, the lessons of the Meridian campaign had to be even more cogent.[37]

Johnston's army remained on the loose and continuing to head south toward the Chattahoochee River. Sherman was convinced that Johnston would never dare dig in with the river at his back. Consequently he rushed his troops forward, hoping to catch his adversary in disarray crossing the waterway. When he entered Marietta and found part of the Union cavalry jammed up in the city streets, he let loose a torrent of expletives at Kenner Garrard, its leader; he tried to swear him and his horse soldiers forward, furious that Johnston might be getting away across the water.

Actually, Johnston had moved only four miles out of Marietta to tiny Smyrna Camp Ground. There, on the Fourth of July, Sherman found O. O. Howard's soldiers, a part of Thomas's army, proceeding slowly because of fear of Confederate entrenchments. "Howard," Sherman said, "you are mistaken; there is no force in your front; they are laughing at you!" "Well, General, let us see," Howard answered skeptically and ordered some skirmishers forward. They were met with vicious musket and artillery fire, and Sherman was forced to admit his mistake. He brought up his entire force and began flanking again. Johnston pulled back once more, Sherman even more convinced he was planning to make an immediate river crossing.[38]

Once again Sherman was disappointed. Johnston pulled back only three miles to a position along the near bank of the river secretly prepared by Brigadier General Francis A. Shoup, a Northern-born West Point Confederate. It was a seemingly impregnable bastion in this campaign of strong fortifications, a six-mile flat horseshoe protecting the railroad bridge with both flanks anchored to the river. Less than ten miles away lay what one Union officer described as the "domes and minarets and spires" of Atlanta. He noted Sherman and Thomas riding up and silently observing the vista, "Sherman stepping nervously about, his eyes sparkling and his face aglow—casting a single glance at Atlanta, another at the River, and a dozen at the surrounding valley to see where he would best cross the River, how he best could flank them."[39]

Sherman was not about to repeat his Kennesaw Mountain mistake; there would be no direct assault on Johnston's fortress. Instead, Sherman looked to river crossings near Roswell sixteen miles upstream and Soap Creek only about ten miles distant. While Howard and McPherson tried to keep the Confederates busy, Schofield sent a division across the river at Soap Creek with such stealth that they made it without a single casualty. Garrard and his cavalry captured Roswell with its factories and female operatives. Sherman created a controversy when he had the women sent away in order to militarize the town. According to one Union soldier, the women he helped guard were happy to be leaving the war area. "Some of them are tough and it's a hard job to keep them straight and to keep the men away from them," he said. Later stories would develop around alleged brutalities to these women, but no convincing facts bear these tales out.[40]

With Union troops across the river, Johnston had no choice but to cross the waterway and enter the outer defenses of Atlanta. On July 9 he left behind his flanked fortress. A jubilant Sherman joined his men in jumping nude into the river to wash away two months of campaign grime. There he stood up to his waist in the water chatting with a teamster sitting atop his braying mule. "Great chance for the boys to get cleaned up for Atlanta," he said, while a watching soldier whispered to a friend what all the soldiers had come to feel: "I'd follow Uncle Billy to hell." Sherman did not hear the comment, but he felt good about himself, too. "I have brought this army to the Banks of the Chattahoochee 130 miles from Chattanooga and no part of it has been a day without ample supplies of food, ammunition[,] clothing and all that is essential." Inside Atlanta, people were beginning to worry. The petulant insistence of the city's press that Sherman was surviving only because he was not fighting fairly (flanking instead of standing and slugging it out) had an increasingly hollow ring.[41]

Sherman did not cross the Chattahoochee immediately. From July 10 to 15, he let his men rest and prepare themselves for the hard fighting that lay ahead. He brought forward his supplies and solidified his forces. He sent his army forward on July 17, the main body reaching Peach Tree Creek, and Garrard's cavalry cutting the railroad east of the city. As Sherman pressed his men forward, Grant warned him, mistakenly it turned out, that Johnston was gathering reinforcements. Rumors also spread that Johnston was in danger of being relieved. A Union picket tried to find out. "Hello, Johnny, who's your commander now?" he asked. A Confederate called back, "Sherman." "How's that?" the Federal said. "Well, when you move we move."[42]

The rumors proved accurate. On July 17 Jefferson Davis, frustrated at the constant backward movement of his long-time antagonist Joe Johnston, fired him in favor of corps commander John Bell Hood. Sherman learned the news in an Atlanta newspaper he read in the shade of a persimmon tree behind his lines. He asked John Schofield, who along with McPherson and Howard had attended West Point with Hood, what sort of person the new commander was. Schofield said "he was bold even to rashness, and courageous in the extreme." Sherman knew what that meant; he could expect no more Confederate retreats. He warned all his commanders to be ready for an attack, stating, "Each army commander will accept battle on anything like fair terms."[43]

Union troops did not have long to wait. The next day, trying to take advantage of a gap in the Union line between Schofield and Thomas, Hood ordered an attack. The plan looked promising, but lack of coordination delayed the assault and allowed Thomas to move all his forces across Peach Tree Creek and into position. Union forces then beat back the Confederates and inflicted heavy losses on them. The battle of Peach Tree Creek was an inauspicious debut for Hood. He fell back into the final defenses surrounding Atlanta—the landscape denuded of vegetation and buildings for a thousand yards to the front to provide a clear field of fire.

Though severely bloodied, Hood was not discouraged. Like Robert E. Lee, whom he admired and tried to emulate and because Davis had appointed him to fight, Hood gave no thought to defense. He launched another furious attack on July 22, this time on McPherson's army east of Atlanta. Again there was Confederate confusion, and the major part of the attack came not on McPherson's flank and rear as intended but against prepared Union lines. The battle raged furiously, the Confederates giving the Army of the Tennessee a serious scare, but Sherman was so confident it would win that he sent no reinforcements from Thomas or Schofield. The Confederate attack failed, and once again the rebels suffered heavy losses. The Battle of Atlanta was another bloody defeat for Hood.

Sherman suffered a serious loss himself. His close friend and leading subordinate James B. McPherson was killed during the battle when he stumbled upon some Confederate soldiers on a road he thought was safe. His body was returned to headquarters, and Sherman cried over his fallen comrade as he tried to keep directing the battle still in progress. He sent McPherson's body to his Ohio home for full military honors. That night he tried to deal with the shock. He told an aide: "I expected something to happen to Grant and me, either the Rebels or the newspapers would kill us both, and I looked to McPherson as the man to follow us and finish the war."[44]

The next day, as a unit of Union soldiers was recovering from the previous day's fighting, the men heard cheering in the distance. They saw General Sherman and his aides come riding up. They too cheered their commander wildly, many throwing their hats in the air in celebration of their recent victories. Sherman removed his own hat and facing the men silenced them for a few moments. He thanked them for their good work and grieved over McPherson's death. Then he rode on to the next unit, and the cheering continued until it faded off over the long length of the Federal line.[45]

Sherman had an even more difficult task than grieving with the army. He had to write to McPherson's fiancée in Baltimore. He had written her once before, and the memory of this first letter must have made his second one even more difficult to compose. In the spring McPherson had told Sherman that he wanted a furlough to marry his beloved Emily, but Sherman had to refuse because of the upcoming campaign. He had written Emily asking: "Would you have us to leave the Rudder of the Ship in the midst of the Angry Sea of War?" Of course not. He counseled patience, saying that when the day of her wedding to McPherson arrived, Emily would "regard him with a high respect & honor that . . . [would] convert simple love into something sublime and beautiful."

With McPherson dead, there would be no wedding day, so all Sherman could do was tell Emily what a fine soldier her fiancé had been and that he would be missed. As for her loss, he wrote: "Better the Bride of McPherson dead, than the wife of the richest Merchant of Baltimore." His words may have strengthened an already existing depression. Emily remained secluded in her room for an entire year and never married.[46]

When Ellen heard of McPherson's death, she also reacted strongly because it brought back all the anguish she and Cump had felt over Willy's passing. The boy had spent his last free day at McPherson's house in Vicksburg. Sherman must have had the same thoughts; losing his favorite son and his favorite colleague in the same year were two horrible shocks.[47]

When McPherson fell in battle, John A. Logan, the southern

Illinois politician turned general, took his place as commander of the Army of the Tennessee. Logan, an excellent corps commander, did an outstanding job when pressed into service as leader of the Army of the Tennessee. He seemed the logical choice for permanent command. Sherman was not so sure as he discussed the matter with George H. Thomas. His old friend threatened to resign if Logan was named. ("If there was a man on earth whom Thomas hated, it was Logan," Sherman later remembered.) Sherman pressed the matter, and Thomas backed off, but Sherman used Thomas's opposition as a good excuse for not choosing Logan, a politican and non–West Pointer. He settled on O. O. Howard, another corps commander and a West Point graduate. When Sherman asked Howard if he would accept such an assignment, Howard reminded Sherman that Joseph Hooker, another corps commander and the former leader of the Army of the Potomac, had seniority. Sherman responded sharply: "Hooker has not the moral qualities that I want—not those adequate to the command; but if you don't want promotion, there are plenty who do." Oh no, Howard replied, he would do anything asked of him. He took McPherson's place.[48]

Logan was disappointed, but Sherman sent him a warm letter on the day Howard received command, and Logan loyally went back to his corps and remained an effective officer, though harboring a grudge into the postwar years. Hooker was more immediately vindictive. He angrily resigned his post. When he reached the North, he insisted that Sherman had made a mess of the Atlanta campaign, and people should expect to hear of a serious setback soon. Sherman ignored the tirade and replaced Hooker with Henry W. Slocum.[49]

Sherman rode out these storms of rank and ego. By July 25, he was plotting how he might finish Hood, planning another flanking movement for two days later. The Army of the Tennessee, now under Howard, would move from its position on the Union left and extend the Union line on the right toward the junction of the Macon and Western and the Atlanta and West Point railroads at Eastpoint. At the same time, Federal cavalry would cut the Macon Road some twenty miles from Atlanta. Sherman also agreed to allow cavalry leader George Stoneman to take his unit to rescue Union prisoners at Andersonville Prison after completing his railroad wrecking task.

Hood discovered these Federal intentions and sent Joseph Wheeler's cavalry after Sherman's cavalry and prepared his infantry to meet Howard. Poor coordination of his forces at Ezra Church once again caused Hood to suffer heavy losses. His cavalry, however, stymied the Union horsemen, and George Stoneman and his cavalry never reached Andersonville. They were incarcerated at Macon.

The fighting at Peach Tree Creek, Atlanta, and Ezra Church was disastrous for the Confederates. Yet Union troops were still outside Atlanta looking in, and the rebel army was still defiant inside. "How many men have you fellows got left?" yelled out a Federal. "About enough for another killin," responded a Confederate. The campaign now settled down into a siege, with Union artillery bombarding the increasingly emptying city. No part of the metropolis seemed safe from Union shells, and because storage areas and other military targets were interspersed with residential areas, shells were landing on houses not previously leveled or damaged by Confederate military activity.[50]

Although matters were going so well, Sherman could not allow himself to feel at ease yet. He worried about soldiers leaving when their enlistments ran out, and he worried that Lincoln and the federal government would fail to enforce an upcoming draft. If adequate replacements were not forthcoming, Hood would win out by outwaiting him.[51]

He expressed his frustration once again in his correspondence. He wrote the governor of Minnesota a scathing letter in response to the governor's complaint about a particularly touchy subject: Sherman's refusal to give a railroad pass to a Minnesota medical commissioner. Sherman reminded the governor that the Union army depended on a single railroad for supplies. "I must accuse you of heartless cruelty to your constituents. . . . You would take the very bread and meat out of your soldiers' mouths that a State Inspector might come & supervise the acts of other medical officers here on the spot commissioned by yourself." He similarly lectured the governor of Kentucky who had complained about martial law in his state. "Have we not, as a people," he queried, "been more forebearing than any people on earth? Did we not bear the taunts and insults of these secessionists until forbearance was cowardice? Have they not tried to coerce you into rebellion and did they not begin to burn the houses of Union men in Kentucky, and carry off the slaves of Union men in Kentucky, when I, poor innocent, would not let a soldier take a green apple, or a fence rail to make a cup of coffee? Why! we have not yet caught up with our friends in the South in this respect for private rights. . . . I pledge my honor when the South ceases its strife, sends its members to Congress, and appeals to the courts for its remedy and not to 'horrid war,' I will be the open advocate for mercy and a restoration to home, and peace, and happiness of all who have lost them by my acts." But as long as the war was on, he said, he would use every harsh measure to try to end it.[52]

Sherman sent similar words to an old friend in Alabama. Yes, he was leading an army of destruction into Georgia, but he was the same person this man had known in 1844 "with as warm a heart as ever, and anxious that peace and plenty shall prevail in this land." If the South would return to the Union "and settle by argument and reason the questions growing out of slavery, instead of trying to divide our country into two angry halves, to quarrel and fight to the end of time," he would "strip himself naked, and my wife and child stark naked." But as it was, he had to battle anarchy, and he would continue to do so until the nation was safe.[53]

These letters vented Sherman's frustrations, and he seemed to be at peace with himself. At his headquarters, with some tent-flies for sleeping and a couple wall tents for offices, he was relaxed and informal. He wore the same clothes he had worn since Chattanooga: a gray flannel shirt, faded blue coat, and military trousers. He had a makeshift table made from a packing crate and sat on a cracker barrel or a simple camp stool. He ate hardtack, bacon, sweet potatoes, and coffee, topped off by cigars and lively conversation. Sherman maintained his simple life-style, though he was now a confident, demanding, controlling, conquering general.[54]

He tried to decide on his next move. Extending his lines any farther toward the Macon and Western railroad would be dangerous, so as he rode the lines, he thought the matter over, "his tall form bent forward until his long nose was 'hob-nobbing' with the horse's ears, looking neither right nor left, evidently deeply absorbed in his own thoughts." Usually when he rode by, he was raising himself up in his stirrups trying to get a good view of the terrain around him. Now he seemed to know the surroundings; he had to decide what to do about them.[55]

He made his decision. He would leave Henry W. Slocum's corps to defend the Chattahoochee bridge and with sixty-thousand men march from his supply line again and "make a circuit of devastation around the town, with a radius of fifteen or twenty miles." If he was cut off from his base of supplies, he warned his superiors, he would march his army to Saint Mark's, Florida, or Savannah, Georgia.[56]

Circumstances quickly changed his mind. He learned that the Confederate cavalry had swung behind him and was attempting to wreck havoc on his supply line. He was confident that garrisons in a series of blockhouses along the railroad could handle the threat and sent his own cavalry to protect his immediate flanks. New cavalry leader Judson Kilpatrick so impressed Sherman that he canceled his plan for the destructive circuit and decided instead to send the cavalry toward the railroad at Jonesboro. "If the cavalry can do what we want," he decided, "there is no need of moving the whole army." Kilpatrick rode all around Atlanta and destroyed railroad tracks near Jonesboro. Within a few days, however, the damage was repaired, and Sherman's anticavalry prejudice was reinforced. He would have to do the job with his infantry after all; he fell back on his original plan.[57]

On August 25, 1864, as Sherman withdrew troops from their entrenchments to march toward Jonesboro, Confederates in the city thought he was retreating; Wheeler must have broken his supply line. They were sure they had won a great victory. As the troops marched, Sherman paced "back and forth in front of his tent, with his hands thrust into his pockets and his eyes bent on the ground, apparently lost in deep thought." He quickly stopped worrying, however, because Union troops were systematically destroying Atlanta's last rail connection with the outside world, beating back William Hardee's corps in the process. The destruction was handled with precision. A regiment marched to the tracks and deployed alongside; the rails were disconnected where the last man on each end of the regiment was standing; the regiment then threw over the rails, ties, and all; they made a pile of the ties, placed the rails across, and started a fire. When the rails began to glow in the middle, the men twisted them so that they could not be straightened without special machinery.[58]

Such destruction made Hood's tenure in Atlanta increasingly tenuous. Sherman told Schofield, "The orders are always to attack. We don't care about Jonesborough [sic], but we want to destroy our enemy." It looked as though he would have his chance. With the city encircled and isolated, Hood exploded and burned all his magazines and left the city to join Hardee's corps at Lovejoy's Station, a few miles below Jonesboro. Slocum and the corps Sherman had left behind to protect the Chattahoochee bridge entered Atlanta, and all thoughts of destroying Hood departed. "We don't care about pushing the enemy any further at this time," he told Howard. "Had we prevented his making entrenchments it would have been well, but, as he has a strong line, I do not wish to waste lives by an assault." He informed Halleck that "Atlanta is ours, and fairly won."[59]

Sherman's decision to spare Hood was ignored in the euphoria over Atlanta's capture. Sherman never doubted that he had done the right thing. In his mid-September campaign report, he said: "The object of my movement against the railroad was therefore already reached and concluded, and as it was idle to pursue our enemy in that wooded country with a view to his capture, I gave orders on the 4th for the army to prepare to move back slowly to Atlanta." It was a mistake. The Confederate army, which had, after all, been his primary objective, was allowed to escape, capable of fighting once more. Clearly Sherman did not want to cause more death and mayhem, satisfied that his capture of Atlanta had given him a major military victory. He was correct, but it was not the victory he might have achieved. He might have destroyed Hood's force and rendered the entire theater of war defenseless. But Sherman abhorred bloodshed, and Kennesaw showed him in graphic terms how much carnage battle could cause.[60]

Sherman's decision to avoid a bloody clash ensured the tremendous success of his campaign. He had kept a huge force tied down, inflicted heavy losses on it, outmaneuvered two of the Confederacy's leading generals, and captured its so-called Gate City. Atlanta was one of the most important Union victories of the war. Not only was it the capture of a major railroad and manufacturing center, but it gave Abraham Lincoln the impetus to hold on to the presidency in the November election.

Despite his huge success, Sherman displayed no more egotism now than he had in camp during the campaign. On September 7, when he arrived in Atlanta, there was "no beating of drums, no flaunting of colors, no firing of salutes, to humble the pride of the conquered." Sherman and his staff quietly rode to his headquarters, those citizens still in the city peeking out from behind closed doors and windows. Soldiers lining the streets exchanged whispers about their commander. Only an old black man seemed to express much emotion. "Lord, massa, is dat General Sherman? . . . I'se glad I'se seen him, . . . I just wanted to see de man what made my old massa run."[61]

Despite his humility, Sherman was the hero of the hour, and congratulations poured in. His brother suggested a Grant-Sherman presidential ticket. His enemy, the press, called him a "genius," "brilliant," and "masterly." Abraham Lincoln, Secretary of War Stanton, Secretary of State Seward, U.S. Grant, famous orator Edward Everett, and many others lauded him publicly. His home town gathered money to buy him a horse to be called Atlanta. In private letters and diaries, individuals like Senator Orville H. Browning, author Henry Adams, Senator Charles Sumner, and Washington socialite Adam Gurowski joined in the chorus. The misspelled words of a Michigan private in a letter home perhaps said it all: "Gen. Sherman is the Courante of his army and he has don a big thing hear this summer[.] he has outwitted and defeated them in every spot and posision."[62]

The praise of one person meant more than all others to Sherman, and that was Thomas Ewing. As he completed his official report, Cump wrote his foster father, wanting to make sure that Ewing understood the significance of the campaign. "You have often said," he wrote Ewing, "that Napoleon had no subordinate to whom he was willing to entrust one hundred thousand men & yet have lived to see the little red headed urchin not only handle an hundred thousand men, smoothly & easily but fight them in masses of tens and fifty thousands at a distance of hundreds of miles from his arsenals and sources of supplies. I feel in this less active pleasure than I know you do." Sherman had achieved something he had strived for: success that he could show off to Thomas Ewing.[63]

He did not rest on his laurels but made a decision that embroiled him in controversy. On September 8, by Special Field Orders No. 67, he ordered that Atlanta "being exclusively required for warlike purposes, will at once be vacated by all except the armies of the United States and such civilian employes as may be retained by the proper departments of government." As he told Halleck, "I am not willing to have Atlanta encumbered by the families of our enemies. I want it a pure Gibraltar."[64]

The outcry was immediate. Stunned city officials asked Sherman to reconsider, painting a bleak picture of the consequences to old women and children. Sherman was sympathetic but said that the order was "not designed to meet the humanities of the case, but to prepare for the future struggles." "The use of Atlanta for warlike purposes is inconsistent with its character as a home for families. . . . Sooner or later want will compel the inhabitants to go. Why not go now, when all the arrangements are completed for the transfer, instead of waiting till the plunging shot of contending armies will renew the scenes of the past month? . . . War is cruelty and you cannot refine it." But Sherman tried to. The 705 adults, 860 children, and 79 slaves who were evacuated were treated so fairly that a Confederate officer wrote him a letter of thanks.[65]

Most Confederates were not pleased. Sherman and Hood were already discussing an exchange of prisoners when they began arguing over the depopulation order. Sherman asked Hood's cooperation, and the Confederate general responded that the order "transcends, in studious and ingenious cruelty, all acts ever before brought to my attention in the dark history of war." Sherman answered that Hood himself "burned dwelling houses . . . because they stood in the way of your forts and men." Besides, he and other Confederate leaders were responsible for bringing on this unnecessary war, which was causing so much harshness. Back and forth it went, the two men slinging words where just a few days before they had been firing bullets. When Hood accused Sherman of using black troops, Sherman became particularly angry, knowing full well that his opposition to the recruitment of black troops was still causing him difficulties in his own camp.[66]

Neither man was converted, but Hood's publication of the correspondence drew considerable attention. Sherman received support from a variety of sources. The usually unfriendly *Cincin-*

nati Gazette said the order "sings like the blast of the war trumpet." A Georgia Unionist in England thought it "was nothing more than a clever ruse to provide 15,000 Missionaries to scatter through the State to beseech their fellow Citizens to lay down their arms." Ellen, whose anti-Confederate bitterness grew throughout the war, told him: "I am charmed with your order expelling the inhabitants of Atlanta as it has always seemed to me preposterous to have our Government feeding so many of their people—their insolent women particularly for they are responsible for the war and should be made to feel that it exists in sternest reality." Most important, the War Department supported him. "Not only are you justified by the laws and usages of war in removing these people," Halleck wrote, "but I think it was your duty to your own army to do so. . . . We certainly are not required to treat the so-called non-combatants and rebels better than they themselves treat each other. Even here in Virginia, within fifty miles of Washington, they strip their own families of provisions, leaving them as our army advances to be fed by us or to starve without our lines."[67]

Sherman never doubted the propriety of his orders, but the criticism stung nonetheless. When the Episcopal bishop of Arkansas, Henry C. Lay, visited Sherman in Atlanta under a flag of truce, the two men discussed recent events over dinner. "To be sure, I have made war vindictively," Sherman said, "war is war, and you can make nothing else of it; but Hood knows as well as anyone I am not brutal or inhuman." He denied aiming at any private dwellings during his bombardment of the city; he insisted that his depopulation orders would actually save civilians from the horror of war; and his strict stance on the exchange of prisoners was in keeping with general Union policy. He particularly contested the bishop's insistence that the two sides could never again live together peacefully. All a person had to do, Sherman said, was watch the opposing pickets to see that, once the war was over, all could return to normal.[68]

Back in Lancaster, Ohio, Ellen had given birth to a son on June 11 and was ill. Mail was sporadic, and Sherman grew increasingly frustrated at having to worry about his wife in the midst of his campaign. When correspondence was restored, he learned Ellen was doing better and determined to move to South Bend, Indiana, to send the children to school at Notre Dame and St. Mary's

Academy. Sherman thought she should stay where she was in Lancaster, but she insisted that, with her mother dead, her father's house was too much of a burden. Thomas Ewing would never allow her to live anywhere else in town, so she better just leave Lancaster entirely. Sherman, who had frequently been exasperated at Ellen's constant desire to visit her father, could not now understand her inconvenient desire to leave him. The expense angered him, but, as always, he gave in, no doubt secretly happy to see his wife freeing herself from her father's influence. Ellen and the children went to South Bend.[69]

An end to the war was not yet on the horizon. "The capture of Atlanta," as a modern historian has put it, "was one of the decisive events of the Civil War. It strongly shook the South's ability and will to continue fighting, it revived the flagging determination of the North, and it assured—perhaps even made possible—Lincoln's reelection." Ironically, while Sherman is usually remembered as the father of total war, the railroad policy and depopulation order exemplifying this philosophy, the Atlanta campaign was really traditional warfare of an earlier age—"a campaign of siege and counter-siege the whole way . . . against fortified positions." The tactics harkened back to an earlier day, but the overall strategy was modern. "Every movement we made from the day we left Chattanooga was an attack upon Richmond," Sherman said.[70]

Atlanta would long be studied in military history courses in the United States and abroad as a model of logistics and movement. To Sherman, it was a personal success. Almost unnoticed, he had become a major general on August 12. Sherman, no longer the dependent ward, had proved himself to his family and to the nation. Atlanta marked a turning point in the Civil War and in Cump Sherman's life. As he had surmised in Louisiana in 1861 and increasingly came to believe throughout the war, his personal success was intertwined with that of the Union.[71]

CHAPTER 13

—— ☆ ——

MARCH TO THE SEA

THE FALL OF ATLANTA in September 1864, the reelection of Abraham Lincoln in November, and U. S. Grant's persistent hammering of Robert E. Lee in Virginia signaled the beginning of the end for the Confederacy. Union military might was exerting its dominance, and Lincoln's political victory over Democratic candidate George B. McClellan indicated that the national will to achieve victory was undiminished. Southerners, however, were determined to continue the battle and equally confident that victory would be theirs. The South's unyielding determination was now the crucial factor. As long as the Southern psyche remained whole, Southerners would support the war effort, no matter the casualties suffered or the territory lost. Northern victory required a defeat of rebel will as much as a string of bloody successes in Virginia. Sherman now saw that the way to restore Union was for him to wage war on the Confederate mind while Grant, Thomas, and Schofield battled Confederate armies. Together they would break the Confederacy militarily and psychologically. Grant and Sherman took their separate paths, but as they had throughout the war, they were moving in the same direction.

Immediately after Atlanta, however, future military activities were not all that clear. Sherman held the city, and Hood, thirty miles away at Lovejoy's Station, posed no immediate threat, so the Federals relaxed, enjoying the plentiful supplies that regularly rolled into the city over the secure railroad lines. One beautiful Saturday night, "the mellow tones of a flute" came "floating through the evening air," and soldiers, sitting in front of their tents, thought of home and not fighting. Blair and Logan were in the North helping Republican candidates in the upcoming November elections, and Schofield traveled to Knoxville on Department of the Ohio business. One lazy early September 1864 evening as Sherman and Thomas sat on an Atlanta veranda, the conversation turned to the possibility of sending supply wagons back to Chattanooga.[1]

Sherman was not so sure all this relaxation was such a good idea. He wanted his units to remain vigilant, though he personally was more concerned about Confederate raiders hitting his supply line than about Hood's army attacking him in Atlanta. When three ex-members of Congress, now Confederates, came to the city under a flag of truce, he tried to convince them to talk Governor Joe Brown into pulling Georgia out of the war. Having seen the war damage in the state, Joshua Hill, Augustus R. Wright, and William King listened attentively as Sherman pledged to spare Georgia further devastation if its officials and people would cooperate. "It would be a magnificent stroke of policy" if it worked, Sherman informed Abraham Lincoln. But it never materialized. Brown withdrew the state militia from Hood's control, but he proceeded no further.[2]

Meanwhile in Virginia, Grant slugged it out with Lee and grew increasingly anxious. He sent a member of his staff, Horace Porter, to coordinate the next phase of the war with Sherman. Porter arrived on September 20 extremely curious to meet the man his commander had told him so much about. He was not disappointed. When he reached Sherman's headquarters, a private home near Court-house Square, he found the conqueror of Atlanta sitting on the porch reading a newspaper, his chair tilted back on its rear legs. Sherman was wearing an unbuttoned coat, a black felt hat pulled down over his forehead, nondescript trousers, and a pair of worn-out slippers. On noticing Porter, he straightened his chair and shook hands. He read the letter Porter handed him from Grant and then launched into a long discussion about the war. Porter watched in fascination. Sherman got up and sat back down several times, toyed with the newspaper and his slippers, and exhibited "a peculiar energy of manner in uttering the crisp words and epigrammatic phrases which fell from his lips as rapidly as shots from a magazine-gun. I soon realized he was one of the most dramatic and picturesque characters of the war."

As always, Sherman impressed a new acquaintance with his personality and manner of speech.

After an informal lunch with Sherman's staff, Porter and Sherman talked further. "I am more than ever of the opinion," Sherman said, "that there ought to be some definite objective point or points decided upon before I move farther into this country; sweeping around generally through Georgia for the purpose of inflicting damage would not be good generalship; I want to strike out for the sea." But before he dare cut himself from his supply line, he wanted to neutralize Hood first and be certain supplies would be waiting for him on the coast. Porter returned North carrying a letter to Grant that exuded confidence: "If you can whip Lee and I can march to the Atlantic, I think Uncle Abe will give us a twenty days' leave of absence to see the young folks."[3]

Hood did not wait for Grant and Sherman to complete their planning. On September 21, 1864, he left Lovejoy's Station thirty miles southeast of Atlanta and shifted his base to Palmetto Station, twenty-five miles southwest of the city on the Montgomery and Selma Railroad. Jefferson Davis's speech to the Confederate troops at Palmetto told Sherman what to expect. Davis once more blamed Joe Johnston and Joe Brown for the region's military problems, but this time he went further. He told the soldiers that Nathan Bedford Forrest was already destroying the Union railroad in Tennessee and that they would soon be doing the same in Georgia. Sherman and his army would either starve or retreat. "To be forewarned was to be forearmed," Sherman later said. He immediately strengthened his garrisons along the railroad and prepared his army to respond to any threat.[4]

Amazingly Sherman and Hood were continuing their correspondence over prisoners of war at the same time as they were preparing for battle. They even worked out an arrangement on September 24 whereby Sherman's St. Louis friend, James E. Yeatman, and his Western Sanitary Commission provided clothing, combs, and scissors for the prisoners at Andersonville. Praise for Sherman's depopulation order also continued rolling in. On a less happy note, Ellen wrote that their three-month-old baby was suffering from asthma. This was bad news, but the imminent threat to the supply line seemed more compelling.[5]

Sherman left Slocum's corps to defend Atlanta and with the

rest of the army, some sixty-thousand men, took out after Hood's forty-thousand-man force on October 3. Cavalry raids on his railroad, like those of Forrest's, presented no long-term threat because he could quickly repair any resulting damage. The infantry was another matter. If Hood's army could capture and hold a crucial section of the tracks, it could choke off Sherman's supplies.

The turning point of this campaign came early. The Union army finished crossing the Chattahoochee River on October 4 and reached Kennesaw Mountain the next day. Hood was already at Dallas, planning to send a division to strike Allatoona Pass. Sherman hurriedly ordered John M. Corse's division at Rome to reinforce the garrison at Allatoona. What followed next was one of those events that fills Civil War folklore. On Kennesaw Mountain, fourteen miles away, Sherman was able to spot the puffs of smoke from the guns of the Confederate division attacking Allatoona and could hear the thunder of its artillery. He hurried additional troops forward and worried whether Corse had received his order and, if so, whether he had actually reached the garrison.

Sherman had a signal officer wig-wag the question by flag. The distance was great, enemy fire at Allatoona was heavy, and visibility was not good; all the signal officer could read from the answering signal flags was something like C, R, S, E, H, E, R. Sherman immediately realized that this meant "Corse Here," and felt better. Still, it was a bitter fight. At 2 P.M. on October 6, Corse wired: "I am short a cheek-bone and an ear, but am able to whip all h—l yet! . . . Tell me where Sherman is." In response to this message, Sherman supposedly signaled, "Hold the Fort! for I am coming," and inspired the Union troops to drive off the attackers. Afterward when he saw Corse's wounds, the story continues, Sherman supposedly joked: "Why Corse they came d—d near missing you, didn't they?"

Though Sherman could never remember sending it, "Hold the Fort, for I am coming" inspired a popular song and numerous stories. His signal flag operator transmitted many messages that day, he remembered, so he probably said something like that. But since Corse's famous message was not received until the following day, Sherman could not have responded to it during the height of the battle. Similarly, Corse did not remember Sherman's ever joking about his wounds. No matter, Sherman laughed in 1887;

"It makes little difference and we had better allow Moody and Sanky's hymn of 'Hold the Fort, for I am Coming' to stand uncontradicted."[6]

Significant as the repulse of the Confederates at Allatoona was, it could not match the impact of Sherman's ability to restore the damaged railroad. Hood's troops had efficiently destroyed eight miles of track between Big Shanty and Ackworth. A Union officer commented: "I suppose they have studied our work in that line, so frequently, they are now nearly as good as ourselves at it." Some ten-thousand Federal soldiers were put to work with the regular repair crews, and the break, requiring thirty-five-thousand new ties and six miles of new rails, was restored within a week. Such engineering magic discouraged the Confederates and served to maintain high Federal morale. "It is wonderful what confidence this army has in Sherman," an Illinois colonel insisted. "Every man seems to think the idea of these rebels being able to do us any permanent harm is perfectly preposterous, and all are in the best of spirits."[7]

The commanding general was so pleased at the Allatoona victory that he issued an effusive order of thanks. Still, he looked "more ugly and surly than ever." A soldier correctly surmised that "he evidently don't like it when Hood sets him to guessing what his next movement will be. . . . Hood cut his haversack strings and he is mad. . . . This having the whip hand—the initiative—is a big thing."[8]

Sherman was indeed unhappy at finding himself chasing Hood across the same ground over which he had fought Johnston. Hood "is eccentric," he complained, "and I cannot guess his movements as I could those of Johnston, who was a sensible man and only did sensible things." He was frustrated to see his troops, which had traveled so lightly before, now burdened by unnecessary equipment and thus being outrun by Hood's army. He ordered all worn-out mules, horses, and wagons sent back to Chattanooga, "together with the sick and wounded, prisoners of war, surplus servants, tents, chairs, cots, and the furniture that now fill our wagons and disgrace the army—in other words, each army will strip its trains to the best teams, loaded only with the essentials for a long march, depending on the country for forage and vegetables."[9]

Hood stayed ahead of Sherman, however, clearly interested in avoiding open battle but hoping to break up the railroad and frustrate Union troops. The farther from Atlanta he moved, the more Sherman's unhappiness grew. By mid-October Hood had taken Dalton, and one of Sherman's officers noted that the Federals were only a day away from Chickamauga, close to their point of departure the previous May. At night when others slept, Sherman bundled up in front of his dying camp fire trying to decide what to do. Often "he would join the sentinel, walk along side of him on his post, and, despite regulations, enter into long conversations with him." He had to do something.[10]

Sherman decided that the only true option was to march to the sea. The decision did not come suddenly. It was, in fact, the result of a lifetime of difficult choices. Throughout his life, Sherman had repeatedly faced desperate situations, and he had always responded by trying something new. He was not afraid of innovation, of taking risks, to try to achieve success. In the process, he had gained experience and abilities that would prove significant in his decision making.

He had learned in his West Point ethics class that war was fought between peoples, not armies, and the Florida Seminoles had taught him the validity of that dictum. During his numerous assignments and travels throughout the South, from Fort Morgan in Mobile, through Fort Moultrie in Charleston, to the Louisiana Military Seminary, he had come to like Southerners and to recognize their prideful stubbornness. He knew it would require the incredible bloodshed of total victory to force them to give up their war effort.

Sherman understood the importance of logistics. He noted with awe how migrants cut themselves off from civilization and came across the barren plains and mountains to California, living off the land as they traveled. He knew what an achievement this was because his army job as supply officer in locales all over the nation and his civilian occupations as St. Louis and Kansas land agent, California and New York banker and entrepreneur, and Louisiana educator dealt with logistics. He knew firsthand that the army—and society as a whole—survived on efficient systems of supply.

When he entered the war, these early lessons were corroborated. He believed the South would fight to the bitter end by any means available. He saw in Kentucky and Memphis how Confederates gained sustenance from the population and how Union commanders had to garrison everything to keep it secure. In Memphis, guerrillas were a bigger problem than the Confederate army, and their activity, he believed, violated the commonly accepted rules of warfare. These guerrillas were seemingly the innocent-looking people he saw around him, but they were the real threat to his cause. They showed him that his earlier opinions were correct: war was between peoples, not armies. Consequently, antiguerrilla activity of the most severe kind was not only acceptable, but it was also essential. By their use of guerrillas, the Confederates had waged a new kind of warfare, and, if the Union army expected to survive, it had to change too.

Sherman believed the Union war effort had to be total. This meant suppression of the press, complete control over all elements of Northern and Southern societies, and warfare that would convince the Confederates to quit. He did not believe that more slaughter on the battlefields was the answer; instead, destruction of Southern land and property to break the South's will made more sense. If he could collapse the enemy's logistical base, the will to keep fighting would deteriorate. All the while, however, he would offer a generous peace. He would make it clear that continuation of war would cause ever greater horror; peace would bring reconciliation.

Sherman had first utilized elements of this strategy in Memphis and later against Jackson, Mississippi, during the Vicksburg campaign. But it was in February 1864 that he first fully applied his formula. During the Meridian campaign, he declared total war against the Mississippi countryside, destroying railroads and property along a wide swath of territory in order to keep guerrillas and regular forces away from the Mississippi River. He cut loose from his supplies, lived off the civilian population in the countryside, terrorized them, and maintained total secrecy over his activities. He believed his raid was a great success. Few people— civilian or military—had died. After his frustrating experience with Johnston and chasing Hood all over Georgia trying to protect his supply line, thereby losing more and more soldiers to garrison duty, he knew he had to return to the Meridian concept, using the terror of destruction to convince the Southern people to give up. The avenue was clear. He had to cut his way through Georgia to the coast.

The major problem was the choice of avenues: Where would it make the most sense to march, and where on the coast could supplies be most easily stockpiled for his arrival? He could march for Charleston or Savannah and then be in position to move north against Lee in Virginia. He might march south toward Albany, Georgia, destroying cotton and liberating the prisoners at Andersonville. "This, however, would leave the army in a bad position for future movements." Or he could move toward Pensacola, Florida, and cooperate with E. R. S. Canby, then in New Orleans, in the capture of Mobile. "In my judgment," he concluded, "the first would have a material effect upon . . . [the] campaign in Virginia, the second would be the safest of execution, but the third would more properly fall within the sphere of my own command."[11]

None of this reasoning considered Hood's army, and Grant wanted it destroyed before Sherman went on any new raid. Sherman disagreed. He thought chasing Hood was a waste of time and energy; he could leave Thomas behind to handle Hood while he raided. He believed the war would drag on forever if it was fought in the traditional way. "If," however, "we can march a well-appointed army right through his territory," he said, "it is a demonstration to the world, foreign and domestic, that we have a power which Davis can not resist. This may not be war, but rather statesmanship, nevertheless it is overwhelming to my mind that there are thousands of people abroad and in the South who will reason thus: If the North can march an army right through the South, it is proof positive that the North can prevail in this contest. . . . Mr. Lincoln's selection [for a second term], which is assured, coupled with the conclusion thus reached, makes a complete logical whole. Even without a battle, the result operating upon the minds of sensible men would produce fruits more than compensating for the expense, trouble, and risk." As he told Grant: "I can make this march, and make Georgia howl!"[12]

Grant reluctantly gave his permission. "If there is any way of getting at Hood's army, I would prefer that, but I must trust to your own judgment." Stanton added the approval of the War Department, and thus Abraham Lincoln, so all seemed set. Grant, however, remained nervous about letting Hood move into Tennessee, while Sherman marched through Georgia to the sea. If

Thomas could not handle the Confederates, Union arms would suffer a tremendous setback.[13]

Sherman realized the chance he was taking and in a revealing moment of psychological projection wrote: "I propose to demonstrate the vulnerability of the South and make its inhabitants feel that war and individual ruin are synonymous terms." Sherman had consistently equated his personal success or failure with the war's outcome. Now he applied the same criterion to his adversary. He would teach them that war would hurt each one individually. In doing this, he would ensure order. Ruin to the South meant restoration of the Union and his personal stature. The South of course, could simply quit and rejoin the Union. Then, everyone, Northerners and Southerners, would escape destruction.[14]

"I am not the heartless Boar I am often represented," he insisted in another letter. "I rarely see my children, but were you to behold them watching for my expected coming, and rush to me with eyes all love, you would not say that I was heartless." Nevertheless, "Let every thought of the mind, every feeling of the heart, every movement of a human muscle all be directed to one sole object, successful war and consequent peace, and you have the ideal I aim at. . . . God will not permit this fair land and this Brave People to subside into the anarchy and despotism that Jeff Davis had cut out for them." Destruction of civilian society would convince the South to forgo anarchy for the peace, security, and order of Union.[15]

Sherman sent George H. Thomas and selected troops to Nashville on September 28, and on October 20 Schofield's corps took position in Tennessee. Thomas had enough soldiers to defend the city, while Schofield was prepared to block Hood's movements from the Confederate's base at Florence, Alabama. As for his Georgia troops, Sherman sent supplies and unfit soldiers back to Chattanooga, and he had the railroad between the Tennessee city and Atlanta destroyed. In the process he invalidated the Confederate strategy of cutting the Union supply line. Sherman himself eliminated his supply line; he was gambling that he could feed his army off the land it crossed and thus make protecting a supply line unnecessary. On November 12 when he reached Cartersville, Georgia, on the way back to Atlanta, he acknowledged a message from Thomas briefly: "Dispatch received—all right." Then he ceased communication to the rear. He had all his army's mail sent to Nashville to try to fool the Confederates into thinking that he was planning to move into Tennessee. He was actually cutting himself off from the rear. All his attention was focused on Atlanta, the sea, and, one thousand miles away, Robert E. Lee in Virginia.[16]

It was a lean, hard army of sixty-two-thousand experienced soldiers that gathered in Atlanta on November 14. Only the most physically fit remained. There were many three-year veterans who had survived hard fighting and disease, their self-confidence evident in their stride and in their appearance. Their spare frames were unburdened with unnecessary equipment. Each man carried a blanket, a few cooking utensils, a shirt and some spare socks, a canteen, a haversack with coffee, sugar, salt, and hard bread, a weapon, and forty rounds of ammunition. Most carried writing paper, and many packed playing cards. A majority came from the Midwest, but there were many easterners too.[17]

As he had done in the successful Meridian raid, Sherman divided these troops into a right wing and a left wing, each consisting of approximately the same number of men. Cavalry patrolled the flanks. He had learned in Meridian that such a formation would allow him to cover a wide front for foraging and destruction. The right (southern) wing was under the command of O. O. Howard, McPherson's recent replacement as commander of the Army of the Tennessee. Henry W. Slocum, a brusque West Pointer from New York, commanded the left (northern) wing. Corps commanders in the right wing were the Fifteenth Corps's Peter J. Osterhaus, a fine German immigrant officer, and the Seventeenth Corps's Frank Blair, the Missouri politician turned general. In the left wing, the Fourteenth Corps's Jeff C. Davis would have plenty of chances to display his colorful vocabulary. Alpheus S. Williams of the Twentieth Corps was a lawyer and had proved himself to be a competent general. The cavalry was commanded by Judson Kilpatrick, notorious for his harsh warfare and womanizing but a man Sherman thought had the necessary flair to provide good cavalry leadership.

Since the army would have no supply line, logistics were crucially important. Sherman's commissary officer, the efficient Amos Beckwith, provided the troops with 1.2 million rations, enough for twenty days, and over three-thousand beef cattle were to be driven along to supplement the menu. The quartermaster officer, L. C. Easton, oversaw the twenty-five hundred wagons, six-hundred ambulances, sixty-five guns, and seventeen-thousand horses and mules. Each brigade established a fifty-man-plus-officer foraging team to scour the countryside for food for man and beast. If stretched out in a line, the army would cover fifty miles along a road; the wagons, another thirty miles.[18]

Considering the magnitude of the undertaking, Sherman's orders were remarkably imprecise. He told the men that he had organized them "for a special purpose, well known to the War Department and to General Grant. It is sufficient for you to know that it involves a departure from our present base and a long and difficult march to a new one." In case anyone was worried, he assured them that "all the chances of war have been considered and provided for, as far as human sagacity can." If they displayed the same "discipline, patience, and courage" they had in the past, the enemy would suffer "complete overthrow." The more detailed orders the next day added little more information, the most intriguing part being the statement: "The army will forage liberally on the country during the march." Soldiers were not to "enter the dwellings of the inhabitants or commit any trespass"; officers alone could order the destruction of property and then only in areas of guerrilla activity.[19]

Amazingly, the officers and men never seriously questioned these nebulous orders. They willingly marched without knowing exactly where they were going and how they would get there. "Sherman, apparently, talked very freely about his intended campaign," a contemporary surmised, "and yet no two men could reach the same conclusion as to his final destination. . . . Every one guessed what the General was intending to do and no one had any misgivings about the success of whatever he might attempt."[20]

Sherman had studied the area well. His army would be marching through a rich agricultural area—as one of Sherman's officers put it, "a perfect garden." Cotton was the major crop, but the war had caused the increased planting of grain, corn, and other vegetables. Cows, beef cattle, oxen, pigs, horses, and sheep were abundant. The typical house was one or two stories high, made of hewn logs with exterior shingles. It sat on low pilings and had a spacious porch. The wealthier the owner was, the grander were the house and its furnishings. Slave quarters were primitive, and barns and other out buildings varied enormously. Forests of tall pine trees surrounded the acreage carved out for agriculture, and the connecting roads "were streaks of red mud or dust across the landscape." There were few large towns—usually only county seats where the grandest houses were located.[21]

A week before departing Atlanta on November 15, Sherman ordered his engineering officer, O. M. Poe, to destroy "all depots, car-houses, shops, factories, foundries, &c. . . . fire will do most of the work." He wanted to avoid having to leave a garrison. Poe went at his task methodically and leveled anything of war-making potential. When he torched one machine shop, shells hidden by the departing Confederates exploded all night, sending sparks onto nearby houses and stores. The next morning, one of Sherman's staff officers "saw no dwelling destroyed, and outside of [the] central business part of town [there was] comparatively little damage. . . . ¼ of area of town destroyed, but this the largest and best built business part." The Confederate view contrasted sharply: "On the night of the fifteenth the torch was applied to Atlanta; and where the merciless commander had already created a solitude he determined to make a conflagration, by the light of which his marching columns might commence their journey to the sea." A Georgian was blunter: "Hell has laid her egg, and right here it hatched."[22]

The story that Sherman had callously burned Atlanta to the ground grew in later years, fanned by the fiery scenes in *Gone with the Wind*. There will perhaps always be controversy as to the exact extent of damage to Atlanta, but the historical facts are clear that the entire city was not destroyed and that Sherman was not solely responsible for the part that was. Hood had destroyed numerous houses during his defense of the city and his evacuation in September. In October one Confederate newspaper, the *Richmond Sentinel*, admitted that its earlier assertion was incorrect: houses in Atlanta had not all been destroyed; the city park had not been turned into a cemetery; and graves had not been desecrated. Hood's army exploded eighty railroad cars filled with ammunition, and, as a later historian has phrased it: "The smoke and the resulting fires [were] partially responsible for the loss of many homes and buildings later said to have been burned by Sherman." Individual Federal soldiers also torched some vacant homes on their own, and civilian looters were active. When Sherman departed Atlanta, however, at least four-hundred buildings stood undamaged.[23]

As he was leaving Atlanta on November 16, Sherman paused briefly to view the woods where McPherson had fallen: "Behind us lay Atlanta, smoldering and in ruins, the black smoke rising high in the air, and hanging like a pall over the ruined city. . . . the gun-barrels glistening in the sun, the white-topped wagons stretching away to the south; . . . [the troops] marching steadily and rapidly, with a cheery look and swinging pace. . . . Some band had, by accident, struck up the anthem of 'John Brown's soul goes marching on'; the men caught up the strain, and never before or since have I heard the chorus of 'Glory, glory, hallelujah!' done with more spirit, or in better harmony of time and place."[24] These words were actually written ten years after the event; Sherman was not exuberant that September 1864 morning. He was suffering from such a bad attack of rheumatism in his right arm he could not write. The difficult task that lay ahead of him was all too clear; no supply line, leading sixty-two-thousand troops three hundred miles through a hostile country to link up somewhere on the coast with a fleet he hoped would be there. He wrote daughter Minnie telling her how much he missed her and the rest of the children, and he told his brother-in-law he was not fighting Jefferson Davis or slavery but "mobs, vigilance committees and all the other phases of sedition and anarchy which have threatened and still endanger the country which our children must inhabit." With dead son Willy on his mind, he told son Tommy that people said he was "a great General." "That is what the People call fame & Glory, but I tell you that I would rather come home quietly and have you & Willy meet me at the cars than to hear the shouts of the people."[25]

The shouts he heard in Georgia were hardly complimentary. General P. G. T. Beauregard, Secretary of State James A. Seddon, Senator B. H. Hill, and six Confederate congressmen implored the state's people to rise up against the invader. "Remove your negroes, horses, cattle, and provisions from Sherman's army, and burn what you cannot carry," the congressmen urged, recommending what they later criticized Sherman for doing. "Georgians, be firm! Act promptly, and fear not!" Senator Hill said. But there was plenty to fear. With Hood in Alabama and Beauregard in Mississippi, the only Confederate troops in Sherman's path were Joe Wheeler's cavalry, Gustavus W. Smith's Georgia militia, and a ragtag mixture of other troops. Together these units perhaps numbered eight thousand men, no match for the Federal juggernaut. Clearly, Sherman had once more outflanked his Confederate opposition. As he embarked on his novel and distinctly modern strategy, he had maneuvered himself into a position where he could bring masses of his troops to bear on fractions of the enemy and achieve his geographic objective without having to fight a battle. Like Antoine Henri Jomini, he believed that "the best way . . . to win battles was more by the movement of troops than by fighting." After the war, he cited Napoleon, Jomini's model, that "the fundamental maxim for successful war is to 'converge a superior force on the critical point at the critical time.'" He went beyond Jomini in breaking the will of the civilian population and psychologically outflanking his opposing army.[26]

As Sherman's army marched out of Atlanta, his two wings followed separate paths, though in four parallel corps columns, covering from twenty to sixty miles in width. The left wing moved down the Georgia Railroad toward Augusta, the right wing along the Macon and Western Railroad to Macon. Sherman hoped to confuse the Confederates over his objective; he was actually aiming for Milledgeville, the state capital, located between the two cities. He asked the War Department to plant false information in the press. The cavalry covered the right wing's flank until Milledgeville, when it moved to protect the left wing against Hood or Lee's sending any troops from the north. The organized foragers, or bummers as they came to be called, soon ignored the strict rules of procedure. They too provided flank protection during their procurement efforts. Interspersed with the bummers on the flanks and even ahead of the main columns were temporary and permanent Union deserters, escaped slaves, Confederate deserters, unscrupulous civilians, and large elements of Wheeler's cavalry, all doing their own plundering. The enormous destruction of the march to the sea had many perpetrators; Union soldiers alone were not responsible.[27]

"Sherman's bummers" quickly became the symbols of the march—villains to Georgians. Each bummer took his foraging job seriously and was ingenious in ferreting out food, horses, and whatever personal effects he took a fancy to. Since so many people fled before the army, he often did his work without a Southerner in sight, but if women and children (black or white) were around, he might be polite or nasty depending on what he thought the situation required. Rarely did he injure anyone, and he did not, as a rule, burn houses, but he did pick many of them clean, leaving behind a trail of destruction. Some Georgians insisted, erroneously, that Sherman received one-fifth of everything the bummers took, and, at least one southern woman charged that Sherman left the South with more than two hundred gold watches.[28]

The main columns themselves foraged extensively, and their arrival was always a frightening spectacle to civilians in the path. "Like demons they rush in!" a Southern woman recorded in her diary. "To my smoke house, my dairy, pantry, kitchen and cellar . . . breaking locks and whatever is in their way." Vandalism was widely practiced. A Union officer told of "soldiers emerging from doorways and backyards" in one town, "bearing quilts, plates, poultry and pigs." "A milliner's establishment was sacked," another Federal recounted, "and gaudy ribbons and artificial flowers decorated the caps of the pretty fellows who had done it."[29]

Sherman and his officers rarely enforced the strict rules he had established. One day early on the march, Sherman caught a soldier "with a ham on his musket, a jug of sorghum-molasses under his arm, and a big piece of honey in his hand." He demanded an explanation. The soldier smiled and replied, "Forage liberally on the country." Another time, Sherman caught a soldier absolutely "covered with plunder. Vegetables were strung all over him, hanging in bunches from his shoulders and belt." From his hand hung a chicken. Sherman cursed him for violating the foraging order. The soldier, not recognizing his commanding officer, swore right back, and the two men faced off in a battle of curses. Finally, Sherman told his antagonist who he was, and the man stopped swearing and introduced himself: "Oh hell, General, I am Abner F. Dean, *Chaplain* of the 112th Massachusetts." At that, he quietly started walking down the road, then pausing to invite his general to dinner that evening. Sherman was furious, but once again he let an offender go.[30]

Sherman opposed plundering in theory; in practice, it helped create the kind of terror he was attempting to instill in the civilian populace. The more havoc he could cause, the less hope these civilians would have and the less trust they would place in their government and army. He did not see civilians as innocent bystanders; they were the enemy too. On the march, he was simply putting into practice his long-held views of collective responsibility. "In war everything is right which prevents anything," he told a dubious aide. "If bridges are burned I have a right to burn all houses near it." A Confederate who had his house destroyed should not complain to him; "let him look to his own people, if they find that their burning bridges only destroys their own citizens' houses they'll stop it."[31]

He often wished there was some other way to achieve his goal, but he had come to believe that, short of the South's surrender, there was none. He wrote an old friend what he told whites all along the route: "I pledge you that my study is to accomplish peace and honor at as small a cost to life and property as possible . . . [and] that I will take infinitely more delight in curing the wounds made by war than by inflicting them." "It is pretty hard on me," he told Ellen, "that I am compelled to make these blows which are necessarily trying to me, but it seems devolved on me and can not be avoided." "I know I grieved as much as any man," he later insisted, "when I saw pain and sorrow and affliction among the innocent and distressed and when I saw burning and desolation. But these were incidents of war, and were forced upon us."[32]

The march quickly developed a routine of its own. Reveille was sounded at daybreak, and the tent cities dotting the landscape came alive with sleepy men cooking their breakfasts. If the foragers had been successful the day before, sweet potatoes and beef might be the fare; if not, hardtack and army bacon. After eating, the soldiers fell into ranks; foragers spread out over the countryside; the day's march began.

The columns covered around fifteen miles a day, destroying railroads, mills, and anything else associated with slavery and the Confederate war effort. Houses and their interiors might or might not be bothered. During rest breaks, the men slept, played cards, snacked, smoked a pipe, or ribbed a passing officer on horseback. A unit of black pioneers kept the roads in repair, but when a road was particularly bad, everyone helped corduroy it so that the army wagons and artillery could keep rolling. River crossings required pontoon bridges and planking on both banks.

There was no stop for lunch, the men eating whenever they could. As the day wore on, the chatter died down in the ranks; the troopers anticipated camp for the night. Foragers began their return, and the men whooped and laughed and applauded the booty. Finally a campsite was reached. The soldiers pitched their tents and ate their only full meal of the day. As night came, camp fires glowed in all directions as far as the eye could see. Men gathered around these fires to cook, play cards, repair clothes, smoke, write in their diaries, and talk. The bummer was the center of attention as he told about his adventures that day. If they sang, the men preferred comic songs over patriotic or sentimental airs. They kept various pets, and game cocks provided regular exciting matches.

Soon the bugler sounded "Tattoo," then "Taps," and the soldiers slowly took to their tents for the night. Chief among those staying up was the commander himself. Stories of Sherman's nocturnal wanderings were legend in his army. Soldiers heard of him "prowling about a camp fire in red flannel drawers and a worn dressing gown." He always seemed to be on the watch, always busy, yet he never seemed distant. "That was Uncle Billy—a great man, a brilliant leader, but still one of them."[33]

Early in the march, Jeff C. Davis's corps, with Sherman along, camped on the plantation of Confederate General Howell Cobb, the famous prewar politician, just outside Milledgeville. The left wing moved into town, where Sherman slept a night on the floor in the governor's mansion Joe Brown had emptied in his dash out of the city. Some of the soldiers amused themselves by holding a mock legislature and rescinding Georgia's secession ordinance. Less humorously, they ransacked offices and the state library, stealing and destroying irreplaceable material.[34]

Meanwhile parts of the Fifteenth Corps on the right wing fought a tragic battle with the outmanned Georgia militia at Griswoldville, ten miles from Macon. After the battle, the Union soldiers found to their horror that the dead in front of their lines were old men and young boys. The only major skirmish of the march was a disaster for the Confederates; they could only fall back before the advancing Union columns. Their frustration resulted in Wheeler's cavalrymen slitting the throats and hanging

In the spring of 1861, Sherman rejoined the U.S. army with some reluctance. He perceived the Union effort as lacking the commitment necessary for victory.

(Francis T. Miller, The Photographic History of the Civil War*)*

His first experience with combat at Bull Run in July 1861 reinforced his reticence and confirmed his fear that the Union government did not take the Confederate threat seriously enough.

(Francis T. Miller, The Photographic History of the Civil War*)*

Ulysses S. Grant. Even though the disorder of the early Union war effort in Kentucky and Mississippi depressed Sherman in the fall of 1861, he found hope in the actions of General Grant, who would become his friend and military commander. *(National Archives)*

On the plains above the Tennessee River in April 1862, the debacle at Shiloh almost destroyed Grant. Sherman's valor and the friendship he proffered afterward helped stabilize Grant and kept him from resigning from the army. *(Francis T. Miller,* The Photographic History of the Civil War*)*

Walnut Hills at Chickasaw Bayou. Sherman suffered a horrendous defeat here in December 1862, when his troops were unable to traverse a watery terrain in order to reach the Confederate entrenchments atop these hills leading to Vicksburg.
(Francis T. Miller, The Photographic History of the Civil War*)*

The press attacked him fiercely, calling him "insane" for the Chickasaw fiasco. He responded angrily by court-martialing New York *Herald* reporter Thomas W. Knox, shown in this portrait. This was one of the most celebrated of Sherman's hostile responses to journalists' presence on the battlefield.
(Ohio Historical Society)

Sherman's troops crossed the Big Black River on pontoon bridges during their May 1863 dash toward Vicksburg, exhibiting Sherman's ability to move troops rapidly. *(Francis T. Miller,* The Photographic History of the Civil War*)*

After the victory at Vicksburg, which catapulted Sherman to national prominence, Ellen Sherman and family, including son Tommy, were able to pay Sherman a long fall 1863 visit at his Mississippi encampment. *(Archives of the University of Notre Dame)*

Although military success was Sherman's lot in 1863, and his domestic situation had never been better, tragedy struck when his first son and favorite child, Willy, died from fever.
(Archives of the University of Notre Dame)

Suffering from this loss, Sherman grew increasingly close to his army family, including the officers pictured here: (1) O. O. Howard, (2) John A. Logan, (3) William B. Hazen, (4) Sherman, (5) Jefferson C. Davis, (6) Henry W. Slocum, (7) Joseph A. Mower, (8) Frank Blair.
(National Archives)

Starting in 1864, Sherman implemented his policy of total war against civilian property as well as Confederate armies. More than the troops of any other general, Sherman's men became expert at tearing up railroads, accomplishing prodigious deeds of destruction in Mississippi, Georgia, and the Carolinas.

(Francis T. Miller, The Photographic History of the Civil War*)*

Those same men were adept at repairing destruction wrought by the Confederates, and performing feats of military engineering—they built this 800-foot railroad bridge across the Chattahoochie River in 4½ days.

(Francis T. Miller, The Photographic History of the Civil War*)*

It was the Atlanta campaign in the summer of 1864 that made clear to the nation Sherman's brilliance as a strategist and his greatness as a commander of armies. His troops, repeatedly outflanking Joe Johnston's army, moved into the elaborate Confederate fortifications (above) and captured guns left behind in the Confederates' hasty evacuation (below).
(Francis T. Miller, The Photographic History of the Civil War*)*

With the capture of Atlanta, Sherman was poised to execute his March to the Sea, which would secure the Union's victory and his own fame.
(Francis T. Miller, The Photographic History of the Civil War*)*

some of the captured Union foragers but then doing their own pillaging and plundering. Many of the women the Federals encountered insisted that their absent husbands had been forced into the Confederate army. They accepted destruction of their own property with, "Well, I don't care, if you will only serve South Carolina the same way for they got us into this scrape."[35]

As the army continued across the Georgia landscape, foraging and destroying as it went, some of what it encountered angered the men and caused them to become increasingly vindictive. They regularly heard stories of slave owners' using hound dogs to chase down fugitive slaves and escaped Union prisoners, so they killed every dog they saw to prevent such activity in the future. They grew increasingly angry at hearing lies being spread about "our uniform cruelty, our killing all the women and children, burning all the houses, forcing the negroes into our army in the front rank of battle, etc., etc." At Millen, Georgia, the men were particularly infuriated when they came upon a pen for Union prisoners. It was nothing more than a three-hundred-yard-square area surrounded by a log stockade with no shelter from the weather and no source of water. They found seven hundred unmarked graves. The Confederate jailers had departed so quickly that they had left several dead prisoners unburied. Escaped prisoners of war from Andersonville also told terrible tales.[36]

Soldiers were aghast to find at a plantation only recently evacuated by a Georgia legislator the man's sick wife and newborn infant. At another place, they found two young girls alone in a cabin and were shocked when none of the neighbors was willing to take the small children in. (The girls eventually were taken North.) And when the army was drawing near Savannah and torpedoes (land mines) blasted off an officer's leg, Sherman expressed army attitude by saying, "This was not war, but murder, and it made me very angry." In retaliation he forced Confederate prisoners of war to sweep the road of torpedoes before his troops passed through.[37]

Such occurrences fed the army's desire to punish the Confederates. The average soldier, like his commander, had come to believe that destroying and plundering were necessary actions for punishing the enemy and ending this terrible war. It was a lot better than charging the entrenchments at Kennesaw Mountain. On the march there was little death or injury to anyone, friend or foe. A lot of fence rails were used for camp fires; pigs and cows and horses, clothes, household goods, and furniture were appropriated or destroyed; houses and barns were often ransacked. In short, a great deal of damage was done, but people were generally left alone. Rape and murder were practically nonexistent. The march to the sea saw a land ravaged by enemy and friendly forces alike and the will of its people broken. Their bodies, however, usually remained whole.[38]

In the North, there was no news from the army except for the propaganda found in the Confederate press reporting that Sherman was on the verge of annihilation. When John Sherman approached Abraham Lincoln for information on his brother, Lincoln replied: "Oh, no, we have heard nothing from him. We know what hole he went in, but we don't know what hole he will come out of." The *Cincinnati Commercial,* which on December 11, 1861, had called him insane, now was confident that "wherever Sherman pleases to go, we have no doubt he can go."[39]

By early December Sherman's army stood poised before Savannah, ready to make contact with the Union fleet and reestablish a supply line. Food and fodder had been plentiful throughout most of the march, but the army ran into scarcity nearing Savannah, where the marsh-infested region produced what one soldier said was "nothing . . . but alligators in the swamp and rice in sheaves in the fields." Even the rice would soon run out because the army was no longer moving forward but taking up positions before the well-entrenched coastal city. A long siege could be disastrous for a hungry army, so action had to be taken quickly. Sherman decided to storm Fort McAllister below the city to make contact with the fleet. The fort was located on the south bank of the Ogeechee River and protected Savannah from ship movement out of the Ossabaw Sound.[40]

Sherman tapped the division led by William B. Hazen to make the assault. Sherman himself had recruited this unit at Paducah, Kentucky, and had led it at Shiloh. It was part of the Fifteenth Corps he had commanded at Vicksburg. He watched the assault from the roof of a rice mill on the opposite side of the river, pacing up and down and increasingly concerned as the afternoon wore away that Hazen would not attack before sundown. Just when he had reached the limit of his patience, he saw a puff of smoke on the horizon, and an American ship appeared on

Ossabaw Sound. A signal flag on the ship asked who he was and "Is Fort McAllister taken?" "Not yet, but it will be in a minute," Sherman signaled back. At that moment, Hazen's troops advanced out of the woods before the fort in perfect order. The small Confederate garrison responded with artillery and small arms fire, the smoke enveloping the attackers. The Federals tried to evade torpedoes hidden in the ground, fought through an abatis, and then charged into a deep ditch filled with spikes and over the final entrenchment into the fort, where fierce hand-to-hand fighting subdued the stubborn garrison. The entire assault took only fifteen minutes and cost only eleven Union lives and eighty wounded. Watching the scene from the rice mill, Sherman's eyes filled with tears. He jumped up and down with excitement.[41]

He climbed into a small boat and was rowed down the river to the fleet. He had dinner with the victorious Hazen, who had also invited the defeated Fort McAllister commander. Major George W. Anderson was shocked to see that one of the waiters was his own slave, a person who only a few hours before had been with him in Fort McAllister. He asked Sherman's permission to address the man. Of course, Sherman replied, "but Bob, remember you are now a free man." Anderson asked Bob if he had joined the Yankees. "Oh! I'm working for Mr. Hazen," the former slave replied. Anderson looked at Sherman and commented: "General, it looks to me as though the game is up." "Yes," Sherman responded, "the game is up. Slavery is gone, and the Southern Confederacy a thing of the past."[42]

Yet many more days of war remained. Hardee's small force still crouched behind Savannah's entrenchments, but now that he had a secure supply line again, Sherman could take his time about squeezing the Confederates out. He was jolted out of complacency by a December 6 letter from Grant found in the backlog of mail his army received. Forget about Savannah, the commanding general wrote. Make a secure base on the ocean, and leave a strong enough garrison to protect it. "With the balance of your command come here by water with all dispatch." "I have concluded that the most important operation toward closing the rebellion will be to close out Lee and his army."[43]

Sherman numbly stared into the camp fire for a long time the night he received Grant's order. He did not want to go to Virginia, back to the conventional war being fought there, but he would obey, and he began preparing Fort McAllister to be the base Grant envisioned. It would take time to assemble the necessary ships to transport his large force, so he determined to capture Savannah before they arrived. On December 17, after Hardee refused to surrender, Sherman began to tighten the noose around the city. There was one escape route still open to Hardee, and though Sherman talked about closing it, he seemed rather nonchalant about doing so. "For some reason unknown to me," a Union officer noted on December 17, "the General has not pushed a heavy or even a small force across the Savannah River, so as to prevent the rebels from escaping in that direction." The northern escape route "remained open to them for at least nine days." Another officer said that the army "concluded General Sherman wanted the enemy to leave and not make a fight necessary."[44]

Hardee abandoned Savannah on December 21 and escaped across the Savannah River into South Carolina. Sherman's soldiers moved into the entrenchments where several discovered a relic of the past: a three-year-old Savannah newspaper announcing Sherman's alleged insanity in Kentucky. No one had the courage to show him the paper so he might savor the irony.[45]

Similar success met Union arms in Tennessee. Schofield defeated Hood at Franklin on November 30, and the combined forces of Thomas and Schofield defeated him at Nashville on December 15 and 16. Sherman had reached the sea while his subordinates had decisively defeated Hood's army. The Confederate cause in the West was doomed. Meanwhile, Sherman convinced Grant that he could march to Virginia as quickly as he would reach there by ship, with his men in better shape from an overland march than they would be after being cooped up in cramped ships.[46]

Once again, things were going Sherman's way. He had captured Savannah after a successful march across Georgia; Thomas and Schofield had defeated Hood in Tennessee; and he had convinced Grant that a march through the Carolinas was the appropriate next move. Yet, as at Atlanta, Sherman had marred his success by allowing the rival army to escape, the only flaw in an otherwise excellent campaign. Sherman never thought these escapes mattered. He had captured Atlanta, and he had taken Savannah, so Hood's and Hardee's escapes made no real difference.[47]

Sherman's priorities allowed the opposing army to withdraw in the face of superior force and did not require the victorious commander to destroy his opponent to be successful. In reality, he followed his own emotions. He hated the idea of killing Southern friends, yet he needed military success to ensure the order necessary for his own personal success. How could he accomplish both? He did it by fighting a war of maneuver (traditional war) yet bringing to the populace a war of destruction (modern war) in which killing or capturing the enemy army was not essential. "Of course I must fight when the time comes," he told his daughter in early 1864, "but wherever a result can be accomplished without Battle I prefer it."[48]

Restoration of the Union was the only legitimate end to the Civil War that mattered to Sherman. "My opinion is that no negotiations are necessary, nor commissioners, nor conventions, nor anything of the kind. Whenever the people of Georgia quit rebelling against their Government and elect members of Congress and Senators, and these go and take their seats, then the State of Georgia will have resumed her functions in the Union." Once the Confederacy quit fighting, things could return to normal. Killing was not necessary to accomplish that.[49]

It was this attitude that caused him anguish at the thought of sailing his troops to Virginia. Fighting Lee meant killing; a march through the Carolinas meant further breaking of the Confederate will with only a few fatalities. Psychological warfare made sense; traditional warfare did not. Carnage had solved little in the past three years; psychological warfare would produce better results. Those who argued that Southerners were "enraged or united by such movements" were simply wrong. Southerners "reason very differently," he believed. "They see in them [marches] the sure and irresistible destruction of all their property. They realize that the Confederate armies cannot protect them and . . . the inevitable result . . . [will be] starvation & misery." Recognizing this, they will quit.[50]

When he entered Savannah, Sherman continued his warfare of the mind. He sent Abraham Lincoln a letter offering the city as a Christmas present.[51] With Savannah captured, its officials and people properly remorseful, and three leading Confederate army officers having left their wives in his care, there was no further need for the iron fist. The velvet glove now made more sense. He had shown the Confederates that resistance guaranteed destruction; now he would demonstrate that surrender and return to the Union would bring peace and security.

When the Union army entered Savannah, it was on its best behavior. Soldiers stopped the city's lawless element from plundering stores and homes; they paid for goods they had previously taken in the countryside. Sherman's favorite regimental band serenaded the city; he held an impressive military review where he startled his own men by appearing in full dress uniform; and he even threw a large party for officers and selected locals. On the owner's invitation, he made his headquarters at the grand home of Charles Green, the father of a Confederate soldier. He welcomed anyone, black or white, who wanted to see him. By official orders he allowed local government to continue functioning and encouraged "usual pursuits." He helped expedite a relief expedition from the North that brought shiploads of food for the hungry city. The streets were safe enough for women and children, and he roamed the city himself and attended Christmas service at the Episcopal church. He governed Savannah as he had run Memphis (not Atlanta), successfully building up Unionism in the area. Residents wondered if he could really be the brute rumor had warned them about.[52]

The city's women were particularly surprised. When the army first entered Savannah and for some time after, women, the majority of the population remaining in the city, kept their shutters closed and stayed off the streets. One night, Sherman arrived to pay a courtesy call on the wife of a Confederate officer, who was also a Union officer's daughter. When he walked in, two little girls (one of them, Juliette, was the later founder of the Girl Scouts of America) became noticeably nervous. Sherman quickly had the children on his knees, joked about being "Old Sherman," and had them giggling. Another Savannah woman refused an introduction to the general, however, and wished "a thousand papers of pins were stuck in . . . [his] bed and that he was strapped down on them."[53]

A Confederate officer from Alabama wrote in his diary that "Attila, Genseric and Alaric were not more cruel to the conquered Romans than the brutal Sherman has been to the defenseless, utterly helpless old men, women and children of pillaged and devastated Georgia." Sherman's days in Savannah resounded with a praise that easily drowned out such Confederate frustration. His mail was filled with letters of congratulations from all over the country. Abraham Lincoln thanked him for the gift of Savannah and admitted he had been wrong in doubting the march to the sea. Grant, Halleck, Porter, and Stanton sent their best wishes. Congress passed a resolution of praise, as did the New York State legislature. A committee in Cincinnati organized a campaign to buy him a house. The governor of California and Dennis Hart Mahan, one of Sherman's former West Point professors, chimed in their good words. His enemy, the press, could hardly restrain itself, the *Chicago Tribune* calling him "Our Military Santa Claus" and comparing his march to "the Anabasis and the best efforts of Marlborough, Napoleon, and Wellington." Even the usually critical British newspapers were uncharacteristically enthusiastic. The *Edinburgh Review* placed the march "with the highest achievements which the annals of modern warfare record." The *London Times* gushed: "Since the great Duke of Marlborough turned his back upon the Dutch and plunged hurriedly into Germany to fight the famous battle of Blenheim, military history has recorded no stronger marvel than this mysterious expedition of General Sherman's route against an unknown undiscoverable enemy." Sherman was so elated that he told Grant: "I don't like to boast, but I believe this army has a confidence in itself that makes it almost invincible."[54]

Once again, though, one man's praise mattered more than the others. Sherman was thrilled to learn of Thomas Ewing's excitement over his success. "Of course I feel just pride in the satisfaction you express and would rather please and gratify you than all the world beside." As he told Ellen, "For his sake I am glad of the success that has attended me, and I know he will feel more pride in my success than you or I do."[55]

In Savannah the army had access to mail and newspapers again, and Sherman tried to catch up on the news. He was stunned when he read in a newspaper that baby Charley had died in South Bend, Indiana, on December 4 and had been buried at Notre Dame on December 7. The shock of the death of his child he had never seen was severe. Once again, personal tragedy choked off savoring a great triumph. This time Thomas Ewing's praise carried him a long way. And when Ellen admitted she should have spent less time in the past on "Father's gratification" and more time and effort on pleasing "those to whom I owed even a greater duty," Cump's satisfaction reached a peak.[56]

Now a serious problem reared up. Throughout the march, slaves had welcomed the Union army enthusiastically; they had acted as spies; they had given directions; and by their exuberant overthrow of their enslavement, they had provided a satisfaction to officers and men. Contemporary accounts of the march are full of slave stories: poignant, funny, insulting, and sometimes all at the same time. "The music of the bands started the young niggers at dancing, . . . the old ones stood with uncovered heads, hands raised, mouths open and eyes turned up; the young negresses stood bowing and curtseying . . . while each negro in his or her own style kept uttering ejaculations of wonder such as 'Lawd, jest look at 'em'; 'whar'd dey cum from'; 'looks like de whole world was comin' &c., &c. Each one expressed his or her wonder in some original and quaint style." One slave succinctly evaluated Sherman's military situation: "Dey got a army behind dat cant catch up with him and de army in front of him cant git out de way."[57]

Every slave, it seemed, had heard Sherman's name and wanted to see him. Sherman always took time to talk to any slave and treated each respectfully, realizing that their information was usually more reliable than any he might get from Southern whites. He usually responded with a variation of the same theme: The war came because their masters disobeyed the law; no master had any power over them anymore, but they should be polite and realize they had to work for themselves; the army would not impress them; in fact, they and their families would be better off not to follow the army but stay where they were and make a new life. The slaves listened politely and then followed the army, thousands of them marching to the freedom they believed awaited them wherever it was the soldiers were going. Sherman and his officers frequently became irritated at this black mass of men, women, and children tagging along, worried that they could not feed themselves and the slaves too.[58]

Army nastiness toward slaves was frequent. Some men plundered slave belongings as much as they did any white's. They freely made racist comments and insulting jokes. But it was Jeff C. Davis, the irascible commander of the Fourteenth Corps, who brought the matter to its ugly head on December 9. Davis, trailed by black fugitives, was crossing Ebenezer Creek near Savannah, with Joe Wheeler's cavalry right behind. When Davis's men completed the crossing, they immediately removed the pontoon bridges, stranding the black men, women, and children on the opposite shore with the Confederates closing in. Panic hit the slaves, and they tried to escape what they feared would be slaughter at the hands of the Confederate horsemen. They began diving into the water, and an indeterminate number drowned in futile crossing attempts, despite the aid of many soldiers. The tragedy created an enormous stir. Sherman, however, stood by his subordinate.[59]

Once again, as he had done in his recruiter letter during the Atlanta campaign, Sherman sent out an antiblack message. What little news filtered back from the march to the sea included the opinion that Sherman's proslavery attitude had kept him from bringing out all the slaves he might have. A Richmond newspaper even quoted him as saying that slavery would survive the war and he would own slaves himself. His reputation for proslavery sentiments was so pervasive in Washington that his lawyer brother Charles, his friend Halleck, and Secretary of the Treasury Salmon P. Chase cautioned him about it. Halleck warned Sherman that he was believed by some to "have manifested an almost *criminal* dislike to the negro," the "inevitable Sambo." Chase criticized "the apparent harshness of your action towards the blacks. You are understood," Chase continued, "to be opposed to their employment as soldiers and to regard them as a sort of pariah, almost without rights." Chase urged Sherman to set a good example for other officers, advice that brother Charles echoed. He warned Sherman not to listen to Thomas Ewing, who was out of step on emancipation.[60]

Sherman did not take the broad hints. He wrote Halleck, who shared his antiblack attitude, "But, the nigger? Why, in God's name, can't sensible men let him alone?" Military success, not protection of "Sambo" was his main priority. He repeated the same point to Chase, this leading antislavery proponent who called for fair play for blacks. "The negro should be a free man," he said, "but not put on any equality with the Whites. . . . the effect of equality is illustrated in the character of the mixed race in

Mexico and South America. Indeed it appears to me," he concluded, "that the right of suffrage in our Country should be rather abridged than enlarged."[61]

This attitude was worrisome enough to get Secretary of War Stanton to pay Sherman a January 11, 1865, visit in Savannah.[62] Stanton asked Sherman about Jeff C. Davis and the pontoon bridges, and the commanding general once more defended his subordinate. The secretary asked for a meeting with area blacks, so Sherman invited about twenty people, mostly ministers, to meet with Stanton at the Green house. Stanton asked a series of questions, and Adjutant General Townsend took notes on the responses.

Sherman thought the idea of consulting blacks was strange, and it was indeed one of the first examples in the postslavery era of a government official's treating freed people with such respect. When Stanton wanted to learn what the black leaders thought of Sherman, he asked him to leave the room. Sherman was insulted. "It certainly was a strange fact that the great War Secretary should have catechized negros concerning the character of a general who had commanded a hundred thousand men in battle, had captured cities, conducted sixty-five thousand men successfully across four hundred miles of hostile territory, and had just brought tens of thousands of freedmen to a place of security." The black leaders gave Sherman their highest praise. "His conduct and deportment toward us characterized him as a friend and gentlemen. We have confidence in General Sherman, and think what concerns us could not be in better hands." Stanton seemed pleased, and Sherman could not help gloating.[63]

Stanton wanted something concrete done for the newly freed fugitives. After a great deal of discussion and several drafts, each carefully edited by Stanton, Sherman issued Special Field Orders No. 15, one of the most famous documents of that era. In this statement, Sherman set aside the abandoned lands on the Sea Islands off South Carolina and Georgia for the former slaves, prohibiting any whites, except official personnel, from going there. He encouraged young black males to enlist in the army, promising they would receive their land after the war. It was a revolutionary document, and it is ironic that someone with Sherman's antiblack attitudes should have issued it. But once he promulgated it and handed over responsibility to a subordinate, he did nothing to further its implementation. In 1866 he told President Andrew Johnson that he had always considered it a war measure with no permanence unless the federal government specifically gave it such. When Johnson then negated the order, Sherman remained silent. Clearly this document was Stanton's more than it was Sherman's. When Sherman told Ellen about the visit, he said the secretary was now "cured of that Negro nonsense." Despite Chase and others' trying to change his mind on the question, Sherman concluded: "I am right and won't change."[64]

In the euphoria of his success, Sherman was blind to the time bomb this issue represented for him and for the nation. As he looked back on his dramatic campaign, the matter of fugitive slaves was hardly foremost in his mind. He had taken an enormous risk in leaving Hood's army behind and marching in the opposite direction. But Thomas had soundly defeated Hood, and Sherman had easily completed his march. He saw no reason to look to the past; he eagerly looked to the future. "Success has crowned my boldest conception," he told Ellen, "and I am going to try others quite as quixotic. It may be that spite of my fears I may come out all right."[65]

Sherman's march to the sea was one of the major events of the Civil War. Contemporaries and later historians have generally concluded that it played a significant role in the Union victory and signaled the future direction of modern warfare. When the Confederacy could not prevent a Union army from moving unimpeded through its heartland, destroying its railroads, taking its food and personal goods, freeing its slaves, terrorizing its people, and shaming its military establishment, its days were numbered. Sherman arrived in Savannah with his army seemingly in better physical shape than its condition on departing Atlanta. He was ready to turn north to join Grant against Lee in Virginia. The impact of the march to the sea on Lee's army was fatal, one Confederate officer stating bluntly that concern for his family in Sherman's path caused his "soul to sink in anguish, and his hope perish." Women in Georgia and later in the Carolinas lost "faith in widely held social and cultural assumptions. So much for the vaunted superiority of Southern civilization—and Southern men."[66]

Clearly Sherman had a profound impact on the Southern mind,

an impact that remains in the late twentieth century. Adherents of the Lost Cause honor Robert E. Lee as their saint and William T. Sherman as the villain. Lee's virtue reflected Southern goodness, the story goes; Sherman's brutality represented Northern evil. He is blamed for destruction in areas where he never marched; he is hated for crimes he never committed.

Sherman never changed his mind about the validity of his actions. His was not the first army to wreak destruction on an opposing society, he pointed out, citing the examples of the duke of Wellington and Napoleon, among others. "I never feel disposed to apologize for or excuse anything," he wrote at another time. "Those people made war on us, defied and dared us to come south to their country, where they boasted they would kill us and do all manner of horrible things. We accepted their challenge, and now for them to whine and complain of the natural and necessary results is beneath contempt." "But for the more manly, who are now engaged in building up," he told another correspondent, "I feel friendship and respect."[67]

CHAPTER 14

———— ☆ ————

PUNISHING SOUTH CAROLINA AND ENSURING VICTORY

SHERMAN'S MARCH ACROSS GEORGIA was the successful implementation of the use of destruction to produce order. Confederate civilians had experienced firsthand the full implication of continued resistance to Union forces—hard, unflinching war against their property and possessions. Sherman thought the campaign had been well executed; an important military victory had been won with minimal human casualties though substantial property loss. Southern lives had been spared so that a chastened people could quit the Confederacy and rejoin the Union. If they refused, he was ready to inflict further lessons in the Carolinas.

Sherman tried to demonstrate the benefits of peace, and Savannah's citizens were surprised and happy at how well he treated them. The City Council passed a Resolution of Thanks for his help in obtaining food. Most people, however, worried, as one South Carolina woman did, that he was "patting them with his cushioned paws, but the claws will soon reappear." But Sherman and his soldiers had no plans to harass the city dwellers; in fact they were impatient to press on. City life was "dull and tame." In the fields and forests on the march, Sherman would escape the Confederate women who were constantly demanding protection for their homes and possessions. In the piney woods, he could avoid the pleas of Northern cotton merchants desperate to protect their profit. He was eager to get back on the move and end this war.[1]

After Grant told him on December 27 that he no longer had to

sail his troops up to Virginia, Sherman began to move out of
Savannah toward Lee's army on the much-preferred overland
march. On New Year's Day 1865, in the course of the celebrations,
Sherman told O. O. Howard, the commander of his right wing, to
move his troops by ship to Beaufort, South Carolina, and then
overland to Pocotaligo on the railroad between Charleston and
Savannah. Meanwhile, Henry W. Slocum's left wing, accompanied by Judson Kilpatrick's cavalry, was to cross the Savannah
River over a causeway and pontoon bridge and establish itself near
Coosawhatchie, South Carolina. Howard had some difficulties,
but Slocum ran into major problems. The worst rains since 1840
had turned the river into a three-mile-wide lake, and Slocum
could not move his wing across until the end of January. Sherman
had to wait impatiently with Howard in Pocotaligo. Noticeably
grumpy to all around him, he complained to Admiral Porter:
"The weather has been villainous, and all the country is under
water, and retards me much. It may be some days yet before I can
cast off, as the roads are under water, and my men are not exactly
amphibious yet, nor the mules either."[2]

Sherman organized as much diversion as possible for his
movement to keep the enemy off-balance. Thomas in Tennessee
organized raids into North Carolina, Alabama, and Mississippi.
The navy made demonstrations along the Atlantic coast, particularly at Charleston. Sherman asked General J. G. Foster, whom he
had left in command of Savannah, to do "whatever you may do to
aid me along the coast." On January 15, 1865, a combined
army-navy force under General Alfred H. Terry and Admiral D.
D. Porter took Fort Fisher at the mouth of Cape Fear in North
Carolina. Meanwhile, Schofield and the Twenty-third Corps were
on their way from Tennessee.[3]

The army organization had not changed from the march to the
sea: two wings consisting of two columns each and a cavalry unit
that rode wherever it was needed. On January 2, Sherman told
Grant how he planned to use this sixty-thousand-man force. He
would have his right wing feint in the direction of Charleston; his
left wing would feint toward Augusta. His actual objective would
be Columbia. The idea was to confuse the Confederates into
protecting Charleston and Augusta, thus leaving the way open to
Columbia. "I don't like to boast, but I believe this army has a
confidence in itself that makes it almost invincible." Actually the

army remained confident in him. "Wherever he goes this Army will go most willingly and faithfully," one officer said.[4]

No substantial Confederate forces lay to Sherman's front. The Army of Tennessee, which had opposed him during the Atlanta campaign and had later been crushed by Thomas and Schofield at Nashville, was licking its wounds at Corinth, Mississippi. William Hardee, Sherman's outmanned opponent during the march to the sea, commanded the Departments of Georgia and South Carolina, but his divisions were scattered. P. G. T. Beauregard, commander of the Military Division of the West, looked to Robert E. Lee for help, but except for a cavalry division under Wade Hampton, Lee had nothing to spare for South Carolina.[5]

Joe Johnston had remained on the sidelines since his replacement as commander of the Army of Tennessee, but he kept a close watch on Sherman, amazed that his army was on the march in the dead of winter through the region's swamps. He later told Sherman: "My engineer officers all reported that it was absolutely impossible for any army to march across the lower portions of the state in winter, and I took it for granted that you would not attempt to advance, unless across the upper hill section of the state."[6]

But Sherman and his army marched across this seemingly impassable terrain, the bulk of the force finally embarking on February 1. He had no easy task, but he believed it was "necessary to the war" and had to be "made sooner or later." Slocum's problems with the flooded Savannah River were only the beginning of the army's difficulties. The area was "traversed by few roads, many deep rivers, innumerable streams, and overflowed swamps," one officer complained. The mud was everywhere, sucking down marching soldiers, artillery caissons, wagons, horses, and mules. The only way to cross some of the swollen streams was to build bridges across them, wading waist deep in the cold water to do so. The only way to move through the water-soaked land approaches was to corduroy them—hard, dirty work that sapped the strength of animals and men. Trees had to be cut down, trimmed of limbs, dragged through muck to the roadway, and laid down one next to another. Sometimes the mud was so watery the logs sank; other times the lumber would float to the surface. All too often several layers of logs were required to conquer the ooze, and even then they would shift and slip, creating traps for wagons and men. Animals suffered enormously trying to pick their way through the muck and lumber, and the soldiers never seemed to dry out. An officer told of seeing a sergeant reaching into the mud up to his elbow, looking for a shoe. Another time Sherman came upon an exhausted soldier carrying his muddy footwear. When the man noticed Sherman, he quickly saluted, forgetting that he still held the shoes in his hand.[7]

Word of Sherman's bemused reaction to this shoe salute and other sympathetic stories of his presence in and among the troops spread throughout the army. He shared his men's hardships. They laughed and joked with him as though he was an old friend. "Don't ride too fast, General," someone would yell out as his horse slipped and slid along a muddy roadside. "Pretty slippery going, Uncle Billy; pretty slippery going." Sherman would smile, when he was not deep in thought, and encourage the soldiers, seeming to know them all by name. They were his "boys," his army family.[8]

Sherman had once more cut his force off from its base of supplies, and once more his men had to forage off the land. "I must risk a great deal," he told Halleck, "based upon the idea that where other people live we can, even if they have to starve or move away." In Georgia, the foragers had been relatively selective in their violence against property. In South Carolina, they showed no such restraint. Like their commander, they blamed the Palmetto State for starting the war at Charleston's Fort Sumter, and they were determined to mete out proper punishment. As the army was poised to enter South Carolina, Sherman told Slocum: "Don't forget that when you have crossed the Savannah River you will be in South Carolina. You need not be so careful there about private property as we have been. The more of it you destroy the better it will be. The people of South Carolina should be made to feel the war, for they brought it on and are responsible more than anybody else for our presence here. Now is the time to punish them." "I almost tremble at her fate," he told Halleck, "but feel that she deserves all that seems in store for her." He had no plans to rein in his army "lest its vigor and energy be impaired." Halleck agreed. He hoped that South Carolina, the "viper nest of the rebellion[,] would be punished and that sternly and severely."[9]

The soldiers needed little encouragement. As they entered the state, a soldier turned to the cheering ranks behind him and yelled out: "Boys, this is old South Carolina, let's give her hell." Houses were burned in much greater numbers than during the march to the sea. "I think I shall never see a distant column of smoke rising hereafter, but it will remind me of Sherman," one officer said. The destruction was thorough, although violence against individuals remained rare. The soldiers embraced Sherman's vision of total war and its implications for civilians. They shared his distaste and bitterness for South Carolinians in particular. Palmetto State residents, a Union officer said, though they had bragged about fighting to the bitter end, were "more cowardly than children, and whine[d] like whipped school-boys. Ridiculously helpless, they sit and groan without making an effort to help themselves," he said disgustedly.[10]

Sherman's soldiers, all veterans, felt a cockiness that was apparent in their disregard for what the elements were doing to their military dress. A black chaplain of the 102d U.S. Colored Infantry described a Sherman man thus: "His pantaloons leg is split half way up to his knee; his face is unshaven and his hair unshorn; the crown of his hat, too, is gone, but he is perfectly oblivious to the eyes that are upon him, or the remarks that are made about him, and with his gun swung carelessly over his shoulder the whole appearance of the man says 'I can hold all the ground that I cover.'"[11]

Stories of the prowess of Sherman's soldiers, especially the bummers, were legend. A slave noted with awe that "these Yankee soldiers have noses like hounds. Massa hid his horses way out dar in de swamp. Some soldiers come along. All at once dey held up dere noses and sniffed and sniffed, and stopped still and sniffed, and turned into de swamp and held up dere noses and sniffed, and, Lord a' Massy, went right straight to where de horses was tied in de swamp."[12]

The bummers provided flank protection and acted as skirmishers all around the main force. In one dramatic incident, they even won an important tactical victory. Howard was moving his wing carefully toward Midway, a stop on the South Carolina Railroad. Suddenly a bummer riding a white horse with a rope bridle and a blanket saddle came galloping down the road toward him. "Hurry up, General," he shouted, "we have got the railroad." "So," Sherman later joked, "while we, the Generals, were proceeding deliberately to prepare for a serious battle, a parcel of our foragers had got ahead and actually captured the South Carolina Railroad, a line of vital importance to the Rebel government." Joe Johnston shared this respect. He later told Sherman: "Your foragers were the most efficient cavalry ever known. They covered your flanks so completely that I never could penetrate through them far enough to feel your column. And the fact that they could be sent so far off from the eyes of the commanding officers and return regularly at night, is proof of the highest state of discipline of your army."[13]

Despite the swamps, rain-soaked roads, the bitter cold, and cavalry leader Joe Wheeler's attempt to obstruct the way with fallen trees, the two wings of Sherman's army made steady progress toward their first juncture on the South Carolina Railroad near Blackville. After the foragers captured the road on February 7, the entire force twisted tracks and incapacitated it. On the eleventh, forward movement began again, and Orangeburg quickly fell to the Seventeenth Corps of the army's right wing. Sherman entered the town with this unit and stayed long enough to supervise the destruction of the railroad tracks, a depot, and cotton bales. He then ordered the columns to turn toward Columbia, having learned that only Hampton's cavalry stood in the way. Sherman's use of what modern scholars call a "strategy of indirect approach" was working. The Confederates were so concerned about Augusta and Charleston that the state capital and its twelve thousand to fourteen thousand people were wide open to the advancing Federals. Meanwhile, Charleston, isolated from the interior by Sherman's advance, fell on February 18.[14]

John A. Logan's Fifteenth Corps of Sherman's right wing took Columbia after a brief resistance from Hampton's cavalry and Confederate artillery. The only Union artillery fire into the city consisted of a few cannon balls to scatter some cavalry and scavengers and harmlessly to strike the unfinished state capitol building. While lead troops were capturing the city, Sherman, as usual, paced up and down, an unlit cigar clamped in his teeth. He would stop to talk to those around him, then step off again, only to sit down and whittle on a stick for a while. Soon he would jump up and begin pacing again.[15]

Sherman and Howard led the way into the city after the mayor surrendered it, the streets littered with broken furniture and other household items left there by pillaging Confederate soldiers and civilians. The railroad depot and a large storage building had been burned to the ground. Bales of cotton piled in the middle of many streets had been torn open, and lint was flying around, catching in trees and bushes. The scene reminded Sherman of a "northern snow-storm." The first Union troops into the city turned to trying to extinguish fires in a number of the cotton bales. So many were burning, in fact, that Cump had to ride his horse along the sidewalk to avoid them.[16]

His welcome was tumultuous. The city's black and white inhabitants plied the weary and hungry Union soldiers with buckets of liquor. Half-drunk, some of these men valiantly formed ordered ranks and cheered their commander. One, outfitted in a dressing gown, stepped forward, lifted his hat, and said: "I have the honor (hic), General, to present (hic) you with (hic) the freedom of the (hic) City." Sherman suppressed a smile, "raised his hat and rode soberly along." Black reaction was even more exuberant. Slaves ran after Sherman, yelling, and dancing, and clapping and loudly thanking God for his arrival. One old black woman grabbed Sherman by the hand when he dismounted in the city square and told him personally that her prayers had been answered. Mayor T. J. Goodwyn was nervous about the fate of his city, and Sherman tried to reassure him. Some bedraggled men pushed their way up to Sherman, and he was excited to learn they were Union prisoners of war freed by his arrival. One slipped him a piece of paper, which he later found was the text of a poem the man had written while in prison, "Sherman's March to the Sea." Sherman and the author, S. H. M. Byers, were to remain friends for the rest of their lives.[17]

Sherman had noted the drunken soldiers and urged Howard, whom he put in command of the city, to discipline them. Meanwhile, Mayor Goodwyn led him to the house he was to use for his headquarters, some seven blocks from the city center. After settling in, he walked all over the community, the mayor introducing him to people they encountered. They went to the house of the daughter of an old acquaintance from Fort Moultrie days and, to his surprise, Sherman found the home and yard completely untouched. The woman credited Sherman for her good fortune. Earlier in the day, some Union soldiers had entered the yard and begun pillaging. The woman showed their leader a book Sherman had inscribed to her in 1845. The sergeant recognized the signature and placed a guard over the property. The young soldier not only prevented damage to the house, but he also helped care for the family's baby.[18]

A tired Sherman returned to his headquarters and napped until a bright light reflecting on the room's wall awakened him. He thought of the smoldering cotton bales and worried that the high wind, which had been whipping the city all day, had rekindled the fires. He sent an aide to investigate and learned that some buildings were indeed on fire and that Union soldiers were battling the flames. The conflagration kept spreading, and at 11 P.M., he went to see for himself.[19]

Fanned by the high winds, the fire had evaded all the Union efforts to extinguish it and spread in all directions. "The very heavens at times appeared on fire. A wide street was no barrier," Howard gasped. "The whole air was full of sparks and of flying masses of cotton, shingles, etc.," Sherman noticed, "some of which were carried four or five blocks, and started new fires." An outraged Southern woman saw it as all the Federals' fault: "The terrified lowing of cattle, the frenzied flight of pigeons circling high above their blazing cotes, the ribald jests and brutal assaults of our drunken conquerors, the dun clouds of despair rolling between us and the pitying eye of God, made up a picture whose counterpart can be found only in the regions of the eternally lost." Some Federals took advantage of the situation to continue their earlier pillaging, while others battled the flames. It was not until 3 or 4 A.M. that the wind died down, and the fire was brought under control.[20]

The next day a dazed population looked out on their city and saw vast destruction. Although two-thirds of the city remained standing that morning, churches, most stores, and many of the most expensive houses were charred ruins. The Union high command did what it could for those in need, providing food and shelter and even providing the mayor with a hundred muskets to maintain order when the army departed. The issue of blame immediately came to the fore, the crux of the argument clear in the debate between Sherman and a committee of women the day after the fire. "Why, then," the women asked, "did you burn our town, or allow your army to do so?" "I did not burn your town, nor did my army," Sherman answered. "Your brothers, sons, husbands and fathers set fire to every city, town and village in the land when they fired on Fort Sumter. That fire kindled then and there by them has been burning ever since, and reached your houses last night."[21]

Southerners then and later were not impressed. They insisted that Sherman was responsible for burning Columbia, some believing that he had issued specific orders. Indeed, the myth grew that Sherman had torched the city and burned it to the ground. There is no evidence. Sherman's diary entry the next day was consistent with his later position: "Columbia burned from high winds. Cotton in the Streets fired by the enemy, and the General animosity of our own men—just distress of People." He blamed Wade Hampton's carelessness with the cotton, in his later memoirs admitting that he did it to place further stress on the Southern mind. Hampton angrily threw the guilt back onto Sherman. An American and British commission established under the 1870 Treaty of Washington absolved Sherman's army of responsibility, but Confederate sympathizers were not convinced. Southern publications like *Confederate Veteran* regularly accused Sherman of incinerating Columbia.[22]

It seems clear now that neither Sherman nor anyone else was solely responsible for the fire. It was an accident of war. Hampton and his soldiers set fire to the cotton bales that fueled the fire, but it was released Southern civil prisoners, former slaves, and some Union soldiers, many of these groups intoxicated by the liquor provided by town's people or stolen from storage areas, who set other fires. The Union high command worked valiantly to extinguish the blazes, but the high winds made their task impossible. "The principal demons in the drama were cotton, whisky, and wind," a later historian surmised. Sherman phrased it more bluntly in later years, refusing to accept the blame for the Columbia fire. "Had I intended to burn Columbia," he said in 1881, "I would have done it just as I would have done any act of war, and there would have been no concealment about it."[23]

Before the Fifteenth Corps left Columbia on February 20, Sherman had it destroy several foundries, the state arsenal jammed with weapons, and a factory that printed Confederate money. The entire right wing then linked up with the left wing at Winnsboro, and the united army turned toward Cheraw and Fayetteville. As they marched along, Sherman conducted a long-range debate with Wade Hampton over foraging. Cump was angry over eighteen dead Union soldiers, several with their throats slit, others with their heads bashed in, and a scrawled "Death to all foragers" pinned to them. Though Joe Wheeler denied knowing about these executions, Sherman warned Wade Hampton that he would retaliate in kind. Foraging was "a right as old as history," he told Hampton, and even if his men committed any wrongdoing, he would not allow Confederates to murder them. Not to be outdone, Hampton said he would shoot two Federals for every Confederate Sherman killed. He refused to admit his men had murdered anyone, but he acknowledged ordering them to shoot any individual burning a house: "This order shall remain in force so long as you disgrace the profession of arms by allowing your men to destroy private dwellings."[24]

Sherman let Hampton's comment pass unanswered. He told Kilpatrick to ignore Confederate complaints about the Union army's "warring against women and children. If they claim to be men they should defend their women and children and prevent us reaching their homes." He was obviously pleased with his army's progress and optimistic about the future. Perhaps he was even able to enjoy what a Confederate deserter said about his generalship. The fugitive Confederate said "Our boys say General Sherman never makes but one speech. When ready for a movement, he says: 'now boys, let's get ready to go; and they get ready,'" both Federals and Rebels, the deserter said.[25]

Sherman's easy entry into Cheraw buoyed his spirits, as did his conversation with a group of area blacks who spoke of whites' running away at the mere mention of his name. "It is not me they are afraid of," Sherman answered, "the name of another man would have the same effect with them if he had this army. It is these soldiers that they run away from."[26]

The march was going so well that Sherman and his staff were able to ride between the columns without any escort. During a gathering of generals, John A. Logan played "Sherman's March to the Sea" on his violin, and the generals joined in the singing. They discovered a large supply of wine and rugs sent there from Charleston for safekeeping, and they enjoyed these too. In a private home Sherman found a cache of Sir Walter Scott novels, his preferred reading during the march, and he helped himself to several volumes he had not yet read, promising to leave others in their place.[27]

An old nemesis ruined his contentment. While examining the contents of the room Confederate general William J. Hardee had used as his Cheraw headquarters, Sherman found a copy of a recent *New York Tribune* announcing that Sherman was actually aiming for Goldsboro, North Carolina, though he seemed to be heading for Charlotte and Raleigh. Sherman was furious at this breach of security and would never forgive Horace Greeley, the newspaper's editor. Ominously, at about this time, Sherman learned that his opponent during the Atlanta campaign, Joe Johnston, had been restored to command of all Confederate armies in the Carolinas.[28]

Sherman's force now entered North Carolina, and a remarkable change came over the marchers. The wholesale destruction they had practiced in South Carolina ceased. Sherman let it be known that he wanted them to "deal as moderately and fairly by the North Carolinians as possible, and fan the flame of discord already subsisting between them and their proud cousins of South Carolina. There never was much love between them. Touch upon the [South Carolina] chivalry running away, always leaving their families for us to feed and protect, and then on purpose accusing us of all sorts of rudeness." But it was more than driving a wedge between two Confederate states that caused Sherman and his soldiers to treat the Tarheel State less destructively. Like their commander, Sherman's soldiers were beginning to see less need for all-out war. Victory seemed to be looming.[29]

The soldiers did not stop all pillaging; they simply toned it down. The bummers continued foraging and even found an exciting new way to cause panic. They discovered that the resin in the tall pine trees of the forests easily caught on fire, and the flames strikingly moved up the tree trunks. This was dramatic enough during the day, but at night these resin fires lighted up the countryside. North Carolinians were already overawed at the size of the force marching through their state, and these smokey fires added to their fears. They complained to husbands, brothers, and husbands in Lee's army, and Lee noted the increase in desertions. Still, North Carolinians were not yet ready to quit.[30]

Soon after taking Fayetteville on March 11, Sherman's army regained contact with the outside world. A steamboat whistle signaled the arrival of a bag full of mail from General Alfred Terry in Wilmington. The two secret couriers Sherman had sent there on March 8 had made it through. Two large Union forces were now in contact, and importantly for Sherman, he once again had a secure source of supplies. Sherman wrote Grant and Secretary of War Stanton excitedly, telling the latter "that I have done all that I proposed, and the fruits seem to me ample for the time employed." He told Ellen that "the importance of this march exceeds that from Atlanta to Savannah." And as he always did, he wrote to Thomas Ewing: "I hope you will be pleased at the plan, execution & effect."[31]

Despite his optimism and excitement, Sherman knew there was still a great deal to be done before the fighting could end. He still had to link up in Virginia with Grant against Lee. More immediately there was Joe Johnston. He worried that Johnston would try to prevent him from joining with Schofield and Terry, who were moving toward him from New Berne and Wilmington, respectively. He needed food and clothing for his bedraggled men, whose battles with the swamps and mud had left their uniforms and shoes in tatters. Schofield and Terry also had to repair the state's railroads from the Atlantic coast to Goldsboro, the concentration point, so he could receive the needed supplies. And they had to relieve him of what he called "twenty to thirty thousand useless mouths" (most of them fugitive slaves). "I can whip Jos. Johnston provided he does not catch one of my corps in flank," Sherman boasted, "and I will see that the army marches hence to Goldsboro in compact form."[32]

Upon entering Fayetteville, Sherman was greeted by a Southerner, a former member of one of his regiments in the pre–Civil War army. The man happily approached his old commander. Sherman returned the smile, then quickly turned stern and hard. "Yes, we were long together, weren't we?" he asked. "Yes," answered the pleased Southerner. "You shared my friendship, shared my bread, even, didn't you?" Sherman persisted. "Indeed, indeed!" the increasingly happy man replied. Sherman stared at him harshly: "You have betrayed it all; me, your friend, your country that educated you for its defense. You are here a traitor, and you ask me to be again your friend, to protect your property, to send you these brave men, some of whose comrades were murdered by your neighbors this very morning—fired on from hidden houses by you and yours as they entered the town. Turn your back to me forever. I will not punish you; only go your way.

There is room in the world even for traitors." The shaken Southerner walked away crestfallen. Sherman sat down for lunch, but he could barely eat. "The corners of his mouth twitched as he continued talking to us of this false friend. The hand that held the bread trembled and for a moment tears were in his eyes." His subordinates were shocked at the depth of his feeling. "We realized as never before," one later wrote, "what treason to the republic really meant."[33]

Sherman destroyed mills, the arsenal, and every other war-making installation in the area as his bummers systematically foraged the farms and houses. "Our smoke house and pantry, that a few days ago were well stored with bacon, lard, flour, dried fruit, meat, pickles, preserves, etc.," one woman said, "now contains nothing whatever except a few pounds of meal and flour and five pounds of bacon." They "spared nothing but our lives," she complained.[34]

Sherman now feinted on Raleigh but rushed his army forward to merge with Schofield and Terry at Goldsboro before Joe Johnston could concentrate his forces against him. Schofield was to become the center of Sherman's army. Howard would remain the right wing and Slocum the left. Sherman wrote Quincy A. Gilmore, commanding Union troops in Charleston, calling for movement from him, too. "All real good soldiers must now be marching. Do not let your command rest on its oars, but keep them going all the time, even if for no other purpose than to exhaust the enemy's country, or compel him to defend it. The simple fact that a man's home has been visited by an enemy makes a soldier in Lee's and Johnston's army very anxious to get home to look after his family and property." In short, he wanted his brand of warfare against civilians intensified, and he was pleased when Grant told him that Lee's army was "demoralized and deserting very fast, both to us and to their homes."[35]

Sherman rode with Slocum and the left wing when it left Fayetteville on March 15. This force encountered resistance from Hardee, and in the brisk fighting that followed, it drove the Confederates back. In the process they captured Colonel Alfred Rhett, a former commander of Fort Sumter and one of the editors of the *Charleston Mercury*. Sherman treated Rhett to dinner and listened to the Confederate's disgust at having been captured without a fight. He then handed him over to Slocum's provost marshal, pleased to hear personally an example of declining Confederate army morale.

Meanwhile, Hardee had dug in near Averysboro. Slocum positioned his troops and followed Sherman's order for a flanking movement on the left. The Confederate line was forced to its rear positions and was soon driven beyond these. When he toured a hospital after the skirmish, Sherman found a Confederate officer, who was the son of one of his Charleston friends from Moultrie days. Federal surgeons had only recently removed the young man's arm, but he had enough command of his senses to recognize Sherman. He asked him to deliver a letter to his mother, once more reminding Sherman that he was fighting friends. Later Sherman talked to a Union officer whom Confederate soldiers had stripped despite his appeal to Wade Hampton himself for courtesy as a fellow officer. Sherman angrily sent word that in retaliation for this outrage, Alfred Rhett should be taken from his horse and forced to walk to prison.[36]

The next day the sound of artillery fire was heard in the left wing, but Slocum sent word that it was only some pesky cavalry. Actually it was Johnston's seventeen-thousand-man army, digging in across the path of Slocum's advance. The left wing entrenched itself, and Slocum sent word to Sherman of his dire predicament. The message arrived so late at night that Sherman was already in his red flannel undershirt and drawers. He told Slocum to hold on. Johnston had surprised Sherman, hoping to annihilate Slocum before the rest of the Union army could concentrate in opposition. Slocum fought furiously, however, and held on until Sherman arrived with Howard's wing. Johnston's army was formed in a V, the town of Bentonville inside the formation. Slocum's wing faced one side of the V, Howard the other.[37]

Slocum's determined stand stymied Johnston. Once again Sherman had an opportunity to destroy an opposing army, and once again, as he had at Atlanta and Savannah, he held back. "I would rather avoid a general battle, if possible," he told Slocum. He remained quiet for several days until one of his division commanders, Joseph A. Mowrer, broke through on Johnston's farthest left flank. Here was a golden opportunity, but Sherman still demurred, refusing to bring on a pitched battle and casualties when his war of terror was working so effectively. Instead of following up with his entire right wing, he ordered Mowrer back.

Sherman told Grant that his men were " 'dirty ragged, and saucy' and we must rest and fix up a little." He later admitted he had thrown away a magnificent opportunity, but at the time he was more interested in merging with Schofield's Twenty-third Corps and Terry's two divisions of the Tenth Corps near Goldsboro than in bloody battle. When he met Schofield and Terry on March 22, he considered the Carolina campaign finished and Lee's days in Virginia numbered. He enjoyed the fulsome praise he received from Grant and Stanton. He called his campaign a "glorious success. After a march of the most extraordinary character, near five-hundred miles, over swamps and rivers deemed impassable to others, at the most inclement season of the year, and drawing our supplies from a poor and wasted country, we reach[ed] our destination in good health and condition." Johnston's army's survival did not overly concern him.[38]

An incident demonstrated just how pleased Sherman was with his army's achievement. His men were in rags from the march. Many trousers were split and tattered from wear, exposing the wearer's legs. As Sherman and his staff watched the bedraggled soldiers passing by, an officer expressed sympathy for these bare legs. "Splendid legs," Sherman jumped in, "splendid legs. Would give both of mine for any one of them." He gloried in his soldiers.[39]

Sherman was pleased with his successful march because the devastation had brought the war closer to completion and made less necessary the killing of people he knew and liked. He had achieved military success without excessive casualties, and he hoped Southerners would recognize his achievement. "I am not the savage and monster that the Southern Press represents me[.] . . . [I] will take infinitely more delight in curing the wounds made by war than in inflicting them." He wrote to the brother of his former St. Louis business partner, Henry S. Turner, lamenting the fact that he and his old friend were no longer close. Perhaps Turner, a pro-Confederate, believed "all the absurd stories" about him, or perhaps he was consumed with grief over the deaths of his two sons. Sherman hotly insisted that Jefferson Davis and other Confederate leaders were the "murderers" responsible for the death of so many young men. He felt no responsibility. In fact, he considered himself "a true friend to the People of the South."

"I feel the same personal friendship as ever—am not conscious of having done anything wonderful further than to persevere in what I deemed the only way to suppress mutiny and sedition in our own Grand Camp."[40]

In his own mind, Sherman was convinced of the wisdom of his march of destruction. He rationalized this thought best to Thomas when he ordered his friend to conduct some diversionary raids: "It is nonsense to suppose that the people of the South are enraged or united by such movements," he insisted. "They reason very differently. They see in them the sure and irresistible destruction of all their property. They realize that the Confederate armies cannot protect them and they see in . . . such raids the inevitable result of starvation & misery."[41]

Clearly, the desires for order and for submission to the Union were the major reasons Sherman continued fighting in 1865. Rebellion in any form could not be tolerated, and his aim was to reimpose Union and stability where earlier it had been threatened. His military ardor and intensity was fueled and reinforced by his personal quest for an orderly and secure situation. Sherman destroyed because it seemed a more direct route to a desired end. He did not try to be cruel; he tried only to convince Southerners to stop the secession and the war. Once they did that, he promised to work as hard at reconciliation as he had at destruction. His strategy was designed to achieve the Union's aims with the least loss of life and the swiftest path to success. Judged on those terms, he could not fault himself—nor could he imagine anyone else faulting him either.

Sherman never thought his campaigns were revolutionary. As late as 1888 he insisted that "all these movements were on a grand scale, strictly in conformity with the lessons of the great masters, and illustrate every branch of the science of war." He would have been baffled by the analyses of the future that crowned him the great innovator of his age. He would have preferred the title of grand strategist. He believed he simply took the war to its commonsense ends. It was a war between people, not just between armies, and it had to be fought that way. What he failed to realize was that efficiently applying military force against civilians on American soil would be seen as revolutionary and morally repugnant. He not only terrified Southerners; he traumatized them. They would remain stunned long after the war was over. Sherman had attacked the Southern psyche, and the wounds he left were slow in healing. Loss in combat allows the vanquished to claim the moral high ground of courage and bravery. Defeat at the hands of Sherman allowed the vanquished only the claim of the victor's moral depravity.

Sherman's perceived brutality lay not in his destruction of Confederate property but in the fact that he, more than any Union general, demonstrated the hopelessness of the Confederate cause. Once he purposefully marched through the interior, letting neither Johnston's nor Hood's armies, distance, logistics, mud, or swamps hinder him, it was all over. The trail of destruction, though not nearly as complete as some claim, was shocking enough to sear the Southern soul. Sherman did not save Southern sensibilities, and this was his real crime.

The end of the march through the Carolinas capped another Sherman success. Beginning in Chattanooga in May 1864, he had captured Atlanta, marched to the sea through Georgia, and swung north through the Carolinas. He was a national hero, one of the military stars of the Union war effort. The unsuccessful business-man of the 1850s, the allegedly crazy commander in Kentucky, and the loser at Chickasaw Bayou had turned his life around. He had shown that his belief about his personal success being tied to Union success was accurate. If he thought about it, he might have realized the significance of a comment he had made to Admiral Porter in late December 1864, before the Carolina campaign. He had confidently said that Charleston, the seat of secession, was "a dead cock in the pit altogether." In the light of his Kansas failure in 1859, he had said: "I look upon myself as a dead cock in the pit, not worthy of further notice." Sherman the failure had become Sherman the hero, even in his own mind. Success was now finally and totally his, and he could see no way anyone could deny it to him or take it away from him either.[42]

CHAPTER 15

☆

FAME TARNISHED

SINCE BEGINNING his Atlanta campaign in May 1864, Sherman had captured the city, marched through Georgia to Savannah, and then made the amazing movement through the water-logged Carolinas. He had rocked the Confederacy on its heels, earned the plaudits of the nation and even the rest of the world, and gained the long-sought-for approval from Thomas Ewing. Cump Sherman felt a self-pride he had rarely experienced before. He had demonstrated that it was unnecessary to kill people to wage successful war, and he believed that everyone now saw it his way too. As he had shown in Kentucky early on and later when he dealt with reporters or recruiting agents or when he adopted war against civilians, he equated his position with the only reasonable reality. If he believed something and asserted it, the argument was over; everyone else had to see it the same way or be guilty of stupidity at best or criminality at worst. His ability to focus made him an effective general, but it also caused him to characterize reasonable differences of opinion as disorderly and harmful. This attitude had prevented him from recognizing problems with reporters and politicians throughout the war and would help cause the greatest crisis of his career, just when he confidently expected to enjoy the fame he had so diligently earned the previous year.

As he sat in his tent in Goldsboro, North Carolina, in March 1865 writing to his wife, Sherman was a contented man. "Thus have I brought the army from Savannah in good order, beaten the enemy wherever he attempted to oppose and progress, and made junction with Schofield and Terry from New Bern and Wilmington on the 21st, one day later than I had appointed before leaving Savannah." He had "no doubt," he told her, that she was "sufficiently gratified to know that I have eminently succeeded." It felt good to see no clouds on his horizon.[1]

His army was equally "cheerful and in high spirits at their success in the last two campaigns." They were convinced that "there never was such a man as Sherman." Among the officers, there was talk that someday their commander would be president of the United States. Oh no, Sherman jokingly insisted, the public was too "fickle" for that. He reminded his supporters of the time when stories of his insanity and Grant's drunkenness had nearly ruined them both. No, he had no eye on the White House.[2]

Just then he was more concerned with supplying his troops, his single-minded military concentration not diverted by his recent success. He impatiently waited for the repair of the railroad from Goldsboro to New Bern, so supplies could reach him. He also wanted to see Grant at City Point, Virginia, to plan their future movements. Until the railroad was ready, however, he had to stay put. In fact, there was no rush. Johnston posed no real threat; "from the character of the fighting . . . we have got Johnston's army afraid of us. He himself acts with timidity and caution."[3]

He wanted to see Grant for personal as well as military reasons. The two men had remained close since before Shiloh, the good feelings between them genuine. In response to a recent rumor of promotion in rank, Sherman had immediately written his brother to quash the possibility, telling Grant that he had no interest in having competition with him. Grant wrote back that "no one would be more pleased at your advancement than I, and if you should be placed in my position, and I put subordinate, it would not change our relations in the least." Grant and Sherman trusted and liked each other. Though different in temperament, they shared a common background of past failure and newly gained success. They stood on the brink of completing the military conquest of the Confederacy, and it would be good to savor the dawn of the final success together.[4]

When the railroad from Goldsboro to New Bern opened on March 25, 1865, Sherman put Schofield in charge and left for the coast. He arrived two days later at City Point on the James River in Virginia, to be greeted at the wharf by Grant and several of his subordinates, some of whom were sure that Sherman was coming to relieve Meade as commander of the Army of the Potomac. Sherman jumped off the ship and hurried toward Grant. "How d'you do, Sherman!" Grant yelled out. "How are you, Grant!" Sherman responded as the two men shook hands warmly. "Their encounter," an officer noted, "was more like that of two school-boys coming together after a vacation than the meeting of the chief actors in a great war tragedy."[5]

The two old friends were soon sitting around a fire, and Sherman was enthralling Grant and all the other officers with stories of his marches. There he sat, "his sandy whiskers closely cropped . . . [with] sharp twinkling eyes, long arms and legs, shabby coat, slouch hat, [and] his pants tucked into his boots." His restless energy was obvious. "Never was a speaker more eloquent," an observer noted, his audience hanging on his every word. He told one anecdote after another about his army's exploits, peppering his comments with self-deprecating humor. One time, he recalled, he told a soldier that he would certainly like to trade his legs for the soldier's. "He sized up my legs with his eye," Sherman said, "and evidently considered them mere spin-dle-shanks compared with his, and then looked up at me and said: 'General, if it's all the same to you, I guess I'd rather not swap.'" The listeners roared in approval, Grant enjoying himself as much as the rest.[6]

After about an hour, Grant told Sherman that Abraham Lincoln was aboard the *River Queen* nearby, and they ought to pay him a visit. Sherman agreed, and the two men started off toward the president's boat. They found Lincoln alone and were soon deep in conversation. Lincoln wanted to know all about Sherman's marches, particularly enjoying stories about the bum-mers and their foraging activities. He kept expressing concern over Sherman's absence from his army, though Sherman con-vinced him that Schofield was more than competent to command.[7]

When Grant and Sherman returned from Lincoln's boat, Mrs. Grant was waiting with tea. She asked about Mrs. Lincoln, and Grant said he had never thought about asking for her, and Sherman said he had not even been aware she was on board the boat. "Well, you are a pretty pair!" Julia Grant scolded. "I do not see how you could have been so neglectful." Grant promised to look to the matter in the morning, and Sherman quickly tried to change the subject: "Let's talk further about the immediate movements of my army," he said. "Perhaps you don't want me here listening to all your secrets," Mrs. Grant said. "Do you think we can trust her, Grant?" Sherman asked jokingly. "I'm not so sure about that, Sherman," Grant responded in equally good humor. Sherman turned his chair in front of Julia Grant and assumed the pose of a stern teacher, asking her all kinds of geography questions. With a straight face, she gave ridiculous answers to his increasingly hilarious inquiries. Finally, Sherman looked at a highly amused Grant and said: "Well, Grant, I think we can trust her." Out came the maps, and the planning commenced, the two men so pleased to be together and buoyed by their military successes that they were almost giddy.[8]

The next day, Grant, Sherman, and Admiral David Dixon Porter met with Abraham Lincoln on the *River Queen* to discuss what they hoped would be the last days of the war. (But first Grant asked about Mrs. Lincoln.) Sherman and Lincoln did most of the talking, and Porter wrote it all down that evening. Lincoln was afraid that Lee might try to break away from Grant, link up with Johnston in North Carolina, and either escape south or try to fight one last great battle. Sherman said he could handle both armies until Grant arrived and completed the conquest. Lincoln hoped that the Confederate armies would surrender; he wanted to give them "the most liberal and honorable terms" so they would return to the Union and obey all its laws again. "My God, my God, can't you spare more effusion of blood?" Lincoln implored. "We have had so much of it!" Sherman responded that within two weeks he could force Johnston to accept any treaty the Union wanted. No, Lincoln said, in two weeks Johnston might get away; give him good terms and get him to surrender immediately. Sherman insisted that Johnston could not escape, but Grant suggested he could use the Southern railroads. "There are no Southern railroads to speak of," Sherman answered. "My bummers have broken up the roads in sections all behind us—and they did it well." Turning to Lincoln, he reiterated his ability to force Johnston's surrender on any terms. Lincoln insisted once again that he wanted to avoid further bloodshed. He even hinted that if the Confederate leaders escaped, it would not upset him.[9]

Sherman was pleased with the meeting, happy that Lincoln agreed with his hard war–soft peace philosophy. He wrote

Secretary of War Stanton that "everything wears a most favorable aspect." He was similarly upbeat to Ellen though much more subdued to Thomas Ewing: "It is perfectly impossible for me in case of failure to divest myself of responsibility[,] as all from the President, Secretary of War, General Grant, etc., seem to vie with each other in contributing to my success." He assured his foster father that he realized that any surrender terms would contain political as well as military terms, and he was "fully conscious of the fact that I would imperil all by any concessions in that direction." He boarded a fast steamship to rejoin his army. The usually cold Stanton wrote him warmly: "God speed you; and that He may have you in his keeping, shield you from every danger, and crown you with victory, is my earnest prayer."[10]

Sherman worked to prepare his force to move toward Grant, expressing little concern about Johnston and emphasizing that Lee was clearly his objective. He told his brother that "the next two months will demonstrate whether we can manoeuvre Lee out of Richmond and whip him in open battle." Yet he also realized the importance of protecting his rear, urging the commander of the Department of the South, headquartered in Charleston, to be sure there was no Confederate resurgence in South Carolina. When he received word on April 7 that Grant had taken Richmond, his optimism rose even higher. "It is to our interest," he wrote Grant, "to let Lee and Johnston come together, just as a billiard player would nurse the balls when he has them in a nice place." He also showered Grant with praise. "You have established a reputation for perseverance and pluck that would make Wellington jump out of his coffin." But he also thought he shared some of the credit. His marches had "produced a marked effect on Lee's army," he believed, causing the Confederates in Virginia to worry about their families back home.[11]

He insisted to an army friend and to the Unionist governor of Louisiana that the South's assaults on the Constitution were the only causes of the war. "If the people had stood by the Constitution, I for one would have fought for the protection of the slavery property, just as much as for any other kind of property, because the Constitution was a contract, signed, sealed, and delivered, and we had no right to go behind it. The right or wrong of slavery in the abstract had nothing to do with the contract made by our forefathers." Once the South broke the pact, they freed their own slaves. As for extending the vote or granting any other rights to the freed people, however, "I for one would be slow in going to such extremes."[12]

He continued to castigate those he considered responsible for the war. When some North Carolina farmers appealed to him for mules and horses to plant a crop, he refused: "I can not undertake to supply horses, or to encourage peaceful industry in North Carolina, until the State shall perform some public act, showing that, as to her, war is over." When he learned that his old friend, Robert Anderson, would be honored at a ceremonial flag raising celebration at Charleston's Fort Sumter, he said: "It looks as a retribution decreed by Heaven itself. . . . But the end is not yet. The brain that first conceived the thought [of secession] must burst in anguish, the heart that pulsated with hellish joy must cease to beat, and the hand that pulled the first lanyard must be palsied before the wicked act that begun in Charleston on the 13th of April, 1861, is avenged." Though he had agreed with Lincoln about ending the war mercifully, he did not seem ready to forgive those he considered responsible for bringing it on and continuing its destructiveness.[13]

So he pushed his troops toward Raleigh and renewed contact with Johnston's army. The telegraph clattered exciting news. On April 9 Lee had surrendered to Grant. The Army of Northern Virginia no longer existed. "Glory to God and our country," he announced to his troops. "A little more labor, a little more toil on our part, the great race is won, and our Government stands regenerated, after four long years of war." "I can hardly know how to express my feelings," he wrote Grant, "but you can imagine them." When the soldiers heard the news, members of the Twenty-sixth Iowa Regiment shouted, waved their hats, and threw them in the air. The band struck up "Yankee Doodle," and even the mules and roosters "seemed to participate in the joys[,] for this crowing and mule braying mingled with the wild demonstrations of the men." Sherman's announcement was read over and over. Another overjoyed unit marching toward Raleigh had its band play "Home, Sweet Home," and the long columns joined in deliriously. "No more would we be called upon to take our place in front of guns," one of the soldiers exulted, "no more killing, or beat of the war drum. It was the happiest day we had seen; peace at last and home again." Ellen Sherman expressed the only critical note: she thought Grant had been too lenient. "I think the rebels ought not to have been allowed their side arms or horses," she insisted, "but I suppose Genl Grant knew best."[14]

Lee's surrender was the collapse of only one Confederate force. Johnston's army was still in the field, as were other Confederate troops all over the South. Until they quit, the war would go on. Jefferson Davis and the Confederate government had evacuated Richmond and were trying to evade capture, and this too was discouraging.[15]

All the omens seemed favorable, however. Once Sherman's forces began moving against Raleigh on April 10, Governor Zebulon Vance opened correspondence with Sherman, first to try to protect the state capital and then in the hopes of opening peace talks. Sherman was amenable to both propositions, even giving special protection to the peace commissioners sent to confer with him. Ex-governor and 1852 Whig vice-presidential candidate William A. Graham, ex-Governor and president of the University of North Carolina D. L. Swain, and three of Vance's staff had dinner with Sherman and spent the night in his camp. They admitted that the Confederacy was dead and that Southerners should return to the Union. Their talks were friendly, Sherman and Graham discussing their experiences as college presidents and lamenting that young men had to go to war. Because Vance had left Raleigh before Sherman's arrival, however, further negotiations were postponed.[16]

Sherman still hoped for a quick peace. No doubt to impress the Confederates, he held a review in Raleigh. In the most concrete way, this display of Union might completed the breaking of the Confederate spirit. Sherman stood at the state capitol grounds while line after line of soldiers marched by, "a sea of bayonets." Carl Schurz, one of Sherman's generals, stood in the crowd of curious North Carolinians. He noticed a young woman daubing her eyes with a handkerchief. She uttered in despair: "It is all over with us; I see now, it is all over. A few days ago I saw General Johnston's army, ragged and starved; now when I look at these strong healthy men and see them coming and coming—it is all over with us!"[17]

Even an inmate at the city's lunatic asylum recognized the extent of Union might. The man asked Sherman for a release order. Sherman counseled patience and "faith in God." "In

God?" the man responded. Yes, said Sherman, "and in His power to take care of all of us." "Well, I think I do believe in a sort of Divine Providence," the inmate said; "but when it comes to the question of power, it strikes me that for a man who has been walking about over the country whipping these cursed Rebels, you have a d—d sight more power than anybody I know of."[18]

Joe Johnston realized better than anyone else how powerful Sherman was. His troops were dwindling, while Sherman's seemed inexhaustible. Lee had surrendered, so the huge Army of the Potomac was now also available for duty against him. Richmond was in Union hands, and the Confederate government was on the run. The situation was hopeless. After conferring with Jefferson Davis, Johnston wrote to Sherman on April 14, asking for "a temporary suspension of active operations" so that "civil authorities" might "enter into the needful arrangements to terminate the existing war." Sherman agreed, offering "the same terms and conditions as were made by Generals Grant and Lee. . . . I really desire to save the people of North Carolina the damage they would sustain by the march of this army through . . . the state." After sending the telegram, he joked to an aide: "The war is over—[my] occupation's gone!" He added, however: "The people here manifest more signs of subjugation that I have yet seen, but Jeff Davis has more lives than a cat and we must not trust him."[19]

Sherman's men erupted with excitement when they learned of Johnston's proposal. Soldiers tossed aside their weapons, and officers threw their hats in the air. One commander characterized the behavior as "more like wild men than old soldiers." Sherman was much more cautious. He believed Johnston was acting sincerely, but he worried that if an agreement was not quickly reached, Johnston's army would break up into roving guerrilla bands. The steady stream of deserters coming into his lines added to his concern. He alerted Grant and Stanton about the peace developments, promising "not to complicate any points of civil policy." He was happy to be doing what he repeatedly had said he wanted to do: turn from destruction to peace making.[20]

Sherman and Johnston agreed to meet on April 17. That morning as Sherman prepared to board the train for Durham Station, the meeting site, he was presented with a numbing telegram: Abraham Lincoln had been assassinated on April 15, and he was also rumored a target. "It fell on me with terrible force," he later remembered. He swore the telegrapher and John A. Logan, who was also there, to secrecy and boarded the train, the awful message in his pocket. At 10 A.M. he completed the twenty-six-mile trip to Durham Station where Kilpatrick had cavalry and spare horses waiting. A trooper with a white flag rode ahead of Sherman and the rest of the detachment. About five miles out on the Hillsboro Road, the Union and Confederate flag bearers met. Soon Sherman and Johnston were shaking hands, Sherman acting cordially to all the Confederate officers except for Wade Hampton, whom he disliked because of his treatment of Union POWs. Sherman and Johnston rode toward a nearby small house belonging to a James Bennett. Arriving there, they asked the farmer's permission to use his dwelling, going inside alone, Sherman bringing in his saddle bag and leather pocket full of paper and pens. Their staffs and escorts waited outside to enjoy the fine weather and the blooming cherry trees.

Once inside sitting at the table, Sherman took his first good look at the gray-headed Johnston, a dozen years his senior. He noted that the Confederate was "short[,] stout and compact" and had his gray uniform "buttoned to the neck." After some small talk, Sherman showed Johnston the telegram announcing Lincoln's death. "The perspiration came out in large drops" on Johnston's forehead, Sherman noticed, and the Confederate condemned the act and worried that his government would be blamed. Oh no, Sherman replied, he did not blame Lee, Johnston, or any other Confederate military officer, but he was not so sure about Jefferson Davis and some other politicians. He was more concerned how his army would react when he told them the news. Someone in Raleigh might say the wrong thing, and violence would erupt.

Johnston suggested that they work out terms not only for his army but also for the entire Confederate military. He thought he could get Jefferson Davis to accede to that. They agreed that if it could be decided quickly, the soldiers could go home to plant corn and potatoes and prevent starvation and crime. The conversation continued in a pleasant vein, but the two men finally decided not to pursue the matter further until Johnston could confer with civilian officials and be empowered to negotiate for all Confederate armies.[21]

Outside the farmhouse, Wade Hampton, the Confederate cavalry commander, lay spread out on a bench, disdainfully ignoring his Federal counterparts. When Kilpatrick tried to be friendly, Hampton let him know that he wanted no part of it. Were it up to him, Hampton said, there would be no peace terms. "I never could bring myself to live again with a people that have waged war as you have done." Kilpatrick reminded Hampton of the Confederate burning of Chambersburg, Pennsylvania, and insisted that the activities of Sherman's army were a response to such Confederate depredations. Hampton ignored that comment, threatening retaliation for Federal harshness. Back and forth it went, until Johnston and Sherman came out at about 2:30. The commanders had had a cordial visit; their subordinates had not. Sherman had to be surprised. War's end would not necessarily end war bitterness, as he had always predicted.[22]

On his return to Raleigh, Sherman announced to his army the assassination of Lincoln, the injury to Secretary of State William Henry Seward, and the threat to other Federal officials. He told his men that he did not blame the Confederate army, but he believed the assassination was "the legitimate consequence of rebellion against rightful authority." "Thus it seems that our enemy, despairing of meeting us in open, manly warfare, begins to resort to the assassin's tools." He warned his men to be on guard and "woe unto the people who seek to expend their wild passions in such a manner, for there is one dread result!"[23]

This order was hardly calculated to calm the army's emotions, and the men were angry. (On the home front, civilians were even more enraged, Ellen Sherman perhaps exemplifying the national mood when she wrote: "I hope President Johnson will have less mercy & more justice in his dealings with traitors.") "Here ninety-nine out of every hundred officers and men believe this to be the act of the Confederate government," an officer insisted. "And it has been with considerable difficulty that the Army has been restrained from acts of revenge." The men were so angry that some hoped that Sherman's negotiations would fail so they could take out their wrath on Johnston's army. "We'll hang Jeff Davis to a Sour Apple Tree" was sung and shouted all night long as crowds of soldiers milled around trying to find a way to express their bitterness. Some two-thousand men, most of them from John A. Logan's corps, began to march on Raleigh. Logan threatened them with artillery, and they angrily turned back. All that night Sherman rode back and forth between the camps, determined to protect Raleigh from his men's wrath. In later years, he said, "Had it not been for me Raleigh would have been destroyed."[24]

That same night and early the next morning, Sherman tried to speak to all his generals to get their advice for his second meeting with Johnston. All worried about having to chase down a disintegrating Confederate army and urged him to negotiate an agreement. They even thought it would be a good idea to allow Jefferson Davis and the politicians fleeing with him to escape. Just end it, they seemed to be telling him. Their soldiers agreed. In late March, one had written home: "My heart sickens at the memories of scenes I have seen enacted, and I sincerely trust God will hasten the day when we shall know 'war no more.' "[25]

When Sherman and Johnston met at 2 P.M. at the Bennett farmhouse, Johnston brought with him the authority to surrender all remaining Confederate armies. He "appealed" to Sherman, "as an old army officer above party feeling, and by reason of my former residence at the South to help him and help them in their terrible strait." He wanted some guarantees about the future political rights of his officers and soldiers. Sherman said that Lincoln's December 1863 amnesty proclamation had said that surrender restored rights to all common soldiers, and Grant, in his agreement with Lee, had extended the same guarantee to all officers. Johnston still wanted something specific and suggested that John C. Breckinridge be invited into the discussion. A suspicious Sherman refused. Breckinridge was Confederate secretary of war, and Sherman would not deal with civilians. Johnston reminded Sherman that Breckinridge was also a Confederate major general, and on that condition Sherman allowed him into the discussions.

Breckinridge reiterated Johnston's position, and then a courier brought the draft of an agreement penned by John H. Reagan, the Confederate postmaster general. Sherman found the terms "general and verbose" and rejected them. He sat down at the table and wrote up his own agreement, promising to submit it to President Andrew Johnson for his approval. In the meantime, there would be a truce. The terms were broad and, despite Sherman's insistence, strikingly similar to those submitted by Reagan. Confederate armies were to take their arms to arsenals in their state capitals and promise to obey federal authority again. Existing state governments were to be recognized and federal courts once again reestablished. The political rights of all individuals were to be guaranteed, and no one was to be punished for his role in the war as long as he obeyed the laws. Finally, "In general terms—the war to cease; [and] a general amnesty." These peace terms were an accurate statement of Sherman's long-held soft peace philosophy, and though they were generous and the nation was in an angry mood because of the assassination, he foresaw no one disagreeing with them. He equated his attitude to that of his army and the nation as a whole. He could not imagine anyone demanding a harsher treaty, and he did not see that, despite his earlier statement to Thomas Ewing, he had indeed made a political statement.[26]

Sherman immediately sent an aide to Washington to obtain the necessary authorization. In the letter of transmittal addressed to Grant and Halleck, he expressed great pride in the agreement. "You will observe," he said proudly, "that it is an absolute submission of the enemy to the lawful authority of the United States." He was particularly pleased that the arrangement "prevent[ed]" Confederate armies from "breaking up into guerilla bands." On the other hand, he pointed out, "we can retain just as much of an army as we please." As for slavery, Johnston and Breckinridge acknowledged it "was dead," so there was no need to discuss it in this agreement. All Southerners of "substance . . . sincerely want peace, and I do not believe they will resort to war again during this century," he said. Sherman was confident he had achieved a great coup. "Influence" Johnson, he wrote Halleck in a separate letter, "if possible, not to vary the terms at all, for I have considered everything and believe that the Confederate armies[,] once dispersed[,] we can adjust all else fairly and well."[27]

Other letters displayed similar uncritical confidence. "I have no doubt," he told his quartermaster, "that I have this day made terms with Johnston that will close the war and leave us only to march home." He told his troops the same thing when he announced the terms to them on April 19. "I can hardly realize it," he told Ellen, "but I can see no slip. The terms are all on our side." Had he been able to read the letters of some of his own generals, however, he might not have been so sure. Slocum and Logan thought the terms would never be accepted in Washington because "they were too liberal."[28]

Sherman's generals recognized the situation more clearly than their enthusiastic commander. His agreement with Johnson ignored the hard facts of war that Sherman never considered as he marched through the South. Both conventional war and that against civilians produce hard feelings that do not evaporate when hostilities cease. Sherman consistently called for hard war and soft peace, and Abraham Lincoln had been of the same mind. Most other Northerners were not. Now Lincoln was gone, and the manner of his death had intensified already inflamed emotions. The nation was in no mood for seemingly lenient terms, not after what its people had been through.

When Sherman's aide delivered Sherman's message to Grant, the general in chief recognized its problems and contacted the secretary of war, Edwin Stanton. The cabinet met at 8 P.M. and immediately rejected the terms. Stanton, especially shaken by Lincoln's death, was particularly negative, "counting" the objections "off on his fingers." Grant was ordered to write Sherman that the terms were unacceptable "and that generals in the field must not take upon themselves to decide on political and civil questions which belonged to the executive and civil service."[29]

Grant immediately wrote Sherman that as soon as he had read the terms he had known that they were inappropriate. The president ordered an end to the truce. "The rebels know well the terms on which they can have peace and just when negotiations can commence, when they lay down their arms and submit to the laws of the United States." Stanton also informed Halleck in Richmond and anyone else who would listen. He had long worried about Sherman's negative attitude toward slaves and freed people and now irresponsibly accused him of throwing "away all the advantages we had gained from the war . . . [and] afford[ing] Jeff Davis an opportunity to escape with all his money." Senator Zachariah Chandler told the president that Sherman "was the coming man of the Copperheads," though Postmaster General Montgomery Blair disagreed vociferously. Meanwhile, Sherman was writing Johnston, clearly demonstrating his assumption that the terms deserved the president's acceptance.[30]

Even Halleck, Sherman's long-time friend, reacted unexpectedly. After Lincoln's assassination, Stanton had ordered Halleck to Richmond, stripping him of his chief of staff position. Perhaps hoping to gain renewed favor with the secretary of war, Halleck wrote Stanton that he had learned from "respectable parties" in Richmond that Jeff Davis was trying to escape with a huge amount of specie and had designs on making "terms with General Sherman or some other Southern commander."[31]

Sherman knew nothing about this firestorm in Washington as he confidently waited for administration authorization and the thanks of a grateful nation. He had no inkling that he had done anything in the least controversial. His agreement with Johnston made perfect sense to him and therefore had to make equally good sense to others. He killed time by reviewing his troops and writing letters, oblivious to Stanton's making public a letter of explanation regarding the terms' rejection. Stanton, who habitually dealt harshly with people anyway, went beyond propriety in rejecting Sherman's terms. Upset over the assassination and worried that the fruits of war might be snatched away by Sherman's leniency, Stanton bluntly accused Sherman of consciously overstepping his authority in dealing with civil matters and giving "practical acknowledgment of the Rebel Government." Furthermore, Stanton said, Sherman's terms guaranteed rebel state governments and consequently endangered loyal ones, especially the new state of West Virginia. The guarantee of property might be construed as a guarantee of slavery. The terms might even mean that the federal government would be held responsible for the Confederate war debt. Sherman had allowed Jeff Davis to escape "with his plunder" by moving one of his units out of his path. Not to worry, however, Stanton concluded," Grant was on his way to North Carolina to take command of Sherman's army and finish off Johnston.[32]

On Sunday, April 23, newspapers published Stanton's rendition of the agreement and put the worst face on it. "It looks very much," the *New York Times* editorialized, "as if this negotiation was a blind to cover the escape of Jeff Davis and a few of his officials, with the millions of gold they have stolen from Richmond banks." Stanton was whipping the nation into an anti-Sherman frenzy, but the target remained ignorant of any controversy, too pleased with his military success to imagine any opposition to his agreement.[33]

Sherman learned of the terms' rejection on April 24, 1865, noting it succinctly in his diary: "Gen Grant came[.] My negotiations disapproved and order to resume Hostilities[.] Notice given[.]" Though Grant's arrival was a shock, he handled the touchy matter diplomatically, calmly explaining to Sherman that the excitement over Lincoln's death had caused the disapproval of the terms. The two men had "a full and frank discussion of the whole case," and Sherman took it well. He immediately wrote to Joe Johnston, terminated the truce, and demanded his surrender "on the same terms as were given General Lee at Appomattox." Grant said nothing about taking over Sherman's command and sympathetically stayed on the sidelines while an appreciative Sherman prepared to renew hostilities. Stanton was not so considerate. He wrote Grant that the Sherman terms had met "with universal disapprobation. . . . The hope of the country is that you may repair the misfortune occasioned by Sherman's negotiations."[34]

Despite his long talks with Grant, Sherman remained unaware of the nation's harsh reaction to his agreement; even his own wife thought his terms were too generous for "perjured traitors." On April 25 he calmly tried to lobby for his position with Stantion. "I admit my folly in embracing in a military convention any civil matters," he said, but he had based his actions on their conversations in Savannah, on Grant's actions toward Lee, and on Union general Godfrey Weitzel's calling of the Virginia legislature. "I still believe the Government of the United States has made a mistake," he said, but it was not his responsibility. What bothered him was that "four years' patient, unremitting, and successful labor" had not earned him sufficient respect to preclude Grant from being sent to take over his army. He wrote a similar letter to Grant, calmly justifying his actions, especially reiterating his fear that "the rebel armies will [now] disperse, and instead of dealing with six or seven States we will have to deal with numberless bands of desperadoes."[35]

Joe Johnston similarly wanted no more combat, so he suggested they extend the truce and modify the original terms. Like Sherman, he also worried about guerrillas. "The disbanding of General Lee's army has afflicted this country with numerous bands having no means of subsistence but robbery, a knowledge of which could, I am sure, induce you to agree to other conditions."

Sherman agreed, met with Johnston the next day, and signed a new agreement based on the Grant-Lee surrender. Grant approved and then immediately returned to Washington. Now at last the imbroglio seemed over.[36]

Sherman was still confident he had accomplished something significant. On April 27 he wrote Johnston an acknowledgment of the Confederate's earlier kind words. "Now that the war is over," he said, "I am as willing to risk my person and reputation as heretofore to heal the wounds made by the past war, and I think my feeling is shared by the whole army." Sherman thought he could now become the peacemaker he had always said he would become once the Confederates quit. "The mass of the people south will never trouble us again. They have suffered terrifically, and I now feel disposed to befriend them." It was a good feeling.[37]

It did not last. Just after Grant left for Washington, Sherman picked up an April 24 New York Times. For the first time, he read Stanton's attack and realized the mess he was in. He was hurt, angry, and amazed. He defended himself, citing his fear of guerrilla warfare as justification for an agreement that would keep the Confederate armies from disintegrating. "We should not drive a people into anarchy," he said, and anarchy was precisely what would happen if the Confederate soldiers formed "bands of armed men, roving about without purpose and capable only of infinite mischief." Once again, as he had in California, Louisiana, Kentucky, and Memphis, Sherman acted to ensure order out of repugnance for anarchy, the condition he considered to be the greatest threat to American society and the greatest threat to his hopes for success. He had fought the war against anarchy; now he believed he similarly had to fight against an anarchic peace.[38]

Sherman was consistent in his position. He had regularly said throughout the war that once Southerners stopped fighting and admitted their mistake, the conflict could end, and they could return to the Union with no questions asked. He viewed the enemy as fallen-away friends who needed chastisement to find their way back but no further punishment. In his single-minded determination to wage this kind of war, he did not understand that most others believed punishment was precisely what the recalcitrant South needed to ensure no future repetition of nation breaking. There was a great deal of animosity toward the South in the nation, and Sherman's leniency seemed shocking. Unless secession and slavery were squashed, many in the North feared, the horrors of the war had been experienced in vain. Sherman's terms did not seem firm enough, so they looked dangerous.

When Stanton branded Sherman a traitor and a threat to the Union, the slur found receptive ears. Republicans in his home town accused him of " 'insanity,' 'drunkenness and insanity' 'rebel sympathy' and being a 'traitor.' " His old nemesis, the press, seemed only too happy to fill column after column with denunciation. No Civil War event except for Lincoln's assassination received such wide coverage. Sherman had frustrated reporters by his ability to silence them during his marches; they seized this chance to gain revenge. "He *may* be a great General," one reporter complained, "but he *is* a great *despot*, in my opinion, and a *dangerous man to trust with power.*" The *New York Tribune* called his terms "a queer bit of diplomacy." The *Chicago Tribune* attributed them to "the hypothesis of stark insanity." The *Washington Star* called it "calamitous mischief," and the *New York Herald* said he had "fatally blundered." "The newspapers are savagely abusing Sherman," a veteran army officer complained. "When the war began he was pronounced crazy, and now he is called crazy again! Nothing is so brittle as popular favor." It was, Ethan Allen Hitchcock said, just as Shakespeare had written in his twenty-fifth sonnet:

> The painful warrior famoused for the fight,
> After a thousand victories, once foiled,
> Is from the book of honor banished quite
> And all the rest forgot for which he toiled.[39]

But Sherman had supporters too. Wing commander Henry Slocum angrily ordered the *New York Herald* burned. Newspapers friendly to Sherman and the Ewing family shot back in his defense. "As to the charge of insanity again made," the *Cincinnati Commercial* wrote, "it is as cruel as it is ungrateful. We wish there were a few more such insane men in the army." The *Louisville Journal* railed against "the most cruel attacks . . . upon the integrity and patriotism of the illustrious soldier." Sherman "did make a mistake" but nothing deserving of such vicious attacks. Back and forth the newspaper charges and defenses flew, the nation closely watching and participating in the debate. Sherman, the magnificent victor, was now being branded a crazy traitor. The controversy grew so vicious that he had to console his distraught daughter. "Be perfectly tranquil," he advised. "You know your Papa is good."[40]

A shocked Sherman gathered his generals in the North Carolina governor's mansion, where he was staying, to discuss his strategy. "He paced up and down the room like a caged lion," the invective against Stanton pouring out of his mouth. "He lashed the Secretary of War as a mean, scheming, vindictive politician. . . . He berated the people who blamed him for what he had done as a mass of fools. . . . He railed at the press, which had altogether too much freedom; which had become an engine of vilification; which should be bridled by severe laws, so that the fellows who wielded too loose a pen might be put behind bars—and so on, and so on." Ten years later when he wrote his memoirs, he was still upset. "To say that I was merely angry . . . would hardly express the state of my feelings. I was outraged beyond measure, and was resolved to resent the insult, cost what it might."[41]

The time he spent with Lincoln's former secretary of the treasury, Salmon P. Chase, by then chief justice of the United States, shocked him even more. Chase, who was in the South preparing for the postwar period, patiently explained to Sherman the impact of Lincoln's assassination on official Washington and also showed him several letters he had written to Andrew Johnson concerning the franchise for former slaves. Sherman said he had never heard any of this before (conveniently forgetting his earlier freed man correspondence with Chase, Stanton, and others.) What it all meant, Sherman decided, was that Lincoln's assassination "had stampeded the civil authorities in Washington, had unnerved them, and they were then undecided as to the measures indispensably necessary to prevent anarchy at the South." Consequently, he decided, he was the scapegoat. Such unchecked official anarchy would only make matters worse, he worried. He still could not consider the possibility that his own inability to see the other side was in any way involved in the imbroglio.[42]

Meanwhile, his army was marching toward Richmond and Washington. To scotch the inevitable rumors, Sherman penned a scorching order castigating the "most foul attempt . . . on his fair fame" made by Stanton and Halleck, the latter who had even telegraphed Sherman's subordinates not to obey him but instead capture Jefferson Davis and the plunder he was allegedly escaping with. Despite such unfairness, Sherman urged his soldiers "to restrain their feelings." The "noble and honest" Grant had salvaged the situation, and a "foul stain on our national Honor" had been avoided. He wrote Chase two letters, continuing to oppose political equality for blacks because it "might rekindle the war." The South was already "pure anarchy," he said, and Northern insistence on black rights would only make it worse; the issue would restart the war. Chase continued to disagree, and he wrote the president telling him so, thereby continuing to keep official Washington suspicious of Sherman.[43]

The army's march north was unlike its movement through Georgia and the Carolinas. Sherman ordered a stop to all foraging and encouraged kindness to the defeated foe; the men responded accordingly. "We are on our good behavior this trip," one officer boasted. "No foraging, no bumming rails, or houses, and nothing naughty whatever. We have the best set of men in the world. When it is in order to raise h— they have no equals in destructiveness . . . [but now] they are perfect lambs. Not a hand laid on a rail this evening with intent to burn, not a motion toward a chicken or smoke-house. . . . They don't pretend to love our 'erring brethren' yet, but no conquered foe could ask kinder treatment than all our men seemed disposed to give these Rebels."[44]

Except for steamy weather, the march was uneventful until the columns reached Richmond. Sherman sent Halleck a telegram that he could not have "any friendly intercourse with you. . . . I prefer we should not meet." Halleck hurriedly responded, professing his long friendship and hoping it could continue. "If in carrying out what I knew to be the wishes of the War Department, in regard to your armistice, I used language which has given you offense, it was unintentional, and I deeply regret it." Sherman was unimpressed. He refused to pass his troops in review for Halleck, though he would march through Richmond. "I beg you to keep slightly perdu," he warned, "for if noticed by some of my old command, I cannot undertake to maintain a model behavior, for their feelings have become aroused by what the world adjudges an insult to at least an honest commander."[45]

Halleck was not beyond his own pettiness. He refused to allow Sherman's soldiers the freedom of the city, although former

Confederates had that liberty. The men grew as angry at Halleck as their commander was. They happily marched by his headquarters "at right shoulder shift, and without saluting [him] in any manner" though Halleck was standing on his portico. Sherman had snubbed his old friend, hoping he would now "think twice before he again undertakes to stand between me and my subordinates." Now he had only Stanton to pay back.[46]

Sherman and his army forgot their animosity as they marched past Chancellorsville and Fredericksburg. They were unimpressed with the fortifications they saw, believing they had faced worse in the West. By May 14 the army was encamped near Alexandria, just outside Washington. "Let some one newspaper know," Sherman told Grant's adjutant, "that the Vandal Sherman is encamped near the Canal bridge half way between the Long Bridge & Alexandria to the west of the Road, where his friends if any can find him. Though in disgrace he is untamed & unconquered." He wrote Andrew Johnson in a more conciliatory tone, expressing his willingness to visit. When the two men met, Sherman was pleased to have the president grasp him cordially with both hands and say: "General Sherman, I am *very* glad to see you—*very* glad to see you—*and I mean what I say.*" Stanton made repeated attempts to end the dispute, but Sherman refused to budge. He could not forgive Stanton, another in a series of individuals in his life who disagreed with him and thus represented a malevolent force. Unquestionably Stanton's reaction to Sherman's terms had been overly harsh, but Sherman could never bring himself to realize that his own actions were not blameless either.[47]

Conciliation was hardly the predominant goal for Sherman. Friends and family were worried that he would lose his temper and do something foolish. Grant tried to calm him, and Robert Anderson's wife, an old friend from Fort Moultrie days, urged him to be careful not to say something he would regret later. Gideon Welles, the secretary of the navy, believed Stanton's actions had been excessive, but he thought Sherman should be more understanding. Brother-in-law Hugh Boyle Ewing was so concerned about Sherman's temper and threats that he pulled John Sherman out of a barber chair at Willard's Hotel and took him and Thomas Ewing, Jr., to Charles Sherman's room for a hastily called strategy session. The relatives decided John better go see Sherman and talk some sense into him. The matter was growing increasingly frightening because Sherman's army was swaggering around town daring anyone to say anything derogatory about their commander.[48]

The Ewings organized themselves to defend Cump as they had done so many times in the past, and the need for their help could not have improved Cump's disposition. On May 1, Tom Ewing, Jr., told him to fight back in a "dignified way on principle" against Stanton, "an infamous and malignant scoundrel." He also published a strong public defense. Stanton's friends were not impressed. Old-line politician Thurlow Weed advised the Secretary of War: "The Shermans are overacting. You can afford to be silent." The president of the National Life and Travellers Insurance Company said Sherman was "taking advantage of the military fame to defame and accuse you," and "I cannot refrain from tendering to you my most hardy approval of your course."[49]

Adding to Sherman's problem was the Committee on the Conduct of War, the congressional watchdog of the Union war effort. Upon his arrival in Washington, Sherman received a May 8, 1865, summons to appear before the committee to explain his agreement with Johnston. He appeared on May 22 and was forceful yet not antagonistic. He insisted that he had acted under the impression that he was fulfilling government policy. He had kept his superiors fully informed and had asked for their approval before implementing the terms. When asked why slavery had not been mentioned in the agreement, he said it was because the president had already freed the slaves in the Emancipation Proclamation. "For me to have renewed the question when that decision was made would have involved the absurdity of an inferior undertaking to qualify the work of his superior." As for the central reason for the terms, it was to prevent the creation of guerrilla bands. He similarly pulled no punches regarding Stanton and Halleck. During his visit to Savannah, he said, Stanton had encouraged him to deal with civil matters. So his attacks were now "an act of perfidy." "I did feel indignant—I do feel indignant," he told the committee. "As to my own honor, I can protect it."[50]

Sherman felt his honor was at stake, and he intended to gain revenge. But how would he do it? It was no small matter that the general of a huge army camped around the nation's capital was threatening the secretary of war. Rumors abounded of an army plot against Stanton. Sherman was even telling Ellen that "Lincoln's assassination was not plotted in Richmond but near his elbow." He told Grant: "Mr. Stanton must publicly confess himself a public libeler or—but I won't threaten." He was even blunter to Ellen: "They will find that Sherman who was not scared by the crags of Lookout, the Ravines of Kenesaw, and [the] long and trackless forests of the South is not to be intimidated by the howlings of a set of sneaks who were hid away as long as danger was rampant, but now shriek with very courage. I will take a Regiment of my old Division & clear them all out." "Though my voice is still peace," he told Logan, "I am not for such a peace as makes me subject to insult by former friends, now perfidious enemies."[51]

The Grand Review of Union troops scheduled for May 23 and 24 helped defuse the tense situation. The celebration of the Union victory was a spectacular success. Though most observers thought the Army of the Potomac looked resplendent on the first day, Sherman noted a number of basic marching errors and too many men, "like country gawks," sneaking looks at the reviewing stand. In reality he was worried about his own soldiers. "Meade," he said to the commander of the Army of the Potomac, "I am afraid my poor tatter-demalion corps will make a poor appearance to-morrow when contrasted with yours." Meade good-naturedly told him not to worry; the people would make allowances. Sherman prepared carefully, refusing the offer of the fancy bands the Army of the Potomac had marched to. He believed his men would step better to the sound of their own musicians. He warned them to maintain their ranks and keep their eyes to the front. Sherman saw his soldiers in direct competition with the eastern troops, and he was determined they would hold their own. And in a final attempt to heal a long-standing wound, he appealed to O. O. Howard's well-known Christianity to let John A. Logan ride at the head of the Army of the Tennessee he had commanded so well for a few days around Atlanta. To assuage Howard, he asked him to ride with him.[52]

The army stepped off at 9 A.M. on that bright May morning, and the soldiers, who were the show, were themselves taken with the scenes around them. "Flags of victory and wreaths of grief [over Lincoln's death]" contested with each other for predominance. Pennsylvania Avenue was jammed, people crowding into the street right up to the flanks of the marching troops. Entire schools had been emptied of children who watched the spectacle and sang for the marching troops. Out of windows, women of all ages fluttered handkerchiefs in greeting. "Some cheered themselves hoarse, others raised their hands to heaven in prayer, sobbing mothers held their little ones aloft, while gray-headed fathers wept with childish joy." The long-striding western troops looked bigger and stepped longer than the easterners. " 'Veteran' was written all over their dark faces, browned by the ardent Southern sun, and health almost spoke from their elastic step and erect figures. . . . they seemed like strangers from another planet." Interspersed with the marching soldiers were bummers, freed people, mules, fowl, and the booty of foraging. It reminded people, Julia Grant noted, of the words in the song "Marching through Georgia"—" 'how the turkeys gobbled' and 'the sweet potatoes even started from the ground.' " Washington had never seen anything like it.[53]

Sherman rode in front of his huge force, proudly wearing a corps badge John A. Logan had presented him. He received a tumultuous reception, his horse weighed down with flower garlands and wreaths. One observer said the crowd was "enthusiastic to the extreme." A newswoman saw "in his eye . . . the proud, conscious glare of the conqueror, while his features, relieved from the nervous anxious expression of war times, assumed an air of repose which well became him." Few could believe that this smiling presence was the same person who had "swept through the confederacy like an avenging Nemesis." His own men laughed to themselves to see him in full uniform, more used to his less formal campaign attire.[54]

As he rode along, Sherman wondered how his troops were doing behind him but dared not look. Finally when he reached the Treasury Building, he swung in the saddle and to his happiness saw that "the sight was simply magnificent. The column was compact, and the glittering muskets looked like a solid mass of steel, moving with the regularity of a pendulum." A little farther along, Sherman dramatically doffed his hat and bowed toward a house on Lafayette Square. Secretary of State William Henry Seward, injured in the assassination plot, sat in a window and returned the salute. Finally, Sherman arrived at the reviewing stand. He got off his horse and walked toward the stairs.[55]

Members of the crowd watched intently, some with field glasses, wondering what he would do when he came face to face with Edwin Stanton. Sherman climbed into the stand and greeted Ellen, her father, and Tommy Sherman, shook hands with the president, with Grant, and with the cabinet. As he approached Stanton, the secretary of war offered his hand. Sherman refused it and passed him by. Sherman had gained his revenge.[56]

When the last soldier and the last mule had passed the reviewing stand at around 3:30 P.M., Sherman could finally relax. His troops had been a smash hit. As one of his officers, the later President Benjamin Harrison, said: "We took the shine off the Army of the Potomac and in marching *altogether* excelled them." Sherman had also gained his revenge against Stanton. He told President Johnson that as far as he was concerned, the controversy was over. He was smiling as he left the platform. The huge crowd pressed up to him, moving up the stairs to shake his hand or present him with flowers. At first he took it all in good spirit, but when the crowd kept pushing up to him, he grew increasingly agitated. He tried to force his way down the stairs and to his horse, at first refusing the outstretched hands, then trying to push his way through and finally shouting, "Damn you, get out of the way! Get out of the way!" The stress of the conflict with Stanton rushed to the surface, and he exploded. He quickly regained his composure, however, and was soon seen smiling again as he rode along down the street.[57]

Sherman had hardly forgiven Stanton or Halleck. Instead of making more threats, however, he expressed ridicule. "I cannot now recall the act," he said in a letter published at this time, "but Shakespeare records how poor Falstaff, the prince of cowards and wits, rising from a figured death, stabbed again the dead Percy, and carried the carcass aloft in triumph to prove his valor. So now, when the rebellion in our land is dead, many Falstaffs appear." Meanwhile, Ellen tried to defuse the situation herself. The day after the review she sent Mrs. Stanton some flowers and later paid the secretary of war a pleasant social call. Cump was not as generous. He remained angry at Stanton until years softened the hard feelings.[58]

The time had come to leave Washington. Sherman was anxious to get his peacetime army assignment in the West. He definitely had no political aspirations. He was a soldier not a politician. "The President has only to tell me what he wants done and I will do it." On May 30, 1865, Sherman issued his farewell. He told his soldiers "that the time has come for us to part. Our work is done, and armed enemies no longer defy us. . . . you have done all that men could do . . . and we have a right to join in the universal joy that fills our land because the war is *over,* and our Government stands vindicated before the world." He urged them to be good citizens. He knew that "if, unfortunately, new war should arise in our country, 'Sherman's army' will be the first to buckle on its old armor, and come forth to defend and maintain the Government of our inheritance."[59]

Further war was hardly Sherman's desire. He looked forward to peaceful days. "I confess without shame," he told a St. Louis friend, "I am tired & sick of war. Its glory is all moonshine. Even success, the most brilliant is over dead and mangled bodies. . . . It is only those who have not heard a shot, nor heard the shrills & groans of the wounded & lacerated (friend or foe) that cry aloud for more blood & more vengeance, more desolation & so help me God as a man & soldier I will not strike a foe who stands unarmed & submissive before me but will say 'Go sin no more.' "[60]

Sherman's aim in fighting the Civil War had been accomplished: The Union was preserved; anarchy prevented; his personal success achieved. No one could deny he had played a major role in the Union's victory—not even the foster father he had so long been trying to please. Yet it all had the same dissatisfying aura of so much of his life. Every time he thought he had found success, it had been snatched away from him. He had been a good banker, but his banks had failed. The coming of the war had negated his excellent work and his future in Louisiana. His fine performance at Bull Run had been marred by his fear for the Union's future and the later insanity accusations in Kentucky. He had not been able to enjoy his resurrection at Shiloh because of political and journalistic accusations of surprise. On and on it went; every time he had reached the pinnacle of success, something out of his control had pushed him back downhill again.

So it was at the end of the war. The victories in the field were stained by the controversy of the Johnston agreement. It was unfair for Stanton or anyone else to paint his actions with the brush of treason, but they did. There was no more loyal Unionist than Sherman, but there was also no better friend to the South and no one more determined to restore peace once the Confederacy was defeated. He was indeed tired of war and killing, but he had felt this way long before he had met Johnston. He had never wanted to fight his friends, but he had seen no choice so long as they attacked the Union and resisted the laws of the land. Punishment was never his aim; ending the war as quickly as possible and with the fewest deaths was. It mattered little what Lincoln might have said or not said at City Point. Sherman, the apostle of a hard war, was also the advocate of a soft peace. His agreement with Johnston was absolutely consistent with everything he had been telling Southerners throughout the war. Stop the fighting, he had kept repeating, and he would become the South's best friend. He tried to be just that.

In his passion for order and peace, Sherman miscalculated. He believed that he could lead and others would follow, in peace as well as war. They did not. Most Southerners considered him a brutal destroyer; many Northerners saw his generous peace terms as offensive at best, treasonable at worst. Sherman, following his own moral imperatives, had failed to hear the voices of others. His dogged pursuit of war would remain his legacy while the same pursuit of peace would be forgotten. Despite his unquestioned military success, Sherman's inner demons continued to threaten his personal peace and stability. He had finished the war as one the nation's major leaders, but this great achievement was marred by yet another imbroglio. Sherman's passion for order seemed always to result in the kind of dissatisfaction he was trying to overcome. So even when he came out of the Civil War with a fame he could only have dreamed of in 1861, that fame was tarnished by the very single-mindedness that had helped him gain it.

CHAPTER 16

— ☆ —

NATIONAL HERO AND THE SOUTH'S FRIEND

THE WAR WAS OVER and the Union was intact, but enormous problems remained. Four years of hard conflict had resulted in over six hundred thousand fatalities and numberless widows and orphans throughout the North and South. Where armies had marched and fought, there was enormous physical damage. Cities and villages mourned the deaths of sons, brothers, husbands, and friends; everywhere men with missing limbs and scarred bodies were evident. The assassination of Abraham Lincoln in the last days of the conflict threw the nation into further shock. Both the war's winners and its losers felt sorrow and bitterness; binding the nation's wounds would not be easy.[1]

In the North, however, there was cause for a celebration despite the hard days of the past and those that still lay ahead. The sacrifices of war seemed validated, and the returning soldiers were greeted as conquering heroes. They had fought the good fight, and they had won the great victory. Even the Grand Review could not express the extent of pride the Northern states felt in their boys in blue.

If the ordinary soldier was a hero, how much more the generals, especially the ones who had become household words during the war. The returning veterans added to the folklore of Grant and Sherman, providing personal stories about them, many no doubt embellished to make the speaker seem more important in the home folks' eyes.

Sherman basked in this glory and particularly benefited from it. His reputation had always been a mixed one, so the public felt more curious about him than it did about the others. The "insane" general of Kentucky and Missouri had redeemed himself at Shiloh with his sterling performance, only to be called crazy again at Chickasaw Bayou. His court-martial of a reporter showed an authoritarian streak, and his hard-nosed attitude toward war in Mississippi, Georgia, and the Carolinas brought shocking but victorious results. Then he tried to let the South off the hook, said the press and politicians. He responded by thumbing his nose at all his tormentors, even snubbing the secretary of war in public. His Indian name was fascinating; people wanted to know more about him. He was no distant ikon, this victorious general, his contemporary photographs showing a no-nonsense, down-to-earth soldier.

His tumultuous receptions at the Grand Review and during a tour he and Ellen took in May and June 1865 demonstrated the nation's affection for and its curiosity about him. When he and Ellen reached New York City in June, the crowds were so large that the police had difficulty controlling them. Soldiers and civilians applauded and serenaded the general and his wife, and Sherman's cousin threw open the doors of his house so all the well-wishers could shake Sherman's hand. It was an impressive sight—the redheaded hero lionized by a grateful nation publicly expressing its thanks.[2]

Leaving New York, Sherman made a nostalgic trip up the Hudson River to West Point. Then he and Ellen traveled on to South Bend, Indiana. His children had attended school there, and the infant son he had never seen was buried on the Notre Dame campus. Everywhere they went the crowds were large and enthusiastic. When he reached Lancaster, several thousand people greeted him at the train station. Claiming no special honor, he once more called upon the victors to be generous in peace to those who had been enemies in war. People liked that, too. The hard-driving general had a heart.[3]

The nation wanted to do more than simply shout and cheer. People wanted to express their gratitude and affection in a more concrete way. The citizens of Lancaster undertook a $100,000 testimonial fund drive throughout Ohio, and within a year, Ohio's governor sent Sherman nearly $10,000 in bonds, the first fruits of the effort. Later, people in St. Louis raised $30,000 to buy him a $24,400 house when he moved there in 1866 and placed the remainder of the money in his bank account. When he became commanding general in 1869, prominent businessmen bought him Grant's former home for $65,000 and banked an additional $37,000. These were enormous sums of money, but Sherman, like the other military figures, took it all in stride as his just due for his wartime exploits.[4]

Even in the South, where he had conducted his destructive warfare, he found people admiring of him. David F. Boyd, his long-time colleague from the prewar Louisiana Seminary days; Willard Warner, a former Union army officer, soon to become senator from Alabama; and George W. Moorman, an ex-Confederate officer, later a sheriff in Mississippi, and the first adjutant general of the United Confederate Veterans, all idolized him and looked to him for help in restoring their section. "The Poor South is ruined," Boyd wrote to Sherman in the early fall of 1865. "There is no help in ourselves—to our *conquerors* we must look for aid & comfort; and upon no one more than yourself does the South rely." If the former Confederacy was treated according to Sherman's 1865 surrender terms, Boyd said, it would "in a short time be thoroughly pacified & be a firm & true supporter of the Constitution." Most Southerners were upset at what Sherman had done to them in war, but they appreciated the lenient peace terms he had offered when the fighting was over. Joe Johnston never forgot, nor did many other former Confederates. Sherman visited the South more than once in the postwar period, and his receptions were always cordial.[5]

Sherman's fame was wider than the North or South. It was international. His Atlanta campaign and the march to the sea had been favorably discussed in European newspapers and magazines, and, as a result, he was considered a great military leader. Six years after the end of the Civil War, he traveled overseas, purportedly to study the Franco-Prussian War but really to get away from the frustrations of political Washington and to bask in his well-earned reputation.

His fame gave him ready entrée everywhere he went. His treatment was at times grandiose. When he was leaving Turkey for Russia, for example, the sultan insisted Sherman travel on the royal yacht. As the ship moved up the Bosporus, "all the Turkish fleet, with their crews on deck, ships dressed up with their colors, and the flagship saluting with twenty-one guns," presented all "royal honors" to Sherman. "The day was perfect," he later reminisced, "and on the whole it was one of the most splendid sights I ever beheld."[6]

Sherman met the major European figures of the age: King Amadeus I and the queen of Spain; Victor Emmanuel II, the king of Italy; Pope Pius IX; Ismail Pasha, the khedive of Egypt; Abdul Aziz, the Ottoman sultan of Turkey; Russian Czar Alexander II, Grand Duke Michael, and Duchess Olga; Francis Joseph, the Austro-Hungarian emperor and his minister of foreign affairs, Count Julius Andrassy; Prussian military leaders Prince Frederick Charles and Helmuth von Moltke; Queen Victoria and the prince of Wales (the future Edward VII); opera singer Jenny Lind; American historian/diplomat George Bancroft and diplomats Charles Francis Adams and Caleb Cushing; Adolphe Thiers, the president of the French Republic, and later president Marshal MacMahon; and H. M. Stanley, the discoverer of David Livingstone in Africa.

Sherman enjoyed himself immensely during the ten months that he traveled throughout Europe and Egypt. He felt at ease among the monarchs, soldiers, and political leaders he met. He showed he was one of them—an important person of great accomplishment. He demonstrated little of the pomposity sometimes associated with fame, and this added to his appeal. While waiting to meet Pope Pius IX (Pio Nono), for example, he learned that it was customary to kneel on meeting the pontiff. His aide said he "would kneel to no man," but Sherman shrugged his shoulders and said he planned to "follow regulations." He felt enough confidence in himself not to make a fuss about protocol, and, besides, as a soldier he understood the importance of deference. Later, he loved to tell how his aide had self-consciously dropped to his knees as soon as the pope had appeared in the doorway.[7]

Everywhere he went, Sherman made a favorable impression. In London, he was the center of attention, soldiers saluting him on the street and civilians discretely pointing him out. The secretary to the American legislation in England, Benjamin Moran, left a description of Sherman's appearance during this period. Sherman, he said, had "a slender figure, a fine manly head, and irregular features, looking much more of the lawyer than the general." But, Moran continued, he had "a will of his own and looks as if he could and would fight. His manners," he said, "are extremely unconventional, and he talks with fluency, ease, and intelligence." Similarly when Sherman visited S. H. M. Byers, then American consul in Zurich, he discussed his campaigns with Swiss military officers there, and Byers noted that "all were greatly impressed with the great simplicity of his talk, [and] his kindness of manner."[8]

During the postwar years, Sherman was thus a major figure in both the United States and overseas, the applause from the admiring throngs deafening in his ears. As he had in the war, he still viewed himself as second only to his friend, Grant, but he showed little interest in building on his elevated status. He had no political ambitions, nor did he want to translate his fame into some civilian profession. He saw himself as a soldier who had given his nation loyal service and wanted only a rest. He entered these years looking forward to no new challenges but rather hoping to enjoy the fruits of his past labor. From this point on he viewed whatever difficulty he encountered through the prism of the glory days of Shiloh, Atlanta, Savannah, and the Carolinas. He remained an important person all his life, but he was never again able to match his war success. However, he was forever more to gain sustenance from that glory.

Throughout the war as he had achieved the success that gave him fame, Sherman had consistently held that once the fighting was over and the Union saved, life in the United States could return to its prewar norm. He had viewed secession as anarchy and Union as order. His had been a hard war–soft peace philosophy precisely to restore matters to the earlier rhythm, not for any revolutionary purposes. To him, the Union was the nation of the 1850s stripped of the controversies over slavery, threats of secession, and disorderly mobs. He had fought the war to preserve the Union and thus to ensure the conditions he held necessary for his personal satisfaction. He certainly saw no reason for an elaborate, possibly destabilizing Reconstruction process.

He believed that his own and the army's role in the South was finished when the Confederate armies surrendered and state governments were functioning again. The army should go back to the prewar tasks of guarding the nation's frontiers against domestic or foreign enemies. He perceived no police or governmental role. His long-held love for the South translated to no desire to serve there in any capacity in the postwar years. Based on his war triumphs, he believed he had the right to choose his own assignment, and he wanted command in the West, with headquarters at St. Louis, his favorite city. Now that the war was over and order was restored, he wanted to go on with the rest of his life.[9]

He was naive, at best, to think that the nation would quietly return to its prewar relationships after so horrible a war and that he could return to the quiet life he remembered being the norm of the prewar army. The nation's problems were too great, and he was too important a person to be left alone. He and the nation were not entering a period of peace. Restoration of the Union on the battlefields had to be matched by the establishment of healed relationships in the political arena, and he had a role to play in that effort, whether he liked it or not.

The nation's major problem was the status of millions of freed slaves. The war had destroyed slavery, but the difficult issue of citizenship remained. Some Americans believed that the freed people should receive full citizenship; others insisted that their freedom should mean a subordinate role in society. Southern governments should remain in white hands, one side argued; the other insisted that the discredited rebel leaders had to be replaced with a new political system based on black voters. Until this issue could be solved, there could be no real peace.

The new president facing these massive problems was not, like Lincoln, a master politician; he was abrasive and stubborn, doing as he pleased, and the public be damned. Congress was split into numerous factions, with little common agreement among them. No one, in the capitol or the executive mansion, had any answer all could agree on.

The lack of precedent was a major stumbling block to a successful mending of the nation. Abraham Lincoln had floated some trial balloons during the war, but he had established no Reconstruction policy. At first Andrew Johnson seemed to favor a harsh restoration, but he soon found himself supporting the very white leadership class that he, a former Southern poor white, had at first wanted to topple. Congress, which was determined to reassert its role after watching Lincoln exert wide presidential power during the war, quickly opposed Johnson's unilateral and increasingly mild policies. The public was unsure what to believe, but because of the vast popularity of its victorious military, whatever these heroes said would be given a respectful hearing.

The politicians knew this, and they looked to the military men for support.

Sherman, however, had no desire to be stationed in Washington or the South or to participate in any political disagreements; he wanted to go out West as far away from politicians as he could go. To his relief, he received his wish. The nation was divided into five military divisions, and Grant, as commanding general, named him commander of the Military Division of the Mississippi, the Trans-Mississippi West, with headquarters in St. Louis. (In 1866, the name was changed to the Military Division of the Missouri.)[10]

Sherman arrived in St. Louis on July 15 and received another of the warm welcomes he had enjoyed everywhere he had been. He was pleased to be there, but all the recent applause had not washed away his anxiety about continued fallout from the peace term debacle. His old fears about being thwarted in his attempt to build a stable and secure personal life returned to haunt him. "It is important that I should get my office and machinery to work," he told Ellen, "for I feel that the War Dept would drop me like a hot potato if possible. Stanton is as vindictive as old satan and is so industrious and has the business of his office so complicated that Mr. [Andrew] Johnson fears to break with him and Grant is not equal to him in energy of thought and therefore will be kept back."[11]

There were national problems to be solved; he recognized, but he tried to imagine he could avoid them. In his role as commander in the West and because so many people wanted to see him, he spoke to many individuals and groups as he traveled the country. The more he heard, the more he came to see that the nation's reconstruction would not be automatic but would require solution of the freed people's role. He heard all the arguments, but nothing altered his firm belief in the superiority of the white race. "The Negros are free and must be treated as such and the U. S. Gov must guarantee & ensure that freedom, but the Negros are not qualified to vote . . . we should aim for the sake of the future to keep power & influence in the hands of the most energetic and stable race, white." In this he continued to share the conservative attitudes of Thomas Ewing, who believed that white supremacy was essential to any approach to the postwar problems. As an important behind-the-scenes adviser to Andrew Johnson, Ewing consistently urged the president to oppose any congressional attempt to impose black-white equality. Sherman reflected his foster father's philosophy and that of his many friends in the South.[12]

But it really mattered very little. He was a military man in the West, not a politician in Washington, and he expected to have little involvement in the whole question. Still, he watched with rapt attention as the drama unfolded. Since Congress was not in session when the war ended in April 1865, Andrew Johnson acted on his own. At the heart of what came to be called Presidential Reconstruction were two proclamations issued in May. First, Johnson established an oath of allegiance for the restoration of full citizenship to most Southerners. Fourteen classes of people were excluded from the oath, however, primarily former Confederate civil and military leaders and large landowners. These had to appeal directly to Johnson for special pardons. Many did, and Johnson readily issued the special dispensations. Next, Johnson established a procedure for the readmission of states into the Union. He named provisional governors who were to call elections of delegates for conventions to write new state constitutions. (Only white men who had sworn the oath or received pardons could participate in the vote.)

Quickly these governments were established, and the old-line leaders, those who had led the Confederacy, returned to local power. They instituted black codes to control the freed people and exclude them from meaningful participation in Southern life. To ensure that the message was clear, violence, the most famous of which were race riots in Memphis (May 1866) and New Orleans (July 1866), erupted against blacks and their white allies. The Johnson governments demonstrated that white supremacy was the rule of the day.

Within the nation and in Congress, concern arose over the unhappy result of Johnson's swift and unilateral actions. His message to the South was that it could return into the Union with its political system unchanged. In December 1865 when Congress convened for the first time since the war's end, Southern states sent ex-Confederate leaders to represent them. Although the Thirteenth Amendment had ended slavery, blacks were still politically, economically, and socially subordinate to the dominant whites, and the arrival in Washington of former war leaders dramatized the fact that little had changed in the former Confederacy. Congress refused to seat these individuals, increasingly concerned that if it did, Reconstruction would be ended and former rebels would be in power and the freed people would not be truly free.

Sherman believed this was as it should be. "You observe," he told his senator brother "that Mr. Johnson is drifting toward my terms to Johnston. He can not help it," Sherman gloated, "for there is no other solution." Unlike John, who grew increasingly critical of Johnson's Reconstruction, Sherman favored seating whomever the Southern states sent to Congress, even ex-Confederate leaders. During an inspection tour of his military division, he addressed a convention of Arkansans who opposed the oath requirement and told them they should take the pledge and stop worrying about it. Concentrate instead on economic development. "Cultivate the soil, set your plantation in order; make every possible improvement; get your local and country affairs in good shape." In short, get back to their prewar normal situation.[13]

Sherman regularly spoke out in support of Johnson, not realizing that his words carried enormous weight in the country. He opposed enfranchising blacks or doing anything for them that might alienate conservative whites, his Southern friends and those he considered the bulwarks for the restoration of an orderly Union. When Johnson asked him about the background and meaning of his famous January 1865 field order providing confiscated land for South Carolina freedmen, he readily displayed his prowhite attitude. It had all been Secretary of War Stanton's idea, he said. At the time, he remembered, the land transfer was strictly a war measure whose permanence the courts had to validate. Johnson understood. He immediately returned the land to its original white owners. Sherman was pleased. Unlike congressional radicals who were "alienating even the well inclined of the South," Sherman said, Johnson was handling matters properly. When Johnson vetoed the Freedmen's Bureau Act, which had established federal relief, labor mediation, and educational opportunity, Sherman's admiration for the president increased. Sherman saw the bureau as an example of the folly of forcing black equality on properly unwilling whites. "To place or attempt to place the negro on a par with the whites will produce new convulsions," he insisted.[14]

As the battle over Reconstruction between Johnson and Congress escalated, Sherman maintained his support for the president because he believed his policies were closest to his own. Thomas Ewing, who was a delegate to Johnson's ill-fated National Union Convention in August 1866, agreed, but Sherman's brother, Senator John Sherman, warned him to stay clear of the president. In late August and early September 1866, Johnson made a disastrous national campaign swing, traveling from Washington to Chicago and St. Louis, then back, attacking Congress all the way. He acted in what even a sympathetic Ellen Sherman called "an undignified manner." He argued with hecklers and insisted that the real traitors were not in the South but in Congress. Sherman and the Ewings began to have second thoughts about Johnson— but not about his Reconstruction policy.[15]

So far, Sherman had been able to stand on the sidelines, willing to comment but not ready to become personally involved. He did not like what he saw—an increasingly complicated disaster in the making—and he had no desire to become involved in it. The politicians were making a mess out of what he was sure his peace terms would have solved easily. The politicians had thwarted him then, so let them pay the price of their stupidity now. Eventually they would see the wisdom of his plan and accept it, but he refused to do any more to help them now.

But he just could not keep quiet. One day, without much forethought, he wrote Andrew Johnson a letter expressing his support of the president's policies. This was a mistake. Johnson was in political trouble, and what better way to extricate himself than by gaining the public support of a war hero. Grant's support would have been better because his fame was greater than Sherman's, but he had not shown himself to be favorable the way Sherman had in his letter. Besides, Grant, it was said, had presidential ambitions. Sherman might help thwart that too by coming out for Johnson. The president decided to make Sherman an active participant in his Reconstruction program. He had increasingly become exasperated with his secretary of war because of Edwin Stanton's increasing alliance with Congress. He decided to fire Stanton and put Sherman in his place. The general would be a valuable ally.

In October 1866 Johnson told Grant to order Sherman to Washington. Sherman was amazed when he realized what was going on. He wanted no part of the secretaryship and all it meant in the climate of political conflict over Reconstruction. He tried to resist, insisting that just because he had written a complimentary letter was no signal he wanted to become a politician. He felt like a fish on the end of a taut line, slowly being reeled in despite his best efforts to escape. He pleaded with Grant to have the orders cancelled, but the commanding general said he could not change a presidential directive. Sherman would have to meet his fate; the stature he had gained in the war had thrust him into this situation. Politics had always been anathema to Sherman, and, with the memory of the war terms imbroglio still fresh in his mind and the animosity over Reconstruction increasing daily, he felt more repugnance than ever for the political arena.[16]

As the battle between Johnson and Congress escalated, Johnson not only wanted to bring Sherman to Washington, but he was also preparing to send Grant out of the capital on a diplomatic mission to Mexico. The French had taken advantage of the Civil War to establish a puppet government there under Maximilian. Now, they were pulling out, but Maximilian talked of staying. In the spring of 1866 Johnson had appointed Lewis D. Campbell, an old-line Ohio politician, to be minister to the emerging anti-Maximilian government, and now he appointed Grant to monitor the military aspect of the French withdrawal. Rumor had it that Johnson hoped to neutralize Grant politically by sending him out of the country with a hard drinker like Campbell so that he might go on a binge and destroy his reputation. Grant refused the Mexico assignment, however. He would obey military orders, he said, but he did not have to take on any nonmilitary tasks.[17]

Grant did not want to go to Mexico; Sherman did not want to be secretary of war; and Johnson was grasping at both straws to try to save himself in the battle with Congress. Much to the president's displeasure, Sherman broke the impasse by offering to go to Mexico in Grant's place. He would save himself from being named secretary of war by going across the border and would allow Grant to remain in Washington, as he wished. He still backed the president's policies, however, telling his brother to be sure that Congress was fair to Johnson and squelch all talk of impeachment.[18]

Sherman and Campbell left New York by ship in early November 1866. "I had to make this trip to escape a worse duty," he told his brother, "and to save another person from a complication that should be avoided." The first several days out, Campbell's alcoholic reputation proved accurate. He drank so much that Sherman had to step in and diplomatically broach the subject to the Ohio diplomat before the other members of the delegation: "Campbell, you and I are fond of our noon toddies, but now we are engaged in a public and delicate mission[,] let us knock off, and compromise on a single glass of sherry at dinner." Campbell agreed and stayed on the wagon until late in the fruitless mission.

He and Sherman futilely chased after Juarez, the new Mexican leader, until Sherman became disgusted and received permission from the president to go home to St. Louis. He had thwarted Johnson's scheme to get him to Washington, at least temporarily. Even more happily he was received "in the most friendly spirit" during a day-long December 1866 visit to Jackson, Mississippi, the site of several of his devastating military campaigns. This experience showed him that the South was friendly to him, and it buttressed his belief that the best policy toward Southerners was to be patient and to avoid extreme measures. He was angry at the president for trying to name him secretary of war, but he continued to support his lenient policy and to see Congress as the major hindrance in Reconstruction.[19]

Sherman's conservative attitude, and perhaps Thomas Ewing's advice, encouraged Johnson to keep trying to get Sherman publicly tied to his administration and policy. In January 1867, "strong family reasons" (Ellen was about to give birth yet again) provided Sherman with a good excuse not to come to Washington. He was increasingly unhappy with Johnson's behavior, particularly his unwillingness to provide legal aid for army officers in the South taken to court by anti-Reconstruction whites, so these repeated calls from the president caused him to become increasingly testy. As always when he saw no way out of a problem, he threatened to resign, to walk away. Grant urged him to be calm. Efforts were obviously being made to draw the two of them into the political situation, he said, and if he could, he would hand over the reins of the army to Sherman and escape to Europe himself. "It would look like throwing up a command in the face of the enemy," however, so he would remain at the helm. Sherman felt relieved; he and Grant had worked well in war; they could cooperate for their mutual benefit again now.[20]

Sherman kept a wary eye on the Johnson-congressional debate from his St. Louis headquarters, watching for any break in the bitter political conflict. The escalating antiblack violence in the South made his pro-Johnson position increasingly difficult. He warned David F. Boyd: "I am in hopes Southern Gentlemen will soon create a public opinion that will at least make it seem mean and contemptible to shoot a negro because he is black. Unless that is done and done soon, it is idle for me or any man to attempt an apology or excuse to ward off the measures of the extreme Radicals." Johnson was trying to do what was right, Sherman continued to maintain, but the violence was undercutting his attempts. The American people would not stand for it. Sherman had not changed his mind about black citizenship, but he believed blacks should at least be treated fairly.[21]

Congress, exasperated by its battle with Johnson over the intransigence of southern state governments, passed the First Reconstruction Act in early 1867. It created five new military districts in the South for the purposes of having the army supervise the restoration of the former Confederate states and of ensuring the rights of freed people in them. A newspaper pointed to Sherman as the leading candidate for command of the district, which included Louisiana. He protested even the possibility of such an order. "I am perfectly willing to take a Regt of cavalry and go out to fight Indians," he wrote, "but to hold an indescribable office of mixed jurisdiction, impossible of logical execution and sure to result in curses from both sides would be a most ungracious task."[22]

Sherman had been so busy worrying about having to go to Washington to the War Department that this new threat blindsided him. Despite all that had gone on in the nation since 1865, he expressed shock that the army could be so used for political purposes; he refused to risk his reputation and his new-found security on such an impossible task. During the war, Sherman had been successful because he had been able to focus on the job at hand and set everything else aside. Such a focus was impossible in the chaotic postwar South. Now he believed his place was in the West, against the Indians, where he had a better chance to accomplish a mission. He refused to go to Louisiana because, he said, he did not believe it was a military assignment. Grant accommodated him in August 1867 by appointing him to the army-civilian Indian Commission established to try to bring peace to the West; he much preferred that to the South. As Reconstruction politics and problems heated up, Sherman became increasingly busy in the West, and that was the way he wanted it.[23]

Yet he continued speaking his mind on the controversies of the day. In mid-November 1867, he publicly condemned congressional radicals in a speech before the Society of the Army of the Tennessee, a veterans' group. He reminded his listeners that the entire nation was responsible for the development of slavery and had long shared in its profits, so Congress "should be charitable and liberal in the final distribution of the natural penalties." If the South was cooperative, it should be welcomed back; if Southerners were recalcitrant, the inevitable "wave of immigration" from the rest of the nation would solve the problem. This speech cheered Johnson and strengthened his desire to bring Sherman into his administration. Sherman naively failed to see why Johnson felt this way and grew confused and angry as a result.[24]

The whole mess and Sherman's part in it now came to a head. As part of its battle with Johnson, Congress passed a Tenure of Office Act on March 2, 1867, requiring congressional approval for any cabinet change. Congress was trying to protect Edwin Stanton from Johnson's open desire to dump him. Johnson saw the law as an infringement on his constitutional authority as president and decided to test it. On August 12, 1867, with Congress out of session, he suspended Stanton from office and, unable to convince Sherman, appointed Grant to the post. Grant took the job to try to protect the army from Johnson's further manipulation. The president was opposing the Reconstruction Act by pressuring army officers not to enforce it. When Congress returned in December 1867, Johnson asked for its consent to Stanton's suspension and Grant's appointment, thinking Grant's popularity would carry the day. Congress refused. Sherman grew concerned about Grant, but he was even more worried that Johnson would somehow still pull him in. So though he wanted to stay out, he became involved for his own and Grant's sake.

The only solution appeared to be finding someone else for the War Department acceptable to Johnson and the Congress. He settled on Jacob D. Cox, the governor of Ohio, a Union veteran, and an opponent of universal black suffrage. Grant and several senators agreed, as did Thomas Ewing. Sherman spoke to the president on January 13, but Johnson showed little enthusiasm. That same day, the Senate voted down Johnson's suspension of Stanton.[25]

Sherman's loyalty to Grant drew him in further. Johnson dressed Grant down before a cabinet meeting for turning his office back to Stanton without first informing him. Sherman demonstrated his support for Grant by accompanying him to a meeting with the president. He hoped that by helping Grant resolve the matter, he would prevent Johnson from turning to him again and once more demanding he take over the War Department. The matter was now a constitutional crisis and dangerous. Sherman, however, personalized it beyond that. He grew furious at Johnson for not accepting Cox, and he similarly thought Stanton's intransigence in hanging on to the post was ridiculous. The two men, he argued, were "strong, stubborn, wilful men, that would embroil the world, rather than yield their point." Sherman saw two egos at work, not a constitutional problem. Ellen, more objectively and no doubt more accurately, thought Grant's presidential ambitions were also a factor. Sherman could not believe this of his friend.[26]

Congress now talked seriously of impeachment, and Sherman grew increasingly upset at finding himself so deeply involved. He appealed to Johnson for his freedom. "I have been tossed about so much that I do really want to rest and make the acquaintance of my family." He wanted to go back to St. Louis and be left alone. Johnson would not hear of it. Increasingly worried about a military showdown with Congress and so recently burned by Grant, Johnson decided to use his power as commander in chief to promote Sherman to brevet general and create a new military district for him in Washington. That way Sherman would be available in any emergency. Thomas Ewing urged him to accept, but Sherman threatened to "get sick or do something very foolish" if the president persisted in his scheme. It particularly bothered him to be placed in potential competition with Grant. He appealed to John Sherman for help. Johnson reluctantly gave up, telegraphing Sherman the cancellation of his order. Sherman was overjoyed: "I cannot express under what deep obligations I am for your concession to my wishes." Once more Sherman avoided becoming a part of the political crisis.[27]

Congress watched Johnson flounder as it proceeded with its deliberations. On February 24, 1868, the House of Representatives impeached the president, and the Senate began preparations for a trial. Sherman took the news calmly—now that he was back in St. Louis. "As to impeachment," he told John Sherman, "I don't know as it will cause much trouble." Because Ben Wade, president pro tem of the Senate, would become president at Johnson's conviction and since his personality was similar to Johnson's, he would soon be quarreling with Congress and be impeached himself. Rather than punishing Johnson for allegedly violating the Tenure of Office Act and then having to repeat the process with Wade, it would make more sense to wait for the Supreme Court to decide the law's constitutionality. Sherman seemed to believe that once the Court ruled, the wrangling between Congress and the president would cease. He saw neither side battling over principles, viewing the Reconstruction battles as mere personal struggles among stubborn men. If they stopped their arguing and left Southern whites alone to reorganize Southern society, he remained sure all would be well.[28]

But Sherman had one more scene to play, a witness at the Johnson conviction trial in the Senate. He had a torturous several days on the stand as the House managers tried to prevent him from buttressing the defense case that Johnson was acting lawfully and only trying to test the constitutionality of the Tenure of Office Act. Every time the defense tried to question Sherman, the proceedings dissolved into a legalistic wrangle over the admissibility of the inquiry. Finally, Sherman was allowed to answer the question about Johnson's purpose in offering him the office of secretary of war. Johnson had told him, Sherman replied, that he wanted the office conducted for the good of the country and the army. "'If we can bring the case to the courts,'" Sherman reported Johnson saying, "'it would not stand half an hour.'" The president's intention had been legal. Johnson narrowly missed conviction because the Senate could not agree that he had committed an impeachable offense. He was able to complete his term of office bowed but unbroken. He never called on Sherman again.[29]

Sherman's behavior during the late 1860s set the tone for the rest of his postwar years. As he had during the war, he continued to recoil from disorder, though somewhat differently now. His reply to the anarchy of war had been sure, hard action. During Reconstruction, he believed forthright action would add to the problem; inaction was the proper response. The South should be left alone so it could reconstruct itself. Any action against it, particularly by helping blacks, would produce further chaos. During the war, he considered himself the South's friend even when he wreaked destruction on it. In the postwar years, he expressed his friendship by trying to remain uninvolved. While he gained fame during the Civil War, he did not use it in his Reconstruction battles. The hard-driving general became passive, but in the change he remained consistent to his opposition to disorder. He had promised his Southern friends a hard war and a soft peace, and he was true to his word—again.

CHAPTER 17

INDIAN COUNTRY CHAOS

WHILE WASHINGTON STRUGGLED to secure the Union in the aftermath of the Civil War, another arena of violent conflict was heating up in the West—the climax of the age-old struggle between the native American's survival and white society's expansion. William T. Sherman was the leading military man involved in trying to find a solution to the seemingly unsolvable problem. He faced it as he faced much else in his life: by trying to bring order to what he saw as an anarchic situation.

The war for survival against and mastery of the native Americans had begun when the first European had set foot on this continent. The European colonists inexorably pushed the Indians back from the Atlantic coastline and quickly pursued them. Presidents Andrew Jackson and Martin Van Buren in the 1830s colonized the eastern tribes across the Mississippi River in land they told them was theirs forever. Leaving their ancestral homelands by way of the tragic Trail of Tears to become "civilized" in "the Great American Desert" was a horrible experience for these Indians. But at least their destination was to be their permanent home, a place where they would be free from further white pressure and forceful eviction.[1]

American guarantees did not hold; the thirst for land was too great. White encroachment on Indian treaty lands began soon after the Indians arrived in their new homes. It continued through the Civil War and escalated after it as huge numbers of former soldiers, eager to start anew, moved West. Under the auspices of the Homestead Act of 1862, which promised 160 acres in return for five years of labor on the land, whites established farms and sheep and cattle ranches. Others searched for precious metals. Though in smaller numbers, newly freed blacks joined the westward movement. The railroad began to spiderweb the region, completing the long-held dream of a transcontinental route. Communities were founded and began to thrive. Alongside the influx of civilians came the military. More and more army forts dotted the countryside. The buffalo, the chief food and clothing supply for the Plains Indians, grew scarce as whites hunted it for profit and sport. The open West that had been promised to the Indians as a permanent home was rapidly being occupied by increasing numbers of white settlers.

As more whites began to settle the West in the post–Civil War years, it became clear that the U.S. government could not tolerate a free Indian presence in the area, yet there was no new frontier to push them to. The treaties, negotiated as permanent, were now ignored or altered, and the Indians pushed onto reservations within specific boundaries. When whites encroached on these reservations, the government shifted the borders to meet their needs. The Indians, feeling betrayed, tried to preserve what little they had. In response, the government turned to the Bureau of Indian Affairs of the Department of the Interior and to the U.S. Army to persuade the Indians or coerce them to acquiesce. It is not surprising that an enterprise so fraught with issues of legality, morality, and loyalty should engender conflict between the agents and the soldiers assigned to accomplish this task.

In July 1865, when Sherman was placed in command of the Military Division of the Mississippi (in 1866 the name was changed to the Military Division of the Missouri), he had jurisdiction over an area that encompassed a huge chunk of what was Indian country—everything from the Mississippi River to the Rocky Mountains, except for Texas. He was pleased to be in the "Great West, where my heart has always been." Although he had to move to Washington, D.C., in 1869 when he became commanding general of the entire army, his interest remained on the frontier. No matter what else he was doing during these years, he hurried back to the trans-Mississippi as often as he could. Here was where a soldier should be—fighting an enemy, not engaged in bureaucratic political battles like those over Reconstruction.[2]

The end of the Civil War resulted in a shift of focus for the army and a change in its perception by the public. The Confederacy was gone, so there was no longer need for a million-man force. But troops were still needed now to enforce Reconstruction and to safeguard the westward migration of American citizens. Only military men seemed to think these tasks required many troops. In July 1866 Congress set the peacetime force at approximately fifty-four thousand men; by the time Sherman became commanding general in 1869, the number was down to around thirty-five thousand and would soon be cut to approximately twenty-five thousand, the size it was to remain for most of Sherman's term in office. This shrinking force had to man 255 posts widely scattered all over the United States in seacoast forts, along the borders, in the South, and throughout Indian country. Sherman constantly received "call[s] for more troops which cannot be granted," he said. In his year-end report to the secretary of war in November 1869, he hoped "Congress may be appealed to not to diminish the military establishment any further." If enough troops were not available, "I believe a condition of things would result amounting to anarchy." He believed that without an adequate army, there could be no national order, especially in the West.[3]

Like many other Americans, Sherman held contradictory views toward the Indians. On the one hand, he felt sorry for them as individuals and insisted that whites should be fair to them; but they exasperated him because of their stubborn opposition to the movement of white society and because of the pathos their condition often engendered. He viewed them as stubborn children who needed disciplining. Their very way of life represented the kind of anarchy he had feared all of his life; their mobility and closeness to nature appeared at odds with stability and order. He did not want to exterminate them, but he hoped they would become productive members of society. And to Sherman, "productive" meant doing things the white man's way. If they did, he would support them, even against white interlopers. If they did not, he would use all the force he could muster to teach them proper behavior. "During an assault," he insisted, "the soldiers can not pause to distinguish between male and female, or even discriminate as to age. As long as resistance is made[,] death must be meted out, but the moment all resistance ceases, the firing will stop and all survivors turned over to the proper Indian agent."

Sherman viewed Indians as he viewed recalcitrant Southerners during the war and newly freed people after: resisters to the legitimate forces of an orderly society.[4]

His attitude was clear when he addressed a graduating class at West Point. He characterized the Indians as lazy; they had an "inherited prejudice . . . against labor." They refused to "earn their bread by the sweat of their brows," preferring instead to depend on "the scanty supply of game, that requires a vast scope of country to range over." Reflecting the idea of Manifest Destiny, the national belief in American superiority and thus the right and duty to expand across the continent, he believed the Indians were barriers to white progress. Twenty thousand Indians, he said, would consider Nebraska "a small range for their substinence, while whites will be able to feed two million off its soil." Indians had to give up their culture and become like whites if they wished to survive. It was "the law of the survival of the fittest," he repeated on numerous occasions, expressing his belief in the social Darwinian philosophy that was so popular in the postwar years.

Sherman saw the Indians as inferior and stubborn, two characteristics that when taken together were particularly troublesome. It was one thing to be found lacking; it was more serious to refuse to recognize it and get out of the way of the obviously superior whites. Such stubbornness created an intolerable disorderly condition; it thwarted progress. The only answer was not reason; it was force. Since the inferior Indians refused to step aside so superior American culture could create success and progress, they had to be driven out of the way as the Confederates had been driven back into the Union. All-out war would quickly end the Indian nuisance as it had finished off rebel arrogance. "All I can say to you," he advised the graduating West Pointers, "is that the inevitable result should be reached with a due regard to humanity and mercy."[5]

Most of the other generals who took a direct role in the Indian wars were, like Sherman, Civil War luminaries. Most also saw the war against the Indians as a new phase of securing the nation against anarchic forces. Their names were familiar from Civil War battles: John Pope, O. O Howard, Nelson A. Miles, Alfred H. Terry, E. O. C. Ord, C. C. Augur, and Edward R. S. Canby. Among the colonels, George Armstrong Custer and Benjamin

Grierson were the most famous. They had already seen war at its worst and did not shrink to use force against the Indians.[6]

The army's enlisted men in the West were mostly urban workers and immigrants—a mixed bag of good and bad, skilled and unskilled, white and black. They earned low pay, a private receiving only thirteen dollars a month. Their training was sparse when it occurred at all, and their units were always under strength. Promotion was slow; discipline was harsh; food was often barely edible; and living conditions were spare. In the average frontier fort the barracks, which housed a company or two, were made of logs, rough lumber, or adobe; they were dusty and dirty and provided little protection against the wind or the sun. Save for the periodic campaign, days were filled with choking dust, extremes of heat and cold, tedium, and the search for an elusive enemy.[7]

Other than Sherman, the most famous Indian fighter was Philip Sheridan, who fought the Indians the way he had fought Confederates in the Shenandoah Valley, all-out. In the public mind, he and Sherman were the two clearest symbols of a harsh Indian policy. Their names were forever tied to that philosophy through their joint linkage to the famous statement: "The only good Indian is a dead Indian." Sherman insisted that the phrase actually went back to colonial days and that "Miles Standish was the author of it." But by his own admission, "Sherman firmly believed in the doctrine."[8]

The 270,000 Indians living in the western territories were divided into over one hundred different tribes, whose cultures varied enormously. Their languages were as diverse as their religious beliefs and forms of government. The Plains Indians depended on the buffalo; those in the desert and mountains subsisted on smaller game; still others farmed. Among themselves, there were intertribal animosities, and even in the face of white encroachment, they continued warring against each other. They used hit-and-run tactics rather than conventional maneuver and mass. In the postwar years, only about one hundred thousand were still actively resisting the white man's advance: the Sioux, Cheyenne, Arapaho, Kiowa, Commanche, Nez Perce, Ute, Bannock, Paiute, Modoc, and Apache.[9]

These one hundred thousand Indian men, women, and children found themselves battling a westwardly expanding United

States, represented and protected by about twenty thousand U.S. soldiers. The army quickly learned that, in order to neutralize the superior mobility of its adversary, it had to stay on the offensive. It established small, visible forts all over the West and used the tactic of converging columns—army units that attacked the Indians from various sides, kept them on the run so they had little time to resupply, and then, ideally, caught them in a box formed by the attackers. Purposely campaigning in the winter when the Indians were with their families, the army destroyed supplies and horse-flesh and all too often killed women and children. Compared to the gigantic battles of the Civil War, the one thousand or so engagements of the Indian wars and the approximately one thousand army losses and three thousand to six thousand Indian casualties were small. The Indian wars consisted of quick skirmishes, not drawn-out battles; even Custer's Last Stand—actually a major Sioux victory—was minuscule compared to Shiloh or Gettysburg. During the Civil War, Sherman and Sheridan had practiced a total war of destruction of property; they had, however, spared the populace. Now the army, in its Indian warfare, often wiped out entire villages. Death and devastation also resulted from disease, starvation, and other casualties.[10]

The ability of the Indians to sustain their resistance to federal land acquisition from 1865 into the 1890s was a testament to their perseverance, but it was also the result of discord among American forces. It is conventional wisdom that the Indians were not able to put aside long-held enmities for racial unity against white society, but it is not often remarked that the whites themselves were far from unified. There was common agreement in American society as to the objective in the West: the Indians had to be moved out of the way. But the means to accomplish this end were in dispute. Should the Indians be driven onto reservations and forcibly kept there by the army, or should they be coaxed on by negotiation and encouraged to stay by the kindness of civilian agents? The policy issue was drawn between the pursuit of military means and war or civilian means and negotiation.[11]

Sherman believed that the first prerequisite for any success against the Indians was to move the Bureau of Indian Affairs from the Interior Department into the War Department, making it subordinate to the army, which could then do its job. In the fall of 1865 he expressed his view to a sympathetic U. S. Grant: "I remember when the Indian tribes were put under the jurisdiction & control of the Interior Dept, and think it was a mistake. Indians always look to the man or men who have soldiers, and the Sooner we regain absolute & unqualified Control of the Indians and all who travel & deal with them the Sooner can we get them under Control." In 1867 Congress discussed the possibility of doing what Sherman and other army men wanted, but the bill failed in the Senate.[12]

Until he became president, Grant had agreed with Sherman about the preferred dominance of the military in dealing with the Indians. From the wider perspective of the executive mansion, he became an exponent of a peace policy that continued civilian dominance but with a new twist. He appointed Ely S. Parker, a Seneca Indian, his prewar friend and military secretary from 1864 to 1866, as Indian commissioner; Parker tried to implement a policy that would be agreeable to both civilians and military men. He devised the idea that tribes on the reservation would be under control of the agents, and those on the outside would be the responsibility of the army. This compromise seemed to have promise, but in January 1870 an army unit attacked a camp of allegedly hostile Piegan Indians and killed one hundred of them. The horror of women and children under military attack was chilling to the hopes for army-agent cooperation. Sherman defended the army before congressional investigators, but the incident reopened the civilian-military split so widely it never healed. "The Indian agents cannot manage the wild Indians," Sherman told Sheridan and testified similarly before a later congressional hearing. The army and the agents continued their unhappy arrangement—military men like Sherman seeing the civilians and their supporters as naive dreamers and the humanitarians considering the military as vicious and cruel.[13]

There was an even more fundamental problem in the command structure of the anti-Indian forces: the disagreement as to the relationship between the secretary of war and the commanding general. This was an old feud; army veterans remembered the harsh words that had passed between Winfield Scott and Secretaries of War William L. Marcy and Jefferson Davis in the 1850s and how, in disgust, Scott had moved his headquarters from Washington to New York. Sherman himself had witnessed firsthand Grant's jurisdictional problem with Secretary of War Edwin M.

Stanton, and he had seen the 1866 letter Grant had written in complaint. "No orders should go to the army, or the adjutant-general, except through the general-in-chief," Grant insisted. Sherman agreed.[14]

When Sherman became commanding general of the army in 1869, Grant was in the White House and another army man, John M. Schofield, was secretary of war. If there was anything Sherman was sure of, it was that Grant would never tolerate his secretary of war treating a commanding general the way Stanton and President Andrew Johnson had treated him. Grant would show these politicians how to run the army properly, Sherman confidently believed. This was confirmed when on March 5, 1869, the day after the inauguration, the War Department issued General Orders No. 11 placing all U.S. Army departments and bureaus under Sherman's command and requiring that "all orders from the President or Secretary of War to any portion of the army, line or staff, will be transmitted through the General of the Army." Sherman was pleased; he would not have to battle the politicians for control of the army the way Grant had. His old friend, chastened by his own problems, had seen to that.[15]

This good fortune lasted less than a month. Schofield, whom Andrew Johnson had appointed as a compromise secretary of war and Grant had continued in office, was replaced by the sickly John A. Rawlins, Grant's former military chief of staff and veritable wartime conscience. Rawlins had backed Grant in the jurisdictional conflict with Stanton but now worried that Sherman had too much power at his expense as secretary of war. He urged Grant to rescind General Orders No. 11. Sherman rushed off a letter pleading against any change. "It would put me in a most unpleasant dilemma because the Army and country would infer your want of confidence," he told the president. It was too late. That same day general orders signed by John A. Rawlins limited Sherman's power to "orders and instructions relating to military operations." Staff bureaus would deal directly with the secretary of war. The commanding general could and would be bypassed. The civilian Rawlins retained ultimate authority over the army, even over its commanding general.[16]

A stunned Sherman rushed to the White House where Grant uncomfortably tried to justify his action. Sherman heard words he never thought would come from Grant's mouth. "Rawlins feels badly about it; it worries him, and he is not well," Grant said. "But, Grant," Sherman replied, "ought a public measure that you have advocated for years, and which he has known you were determined upon, to be set aside for such a reason? Ought he not acquiesce in what he knew was your fixed purpose, and what was done before he entered the War Department?" "Yes, it would ordinary [*sic*] be so," Grant answered, "but I don't like to give him pain now; so, Sherman, you'll have to publish the rescinding order." "But Grant," Sherman responded, "It's your own order that you revoke, not mine, and think how it will look to the whole world!" "Well, if it's my own order, I can rescind it, can't I?" Grant retorted. Sherman stood up, bowed, and walked away: "Yes, Mr. President, you have the power to revoke your own order; you shall be obeyed. Good morning, sir." He left in his wake a strained friendship and went back to a suddenly crippled command.[17]

Sherman and Grant continued to be polite to each other, but they were never close again. "Yet to me he is a mystery," Sherman recounted sadly, "and I believe he is a mystery to himself." Sherman never got over the hurt of Grant's political turnabout. He felt sorely betrayed. He believed that Grant had succumbed to political pressure and hurt the army in the process. He was no longer the no-nonsense general Sherman had come to depend on during the war. It was sad, and it frightened him.[18]

Rawlins attempted to soften the blow by voluntarily forwarding all orders to the army through Sherman, sometimes apologizing when he forgot, but he maintained his office's superiority. When he died in September 1869, Sherman thought he had another chance to regain his lost status. Grant made him interim secretary of war, momentarily uniting the two contending offices. Sherman hoped this merger might be the permanent solution to the imbroglio. It could not; the political system would never tolerate a sitting general holding a civilian office at the same time. The best Sherman could hope for was a secretary of war who would share power with him. Grant asked his advice, and Sherman happily suggested, among others, W. W. Belknap, an internal revenue collector in Iowa and formerly a brigade commander in Sherman's Civil War Army of the Tennessee. When Grant made Belknap his secretary of war, Sherman was relieved and promised "every assistance." He was sure his former subordinate would pay him proper deference. "Of course, Belknap's appointment is perfectly satisfactory to me," he enthused to a friend. "I don't see why with his youth and business qualifications he may not achieve a real fame."[19]

It did not take Sherman long to see that once Belknap took office, he was not only determined to maintain the secretary of war's dominance over the military, but he was also prepared to expand his powers, at Sherman's expense, even over the line units in the West, involved in the Indian wars. Sherman saw Belknap's actions as worse than Rawlins's, an explicit attempt to undercut the rightful authority of the commanding general with the resulting loss of operational efficiency. Less than a year after Belknap had taken office, Sherman made a formal protest. "Leaves of absence are granted, the stations of officers are changed, and other orders are now made directly to the army, not through the general, but direct through other officials and the adjutant-general. So long as this is the case I surely do not command the army of the United States, and am not responsible for it." He urged Belknap to support new regulations that would guarantee the commanding general his legal due, ominously pointing out that Jefferson Davis as secretary of war had made the office of commanding general meaningless for his own obvious "purpose." Sherman also appealed to Grant, and the president soothingly responded that he was confident that "the relations between the Sec and yourself can be made pleasant." Sherman still wanted to trust his friend and "promise[d] to submit to whatever decision" Grant made.

Grant, however, was increasingly dependent on Washington insiders and did nothing, and Sherman's position continued to erode. He sought refuge in a two-month inspection tour of the Indian country out West in the spring of 1871. He began threatening, as he had the previous year, to move his command out of Washington to St. Louis as Scott had moved to New York in the 1850s. When he returned from the West, nothing had changed, so he spent the summer vacationing with his children. In the fall, he jumped at the chance to go to Europe and stayed abroad for nearly a year. The secretary of war was commanding the army, anyway, he thought, so why should he stay around Washington and feel slighted and embarrassed. He refused to fight Belknap politically because he saw it as beneath him and envisaged no chance for success without Grant's support; in frustration, he sailed away.[20]

When he returned in the fall of 1872, the problem had not gone away as he seemed to hope it had. Once more he wrote Belknap: "I am really at a loss to know what is my true field of duty." He asked for a separate adjutant general and chief engineer for himself, over and above the heads of those bureaus whom he could not command. His adjutant, he said, would receive "all reports and returns that should come to me, and . . . make all orders that I have to make." The chief engineer would "consolidate" and "report" information received from army units "concerning the geography and resources of the country." Sherman wanted to move out of the War Department into some "separate building." Clearly this was all a surrender. Sherman was willing to give in to Belknap for a few face-saving crumbs.[21]

He got his adjutant and engineer but then was handed another setback. Previously when the secretary of war had been absent for any extended period of time, Sherman had acted as his temporary replacement. The attorney general now ruled that since the secretaryship was a civil office, no military man could hold it. The Grant administration, unlike others before and after, seemed determined to maintain total civilian control over the military even with the Indian wars in progress. In response, Sherman's annual report was unusually brief: "No part of the Army is under my immediate control, and the existing Army regulations devolve on the Secretary of War the actual command of the military peace establishment, and all responsibility therefore, so that I forbear making any further recommendations or report."[22]

If Sherman believed that such petulance would resolve matters, he was disappointed. It did not. He had to play his last card. In the spring of 1874, he asked Belknap for permission to move his headquarters to St. Louis in October, citing Winfield Scott's action as precedent. Belknap was only too happy to agree, realizing that Sherman's departure from Washington meant his complete surrender to civilian control. As President Grant was now the head civilian, Sherman's departure meant that another potentially troublesome military voice of protest was silenced. Just to be sure, Belknap reminded Sherman that, as had been the case with Scott, "no material change shall be made in the stations of troops or commanders without previous approval by this Department."[23]

The news of Sherman's imminent departure shocked his fellow army officers. Former aide C. B. Comstock said his departure would "only diminish his power in the Army and give [the] Sec of War even more power." Nelson A. Miles called it a "fatal mistake," and Phil Sheridan agreed. Sherman refused to change his mind. "I will do it," he told Comstock, even "if it results in the abolition of my office." The whole thing was "beneath the dignity of my office and character," he complained to old army friend E. O. C. Ord, and "though willing to make as much personal sacrifice as anybody," he could not stand it any longer. He told Sheridan, "Of course I have felt humiliation," but he could have tolerated it had Grant been supportive. "My faith in his friendship is shaken," he sadly admitted to a magazine editor, "and when again he wants it, it may be less than he supposes."[24]

The official order was published in early September; Sherman and his family moved to St. Louis, carrying with them a match holder Belknap had unaccountably given Sherman as a going-away present. The family remained in Missouri for nineteen months, Sherman continuing as commanding general but spending almost all his time working on his memoirs. He played practically no role in army management, and neither Grant nor the secretary of war protested his self-imposed exile. Belknap administered the army without him, pleased to have his own way. When Belknap was put on trial in early 1876 for receiving kickbacks from sutlers (post traders), Sherman felt a sense of justification. But Grant named Ohio lawyer and jurist Alfonso Taft as the new secretary of war without asking Sherman's advice. John Sherman urged Cump to return to the capital, but Cump said he would come back only if "Secretary Taft is willing to trust me to execute and carry into effect his orders and instructions." When Taft agreed to ask Sherman's advice before taking any action, Sherman returned to Washington in late March 1876. On April 6, 1876, Grant issued an order placing the adjutant general and inspector general under Sherman's command and indicating that all War Department orders "shall be promulgated through the General of the Army." The other staff bureaus maintained their independence of the commanding general, but Sherman's situation was vastly improved. The principles of the dispute remained unresolved, but Taft, in the wake of the Belknap scandals, his own military inexperience, and an unassertive personality, was willing to allow Sherman a greater role in army management.[25]

Taft and later secretaries treated Sherman with more respect than Belknap had, but Cump remained unhappy with his position. He continued to insist he should have total control over all the army, but civilian secretaries of war and encrusted army staff bureaus continued to insist on civilian authority. The problem of the relationship of the commanding general and secretary of war outlasted Sherman and was repeated numerous times until it was finally resolved with military reform in the early twentieth century.

Such long and complicated discord at the highest levels of the military made coordinated activity against the Indians difficult, especially within the context of the army-agent conflict. Throughout most of the post–Civil War years, however, despite such conflicts, the army was able to maintain its ascendancy over the Indian tribes. Its control was never universal, and every so often, the Indians would shock the nation with a surprise victory. Such an event would enrage Sherman and the military, and their usual response was to press the war even more harshly. As early as December 21, 1866, during the Johnson presidency, the Sioux under Red Cloud killed all eighty members of a unit commanded by Captain William Fetterman near Fort Kearny, Nebraska. Sherman angrily said the Indians had to be punished "with vindictive earnestness, until at least ten Indians are killed for each white life lost." He insisted that the only answer to the Indian problem was all-out war—of the kind he had utilized against the Confederacy.

Instead, President Johnson, under congressional mandate, established the so-called Sanborn commission. This body reported in June 1867 that the Sioux Indians were simply angry at the army for occupying the Bozeman Trail, which ran through their country. It recommended negotiations, not military activity, to move them onto a reservation. In July 1867 Congress ordered the president to appoint a commission to negotiate such treaties with the various tribes.[26]

Sherman disagreed completely. Force, not negotiations, was the solution. But no one listened. A Peace Commission of eight members was established. Four favored the treaty procedure:

Indian commissioner N. G. Taylor; Senator John B. Henderson, the chairman of the Senate Indian Affairs Committee and later the recipient of Sherman's famous refusal to run for the presidency; former Indian agent Samuel F. Tappan; and General John B. Sanborn. Favoring force were army men: Sherman, Alfred H. Terry, C. C. Augur, and the old veteran W. S. Harney. Sherman promised to be cooperative, but he gave the commission little chance to succeed. Indians and whites could not live together, he insisted. "In the end they must be removed to small and clearly defined reservations or must be killed."[27]

The Peace Commission went West in August 1867 to negotiate appropriate treaties for northern and southern reservations, as well as for the opening of the vast middle of the West to the railroad and white settlement. The army promised not to carry on any offensive operations in the meantime. Sherman found the civilian commissioners to be congenial companions, but his goals were different from theirs. "I dont care about interesting myself too far in the fate of the poor devils of Indians who are doomed from the causes inherent in their nature or from the natural & persistent hostility of the white race. All I aim to accomplish is to so clearly define the duties of the Civil & Military agents of Govt so that we wont be quarrelling all the time as to whose business it is to look after them." As far as Sherman was concerned, the Peace Commission would make peace among the whites, not between the whites and the Indians.[28]

In mid-September in Nebraska, the commission met with spokesmen for several tribes, but not Red Cloud and his Sioux. After hearing from these representatives, Sherman made clear that he had little tolerance for their demands. Whatever they said or did, they were doomed. The United States, with its expanding population, its railroads, and its army, was the face of the future. Their only option was to choose good sites on the reservations and begin living like white people. They should not expect any protection from the old treaties. "I am afraid they did not make allowance for the rapid growth of the white race." And if the Indians refused to see reason and cooperate, Sherman threatened them with military force. "This Commission is not only a Peace Commission but it is a War Commission also." They had until November to make up their minds.[29]

Although Andrew Johnson urged Sherman to return to Washington at this time to aid him in his battle against Congress, Sherman procrastinated and was able to participate in the signing of several treaties that placed some, though hardly all, tribes on reservations. With winter rapidly approaching, however, the commission delayed negotiating other agreements until 1868. Congress, caught up in the impeachment proceedings, delayed ratifying the agreements, and the cooperative Indians paid the price. They gave up their old hunting grounds before Congress appropriated funds to care for them on their new reservations, and they suffered terribly. Meanwhile the army did nothing to prevent further white encroachment. Finally Congress voted the promised money and then appointed Sherman to do the disbursing, putting him in charge of the special agents it hoped would do the work. Sherman saw this as a political job and only reluctantly agreed to do it. He tried his best, but the $500,000 proved insufficient. Once again the Indians felt betrayed, and before long they and the army were at war again.[30]

The results of the Peace Commission's efforts reflected the conflicting views and tensions surrounding the Indian question. Sherman and one of the civilian commissioners, Samuel F. Tappan, exchanged a series of increasingly bitter letters, expressing their dissatisfaction with the whole procedure. Tappan called the Indian wars part of a conspiracy to draw troops from Reconstruction. Sherman and his army men were guilty of using excessive force. Sherman expressed support for the commission's activities only because he knew they would lead to the failure of the peace policy and allow the government to use force again. "I have no hope of civilizing the plains Indians," he said. "One thing is demonstrated," he insisted, "either the Indians must give away or we must abandon all west of the Missouri River and confess as you say that forty millions of whites are cowed by a few thousand savages." The Peace Commission "provided liberal homes for these savages" on the reservations, he insisted, and their response was to "laugh at our cordiality, rape women, murder men, burn whole trains with their drivers to cinders, and send word that they never intended to keep their treaties." Sherman had little compassion for the Indians and no guilt about the failure of the United States to live up to its treaty obligations.[31]

The construction of the transcontinental railroad made the Indian issue particularly conspicuous. Sherman had long thought about such a road, investing $10,000 of his bank's money and working toward it during the 1850s in California. In the Civil War he had fought the Atlanta campaign anchored to a thin line of tracks. He marveled at the railroad then and was now even more in awe of the possibility of its construction across the continent. He was confident that its chief engineer, Grenville Dodge, and the other laborers, who had pulled off railroad miracles for him in Civil War Georgia, could accomplish the transcontinental feat. However, the railroad could not be completed across the West if the work parties were subject to constant Indian attack. Thus, Sherman was very enthusiastic about the creation in 1866 of a separate Army Department of the Platte to protect the road's construction. He considered the rails as important as the white settlers. "Of course you are right in saying," he told one of his subordinates in 1870, "that the safety of the Line of the Pacific Railroad . . . is your first consideration."[32]

He assigned army units to protect the work crews, and he regularly visited the sites himself. He was close friends with Dodge, and he was pleased to hear the laborers, many of them his former soldiers, yell out "Uncle Billy" as he walked by. He urged his senator brother to support government aid for the roads, a key to continued national expansion. The railroad would unify the Atlantic and Pacific coasts, preventing the necessity of long ocean voyages. During the Civil War he had learned about railroads, and he believed they could be militarily significant in the wide expanses of the West. He personally preferred the speed and dependability of the train over the uncertainty of the river steamboat.[33]

According to chief engineer Dodge, Sherman's personal interest in protecting the railroad was instrumental in its completion. In 1869, when the pounding of the last spike at Promontory, Utah, was carried by telegraph all over the nation, Sherman excitedly listened in the War Department offices. He appreciated Dodge's telegram thanking him for his "continuous active aid," which permitted the road's completion "in so short a time," excitedly responding to what he called the "mystic taps of the telegraphic battery." He promised to ride the rails their full length to California soon, reminiscing about how different it would be from his 196-day trip by ship in 1846.[34]

The more experiences he had with the four transcontinental

railroad routes across the nation and the connecting lines, the more he came to appreciate their importance. In an annual report to the secretary of war late in his term of office, he said that the railroads had "completely revolutionized our country" and "imposed[d] on the military an entire change of policy." Previously the army had maintained small forts along wagon and stagecoach roads, but the railroad made many of these outposts unnecessary. Now army units could be "concentrate[d] at strategic points, generally near the national frontier or where railroads intersect, so as to send out detachments promptly to the districts where needed." This would allow for more permanent installations, and thus more comfortable quarters for the officers and men. But it would also have an educational impact too. The railroad, along with the telegraph, broke down the army's isolation and allowed every military man "to keep up with the times." "The completion of the transcontinental railroad is as great a victory as any in the war," he said.[35]

Throughout the 1870s, Sherman maintained a constant pressure for a military solution, determined to keep the Indians on the reservations so railroads and white settlements could continue. Upset as he was over problems with the Indian agents and the secretary of war, he regularly left his office in Washington to make inspection tours of the West. A year did not pass that he did not make one or more visits to the trans-Mississippi region, inspecting forts and army units, riding the railroad and watching its progress, studying the geography of the region and its rocks and fauna, and interviewing the local populace. He left the political discord of Washington for the calm and tranquility of the sparsely populated frontier. "I confess," he told Ellen, that "in this wild roving about, camping by the side of some stream with pickets out to give alarm if necessary & mules picketed close in them is a charm that cannot be described or reasoned about."[36]

Sherman remained most at ease when he gathered around the camp fire or anywhere else late into the night swapping tales with fellow army officers about friends and enemies from the war or discussing the military campaigns of Alexander, Caesar, Napoleon, Cromwell, Wellington, and Washington. There was the "twinkle of his eye, the jocular toss of his head, and the serio-comic twitch of his many-wrinkled features" as he told a story, all the while a circle of cigar smoke surrounding him. "The puffs came fast and furious, and shot from his mouth as though he were firing off a pistol." He "kept up that everlasting long stride of his . . . , with his hands deep in his trowsers' pockets, as if he would never weary." He visited Kit Carson, whom he had first met in 1840s California. "These Red Skins think Kit twice as big a man as me," he joked one time, impressed at his friend's ability to fathom the Indians. Carson's poverty appalled him, however, and he used part of a scholarship from Notre Dame to try to educate one of Kit's sons.[37]

It was during one of his many tours West that Sherman experienced the violence that was an integral part of the army-Indian conflict in the West. Texans had long been complaining about the extent of Indian depredations on the frontier, but humanitarians like Tappan argued that it was all a subterfuge to draw troops away from protecting freed people in the South. On April 23, 1871, Sherman, several staff members, and Inspector General Randolph B. Marcy went to Texas on one of Sherman's regular western tours to see for themselves. They left San Antonio in wagons on May 2, escorted by seventeen soldiers from the black Tenth Cavalry Regiment, moving slowly north toward Fort Sill in Oklahoma. They saw evidence of burned-out ranch houses indicating that the Indians had carried out successful raids against white settlers. As they approached Fort Richardson, near Jacksboro, Texas, they crossed the Salt Creek Prairie under the watchful eyes of some one hundred Kiowa braves led by Satanta, Satank, and Big Tree. A medicine man, the story went, had interpreted the hooting of an owl to mean that the warrior band should let the first group it saw pass unmolested and attack the second. The Kiowas let Sherman's columns pass and then attacked a ten-wagon civilian supply train that followed a few hours later. Seven wagoners and three Indians died; five whites escaped to tell the story.

Sherman arrived at Fort Richardson and learned of the ambush from one of the escapees. He ordered troops to the scene in hopes of catching the marauders, but heavy rain impeded the search. Notwithstanding the danger, Sherman's party moved on toward Fort Sill the next day, arriving on May 23, 1871. He and the fort's commander, Colonel Benjamin Grierson, immediately conferred with reservation Indian agent Lawrie Tatum, a Quaker who had come to support the use of force against the Indians. When the Kiowa leaders arrived for their rations on May 27, Tatum asked Satanta if he knew anything about the ambush. Of course, Satanta replied; he had led it personally, in protest against the illegal building of the railroad across Indian land and the enforced reservation policy. "If any other Indian claims the honor of leading that party, he will be lying to you. I led it myself."

Tatum reported to Sherman and urged the Indian's arrest and trial in Jacksboro. Sherman set a trap, perhaps remembering his two California adventures in capturing Alcalde John H. Nash and the group of army deserters. When Satanta arrived with a number of his followers, he proudly repeated his story to Sherman, who was standing on the fort commander's porch. Sherman lectured Satanta on what he called his cowardly attack and ordered his arrest. Satanta now had second thoughts. Actually he had not led the attack, he said; he had only watched. Sherman was unimpressed. He had Satanta, Big Tree, and Satank placed in handcuffs. Satanta begged to be shot on the spot rather than be returned for trial to Jacksboro. Kicking Bird urged compromise, but Sherman stood firm.

Meanwhile, Lone Wolf came riding up, handed a bow and arrows to one brave and a rifle to another, and sat down on the porch, a cocked Winchester across his lap. A gunfight between the Indians and the mounted armed black soldiers who appeared on signal seemed certain, and Sherman would be caught in the crossfire. The shutters on the veranda were thrown open, exposing more black soldiers with leveled rifles. Grierson courageously grabbed Lone Wolf's weapon and shouted to the other Indians through an interpreter that they had no chance and should surrender. Some distance from the porch, four or five braves charged some other soldiers; one was killed and another wounded.

The sixty-year-old Satank was determined not to suffer the shame of trial. As the wagons with the shackled Indians left for Jacksboro, Satank began moaning. The soldiers found his behavior humorous, but the other Indians recognized it as a death chant. In words unintelligible to the whites, he said that he would die at the side of the road and wanted his people to gather his bones. "I shall never go beyond that tree," he said, pointing ahead. He chanted: "O Sun, you remain forever but we Kaitsenko must die; O Earth, you remain forever but we Kaitsenko must die." He repeated the phrases several times until he reached the designated tree. He slid out of his handcuffs, pulled out a knife he had hidden under his blanket, and attacked one of the guards sitting next to him in the wagon. Both guards tried to get away, and he grabbed a rifle but was unable to load it. A soldier in another wagon shot him twice, then threw his body out alongside the road. The column of wagons continued on its way.[38]

Sherman took this threat to his personal safety calmly, and he expressed no sorrow over Satank's violent death. As always, he had been cool under fire, but he was angry over the disorder this incident demonstrated. Satanta, Satank, and the Kiowa were reservation Indians, who, because of "their natural propensity to steal horses and kill people," "commit[ed] all these murders and robberies, using the Reservation" as a safe haven. Whites in the surrounding area had long complained about such behavior. "I am satisfied that many of these murders and depredations have been done by Indians from this Reservation, and that a system exists of trading the stolen horses and mules to Kansas and New Mexico for arms and ammunition." This incident reinforced his hostility to the peace policy. The Kiowas had been on the reservation for two years, but none were farming and no children attended school. "Their progress in Civilization is a farce," he concluded. "The Kiowas need pretty much the lesson you gave Black Kettle and Little Raven," he told Sheridan. They needed a military drubbing. Sounding like he did during the Civil War when he was speaking about Southerners, he told his son: "I know Indians well enough to believe that they must be made to feel the power of the United States, before they cease their murders & robbery."[39]

Meanwhile, Satanta and Big Tree faced civil trial in Jacksboro, an unusual occurrence for Indian chiefs. They were found guilty and sentenced to be hanged. The legal proceedings were a national sensation, humanitarians arguing that the court lacked jurisdiction and that the Indians had not received a fair hearing. Even agent Tatum and the trial judge urged Texas governor Edward J. Davis to commute the sentence. Under pressure from Grant and the secretary of the interior, Davis reluctantly agreed. On August 2, 1871, the two Indians were sent to prison, where they remained for the next two years. Commissioner of Indian

Affairs Francis A. Walker told the Kiowas that Satanta and Big Tree would be freed if they promised to behave. Favorable press reports had made the two men martyrs, and the Grant administration thought their pardon would be politically wise. At a meeting at Fort Sill, federals pressured the Texas governor, and he agreed to release the Indians.

There was an avalanche of criticism. Agent Tatum resigned in protest, and Davis tried to put the onus where it properly belonged—on the federal government. Sherman, especially angry, issued a series of scathing statements. He told the secretary of the interior: "I hope when Satanta is released, and when he is actually killed at the head of a raiding party off his Reservation (as certain as next year comes) you will simply decree that the Kioways [*sic*] are outlaws, their property confiscated, and their most valuable Reservation restored to the Public Domain. Such an example will be worth the experiment." He told the House Military Affairs Committee that the next time the two Indians led a raid, he would not be upset if they scalped Governor Davis first. Davis tried to defend himself, but Sherman was in no mood to listen, his anger hotter because of the recent death of General E. R. S. Canby during the Modoc war. "I believe," he told Davis, "[that] in making the tour of your frontier, with a small escort, I ran the risk of my life, and I said to the Military Committee what I now say to you, that I will not again voluntarily assume the risk & in the interest of your frontier; that I believe that Satanta and Big Tree will have their revenge, if they have not already had it, and that if they are to have scalps, that yours is the first that should be taken." He was not interested in any promises civilians may have made Davis; that was not his concern. He told Sheridan "to act with vindictive earnestness and to make every Kiowa & Comanche knuckle down."[40]

Sherman saw himself in a state of war with the Indians, the uncivilized elements battling against society. As far as he was concerned, he had proved in the Civil War that the only way to deal with anarchic forces was to apply all-out war against them. In war, there was no place for compassion, because such sentiment prolonged the conflict. What frustrated Sherman so much was his inability to convince his civilian superiors of the correctness of his views.

Events eventually pushed the nation toward his philosophy. On

June 25, 1876, there occurred the most famous army-Indian battle of the post war years: Custer's stand at the Little Big Horn River. Sherman had always considered George Armstrong Custer to be "*very* brave, even to rashness," but thought, as others did, that only Custer's celebrated luck had regularly saved him from the disaster of his foolhardiness. His encounter with Sitting Bull and the Sioux at the Little Big Horn in Montana in late June 1876 was to be his last. Custer's impatience to bring on battle without proper reconnaisance and without waiting for approaching support units led to his military defeat and death. The Indians deceived him as to their location and their superior size and then beat him in the pitched battle that he unwisely initiated.[41]

The public was shocked that the Indians could so resoundingly trounce the U.S. Army, especially on the eve of the hundredth anniversary of the Declaration of Independence. When he addressed the Society of the Army of the Cumberland, which was meeting in Philadelphia as part of the Centennial celebration, Sherman knew only what he had read in the newspapers. "I suppose poor Custer, at the head of his command—for he was as gallant an officer as ever lived—dashed down through that gorge of hell, with imps of Satan on the right of him, with savages on the left of him. And he will never come back to tell the story." Sherman did not know all the details yet, so he could not comment further, but his anger was clear: "Those Indians must submit to the common laws of humanity and of our country."[42]

Wendell Phillips, the famous prewar abolitionist and postwar humanitarian, took the occasion of the nation's shock over Custer's debacle to protest yet again, this time in the *New York Herald,* about the army's harsh treatment of the Indians. He accused Sherman, the clearest symbol of that philosophy, of supporting extermination. Sherman responded through a private letter, soon published, denying any espousal of extermination but expressing forthrightly his views that the Indians had better become like white men and stop protesting the process or face dire consequences. "Peaceful Indians have by me, and by all the army, always been treated with the utmost kindness, but the hostile savages like Sitting Bull and his band of outlaw Sioux . . . must feel the superior power of the Government, before they can realize that they must not kill, must not steal, and must not continue to carry into practice their savage instincts and customs."[43]

His most extended public statement on the battle of the Little Big Horn came in an annual report to the secretary of war. Here he discussed Indian matters more calmly. He reprinted verbatim the reports of Alfred H. Terry, the commander of the Department of Dakota, and Marcus Reno, the senior surviving officer of Custer's unit, and indicated the army's plans for capturing the victorious Indians. It was all very rational, as was the letter he wrote to Sheridan in August discussing the tactics of the battle. By February 1877 he was finding fault with the presence of newspapermen on the expedition and the insufficient military pressure on the Indians to keep them off Custer. "Surely in grand strategy," he revealingly complained, "we ought not to allow savages to best us, but in this instance they did." Sherman knew there had been no massacre; the Indians had simply whipped Custer and his soldiers, a disconcerting realization.[44]

The convincing Indian tactical victory was to presage their ultimate defeat. The angry army chased down the Sioux and other tribes and forced them from their free-range hunting existence to the dependency of the reservation. Generals Ord, Miles, and Crook urged "hot pursuit" into Mexico against the Apaches, but Sherman worried about international law and Mexican reaction. Several American units penetrated into Mexico anyway, but full-scale operations proved unnecessary. As early as July 1879 Sherman said that "time is working so beautifully in our favor that it is folly to precipitate trouble with the Indians." Though the Indian wars continued into the 1890s, they were never again as intense as they had been earlier. The noble Chief Joseph of the Nez Perce and Geronimo of the Apaches were yet to be heard from, but the 1890 tragedy at Wounded Knee Creek in South Dakota was the real symbol of the post-Custer era. "No government on earth has expended as much money, so much charity, so much forbearance in this great problem," Sherman insisted in 1880, "as has the Govt of the U.S. and if the Christian policy has failed it had not been for want of effort but because the problem is insoluble—unless the Indian will change his nature & habits, select his spot of earth, and become as a white man he is doomed. It is not because the white man is cruel, inhuman and grasping but because it is the Law of Natural Change & development—the wrong began at Plymouth Rock and will end in the Rocky Mountains."[45]

It was inevitable, Sherman had thought all his life. Just a few months before his death, he gave once again his long-held solution to the problem of the American Indians: Exclusive control of the Indians should have been given to the army under its military leaders early on, and civilians should have stayed out of the army's way. "This country had no room for wild marauders," he concluded, and without civilian interference, the army would have gotten rid of them all.[46] Unfortunately, he held, chaotic policy had exacerbated anarchic conditions. If he had only been able to have complete control over the army and been able to use unlimited military force on the Indians as he had in the South during the Civil War, he believed he could have produced the solution that the disorderly situation required.

CHAPTER 18

———— ☆ ————

THE ANCHOR OF HOME

DURING THE IMMEDIATE YEARS after the Civil War, while he jousted with Andrew Johnson and fought the Indians on the Great Plains, Sherman pursued a busy social life befitting his status as Civil War hero and commanding general. He was invited to social gatherings all over Washington, and he traveled throughout the nation as well. He was a regular visitor to the White House; during the Hayes administration he joined in the Sunday evening hymn singing and escorted Mrs. Hayes to social functions when the president was busy. He frequently played whist with other Washington dignitaries at the home of Senator Justin S. Morrill. He corresponded with a variety of people in all walks of life, freely chatting on whatever interested him. He seemed to know everyone—writers, diplomats, businessmen, royalty, and the important politicians.[1]

He went to West Point for the June graduation ceremonies whenever he could, and his off-the-cuff remarks were usually the hit of the day. He was also the recipient of formal honors from other universities. Dartmouth (1866), Yale (1876), and Princeton (1878) conferred honorary Doctor of Laws degrees. Notre Dame awarded him a twenty-five-year scholarship, which he used to send Kit Carson's son to South Bend.[2]

These relationships with the important people of his day did not cause any change in his demeanor; he remained an approachable, outgoing person. When his son, Tom, graduated from Yale in 1876, the school made Sherman a guest of honor and sat him next to President Noah Porter at all the ceremonies. Sherman put up with all the pomp for awhile, but then he slipped away, much to his hosts' chagrin. They frantically searched until they found him on an outdoor bench sitting next to a recently discharged black inmate of the local workhouse, the two men contentedly puffing away on several of Sherman's favorite Havana cigars. Sherman was surprised at the fuss. He wanted a smoke and had come outside by himself. He found this man more interesting than the stuffy speakers inside, so he felt no compunction about sitting with the lowly rather than being bored by the famous.[3]

Sherman seemed able to get along well with everyone he met; he had what later Americans would call charisma. "No American knew so many people by face and by name," a friend insisted, and because he was a marvelous conversationalist, loved to tell stories, and had a quick wit, people were attracted to him. He was never at a loss for words. He frequently gave speeches to groups, and had he wanted to, he could easily have made a great deal of money going on the professional lecture circuit. His fame and his personality would have ensured him large audiences all over the country.[4]

No doubt he was tempted; the money would have been good, and if there was anything that Sherman worried about, it was money. The subscription drives immediately after the war netted him significant sums, and the house purchases in St. Louis and Washington were substantial. By 1869 he had received property and money worth close to $145,000, an incredible sum of money in those days when congressmen made only $5,000 a year. His own salary of $15,000 per year was itself substantial. He never had to fear for housing or day-to-day expenses, though he regularly complained about being monetarily pinched. The problem was that he hobnobbed with the wealthiest members of society—individuals whose fortunes overshadowed even his substantial worth. Due to his stature, he came to expect that he had to live well, and Ellen agreed, or lose face with the rich and famous. In the back of his mind, too, the example of his destitute father—a successful man of substance who had made a major mistake and lost it all, leaving his family penniless—always loomed. Through-out the pre–Civil War years, Sherman had lived with that worry, the war obscuring but never really removing it. In the postwar years, this obsession came crowding back to the surface again. He could not leave his family penniless, dependent on charity, as his father had. "That has been the dread of my life," he confessed to a friend.[5]

Every member of the family had stories of Sherman's complaints about their spending habits, but it was Ellen who took the brunt of the financial frustration. "My father continually and bitterly complained of my mother's extravagance," and predicted the family would end up in the poorhouse, son Cumpy later remembered, but Ellen "commonly pooh-poohed" such comments. Her more casual attitude toward money stood in direct contrast to his deeply felt need to manage it carefully. "Ellen demands more money than my salary to keep up the house, for schools, churches, &c," he exaggeratingly complained to her brother.[6]

Despite such complaints, his busy social life, and a heavy traveling schedule during his years as commanding general, Sherman always looked to home, to his wife and family. They were always there and when he was not physically present, he kept in close touch through the mails telling them of his adventures and seeking out information about their activities. Ellen was the glue of the family, the one who kept it all together while he pursued his career and social obligations. Sherman recognized this fact and deferred to her on domestic matters. "I have my hands full running the Army," he said.[7] She raised their substantial family in his frequent absences, demanding regularly that he provide the financial means she and the children required while ignoring his complaints that she was spending too much.

Cump and Ellen clearly had an understanding, and both seemed content with it. Theirs was no story-book romance, but they loved and respected one another in their own ways. Sherman looked to Ellen to be there always, to serve as a sounding board, to steady him when he felt off-kilter, and to leave him alone when he needed his freedom. He expected her to follow him and take care of the family when duty moved him from city to city. He wished she were more outgoing, that she would share more of his social life, and that she was less attached to her church and religion, but he grew to accept her the way she was.

Ellen was always proud of her famous husband and guarded his reputation with a zeal and tenacity that was untiring. She saw him as a great man—but not as great as her father, and not as great as he might have been had he accepted the Catholic faith. Despite his fame and office, she wished he had settled down in a less imposing profession, in Lancaster, Ohio, near her family. She found the constant moves difficult, but she accepted them as part of her duty as his spouse. She increasingly refused, however, to share in his social life. She saw attendance at parties and receptions as his professional duty and did not consider that as part of her responsibilities as his wife.

By 1865 they had been married for fifteen years and had shared the glory of Civil War victory and the sadness of personal grief. They lost two children during the war: Willy in 1863 in Memphis and the infant Charles at Notre Dame in 1864. Their first-born, Minnie, had spent most her early years with the Ewings as ransom to ensure their presence close to Lancaster. The other children had come at regular intervals, bringing the joy and stress of a large family. In 1865 Minnie was fourteen; Mary Elizabeth (Lizzie), thirteen; Tommy, nine; Eleanor Mary (Elly), six; and Rachel, four. In 1867, P. Tecumseh Sherman (Cumpy) completed the brood. They all resembled each other, their red hair like their father's. A maid once joked that should Sherman die, Ellen would only have to put the children "out on the rail fence and the woodpeckers would feed them."[8] As Cump and Ellen watched these children grow to maturity in the 1860s and 1870s, they frequently expressed pride and gratification in them.

Sherman took a genuine interest in his children. He favored legal studies for his sons, and for his more numerous daughters "he wished them to be educated cultivated women, fitted for faithful wives and mothers, if Providence so ordained, but not 'blue stockings.' " He spent time with each of them. He took them riding or out to visit farms. When they grew older, he escorted them to social functions, taking Minnie, for example, to dinner with Andrew Johnson in the White House. He watched with pleasure as six-year-old Cumpy tended his garden and chickens. When Tommy was seventeen, he bought him a pistol and taught him to shoot. He took his children and later grandchildren to minstrel shows, operas, the theater, the circus, and the Buffalo Bill Wild West Show. He bought Cumpy a pony and helped direct his intellectual growth by listening to him read aloud. Cumpy read his father's memoirs as a very young child, with Sherman explaining the battles on some large maps in his office. The family also read aloud Shakespeare, biblical histories, and authors such as Longfellow and Cooper, and they put on parlor plays.[9]

Meals were a favorite family time. Sherman joined them for breakfast wearing old slippers and a well-worn morning coat, though quickly leaving the table to read the newspaper. Dinners were less rushed. Sherman presided as carver, until Cumpy grew old enough to take over the task. Food was served according to a diner's age and status, and any protest was met with Sherman's admonition to "take what you can get and thank the Lord you've got it." Sherman was a light eater himself, though his time in California had given him a taste for red pepper dishes. He rarely ate desert unless it was one of his favorites: apple dumplings, plum or fig pudding, or sponge cake with Ellen's wine sauce. (Daily he consumed two bourbons with water.) Table discussions wandered over a variety of religious, political, literary, and domestic issues, and sometimes the conversation got as hot as one of Sherman's red peppers. Ellen held her own with her famous husband, no matter the issue discussed.[10]

During the summer months in the 1870s, dinner was served early, at 5 P.M., so that the family had enough time before dark to take a carriage ride around Washington. Then they retired to the benches Sherman had placed in the yard. He sat under a fig tree, and Cumpy brought out a song bird in a cage to hang in its boughs. "There we all congregate," Ellen said. "The old folks reading the papers, the young people playing croquet, the children frisking about, the humming birds dipping into the flowers and the canary singing overhead."[11]

On such evenings, friends and relatives might drop by. Ex-Confederate general Joe Johnston and his wife often spent an evening on the Sherman lawn. When in town Phil Sheridan was a favorite of the children because he joked and teased with them—once laughingly comparing his short legs to those of the very young Cumpy. David F. Boyd, Sherman's friend from Louisiana days, paid a visit to the Sherman house, as did John Bell Hood and S. H. M. Byers. A Sioux delegation came once too; their imposing stature and interest in Cumpy's red hair frightened him.[12]

Minnie's wedding was an especially important occasion for the family. Ellen, who had not been married in the full pomp of Catholic ceremony because of Sherman's lack of faith, was determined that her eldest daughter would not be similarly deprived. She would show Protestant Washington and the country as a whole how impressive Catholic worship could be.[13]

Archbishop J. B. Purcell of Cincinnati officiated when Minnie and Thomas W. Fitch of the U.S. Navy exchanged vows. President Grant, cabinet members, Supreme Court justices, hosts of generals and admirals, the bishop of Philadelphia, the president of Georgetown University, and international diplomats were part of the congregation of some two thousand people jammed into and around St. Aloysius Church to see the famous general's daughter's wedding. Eight bridesmaids and groomsmen flanked the young couple. Afterward some one thousand guests attended the reception at the Sherman home. The *New York Herald* called the event "the most sumptuous wedding which America had known in a generation," and the *Philadelphia City Item* described it as "the most brilliant and impressive affair of the kind ever beheld in this city." Even Sherman was swept up in the occasion and stood in the receiving line, instead of informally mingling, as was his usual custom. Ellen was thrilled to hear later that a friend had sent a brief comment about the wedding to the pope, and he had directed its printing in an Italian newspaper. The Shermans had done themselves proud, befitting his stature as commanding general.[14]

Such public spectaculars were rare; most of Cump's and Ellen's home life was private. One important hallmark of their personal relationship was their openness with one another on most matters. In the mails and when together, they told each other exactly how they felt. The exchanges could be sharp, but, in the end, the point of contention was resolved. Usually the discussion was over nothing more than some normal domestic matter, but when it came to religion, finances, or the children's education, the debate could be long and drawn out. In the end, Ellen usually had her way. She wore her husband down, and he gave in. If it was a particularly hot debate, he would manage to find a trip to take and then go away for awhile. A more minor disagreement might result in an evening out with friends or acquaintances. It never seemed to last very long; Ellen and Cump seemed to have a close and workable spousal relationship.

There was one major source of division between Cump and Ellen that was not settled definitely until 1871, when Thomas Ewing died. Despite the close communication between Ellen and Cump, Ewing was an unspoken source of discord. For most of their married life, Ellen looked to her father more than to her husband. She went home at every chance, leaving Cump and children behind. Sherman spent much of his early life seeking the great man's approval but not finding it until his Civil War victories gave him the status he needed to see himself on his foster father's level. Similarly it was not until then that Ellen began to break away and live her life with her husband, free from Ewing's pull. Sherman often joked that if he blindfolded Ellen and spun her like a top, "she would make a direct line for Lancaster."[15] It was no joking matter, of course; it was a serious strain on their marriage.

Ewing's 1871 death changed this situation. At first, it thrust Ellen into a deep depression. Although by this time she had freed herself from much of his influence, his death brought all the old feelings flooding back. Ellen was crushed, and her lament demonstrated the extent of Ewing's influence on her despite twenty-one years of marriage to Cump. That "he the greatest object of my love on earth should be beyond my sight & intention," she said, was too much to take. "Life will seem long now I fear and purposeless," she cried. "The zest has gone out of everything & the comfort & strength from my heart."[16]

Sherman's correspondence indicates no such reaction to Ewing's death, and not even much comment. "He was a grand old man, of classic taste and wit, and one of the strongest lawyers in our country for many years prior to his death," he wrote. That was about it. Sherman rarely mentioned Ewing again in the years following his demise.[17]

This cool response to the death of a man who had played so substantial a role in Sherman's life seems strange at best, disrespectful at worst. Thomas Ewing had taken Cump in as an orphan and raised and educated him as his own. He gave him his daughter for a wife. He pulled strings to aid Cump throughout the 1850s and 1860s. But he had also tried to organize Cump's life for him, to keep Ellen close by, in Lancaster, and Cump at work for the family interests. It had been all done with affection, but it had wounded Cump deeply. He had always wanted the old man's respect, but he had wanted freedom from his influence too. Ewing held the affection of Cump's wife, and, for a time, he even held his first-born child. Ewing was economically secure, while Cump seemed always to have to struggle to keep financially afloat. Even after the Civil War, after Cump had gained Ewing's approval for his war successes and after his finances were stronger, Ewing remained a major influence on him publicly and privately.

Sherman never stopped admiring the great man and being thankful for all he had done for him, but as long as Ewing was around, he was a reminder of Sherman's orphanhood and his financial failures in the 1850s; he reminded Cump of his vulnerability. His very desire to help and advise Cump and to maintain his hold on Ellen's affections gnawed at Sherman's confidence. The death of Thomas Ewing meant a freedom to Cump Sherman that he had sought all his life. But he could hardly rejoice, not when his wife grieved and he loved the old man himself. He dealt with his ambivalent feelings through silence. He went on with his life, quietly accepting the release his foster father's death provided him. Soon after, he went to Europe, where he enjoyed being feted by monarchs and potentates, seeing that he certainly was his dead foster father's equal now. Thomas Ewing's death lifted a burden Sherman had carried since his childhood.

Ellen's depression did not last long either, but her recovery was for an entirely different reason than Cump's silence. On his death-bed, Ewing had accepted the Catholic faith, and Ellen joyfully thanked God for guaranteeing her father's eternal salvation at this last moment. Since she believed life was a preparation for eternity, she felt relieved. The great man she had so adored and prayed for all her life had embraced Catholicism, and she could now be sure he was saved. Her faith overwhelmed her depression.[18]

She wished even more that Cump would see the light and follow her father's example. She had hinted, cajoled, insisted, argued, and tried every device she had known throughout their years together, but nothing would budge his stubborn refusal. Clearly she hoped that Ewing's last act would influence him, blind to Cump's deep feelings. Sherman would hardly become a Catholic when he was experiencing his newly gained status of freedom. He saw religion as a form of tyranny. He believed in God, all right, but not the God of the Catholic religion or any other sectarian church. Rival religions produced chaos with their denominational debates, and he wanted no part of that—Ellen's desires or Ewing's example notwithstanding. If people just left each other alone to worship God as they saw fit, the world would be a much more orderly place. In his own family, if Ellen would stop her proselytizing and stop spending so much money on Catholic education or other church causes, they would all be better off.[19]

Most of the time, Cump ignored Ellen's religious appeal and let her practice her faith so long as it did not interfere with him too much. It was a waste of time and money, he believed, for eldest son Tommy to attend Georgetown University, for example, but since he also went to Yale and then to Washington University Law School in St. Louis, his time in Catholic schools did not matter much.

Of all his children, Tommy became increasingly important to Sherman. Next to Cumpy born in 1867, Tom was his only son. One of the major sadnesses of his life had been Willy's death in 1863, and one of the ways he had come out of his grief was by turning to Tommy and placing all his hopes in him. As the young man matured, Sherman increasingly saw him as the solution to another of his long-held fears—the worry of financial collapse. Sherman decided sometime in the 1870s that Tommy's role in life would be as manager of the family finances. Once he became an attorney and accepted a position with a prestigious St. Louis law firm, he would free Sherman from management of the family properties and moneys. Sherman would advise, but Tom would have ultimate responsibility. Deep down, Sherman would then be freed from the weight of his father's failure. He would hand over his assets to Tom and feel he had done his job by ensuring his family's stability. If he died, he could go in peace—not with religion the way Thomas Ewing had but with financial satisfaction the way he wished his father had.

With Tom in financial command, there would be no groveling for government pensions; there would be no breakup of the family and no children forced to accept the charity of neighbors and relatives, as Cump had been forced to do as a nine year old. Tom was increasingly lightening his father's deeply felt family burden. "You know how much the Future of the Family rests with you," Sherman told him in 1874. "All speak of him as one of the most promising youths of the country," he bragged to a friend, "thoroughly educated, and of excellent private character." "There is not the shadow of doubt that you are on the Right Road," he praised Tom. Fortunately, Catholic education had not ruined Tom, and he was preparing to do his duty.[20]

The son seemed similarly pleased with his life. He joked with his father about his alleged interest in a certain young woman, and he reported that he was "more & more interested" in his law studies. In fact "I assure you I am as happy and contented as I ever want to be." When he graduated from the St. Louis Law School (the Law Department of Washington University) on May 13, 1878, Sherman was thrilled. His family's future seemed secure.[21]

As he tore open the envelope and began reading Tom's May 28, 1878, letter, however, the words shattered Sherman's world. Tom's long letter announced that he was not going to be a lawyer after all, nor did he plan to spend the rest of his life caring for his mother and sisters. He had decided to become a Jesuit priest. He knew this decision would hurt his father, he said, but he had been thinking about it since graduation from Georgetown. He had gone to Yale and to law school only out of paternal respect. He had struggled on alone, saying nothing to father or mother, held back from his final decision by only one consideration: "worry that I will wound and grieve the kindest and tenderest of fathers." But he finally decided he had to live his own life. He planned to go quietly to a European seminary because he worried that Sherman would be "somewhat ashamed" and would not want the public to know that his son was becoming a Catholic priest.[22]

Tom waited in St. Louis for his father's answer from Washington, he and the rest of the family living "in dreadful suspense." Sherman wrote back separately to Ellen and Tom, but the letters were apparently so hostile that they were not preserved. Simultaneous letters to friends demonstrated the depth of his anguish. "Again am I in deep affliction and as of old I turn to you for sympathy if not for help," he wrote to old St. Louis friend Henry S. Turner. Tom was going to "abandon, to desert" him because the Catholic church had "poisoned his young mind, wound its tendrils around his heart and weaned him from his Father who has never denied him anything." The world was in a dangerous state, he reminded Turner, and his family needed Tom "in a contingency not unlikely of my death or downfall. This duty he has no right to throw off, [not] even to save his own Soul or the Souls of others. His own peace of mind must be secondary to his duty to others." Without Tom to help him with the family, "so far as I am concerned the whole world offers me no safe place of refuge." He felt "like an actor on the stage rehearsing [*sic*] words," he told friend S. H. M. Byers, "and yet with no heart in the play." His financial worries would not be assuaged; the fear of financial failure remained on his shoulders, his one hope of relief gone.[23]

Even more, Tom's decision demonstrated that his long-held fears of Ellen's insistence on Catholic education had been accurate. He had gone along with her because he never thought it mattered. Now he knew it did, and it cost him his eldest son. It was embarrassing too. What would the secular world he lived, worked, and played in think of the great General Sherman's losing his son to the Catholic church?

Sherman demanded that Tom write a public letter explaining that though his father had provided him with a first-rate education and opposed his decision, he was going to the Jesuits. Meanwhile, Sherman wrote to his former Civil War aide, Henry M. Hitchcock, and released him from his promise to provide a position for Tom in his St. Louis law firm. Tom agreed to come East and discuss the matter with his father face to face. Ellen felt sure that this meeting would solve everything, hopeful that it would "bring a great and overwhelming grace" to Cump. She believed that this event that was so hurtful to her husband would, like her father's death, accomplish her long-felt desire: his acceptance of the Catholic faith.[24]

Nothing could have been further from reality. Sherman had only one thought: to convince Tom of the error of his ways. They met early in the morning on June 3, and the result was a compromise, or, more properly, arbitration. The two men agreed to allow New York's John Cardinal McCloskey to make the final decision. Considering how upset Sherman was, his "heart cold as lead" as he told Schofield, his agreement to allow a third party, particularly a prince of the church, to make the final decision is unusual. Perhaps he decided that only someone of McCloskey's religious stature could convince Tom that his decision was misguided. In his panic, he could not see how anyone, even a cardinal, would not see things his way. He bitterly explained to McCloskey by letter how much he needed Tom. The church had "plenty of recruits and priests," but he had only one adult son. "My life is precarious," he insisted, and Tom's "mother and sisters must soon depend [on him] for those necessities imposed on all mankind by God himself." If Tom left for Europe, "it severs [us] forever. I am a soldier by profession and nature and it looks to me like 'Desertion.'" Tom had a duty to him as any soldier had a duty to his unit or his country. If Tom refused to follow orders as Sherman expected any private to do, he committed the ultimate sin in a military man's mind: desertion.

He waited for word of Tom's decision, sensing a final defeat. He felt that his family was crumbling as his childhood had in the distant past. As he had turned to "the Great family of the Army" as a young man at West Point, he looked again to his army family. But the army itself was in turmoil in the chaotic postwar world, so it provided little real comfort. When he received the dreaded word that the cardinal had sided with Tom, he cried out to his old friend Turner: "My love for Saint Louis and desire of securing there a home in my old age have vanished and I am once more adrift." "Henceforth," he told his daughter, "my thoughts will go out more and more to my Army comrades, because they now compose my family."[25]

Sherman sank deeper into depression. He told Sheridan that he would try to do his job but his heart was "sad & weary." In his anger and disappointment, he so vilified Tom that his son-in-law who had seen the young man off at a New York pier carefully remonstrated with Sherman on Tom's behalf. Sherman told a daughter: "Since Tom's defection of which I cannot yet think with composure[,] I am all at sea about the changes made necessary by his actions." He thought once more of dealing with his problems by running away, and he turned his thoughts again to California. It was only his concern that former rebels in Congress would take over the army that kept him in Washington, he said, but he seemed to realize the finality of Tom's decision. He asked a St. Louis friend to take over management of his property there and with a heavy heart replaced Tom with an agent. Responsibility for his family's financial security was again in his hands alone. He could not see that in his anger, he was placing his personal needs above those of his son. He called Tom a deserter and selfish, but he was being autocratic and unfeeling himself, ignoring the fact that if it had been necessary for him to seek his freedom from Thomas Ewing, his son certainly had the right to choose his own career and life. He was treating Tom as though the young man was under orders to follow his wartime strategy, and Tom's refusal to fight alongside him was the worst form of disloyalty. To Sherman, financial perils were as dangerous as any enemy, and their battle required the same kind of loyalty.[26]

During the next months, Sherman continued to grapple with his feelings, writing letters full of woe to friends and relatives. In late July, he still felt depressed: "I can hardly stand it because I miss Tom." "He was the keystone of my arch, and his going away lets down the whole structure with a crash." He made one final desperate bid to try to bring him back. He wrote to Adam Badeau, an old army acquaintance living in England, to visit Tom and see how he was doing. Badeau found the young seminarian upset that his father was still angry at him and still refusing to write but happy to see someone he had sent. The subject of his return home, however, never came up. Sherman was glad to learn about Tom's good health but disappointed at the failure of the Badeau mission. He said he remained willing to welcome him back at any time, but, "if he must be a Priest, it separates us for life."[27]

Unable to take the strain any longer, Sherman escaped west on an extended tour. As always, he enjoyed the rugged landscape and the military comradeship. His army family greeted him warmly everywhere he went. It was all reassuring, but when he returned to Washington, journalists had gotten word of the family strains, and newspapers rang out with rumors that Sherman blamed his wife for Tom's entrance into the Jesuit order.

Throughout this imbroglio, Ellen was living in St. Louis with their children while Cump was in Washington or on tour. She repeatedly told him that she worried about his depression and anger. Minnie later remembered Ellen being "nervous and a little broken down." Still, Ellen could not hide her happiness at her son's decision. "Her heart was full of thanksgiving to the Lord who had answered her prayers," Minnie said. Sherman quietly blamed his wife for his son's departure, but he never verbalized that feeling, not even in the bluntest letters to friends and family. When eleven-year-old son Cumpy and seventeen-year-old daughter Rachel were placed in Catholic schools in Baltimore and Ellen moved there to be closer to them, Sherman was displeased but said little. The press attacks continued, however, so he wrote a public letter denying any marital problems over religion, pointing out that he and Ellen would be traveling to St. Louis shortly, and the entire family would be together in Washington for the winter. That seemed to clear the air; Sherman stopped talking about Tom.[28]

This was only a brief respite. In mid-December Sherman called Tom a monster for shirking his family responsibilities and ruminated over the story of a man who had killed himself in despair over his family's "unnatural fascination for the Church." A short time later, he and Ellen exchanged harsh letters over her deficiencies as his social mate. She could not constantly run away from such obligations, he scolded. She retorted that she had always done her best. That Christmas Ellen and the children were in Baltimore; Sherman spent the holiday alone in Washington just ninety miles away. "Offices [were] closed," he sadly wrote Turner, "streets abandoned and dinners at home. I have no home," he concluded, "and am therefore sort of vagabond."[29]

His family life was in shambles, and meanwhile, two of his closest military friends, Sheridan and Schofield, disagreed with him over the passage of an army reform bill. Beaten down and unwilling to battle back because he insisted there was nothing he could do, he once more took to the road, this time to the south. Surely his former enemies could not treat him any worse than his personal and army families had. Tom's decision to become a Jesuit was proving more than a disappointment to his father; it symbolized a whole complex of long-held, deep-rooted fears.[30]

It was not until the spring of 1880 that Sherman began writing Tom again. In late August 1880, the seminarian returned to the United States, and when Sherman saw him for the first time, daughter Rachel reported, "With a cry my father threw his arms around him." Tom was thrilled. "Papa has let his grand heart get the best of past disappointment, received me most affectionately, and shown no signs of displeasure." On the surface the conflict was resolved, but in a letter to Minnie, Sherman said he remained "amazed" that Tom would "subject himself to such an absolute and worn out order of Priests." For the rest of his life he never forgave him, nor did he forgive the church, which, he continued to insist, had stolen him away. Sherman could hold a grudge a long time when someone, even his son, created disharmony in his life.[31]

Minnie and her husband discovered this fact when they disagreed with Sherman over another deeply felt matter. During his overseas trip in 1872, Sherman had visited Egypt and become friends with its leader. When the khedive learned of Minnie's wedding, he sent her earrings and a magnificent diamond necklace, large enough to cover most of her chest. Sherman immediately forwarded profuse thanks, but then he realized he had a major problem on his hands. Article 1, section 9 of the Constitution prohibited government officials from receiving gifts from foreign heads of state without Congress's consent, so he was not sure what he ought to do about this present. He could return it, but he did not want to insult the khedive. For the time being, he put the diamonds on deposit with the government, worrying all the while how long he could restrain Ellen and Minnie from trying to get their hands on something as beautiful and valuable.[32]

The diamonds remained in government vaults while Congress passed a law allowing Fitch to receive them, but then the secretary of the treasury declared them subject to duty. Congress now had to pass a duty exemption, but it was too late in the session for that, so the jewelry had to remain in government hands still longer. Meanwhile, Sherman decided that the gift had really been sent to him, not to Minnie, so all four daughters should share in it. In order to get Minnie to agree to the split and to promise not to sell any part of it during the khedive's lifetime, he offered to pay her a hundred dollars a month, asking her to sign an agreement to that effect.[33]

Minnie refused. If the diamonds belonged to him, she responded, he could do what he wanted with them; if they belonged to her, she had exclusive ownership. Then she changed her mind. She agreed to a settlement on the condition that she receive half the necklace and the other sisters split the rest. Sherman was hurt. "I fear those diamonds surpass in value the measure of Mr. Fitch's virtue," he decided, concerned that his son-in-law planned to pawn them for the money. Ellen became so upset at the machinations that she warned Minnie that she "better pray for the mountains to cover" her from the wrath of God for her selfishness. She followed that biblical threat with another, warning Minnie about "violating God's commandments against your Father & your Mother." This use of religion did the trick; Minnie caved in: "I hope God may forgive me. I feel now I sorely need his help." Sherman sent two agreements, one assigning the diamonds to him as trustee and the other promising to pay Minnie a hundred dollars a month against her share. She signed. When Congress passed a bill allowing the diamonds into the country duty free, Sherman told Tiffany jewelers to split them four ways. It took a great deal more soul searching and bureaucratic maneuvering, but the diamonds were divided into four parts—one-quarter for each of the Sherman daughters. About this same time, word reached the United States that the khedive had bankrupted his country.[34]

Sherman believed that maintaining the diamonds was a question of personal honor, the khedive's financial problems only intensifying this insistence. The whole experience bothered him. His son had abandoned him for the priesthood right on the heels of his daughter's demonstrating an unexpected streak of greed. And the powerful and wealthy khedive was in financial trouble despite his apparent wealth, so obvious in his ability to give such impressive gifts. Money, family, friends, religion—all were in chaos.[35]

But there was still Ellen. She was involved in much of his problems, but he could not stay away from her for long. She had always been his anchor, the constant in his life, and he needed her. He could not imagine his life without her, though he spent so much time away from her and despite their disagreements on religion, finance, and social life. Their lives usually proceeded at a normal rhythm unless interupted by crisis like Tom's entering the Jesuits or Minnie's wanting the diamonds. Beneath the usual normality of husband and wife, however, was another complication. Sherman constantly placed himself in situations where he had the opportunity to philander.

Soon after the war, Grant and Sherman were traveling somewhere together, and Grant jokingly asked his friend what kind of hobby he planned to have now that the war was over. He had not thought about it, Sherman replied, but what difference did it make? He had to have a hobby, Grant replied, or the press would invent something for him—something he might not find palatable. He planned to make a hobby of his horses, Grant said. That was fine, Sherman mused, but he was not sure what he would do. "Let me see—Let me see; what shall it be? I have it! You may drive your fast horses, and I will kiss all the pretty girls. Ha! ha! that shall be my fad."[36]

During the postwar years, he kissed every young woman he

encountered. The wife of General W. B. Hazen described his approach as one of "cunning." "He always made believe he [was] absent minded, and if a woman was young he made a habit of kissing her in an off-hand way everytime he met her." Mrs. Hazen pulled back after his repeated approaches, and "he looked queer, but was amused." " 'God bless my soul,' " he said, " 'Hazen is one of *my* boys and I'm old enough to be your grandfather.' " Mrs. Hazen said they would debate that later, but "until it was settled we would defer courtesies." Sherman stopped the kissing, but later he became so engrossed in conversation with her that he backed her into a corner until she "called a halt."[37]

Most women seemed only too happy to accept Sherman's attentions. "I never saw a man so run after by womankind in my life," a friend marveled. Ellen did not seem to mind, joking on one occasion that she had no objection to his kissing young women, but she drew the line at widows. She just wanted him to remember that she was the only love of his life, and she knew that he "was true" to her "in heart and soul." Had she stopped there, these words would have been a touching expression of love. But she continued. His "[religious] prejudices" did "run away" with him at times, she said, and they really ought to be thinking of their eternity. As she had done all their lives, she qualified her love for him because he would not embrace the Catholic faith.[38]

Sherman had become accustomed to Ellen's religious preoccupation and her lack of interest in social life, and as he kissed his way across the country, he complained but increasingly without much emotion. It was just the way things were, and he knew it. Occasionally, though, he expressed a desire for something more. When Phil Sheridan was about to marry, Sherman sent him a congratulatory letter on his good fortune in finding someone "whose whole heart and interest will be yours who will take a Great pleasure in conforming to your wishes and plans and who can go with you to the camp or a palace with equal grace and happiness." He followed that revealing statement with the sentence: "I know that Mrs. Sherman will come [to the wedding] if possible. I will come anyhow." Clearly Sherman wished for a wife who shared more of his life.[39]

Sherman knew many women, some very well. Late in his life, he met the young Mrs. Grover Cleveland, and the two became fast friends. Suspicious newspapers headlined GEN. SHERMAN FALLS IN

LOVE, and Ellen was concerned enough to send him a clipping and ask for an explanation. There was nothing to explain.[40] There were, however, two other young women in Sherman's life: the sculptor Vinnie Ream and Mary Audenreid, the widow of his deceased military aide. Their relationships were much more complicated.

It is unclear when Sherman first met Vinnie Ream, but he came to know her well when she made application to win the commission to fashion the statue of the deceased Admiral David Farragut. Sherman was on the selection committee. She was so attractive that by this time, there was suspicion that her beauty, not her skill, had won her a number of previous government commissions. The acerbic newsman, Donn Piatt, satirized the situation by describing her on a scaffold wearing a tight dress and carving a statue of Venus. Around her, he said, stood a group of enraptured congressmen: "What infinite grace! Divine waist! Ravishing lips!" —and it was obvious the politicians were speaking about her, not the statue.[41]

The correspondence between Vinnie and Cump began in 1873, was steady for about four years, and continued intermittently until Sherman's death. At first Sherman merely gave her advice on how best to secure the Farragut commission, but the letters became increasingly friendly. In April 1873 Vinnie had to leave Washington for several days, and he told her: "I miss you more than I thought possible, and your little foolish ways." Then after advising her how to win friends among other artists, he concluded: "Is it not so, my foolish little pet?" He told her to write him freely and often because no one else saw his mail, and, besides, Ellen was away. "I destroy your letters," he told her. "You must do the same of mine for in wrong hands suspicion would not stop short of wrong—which we must not even think of."[42]

Sherman clearly had more than a statue on his mind. One time he offered to take Vinnie for a ride in his carriage; they could have "the back seat all to ourselves." On another occasion, he took her handkerchief, mistakenly he said, and used the occasion to tell her how bored he was in his office and how he really wanted to come see her so she could sing for him as she often did. When, through Sherman's active support on the selection committee, Vinnie received the Farragut commission, he told her he knew she would "put in that statue your own earnest nature and heart." "I often think of your studio," he sighed, "and my precious moments there and wonder if you miss me and who now has the privilege of toying with your long tresses and comforting your imaginary distresses." Ellen apparently suspected nothing because she joined Cump in decrying women who opposed Vinnie because of her good looks. Ellen was not envious, Sherman told the sculptor, "for she thinks you are wedded to your marble statues." Nonetheless he warned her to be careful because Ellen now frequently saw his mail.[43]

He continued to express his own feelings, apparently unconcerned about anyone reading his letters. In August 1875 he thanked her for sending him a photograph, "though it was unnecessary to recall your appearance for I prefer to think of you in your artists garb, plain & simple." In December 1877 after unsuccessfully trying to call on her several times, he wrote that he "especially" wanted to see her "in that white dress with the Harp that will make an exquisite picture, even without the music which cannot fail to be inspired."[44]

In 1878 the relationship changed. Vinnie married navy lieutenant Richard L. Hoxie, and Sherman said he was "prepared to act as your Father to give you away in marriage." The correspondence then fell off until the mid-1880s, when Hoxie became ill and died. Now Sherman's letters were full of advice and commiseration. In 1887 some of the old fervor returned. "You have a sick husband, and I a sick wife," he said. "I sometimes think the Mormons are right and that a man should have the right to change—tell Hoxie I will swap with him." Was this humor or wishful thinking?[45]

In the early 1880s Sherman became involved with another young woman, the wife of his aide, Joseph C. Audenreid. The two men had known each other for a long time, Audenreid first beginning his service with Sherman in 1863. Mary Audenreid had no special relationship with her husband's boss, but this changed in mid-June 1880 when Audenreid died after an extended illness. "Poor Mrs. Audenreid is so dumb founded—so stunned, poor little lady that I feel deeply for her," Sherman said. "I have acted as a father to her." He filled his letters to her with advice about how to get over her depression so she could continue raising Florence, her daughter. He took her and his daughter Rachel with him when he accompanied President Hayes on a tour to the Pacific. She long continued despondent but roused herself enough to send him gifts at regular intervals. She began to view him romantically.[46]

Sherman reacted with mixed feelings. He wanted her to marry again, but when suitors arrived, he knew he would be "jealous." "Of course you must marry again, and it is the veriest nonsense for you to talk about an old man." Still, "I will envy the man who gets you as wife." Obviously he was struggling with words, trying to express his ambivalent feelings. "As the wife of my aid you were of my family, and I really feel to you as I do to Elly or Rachel, to caress and love you as a child rather than as a woman. If I were twenty years younger, I would not even trust myself with you, in the close intimacy in which you hold me but you know that my reasoning faculties are so strong that I look away ahead for your future and not to gratify my present vanity."[47]

Mary was not discouraged; she continued her suit. Once more he warned her of their age discrepancy. "Your life is too young and too precious to waste on an old man," he said. "All I could or ought to suggest is that any partiality for old men may keep off suitors more worthy of your love and esteem." She continued unconvinced. "I am very fond of you and want your love, affection, and veneration," Sherman responded again, "but nothing which can cast a shadow on your after life. . . . You will always have a warm place in my affections but I realize that I must play the part of father, not that of lover."[48]

He tried to play the part of father to Florence Audenreid, an obstreperous teenager. The young girl sneaked away from her boarding school to see a boy and then refused to admit she had done anything wrong. Sherman tried to force her to see reason, but he failed. Worse, Ellen found one of Mary's letters and blamed her for threatening her daughter's soul by taking her side in the school dispute. Ellen angrily destroyed all the letters Mary had sent to Cump, although he thought she had read only the last one. Sherman defended Mary and then, to his consternation, heard nothing from her for months. The problems with Florence had split them apart. There seemed to be no further expressions of affection. On Sherman's seventieth birthday, however, he traced an unmarked present, "the nicest one," to her. Mary Audenreid had not forgotten.[49]

Since Sherman was so open with his flirtations and he had a reputation for kissing young women, no one ever accused him of having a serious affair. Clearly though, he enjoyed younger women, and there must have been some flings. A famous person like Sherman, so powerful yet so outgoing and approachable, attracted women without much effort, and his constant need for approval and Ellen's unwillingness to share his social life made him reach out to them. During his youth, he avoided any written comments on sex, even in response to statements in Ellen's letters, but the extent of such prudery and its continuance into his later years is problematical. Certainly the nature of his relationships with Vinnie Ream and Mary Audenreid and his aggressive behavior with Mrs. Hazen indicate that he was reaching out for feminine intimacy here and, no doubt, in other cases. His need for Ellen, however, precluded any permanent dalliances. A serious attachment would have produced disorder in his life, would have meant giving up all the support Ellen provided him. He could never bring himself to do that; she represented too much to him.

In the end, Sherman settled for flirtations, public kisses, and perhaps brief liaisons when he went out on the town. Then he returned home to the security of Ellen and the family. He received the adulation he required in the outside world, and at home he had the ballast he needed to stay on an even keel. He maintained the best of both worlds, each supplying what he could not find in the other. The relationships inside and out of the home helped make sense out of the disharmony he too frequently found in both.

CHAPTER 19

———— ☆ ————

COMMANDING GENERAL VERSUS THE POLITICIANS

BEING COMMANDING GENERAL was not easy. As soon as Sherman had gained the office in March 1869, he had found himself battling politicians in Washington and Indian agents in the West. Even his Civil War comrade, U. S. Grant, the new president, proved to be undependable, supporting his new friends, the politicians, instead of his old friends, the army and its new leader. Within the military itself, the independent staff bureaus fought against being placed under his command, preferring the wide latitude they enjoyed under civilian direction. In the West, the Indians proved more disorderly than he imagined, and he did not have the power to deal with them as he wanted. These were frustrating times for one of the great heroes of the Civil War who had come to expect much better from a nation he had helped save and a president who had been his comrade in arms.

As the 1876 presidential campaign began, he found himself looking forward to a new occupant of 1600 Pennsylvania Avenue, something he could not have imagined when Grant took office in 1869. Sherman thought Grant would always be the soldier he remembered from the Civil War. When Sherman had been depressed after the insanity controversy in Kentucky and Missouri, it was Grant's successes that had given him inspiration and hope. At Shiloh, Grant had shown Sherman how far dogged tenacity could carry an individual and an army even in the face of the most discouraging odds. Sherman was awestruck. When Grant himself almost succumbed to the attacks of newsmen and the pettiness of Halleck after Shiloh, Sherman provided important support. He helped convince Grant not to quit and built up his own self-confidence in the process. These reciprocal events were the defining moments in the two men's relationship. Sherman explained their friendship by saying: "He stood by me when I was crazy and I stood by him when he was drunk; and now, sir, we stand by each other always."[1]

As Grant's star rose during the war, Sherman's followed in its light until the two men were the major military leaders in the Union war effort. They could always depend on each other, confident that neither would hurt the other for personal gain. They were a team, working together for the good of the Union and to become the successes they had never been before. They were totally different personalities, and their approaches were different. The taciturn Grant and the voluble Sherman complemented each other and in the process carried war to a new level of victorious violence. Neither Grant's war of attrition in Virginia nor Sherman's destructive war in the interior would have achieved such success without the other. At war's end, their names were indelibly written together in the history books as the co-fathers of modern war. And their friendship was secure.

Sherman believed it would always be so. He and Grant would maintain the same relationship in peacetime they had formed in war. They would work together to ensure the nation's future by securing a stable place for the army in the postwar world. In that way they would ensure their own continued security too. And so it was while Grant remained in the army. Then Grant became president, and to Sherman's disbelief, he did not remain the soldier he had been in the war; he joined the enemy—he became a politician.

Sherman watched in sadness as his friend acted as the nation's chief politician rather than, as he had hoped, an honorable independent, the same straightforward person he had been during the war. Sherman grew increasingly disillusioned when Grant gave into Rawlins and, Sherman thought, hurt the army in the process. He was cut even more deeply when Belknap progressively shunted him aside, and Grant meekly promised fairness but never delivered. By the end of Grant's second term, Sherman considered his presidency "a failure." He thought Grant had made a grievous error by not supporting the army more strongly, but he was particularly upset at his policy toward the South. The "great mistake" had been made, Sherman said, "in putting all the political power of the Southern states in the hands of the ignorant, and substantially disfranchising the intelligent classes." This, of course, had not happened, but Sherman thought any attempt at black enfranchisement was an attack on white control. Since Grant did not agree, it was, in Sherman's mind, the result of Grant's unwillingness to stand up to the politicians. He believed, in 1875, that "the South was in worse condition than at the close of the war," because its "public affairs . . . could not have been much worse managed." He also thought Grant's Indian policy had been naive, undercutting the army for a peace approach implemented by ignorant civilians. Grant was not the soldier and comrade he had known in war. His friend had changed, Sherman believed, and the result was the disruption of the relationship that had forged victory over the Confederacy.[2]

Sherman did not realize as Grant did that in the postwar world, the commanding general's job was political more than it was military. Political opponents of the army understood this well, and they pushed their power as far as it would go. Instead of battling back, Sherman usually only complained to the press or to friends in conversation and correspondence. During the Civil War, he had boldly marched through the South toward his objectives, and thus victory, but now he walked away from his political problems, substituting complaints for effective lobbying. Sherman's talent lay in his ability to focus on an objective, decide on the means to get there, and then move toward it inexorably. Now he balked at becoming part of what he viewed as the disorder of participatory democracy, the complicated, uncertain process of trying to convince others to do his will, which in war took only a command. He still did not recognize that the war was long over and that he had to exhibit new skills if he wanted to repeat in Washington the successes he had enjoyed on the battlefield. It bothered him that Grant did not see it his way. Grant, the politician: the very words stuck in Sherman's throat. Grant was now one of the enemy, one of those Sherman saw as a barrier to an orderly society. Grant, the pillar of strength and success, the one individual to whom Sherman could most attribute his fame, was gone. In his place was an agent of disharmony and disorder.

Despite it all, however, Sherman maintained a soft spot in his heart for his old captain, calling him "an extraordinary man" who had "rendered great service in war, and in peace." He looked forward to the day Hayes took office so Grant would become a soldier again. Then Grant would see things as he once had, and their relationship could return to what it had been during those days of glory.[3]

The core of the problem was that politics was anathema to Sherman. He viewed politicians as venal adversaries he was forced to tolerate but refused to work with. Arriving at his office on the third floor of the War Department sometime between 9 and 10 A.M. each day, he kept gentlemen's hours. He took care of his paperwork, had whisky and sandwiches for lunch, spent the afternoon on more paperwork and meetings, and left by 4 P.M. Until dinner at 6 P.M. he visited government offices and the homes of acquaintances and then spent evenings with his family at home or attended social functions in the city. He was absent from Washington regularly, taking long tours of military posts in the West. He kept busy but neglected the necessary political machinations and battles that the army required from its commander if it was to thrive.[4]

As he pondered Grant's eight years in office and lamented their lost friendship, Sherman stubbornly expressed continued support for positions he had expressed in earlier years, positions that had helped separate him from Grant. He believed that an activist restoration of the South had proved to be the disaster he had predicted it would be. If only his peace terms had been accepted in 1865, there would not now be the chaos there was in the Southern states. If only Grant had understood.

He best expressed this attitude back in 1871 when he spoke out regarding the Ku Klux Klan, the secret society for white supremacy. Hooded men rode over the Southern countryside using terror tactics against blacks in punishment for political, economic, or educational aspirations. Whippings, mutilations, burnings, and murders were so numerous and so gruesome that Congress held hearings, which resulted in the passage of two Ku Klux Klan Acts in 1870 and 1871 that Grant enforced. Sherman thought the threat was overblown. Agreeing with former Confederate general Joe Johnston, who told him that the Klan was made up of the same kind of individuals "that compose our mobs and vigilance committees," Sherman said that because Reconstruction had wrongly given power to blacks and their white allies—"the ignorant and depraved"—the mass of the people had become frustrated and taken the law into their own hands. "If Ku-klux bills were kept out of Congress, and the army kept at their legitimate duties, there are enough good and true men in all Southern States to put down all Kuklux or other bands of marauders," he told a New Orleans audience in 1871 on his way home from a visit to his old military seminary. Had there been no organized Reconstruction, had the politicians, Grant included, simply followed the example of his treaty with Joe Johnston, then the nation would now be reunited and orderly.[5]

White Southerners were ecstatic. The commanding general of the army, the nominal coordinator of the military reconstruction Congress had established in 1867, was saying it was all unnecessary. The scourge of Atlanta and the Carolinas was expressing their deepest feelings. Newspapers around the region trumpeted him for the presidency. A former Mississippi governor wrote him a personal letter urging him to run, and his Mississippi correspondent, George W. Moorman, sent him favorable press clippings and praised his KKK comments. "I have never seen, nor heard of any such organization as the Ku Klux," Moorman said.[6]

As he had during the Johnson presidency, he continued to urge caution; the army should avoid anything political, and he certainly had no interest in the presidency. In mid-1870, for example, General Alfred H. Terry had asked Sherman what he should do in Georgia about black complaints that they were never allowed to serve on juries. They had a just grievance, Terry said, because all-white juries were usually not fair to them. But should he, as blacks insisted, issue an order integrating the judicial process? It was up to the people themselves to establish their own judicial system, Sherman responded, and if it proved unfriendly to black people, "these will gradually move to a more favored region and the prosperity of the State will fall away." Similarly the army should not take any stand on the legality of a recently established state government. The matter belonged to the attorney general. The best thing for Terry or any general to do was nothing.[7]

Sherman gave similar advice to General Joseph A. Mower in Louisiana. Mower should take action only when "the Civil Authorities confess themselves powerless," that is, when law and order were in jeopardy. When George Moorman told him that General Adelbert Ames in Mississippi was being rumored as a candidate for governor or senator, Sherman warned Ames of the dangers of politics. He thought Ames had "too much professional ambition and pride to give up the [army] commission . . . for Civil office." When Phil Sheridan was preparing to take command in Louisiana in 1875 to try to deal with the violence there, Sherman reminded him that problems throughout the South were "deep seated" and would "hardly disappear till a new Generation is born and reach maturity." When the impetuous Sheridan tried to act forthrightly to prevent further violence, he stirred up a hornet's nest, and Sherman insisted he could have predicted it. Sheridan "was sent . . . to prevent Collision but he wanted to anticipate & prevent conflict—by anticipating it—but that is not the function of the Military." And since Grant was involved in all of this and had given up his commission for the presidency, Sherman could only sadly declare his disappointment in his old friend.[8]

So while Sherman castigated Grant's Reconstruction policy throughout the 1870s, what actually happened was that individual Southern states reentered the Union under old-line white leadership and with blacks firmly suppressed. Army units stationed below the Mason-Dixon line were withdrawn, and local white leaders were firmly in charge. By 1876 only Louisiana and South Carolina remained under any significant semblance of federal military control, and even this was tenuous. During the 1876 presidential campaign between Ohio Republican Rutherford B. Hayes, a former Union general, and New York Democratic attorney Samuel J. Tilden, rumors spread that there would be violence at the polls and another civil war. It sounded all too familiar to Cump. "As in 1861, some faction will not submit to the result of a vote and appeal to arms." He readied troops in case of any trouble. Sherman favored Hayes, but he kept his choice to himself, insisting that it was not proper for a military man to take public sides.[9]

Election day, November 7, 1876, came, and there was no clear-cut winner. Both sides claimed victory in Louisiana, South Carolina, and Florida. On November 10 a worried Grant told Sherman to be sure that troops on the scene protected canvassing commissions as they tried to unravel the impasse. A week later, Sherman quietly stationed four companies of artillery in Washington, afraid that "these Politicians may again embroil us in Civil War."[10]

Sherman believed that both sides were guilty of electoral

corruption, and he was correct. He continued to hope Hayes would be chosen, but he told a friend that he was ready to support "the lawfully constituted President, be he Hayes or Tilden." Some Democratic veterans led by John M. Corse, one of his former generals, wrote him an open letter insisting that the army remain neutral or it would invite extinction. Judson Kilpatrick and at least one other veteran said they were ready to support Hayes, with force if necessary. Sherman had no plans to mobilize the veterans, but under Grant's prodding, he made plans to provide the four thousand men the president thought necessary to protect Washington.[11]

Meanwhile, Sherman carried on a detailed correspondence with two other generals, John M. Schofield and Winfield Scott Hancock. The latter reminded Sherman that in case no president was chosen by inauguration day, March 5, 1877, he might well be the only recognizable power in his position as commanding general and have to direct the army, the "bulwark in defense of the people and the law," to save the nation. For the present, however, Hancock urged moderation and no sudden military activity that might bring on the violence everyone hoped could be avoided.[12]

Congress established a joint commission, consisting of five senators, five representatives, and five Supreme Court justices, to decide the legal victors in the disputed states. The decision of the commission would be final unless both houses of Congress disagreed. At the same time, secret meetings were being held among political insiders that ensured the support of Southern Democrats for the commission's decisions. Republican negotiators pledged they would end Reconstruction (remove the last troops from the South), appoint a Southerner to the cabinet, and provide funds for internal improvements in the South, particularly the Texas and Pacific Railroad.[13]

Sherman knew nothing about the secret negotiations, but he was extremely pleased with the commission idea. It was clear, however, that, in Louisiana at least, local issues of black-white control were more important than the presidential election. Consequently Sherman worried about violence no matter who was chosen. He told General C. C. Augur in New Orleans to "keep perfectly cool and always depend on me as far of [sic] my influence goes to sustain you in the Right." When Grant signed the bill establishing the commission on January 29, 1877, however, Sherman began to relax. "The probabilities are," he told Sheridan, "that you will not be called on for any troops."[14]

The day the two houses of Congress met to make the presidential electoral count, Sherman was in attendance. He found the count "dull" until Florida, the first of the disputed states, was reached. The special commission was formally given its arbitration task, and the count was delayed pending its deliberations. Sherman confidently awaited the final result, and when it came he approved the commission's choice of Hayes. "I believe General Hayes to be a conscientious, good man, of good intellect, and desirous to produce happy results," he wrote his friend Boyd. "I think he wants the substantial people of Louisiana to govern the state." The new president, Sherman was confident, would justify the Sherman-Johnston terms and Andrew Johnson's administration. Unsaid was Sherman's belief that he would be a better president than Grant. He was momentarily taken aback, however, when Hayes seriously considered Joe Johnston for secretary of war. Sherman respected his old foe but opposed any former Confederate's holding such a delicate post, particularly with jurisdiction over him. That aside, he was convinced that Hayes would "do what seems right and proper."[15]

Sherman was even happier when Hayes ordered the few troops in New Orleans and Columbia, South Carolina, into garrison. Reconstruction was over; he and his army were now free of a political burden. All over the South, the traditional white elites Sherman had supported were back in control, and black rights were being effectively suppressed. He thought the future under Hayes's leadership looked promising.

He quickly learned how wrong he was. The resolution of the election dispute created more problems for Sherman as the losing congressional Democrats lashed out at a convenient scapegoat—the army.[16] In early 1876, Henry Banning, Ohio Democrat and former Union general and the House Military Affairs Committee chairman, had almost pushed through an army reduction bill, but the Custer debacle in June had stymied his efforts. A commission under former Secretary of War J. D. Cameron had then been established to recommend changes, but inability to come to any agreement and the disruption of the election crisis prevented any decision. Congressional Democrats then decided to push through a reorganization-reduction bill soon after Hayes took office. It too failed. Undaunted, they called for a reduction of the army from twenty-five thousand to seventeen thousand men and a ban on future use of military units to enforce civil order—that is, to prevent any further military activity to ensure fair elections in the South. They added these proposals as a rider to the army appropriations bill, and when Congress could come to no agreement, it adjourned without appropriating any funds for the army.[17]

This was nothing new. Every year since the Civil War, it seemed, there was some attack on the army. Genuine reformers, economizers, Southern sympathizers, supporters of volunteer troops, and a host of other congressional critics believed the army was too large and too generously paid. During 1869–1870, the attack had been particularly severe and upsetting to Sherman because it had been led by one of his own former generals, John A. Logan, then House Military Affairs chairman.

Logan introduced a bill to shrink the army and cut its appropriations, promising a savings of $3 million out of the $37 million annual military budget. Expressing his intense dislike of professional soldiers and his enthusiastic support for volunteers, he criticized the preponderance of West Pointers in the service. Then he went after Sherman's $19,000 pay. "I am willing he should have all the credit to which he is entitled," Logan shouted on the floor of the House. "But because I am willing to give him credit as a great general, that is no reason why I should tax the wooden-legged and one-armed men, and the widows and orphans." Angered and hurt at this low blow, Sherman stomped out of the chamber. Other army men were equally stunned. George H. Thomas despaired that the bill displayed "more heartlessness than I supposed one Congress could be guilty of."[18]

When the Senate took up the matter, Henry Wilson, that chamber's Military Affairs Committee chair, asked Sherman for his opinion, and Sherman sent back a detailed response. He disagreed with all Logan's assertions and, returning to the Civil War for inspiration, threw in his favorite argument besides—his own version of the bloody shirt. During the war, he said, "nothing was too good for the valiant officer and soldier, *now* how changed." "Whilst the cry goes forth extending Liberty and the Franchise to all races and to all kinds of men[,] it is proposed to deny them to the very soldiers who sacrificed their limbs and their bodies to attain this result." As for officers' salaries, he had been vastly underpaid during the war but had never complained. "I do believe that my present pay is not wholly for present work but is in great part for past services." The same was true for most other officers. "What money will pay Meade for Gettysburg? What Sheridan for Winchester and the Five Forks & what Thomas for Chickamauga, Chattanooga or Nashville? Few Americans would tear these pages from our national history for the few dollars saved from their pay during their short lives." And if some were critical of the quality of men in the enlisted ranks, Sherman responded: "Well, madame, you surely can't expect the possession of all the cardinal virtues for thirteen dollars a month."[19]

Other than writing the Wilson letter, Sherman made little effort at lobbying against the bill. Congress passed a modified version on July 7, 1870, reducing the number of generals by retirement and death rather than by immediate expulsion. Generals lost pay; Sherman now would earn $13,500 plus allowances rather than his previous $19,000. Junior officers received slight increases. Once again Sherman felt betrayed. The nation he had fought for so totally was now diminishing his value. He ignored the fact that even his lower salary was substantial. An enlisted man made only $200 a year and a civilian engineer $7,000. While it was true that the president earned $25,000, a Supreme Court justice made but $7,500 and the vice-president and members of Congress made only $5,000. Sherman's $13,500 was hardly as insignificant as he seemed to think.[20]

When Congress adjourned in 1877 without passing an army appropriation bill, Sherman should have placed their inaction within the perspective of such earlier congressional animosity. He did not. He could not imagine Congress's not passing an appropriation soon and told Schofield: "On the whole the Army has come out of the past three months conflict of opinion with reputation second to none in the Public Esteem." As for the appropriation impasse, "It was always thus. In war the army is petted, but in peace it is always slighted and neglected. This year it is worse than usual." He still did not understand that the status of the army, like any other institution in a democracy, was influenced not only by the military situation at the time but also by public opinion and political forces. He continued to believe such factors were devious and thus anarchic. The army, he thought, should be above politics, but it was not.[21]

The political stalemate kept Congress from meeting in May, as planned, to deal with the necessary appropriations. No one—from General Sherman to the lowest private—could receive any pay. "All over the Army now comes the cry of distress," Sherman wrote Ellen in early May 1877. The officers and men were asking him, "How can we live, maintain our families, send children to school &c &c without pay?" and he had no answer except to tell them that it was "a question between disbandment or temporary suspension of pay. I suppose disbandment will come at last, and we might as well look the danger in the face." Sherman gave a mid-May speech before a New York Chamber of Commerce banquet reminding the merchants that the army and navy were "the great High Sheriffs of the nation" and their protection of law and order allowed businessmen to function. He concluded: "I know there is a soft place in the heart of every true American, which will, in time, frustrate any harsh or unjust treatment." But in private letters he was not so generous. "Our enemy is not now the Indians but Congress." Appearing before congressional committees, he could hardly contain his disgust. He confided to his son, "It is simply shameful that our pay and our Army organization should depend on the very men we whipped 12 years ago—Such however is the manner of a Representative Government."[22]

An appropriation bill was not passed until a special session in October. Congress then met in regular session in December 1877, and Henry Banning and his House Military Affairs Committee once more pushed for reduction. Banning proposed that when Sherman and Sheridan retired, their ranks should retire with them. In the meantime, Sherman's salary should be reduced to $12,000, and other officers should be affected proportionally. Should Congress not appropriate funds during a regular session, the army would be disbanded. Banning's bill contained some genuine reform provisions—promotion boards, mandatory retirement, the three-battalion regiment, noncommissioned officer pay increases, and commanding general control of the staffs—but these positive aims were buried by the more sensational reduction scheme. Army supporters were baffled. Banning was proving again that even he, a perceived enemy of the army, supported

SANTA CLAUS SHERMAN PUTTING SAVANNAH INTO UNCLE SAM'S STOCKING.

The successful completion of the March to the Sea and the capture of
Savannah excited the nation's imagination. Sherman achieved a celebrity
second only to Grant, and was accorded the status of national hero.
(Library of Congress)

Despite the acclaim, notoriety attached to his armies' actions in the field. The foraging and plundering of Southern civilians' possessions by Sherman's "bummers" and the poor treatment of the contrabands–runaway slaves who followed his army–continued to provoke controversy long after the war's end. *(National Archives)*

In the closing days of the war, Sherman (shown here at center), contrary to his ferocious image, negotiated lenient terms for the surrender of General Joe Johnston, which pleased the South but aroused opposition in the North. *(Henry Davenport Northrup,* Life and Deeds of General Sherman*)*

The Grand Review of Union Armies in 1865 celebrated victory and the completion of the war.
(Francis T. Miller, The Photographic History of the Civil War*)*

With the war over, Sherman confronted at age 45 the question of how to shape his future. *(Library of Congress)*

Ellen continued to provide stability at home while Sherman went out to find his way in the political world. *(Ohio Historical Society)*

General Grant (center, in white hat), aspiring to be president in 1868, took Sherman (far right), considered a political asset, on a western tour. Sheridan is on the left.

(National Archives)

As commander of the Army of the West, Sherman waged war against the Indians, whom he saw as another rebellious threat to the national order. Satank of the Kiowa Nation (top) was killed trying to escape after being captured by Sherman, who preferred force to negotiation in dealing with the Indians. Nonetheless, Sherman (below, left of center) was coerced into serving on a Peace Commission, in which he had little faith. *(National Archives)*

While he traveled, his family stayed behind and continued to grow. Behind four grandchildren are seated (left to right) Mary Elizabeth Sherman (Lizzie); Thomas E. Sherman; Rachel Sherman; Ellen Sherman; Eleanor Sherman Thackara (Elly); P. Tescumseh Sherman (Cumpy); and Maria Sherman Fitch (Minnie). *(Archives of the University of Notre Dame)*

As Ellen became increasingly sickly and reclusive, Sherman found feminine companionship in the person of sculptress Vinnie Ream Hoxie. *(Library of Congress)*

His loyal devotion to Civil War veterans' gatherings kept his army family intact throughout his post-Civil War life. Here Sherman sits front row, center. *(Library of Congress)*

Sherman died in New York in 1891 and was honored with a huge procession. Here, in Saint Louis, a funeral cortege escorts his body to his final resting place in Calvary Cemetery. *(Ohio Historical Society)*

His military monument stands to the left of his wife's imposing cross and Willy's smaller stone. *(Archives of the University of Notre Dame)*

William Tecumseh Sherman's passion for order left its imprint on the history and future of his country. He had lived according to deeply held values, which emphasized the preservation of the Union and the perpetuation and continued growth of his nation.
(Archives of the University of Notre Dame)

reform. The problem was how to get the needed improvements without gutting the military.[23]

The issue struck at the very core of Sherman's being: his role as a military commander. It was also an example of the politics he did not understand. Instead of debating the issues, he personalized the conflict. He opposed the bill by attacking the author. He reminded Cameron that Banning had not regularly participated in Cameron commission meetings and certainly had never made any suggestions. "But now alone he submits a bill containing much that is valuable, with much that is disorganizing and unjust, and is, I am told, astonished that there should be objection." Then he bluntly lectured Banning himself. It was simply inaccurate to contend that the army was too big; actually it was too small. Disbanding it if Congress failed to appropriate gave the legislature authority that violated the traditional three branch power over "institutions established by law." Sherman said he agreed that there was need for reform and that the South deserved representation in all army ranks, but the way to accomplish these desires was not "to turn out meritorious officers who aided in suppressing the rebellion to make room for those who were engaged on the other side." The best solution, Sherman concluded, was to allow a "Board of General Officers, line and staff, to mature a scheme and submit it to Congress." Sherman repeated these arguments in a no-holds-barred interview and a letter to the editor published in the *Washington Post* and reprinted all over the country.[24]

Congressional debate continued until a compromise was finally reached in June 1878 leaving the army size unchanged at twenty-five thousand but establishing a joint committee to propose acceptable reorganization. Meanwhile James A. Garfield, who led the anti-Banning forces in the House, published, with Sherman's detailed statistical and narrative help, two magazine articles staunchly reiterating Sherman's arguments that reform was necessary but not at the expense of dangerously shrinking the army and preventing it from meeting its responsibilities on the border, in the West against the Indians, in protection of public property, and against riots or rebellion. The articles bemoaned the growing congressional animosity toward the military. In a Decoration Day address in New York City, Sherman defended his earlier chamber of commerce speech. Despite accusations to the contrary, he had never said that the army prevented the people from becoming a mob. The army's role in suppressing labor strikes in the summer of 1877 reinforced what he had meant—that the army was there to shield the nation from domestic violence. (Ironically he had been on a western tour at the time and had not wanted to come back despite Hayes's order.) He concluded passionately, "The armies that were disbanded in 1865 still live in the spirit, and these will never, in my judgement, permit this Government to drift into anarchy." Congressmen were attempting to weaken the army; if they were successful, disorder would be the obvious result.[25]

Sherman saw little hope for the army's future with the new joint committee. He ignored the fact that its chairman was Rhode Island Republican senator Ambrose E. Burnside, the former commander of the Union Army of the Potomac and a person interested in genuine reform. Sherman was unhappy that his nemesis Henry Banning was a member of the committee, as was Wisconsin's Edward S. Bragg, another former Union general and antiarmy Democratic congressman. Tennessee's Democratic representative George Dibrell and South Carolina's Democratic senator and ex-Confederate general Matthew C. Butler were the lone Southerners; Kansas Republican senator Preston Plumb and Republican congressmen Horace Streight and Harry White completed the panel. "The Committee entrusted with the Reorganization of the Army is composed of the open proclaimed enemies of the Army," Sherman erroneously insisted. Such a group would either reduce the army or disband it entirely, he pessimistically predicted.[26]

The Burnside committee began work in Washington in July 1878 but soon moved to a cooler locale, White Sulphur Springs, Virginia. Because of the delicate nature of the deliberations, the committee maintained secrecy during its ten-day July session and its late November New York City gathering. Sherman not only wrote Burnside a detailed letter expressing his position but appeared before the panel. "I will not for an instant yield to the naked assertion that the country wants or expects a further reduction of our already attenuated Army." What the people wanted was strict economy. He supported a wise use of government funds but opposed any further cuts in army appropriations. He responded similarly to Senator Butler's inquiry and naively insisted that army reorganization "ought not to be a political question." The army obeyed orders but had "no voice in any elections." Without it, however, "an executive would be the laughing stock in any civilized government." The army stood ready to accept whatever the committee recommended: "I am perfectly willing it should sweep away any and every drone found in it—but *spare the fighting force.* This is all I contend for, and will contend for, before any and every tribunal open to me." The army had defeated the disorder of secession during the Civil War and ensured the existence of the nation. Sherman could not imagine the viability of the United States without such a shield.[27]

Congress received the Burnside committee's massive 724-section report on December 12, 1878. It was a compromise. The army was left at twenty-five thousand men, and there would be two major generals and four brigadier generals, Sherman's and Sheridan's higher ranks expiring with their retirements. Some 333 other officers would be eliminated through attrition. The adjutant general and inspector general bureaus would be merged into a general staff containing six fewer officers. Other bureaus would remain separate, but all would have fewer officers and be placed under the control of the commanding general, who would serve at the pleasure of the president. The mandatory retirement age would be pegged at sixty-two years for officers, except for generals, who could stay on until age sixty-five. Officer promotion would now be accomplished by branch rather than by regiment and through a three-officer board oral examination.[28]

Many officers opposed the bill, but Sherman cautiously endorsed it. "I confess it is less damaging than I feared," he confided to Burnside, but to Sheridan he said: "I have given my emphatic approval to the whole Bill if not mangled in the amendments." What worried him, however, was that it "is so infernal long, that it offers a vast surface for attack." He grew angry at the staff bureaus for selfishly trying to torpedo it and was taken aback when both Schofield and Sheridan criticized it for loftier reasons. He insisted that "if the Army by opposition defeats this Bill[,] we will get another and a worse one next year." "We must fight this Battle in public and not in secret," he told Schofield, but he soon backed off. "I shall not advocate the Bill or oppose it, but shall conform my action, official and personal, to the conclusion of the Law Making Powers of Our Government."[29]

Once more, instead of waging all-out war against the politicians who threatened his views of the military's role in society, Sherman left Washington and went on tour. Depressed over his eldest son Tommy's departure for the Jesuits and the conflict it provoked within his marriage, he made a month-long tour of the South, allegedly inspecting military installations but actually revisiting Civil War battle sites. "I would not go if I thought I could do any good by staying," he insisted to Schofield, "but I am satisfied that other influences than the good of the Army or of the Country now predominate, and we are powerless." He feared that the nation had lost the unifying influence of the Civil War. He blamed Grant for not putting things on a right course in 1869 when he might easily have done so. The evil influence of Grant's selling out to the politicians was hurting the army still.[30]

The wrangling in Congress was bitter. The bill was defeated in the House 95 to 90 in early February 1879 even before Burnside could bring a shortened version to a vote in the Senate. Banning took what was left—the seventy sections dealing with reorganization—and attached them to the army appropriation bill. It passed 101 to 91. The Senate, however, refused to go along, voting 45 to 18 in late February that time was too limited before adjournment for serious consideration. Later in 1879 Congress took up the battle in the context of the army appropriation bill, but it now no longer debated reform but the matter of the army's role in safeguarding elections, the Democrats' favorite issue. In mid-April Hayes vetoed a funding bill that included a provision forbidding the use of the army or federal marshals at elections, this provision the direct result of Southern anger at the army's role in Reconstruction and the Hayes-Tilden election. In May Hayes vetoed a bill prohibiting the use of the army unless at state request. Three more times Congress passed similar bills, and each time Hayes said no. In mid-June 1879 he finally accepted a bill prohibiting the use of the army as a police force at any polling place. That ended the wrangling. Future congresses did not try to reduce either the size or the pay of the army. Congress grew tired of the yearly ritual; army reform was dead until 1903.[31]

Sherman paid little attention to this debate while touring through Dixie, but once he returned in early March 1879, he went to the House often to listen to the argument. It bothered him that Democrats, especially those from the South, wanted to prohibit the president from sending the army to maintain electoral order and used states' rights arguments he "thought the war had settled." Besides, the recent riots had shown that the states could not handle such crises without the army. The whole matter smacked of Southern "want of appreciation" to President Hayes for giving them "untrammeled control of their own section." Sherman correctly diagnosed Southern animosity toward the military, but he erred in believing it was solely responsible for congressional reduction attempts. Economy-minded Republicans, true reformers, and angry haters of the military also were involved. It was a complicated, not-always-clear matter, and the villains were not as obvious as Sherman seemed to think they were. No matter. Other than complaining to Grant, once again a civilian, he did little; he just could not deal with political questions. In late June and early July 1879 he took a three-week inspection tour of the Great Lakes and later accompanied President Hayes on the first presidential tour in history to the Pacific Coast.[32]

Despite all the trouble with Congress, Sherman's and Hayes's relationship had remained excellent throughout his presidency. Hayes was a former Civil War army officer whom Sherman enjoyed socially and whose policy toward the South he approved. Unlike Grant's presidency, Hayes's four years had seen no army involvement in the South, and Hayes's agreement with Sherman was that that was the way it should be. Even friendship and general agreement on issues could not prevent a rupture between the two men over army matters, however, Hayes becoming upset at the way Schofield, with Sherman's strong support, handled the April 1880 case of West Point black cadet Johnson C. Whittaker. Schofield, Sherman, and most military men refused to believe Whittaker that he had been attacked during the night and instead blamed him for mutilating himself in order to escape an examination and then in order to gain revenge on white cadets who had ostracized him because of his race, trying to shift the blame to them. When a shocked public made this a national cause célèbre, Hayes responded to the widespread criticism of West Point practices by replacing Schofield with O. O. Howard, of Freedman's Bureau fame, as West Point superintendent. "I was not consulted," Sherman reported to Sheridan, "and wash my hands of the whole thing." When Sherman recommended that Irvin McDowell be retired and E. O. C. Ord be retained, Hayes did just the opposite for what Sherman considered were political reasons. In his last annual message, Hayes also recommended that Grant be given a new rank, captain general, and once more Sherman felt threatened. Grant's superior rank would demote Sherman's stature, and Grant was no longer the war comrade whom Sherman could implicitly trust. Hayes meant no insult to Sherman by any of these actions, but Sherman's sensitivity toward politicians made him suspicious. Obviously upset, Hayes came to Sherman's office in early February 1881. He "made almost an apology," Sherman told his daughter approvingly; he was happy to have finally bested at least one politician in the only way he understood—not politically but personally.[33]

Although he took no part in the 1880 presidential election, Sherman looked forward to the inauguration of his long-time confidant, James A. Garfield. The president-elect had been one of the army's staunchest defenders over the years, and he and Sherman were intellectually and personally close. Sherman saw days of cooperation ahead, but he forgot that he had felt the same way at Grant's and Hayes's inaugurations too. Once more he was disappointed. This time an assassin's bullet intervened. Charles J. Guiteau, a disappointed officer seeker, whom Sherman labeled "a fool, madman, or criminal," shot the president on July 1, 1881. The explanatory note, which he insisted be entrusted to Sherman, whom he knew only through reputation, said the shooting was a "political necessity." In his shock, Sherman worried about "political confusion" and did all he could to prevent it. He regularly telegraphed army commanders all over the country keeping them informed of Garfield's condition. He was determined not "to allow" the assassin "to be the victim of mob violence," and he responded firmly.

By mid-July Sherman reported "all apprehensions" about Garfield's survival "seem to have vanished, so that the appearances about the White House and on the Streets are as of old—guard withdrawn—and gates open—A stranger would see no signs of the recent catastrophe." Sherman felt so confident about Garfield's health that he visited his senator brother in Mansfield, Ohio, and then took a trip to Yellowstone Park. By late August, Garfield's health worsened. The adjutant general of the Washington militia offered his unit's services in case a mob tried to lynch Guiteau (an idea John Sherman found acceptable), but

Sherman believed the regulars could handle things on their own. Publicly he urged calm, but privately he was deeply worried, comparing this crisis to the vigilante days of 1850s California. When quizzed by Secretary of War Robert T. Lincoln and Secretary of State James G. Blaine as to military preparations, he agreed to bring into Washington four additional companies, giving him 650 soldiers and marines to meet any emergency. He personally inspected the jail. "I saw the man Guiteau as I passed his cell door, a poor miserable wretch, whose life is not as valuable as that of a chicken, but if that life is taken, it ought to be by 'due course of law.' A mob in Washington would disgrace us all as a people." He was determined there would be no extra legal hanging as he had witnessed in vigilante California. Garfield fought for life into late September, and when he died, no mob appeared to lynch Guiteau who was later tried, convicted, and executed. Vice-President Chester A. Arthur quietly became president, and no crisis developed. Sherman's firm actions in a clear-cut situation, unlike his tepid response to complicated political problems, demonstrated that he had not lost his ability to act when the objective was clear. Unfortunately, politics rarely is uncomplicated. Sherman never learned how to deal with such uncertainty.[34]

As Sherman endured his battles with secretaries of war and Congress, toured the world, fought the Indians, and provided stability in time of crisis, a host of other military matters kept him simultaneously occupied and intellectually stimulated. He reached out in all directions eager to see and learn. Sherman maintained regular contact with former Union general Charles P. Stone, now a military adviser in Egypt. When a government change forced Stone to leave that country in 1883, Sherman obtained a job for him in the United States as engineer in charge of building the pedestal for the Statue of Liberty; he personally chose Bedloe's Island as the site. In 1873 it looked as though war might break out with Spain over the *Virginius* affair, the case of a gun-running Cuban ship illegally flying the American flag. When the Spanish captured the ship and executed as pirates fifty-three of the men they found on board, including a number of Americans, war fever briefly swept the United States. Offers to serve in the predicted war against Spain poured into the War Department, including an application from Sherman's old enemy, Nathan

Bedford Forrest. Sherman enthusiastically endorsed Forrest's letter. Sherman also served on O. O. Howard's court-martial for alleged Freedman's Bureau misconduct and spent a great deal of time on the military law problems of Fitz-John Porter, W. B. Hazen, D. S. Stanley, and George Armstrong Custer. He worried about a nasty disagreement between Grant and Winfield Scott Hancock and similar problems among John Pope, John Gibbon, and Philip Sheridan. He made sure a nephew charged with embezzlement did not get favored treatment because of their relationship. He curtly told a Georgia congressman that he would close down an Atlanta fort rather than prohibit band music on Sundays as the politician insisted. He played detective to try to decide whether an army officer was a bigamist, and he unsuccessfully played matchmaker between a young woman and another soldier. More intellectually, he exchanged letters with U.S. Supreme Court justice Stephen J. Field about California history and the preparation of a journal article on military law.[35]

He even developed a warm feeling for Washington, D.C. One night during the Garfield death watch, he walked east of the U.S. capitol and sat on a bench next to a reporter already there. At sixty-one years, Sherman was still "a tall, slight soldier-like man . . . spare in build, but sinewy and well knit in figure," the reporter noted. "Young man," Sherman said, "you are looking at one of the grandest sights that civilization affords. I have seen St. Paul's and St. Peter's but for grandeur and dignity of architecture this structure excels them [all]. . . . I can not see how any American can view this Capitol without feeling prouder of his country than he was before."[36]

A favorite task for Sherman during his years as commanding general was to visit West Point. He took part in the graduation ceremonies there whenever he could, reminiscing about the good old days and encouraging the cadets about their military futures. He loved the young men, and they loved him. Once in company with some foreign dignitaries, he visited his old room in the barracks, and some of the rascality he had then come out again. To the horror of the present room's occupants, who stood at rigid attention, he wondered if they kept contraband food hidden in the chimney as he had in his day. He took a cane from one of the party and poked around until "a whole shelf of delicatessen came tumbling down." Settling down the terrified cadets, he told them the officers watching the scene "were not on duty and therefore had seen nothing."[37]

Another time he gave the cadets the hospitality of his Washington home. Two hundred fifty of them took part in Grant's second inaugural festivities in March 1873. It was an extremely cold, windy day, but after completing their presidential duties, the cadets marched to their commanding general's house and put on a dress parade in his honor. They were invited in and joined the reception in progress. Ellen Sherman had punch and cigars ready, but Emory Upton, the West Point commandant, disappointingly insisted that the cadets not drink any alcohol. Ellen prepared coffee, but the cadets were clearly more interested in the punch. Tom Sherman emptied several bowls, filling their glasses while they packed in around him so Upton could not see what was happening. Sherman allegedly did not notice either, but considering his own cadet days, his ability in Louisiana to thwart student pranks, and his affection for the cadets, he knew very well what was going on.[38]

As a satisfied product of the institution ("the best Military College in the civilized world," he once insisted), Sherman loyally opposed any changes at the academy. John A. Logan's legislative attacks on it enraged him; he supported Emory Upton during his days as commandant and John M. Schofield when he was superintendent. Except for backing the move to allow nonengineers to be superintendent, he encouraged Upton, Schofield, and other administrators to do no more than make better what he considered already good. He opposed any increase in admission standards, for example, and, no doubt because of his own mischievous youth, admitted: "I of course have too abundant (too much) leaning towards boys called bad."[39]

He firmly believed that no one could be an effective officer without a West Point education. "Men who profess the Law, Medicine, Machinery, or the Arts must first acquire a professional education. How much more necessary with us who hold in our hands the lives of so many people and the honor and good name of the country itself." At the same time, however, as he told the 1869 graduating class, "The only schools where war and its kindred sciences can be properly learned are in the camp, in the field, on the plains, in the mountains, or at the regular forts where the army is." He told Schofield when his friend was West Point superintendent: "All I expect is that you will perfect what is already so good, in giving preference only to the Studies and exercises which will make good officers—Our country abounds in Scholars. We want men of action."[40]

The man who took this practical versus intellectual position was the same individual whom historians credit with being the most forward military thinker of his age. Called "one of the most cerebral and innovative of all," Sherman did push development of professional education for officers; he sent army officers to land grant colleges as instructors; he encouraged military scholars such as Emory Upton and Francis V. Greene to travel overseas and write books; and he supported professional publications like the *Army and Navy Journal* and the *Journal of the Military Service Institution.* When in 1880 he addressed the Artillery School, which he had helped invigorate, however, he clearly showed his conservative nature regarding military science. He admitted that technology had given the soldier "at least twelve times the power of one in 1779" and that each individual must "keep well up in the scientific developments of our own and other lands." Still, "To know men—their nature, strength, powers of endurance—the influences which impel them to action, is even a higher branch of knowledge than that of their armament and equipment, and the best possible of all schools is that of Actual Field and Garrison service." Professional schools were essential, but as he explained to Sheridan about the School of Application for Infantry and Cavalry he had founded on May 7, 1881, at Fort Leavenworth: "The School should form a model Post, like Gibraltar with duty done as though in actual war, and instructions by Books be made Secondary to drill, guard duty and the usual forms of a well regulated garrison."[41]

It is not even clear that Sherman founded Leavenworth solely for the highest professional purposes. He gave a more mundane justification: "I confess I made the order as a concession to the everlasting demand of friends and families to have their boys detailed to Signal duty, or to the school at Fort Monroe to escape company duty in the Indian Country. This school at Leavenworth may do some good, and be a safety valve for those who are resolved to escape from the drudgery of Garrison life at small Posts. We must aim to get our Regiments into large Posts."[42]

Still, he had a firm commitment to military professionalism, and this belief only intensified his postwar battles with politicians and an unconcerned nation over the army's survival. No one, it seemed, respected military men for the professionals he believed they were, and the disrespect worsened as each year dimmed the Civil War's import. Why fund a standing army when a militia could do as well? too many people argued. Pay remained low; promotion was slow; and duty at distant posts was dull. The Civil War remained the model, and that war seemed to prove to many observers that volunteers could do very well indeed. The criticism forced Sherman to look within and see the military's problems. Reform was indeed necessary, but Sherman viewed it as reaching back to the glory days of the Civil War rather than looking forward to the future. He had played a major role during the Civil War and had been treated as a conquering hero immediately after. Now he was generally ignored by the politicians because he never used his fame to battle them effectively. He encouraged Emory Upton "to direct your argument to the great proposition that war is a science needing education, training, and practice, and that the rank and file must be drilled, instructed, and habituated to the duties of war, before being subjected to 'fire.'" He believed that professional soldiers, not volunteers, were the answers to the nation's military needs. But he had said the same thing in 1861.[43]

In many ways, Sherman, like Winfield Scott before him, tried to hang on rather than innovate. His actions in establishing Leavenworth and encouraging Upton were later to produce important army reform, but there is little to indicate that reform was his purpose. Sherman had always been restlessly curious and encouraged intellectual pursuit in himself and by others, but he remained convinced that such inquiry would only buttress what he already knew. Upton's writings supported Sherman's belief that the army ought to be left in the hands of professionals like him—not politicians and not the militia. Leavenworth would give young officers a chance to gain practical experience that they could not gain except in war: "limit the quality of study of books and . . . encourage out of door education with the horse, the rifle, and of the usual Field exercises." Sherman's position on military education was that whatever convinced a hostile nonmilitary world that army officers were professionals, worthy not only of existence but also of respect and good pay, was worthwhile and should be encouraged.[44]

No matter what he said or did, he could not achieve what he wanted: control over the army free of political interference. During the Civil War and afterward, he never fully appreciated that the military was part of the democratic political process and was subject to the vicissitudes of national politics. Sherman castigated and tried to ignore the politicians instead of seeking ways to work with them. In 1876 he said: "I can not and will not condescend to importune members [of Congress] to obtain any special end, however desirable."[45] Unlike his posture during war, his solution to most of his problems with politicians was to complain, make a few perfunctory thrusts, and walk away. He would take a trip, some tour somewhere, thinking that the obvious disdain his absence demonstrated would convince his opponents of his position and cause them to leave him alone. They did not, of course, and the disagreements remained, frustrating him even more. It was not easy being commanding general—not when there was no war to fight and when one's closest friend from the great war had become one of the enemy.

CHAPTER 20

—— ☆ ——

RETIRING FROM THE ARMY AND REFUSING THE PRESIDENCY

THROUGHOUT THE CIVIL WAR, whenever Sherman had felt particularly upset, he had threatened to quit and go home. Afterward as commanding general, he regularly took long tours when things were not going his way. Increasingly in the late 1870s and regularly in the early 1880s, he talked of retiring from the army. The frustrations of working with the politicians were simply too great, and the older he became, the less he wanted to put up with them. He had grown concerned too that unless he left, he would stand in the way of Schofield and other officers mired in their jobs awaiting an office proper to their ranks. What finally convinced him to leave, however, was Congress's willingness to let him retire at full pay and benefits for the rest of his life. In October 1883, he suggested to the secretary of war that, although he would not become sixty-four until February 8, 1884, he wanted to turn over his command to Sheridan on November 1, 1883, take his staff to St. Louis, and await the formal retirement date. President Chester A. Arthur agreed.[1]

Sherman took the opportunity of his impending departure to put matters in order. He exchanged letters with John A. Logan, his Civil War colleague and later congressional nemesis, clearing the air of their long-held animosities so that they might return to the good relations they had enjoyed during the conflict. He responded to the best wishes of a former Confederate officer by hoping that some day "the people of the South will thank us for preventing them from committing suicide." He took a final tour of the nation "to observe the great changes which have occurred during the period of my command of the Army," and his nostalgic farewell address at West Point brought tears to the eyes of many of the listeners. His final report as commanding general was less emotional, calmly praising West Point, the Artillery School at Fort Monroe, and the Cavalry and Infantry School at Fort Leavenworth. He regarded "the Indians as substantially eliminated from the problem of the Army," not simply because of military operations but especially because of the coming of the railroad. This engineering marvel made it possible to construct larger forts at strategic sites and make the life of the soldier more comfortable. He "purposely abstained from making any recommendations for the future," but he did suggest the adoption of the twelve company–three battalion regiments for all service arms. Finally, he urged Congress to provide for the regular rotation of troops from the frontier to more established posts. It was a quiet, orderly end to a controversial and distinguished career.[2]

In personal letters, he was more expansive. He told his daughter Elly: "If I had done nothing else than aid the development of the Great West, the Mississippi and Pacific to make it accessible, and susceptible of settlement by peaceful families, I will rest content quite as much as if I had attended church every day of every year of my life." In supporting a pension for a military widow, he called himself "the Father of the Army," obviously reveling in the stature he had reached in his long-held profession. He told his old colleague O. O. Howard that "in History I must stand as the 'Soldier' and I am proud that those who were nearest to me in times of danger and battle are the first to manifest their love."[3]

On February 8, 1884, Arthur issued the formal order of retirement expressing what he called the people's "mingled emotions of regret and gratitude." "I can only say that I feel highly honored and congratulate myself in thus rounding out my record of service in a manner most gratifying to family and friends," Sherman responded. "I feel sure that when the orders of yesterday are read on Parade to the Regiments and Garrisons of the United States, many a young hero will tighten his belt and resolve anew to be brave and true to the Starry Banner."[4]

Once he left the service, Sherman rarely looked back to his time as commanding general. He bragged to Commanding General

John M. Schofield in 1888 that "I don't believe I have in a single instance meddled with army matters since I voluntarily relinquished the command in Novr 1883." He did insist that the army provide him with a clerk to handle his huge correspondence and an office in New York where he might read it, when he moved there in 1886 to be nearer his grown children. He did defend the army against what he considered a slight in the 1890 centennial celebration of the Supreme Court. Otherwise, except for veterans' activities, he remained aloof. He never showed interest in what the army was doing or what was happening to it. In his heart, his army would always be the force that fought the Civil War. It was the source of his success; it had restored order out of the anarchy of secession. He could not say the same for the army of the postwar years. It and the society in which it functioned never achieved the order and definition he had hoped for. These were years he had no wish to dwell on.[5]

Sherman had no specific plans except to live in St. Louis free from the politicians who had made his life so miserable since 1865. The house at 912 Garrison Avenue, which Missouri citizens had purchased for him in 1865 and where he had lived during his nineteen-month hiatus from Washington, was to be the permanent family homestead. It was an impressive edifice, and Sherman was sure it would serve the family well. The red-brick two-story mansion had a large hall running the length of the first floor, dividing three parlors on one side from a dining room, pantry, and Sherman's office on the other. The kitchen was in the cellar, and six bedrooms were located on the second floor. The attic had two servants' bedrooms and space for guests. Cumpy, Lizzie, and Rachel were the only children still home, so there was plenty of room and plenty of quiet. In St. Louis, he anticipated a pleasant change from the sometimes hectic, usually unfulfilling life of commanding general in Washington.[6]

Once again, Sherman miscalculated, and once more the politicians were the culprits. He should have realized that his fame would no more allow him to stay out of the public eye in 1884 than it had in 1865, but he once more ignored that fact. He thought that he had made it abundantly clear to everyone that he abhorred politics and that being a politician was the worst catastrophe he could imagine for himself. "It is too like the case of the girl who marries a drunken lover in the hopes to reform him. It never has succeeded and never will; the same of any individual trying to reform the government, he will be carried along and involved in its scandals and unavoidable sins." To become president, to sit at the pinnacle of political power, was especially unimaginably awful. "I would rather at once commit a forgery, or homicide to entitle me to a term in the Penitentiary."[7] Sherman enjoyed power but not the kind politics offered. He demanded absolute authority—the hierarchy that the military offered. Political power was too chaotic, the give and take of democracy frustrating and impossible of allowing the kind of control he needed to function. He saw no hope for achievement in the White House under such disorderly conditions. Look at what the presidency had done to his friend Grant. It had made him turn against his best friends and mired his reputation in the mud of political corruption.

Yet his frequent public speeches and comments and his acquaintance with the nation's power brokers prevented him from convincing the public that his aversion to politics was real. The public revered stories of his Civil War successes, his direct, no-nonsense approach to everything, and his refusal to set himself above the common soldier. He had been "Uncle Billy" to his "boys," and now the nation saw him in the same way, a reminder of the excitement of the war days, which time made increasingly nostalgic. He had a charisma about him that the public and the politicians found irresistible. The chaos of the postwar years was hard, and the nation looked for someone to draw some sense out of it. Sherman symbolized the successful struggle for the Union and the willingness to reunite the nation through mutual understanding, not divisive politics. He had been a strong man during a time of weak political leadership. He seemed just the person to lead the nation and just the individual to keep the Republican party in power. At the approach of every presidential election between 1868 and 1892, someone or some group started a boom, determined that he become a candidate. Typically it was the Republicans, the party of Union, who pursued the soldier, but Democratic party politicians inquired too. In 1868 former Democratic president James Buchanan broached the idea, and the so-called Soldiers and Sailors Convention offered Sherman the Democratic nomination on a platform supporting the results of the recent war. In 1871 after he made a pro-Southern speech in New Orleans, numerous Southern newspapers and politicians boomed him for 1872. In 1875 his brother said his election would be "the only guarantor of the results of the war."[8]

Sherman's answer was always the same: he would not consider any presidential bid. In 1868, he said: "I have long since made up my mind never under any state of facts to be drawn into politics." In 1871, in words reminiscent of his later famous quotation, he said: "If nominated by either party, I should peremptorily decline, and even if unanimously elected, I should decline to serve." In 1876 he insisted: "I never have been, am not now, and never will be a candidate for the high office of President before any convention of the people."[9]

The string of strong statements did not prevent the same insistent requests from being repeated election after election. As long as he was general in chief of the army, he stood behind his military obligations, but when he retired in February 1884, he found himself besieged even more forcefully. The Republican winner in 1880, James A. Garfield, had been assassinated soon after taking office, and Vice-President Chester A. Arthur, his replacement, was beatable. There were plenty of other possibilities, too—James G. Blaine, John Sherman, Senator George S. Edmunds, Indiana governor Benjamin Harrison, Senator Walter Q. Gresham, Secretary of War Robert T. Lincoln, and Senator John A. Logan—but each had liabilities. Sherman would easily carry the important veterans' vote, and he had friends in all the Republican camps. The public seemed ready for a candidate of his standing. This made him politically appealing.

Sherman felt the pressure beginning in November 1882. Letters flooded in from politicians, old army colleagues, and newsmen, all urging him to run. Brother John, a perennial candidate himself, joined in the chorus, recommending that Cump not declare openly but simply accept the nomination and election when it came his way. General John M. Schofield agreed. By 1884 an Atlanta journalist and war Democrat reported "a sort of epidemic," "a feeling *creeping* over the people of the *entire* country" that Sherman should be the next president. The sheriff of Rockingham County, New Hampshire, was, in proper New England fashion, more subdued, but he too expressed hope that Sherman would run. Chicagoan Isaac N. Arnold was more insistent: "You have never refused the call of duty and you would not now. If the people ask you to be President, you cannot refuse." But Sherman continued to say no. In November 1882 he told a brother-in-law: "No earthly consideration shall ever induce me to consent to have my name bandied about as a Candidate. I treat the suggestion now with ridicule, but if any unauthorized party uses my name in this connection I shall answer in such a way as to leave no room for doubt."[10]

Such definitive comments did not deter the 1884 presidential boom. The public and the politicians viewed his comments as part of the political game—appealing statements of his humble unwillingness to grasp for power. Sherman could be trusted to work for the good of the country because he certainly did not want the presidency for his own gratification. Letters poured into the Sherman house in St. Louis entreating him to run or, at least, not to slam the door on a possible candidacy. Rumors spread that Sherman was planning to ignore the Republican call and run as a Democrat. John Sherman continued to urge his brother to accept the Republican nomination "if it comes unsought and with cordial unanimity." One of his old soldiers put it more bluntly: "As we did not desert you before[,] we ask that you now stand by us and be our leader if we succeed in selecting you [now]." Sherman responded that he valued the "love and confidence" of his old soldiers "more than Gold and Riches," but he thought they should "concede" to him "the simple privilege of living out my own time in peace and comfort."[11]

These entreaties were only preliminary to the major boom that occurred in the last days of May 1884, just before the opening of the Republican National Convention. James G. Blaine, Ellen's relative and a frequent visitor to the Ewing house in Lancaster during Cump's youth there, was clearly the front-runner for the Republican nomination, but many leaders were unconvinced of his electability and pined after Sherman. Blaine himself was unsure if Sherman was truly serious about his demurrals, so on May 25, 1884, he wrote Sherman a secret letter urging him to remain silent but accept the nomination if it were tendered him. It was not a matter of politics, Blaine insisted; it was "a call of patriotism," and Sherman could "no more refuse [it] than you could have refused to obey an order when you were a lieutenant in the army." Newsman Murat Halstead believed Blaine wanted a Sherman and Robert T. Lincoln ticket because he knew he could not be elected himself. Significantly, however, Blaine never withdrew his own candidacy. Whether his letter was genuine or a ploy to neutralize a dangerous opponent is uncertain, but, in any case, he had wasted pen and ink. Sherman immediately responded that "I will not in any event entertain or accept a nomination as Candidate for President by the Chicago Republican Convention or any other Convention for reasons personal to myself." "Patriotism does not demand of me," he concluded, "what I construe as a sacrifice of judgment, of inclination and of self-interest." In case that was unclear, that same day he said that his answer was "the simplest one which I learned when I was a Banker, *No.*"[12]

Blaine carefully flew a Sherman-Lincoln trial balloon at the 1884 convention, but his supporters quickly, and no doubt to his relief, shot it down. Still, Sherman's candidacy remained a topic of conjecture. When his friends among the delegates and visitors insisted that he was indeed determined not to run, they were "laughed at for so protesting." Every candidate had to play this game. Even ex-Missouri senator J. B. Henderson, Sherman's neighbor, his representative at the convention, and the meeting's chairman, began to have doubts about Sherman's true intentions despite their frank talk before his departure. "Write me in strict confidence tonight what I shall say in case of a break to you," he telegraphed from Chicago on June 2. Sherman responded that he hoped the convention would unify behind a willing candidate and his name would not even come up. If it did, however, Henderson was to say that Sherman "would answer no with an emphasis that might do harm to the Party and to myself."[13]

Mysteriously Sherman's letter did not reach Henderson, so the Missouri politician telegraphed again on June 3 asking for more instructions. Sherman wired back that if his letter had not arrived, "please decline any nomination for me in language strong but courteous." Meanwhile, Wisconsin Democratic senator James R. Doolittle added his voice to those pressuring Sherman, writing a long letter on June 3 insisting that Sherman's nomination and election was necessary to halt Reconstruction abuses—"this trampling under foot of the Constitution," this "march towards Centralized Despotism." Although he was a Democrat, Doolittle said, he would be happy to see the Republicans come to their constitutional senses by nominating Sherman, a man who held correct views on the relationship of federal and state governments. Those who wanted to ensure the fruits of the Civil War and had supported Reconstruction and those who saw Reconstruction as a perversion looked to Sherman. So did the mass of old soldiers. Professional politicians increasingly saw in him their best chance for a continuation of Republican dominance in the White House.[14]

He seemed like the perfect candidate, but he had warts too. His outspoken independent streak was well known, and he might not prove as malleable as the politicians hoped. He clearly disliked the electoral process, and some worried he might try to rule the country by martial law. But the biggest problem was the Catholicism of his family. Ellen Sherman was nationally known for her willingness to speak out for her religion. Tom Sherman's entrance into the seminary had been similarly widely publicized. The Catholic issue, a perennial focus of American prejudice, had caused major problems for those pushing him to run in 1876, and now it caused serious opposition to Sherman's candidacy in New York and Massachusetts. As one politician told Senator George Frisbie Hoar: "Our people do not want a Father Confessor in the White House."[15]

Despite this problem, many delegates still remained interested in mounting the Sherman bandwagon. Henderson felt such pressure that he went to bed with a sick headache, but not before telling the convention that no matter what they had heard, Sherman was still available. Sherman's letter and telegram had been delivered to the wrong hotel and then appeared opened at the Palmer House. His refusal to run was known all over town. Still, several state delegations were on the verge of publicly supporting him, Mrs. Henderson reported, and a constant stream of delegates was pouring into their hotel room to get corroboration of Sherman's real position. A rising young politician named Theodore Roosevelt hoped to be able to nominate Sherman and was particularly distressed. Letters from nephew Henry F. Sherman and son-in-law Thomas Fitch said that Sherman would be nominated unless he declined himself. They ominously warned that Henderson was "acting with a clique" to use the boom for unstated "personal ends."[16]

Telegrams flew back and forth from Chicago to St. Louis and back again, and unfortunately not all have been preserved. What transpired, however, was one of the most famous scenes in American political history, and Sherman's two sons were present at their father's side to record it. The three men were in conversation at home in St. Louis when yet another telegram came from Henderson, almost hysterically insisting that Sherman accept the impending call of the convention. Since this was only one of many such letters and telegrams pouring out of Chicago, its arrival caused little reaction from Sherman. Chomping down on the cigar he held between his teeth, he penciled one of the most quoted (and misquoted) statements in American history: "I will not accept if nominated and will not serve if elected." He read the words to his family, handed the paper to the messenger, and then returned to his conversation as though nothing had happened. Soon after another telegram arrived, this one from James G. Blaine in Augusta, Maine, urging Sherman to accept the convention's nomination if it came. Sherman repeated the famous words to Blaine. A newspaper finally got the message. "He will not accept a nomination and he would not serve if elected. That certainly ought to 'settle it,'" the newspaper concluded. Sherman's name was never put into nomination and, though he received a handful of votes on the first three ballots, Blaine won on the fourth.[17]

Sherman was in fine spirits after the Republicans selected Blaine, immediately sending the nominee a high-spirited congratulatory letter. He was writing, he said, because he understood "that the proper thing to do is for rival candidates after the contest to shake hands and for the defeated to congratulate the victor. I will now admit that I was a Candidate, . . . but am nevertheless willing to congratulate you on your brilliant success." Some later historians, reading only these words, have considered them proof that Sherman had wanted the nomination. But Sherman was only joking. In the same letter he told Blaine that "certain injudicious friends were determined in case of a 'break' to use my name and I was equally determined to decline it." Thankfully, he concluded, Blaine's victory had saved the day. He was similarly more bemused than angry when the son of some wealthy New York friends offered him $10,000 to become an independent presidential candidate. Multiply that sum "by a million," he answered, "and add thereto the wealth of all the Vanderbilts, Astors, Goulds &c with the contents of the U.S. Intl Treasury," and he still would not run.[18]

Sherman's determination to stay out of presidential politics was genuine. Grant's negative experience was a consideration, and he knew better than anyone else that, if he ran, he would have two major problems to grapple with and both centered on his wife: Ellen's aggressive Catholicism and her abhorrence of social obligation. He had long ago learned how to work around her unwillingness to be a public figure, but he had never been able to deal with her Catholicism. Even those who urged him to run recognized this problem, but in their enthusiasm for his candidacy they tried to ignore it.[19]

Ellen begged her husband not to become a candidate: "The newspaper abuse which would be heaped upon you and me and each and every child we have would be intolerable to you and they would dig the dead from their graves to vilify them and what is more you could not be elected by reason of your family being Catholic." When John Sherman later discussed the matter with another senator, he said that Ellen's religion was the major reason for his brother's refusal to run. Perhaps.[20] But even had Ellen been a Protestant, Sherman would not have become a candidate. He abhorred politics and tried to stay clear of it all his life, not even voting in any presidential election, except in 1856 for Buchanan. He never took a public stand on any candidate, though privately supporting Republican candidates because they were usually army men. In 1880, however, since both Garfield and Winfield Scott Hancock had military backgrounds, he had remained neutral. He repeatedly pointed out how the office had beaten down previous military presidents like Harrison, Taylor, and Grant, seeing Grant's experience as an especial horror story, proving the correctness of his antipolitical prejudice. Why would he want to trade his peace of mind for the disorder of the presidency when there were so many others—his brother for example, who pined for the office and were better qualified to hold it?[21]

He probably expressed his views toward the presidency most dramatically one day in later years while traveling on a New York ferry boat with a friend. "What? Do they think I am a damned fool? I am a happy man now. Look at Grant! Look at Grant! What wouldn't he give now if he had never meddled with politics? No, they must let me alone. They can't bedevil me!"[22]

But they never gave up trying. In 1886 the entreaties began again, and in a pique over former Confederates' being appointed to the Supreme Court, he exaggeratingly threatened to "risk the obloquy and drudgery" of the presidency. But he was only engaging in loose talk and never seriously thought of running. He refused the 1888 nomination. Only his death saved him from yet another presidential boom in 1892.[23]

Having escaped his most serious encounter with the politicians and having retired from the military, Sherman turned his foremost attention to a worry he could not so easily escape—finances. Tom's decision to join the Jesuits meant he still had the family burden on his own shoulders, and though his retirement pay would remain the same $15,000 he had earned while in office, he was not at ease. He took no outstanding debts into retirement, and he held "about $40,000 in good cash assets and about $60,000 in good productive property," but it did not impress him as being enough.[24]

He spent a great deal of his retirement time bemoaning his financial situation and trying to improve it. In June 1885, for example, in complaining about Ellen's inability to understand his money problems, he provided some figures to support his pessimism. His salary was $1,250 a month, he pointed out, and, out of this amount, Ellen required $800 to run the house (food, servants, and so forth). The coachman cost $35 a month, a helper at another property $40, "water sprinkler" $4.60, carriage repairs and horse shoeing $30, taxes $100, and subsidy to Minnie's family $200. The total was $1,209.60, leaving him $40 for his personal expenses, charity, social engagements, and so forth. Two years later he concluded that his total outlay for 1887 had been $17,194.02, a deficit of $2,194.02 on his salary. Fortunately, rents on his properties grossed $5,534, less taxes and repairs of $2,511.88. Applying the remainder to the salary deficit resulted in a surplus for the year of $828.10.[25]

He never wanted to include his significant revenue-producing property in his income, considering it too unstable to count on for the monthly expenses. He was constantly buying and selling houses and land, so his worth varied from year to year. By the 1880s, he owned several properties in St. Louis: 912 Garrison Avenue, five acres and a house at Cote Brilliante Place, a house and lot on Exchange Place, and two houses and lots on Lucas Avenue. He also owned a ninety-two-acre farm with house in Madison County, Illinois. Late in his life, he bought a house in

New York and rented all the other property. In addition he had intermittent income from literary royalties. In 1888 he estimated his estate at around $107,000, including $15,000 in cash. In 1889 he estimated the value of his memoirs and manuscripts at $50,000, added in this amount and the value of his newly purchased New York House ($35,000 less the mortgage of $17,500), and concluded that his net worth was about $165,000. Sherman was well off by the standards of his day, but comparing himself to Andrew Carnegie and the other millionaires he associated with, he never felt financially satisfied.[26]

Sometimes he joked about it: "It will require on my part as much financing to provide for my family as it did to fund 100,000 men [in the Civil War]." Most other times he worried that Congress would slash his salary. Old soldiers constantly called on him for financial help, and he wished there was some way he could stop this drain on his pocket. When his daughters married, the weddings were expensive, and afterward he felt obligated to help their husbands begin their businesses. Ellen's extensive charity activity for the Catholic church eventually used up the significant St. Louis and Ohio property Thomas Ewing had deeded her over the years.[27]

Sherman was determined to have his family financially secure no matter what happened to him. His lifelong dread of his father's example was intensified as he watched the families of deceased military men trying to survive on the dole of friends or on inadequate government pensions or jobs. He shuddered when he observed Grant's financial crisis in the 1880s—the old soldier slowly dying from cancer, penniless because of some unwise investments. "I hope you and all my children now realize," he told Elly, "why I have been so mean in the past. We have lived on what we had, and now owe no man a cent, and as long as I live you all have a safe home in St. Louis." But he feared that despite all his best efforts, something might go wrong. "The old memories of 1856 came back," he told a brother-in-law. He remembered how he had saved and invested money in California and then had to use it up repaying his army friends for bad investments. Ellen still thought (correctly) that he exaggerated the plight of their finances and insisted they could always borrow if matters became too tight. He totally opposed the idea. "I will steal, rob, murder—any thing rather than borrow. Debt & credit are greater crimes than murder and robbery." So he fretted while Ellen spent. "I think we could economize about this House," he told Minnie, "but your Mama says *No* and Lizzie seems to concur. I know I could stop some leaks, but your Mama likes to handle the money and utterly ignores the fact that I cannot get all the money I want."[28]

Sherman also experienced financial problems because of Minnie and her husband. Soon after he married Minnie, Fitch took Sherman's advice and left the navy to join the Harrison Wire Company in St. Louis. Sherman purchased $10,000 of the company stock, dividends assigned to Fitch, and encouraged some friends to invest too, thus securing for his son-in-law a place in the management with an annual $2,500 salary. He then regularly encouraged the chronically worried entrepreneur, who invested more heavily in the enterprise and expanded its operations. Meanwhile, Fitch, Minnie, and their growing family lived in a house Sherman owned in Cote Brilliante, and in 1884 Sherman was pleased to be able to tell a friend that Fitch was a partner in two businesses and had "not asked for help in years."[29]

It turned out that Fitch was keeping the truth from his father-in-law. By the summer of 1884, the Harrison Wire Company was a million dollars in the red, with Fitch and two silent partners each in debt over $300,000. Amazingly Sherman did not blame his son-in-law; he blamed himself, seeing a repetition of his father's financial failure as tax collector and his own banking collapse in the 1850s. He had done all he could to help Fitch, yet failure had come again. It was all terribly frightening and depressing. Fitch went bankrupt, temporarily left Minnie and the children in St. Louis, and traveled to Pittsburgh in the hopes of starting over again. He organized a new business, while Sherman provided monthly checks to keep the family afloat. "God knows I wish you & yours every possible blessing," he told Minnie, "but my means and power are overtaxed." Fitch's new wire mill proved profitable, and by 1888, much to Cump's relief, the family seemed financially secure.[30]

Feeling as strapped as he did, Sherman looked for additional sources of income. He published his memoirs in 1875, and he hoped it would be profitable, but his financial returns were not as great as he hoped. Conventional wisdom holds that Sherman made $25,000 on his memoirs; Grant told Mark Twain that Sherman had said so. Since he paid for the printing plates and had other expenses, it is not clear if the $25,000 was gross or net profit. The publisher printed a first run of ten thousand copies, but the extent of sales and further printings is unknown. Sherman, who freely discussed his finances with family and friends, never mentioned receiving any large royalty payments. In fact he intimated just the opposite in 1889. "I have watched the course of trade in Books, and don't know of any War Memoirs except Grants which have resulted satisfactorily to the Authors and in Grant's case the feeling of charity came in to help his distressed family." In 1890 he stated flatly: "My annual receipts from Sherman's Memoirs don't pay one-quarter of traveling expenses *demanded* at the Army Reunions each year."[31]

Cumpy later called the first edition "highly profitable" and said the second version "also yielded a substantial return." He never provided any concrete figures to support these assertions, however. Sherman arranged with Mark Twain's Charles L. Webster & Company to put out a new edition so that his memoirs and those of Grant and Sheridan could stand together under the same commercial roof. He died before this new version was printed, but his family rushed it out complete with a sketch by Tom Sherman and a brief "Tribute" by James G. Blaine. The edition sold around 17,000 copies at a loss of fifty cents a set. The family received a bill for half the loss, $4,200 (on top of the $3,500 they had previously invested in the venture). Complicated legal maneuvering resulted in the volumes going back to Appleton's, but the financial problems were never resolved, and Webster went bankrupt anyway. Appleton's later republished the 1886 edition, but any family profit is unknown. Perhaps Sherman's own statement late in his life was an accurate assessment of the book's financial history: "If the Publishers don't bring me into debt I will be content."[32]

With such a publication experience, Sherman was not eager to accept offers from magazines. When Grant was on his deathbed, editors intensified their pressure for a piece about his friend, but Sherman continued to resist, additionally worried about the sensationalism involved. Over time he gave in to the editors' entreaties, however, and published articles in the *Century, North American Review,* and other magazines, his perceived financial needs overcoming his scruples. He was paid well, receiving from $120 to $1,000 per article, but the mixed critical reaction that greeted his efforts upset him. Editors continued to press, but he refused to do any more writing. "Knowing full well that it is not the subject matter these gentlemen want but my name—I am resolved not to compromise my good name by any further publication.[33]

Tour agents regularly tried to sign him as a client, promising large fees. In 1885 he was offered a retainer of $12,500 for a series of winter lectures, and some London businessmen offered him $10,000 plus expenses to preside over a commercial gathering. He refused every offer. "To me," he said on one occasion, "the mere thought of traveling round like the Circus repeating the same tricks is humiliating[,] and a million dollars cannot tempt me." On another occasion he was even more forthright. "My regular charge for 'Lecturing' is a million of dollars for outsiders —for my soldier comrades once a year nothing."[34]

The truth of the matter was that Sherman was not financially pressured enough, despite his complaints, to brave the chaotic reaction to speeches and writing for a fee. He thought that if he refused offers, he could escape the criticism such endeavors would bring on. Once more he was wrong. Not only did he not avoid prose and rhetoric, but he actually spent much of his retirement time engaging in it and often inciting the very criticism he wanted to avoid. He believed that he had as much of a duty to ensure the true history of the Civil War as he once had to fight in it. Unless the true history of the war was preserved, the conflict itself would have been in vain. Sherman could well have been president, but he found that possibility distressing. Standing in defense of the Civil War was a much more valuable vocation. It would not make him rich, but it would ensure the accurate remembrance of the events that had given him the success he could never hope to repeat in the White House.

CHAPTER 21

SAFEGUARDING HISTORICAL ORDER

SHERMAN LOOKED BACK to the Civil War as a time of glory that achieved the Union's preservation and his personal success. He had played a leading role in overwhelming the anarchy that had threatened to destroy the nation and his own future, and, in the process, he had become an internationally known celebrity. He thought this accomplishment was permanent, and in the technical sense it was because secession was destroyed as a legitimate political device. In another way, however, the Civil War never ended, and Sherman participated in the continuing battle for the rest of his life. He worked to ensure an accurate historical remembrance of the events of the 1860s, worried that if the Confederate view of the war as the Lost Cause prevailed, his success would be taken from him. The problem was that he proved incapable of the precision of language necessary for his self-appointed role. Personal feelings proved more compelling than the search for truth.

He devoted a good portion of his life after the war to clarifying and securing his place in history. He was an impatient supporter of the government's publication of the *Official Records* of the Civil War, convinced that these volumes were the only genuine hope for an accurate account of that conflict. When former Confederate general John Bell Hood tried to sell his personal war papers, Sherman willingly helped, not only out of sympathy for Hood's financial problems but also because of his concern for the history the papers contained. He saw the need for a comprehensive, definitive study of the war and provided factual information and insight on the western war for Columbia University professor John W. Draper's three-volume history. He similarly offered advice, sometimes of the most detailed sort, to Adam Badeau for his book on U. S. Grant. He pushed his engineering officers to prepare the maps of his march to the sea for publication. He advised military thinkers, encouraged military officers to write books, and critiqued a host of publications that crossed his desk. He recommended the collection of oral histories to preserve the war as it was truly fought.[1]

He knew that his own legacy was secure because of the Atlanta campaign and his 1865 restoration of civilian authority to the South. What worried him, he said, was the future's evaluation of the Union cause. If advocates of the Confederacy controlled the history books, they might distort the great Unionist achievement in preserving the nation. "The Great Lessons of our Civil War," he told the principal of the Harvard Grammar School, "are that each youth must be faithful to his whole country and not a part, that each must stand ready to do his manful part, that wars are as much a part of God's Providence as the Thunderstorm, and that War's legitimate object is more perfect peace." Consequently, he believed that Unionists should write the Civil War histories: "We the victors must stamp on all history that we were right and they wrong—that we beat them in Battle as well as in argument, and that we must give direction to future events."[2]

In pursuit of that aim, sometime in the early 1870s he decided to write his memoirs. No other Civil War general had done so yet, but Sherman's frustration with his bureaucratically constrained role as commanding general of the army encouraged him to look back to the Civil War, a more fulfilling time, and preserve his role for posterity. In mid-August 1874 he cryptically wrote John W. Draper that he had "written something not for publication but for his children and to help someone writing a history of the war." The Columbia University professor read the manuscript and urged its publication.[3]

Sherman thought about it some more and decided to seek a publisher. Living in St. Louis, away from Washington and most official duty, he opened negotiations with several companies and signed a contract with an eastern firm. He told a brother-in-law, "I have just done a thing that I may regret all my life, committed to the Appletons of New York the manuscript of two volumes mostly on the Civil War that may bring me some profit but more controversy." The three-year contract called for Sherman to pay

$2,000 for the printing plates and thus "absolutely own the work." He would earn $0.40 a volume, the two-volume set selling for $5.50. Of more concern than the money was his determination that nothing in the memoirs alienate anyone. "In my book I have taken great pains to avoid objects of controversy," he told his brother, "but have explained causes and reasons, so that the Real Historian will find less trouble to account for actual events."[4]

The massive tome appeared in May 1875: two blue-covered volumes with gold lettering, twenty-four chapters, and 814 pages. The first seven chapters detailed the period from 1846 to 1861, from California to Louisiana, and the last seventeen chapters dealt with the Civil War. The text had a rambling quality about it, frequently interrupted by letters to and from the memoirist at the time of the events under discussion. The account was by turns very personal, as when Sherman described his role during the California gold rush, or very factual, as when he included page upon page of official correspondence and after-battle reports. His final chapter, "Military Lessons of the War," contained too little insight into his philosophy of war,[5] and in other places there was perhaps too much on petty animosities that might have been better unsaid.

Behind the torrent of words, Sherman the man shines through. He places himself at the center of the major events of the war, reflecting his personal view of the conflict. Other than Grant, most other generals on both sides receive their share of criticism in a matter-of-fact style that was Sherman's. He described the war from his perspective, as any memoirist must, but, in so doing, he downplayed the role of others. He did not do so out of conscious spite, but simply because he saw it that way and saw no reason to embellish his view to please someone else. If someone was not pleased with the place Sherman assigned him in a war event, he could write his own memoirs. Sherman clearly wrote his remembrances to show the world how well he had done in the conflict. He admitted the insanity imbroglio but, despite it and other problems, he did great things at Atlanta and on the marches. He saw himself as a great general, and he wanted the world to agree.

Sherman wrote with as much ease as he talked. He allowed his pen to ramble, giving the memoirs a charm and a worth; its tone is that of Sherman telling his story around a camp fire, forthrightly presenting his view of the nation's great domestic crisis to friends and admirers, comrades and family, former enemies and current critics.[6]

As soon as the memoirs appeared, Sherman's fears were realized. He and his book were engulfed in a firestorm of criticism, unlike anything any other Civil War memoirist ever faced. His mail, the newspapers, and magazines were filled with commentary, some of it reopening war wounds and long-held personal animosities. Friends rallied in defense of the embattled general; enemies gleefully tried to take advantage. Sherman spent the better part of the following year defending his words and trying to deflect the criticism.

Reviews appeared in all the major magazines and newspapers in the United States and overseas, and in most of the lesser ones too. Most commentaries were long synopses, concluding that the volumes were a great contribution to the knowledge of the Civil War. In 1876 Captain A. von Clausewitz translated the Atlanta campaign chapter and published it in a German military journal as "Ein Eisenbahnkrieg im amerikanischen Sezessions-Krieg." Others were critical and questioned Sherman's war effort. Those who liked the book echoed the words of a small newspaper in New York State that concluded: "He is as dexterous and trenchant with the pen as with the sword." Those who disagreed concluded that "his military deeds, while in the main highly beneficial to his country, have not been marked by the exhibition of the loftier attributes of a great captain." Sherman's use of destruction was too radical to include him among the classic generals in history. Southern reviews were similarly mixed. The *Louisiana State Register* said he had "told the truth . . . and if he has touched some people in a tender spot, they deserve it." Defenders of the Lost Cause, however, had a field day, former Confederate General Dabney H. Maury perhaps producing the most ingenious critique. Sherman's memoirs, he said, were full of "vain glory and self conceit," but, like fertilizer which helps plants grow, the memoirs would stimulate other participants to publish accurate accounts of the war.[7]

A host of readers expressed their evaluations to Sherman personally. Military scholar and Sherman pet Emory Upton called the memoirs "a contribution to history, which will enhance your reputation but . . . will [also] attract the attention of Europe . . . and open up a fertile field of illustration to the future students of strategy and grand tactics." Future president and friend James

A. Garfield enthused about "the fresh and vivid style [and] the graphic description of persons and events. . . . I do not believe that a just criticism will charge you with doing any intentional injustice to anyone." Charles P. Stone wrote from Egypt: "The book reads like romance and bears on its face the impress of exact truth and candor."[8]

Others found the memoirs lacking. Fighting Joe Hooker and John A. McClernand, two generals who had never gotten along with Sherman (or many other people) during the war, were angry at the way he had written about them and just about everything else in his book. Montgomery Blair was indignant that Sherman had castigated his brother Frank for his wartime political activities, and Senator and Mrs. John A. Logan agreed that Sherman had been unfair to Logan. Civil War newsman Franc B. Wilkie thought Sherman was too harsh on the journalistic fraternity. Don Carlos Buell believed he and the Army of the Cumberland had not received their just due for their role at Shiloh. California's John A. Sutter thought Sherman had done a good job on the gold rush chapters, but he disagreed with Sherman's characterization of him as "tight" during the famous Fourth of July party in 1848. The most insistent critic was General William (Sooy) Smith. He and Sherman carried on a two-month debate over the accuracy and fairness of Sherman's accounting of Smith's ill-fated cavalry role in the 1864 Meridian campaign. The most honest critic was brother John. He predicted that Grant, Halleck, and Hooker, among others, would not like what they read. The book's ending was "also rather abrupt," and it needed a discussion of his life before California. Still, John concluded, this effort showed that Cump could write and in the future he should take on "broader historical themes."[9]

Henry Van Ness Boynton, a brevet brigadier general in the Army of the Cumberland and, after the war, the Washington correspondent for the *Cincinnati Gazette,* wrote the most scathing and extended critique of the memoirs. It was entitled: *Sherman's Historical Raid. The Memoirs in the Light of the Record.* Boynton stated the thesis in the Preface: "Judged by the official record, the verdict must be that the work [memoirs] is intensely egotistical, unreliable, and cruelly unjust to nearly all his distinguished associates." In the text, Boynton purported to use documentation to buttress his position, but all too often unfounded accusation and debatable opinion are the basis for the argument. The tone is sensationalistic. Boynton insisted that Sherman tried to take due credit away from Grant, Thomas, and other worthy colleagues. He had never done anything right during the war, Boynton argued, and in his memoirs he was trying to cover his tracks. He had not conceived the march to the sea; Grant had. He had never properly supported Thomas and the Army of the Cumberland, yet Thomas had won the glorious victory at Nashville in December 1864 that had saved Sherman and the nation from disaster. Thomas had similarly carried the day at Chattanooga after Sherman had almost lost it. Conversely, Sherman unfairly blamed Sooey Smith for his actions during the Meridian campaign. As for Sherman's peace negotiations with Johnston, he had accepted "terms drawn up by a member of the rebel Cabinet."[10]

Sherman was infuriated. Initially, he believed he could best defend himself by ignoring the *Historical Raid*, but he could not restrain himself. He could not stand by and allow a hated reporter to attack his views of the Civil War and to destroy his place in its history. He organized a counterattack. Jacob D. Cox, a former Sherman general who would later write books on the Atlanta campaign and the march to the sea, agreed to compose an extended review of Boynton's book for one of the country's major magazines, the *Nation*. Charles W. Moulton, Sherman's brother-in-law and an experienced journalist, published at Sherman's expense *The Review of General Sherman's Memoirs Examined, Chiefly in the Light of Its Own Evidence*. Samuel M. Bowman, the author of an 1865 Sherman biography and long-time California lawyer, was hired to help coordinate all the activity and work with a former Sherman aide, St. Louis lawyer Henry Hitchcock, on the possibility of a new edition of the memoirs. Meanwhile, in the press, Judson Kilpatrick, Sherman's former cavalry leader, was independently debating James H. Wilson, another Union cavalryman. Sherman organized this all-out attack on the detractors. His version of history was too important to be doubted or mired in controversy. He rose to the fight, and ultimately the controversy died away.[11]

The real turning point in the imbroglio came on January 29, 1876. President U. S. Grant had remained publicly silent, Sherman afraid that the silence was the result of their postwar coolness toward each other and indicated Grant's disapproval of the volumes. During the annual meeting of the Society of the Army of the Cumberland, however, Grant confided to Sherman, in Senator Roscoe Conkling's presence, that he had read the memoirs and had found nothing to criticize about them. He promised Sherman a written statement. Based on all he had heard, Grant said, he had "commenced the reading with great prejudice," but he had come away pleasantly surprised. He wished Sherman had not been so critical of Burnside's Knoxville activities and Blair's and Logan's politics, and he had unnecessarily brought up the matter of the origin of the idea for the march to the sea. Similarly, Grant said, he, not Halleck, had originated the movement against Fort Donelson. Still "I will repeat that I do not believe a more correct history can be given of the events recorded by you in the 'Memoirs.'" Sherman was thrilled; he had won a major victory. With Grant for him, it mattered little what anyone said against him. It felt good to be linked with Grant again, even if only briefly.[12]

Four years later during an 1880 interview with the *Cleveland Leader,* Sherman attacked Boynton's book and the author himself: "You could hire him to do anything for money. Why, for a thousand dollars he would slander his own mother." Boynton cautiously suggested that Sherman must have been misquoted. No, Sherman replied, the quotation was accurate. "This is a hard thing to say of any man, but I believe it of you."[13]

The controversy returned, now centering not on Sherman's historical veracity but on Boynton's integrity. Charges and countercharges reverberated in the press and in the mails again. When Boynton publicly demanded Sherman be court-martialed for slander and conduct unbecoming an officer, Sherman wrote to the secretary of war insisting on civil action instead. He hired Senator Matt H. Carpenter to serve as his lawyer, but the War Department ruled that the military had no jurisdiction over the matter. Boynton was leery of civil action, but Sherman refused to let him off gracefully. He told O. O. Howard: "I regard this man as an enemy of mankind and will spare no efforts to bring him to condign punishment." The public debate once again faded away, and Sherman was soon crowing in victory. "Boynton has simply subsided—swallowing whole the insult I put on him." Years later, Sherman was still angry enough at Boynton to call him a "yellow cur."[14]

After his retirement and the 1884 presidential furor, Sherman took up the matter of revising the memoirs. Moulton did the work, and by July, Sherman and his clerk were reading the final page proofs. Sherman procrastinated, waiting for the forthcoming publication of Grant's memoirs. He still worried about Grant's saying something in his book that would require comment in his revised edition, the implicit confidence the two men had enjoyed during the war no longer in evidence. Fortunately, Grant's volumes supported Sherman on all the major issues. They were "as near the truth as man can make it," Sherman concluded.[15]

Sherman's revised edition appeared in 1886. The new Preface emphasized the argument he had used consistently in answer to criticism of the first edition. He was not a historian, he wrote, but was merely presenting his views for later scholars. He had done his best and would "publish no other." "Of omissions there are plenty," he concluded, "but of wilful perversion of facts, none." He expanded the text by adding a new first chapter discussing his life before 1846 and a new final chapter detailing his post–Civil War career. Two appendixes contained letters and excerpts from the many critics of the first edition, and this edition featured an index. Despite the debate and argument, the second edition was an almost verbatim transcription of the first version. Sherman stood by his words. Most of the fifty or so changes were minor corrections of fact. Sutter was now characterized as "enthusiastic" rather than "tight," and McPherson at Resaca was called "cautious," not "timid." Sherman also toned down an earlier comment regarding the 1861 insanity charge and softened a reference to Hooker. All the other controversial statements, such as the comments about Grant, Thomas, Blair, and Logan, remained. Public reaction was minimal; there was no repetition of the hoopla surrounding the publication of the original version.[16]

Deep in his heart, Sherman was proud of his literary achievement, but, as on the Civil War battlefields, he once more demurred to Grant. "Grant's book will of course survive all time," he told a friend. "Mine, Sheridan's and a few others will be auxiliary, but the great mass of books . . . will be swept aside." Sherman saw his memoirs as second only to Grant's—exactly as he ranked himself in Civil War military history.[17]

With retirement in 1884, Sherman had more time for promulgating his views of the Civil War, increasingly now on the speaker's podium. He spent an enormous amount of time giving formal and informal addresses at a variety of banquets and meetings, most of them at veterans' gatherings where the war was especially revered. The only time he missed the annual meeting of the Society of the Army of the Tennessee in the postwar years was during his European tour. He attended many yearly meetings of the Society of the Army of the Cumberland, the Society of the Army of the Potomac, the Grand Army of the Republic, and the various Societies for New England. In addition, there were public ceremonies, convention banquets, and private dinner parties. He was one of the era's most prolific and popular after-dinner speakers. He had an incredible ability to entertain and move people with his words, so he was always in demand. He never kept a record of how many speeches he gave, but it ran into the thousands. The image many Americans had of William T. Sherman was not simply a military genius of the Civil War but also an entertaining and instructive master of the spoken word.

His favorite element was the veterans' reunion, where he felt most comfortable around his "boys." He was president of the Society of the Army of the Tennessee for twenty-two years, and he regularly presided over and spoke to this organization of former officers dedicated to preserving the memory of their army's role in combat. The meetings had a predictable rhythm. The opening sessions dealt with business, but once that was completed and the main address delivered, there ensued the so-called bummers' meeting. The audience would shout out the names of favorite individuals, demanding a speech. This would go on until Sherman, as presiding officer, cut off the raucous give and take.

A major duty of his presidency was to preside over the yearly business meeting and banquet, and Sherman was a benevolent dictator, much to the amusement of the participating veterans and the onlooking public. A newspaper reporter one year caught the essence of his presidential manner: "Gen. Smith—Did I see Gen. Smith rise?" (a voice: "He's gone for a moment.") "Well, never mind; it's all the same. Gen. Smith moves the appointment of a committee on Resolutions and will consist of (taking a list from his right vest pocket) Gen. So-and-so. (looks blank.) That's not the committee, either. The list I just read is another committee, and it will be moved later. Here's the right one (Reads it.) You see, gentlemen, we get our young staff officers who have nothing else to do to fix up these things in advance."[18]

As master of ceremonies at the yearly banquet, he dispatched business at lightning speed and was as ruthless with parliamentary rules as he had been with red tape during war. "We have a long list before us," he reminded the listeners in characteristic fashion one year, and he wanted absolute silence so every speaker could be heard. He complimented the musicians but told them to keep the music brief. "Make it, as it were, a loop between the speeches." As for the presentations themselves, "Each speaker is requested to speak as long as he holds his audience. [Some laughter and cheers.] As to applause, gentlemen, recollect that that takes a good deal of time. A good, hearty laugh and marked applause are all right, but don't drawl it out into a long giggle, or into a noise. Let the applause be short and emphatic. [laughter.]" Then he introduced the speakers and kept the program moving along. When the end was reached, he concluded with something like: "It is now 2 o'clock A.M., time for me to quit and I think you had better quit too!"[19]

Sometimes Sherman could be cutting, and not everyone found him amusing. Once during a bummers' meeting, a nonveteran yelled for a civilian to speak. Sherman showed no mercy: "Sit down, young man! We are willing you and your friends should stay here and listen; but this is our meeting, and we propose to run it!" Sherman ran the meetings, and he brooked no opposition to his benevolent but firm rule. On at least one occasion, a veteran grew incensed at Sherman's high-handed manner. He tried to offer an additional toast at the end of a banquet, but Sherman declared him out of order and adjourned the festivities. The wronged officer stopped Sherman outside and waved his fist under the startled presider's nose until some bystanders led him away.[20]

At almost every meeting he attended, Sherman gave some sort of speech. Often it was the major oration of the evening and/or it was a response to a toast to the army and navy, to the flag, or some Civil War topic. He wrote out his formal speeches on legal-sized paper and read them to his audience, more or less sticking to the text.[21] Often, however, he spoke extemporaneously. The words flowed from his mouth in a torrent just as they did in conversation or from his pen onto his stationery. He used stories and humor effectively, evoking patriotic and nostalgic emotions. His accompanying body movements and gestures helped drive home his message. "He leaned forward," one observer wrote, "gesticulated forcibly with his long right arm, looked his hearers full in the eyes, and seemed to be speaking into the particular ears of each individual before him." It mattered little whether he was speaking from behind a podium at a society dinner, from an open-air speaker's stand adorned with faded and torn battle flags, or on top of a chair at the edge of a hotel balcony; he had an uncanny ability to touch his audiences.[22]

The content of his speeches varied enormously, but his predominant theme was that of national achievement and pride. The Civil War, which achieved an era of social and material progress, was the overriding subject of his presentations, and his attitude toward it never changed. In 1871 he called the war "a holy cause"; in 1887 he told a Grand Army of the Republic post: "The war in which we were engaged was a holy war. They may call it otherwise, but it was a holy war, a war in the interests not only of America, but of the whole human race." Those men who took up arms for the Union were special. "It was one of the proudest points in our history that our young men regardless of party and other former associations rushed to the rescue of that flag which is the symbol of our nation." "Bring up your children," he told another audience, "to love and venerate the old soldiers who fought in 1861 and 1865, and make them uncover their heads" before the flag.[23]

Most of these speeches discussed the historical aspects of the war, not its results. He tried to present his side, not only in opposition to advocates of the Lost Cause, who argued the moral superiority of the Confederate army despite its defeat, but also because some Union generals or their supporters might present an incorrect view—one that downplayed Sherman's role. He gave extended speeches on Shiloh, the march to the sea, the City Point meeting with Lincoln, Grant, and Porter, the Grand Review, Atlanta, and Kentucky. In each instance, he hammered away at his side of a controversy, such as insisting that there had been no surprise at Shiloh and that reporters far from the scene of the action had published false information about it.[24]

When he was not speaking about the Civil War, he was writing magazine articles on it. He most expansively expressed his ideas about the war in an 1888 essay, "The Grand Strategy of the War of the Rebellion," in which he surveyed the war's battles. "Many of us in our civil war did not think of Napoleon, Wellington, Hamley, or Soady, yet as we won the battle, we are willing to give these great authors the benefit of our indorsement." Sherman did not emphasize the modernity of his own strategy, but he insisted, in answer to those who criticized his methods of war, on its classic nature. He said little about revolutionary aspects of the march to the sea, stating that it "was only a shift of base for ulterior and highly important purposes," namely to get his army in position, after the capture of Atlanta, for his movement north against Lee in Virginia. When commenting on the march through the Carolinas, he still insisted that Lee's army was his objective, and he linked the movement's psychological aspects to that. "This march was like the thrust of a sword towards the heart of the human body; each mile of advance swept aside all opposition, consumed the very food on which Lee's army depended for life, and demonstrated a power in the National Government which was irresistible." His marches were orderly in purpose and execution, not chaotically destructive as critics argued. The Union cause, its leaders, and the way the Federals successfully fought the war were all superior to the Confederate effort and its leaders, even Robert E. Lee. Grant was the greatest military leader of the war, Lee not his equal because "he never rose to the grand problem which involved a continent and future generations." "His Virginia was to him the world," Sherman said in a later article. "He stood at the front porch battling with the flames whilst the kitchen and house were burning, sure in the end to consume the whole."[25] Like so much else in his life, Sherman's historical effort was a highly personal activity. The truth as he saw it had to be preserved so that disorder could never threaten the Union, or him, again.

Sherman felt little animosity for white Southerners, early insisting "that the period of suspicion natural to an internecine war, has died away." He remained friendly with ex-Confederate leaders John Bell Hood, Braxton Bragg, Joe Johnston, James Longstreet, and Gideon Pillow, even recommending to E. O. C. Ord in 1876 that Bragg receive a job in the army subsistence department and supporting Johnston, Longstreet, and Pillow for midlevel political office in the restored Union. Former Confederate vice-president Alexander H. Stephens asked Sherman's help for a Southern West Point cadet, and Confederate cavalryman Joe Wheeler, in 1886 a congressman, invited Sherman to his house for a large party. When Southerners asked him to support the establishment of a federal home for former Confederate soldiers, Sherman suggested that the needy ex-Confederates share the homes already provided for former Union men.[26]

In 1879 when Sherman toured the South, retracing his famous campaigns, he was pleasantly received everywhere, "hundreds professing friendship," he reported, "and thousands every variety of curiosity." In Atlanta he socialized with the city fathers and toured the city's length and breadth, pleased at its prosperity. In New Orleans, he was special guest during Mardi Gras, receiving a warm welcome every place he appeared during the festivities. The only awkward moment occurred on a train in Mississippi. A Southern friend asked Sherman to greet Jefferson Davis, sitting in another car. Sherman politely refused.[27]

The ex-president of the Confederacy was Sherman's bête noir throughout the postwar period. Both men were stubborn, outspoken, easily angered, and slow to forgive and forget. Sherman despised anyone who continued to insist that the South had been justified in warring against the United States, and Davis was the leading exponent of that view. Similarly, Davis castigated anyone who upheld the Union side. The two men were in perfect opposition on matters close to their hearts and their egos: the history and meaning of the Civil War. Throughout the postwar years Sherman viewed Davis as "a simple monomaniac," "the impersonation of all that was wicked" in the war.[28]

Davis felt a similar animosity toward Sherman and indulged it fully in 1881 when he published his defense of the Confederacy, *Rise and Fall of the Confederate Government.* He labeled Sherman a hypocrite and a liar, charging that the march to the sea had been "an act of cruelty which only finds a parallel in the barbarous excesses of Wallenstein's army in the Thirty Years' War." His depopulating of Atlanta was the worst savagery "since Alva's atrocious cruelties to the non-combatant population of the Low countries in the sixteenth century." He later told a reporter that Sherman's "so-called march to the sea, 'so much lauded,' was really the most absurd of military maneuvers ever undertaken in all the tide of time. It was right in the teeth of all the rules of war," and the only reason it succeeded was because of the Confederacy's weakness.[29]

"I am now convinced," Sherman said of Davis, "that he is the type of a class that must be wiped off the face of the earth, and unless I was convinced that his book will accomplish this end, I would favor starting in again, and not stopping until the thing was complete." By August, he felt calmer, concluding that "nobody seems to read "Davis' two ponderous volumes," so it was a waste of time to critique them. However, when Sherman visited the Atlanta International Cotton Exposition in November (inadvertently on the anniversary of his Civil War visit), his reception was still polite but now cool. The newspaper that had been so friendly just two years previously now reprinted Davis's attacks, and other papers expressed unhappiness at his insensitive timing. Sherman "was more amused than alarmed," referring to himself as "the Vandal Sherman." When he supported the attempt to get an army barracks for Atlanta, the city council passed a warm resolution of thanks, and the mayor added his "sentiments of high esteem for you officially and personally."[30]

At the opening of a new headquarters for a St. Louis Grand Army of the Republic post several years later, Sherman reopened his conflict with Davis. He said the Civil War had been neither a rebellion nor secession. It had been a conspiracy. Jefferson Davis had been part of the national government when he had begun plotting to destroy it. Sherman said he remembered seeing a wartime letter from Davis to a Confederate governor, now a U.S. senator, threatening to use Lee's army against this official's state if it tried to secede from the Confederacy. Newspapers around the country picked up the sensational story. Davis was outraged. He wrote the editor of the *St. Louis Republican:* "If General Sherman has access to any letters purporting to have been written by me which will sustain his accusation let him produce them or wear the brand of a base slanderer."[31]

Sherman had captured piles of Davis's papers and remembered seeing letters containing Davis's threats against any state seceding from the Confederacy. Most of these letters had been sent to Chicago for storage, he said, and they were later destroyed in the Great Chicago Fire of 1871. Sherman made an intense effort to find the letters, but he failed.

The controversy seemed to be fading from the public eye when it exploded on the floor of the U.S. Senate in mid-January 1885. Connecticut senator Joseph R. Hawley, a former Union army officer, introduced a resolution calling on the president to send the Senate what he said was Sherman's report on the activities of the Confederate Executive Department. This request stirred a heated debate. Southern Democrats tried to kill the resolution, and John J. Ingalls of Kansas accused them of choosing Davis over Sherman. "Well sir, as between William T. Sherman and Jefferson Davis, I am for William T. Sherman; and . . . the loyal men of this country, the loyal men of the North particularly, will always be in favor of William T. Sherman as against Jefferson Davis." John Sherman agreed. L. Q. C. Lamar of Mississippi insisted that General Sherman had been wrong in attacking Davis in the first place. The next day the Senate voted 52 to 14, with 14 absent, in favor of Hawley's resolution. Sherman's response to Davis would become an official Senate document.[32]

Sherman insisted in this statement that the Civil War was the result of a conspiracy headquartered in Washington. He himself had been approached by a member of the Knights of the Golden Circle just before the war. He could not, however, produce specific letters because they had been lost. Instead, he included a letter from Alexander H. Stephens accusing Davis of changing his states' right position and "aiming at absolute power." He also included an appendix with other documents purporting to prove Davis's dictatorial ways. As far as he was concerned, he had shown that Davis "had enrolled his name with those of Arnold and Burr."[33]

Davis did not respond immediately. A year later, in September 1886, he wrote to a Southern historian, who published the comments in the *Baltimore Sun* and the *Southern Historical Society Papers.* Reading like a legal brief, this reply categorically denied all Sherman's accusations and ridiculed his claim that incriminating letters existed but could not be found. All his papers, Davis said, had been carefully studied after the war, yet no one but Sherman had ever seen the letters in question. "Every fair-minded man must therefore conclude that General Sherman stated at the Grand Army Post a willful and deliberate falsehood, and that his motive had its inspiration in that mean malice which has characterized his acts and writings in other respects towards the Southern people."[34]

The comments completed the debate. Supporters of Sherman did not appreciate the force with which Davis ridiculed Sherman's argument, but they kept quiet, as did Sherman. He continued to view Davis as "the impersonation of treason and hate," but he admitted to a friend that he and Davis had "both indulged in too much personality." He long continued belittling Davis every chance he had.[35]

He grew equally furious at a former Union general who disagreed with his perceptions of the Civil War and, worse, tried to argue that Sherman was trying to elevate his reputation at the expense of Grant, whose recent death prevented him from being able to defend himself. James B. Fry had been an officer in the Army of the Cumberland and a lecturer and writer in that army's interests. Sherman was a champion of the Army of the Tennessee, so it was inevitable that the two men should clash whenever Fry too boldly criticized Sherman's version of the war.

In 1884 just before Sherman became embroiled with Jefferson Davis, Fry had published *Operations of the Army Under General Buell*, in which he said that Buell's army had "rescued Grant's army at the Battle of Shiloh and converted the disaster of the first day into a victory on the second day." Sherman had become so angry that he accused Buell and the Army of the Cumberland of deliberately arriving late to avoid the first day's bloody fighting. Fry shot right back, and the only thing that had stopped the postal war of words had been Sherman's emerging conflict with Jefferson Davis and the fact that Grant had published a magazine article that mirrored Sherman's Shiloh view.[36]

By late 1885, Grant was dead and Fry went on the offensive. In the December issue of the *North American Review* Fry wrote: "General Sherman goes so far as to have said since Grant's death that 'Had C. F. Smith lived, Grant would have disappeared to history after Donelson.' "[37]

Instead of calmly considering that there was some truth to the assertion that Grant *might* never have obtained his early leadership opportunities except for the death of his superior, Sherman became furious. He demanded Fry substantiate the quote, but Fry cleverly refused to do so unless Sherman denied it. Otherwise he would let it stand. Sherman felt trapped. He wrote many letters, often carelessly, and did not always keep copies. He might have made such a comment in passing. He could not be sure.[38]

The impasse continued for three months, Sherman increasingly desperate that his treasured Civil War bond with Grant was in danger. He and Grant might have had a falling out over politics after the war, but their wartime affections had never wavered, witnessed by their postwar agreement on Sherman's memoirs and Grant's Shiloh article. Sherman demanded the secretary of war force Fry to disclose his sources. Of course, there was nothing the department could do, so Sherman plotted all sorts of other schemes to thwart Fry, personally if possible. Finally the word came out that Sherman had actually used the quoted words, in an offhand manner, in a letter to the army officer editing the *Official Records* of the Civil War. Fry had a copy of that letter, and it was the source of his accusation. Fry published a six-line extract in the *North American Review,* and a shaken Sherman fired back with a long explanation in the *Review* and a personal letter to the Grant family. He denied any intent to hurt Grant, arguing that the entire letter "breathes my real love and respect for your Father's memory."[39] Fry was a villain for stirring matters up unfairly.

Once more Sherman came out of a historical controversy second best. Once again he allowed his looseness of pen and voice to get him in trouble, and his insistence on pushing the controversy to its limit made it worse. He waged all-out war on Fry instead of utilizing political skills to defuse him. Once again Sherman showed that politics was not his forte, and his inability in this arena was a real handicap to his historical purposes.

Ironically, it was a casual remark like the ones that had caused trouble with Jeff Davis and Fry that ensured his permanent place in the American historical vocabulary. Not one of his speeches ranks with the great orations of American history. Sherman is most famous for three short words: "War is hell."

Sherman accompanied Rutherford B. Hayes to a Grand Army of the Republic encampment in 1880 at the old Ohio State Fair Grounds, later Franklin Park, in Columbus. The president spoke first as rain began to fall. Undaunted, the crowd, numbering between five thousand and ten thousand people, began to call for Sherman. He went to the podium with no prepared speech as he had done and would do at so many similar reunions. He looked out over the assembled veterans and joked about how often during the war they had braved the rain. He was there only as the president's escort, to see them, and to "let the boys look at old Billy again. We are to each other all in all as man and wife, and every soldier here today knows that Uncle Billy loves him as his own flesh and blood." He knew that they understood all about war. "You all know this is not soldiering here. There is many a boy here to-day who looks on war as all glory, but, boys, it is all hell." Then he joked once more about the rain, congratulated them for their role in giving the nation peace, and sat down. A local reporter captured his words for the larger audience. The *New York Times* wrote a long editorial on his wisdom in condemning war so forcefully, but most people, including Sherman, saw nothing special in what he had said.[40]

Sherman had used similar words before and he would use them again later. He allegedly said "war is hell" near Jackson, Mississippi, in 1863 and in an 1879 speech before the Michigan Military Academy. In 1864 he told the mayor and city council of Atlanta: "War is cruelty, and you can not refine it." In 1882 he said, "War is violence." In 1884 he told war veterans to "paint the hardships and cruelty of war" that no one would pursue it easily. When asked later in his life whether he had ever said "war is hell," Sherman admitted he had many times—before, during, and after the Civil War.[41]

"War is hell" well expressed Sherman's feelings toward violent conflict. He hated the killing and mayhem of battle, yet he still believed that war frequently was a necessity. He regularly characterized the Civil War as "hell," but he also believed it had been a necessity to preserve the nation's integrity. The second sentence that followed the famous one was: "I look upon war with horror, but if it has to come I am here." Or as he put it in a little-known speech three years after his Columbus effort: "Wars are not all evil; they are part of the grand machinery by which this world is governed; thunder storms, which purify the political atmosphere, test the manhood of a people, and prove whether they are worthy to take rank with others engaged in the same task by different methods." Sherman is not remembered either for "wars are not all evil" or "wars are inevitable," though these expressions more nearly expressed his views.[42]

Sherman persisted in his attempts to ensure his proper place in the history of the Civil War. But he had no cause to worry. As long as history books are published discussing that conflict, his name and exploits will be there. Whether later generations disliked him or not, they could not take away from him what he sought from history: acknowledgment of his critical role in preserving the Union. However, Sherman's postwar comments caused Southern apologists like Davis, Wade Hampton, and the editors of the *Southern Historical Society Papers* to attack him. Sherman spoke and wrote his mind, often with little forethought. This made him more enemies in the South than any other activity of his life and helped guarantee Southern animosity in the twentieth century. Looseness of expression overwhelmed fact and historical order. He never really considered the possibility of that happening. After all, he and the Union had clearly been in the right, and only the stubborn could continue to deny it after he explained it to them so clearly and so often in so many printed and spoken words.

CHAPTER 22

——— ☆ ———

A FULL LIFE ENDS

RETIREMENT BROUGHT MAJOR CHANGES to Sherman's life, the most significant being his freedom from politicians. It did not, however, slow him down; he continued to live his life at full throttle. The lack of official duty gave him the opportunity to fill his voracious intellectual appetite more completely, spend time on his defense of the Union war effort, and enjoy the adulation of his old soldiers and the general public. Grant died in 1885, so for most of his retirement he was the leading survivor of the Union war effort. Everywhere he went, he was a celebrity. He was never free of an inquiring public looking to him for words of wisdom and former soldiers seeking another glance, perhaps their last one, at their Uncle Billy. He had achieved the status he had battled for all his life; he was universally viewed as one of the elite of late nineteenth-century American society.

He was sought after by various organizations. He served several terms as a regent of the Smithsonian Institution both before and after retirement: 1871 to 1875 and 1878 to 1886. After retirement he belonged to Washington's Scientific Club and was given honorary memberships in the St. Louis Commercial Club and the St. Louis Club. The Missouri National Guard offered him its highest command, which he declined, and it took Grover Cleveland to defeat him narrowly for election to the board of trustees of the prestigious Peabody Fund. He was president of a theater group, the McCullogh Club, and one of the founders of the more famous Players Club. He was given a membership in the Theta Chi fraternity at Norwich University in Vermont. He headed the New

York City Executive Committee of 100 to aid the sufferers of the famous Johnstown flood. In 1888 he joined New York's Union Club and became a nightly fixture in its clubrooms. Persons in all walks of life knew that association with him gave them and their organizations a stature they would otherwise not have, so they were pleased when he added his name to their rosters.[1]

Sherman joined these and other groups gladly because he enjoyed being among others and because it gave him experience with a changing variety of professions and individuals. His voracious curiosity pushed him forward to become involved in all he could. He even joined the politically oriented Grand Army of the Republic, helping to found the Ransom Post in St. Louis. Initially he hesitated because of the organization's involvement in politics, but he enjoyed the Civil War camaraderie the group fostered. He steadfastly refused repeated offers to be its president, preferring to be a mere delegate to national encampments. His fame, however, sometimes forced him to speak up anyway. Once some members of the organization, angry at President Grover Cleveland for ordering the return of Confederate battle flags (the order later withdrawn) and for vetoing veterans' pensions, threatened to snub him if he attended the 1887 encampment. Sherman called the threat of disrespect to the president "monstrous," and when Cleveland decided not to come, the matter blew over, and Sherman could return to the political silence he preferred.[2]

Chief among Sherman's public interests, besides his veterans and all their reunions and meetings, was the theater. He had seen his first performance in New York City on his way to West Point in the 1830s, and he never got over the sensation. He attended stage shows in San Francisco in the 1850s and in Memphis, Vicksburg, Nashville, Savannah, Chattanooga, and other places during the war. The theater relaxed him, and late in life he credited it as being "a potent factor" in his "health & cheerfulness." In 1887, in responding to a toast at a dinner of theater dignitaries, he said that "the stage contributes as much to the happiness and to the education of our people as almost any profession in life."[3]

Sherman was drawn to the theater because of the enjoyment he received from viewing the wide variety of productions available and hobnobbing with theater people. He loved Shakespeare, but there was much more to see than the Bard. New York was already the mecca of a thriving entertainment business. Melodramas, comedies, romances, and historical tragedies by American playrights abounded, and European imports were still in evidence. Costuming was extensive, often garish, and the backdrops and staging could be spectacular. The theater of Sherman's retirement years did not aim at the intellect as much as it enticed the wider masses through more popular, and thus less critically correct, productions. Even Shakespearean plays, Sherman's favorites, were sometimes altered to appeal to a wider audience, but Sherman never complained. He seemed captivated by the productions and by the show people, impressed with their ability to use the imagination in such a structured manner. As a military man who understood the importance of disciplined imagination, he found the work of the show people impressive.[4]

He attended plays regularly throughout the postwar years, and the older he became, the more he seemed drawn to them. He kept charge accounts at the major New York show places and dropped in regularly, sometimes with a group but often alone. He rarely sat through an entire play, seeing half one night and the rest the following evening, his restlessness and desire to do and see everything preventing him from remaining in one place too long. His appearance in the audience often produced a standing ovation, and he was a frequent visitor backstage, chatting with the actors and actresses, many of them personal friends. He was particularly close to Augustin Daly, the entrepreneur of one of the city's leading theaters and a major influence on popular theater, well-known actors Edwin Booth and Joe Jefferson, and beautiful actresses Mary Anderson and Ada Rehan, the latter Augustin Daly's leading lady. On one occasion in 1887, when Daly hosted a postplay dinner party on his stage, he asked Sherman to be his master of ceremonies. The party lasted until 5 A.M.[5]

Sherman was friendly with Buffalo Bill Cody from the days Cody served him as a scout in the fall of 1865. He attended Buffalo Bill's Wild West Show every chance he had, enjoying the staged sights and sounds of his beloved western frontier. "That man's a genius," he said to a friend once, so impressed was he with Cody's show business acumen. When Cody traveled to Europe, he took a letter of introduction from Sherman and kept Sherman informed of his activities, profusely thanking him for his interest and support. Sherman was a devotee of the circus, enjoying personal attention from the famous showman, P. T. Barnum, every time he attended. A reporter watching him during one of these visits noted how excited he was at everything he saw. He particularly seemed to enjoy Jumbo the elephant, the horses, the tumblers, the midgets, the giant, and the clowns. His laugh was loud and infectious. "He starts in a mouthful of wind," the reporter wrote, "which he expands in three or four short, jerky semi-guttural aspirations. It has a Scotch sound, something like 'Eh, hech! hech! hech! hech!' "[6]

His musical tastes remained common too. He occasionally attended the opera but generally disliked it and most formal chamber music, preferring Stephen Foster and songs taken from around the camp fire or a minstrel show. "Whether fashionable or not I intend to be honest and declare that I prefer 'Old Shady,' 'the Gum-tree Canoe,' 'Tramp, tramp, &c' to possess more music to my soul than the Trilogy of Wagner with the 'Dunder & Blitzen,' 'Gotter damerung,' and the *three* days of noise and banging without a single note of music like the last rose of summer.'" He grew sick of hearing "Marching Through Georgia," which every band felt it had to play in his honor, preferring the "Battle Hymn of the Republic."[7]

Although he never took up the painter's brush he had put down at Fort Moultrie in the 1840s, he maintained his love of the art. G. P. A. Healy and Daniel Huntington were among the famous artists who made portraits of him, and he sat for renowned sculptor Augustus Saint-Gaudens. He had numerous photographs made of himself and kept an album of likenesses of family and friends. He collaborated with Healy on *The Peacemakers*, a famous artistic rendition of the 1865 City Point meeting. Works by such other important painters like Albert Bierstadt hung on the walls of his homes and offices.[8]

He corresponded with a wide range of artists and freely commented on their work, advising them how he thought they might improve their art. When Newbold H. Trotter sent him his painting of an elk, Sherman advised the artist that the background was too clear for proper perspective and the snowline on the lower hills did not match that on the mountains. "A few dashes of snow in the lower ravines of the larger mountains will correct this," he concluded. One day, while a sculptor was working on the clay model for a bust of Grant, Sherman began making suggestions; then he ran his fingers over the moist clay and finally took a tool to reshape part of the model. It was characteristic of his curiosity and his talent in a variety of skills that he knew what to do. The artist almost panicked. Sherman also worked with James E. Taylor as the artist painted the Grand Review and the Union army's crossing of the Big Black River during the Vicksburg campaign. "Pictures like these . . . in one glance give a better idea than a hundred pages of the best descriptive writing," he said.[9]

He loved to ride, early in his life on horseback, later in a buggy or carriage. Every Sunday when he could, he explored the countryside. He always seemed to know where he was, even when he frequently cut across a field or encountered a more formidable obstacle, his memory for geography still sharp. He would stop at a friend's house for dinner and enjoy the fresh air and the farm talk. Inside the city, he used public transportation, unperturbedly jostling with all classes, not allowing his fame to prevent him from being among the common people.[10]

He read a great deal, owning a substantial library he purchased with government and personal funds. He kept close by such standard reference books like the sixteen volumes of the *American Cyclopaedia,* twelve volumes of the *Despatches of Wellington,* two volumes of Shakespeare's works, Buckle's three-volume *History of Civilization in England,* Bancroft's nine-volume *History of the United States,* the Bible, Colton's *Atlas,* and a book listing the public libraries in the United States. He perused these books frequently as he wrestled with his own writing and speeches or inquiries from old soldiers.[11]

He tried to read everything written on the Civil War, in book and magazine form, and he had a general interest in history. He thought John W. Draper's and the Comte de Paris's volumes on the war best told the story, and he admired Grant's *Memoirs.* He respected the historian Bancroft. His favorite author, however, was William Shakespeare. He attended his plays and frequently quoted him. But he admired other writers too. "Often have I hung on the mellifluous lines of Walter Scott, the impassioned lines of Lord Byron, and the inimitable verse of Robert Burns," he said. He read to his young children from Charles Dickens, Washington Irving, and Walter Scott and later in life advised Minnie that "Scott, Dickens, and Washington Irving [were] as necessary to fix the tastes of the young as was the Bible and Shakespeare" and "no home was complete without" them. "Every character of Dickens was an acquaintance of his," his daughter later remembered. Despite his love for the popular theater, he abhorred dime novels, newspaper comics, and what he called "trashy literature." He disliked Tolstoi's later realism but enjoyed reading Benjamin Franklin's advice to a young man on choosing a mistress when he discovered the essay in 1887.[12]

He did his writing and reading and even the greeting of most of his guests in the office he always maintained in every one of his houses. When he and the family lived in New York's Fifth Avenue Hotel from 1886 to 1888, he insisted the government provide him an office in the army building and a clerk to help him deal with the large number of inquiries he regularly received about the Civil War and other military matters. But he much preferred an office in his home, taking his clerk with him there when he purchased a house in New York in 1888.

He always put up a little tin sign in the window announcing: "Office of General Sherman." His desk, one reporter thought, had the "barren simplicity of a camp table." Photographs adorned the walls and mantels, three particularly prominent— Grant, Sheridan, and Sherman. Piles of books, papers, maps, and mementoes were everywhere. Here Sherman received callers, opened his mail, wrote, and talked at the same time, all without missing a beat. In later years he wore large, round, tortoise-shell reading glasses, presented to him by the Chinese minister, peering over them to see his caller or pushing them out of the way on his forehead.[13]

By the time he retired, his family had shrunk to half its previous size. Minnie married in 1873, Elly in 1880; Tom had joined the Jesuits in 1878. Still living at home were Lizzie who in 1884 was thirty-two, Rachel twenty-three, and Cumpy seventeen. Cumpy attended Catholic schools and then went to Yale, before becoming a lawyer and helping his father with family finances. He fulfilled the role Sherman had set for Tom, but his father regularly worried about any unspoken religious motivations he might have. Lizzie and Rachel served as Sherman's social aides, frequently taking Ellen's place at dinners, parties, and receptions. They became adult partners rather than children, though they always treated their "Papa" with the utmost respect. Their love for him was open and genuine, and he reciprocated in kind.

The older Ellen became, the less socially involved she became. She was particularly averse to the theater, Sherman's favorite pastime. She had developed the fear of theater fire and refused to enter a theater if she could help it. Sherman either took one of his daughters, some male or female friend, or he went alone. He had regular female companionship, but there was no Vinnie Ream or Mary Audenreid. If there were any serious flirtations, he kept them hidden.

Ellen had complained of illnesses all her life and, real or imagined, she used them as excuses for not participating in a wide variety of activities. In the prewar years and during the war itself, this created no major problem because she and Sherman were separated so much. But in the postwar period, especially while Sherman was commanding general of the army, he expected Ellen to be his partner in the social responsibilities that went with the job. On occasion she tried, but increasingly she balked. She wanted "peace and repose," he said, while he was "forced to mingle with the active elements of Government." He found it embarrassing to keep telling people she was sick when he knew she was not. Sherman suffered his own health problems, particularly asthma and a streptococcal inflammation called erysipelas. He had bouts of malaria and constipation. These rarely slowed him down, however, and he found it increasingly difficult to understand why Ellen could not be as resolute. He regularly accused her of being "lazy & hypochondriacal."[14]

All her life, going back to her youth, Ellen had suffered from large boils all over her body, and she regularly took medication against them. Whether it was the boils, the medicine, heart disease, a psychological problem, or a combination of all, Ellen grew increasingly stouter and slower moving. Her normal unwillingness to exercise increased and resulted in more weight and further lassitude. Her lifelong obsession with an afterlife intensified. "As I am incapable of taking any useful part in life & as I am drawing to the time of my departure from this world I must ask to be so situated as to be able to assist at Mass of mornings." By 1887 she was regularly complaining of breathing difficulties, at first insisting that living in New York's Fifth Avenue Hotel was responsible. Sherman solicitously took her to a hotel in the countryside but insisted it was not New York "but fat about the heart" that was the problem. Her doctor prescribed fresh air and exercise, but she steadfastly refused to rouse herself and kept looking for a better place to live. Sherman grew increasingly discouraged about her search.[15]

Her complaints drew no sympathy from him, and she was unhappy at his lack of understanding. She came to insist that, like him, she was actually suffering from asthma (how could he of all people not sympathize with her over that?). She told him she was not overweight. One afternoon in 1869, she pointedly remembered, she and Mrs. Grant had weighed themselves on a White House scale. She had weighed 150 pounds, Julia Grant, 175. Her present weight was only 165, "so I am not a monstrosity even yet, nor in danger of dying of mere fat." Sherman was not convinced. She might think it was asthma, but he knew it was being "stout."[16]

During this same period, asthma kept his throat and bronchial tubes regularly sore, and he had at least one rheumatism attack severe enough to force him to bed. He was fitted with a dental plate, had a wart removed from his face, and experienced a dizzy spell during an official function. He kept going, however, and he failed to see why she could not. But her constant demands and unwillingness to help herself, increasingly distressed him. Her boils kept returning; her breathing grew increasingly labored; and her ankles and feet were swelling. She complained more: "I have wondered how Job ever recovered & I have prayed to him to get me patience resembling his." She hoped she could live to see Tom ordained. She believed she was seriously ill; he refused to agree, disregarding the obvious facts before him.[17]

It particularly bothered Sherman that while they were grappling with this problem, Ellen was living in New Jersey, and he was in New York. "We should be together for better or worse, and I know of no better place *now*, than the Fifth Avenue Hotel." Sherman became convinced she was "a confirmed invalid—i.e., prefers to be sick and cannot or will not take exercise enough to be well." He thought she was doing as well as she had for the past twenty years. Ellen grew infuriated with his attitude, telling a brother "never [to] trust to his [Cump's] account of my condition in *any respect.*" "I am extremely weak," she said, "I certainly am not robust as Cump reports."[18]

The summer of 1888 saw no improvement. Her indigestion worsened, and Sherman grew frustrated when she decided to spend her time in Woodstock, Maryland, where Tom was stationed at the Jesuit house. To try to get her back, he decided to find a house in New York City. She seemed happy with his decision, but when she learned he planned to put the house in Cumpy's name, she exploded. What if he died? she demanded. Cumpy might marry and his wife would become "the mistress of the home I would have. How long do you think I would stay there? I would go to the Little Sisters of the Poor first." Sherman resolved the matter and bought and furnished the house, and Ellen happily moved in on September 24, 1888.[19]

The house, located at 75 West Seventy-first Street near Central Park and the Sixth Avenue elevated railroad, was a large, four-story brownstone. A basement contained a kitchen, storeroom, and Sherman's office. The first floor had two parlors, a dining room, and a hall. Cump's and Ellen's rooms were on the second floor; Lizzie's and Rachel's on the third floor; and Cumpy's and the servants' on the fourth floor. The family excitedly moved in, hoping the new surroundings would help Ellen feel better. Sherman tried to continue his busy round of correspondence, meetings, and the theater as he had all his life, trying to live with an increasingly sick wife whose illness he refused to acknowledge.

The strain had been proving too much for him for some time. Where previously he had clearly enjoyed his hectic schedule, now he began to complain about it. Ellen's illness and the deaths of Grant, Sheridan, and most of the other Civil War luminaries caused him to have to face his own mortality. He began to see himself as the "Last of the Mohicans," and the overwhelming number of insistent invitations from all over the country began to grate on his nerves. Sometimes he joked about it, as when he stood before the Society of the Army of the Potomac in 1887 and told a story about an old soldier named Benjamin deBonneville immortalized by Washington Irving. According to Sherman, Bonneville stayed away from the official army for two years and then reappeared before the adjutant general to collect his pay. The adjutant said: "Bonneville is dead." He responded: "I am not dead." "Oh, yes," insisted the adjutant, "you are dead; you are dead as a mackerel. Go away from here and don't disturb the record." That's just what he wanted, Sherman concluded. "Mark me dead and I won't turn up. . . . Let me alone and I will have some peace the rest of my days."[20]

But people continued to call on him as they always had, and he grew increasingly tired of it, feeling as though he was "on the go all the time" and could "expect little rest till I reach the cemetery." "These army meetings are becoming to me most oppressive and distasteful, because spite of my wishes they advertise me and exhibit me as a prominent animal in Barnum's show." He especially grew tired of listening to "Marching Through Georgia." During a Grand Army of the Republic (GAR) encampment, for example, every one of the 350 musical units that passed in review broke out into its strains. Sherman grew so exasperated that he said he would never come to another encampment until every band in the United States pledged not to play the song again.[21]

Sherman's growing unhappiness with his public life was a direct result of his problems at home. He continued to insist that Ellen was not sick, that she had chronically complained about her health as long as he had known her, and it was no different now. Deep down he knew better. Ellen was seriously ill, but he could not face that reality. If only she roused herself, she would get better, he kept saying. He tried all he could to talk her back to health, as he tried to talk and write his views of the war into reality. Nothing helped. Even the new house failed to revive her.

If anything, she grew worse. Her physician decided, in November, just two months after the move, to bring in a specialist from Philadelphia. Sherman agreed but still refused to believe her condition was serious. "Her father was exactly so for twenty years and lived to 83 yrs," he insisted. It was not until November 27 that he came to his senses. He telegraphed his brother John. "The doctors pronounce Ellen in a most precarious situation and I am forced to the same conclusion." He had already hired a nurse, but it was still difficult for him to accept the inevitable. On November 28, as he was reading in his office, the nurse called down to him that Ellen was dying. He ran up the two flights of stairs to her room calling out in anguish: "Wait for me Ellen, no one ever loved you as I loved you." It was too late; she was gone.[22]

Since he had never come to terms with Ellen's illness, her death came as a great shock. He became extremely depressed. A day after the funeral, asthma almost closed his throat, and soon after he failed to stir himself to escape the poison gas coming from a blown-out lamp. Condolences poured in from Presidents Hayes and Harrison, from old army friends in the North and South, from William Henry Seward, James Cardinal Gibbons, and even Vinnie Ream and her husband. There was a constant stream of visitors to his basement office, where he and his clerk, James M. Barrett, worked on acknowledgments. Grant's son Fred was a welcome visitor, as were hosts of Sherman's theater friends who lured him back to the plays. He told his former aide, John E. Tourtelotte, that of all the many deaths he had witnessed in his life, "hers was the easiest of all. In the last hour she seemed twenty years younger exactly like the Healy portrait . . . and as such I shall ever remember her. To her the world was a day—Heaven Eternity—and could I, I would not bring her back." Despite it all, Cump still loved Ellen, and he had, in her death, finally reconciled himself to her religious view of reality.[23]

But it was difficult. He missed having her always there, whether in person or the mails. Her passing resurrected in him the same urge toward suicide he had felt during the dark days of 1861–1862 in Kentucky and Missouri. Concern for his children had stayed his hand then, as it did now. "I see no reason to resort to suicide when I have children and grand children dependent on me, and when I seem to possess my usual faculties." Nostalgically, he recalled for an Ohio friend his childhood, his mother and his father, his grandmother, and Thomas Ewing. His mother "was a strong Presbyterian to the end," he remembered, "but she loved my Ellen, and the love was mutual. All my children inherit their mother's faith, and she would have given anything if I would have simply said Amen; but it was simply impossible." His thoughts ran to his old Civil War army, once more linking them to his personal family. He developed a sore throat and hoarseness in mid-December, and his shaky handwriting during this period displayed his feelings better than any words. His anchor was gone, and he wondered how he could continue without her.[24]

Slowly Sherman pulled out of the shock over his wife's death. His correspondence returned to more usual topics; he began going to public functions and the theater again, and in February Lizzie organized a series of dinners in honor of his sixty-ninth birthday. An even greater round of celebrations occurred in 1890 on his seventieth birthday. Sherman returned to the social whirl that made up so much of his life in the postwar years. He missed the security Ellen's presence gave him, but his life went on: touring, socializing, attending veterans' reunions, and remaining among the nation's leading personalities.

Increasingly, however, he began to show signs of reckoning with his own mortality. One day a young man excitedly rushed up to him. "You've been a landmark to me all my life," he said. "I've read about you in history." Sherman politely listened but later expressed his exasperation. "Lord! he looked at me with reverence and bowed down before me, and it was all I could do to be civil to him. Read about me in his history, indeed! as if I were Moses!" Sherman recognized his age and his physical limitations, but he did not want to believe his life was behind him. He saw himself as a "restless spirit"; he had much left to do and was not ready to be honored as a dead hero. In early February 1891 he was averaging four private or public dinners a week, answering his usual volume of mail, visiting family and friends, going to the theater, and exchanging conversation and gossip at the Union League Club.[25]

Still, he began referring to his inevitable demise. He saw time "fleet[ing] by with race horse speed" and on more than one occasion openly talked about the approach of death. When Schofield warned him in early 1891 that, considering his asthma problems, he should protect himself against colds, Sherman nodded gravely. "Yes," he said, laying a tightened fist against his chest. "It will catch me like that sometimes, and I will be gone." To General C. H. T. Collis, he was even more prophetic. "I feel it coming sometimes when I get home from an entertainment or banquet, especially these winter nights. I feel death reaching out for me, as it were. I suppose I'll take cold some night and go to bed never to get up again." And more tenderly, he told his dinner mates at a banquet in New York. "With me the warfare is nearly ended, and within a short time I shall join those who have gone before me." And then with tears in his eyes, he concluded: "In a little while, I will be sleeping with my wife and my soldier boy Willie."[26]

These premonitions did not, however, cause him to slow down. He continued his frenetic social activities. "Indeed for a 71 year old colt I manage to get a good deal of fun." At a January 31, 1891, Press Club dinner honoring H. M. Stanley of African fame, he responded to the toast to the "Old Army." In this last formal talk of his life, he discussed the ties of army history to the history of the nation. He told about an old officer he had served with at Fort Moultrie in the 1840s, who foolishly held on to the past until the day he died. "He is gone," Sherman concluded, "like nearly all of his type, but we realize that new boys are born as good as those in the past; they grow up into stout manhood and will take our places and be none the worse for the old traditions of courage, manhood, and fidelity passed down to them legitimately by the "old army." Sherman seemed to be preparing his audience and himself for the inevitable.[27]

Five days later, on Wednesday, February 4, Sherman attended the theater. He went home in fine spirits, but the next morning, he had a severe cold. Though coughing and complaining of his symptoms, he attended a wedding that afternoon. On Friday he felt worse, his throat now severely sore, and he canceled a dinner engagement at the Union League Club with the actor Lawrence Barrett. On Saturday morning, he broke out with an old problem, a streptococcal inflammation that turned his face and nose deep red. He also had a fever. He called army surgeon Charles J. Alexander, his longtime physician, but Alexander provided no relief. By Sunday, his seventy-first birthday, the redness had spread over his face and neck, and he had difficulty talking. He spent most of the day reading one of his favorite authors, Charles Dickens: *Great Expectations.* On Monday, Alexander called in a consulting physician, but Sherman's cold and the inflammation had so worsened his chronic asthma that his family was called to his bedside. His face was now badly swollen and painted with iodine. He became so excited at the first-arriving children that the doctor asked the late-arriving eldest daughter, Minnie, not to go in and overstimulate her father again. When Cump noticed his brother, John, he grew upset, but the assurance that the senator was in New York on business calmed him. Meanwhile hectic attempts were being made to reach Father Tom Sherman aboard an ocean liner sailing to the United States.

Sherman grew increasingly weak; every movement was painful, and he was taking only whiskey and milk for nourishment. On Tuesday the nation's press announced his illness and began publishing regular bulletins. Wednesday to Friday, February 11 to the 13, his condition momentarily improved as the inflammation subsided, but his long-time enemy, asthma, increasingly ravaged him. On Thursday, he was unconscious, and his family, despite his lifetime of refusal to accept Catholicism, had a priest administer the last rites of the Catholic church and lead them in praying the rosary. Like their mother, they believed that, otherwise, his soul would be lost. That afternoon and evening he rallied, getting out of bed and walking to a nearby chair, momentarily clearing his lungs from the pneumonia that had settled there. Now and then, despite his swollen tongue and stiff jaw, he said a few words to those around him, but it was never clear whether he recognized anyone. His most emphatic words were those he wanted inscribed on his monument. "Faithful & honorable; faithful & honorable," he insisted several times.

On Sunday, February 14 at 4 A.M., his family gathered in his room. Two hours later he began to experience breathing problems, the chloroform plasters on his chest proving ineffective. He battled on though. About 1:30 P.M., his extremities began growing cold. His head was lowered from his large pillow to try to help him breathe more easily, but his lungs were filled with mucus, and he was suffocating. At 1:50 P.M. he sighed and died. His left hand lay across his chest as though he was giving the familiar sergeant's salute. Watching in sadness were Cumpy, Minnie, Elly, Lizzie, and Rachel; his two sons-in-law, Fitch and Thackara; John Sherman; Tom Ewing, Jr.; Dr. Alexander; and nurse Elizabeth Price. Generals Slocum and Howard waited in another room. As soon as Sherman breathed his last, one of his servants stepped outside and told the waiting crowd that had gathered in the street: "It is all over." That evening sculptors Daniel Chester French and Augustus Saint-Gaudens made a plaster cast of his face.[28]

Telegrams and letters poured in from all over the nation in response to news of Sherman's illness. Among the most famous well-wishers were Mark Twain; President Benjamin Harrison, a regimental and brigade commander under Sherman during the Atlanta campaign; Vinnie Ream Hoxie; Mrs. Robert Anderson, the widow of the hero of Fort Sumter; and England's imperialist statesman, Joseph Chamberlain. Newsman Murat Halstead suggested Pond's Extract for Sherman's inflammation; an Episcopal clergyman offered his services, knowing, he said, that Sherman was not a Catholic.[29]

Even in his death, Sherman provoked his old antagonists, the press, into controversy. A *New York Times* reporter insinuated that the family had taken advantage of John Sherman's momentary absence to sneak in a priest, have him administer the last rites, and thus be able to claim that the general was a Catholic. The normally calm John Sherman became so upset at this political and personal attack that he fired back a sharp response. Everyone knew that he and the general were not Catholics, though Ellen Sherman had practiced that faith and had raised the general's children in her religion. Sherman was "too good a Christian and too human a man to deny to his children the consolations of their religion," John insisted. Had he been conscious at the time, he would still have agreed to the rites for his children's sake. If he had been there himself, John Sherman concluded, he would have similarly agreed. Besides, newsmen should stop intruding on a grieving family's privacy.[30]

Newspeople could hardly ignore the story of the last days of a national hero and provided the minutest details of Sherman's demise. The day he died, President Harrison issued an official announcement, and Congress adjourned for the day. Several senators and representatives, a number of them Sherman's former soldiers, gave eulogies in his honor. State legislatures held memorial sessions, as did the Grand Army of the Republic, the Military Order of the Loyal Legion of the United States, churches, schools, and political clubs. The William Lloyd Garrison Local Assembly No. 8266 of the Knights of Labor and the GAR post in Augusta, Georgia, passed memorial resolutions. Sherman's own GAR unit, the Ransom Post in St. Louis, prepared to fulfill the duty he had given it just the year before: to escort his body to its final resting place next to his wife and children in St. Louis's Calvary Cemetery.[31]

Personal condolences flooded into the family home in New York. There were leading political figures like the president, ex-president Rutherford B. Hayes, Secretary of State James G. Blaine, Missouri governor David R. Francis, chief justice of the United States Melville W. Fuller, Justice John Marshall Harlan, former Union officer and ex-Alabama senator Willard Warner, and former secretaries of state William Henry Seward, Hamilton Fish, and William M. Evarts; former military colleagues Grenville M. Dodge, J. E. Tourtelotte, John M. Corse, J. D. Cox, George Meade, John Pope, Fitz-John Porter, Henry W. Slocum, John M.

Schofield, O. O. Howard, the West Point Corps of Cadets, George Armstrong Custer's widow, old Confederate adversary Joseph E. Johnston, and survivors of the First Battalion of the Thirteenth U.S. Infantry, the beloved unit Cump had promised never to forget for befriending Willy Sherman; newspapermen Murat Halstead, Whitelaw Reid, H. M. Stanley, and the New York Press Club; Archbishops Peter Richard Kenrick of St. Louis and Michael Corrigan of New York; Edward Sorin, the president of Notre Dame; actor Lawrence Barrett, Buffalo Bill Cody, and members of the Players Club, a theater group Sherman had helped organize; artist George Healy; Civil War historian the Comte de Paris; old friend from Louisiana days, David F. Boyd; and Blakely Durant, the former slave Sherman had known during the war and helped immortalize in popular song as "Old Shady."[32]

Newspapers all over the nation gave extended coverage to the death and funeral, as well as to the contributions of the deceased. Most ranked him high as a soldier and a human being. The *Chicago Herald* called his march to the sea "the first colossal demonstration of the superior intellectual acumen and moral strength of the northern leadership." The *New York Herald* said, "He will live forever in the 'mansions not made with hands,' and live forever in the hearts of a grateful people." The *San Francisco Examiner* printed three columns of praise, proudly noting his California ties. The *Minneapolis Tribune* said he was an "IMMORTAL HERO," while the *Cleveland Leader* called him "A GRAND, NOBLE, AND LOVABLE CHARACTER."[33]

Even the South joined the eulogizing. The faculty of his old school, Louisiana State University, published in the Baton Rouge press their resolution that, in Sherman's passing, "the nation has lost a distinguished soldier and prominent citizen . . . [and] a staunch friend to this Institution and to the cause of education in general." In New York a group of former Confederate soldiers, the Confederate Veteran Camp, held a special meeting and appointed a delegation to attend the funeral. In the Senate, John Tyler Morgan of Alabama said: "We differed with him and contested campaigns and battlefields with him to the bitter end, but we welcome the history of the great soldier as the proud inheritance of our country. We do this as cordially and as sincerely as we gave him welcome in the South." In the House, Sherman's former Confederate cavalry antagonist, Joe Wheeler, now U.S.

representative from Alabama, finished his extended tribute by saying: "Mr. Speaker, I will not dwell longer, further than to say that I feel that the entire country, the South together with the North, the Confederate with the Federal, forgetting all of the feelings of the past, join in the deep grief which has befallen our country in the death of this distinguished man."[34]

Even elements of the Southern press shared these good feelings. The *Atlanta Constitution* said that "when all is said that can be said, the fact looms up that this man was one of the greatest soldiers of the age. . . . But when the business of war was over— when he had accomplished his mission—he showed a softer side, and men and women, even among his former foes, found him a very lovable man." The *Louisville Times* was not similarly kind. "The death of General Sherman will occasion no pang at the South," it insisted. "Under his generalship war became rapine." The *Richmond Times* agreed that the South could not forget "the useless vandalism and inhumanity which marked his progress," but, then again, he "did nothing to add to the humiliation of this section." The *Knoxville Sentinel* noted that the march to the sea was "to some a term of endearment, to others one of bitterest regret," but "as a military chieftain . . . [he had] few equals . . . and the Nation may mourn [his death] in profound sympathy."[35]

The acclaim from Europe was similarly laudatory. Newspapers and magazines all over the Continent published long articles detailing Sherman's life and praising his military brilliance. Prussian general Helmuth von Moltke said that by virtue of his march to the sea, Sherman "stood brilliantly to the front as a strategist," while Britain's J. F. Maurice praised his Atlanta campaign. A coterie of other European military leaders agreed, sometimes in grandiose words.[36]

While his contemporaries discussed his legacy, plans for his internment proceeded. He had long insisted that he wanted a simple funeral, so the family politely rejected the president's suggestion that his body lay in state in the U.S. Capitol rotunda. Original plans called for no wake. His body was simply to be placed in the casket he himself had chosen (just like Ellen's) and then immediately be sent to St. Louis for burial, under supervision of the military. Sherman was, however, too important a figure to be buried that quietly. At the request of old friends, neighbors, and a variety of acquaintances, the casket was opened and placed in the first-floor drawing room of his home for public viewing. For two days a steady stream of mourners of all ages and social classes passed through the room perfumed by a large mass of flowers and lighted by six flickering candles. An American flag draped the casket and upon it were Sherman's hat, his spurs, a sword, and a scabbard. A simple engraved silver plate noted his full name, his rank, and his birth and death dates. The body was dressed in full uniform, including the sash of the Legion of Honor. Only his normally stubby beard appeared longer than usual.[37]

Sherman's children and his brother asked two of his closest living military colleagues, O. O. Howard and Henry W. Slocum, to organize the logistics of the funeral. Former Confederate general Joseph E. Johnston was an honorary pallbearer. On Thursday, February 19, after a brief Catholic ceremony conducted by Father Tom Sherman, just arrived from Europe, the casket was slowly carried down the house stairs to the street. The pallbearers, Johnston among them, stood with bare heads in the brisk wind. Someone expressed concern for Johnston, whose own health was weak: "General, put on your hat, you will take cold." The old Confederate refused. "If I were in his place and he standing here in mine he would not put on his hat," he said. He died five weeks later.[38]

Sherman's funeral procession slowly wound its way through the streets of New York. In the line of march were the family, political and military dignitaries, and ordinary former soldiers from all over the country. The day was crisp and sunny, and the crowds numbered in the tens of thousands as the procession turned onto Fifth Avenue. People climbed trees and signs and lamp posts to see better. House tops and balconies were crowded, and the throng spilled out into the street, making it difficult for the police to keep a path open for the procession. There was an eerie silence as people bared heads, bowed, or saluted in tribute to the passing casket, drawn on a caisson by four artillery horses. Only the sound of the muffled drums, the funeral dirge, and the slowly tolling bells broke the silence. Observers could only point to Grant's funeral five years previously to think of any rival to this impressive event.[39]

Sherman would have appreciated the procession's military precision as it bore his body to the tip of Manhattan for ferry transport to the waiting Pennsylvania Railroad train in Jersey City. It probably would have reminded him of his pride for his troops during the Grand Review of Union armies in 1865. And he certainly would have agreed with the disdain, an Irish woman, with a heavy brogue, expressed at some passing politicians. Noting former President Grover Cleveland in his open carriage, she spoke out above the otherwise silent crowd: "AND WHAT IS HE DOING AT SUCH A DACANT MAN'S FUNERAL!!"[40]

The eight-car train left Jersey City on schedule. In keeping with Sherman's wishes not to have "his body taken about like Gen. Grant's had been,"[41] the train took a direct route to St. Louis and stopped only when necessary. In Philadelphia, the car containing the president and his party was uncoupled, and the train proceeded with seven cars. First in line was the heavily draped funeral car, its door opened so waiting crowds could see the casket inside. From the ceiling hung a lamp casting a dim shadow on the flag-drapped casket, the mass of flowers, the saddle, boots, and spurs. The honor guard inhabited a separate compartment in the same car. The family, pallbearers, military escort, and various other dignitaries filled five cars.

The train sped its way across country past crowds along the tracks, making no stops. Those aboard saw a nation in mourning. "Now they saw a farmer and his family with bared heads before their home in the midst of the fields; now it was a line of men at a village station; again it was thousands upon thousands drawn up in the cities with presented arms. Above the rattle of the wheels could be heard sometimes the roll of a drum, the peal of a church bell; sometimes the heavy solemn music of a band playing a hymn; sometimes the boom of a cannon." In Pittsburgh where the train changed engines, the tracks were lined with people all the way through the city, and at the station, veterans placed faded and torn battle flags around the casket.

In Ohio, there seemed to be decorations on every building, and school children could be heard singing as the train rushed by. In Columbus, twenty thousand mourners filled the station. The fresh engine carried Sherman's picture above its headlight and below: "Ohio's Son, the Nation's Hero." The caravan traveled through the Buckeye State and then into Indiana and Illinois. Everywhere it passed, people paid their respects. Ex-president Rutherford B. Hayes noted that "the faces of all [were] solemn and full of sympathy [and] some [were] weeping." The train arrived in St. Louis to the roar of cannons.[42]

The funeral procession in St. Louis rivaled that in New York, the large crowds equally solemn and respectful. Sherman's former staff member, Henry M. Hitchcock, and Western Sanitary Commission leader, James E. Yeatman, had organized the proceedings, and General Wesley Merritt handled the military, the Ransom Post GAR playing a conspicuous role. A little-known poet caught the essence of the event in a verse of one of the many popular poems composed about Sherman's passing:

> The tramp, tramp, tramp of soldiery,
>   is heard upon the street,
> The death march they are treading now
>   with slow and reverent feet,
> The bells in mournful monotone
>   their funeral dirges toll—
> The muffled drums their throbs of woe,
>   upon the soft air roll.
> Once more the bugle blast is heard
>   resounding through the air:—
> It calleth not to action now—
>   but to repose—to prayer.
> A few who bravely followed
>   in that long march to the sea,
> With silvered locks, now bear their chief,
>   in state, to Calvary.[43]

When the procession reached the cemetery, the military units formed a pathway of two columns for the casket and main body of mourners. Near the grave site, eight husky soldiers bore the flag-draped casket on their shoulders to its final resting place. Father Tom Sherman conducted the Catholic ceremony for the dead, displaying such self-control that O. O. Howard later asked him how he had avoided tears. The priest, a true son of his father, smiled and responded with a question of his own: "General, do you know what it is to obey orders?"

As the solemn religious words disappeared into the vastness of the crowd and surrounding landscape, riflemen from Sherman's Thirteenth Infantry fired a volley of three shots, responded to by a battery of distant artillery. A lone musician stood next to the grave site, and sounded "Taps" over the remains. The mourners noted Ellen's monument with the words "In Thee, O Lord, have I hoped" chiseled in the stone beneath her name and dates. Nearby were the monuments to the two deceased children: "Little Sergeant Willie" and Charles Celestine. Soon standing there would be the simple ten-foot monument to Sherman containing his name, dates, and, as he had insisted, the words: "Faithful and Honorable."[44]

He was that. He adhered to his nation, his profession, his wife, and his family. He was true to his word, in war and in peace. He was genuine, never losing the sense of his true self no matter how difficult the times or how important he became. He was constant and devoted, trustworthy and steadfast. He was not perfect—far from it—but he was not the brute of popular legend either. He was a complicated individual who despite his shortcomings did great things and became deserving of respect, admiration, and allegiance. He brought distinction and integrity to whatever he did, whether he ultimately succeeded or failed. In his later years, he was one of the era's most distinguished public figures, and the public adulation he received was a mark of a nation's genuine deference and affection.

William Tecumseh Sherman chose his own epitaph, "Faithful and Honorable," and it was an accurate assessment of a life that had never been easy but was accomplished. He never attained the order he so passionately strove for, but in the search, he achieved a fame given to few people. He remained a soldier always, the Civil War the defining moment of his life. Here he attached himself to his nation and its cause. Without his presence on its battlefields, the United States might not have remained whole. Without it, he might never have found himself. His epitaph finally came down to this: He helped preserve the Union; he was proud of it; and he wanted even those who disagreed with him then, and those who came after him later, to honor his faithfulness to its preservation and to himself.

NOTES

---- ☆ ----

ABBREVIATIONS

Adec	Andre de Coppet Collection
AJ	Andrew Johnson, Andrew Johnson Papers
AL	Abraham Lincoln
BC	Bowdoin College Library
BL	Bancroft Library, University of California, Berkeley
BLY	Beinecke Rare Books and Manuscripts Library, Yale University
CE	Charles Ewing, Charles Ewing Papers
CHH	Clinton H. Haskell Collection
CHS	California Historical Society, San Francisco
CRS	Charles R. Sherman
CU	Columbia University, Rare Books and Manuscripts Library
CWM	Charles W. Moulton
DFB	David French Boyd, David French Boyd Papers
DDP	David Dixon Porter, David Dixon Porter Papers
DU	Duke University, Special Collections Department, William R. Perkins Library
EFP	Ewing Family Papers
EMS	Edwin M. Stanton, Edwin M. Stanton Papers
ER	Elizabeth Sherman Reese
ES	Ellen Boyle Ewing Sherman
ESF	Eleanor Sherman Fitch
EST	Eleanor Mary Sherman Thackara (Elly)
GAR	Grand Army of the Republic

GMG	G. Mason Graham
G.O.	General Orders
HB	Hiram Barney Collection
HBE	Hugh Boyle Ewing, Hugh Boyle Ewing Papers
HL	Huntington Library
HLH	Houghton Library, Harvard University
HMH	Henry M. Hitchcock, Henry M. Hitchcock Papers
HPC	Rutherford B. Hayes Presidential Center
HSPa	Historical Society of Pennsylvania
HST	Henry S. Turner
HWH	Henry W. Halleck, Henry W. Halleck Papers
IHS	State Historical Society of Iowa
ISL	Illinois State Historical Library
JAC	James A. Connolly
JAG	James A. Garfield, James A. Garfield Papers
JAH	James A. Hardie, James A. Hardie Papers
JAL	John A. Logan, John A. Logan Papers
JAR	John A. Rawlins
JEJ	Joseph E. Johnston
JGB	James G. Blaine, James G. Blaine Papers
JMS	John M. Schofield, John M. Schofield Papers
JS	John Sherman, John Sherman Papers
JTD	John T. Doyle
JWD	John W. Draper, John W. Draper Papers
LC	Library of Congress
LSU	Louisiana State University, Louisiana and Lower Mississippi Valley Collections, LSU Libraries
MA	Mary Audenreid
MaHS	Massachusetts Historical Society
MBE	Maria Boyle Ewing
MES	Mary Elizabeth Sherman (Lizzie)
MiHS	Minnesota Historical Society

MoHS	Missouri Historical Society
MOLLUS	Military Order of the Loyal Legion of the United States
MSA	Mary Elizabeth Sherman Fitch Armstead
MSF	Maria Ewing Sherman Fitch (Minnie)
NAM	Nelson A. Miles, Nelson A. Miles Papers
NARS	National Archives and Records Service
NCDH	North Carolina Division of Archives and History
NYPL	New York Public Library, Astor, Lenox and Tilden Foundations, Rare Books and Manuscripts Division
NYT	*New York Times*
OHS	Ohio Historical Society
OOH	Oliver Otis Howard
Ord	E. O. C. Ord
O.R.	*War of the Rebellion . . . Official Records of the Union and Confederate Armies*
PBE	Philemon Boyle Ewing, Philemon Boyle Ewing Papers
PHS	Philip H. Sheridan, Philip H. Sheridan Papers
PTS	P. Tecumseh Sherman
PU	Princeton University Library
RA	Robert Anderson, Robert Anderson Papers
RST	Rachel Ewing Sherman Thorndike
R.G.	Record Group
SCL	South Carolina, University of, South Caroliniana Library
SCW	Schoff Civil War Collection
S.F.O.	Special Field Orders
SFP	Sherman Family Papers
SH	Sherman House, Fairfield Heritage Association
SHMB	S. H. M. Byers, S. H. M. Byers Papers
S.O.	Special Orders
ST	Sherman-Thackara Papers
TE	Thomas Ewing, Thomas Ewing Papers
TE, Jr.	Thomas Ewing, Jr.

TS	Thomas Ewing Sherman
UNDA	Archives of the University of Notre Dame
USMHI	United States Military History Institute
USG	Ulysses S. Grant, Ulysses S. Grant Papers
USMA	United States Military Academy Library, Special Collections Division
VFM	Vertical File Material
VHS	Virginia Historical Society
VRH	Vinnie Ream Hoxie
VU	Villanova University, Falvey Memorial Library
WLC	William L. Clements Library, University of Michigan
WLF	Walter L. Fleming Papers
WRHS	Western Reserve Historical Society
WTS	William T. Sherman, William T. Sherman Papers
WTS, Jr.	William T. Sherman, Jr. (Willy)
WW	Willard Warner, Willard Warner Papers
WWB	W. W. Belknap
YL	Yale University Library, Manuscripts and Archives

CHAPTER 1 UNSTABLE BEGINNINGS

1. TE to ES, February 13, 1865, cited by Paul I. Miller, "Thomas Ewing, Last of the Whigs," (Ph.D. diss., Ohio State University, 1933), 13.

2. Information on Sherman family genealogy is located in *John Sherman's Recollections of Forty Years in the House, Senate and Cabinet* (Chicago, 1895), 1:1–14; WTS, *Memoirs of General W. T. Sherman* (New York, 1990), 1:9–11; Thomas Townsend Sherman, *Sherman Genealogy* (New York, 1920), 14; undated, untitled notes, Box 6, SFP, UNDA; De B. Randolph Keim, *Sherman, a Memorial* . . . (Washington, D.C., 1904), 126–29.

3. WTS may also have been related to General Winfield Scott through his mother's line. See Arthur Maynard to ESF, May 31, 1952, and undated, untitled typed sheet following this letter, Box 10, SFP, UNDA. WTS never claimed Scott and even regularly denied any significant tie to Roger Sherman. See WTS to PTS, March 15, 1888, two letters, WTS, OHS; WTS to JTD, March 22, 1886, WTS, CHS.

4. Information on CRS is found in William R. Reese to Tom O. Edwards, January 1, 1872, Sherman-Ewing Pamphlets, vol. 1, OHS; JS, "Memorandum of Life of Charles R. Sherman & Pedigree of Hoyt family," February 1847, unpublished, SFP, UNDA; *John Sherman's Recollections*, 1, 15–23; Charles Wiseman, *Centennial History of Lancaster Ohio and Lancaster People* (Lancaster, 1898), 53–57.

5. Taylor Sherman to CRS, August 24, 1810, copies in CRS, OHS, and SFP, UNDA.

6. The sketch of Lancaster and Fairfield County is based on the following sources: Charles M. L. Wiseman, *Pioneer Period and Pioneer People of Fairfield County Ohio* (Columbus, 1901); Hervey Scott, *A Complete History of Fairfield County, Ohio,* (Columbus, 1877); A. A. Graham, comp., *History of Fairfield and Perry Counties, Ohio* (Chicago, 1883); Charles C. Miller, *History of Fairfield County, Ohio and Representative Citizens* (Chicago, 1912); Norris F. Schneider and Clair C. Stebbins, *Zane's Trace* (Zanesville, Ohio, 1973); Laura E. Kerr, *Campfire to Courthouse, An Early History of Fairfield County, Ohio* (Lancaster, 1981). The initial quotation is from S. Winifred Smith, "The Sherman House," *Museum Echoes* 29 (September 1956): 67.

7. CRS to R. J. Meigs, August 24, 1813, CHH, WLC.

8. John J. Patrick, "John Sherman: The Early Years, 1823–1865" (Ph.D. diss., Kent State University, 1982), 6–7.

9. Author's tour of Sherman House, June 1984; Sherman House brochure, Fairfield Heritage Association; Smith, "The Sherman House," 67–70; WTS, "Autobiography 1828–1861," unpublished manuscript, 1–2, WTS, OHS; WTS, speech, April 7, 1888, in James H. Kennedy, *History of the Ohio Society of New York* (New York, 1906), 60.

10. Reese to Edwards, January 1, 1872, WTS Pamphlets, OHS. All the evidence indicates that CRS never met Tecumseh. WTS to William Stanley Hatch, November 22, 1872, WTS, ISL; E. K. Burnett to ESF, March 22, 1945, SFP, UNDA.

11. WTS, *Memoirs*, 1:12; Reese to Edwards, January 1, 1872, WTS Pamphlets,

OHS; WTS to Dewitt Talmage, December 12, 1888, copy, Box 6, SFP, UNDA; WTS, "Autobiography," 2–3; Jared Young, "General Sherman's Puritan Heritage," *Eugenical News* 13 (August 1928): 109.

12. WTS, "Autobiography," 3–4.

13. Henry Stoddard to E. Schofield, P. Beecher, C. King, TE, and other friends of CRS, June 25, 1829, Henry Stoddard to Mary Sherman, June 29, 1829, copies, SFP, UNDA.

14. *John Sherman's Recollections*, 1:28–29; WTS, "Autobiography," 4–5; Sherman, *Sherman Genealogy*, 319–26; WTS to MSF, June 23, 1887, WTS, OHS.

15. A convenient compilation of important literature on a father's influence on his children is Michael E. Lamb, ed., *The Role of the Father in Child Development* (New York, 1981).

16. Unless otherwise noted, the following information on TE is derived from Paul I. Miller, "Thomas Ewing, Last of the Whigs" (Ph.D. diss., Ohio State University, 1933); Clement L. Martzloff, ed., "Autobiography of Thomas Ewing," Ohio Archaeological and Historical Society, *Publications* 22 (1913): 126–204; TE, "Autobiographical Sketch," in Charles M. Walker, *History of Athens County, Ohio* (Cincinnati: 1869), 395–404; *A Biographical Record of Fairfield and Perry Counties* (New York, 1902), 352–58; Silvia T. Zsoldos, "The Political Career of Thomas Ewing, Sr." (Ph.D. diss., University of Delaware, 1977).

17. John Bownocker, *Salt Deposits and the Salt Industry in Ohio*, in *Report of the Geological Survey of Ohio*, (Columbus, December 1906), vol. 9, pamphlet 8, p. 12.

18. TE to MBE, January 12, 1833, TE, LC.

19. MBE to TE, December 4, 7, 1832, EFP, UNDA; Cincinnati *Enquirer*, n.d., in EFP, UNDA.

20. WTS to T. Dewitt Talmage, December 12, 1888, copy, SFP, UNDA; WTS, speech, February 19, 1890, in James H. Kennedy, *History of the Ohio Society of New York* (New York, 1906), 91; NYT, February 20, 1890.

21. ESF, undated notes, MSF; "Tribute to Ellen Ewing Sherman," unpublished 1892 manuscript, SFP, UNDA.

22. ES, "Recollections for My Children," unpublished manuscript, October 28, 1880, WTS, OHS; Ellie Ewing Brown, "Notes on the Boyhood of Philemon Beecher Ewing and William Tecumseh Sherman," unpublished manuscript, c. 1932, SFP, UNDA.

23. TE to MBE, December 9, 1831, cited by Miller, "Thomas Ewing," 14. Edward Chase, *The Memorial Life of General William Tecumseh Sherman* (Chicago, 1891), 11.

24. See, for example, WTS to TE, January 16, 1832, January 4, 1833, EFP, UNDA, and March 4, 1832, in Joseph H. Ewing, ed., "Sherman Bashes the Press," *American Heritage* 38 (July–August 1987): 24–25, and April 22, 1832, TE, LC; TE to MBE, January 29, 1828, March 5, December 9, 25, 1831, copies, SFP, UNDA; Alice M. Jordan, *From Rollo to Tom Sawyer* (Boston, 1948), 61–71; Jane Bingham and Grayce Scholt, *Fifteen Centuries*

of Children's Literature (Westport, Conn., 1980), 169–70; Anne Scott MacLeod, *A Moral Tale: Children's Fiction and American Culture, 1820–1860* (Hamden, Conn., 1975), 24–25, 37–46.

25. MBE to TE, January 3, March 16, 1832, EFP, UNDA: Brown, "Notes."

26. MSF, "Tribute," SFP, UNDA; HBE, "Autobiography of a Tramp," manuscript, HBE, OHS.

27. WTS, "Autobiography," 1, 3–4, unpublished manuscript, WTS, OHS.

28. Ibid., 1, 5; MBE to TE, December 26, 1833, January 12, March 26, 1834, PBE to TE, April 23, 1834, SFP, UNDA; MBE to TE, December 6, 1833, EFP, UNDA; E. V. Smalley, "General Sherman," *Century* 5 (January 1884): 452; J. P. Thompson, "Major-General William T. Sherman," *Hours at Home* 1 (November 1865): 12.

29. Grenville M. Dodge, *Personal Recollections* . . . (Council Bluffs, Iowa), 133; MBE to TE, January 3, 1832, EFP, UNDA; Brown, "Notes."

30. WTS to TE, January 16, 1832, MBE to TE, February 12, 1831, EFP, UNDA; Brown, "Notes"; HBE, "Autobiography," 12; Albert G. Brackett, "General William T. Sherman," *United Services Magazine* n.s. 5 (June 1891): 580.

31. WTS, "Autobiography," 4–5.

32. Dodge, *Personal Recollections*, 132–33, NYT, February 20, 1890; Brown, Notes; HBE, "Autobiography," 12. The composer of "Dixie," Daniel Decature Emmett, allegedly grew up with WTS in Lancaster. H. A. Smith, "The Culture of 'Dixie,'" *Confederate Veteran* 40 (1932): 17. WTS never mentioned Emmett.

33. Brown, "Notes"; HBE, "Autobiography," 9–10.

34. Charles C. Miller, *History of Fairfield County, Ohio and Representative Citizens* (Chicago, 1912), 325; Brown, "Notes"; HBE, "Autobiography," 6–7.

35. HBE, "Autobiography," 7.

36. WTS to T. Dewitt Talmadge, December 12, 1888, copy, SFP, UNDA; WTS to William Henry Smith, June 26, 1885, WTS, LC.

37. Brown, "Notes"; HBE, "Autobiography," 33–34.

38. MBE to TE, December 1834, copy, SFP, UNDA.

39. WTS to HBE, July 2, 1873, SFP, UNDA; Frederick Capaldi and Barbara McRae argue that "many stepchildren feel caught between their feelings of love and identification with the natural parent who is absent and their growing respect (possibly even love) for and identification with the stepparent. For most, it is often described as an either/or proposition. They are caught in 'the middle.'" Frederick Capaldi and Barbara McRae, *Stepfamilies: A Comparative Responsibility* (New York, 1979).

40. A measure of nineteenth-century success, one author points out, "was to do better than your father." Richard M. Huber, *The American Idea of Success* (New York, 1971), 81.

41. WTS, speech, in *Proceedings of 8th Reunion of the Army of the Cumberland*, September 16, 17, 1878, p. 86.

42. TE to MBE, December 22, 1833, TE, LC.

43. TE to Louis Cass, August 1, 1835, SFP, UNDA.

44. TE to Cass, March 6, 1836, Mary Sherman to Cass, April 4, 1836, WTS to C.ass, April 4, 1836, SFP, UNDA. See also WTS Application Papers, R.G. 94, NARS.

45. WTS, *Memoirs*, 1:14; Harry N. Scheiber, *Ohio Canal Era . . .* (Athens, Ohio, 1969), 102; Silvia T. Zsoldos, "The Political Career of Thomas Ewing, Sr." (Ph.D. diss., University of Delaware, 1977), 12.

46. Unless otherwise indicated, this account of WTS's journey to West Point is based on his *Memoirs*, 1:14–15.

47. WTS to MBE, June 2, 1836, WTS, UNDA.

48. *Boston Globe*, January 22, 1888, in SFP, UNDA; WTS, "Autobiography, 1828–1861," 7, unpublished manuscript, WTS, OHS; WTS, speech, April 7, 1888, in James H. Kennedy, *History of the Ohio Society of New York* (New York, 1906), 61; WTS to ES, July 15, 1873, TE Memorial, OHS, p. 68.

49. WTS to HBE, January 25, 1844, HBE, OHS. This letter is also in John F. Marszalek, ed., "William T. Sherman on West Point—A Letter," *Assembly* 30 (Summer 1971): 14–15, 38; and in *Civil War Times Illustrated* 10 (January 1972): 22–23.

50. Stephen E. Ambrose, *Duty, Honor, Country: A History of West Point* (Baltimore, 1966), 148; WTS to PBE, February 17, 1839, PBE, OHS.

51. Ambrose, *Duty*, 90, 124; James L. Morrison, Jr., "Educating the Civil War Generals: West Point, 1833–1861," *Military Affairs* 38 (October 1974): 108.

52. John W. Brinsfield, "The Military Ethics of General William T. Sherman: A Reassessment," *Parameters* 12 (June 1982): 39–40.

53. James L. Morrison, Jr., *"The Best School in the World": West Point, the Pre–Civil War Years* (Kent, Ohio, 1986), 47–51; Ambrose, *Duty* 91–102; Sidney Forman, *A History of the United States Military Academy* (New York, 1950), 52–53; Thomas J. Fleming, *West Point: The Men and Times of the United States Military Academy* (New York, 1969), 111; WTS to Robert W. Weir, July 21, 1876, WTS, LC.

54. Morrison, *The Best School*, 40–42; Fleming, *West Point*, 91–97; Ambrose, *Duty*, 125–26; WTS to PBE, October 15, 1838, SH.

55. Morrison, *The Best School*, 71; Ambrose, *Duty*, 152; Forman, *History*, 96–97.

56. Ambrose, *Duty*, 153.

57. Ibid., 154; Morrison, *The Best School*, 77–78; Freeman Cleaves, *Rock of Chickamauga: The Life of General George H. Thomas* (Norman, Okla., 1949), 11–12.

58. WTS to PBE, May 18, December 1, 1839, PBE, OHS.

59. Ambrose, *Duty*, 163–64; Fleming, *West Point*, 92–93.

60. WTS to TE, June 21, 1836, TE, LC; WTS, *Memoirs*, 1:16; "Register of Delinquencies, 1834–1839," "Reports of Merit, 1836 to 1853, No. 2," USMA; WTS to PBE, July 11, 1837, PBE, OHS; WTS to PBE, October 15, 1838, January 26, 1840, SH.

61. WTS, 1885 speech, in James Grant Wilson and Titus M. Coan, eds., *Personal Recollections of the War of the Rebellion* (New York, 1891), 109.

62. James G. Wilson, "William T. Sherman," William P. Palmer Collection, WRHS; Bernarr Cresap, *Appomattox Commander: The Story of General E. O. C. Ord* (San Diego, 1981), 19.

63. WTS to PBE, November 5, 1837, PBE, OHS; Morrison, *The Best School,* 81–82; WTS to ES, August 30, 1837, SFP, UNDA. William S. Rosecrans' comments on Sherman the hashmaker appear in W. Fletcher Johnson and O. O. Howard, *The Life of Gen'l William Tecumseh Sherman* (Philadelphia, 1891), 586–7; WTS to JMS, January 6, 1880, HB, HL.

64. Ambrose, *Duty,* 102; Johnson and OOH, *Life of Sherman,* 588; D. H. Mahan to Editor of *Evening Post,* March 8, 1866, unlabeled newspaper clipping, scrapbook, WTS, OHS.

65. WTS to PBE, December 15, 1838, PBE, OHS; "Library Circulation Records, 1836–1841," USMA; Morrison, *The Best School,* 76–77.

66. WTS to ES, October 22, 1837, SFP, UNDA; WTS to PBE, October 15, 1838, January 26, 1849, SH; WTS to JS, April 13, 1839, WTS, LC; WTS to PBE, December 1, 1839, January 26, 1840, PBE, OHS.

67. WTS to ES, February 20, 1838, SFP, UNDA; WTS to JS, June 9, 1839, WTS, LC.

68. WTS to ES, August 21, 1839, SFP, UNDA. In 1836 he had asked MBE for five dollars so he could buy a pair of warm gloves. WTS to MBE, October 15, 1836, TE, LC.

69. WTS to Mary Sherman, September 30, 1839, WTS, LC.

70. WTS to ES, July 10, 1837, WTS, LC; WTS to PBE, July 11, 1837, PBE, OHS; WTS, "Autobiography," 7; unlabeled newspaper clipping, scrapbook, WTS, OHS.

71. WTS to JS, January 14, 1840, September 15, 1838, WTS, LC; WTS to PBE, September 15, 1838, PBE, OHS; WTS to ES, September 1, 1838, TE, LC.

72. WTS to PBE, February 17, 1839, PBE, OHS; invitation dated August 10, 1838, signed by WTS, WTS, USMA.

73. WTS to ES, August 21, 1839, SFP, UNDA.

74. Albert G. Brackett, "General William T. Sherman," *United Services Magazine* n.s. 5 (June 1891): 577; WTS to PBE, February 17, 1839, PBE, OHS.

75. WTS to PBE, September 15, 1838, PBE, OHS; WTS to JS, January 14, March 7, 1840, WTS, LC; WTS to ES, November 1, December 8, 1839, SFP, UNDA.

76. PBE to MBE, June 21, 1840, SFP, UNDA; WTS, "Autobiography," 17–19.

77. WTS to ES, May 4, 1839, SFP, UNDA.

78. WTS, *Memoirs,* 1:16; In his somewhat longer account in his unpublished "Autobiography," on p. 16, he justified his brevity on the fact that "the experience of all cadets is about the same and hardly worthy of notice. It is simply four years devoted to hard and well deserved study."

79. WTS to ES, November 1, 1839, SFP, UNDA; WTS to TE, February 20, 1844, TE, LC; E. V. Smalley, "General Sherman," *Century* 5 (January, 1884): 453.

CHAPTER 2 MAKING SOUTHERN FRIENDS

1. Gail Hamilton, *James G. Blaine* (Norwich, Conn., 1895), 582; Anna S. McAllister, *Flame in the Wilderness* . . . (Notre Dame, Ind., 1944), 25–27; WTS, "Hon. James G. Blaine," *North American Review* 147 (October 1888): 616.

2. WTS to PBE, October 24, 1840, PBE, OHS; WTS, *Memoirs*, 1:17; Richard Delafield to Joseph G. Totten, September 22, 1840, Totten to Delafield, September 26, 1840, SFP, UNDA.

3. WTS to MBE, October 2, 1840, SFP, UNDA; OOH, "William T. Sherman," in *22nd Annual Reunion, June 12, 1891, of the Association of Graduates of the United States Military Academy* (Saginaw, Mich., 1891), 51.

4. The following sketch on the Second Seminole War is based on John K. Mahon, *History of the Second Seminole War, 1835–1842* (Gainesville, 1967), and Charlton W. Tebeau, *A History of Florida* (Coral Gables, 1971), 151–70.

5. Edward Coffman, *The Old Army* . . . (New York, 1986), 50.

6. Mahon, *History*, 303.

7. WTS, *Memoirs*, 1:18–19; WTS to PBE, October 24, 1840, PBE, OHS.

8. WTS to JS, March 30, 1841, WTS, LC.

9. WTS, *Memoirs*, 1:18–19; WTS to PBE, October 24, 1840, PBE, OHS.

10. WTS to JS, March 20, March 30, July 14, 1841, WTS, LC; WTS to ES, September 7, 1841, SFP, UNDA; WTS to PBE, April 10, July 11, 29, 1841, PBE, OHS; OOH, "William T. Sherman," 51. For WTS post–Civil War career, see chapter 17.

11. WTS, *Memoirs*, 1:20–21; WTS to PBE, November 11, 1841, PBE, OHS; Powhaten Clarke to Leroy Boyd, May 21, 1903, copy, SFP, UNDA.

12. WTS to PBE, April 10, June 1, 1841, PBE, OHS; WTS to "Dear Sister," January 16, 1841, WTS, LC; WTS to JS, December [?], 1841, SFP, UNDA; William B. Skelton, "The Army in the Age of the Common Man, 1815–1845," in Kenneth J. Hagan and William R. Roberts, eds., *Against All Enemies* . . . (New York, 1986), 104.

13. Mahon, *History*, 248–49, 286.

14. In his *Memoirs*, WTS said that Colonel William J. Worth had succeeded Zachary Taylor as commanding officer in Florida. Actually Walker K. Armistead succeeded Taylor; Worth did not take command until May 31, 1841. WTS also said that Taylor was commanding officer when he arrived in Florida. Actually Armistead was. WTS, *Memoirs*, 1:22–26; Mahon, *History*, 289–300; WTS to PBE, May 8, 1841, PBE, OHS.

15. WTS to JS, July 14, 1841, WTS, LC; WTS to PBE, July 11, 1841; WTS to JS, October 11, 1841, WTS, LC.

16. WTS to PBE, April 10, 1841, PBE, OHS; EBE to MBE, copy, November 4, 1841, TE, LC.

17. WTS to PBE, July 11, 23, 1841, PBE, OHS.

18. Ibid., January 11, 28, 1842, PBE, OHS.

19. E. D. Keyes, *Fifty Years Observation* . . . (New York, 1884), 163; WTS, untitled speech, December 1870, WTS, LC.

20. WTS, *Memoirs*, 1:26.

21. WTS to ES, January 13, 1842, SFP, UNDA; WTS to PBE, January 11, 1842, PBE, OHS; WTS to ES, January 13, 1842, SFP, UNDA; WTS to PBE, January 11, 1842, PBE, OHS; WTS to ES, September 7, 1841, SFP, UNDA.

22. WTS to JS, February 15, 1842, WTS, LC; Tebeau, *History,* 168.

23. WTS to PBE, March 11, 1842, PBE, OHS.

24. WTS, *Memoirs,* 1:27; WTS to PBE, March 11, 1842, PBE, OHS.

25. WTS to ES, April 7, 1842, SFP, UNDA; WTS to PBE, March 11, April 23, 1842, PBE, OHS; WTS to JS, May 11, 1842, WTS, LC.

26. WTS to PBE, April 23, 1842, PBE, OHS; WTS to ES, April 7, 1842, SFP, UNDA.

27. WTS to ES, April 7, 1842, SFP, UNDA.

28. WTS to PBE, March 11, April 23, 1842, PBE, OHS; WTS, *Memoirs,* 1:27; WTS to JS, May 11, 1842, WTS, LC.

29. WTS to ES, April 7, 1842, SFP, UNDA; WTS to PBE, April 23, 1842, PBE, OHS.

30. WTS to ES, April 7, 1842, SFP, UNDA.

31. WTS to PBE, June 10, July 23, 1842, PBE, OHS; WTS, *Memoirs,* 1:28.

32. WTS, *Memoirs,* 1:27–28, 34; WTS to PBE, June 10, 1842, PBE, OHS; Edward M. Riley, "Historical Fort Moultrie in Charleston Harbor," *South Carolina Historical Magazine* 51 (1950): 69; WTS to PBE, July 3, 1842, PBE, OHS; WTS to H. W. Benham, July 20, 1842; H. W. Benham Papers, SCL.

33. Anne Chapman, "Inadequacies of the 1848 Charleston Census," *South Carolina Historical Magazine* 81 (1980): 29; WTS to PBE, November 5, 1842, PBE, OHS.

34. WTS to HBE, May 31, 1845, HBE, OHS; WTS to ES, June 9, 1845, SFP, UNDA; WTS to JS, May 23, 1843, WTS, LC.

35. WTS, Untitled speech, December 1870, WTS, LC; Keyes, *Fifty Years Observation,* 170; Freeman Cleaves, *Rock of Chickamauga: The Life of General George H. Thomas* (Norman, Okla., 1949), 22; WTS, "General Sherman's Last Speech. The Old Army . . . January 31, 1891," *Century* n.s. 20 (June 1891): 191.

36. WTS to JS, May 23, 1843, WTS, LC; WTS to PBE, July 3, 1842, PBE, OHS.

37. WTS to PBE, November 5, 1842, PBE, OHS; WTS to ES, March 12, 1843, SFP, UNDA; Jane H. Pease and William H. Pease, "Intellectual Life in the 1830's . . . Charleston," in Michael O'Brien and David Moltke-Hansen, eds., *Intellectual Life in Antebellum Charleston* (Knoxville, 1986), 253.

38. WTS to ES, March 12, 1843, SFP, UNDA.

39. WTS to JS, May 23, 1843, WTS, LC.

40. WTS to MA, April 11, 1886, WTS, HPC; WTS to ES, November 28, 1842, June 14, September 17, 1844, April 6, June 9, 1845, SFP, UNDA; WTS to PBE, August 25, November 5, 1842, May 7, 1843, October 20, 1844, March 17, 1846, PBE, OHS; WTS to JS, April 4, May 1, 1845, January 4, 1846, WTS, LC.

41. WTS to ES, November 28, 1842, SFP, UNDA; WTS to PBE, December 13, 1845, PBE, OHS. Unfortunately none of WTS's Fort Moultrie paintings has survived.

42. WTS to ES, November 28, 1842, September 17, 1844, SFP, UNDA; WTS to

PBE, October 20, 1844, PBE, OHS; WTS to JS, October 24, 1844, PBE, OHS.

43. WTS to ES, September 17, 1844, SFP, UNDA; WTS to PBE, October 20, 1844, PBE, OHS.

44. WTS to ES, September 17, 1844, June 9, 1845, January 31, 1846, SFP, UNDA; WTS to PBE, December 13, 1845, PBE, OHS; WTS, "Memorial Tribute for Major-General George H. Thomas at House of Representatives, April 6, 1870," untitled newspaper clipping, scrapbook, WTS, OHS.

45. WTS to PBE, June 10, 1842, September 9, 1845, PBE, OHS; WTS to JS, January 4, 1846, WTS, LC.

46. WTS to ES, February 8, 1844, SFP, UNDA; WTS to JS, August 29, 1845, WTS, LC.

47. U.S., *Statutes at Large,* 5, 512–13; WTS to PBE, April 25, 1844, PBE, OHS; WTS to HBE, March 10, 1844, WTS, OHS. For WTS postwar battles with Congress, see chapter 19.

48. WTS, diary, November 20, 21–25, 29, December 4, 6–9, 13–16, 19–20, 24–27, 1843, SFP, UNDA; WTS to JS, January 19, 1844, WTS, LC; WTS to PBE, December 28, 1843, PBE, OHS; WTS, *Memoirs,* 1:28–29.

49. WTS to JS, January 19, 1844, WTS, LC.

50. WTS, *Memoirs,* 1:29–30; WTS to TE, February 19, 1844, TE, LC: WTS to HBE, March 10, 1844, copy, WTS, OHS.

51. WTS, diary, March 3, 16–23, 1844, SFP, UNDA; WTS, *Memoirs,* 1:30; PTS to Gherardi Davis, August 2, 1938, copy, SFP, UNDA; E. V. Smalley, "General Sherman," *Century* 5 (January 1884): 454; SHMB, "Some Personal Recollections of General Sherman," *McClures* 3 (August 1894): 218.

52. WTS to PBE, August 25, 1842, PBE, OHS; WTS to ES, March 12, 1843, SFP, UNDA.

53. WTS to ES, February 8, 1844, WTS, diary, March 5, 1844, SFP, UNDA; WTS to TE, June 17, 1844, TE, LC.

54. WTS to ES, February 8, September 17, 1844, SFP, UNDA.

55. WTS to HBE, March 10, 1844, WTS, OHS; WTS to JS, June 11, 1843, WTS, LC.

56. WTS to ES, June 14, 1844, SFP, UNDA; WTS to PBE, October 20, 1844, PBE, OHS; WTS to TE, February 19, 20, June 17, 1844, TE, LC.

57. WTS to PBE, June 12, 1844, PBE, OHS; WTS to ES, September 17, 1844, SFP, UNDA; WTS, diary, 1845, SFP, UNDA.

58. WTS to ES, November 19, 1845, SFP, UNDA.

59. Ibid.; February 8, 1844, January 31, 1846, SFP, UNDA.

CHAPTER 3   GOLD RUSH SOLDIER

1. WTS to JS, April 2, 1846, WTS, LC; WTS to Roger Jones, December 19, 1845, SCL; WTS to Jones, January 15, 1846, T. W. Norris Collection, BL.

2. WTS, *Memoirs,* 1:35–36; WTS to ES, June 11, 1846, SFP, UNDA.

3. WTS to JS, June 12, 1846, WTS, LC.

4. Ibid., April 2, 1846, WTS, LC; see also ibid., June 12, 1846, WTS, LC.

5. WTS to ES, June 11, 1846, SFP, UNDA; WTS, *Memoirs,* 1:36; E. O. C. Ord to WTS, June 18, 1846, PBE, OHS.

6. WTS, *Memoirs,* 1:36; WTS to JS, June 23, 1846, WTS, LC.

7. WTS, *Memoirs,* 1:37; WTS to PBE, June 29, 1846, PBE, OHS.

8. WTS to ES, June 30, 1846, SFP, UNDA.

9. WTS, journal, July 12, 1846, WTS, LC; WTS to PBE, July 3, 1846, PBE, OHS; WTS to R. C. Schenck, July 3, 1846, Boston Public Library.

10. Hubert Howe Bancroft, *History of California* (San Francisco, 1886), 5:518–19. For Ord's account of the voyage, see Bernarr Cresap, *Appomattox Commander: The Story of General E. O. C. Ord* (San Diego, 1981), 23–25.

11. Winfield Scott to Christopher Q. Tompkins, June 20, 1846, WTS, LC.

12. WTS to ES July 12, 1846, August 3, 1846, SFP, UNDA.

13. K. Jack Bauer, *Surfboats and Horse Marines: U.S. Naval Operations in the Mexican War* (Annapolis, 1969), 259; WTS to ES, August 3, 1846, SFP, UNDA.

14. WTS, *Memoirs,* 1:38; WTS, journal, July 26, 1846, WTS, LC.

15. WTS to ES, July 12, August 27, October 27, 1846, SFP, UNDA; WTS, *Memoirs,* 1:39; NYT, December 29, 1880.

16. WTS to TE, May 3, 1862, Joseph H. Ewing, ed., "Sherman Bashes the Press," *American Heritage* 38 (July–August 1987): 30.

17. WTS to ES, August 3, 1846, SFP, UNDA.

18. Ibid., October 27, 1846, SFP, UNDA.

19. WTS, journal, October 24, 1846, WTS to ES, October 27, 1846, SFP, UNDA.

20. WTS to ER, November 10, 1846, WTS, LC.

21. WTS, journal, August 28, 1846, WTS, LC; WTS to ES, August 28, 1846, SFP, UNDA.

22. WTS, journal, July 30, 1846, WTS, LC.

23. WTS, *Memoirs,* 1:39; WTS to ES, September 5, 1846, WTS, journal, September 21, 1846, SFP, UNDA.

24. WTS to ES, September 12, included with September 5, 1846, SFP, UNDA; WTS, journal, September 21, 1846, WTS, LC.

25. WTS to ES, September 5, 1846, SFP, UNDA; WTS, *Memoirs,* 1:39–40.

26. WTS to ES, September 16, 1846, SFP, UNDA.

27. WTS, journal, September 21, 1846, WTS, LC.

28. WTS to ES, September 16, 1846, SFP, UNDA; WTS, journal, September 21, 1846, WTS, LC.

29. WTS to ES, September 16, 1846, SFP, UNDA; WTS, journal, November 12, 1846, WTS, LC; WTS to ES, October 27, 1846, SFP, UNDA.

30. WTS, journal, November 28, 1846, WTS, LC; WTS to ES, December 5, 1846, SFP, UNDA.

31. WTS to ES, January 25, 1847, SFP, UNDA.

32. WTS to EBE, January 25, 1847, SFP, UNDA; WTS, journal, November 28, 1846, WTS, LC.

33. WTS to ES, December 5, 1846, SFP, UNDA.

34. Ibid., January 26, 27, 1846, SFP, UNDA.

35. WTS, *Memoirs,* 1:43.

36. Unless otherwise indicated, this chapter's discussion of California in the Mexican War is based on the following works: Hubert Howe Bancroft, *History of California, vol. 5, 1846–1848*, vol. 22 of *Works of Hubert Howe Bancroft* (San Francisco, 1886); K. Jack Bauer, *The Mexican War, 1846–1848* (New York, 1974); Theodore Grivas, *Military Governments in California, 1846–1850* (Glendale, Calif., 1963); Neal Harlow, *California Conquered: War and Peace on the Pacific, 1848–1850* (Berkeley, 1982); Allen Nevins, *Frémont, Pathmarker of the West* (Norman, Okla., 1961); Otis Singletary, *The Mexican War* (Chicago, 1960).

37. WTS, *Memoirs*, 1:43.

38. WTS to ES, January 27, 1847, SFP, UNDA; WTS, *Memoirs*, 1:44; Richard B. Mason to R. Jones, September 18, 1847, WTS, LC.

39. WTS, *Memoirs*, 1:48–49.

40. Nevins, *Frémont*, 315; WTS, *Memoirs*, 1:50, Stephen W. Kearny to W. L. Marcy, April 28, 1847, WTS, LC; WTS to ES, March 12, 1847, SFP, UNDA; Nevins, *Frémont* 317, 320–21.

41. WTS, *Memoirs*, 1:50.

42. WTS to Richard C. McCormick, copy, February 17, 1890, WTS, LC. WTS shared shirts, socks, and underwear with HST and W. H. Warner, who had used up most of theirs in the overland trek with Kearny. From that point on, HST and WTS became lifelong friends and, in the 1850s, business associates. WTS, *Memoirs*, 1:49–50; Thomas T. Gantt, "Henry Smith Turner," Thirteenth Annual Reunion, June 12, 1882, Association of Graduates, United States Military Academy, 57–63.

43. WTS, *Memoirs*, 1:54; WTS to PBE, April 25, 1847, PBE, OHS; WTS to ES, May 30, 1847, SFP, UNDA.

44. WTS to ES, May 30, 1847, SFP, UNDA; Mason to R. Jones, June 18, 1847, WTS to J. E. Tourtellotte, January 3, 1883, WTS, LC.

45. WTS, *Memoirs*, 1:45–46; WTS to ES, March 12, 1847, SFP, UNDA; WTS, journal, February 15, 1847, WTS, LC.

46. WTS, journal, February 23, 1847, WTS, LC; WTS to ES, March 12, 1847, SFP, UNDA.

47. WTS to ES, March 12, 1847, SFP, UNDA.

48. WTS, *Memoirs*, 1:46–48; WTS, Journal, March 11, 21, 22, 1847, WTS, LC; WTS to ES, March 12, May 1, 1847, SFP, UNDA. For Ord's view of this tour and army life in Monterey, see Bernarr Cresap, *Appomattox Commander: The Story of General E. O. C. Ord* (San Diego, 1981), chap. 3.

49. WTS to ES, October 8, 1847, SFP, UNDA.

50. WTS, journal, July 27, 1847, WTS, LC, and WTS, *Memoirs* 1:55–62. WTS had little respect for the alcaldes. He told, for example, about the case of a woman having a miscarriage brought on by fright at the sudden appearance of horses and riders racing through town streets. The woman sued the racers, and the alcalde ruled that "the Judge of the race should restore the woman to her original condition, and that the others should pay the costs." WTS added: "How far the sentence has been executed I have not learned." WTS to PBE, April 16, 1848, PBE, OHS.

51. WTS to ES, April 10, 1848, SFP, UNDA; WTS, *Memoirs*, 1:62; WTS to ES, October 8, 1847, SFP, UNDA.

52. WTS to ES, October 8, 1847, SFP, UNDA; WTS to John Burten, September 6, 1847, WTS, HLH.

53. WTS to ES, November 10, 1847, February 3, 1848, SFP, UNDA.

54. Ibid., February 3, 1848, SFP, UNDA; JAH to WTS, January 16, 1848, WTS, LC; WTS to ES, February 3, 1838, SFP, UNDA.

55. WTS to ES, November 10, 1847, SFP, UNDA; WTS to JS, April 18, 1848, WTS, LC.

56. WTS, *Memoirs*, 1:70–71. The mail rider from Monterey south was the fabled black trapper, explorer, and Indian chieftain, James Beckwourth. WTS considered him "one of the best chroniclers of events on the plains that I have ever encountered, though his reputation for veracity was not good." WTS, "Old Times in California," *North American Review* 148 (February 1889): 271.

57. WTS, *Memoirs*, 1:64–65; Mason to J. A. Sutter, May 5, 1848, in Rodman W. Paul, ed., *The California Gold Discovery* . . . (Georgetown, Calif., 1967), 81–82. WTS's West Point textbooks that included information on gold were James D. Dana, *Manual of Mineralogy* . . . , rev. ed. (New Haven, 1866), 312–13, and Robert Bakewell, *An Introduction to Geology* . . . , 3d ed. (New Haven, 1829), 310.

58. *San Francisco Californian*, May 29, 1838, in Frank Soule, et al., *Annals of San Francisco* (Palo Alto, 1966), 204; WTS, *Memoirs*, 1:65; Joseph A. Folsom to WTS, May 29, 1848, WTS, LC.

59. WTS, *Memoirs*, 1:70.

60. Ibid., 1:70–80; WTS to HST, August 25, 1848, Mason to R. Jones, August 17, 1848, WTS, LC. WTS wrote the Mason letter. Erwin G. Gudde, *Sutter's Own Story* (New York, 1936), 214–15.

61. WTS, *Memoirs*, 1:80; WTS to George Gibson, August 5, 1848, WTS, BL, also published as *A Letter of Lieut. W. T. Sherman Reporting on Conditions in California in 1848* (Carmel, Calif., 1947); WTS to J. D. Stevenson, August 26, 1848, in *A Letter from Sherman to Colonel Stevenson* . . . *from the Collections of the University of California, Los Angeles* (Los Angeles, 1960).

62. WTS to HST, August 25, 1848, WTS, LC.

63. WTS to ES, August 28, 1848, SFP, UNDA; WTS to JS, August 9, 1848, WTS, LC.

64. WTS to JS, August 9, 1848, Mason to Jones, August 17, 1848, James K. Polk, Special Message to Congress, December 5, 1848, WTS, LC; WTS, *Memoirs*, 1:81. For a copy of WTS's sketch map of the gold region deposited in the NARS, see Theresa Gay, *James W. Marshall, the Discoverer of California Gold: A Biography* (Georgetown, Calif., 1967), 201; WTS to ES, August 28, 1848, SFP, UNDA.

65. WTS, *Memoirs*, 1:82–83; Norman S. Bestor to W. H. Warner, November 3, 4, 1848, WTS, LC; *San Francisco Star and Californian*, December 9, 1848; Warner to WTS, December 11, 31, 1848. Ed Gilbert to WTS, January 29, 1848, Bestor to WTS, March 4, 1849, WTS, LC; WTS to Ord, October 28, November 14, 1848, WTS, BLY; Gay, *James W. Marshall*, 231–32.

66. WTS, *Memoirs,* 1:85–89; WTS to Arthur B. Stout, May 29, 1874, in NYT, June 21, 1874; WTS to P. S. Smith, February 26, 1849, G. O. No. 3, Hqs., 3d Division, February 27, 1849, WTS, LC. WTS to John S. Griffin, January 10, 1849, in Viola Warren, ed., "Dr. John S. Griffin's Mail, 1846–53," *California Historical Society Quarterly* 34 (March 1955): 341. Regarding the "Castanares" nickname, see José Antonio Jimeno to WTS, Porfirio Jimeno to WTS, November 9, 1850, and WTS's handwritten comment on the back that "Catanares" was his California nickname. According to a Spanish-English dictionary, there is no such word, but the word *castana* means "chestnut" and the phrase *dar a uno para castana* means "to play a trick on someone." Therefore, WTS's nickname might have referred to his red hair or his prankster nature.

67. WTS, *Memoirs,* 1:89–92; William H. Thomas, speech, Fourteenth Meeting of the Associated Pioneers of the Territorial Days of California, January 9, 18, 1889, HL.

68. ES to WTS, January 19, February 5, May 22, 1849, SFP, UNDA; WTS to Ord, October 28, 1848, BLY; WTS to ES, March 5, 1849, SFP, UNDA.

69. WTS, *Memoirs,* 1:93–95. Later Civil War General E. R. S. Canby was one of the pursuers. See Max L. Heyman, Jr., *Prudent Soldier: A Biography of Major General E. R. S. Canby, 1817–1873* (Glendale, Calif., 1959), 78.

70. S.O. No. 12, Hqs., Pacific Division, May 15, 1849, R. Jones to P. F. Smith, May 21, 1849, WTS, LC; WTS, *Memoirs,* 1:96–100; Bestor to WTS, June 7, 1849, Sutter to WTS, June 28, 1849, property deed, October 8, 1849, WTS, LC.

71. WTS to Smith, June 12, 1849, two letters, WTS, LC.

72. WTS, *Memoirs,* 1:100–101.

73. Ibid., 1:101–102.

74. Ibid., 1:79–81; W. C. Carrie to WTS, December 2, 1848, Daniel M. Martin to WTS, January 19, 1849, Tom Edwards to WTS, December 9, 1849, HBE to WTS, December 21, 1848, August 11, 16, 1849, WTS, LC; WTS to HBE, June 30, August 3, 1849, HBE, OHS; JAH to WTS, April 9, 1849, with enclosure of *Rochester Daily Courier,* February 1, 1849, WTS, LC; WTS to TE, April 28, 1849, TE, LC; T. P. Effinger to "My Dear Mother," October 3, 1849, Robert Effinger Papers, CHS; WTS, "Graduation Address, USMA 1869," *Army* 16 (June 1966): 65.

75. S.O. No. 22, Hqs., Pacific Division, November 8, 1849, SFP, UNDA; HBE, autobiography journal, January 1, 1850, HBE, OHS; Cresap, *Appomattox Commander,* 31.

CHAPTER 4   SETTING DOWN ROOTS

1. WTS, *Memoirs,* 1:104–5.

2. Ibid., 1:105.

3. February 8, 1850, endorsement by Winfield Scott on P. F. Smith to W. G. Freeman, October 7, 1849, WTS, LC.

4. Anna McAllister, *Ellen Ewing, Wife of General Sherman* (New York, 1936), 62.

5. WTS, *Memoirs*, 1:105. There appeared an apocryphal story about Zachary Taylor's sending WTS on a one-year inspection tour of the New Mexico, Arizona, and Southern lands gained from Mexico after the Mexican War. When WTS returned, the story goes, he told Taylor the United States would have to fight another war with Mexico—"to make'em take the d—d country back!" Eli Perkins, *Kings of the Platform and Pulpit* (Chicago, 1891), 550; S.O. No. 17, Hqs. of the Army, February 28, 1850, SFP, UNDA; WTS to Adjutant General of the Army, March 15, 1850, WTS, LC.

6. WTS, petition, unaddressed, April 22, 1850, SFP, UNDA; WTS to Adjutant General of the Army, March 26, 1850, WTS, LC.

7. WTS to ES, March 27, 1850, SFP, UNDA.

8. Ibid., March 29, 1850, SFP, UNDA.

9. Ibid., March 27, 29, 1850, SFP, UNDA.

10. WTS to PBE, March 15, 1850, PBE, OHS. According to ES, TE wanted WTS to remain in the army as long as the Ewing family remained in Washington. ES to PBE, March 18, 1850, SH.

11. WTS to JS, April 29, 1850, WTS to ER, October 31, 1849, ER to JS, January 15, 1850, WTS, LC; WTS, power of attorney, May 22, 1850, SFP, UNDA; WTS to JS, June 16, 1850, John A. Reese to WTS, July 1, 1850, WTS to JS, July 1, 1850, WTS, LC; ES to WTS, August 24, 1850, SFP, UNDA.

12. WTS to ES, March 27, 29, 1850, SFP, UNDA; WTS to PBE, March 29, 1850, EBE to PBE, April 12, 1850, PBE, OHS; WTS to PTS, January 19, 1888, WTS, OHS.

13. McAllister, *Ellen Ewing*, 62–65; WTS to JAH, April 12, 1850, JAH, LC; WTS to P. F. Smith, August 4, 1850, WTS, HSPa, published as Roy F. Nichols, ed., "William Tecumseh Sherman in 1850," *Pennsylvania Magazine* 75 (October 1952): 424–35; *Baltimore Patriot*, May 2, 1850, in *Lancaster Gazette*, May 10, 1850.

14. WTS to Ord, May 1, 1850, WTS, James S. Copley Library; McAllister, *Ellen Ewing*, 64–68; ES to PBE, May 6, 1850, PBE, OHS; TE to PBE, May 26, 1850, TE, OHS. In SFP, UNDA, there is a copy of such partnership, though no Reese name appears. "Indenture and Agreement May 24, 1850 between Mary E. Sherman and sons . . . ," SFP, UNDA.

15. MBE to ES, May 4, 1850, TE, LC; TE to ES, May 5, 20, 1850, MBE to ES, May 21, June 8, 1850, copies, SFP, UNDA; ES to PBE, May 6, 1850, PBE, OHS; ES to MBE, May 22, 1850, copy, SFP, UNDA.

16. WTS, *Memoirs*, 1:106.

17. Ibid., 1:106–7; WTS to JS, July 16, 1850, WTS, LC.

18. WTS, *Memoirs*, 1:107–8; ES to PBE, July 26, 1850, PBE, OHS.

19. WTS, *Memoirs*, 1:108–9; Craig R. Smith, "Daniel Webster's July 17th Address: A Mediating Influence in the 1850 Compromise," *Quarterly Journal of Speech* 71 (August 1985): 349–61; untitled Pittsburgh newspaper clipping, February 10, 1890, WTS, OHS; WTS to Robert C. Winthrop, October 13, 1886, Robert C. Winthrop Papers, MaHS, copy in WTS, LC.

20. WTS, "Personal Recollections of California," WTS, LC.

21. S.O. No. 7, Hqs., Third Artillery Regiment, June 17, 1859, SFP, UNDA;

HST to WTS, July 4, 1850, WTS, LC; Charles H. Hoyt to WTS, July 21, 1850, SFP, UNDA; Ord to WTS, August 21, 1850, WTS, LC.

22. TE to WTS, September 12, 1850, TE, LC; WTS to JS, September 7, 1850, WTS, LC; WTS to ES, September 17, 1850, SFP, UNDA.

23. WTS to ES, September 22, 1850, UNDA.

24. Ibid.

25. WTS to ES, September 24, 25, 1850, SFP, UNDA.

26. P. F. Smith to WTS, September 27, 1850, WTS, LC; WTS to ES, October 8, 1850, Adjutant General Certificate of Commission, October 14, 1850, SFP, UNDA.

27. WTS to ES, October 23, 1850, SFP, UNDA.

28. WTS to JS, November 12, 1850, WTS, LC; WTS to ES, November 1, 1850, SFP, UNDA.

29. MBE to TE, December 11, 1850, TE, LC: WTS to HBE, January 5, 1851, WTS, OHS; WTS to ES, December 28, 1851, SFP, UNDA.

30. WTS to ES, January 30, 1851, SFP, UNDA; ES to HBE, February 22, 1851, copy, WTS, OHS.

31. TE to MBE, copy, February 25, 1851, WTS to TE, March 11, 1851, TE, LC.

32. WTS to ES, March 1, 1851, ES to MBE, April 10, 1851, copy, SFP, UNDA; ES to HBE, May 18, 1851, WTS, OHS.

33. ES to MBE, February 11, 1852, copy, SFP, UNDA; ES to HBE, December 16, 1851, copy, WTS to HBE, May 6, 1851, December 8, 1851, WTS, OHS.

34. ES to HBE, February 1, 1852, copy, WTS, OHS; ES to MBE, January 28, 1852, copy, SFP, UNDA.

35. WTS, *Memoirs*, 1:110; TE memorandum, October 19, 1868, EFP, UNDA; WTS to HBE, December 8, 1851, WTS, OHS; WTS to JS, September 23, July 16, August 19, 1851, WTS, LC; TE, Jr., to PBE, September 22, 1851, PBE, OHS; WTS to PBE, November 21, 1851, SFP, UNDA; WTS to JS, May 19, December 19, 1851, WTS, LC. For WTS discussion of Amos Stoddard, see WTS, speech, New England Society of Pennsylvania, 1882, in PTS, Scrapbook, WTS, OHS.

36. ES to HBE, February 1, 1852, copy, WTS, OHS; MBE to ES, September 23, 1851, copy, ES to MBE, May 3, 1852, copy, SFP, UNDA; ES to TE, Jr., March 20, 1852, copy, WTS, OHS.

37. ES to HBE, February 1, 1852, copy, WTS, OHS; WTS to JS, September 23, 1861, WTS, LC; TE to ES, February 26, 1852, SFP, UNDA; WTS to HBE, May 6, 1851, WTS, OHS; WTS to ES, November 4, December 2, 1852, SFP, UNDA; WTS to HBE, June 15, 1852, WTS, OHS; WTS to TE, December 19, 1851, TE, LC.

38. WTS, *Memoirs*, 1:112; ES to MBE, May 3, 1852, copy, SFP, UNDA.

39. WTS to ES, May 21, 1852, May 30, 1852, SFP, UNDA.

40. Ibid., August 14, 1852, SFP, UNDA; WTS to TE, Jr., September 7, 1852, TE, LC; WTS to HBE, January 5, 1851, WTS, OHS; WTS to TE, Jr., August 30, 1852, TE, LC.

41. WTS to ES, September 30, 1852, SFP, UNDA.

42. WTS, *Memoirs*, 1:113; WTS to ES, October 29, 1852, SFP, UNDA; JGB,

"Some Personal Traits of General Sherman," in WTS, *Memoirs*, rev. ed. (New York, 1891), 2:appendix.

43. WTS to JS, November 17, 1852, WTS, LC; WTS to PBE, October 13, 1852, WTS to ES, November 4, 10, 1852, SFP, UNDA.

44. WTS to ES, November 10, 1852, SFP, UNDA; WTS to JS, November 17, 1852, WTS, LC; WTS to ES, December 2, 10, 14, 1852, SFP, UNDA.

45. MBE to WTS, November 18, 1852, WTS to ES, December 2, 10, 1852, SFP, UNDA.

46. WTS, *Memoirs*, 1:113–15; WTS to JS, November 27, 1852, WTS, LC.

47. HST to WTS, December 7, 1852, Lucas and Simonds to WTS, January 4, 1853, WTS, LC; WTS, *Memoirs*, 1:113–14.

48. HST to WTS, January 15, 19, 1853, Robert M. Renick to WTS, January 31, 1853, WTS, LC; WTS to George Gibson, January 20, 1853, copy, SFP, UNDA; Lucas and Simonds to WTS, January 27, 31, 1853, WTS, LC; TE to MBE, copy, February 1, 1853, TE, LC; WTS, *Memoirs*, 1:113–14.

CHAPTER 5   THE DISORDER OF FINANCIAL LIFE

1. WTS, *Memoirs*, 1:116–20; WTS to ES, April 12, 1853, SFP, UNDA; Mildred Brooke Hoover, *Historic Spots in California* (Stanford, 1966), 185.

2. Dwight L. Clarke, *William Tecumseh Sherman: Gold Rush Banker* (San Francisco, 1969), 3; WTS to JS, June 3, 1853, WTS, LC; WTS to ES, April 12, June 30, 1853, SFP, UNDA; WTS, *Memoirs*, 1:121.

3. Clarke, *Sherman*, 8–9; WTS, *Memoirs*, 1:121–22.

4. WTS to ES, April 12, 15, May 11, 1853, SFP, UNDA; WTS to JS, June 3, 1853, WTS, LC.

5. ES to WTS, June 23, 1853, WTS to ES, June 30, July 14, 1853, SFP, UNDA.

6. WTS to ES, July 14, 1853, SFP, UNDA; WTS, *Memoirs*, 1:122; WTS resignation, September 3, 1853, WTS, LC.

7. TE to WTS, February 1, 1853, MBE to ES, February 27, 1853, ES to MBE, December 12, 1853, copy, WTS to PBE, March 30, 1854, SFP, UNDA; TE, Jr., to MBE, September 21, 1853, copy, TE, LC.

8. WTS to TE, August 22, 1853, TE, LC.

9. WTS to HBE, September 29, 1853, ES to MBE, October 31, 1853, copy, WTS, OHS; WTS, *Memoirs*, 1:122–23.

10. ES to MBE, October 31, 1853, WTS, OHS; WTS to PBE, January 31, 1854, SFP, UNDA; ES to MBE, November 11, 1853, copy, WTS, OHS; ES to MBE, November 19, December 4, 8, 12, 23, 1853, copies, SFP, UNDA.

11. TE to WTS, September 29, December 23, 1853, WTS, LC; WTS to TE, September 29, 1853, TE, LC.

12. WTS, *Memoirs*, 1:124–25.

13. ES to MBE, November 19, December 4, 12, 1853, January 23, February 26, 1854, copies, WTS to PBE, March 30, 1854, SFP, UNDA; ES to HBE, April 3, 1854, copy, WTS, OHS; Freeman Cleaves, *Rock of Chickamauga: The Life*

    of General George H. Thomas (Norman, Okla., 1949), 52; WTS to Martin Breen, February 1, 1887, copy, WTS, LC.

14. WTS to PBE, June 15, 1854, SFP, UNDA; WTS to HST, June 15, 1854, WTS, OHS; WTS to TE, Jr., July 15, 1854, TE, LC.

15. WTS to PBE, June 15, 1854, SFP, UNDA; WTS to HST, July 31, 1854, WTS, OHS; WTS to JS, November 30, 1854, March 20, 1856, WTS, LC.

16. WTS, *Memoirs*, 1:124–26; WTS to HST, June 15, August 31, September 29, 1854, WTS, OHS; WTS to HST, January 23, 1855, copy, SFP, UNDA; WTS to JAH, October 11, 1854, JAH, LC; WTS to HST, January 31, 1855, WTS, OHS.

17. Unless otherwise indicated, the following account of the panic is based on WTS, *Memoirs*, 1:128–36, and WTS to HST, February 25, 1855, copy, SFP, UNDA.

18. Clarke, *Sherman*, 60–61; JS, "An Address Commemorative of General William T. Sherman," New York Commandery, MOLLUS, April 6, 1892, 21–22; Braxton Bragg to WTS, June 3, 1855, in SHMB, ed., "Some Unpublished War Letters . . .," *North American Review* 144 (May 1887): 377; Cleaves, *Rock of Chickamauga*, 52; E. A. Hitchcock, *Fifty Years in Camp . . .*, ed. W. A. Croffert (New York, 1909), 407–10.

19. WTS to W. M. Gardiner, July 27, 1855, in "The Memoirs of Brigadier General William Montgomery Gardner of the Confederate Service," ms. copy, USMA, also published in *Memphis Commercial Appeal*, June 30, 1912ff.

20. WTS to Daniel Ammen, December 4, 1884, Daniel Ammen Papers, UCLA.

21. ES to TE, February 25, 1855, WTS to HST, February 25, 1855, copy, SFP, UNDA.

22. ES to MBE, March 8, 1855, copy, SFP, UNDA; WTS to HST, March 8, 1855, WTS, OHS.

23. WTS to ES, May 8, 31, 1855, SFP, UNDA; WTS, *Memoirs*, 1:136–37; ES to TE, February 7, 25, 1855, WTS to HST, March 28, 1855, SFP, UNDA; WTS to ES, September 18, 1855, July 14, 1855, SFP, UNDA.

24. ES to WTS, May 13, 1855, WTS to ES, June 16, 1855, SFP, UNDA.

25. ES to WTS, April 21, July 14, 21, 30, October 10, 1855, SFP, UNDA.

26. WTS to PBE, October 5, 1855, SFP, UNDA; WTS to HST, May 16, 1855, WTS, OHS; WTS to ES, May 31, 1855, WTS to ES, August 17, 1855, June 16, 1855, SFP, UNDA. "Surmounting the Sierras," *California Historical Society Quarterly* 7 (1928): 3–19. There was another WTS in San Francisco who was elected city comptroller on the Know Nothing ticket. Dorothy Huggins, *Continuation of the Annals . . .* (San Francisco, 1939), 21.

27. W. C. Little, "The Sherman of Early Days," *Overland Monthly* 17 (April 1891): 358–59; C. Turner to James H. Lucas, July 30, 1855, James H. Lucas Papers, MoHS.

28. WTS to ES, March 31, May 31, September 18, 1855, SFP, UNDA.

29. ES to MBE, December 4, 1855, copy, SFP, UNDA.

30. WTS to HST, December 3, 1855, WTS, OHS; WTS to HST, January 5, 1856, copy, SFP, UNDA.

31. WTS to HST, April 5, 1856, copy, SFP, UNDA; WTS to J. B. Crockett,

April 19, 1856, G.O. No. 1, Hqs., California Militia, April 30, 1856, WTS, LC; WTS to HST, March 4, 1856, copy, SFP, UNDA; WTS to JS, March 20, 1856, WTS, LC.

32. ES to MBE, January 14, 1856, copy, February 17, 1856, copy, ES to TE, January 3, 1856, copy, SFP, UNDA; WTS to HBE, April 30, 1856, WTS, OHS; ES to MBE, March 16, 1856, copy, SFP, UNDA.

33. Robert M. Senkewicz, S.J., *Vigilantes in Gold Rush San Francisco* (Stanford, Calif., 1985), 105, 189. This is the most cogent analysis of the California vigilantes of the 1850s.

34. Unless otherwise indicated, the following account of the vigilante crisis is based on: WTS, *Memoirs*, 1:137–50, and ES to TE, May 18, 1856, SFP, UNDA. ES copied WTS's account of the events for her father's benefit; WTS to Stephen J. Field, February 25, 1868, in "The Vigilante Committee of 1856," *Overland Monthly* 12 (February 1874): 106–16; WTS to HST, May 18, 1856, WTS, MoHS; WTS to TE, May 21, 1856, TE, LC. Hubert Howe Bancroft in his favorable account of the vigilantes attacked WTS's statements "impeaching the integrity of California's purest and best citizens." Bancroft, *The Works of Hubert Howe Bancroft* (San Francisco, 1886), 37:284–89.

35. Senkewicz, *Vigilantes*, 8.

36. ES to MBE, May 20, July 4, 31, 1856, copies, SFP, UNDA.

37. ES to TE, May 18, 1856, ES to MBE, July 4, 1856, SFP, UNDA; WTS to JS, December 4, 1856, WTS, LC.

38. J. Neely Johnson to WTS, June 2, 5, 1856, WTS, LC.

39. WTS, *Memoirs*, 1:145–50; Johnson to WTS, June 5, 1856, WTS to TE, June 16, 1856, WTS, LC; John E. Wool to Johnson, June 5, 1856, Wool to WTS, June 6, 1856, Johnson to WTS, June 6, 1856, WTS to Wool, June 6, 1856, Johnson to WTS, June 7, 10, 1856, WTS, LC.

40. WTS to TE, June 16, 1856, WTS to Johnson, June 7, 1856, WTS, LC; order calling out militia, June 4, 1855, and undated newspaper clipping, WTS, scrapbook, WTS, OHS.

41. WTS to TE, June 16, 1856, Johnson to WTS, June 10, 1856, WTS, LC; WTS to HST, July 2, 1856, copy, SFP, UNDA.

42. WTS to HST, July 2, August 18, 1856, copies, SFP, UNDA.

43. TE to ES, July 1, 1856, TE to WTS, July 1, 1856, SFP, UNDA; WTS to W. A. Scott, November 17, 1856, William A. Scott Papers, BL; WTS to JS, August 3, 1856, WTS, LC.

44. ES to MBE, July 4, 1856, copy, SFP, UNDA; JS to WTS, July 15, 1856, WTS to JS, August 19, December 4, 1856, WTS, LC; WTS to HST, October 19, 1856, copy, WTS, OHS.

45. ES to MBE, July 31, 1856, copy, TE to WTS, July 2, 1856, SFP, UNDA; WTS to MSF, October 19, 1856, copy, WTS to HST, October 19, 1856, copy, WTS, OHS; ES to MBE, January 4, 1857, copy, SFP, UNDA.

46. WTS to HST, December 18, 1856, copy, SFP, UNDA; statement closing bank, December 15, 1856, WTS, LC; WTS to TE, January 3, February 19, 1857, TE, LC; WTS to HST, January 18, 1857, copy, SFP, UNDA; WTS to HST, July 3, 1856, WTS, OHS.

47. WTS to A. R. Shepherd, April 24, 1888, WTS, LC; ES to MBE, February 3, 1857, copy, TE to ES, February 27, 1857, MBE to ES, March 15, 1857, copy, ES to MBE, March 20, April 5, 1857, copies, SFP, UNDA.

48. WTS to HST, April 2, March 4, 1857, WTS, OHS.

49. WTS, *Memoirs*, 1:153; WTS to ES, July 13, 1857, SFP, UNDA; WTS to HST, July 24, 1857, WTS, LC; co-partnership notice, July 1, 1857, enclosed in WTS to Riggs and Company, October 20, 1858, CHH, WLC; WTS to HST, April 2, 1857, WTS, OHS; TE to ES, February 1, April 1, 1857, WTS to HST, May 4, 1857, copy, SFP, UNDA; ES to WTS, July 12, 1857, SFP, UNDA.

50. WTS to James H. Lucas, July 21, 1857, letterpress copy, WTS to HST, July 24, 1857, WTS to HST, July 30, 1857, letterpress copy, WTS, LC; WTS, *Memoirs*, 1:153–54; *Proceedings of the Society of the Army of the Tennessee*, 1882, 73, in WTS, pamphlets, WTS, OHS; WTS to HST, August 13, 1857, WTS, OHS; WTS to HST, July 1, 1857, copy, SFP, UNDA; WTS to HST, July 29, 1857, WTS, OHS; WTS to Benjamin R. Nesbit, August 4, 1857, letterpress copy, WTS, LC.

51. ES to WTS, July 26, 1857, SFP, UNDA.

52. WTS to ES, July 29, 1857, SFP, UNDA; WTS to HST, August 10, 1857, WTS, OHS.

53. WTS to HST, January 3, 1858, WTS, OHS; WTS to Nesbit, August 4, 1857, letterpress copy, WTS to W. H. Brooke, August 3, 1857, letterpress copy, WTS to Nesbit, August 14, 1857, letterpress copy, WTS to JS, September 4, 1857, WTS, LC; ES to WTS, September 1, 1857, SFP, UNDA; WTS to J. G. Barnard, December 8, 1858, letterpress copy, WTS, LC; JS, "An Address."

54. WTS to Nesbit, August 14, 1857, letterpress copy, C. F. Ruff to WTS, December 11, 1857, W. G. Freeman to WTS, December 15, 1857, WTS, LC; WTS to HST, January 3, 1858, WTS to HST, September 20, 1858, copy, WTS, OHS; E. A. Hitchcock to WTS, September 1, 1858, WTS to JS, August 22, 1857, WTS, LC.

55. WTS, *Memoirs*, 1:155–56; WTS to Nesbit, September 5, 1857, letterpress copy, WTS, LC; WTS to HST, October 6, 1857, WTS, OHS; WTS to Nesbit, October 7, 1857, letterpress copy, WTS to JS, October 12, 1857, WTS, LC.

56. WTS to JS, September 4, 1857, WTS, LC; WTS to ES, October 6, 1857, SFP, UNDA; WTS to Nesbit, October 7, 1857, letterpress copy, WTS to Lucas, October 7, 1857, letterpress copy, WTS to JS, October 9, November 5, 1857, WTS, LC.

57. WTS to HST, October 10, 1857, WTS, OHS; WTS to JS, October 12, 1857, WTS, LC; WTS to ES, October 23, 1857, WTS to PBE, October 27, 28, 1857, SFP, UNDA; WTS to JS, November 5, 1857, WTS, LC; *Memoirs*, 1:156; WTS to TE, November 17, 1857, TE, LC.

58. WTS to JS, December 16, 27, 1857, WTS, LC; WTS to Samuel Cooper, December 16, 1857, AdeC, PU; Cooper to WTS, December 24, 1857, WTS, LC; WTS to HBE, November 26, 1857, WTS, LC; WTS, *Memoirs*, 1:157–58.

59. NYT, September 10, 1885.

60. WTS to JS, February 4, 1858, WTS, LC; WTS to HST, February 18, 1858, WTS, OHS; ES to WTS, November 29, 30, 1857, SFP, UNDA; WTS to Johnson, February 6, 1858, letterpress copy, WTS to E. D. Baker, February 24, 1858, letterpress copy, WTS, LC; WTS to HST, February 18, 1858, WTS, OHS; WTS to T. H. Stevens, March 21, 1858, letterpress copy, WTS to Meyers, February 19, 1858, letterpress copy, Lucas to WTS, March 15, 31, April 31, [sic] 1858, WTS, LC.

61. WTS to TE, March 3, 1858, TE, LC; WTS to HST, March 4, 21, 1858, copy, WTS, OHS.

62. WTS to TE, April 2, April 15, 1858, TE, LC.

63. WTS, diary, July 7–9, 1858, SFP, UNDA; WTS to Lucas, July 16, 1858, letterpress copy, HST to WTS, August 12, 1858, WTS, LC.

64. WTS, Memoirs, 1:158–61; WTS to TE, Jr., August 9, 1858, WTS to B. R. Alden, July 16, 1858, copy, WTS to JS, August 9, 1858, WTS, LC.

65. WTS, Memoirs, 1:158, ES to WTS, September 12, 15, 1858, WTS to ES, September 14, 18, 25, 1858, SFP, UNDA.

66. WTS, Memoirs, 1:159–60; WTS to ES, September 18, 25, 1858, SFP, UNDA; WTS to TE, Jr., September 18, 1858, TE, LC; Silvia T. Zsoldos, "The Political Career of Thomas Ewing, Sr." (Ph.D. diss., University of Delaware, 1977), 251–52.

67. WTS, Memoirs, 1:161; business card, SFP, UNDA; Leavenworth Conservative in Cincinnati Commercial, February 18, 1865, in Daniel O. Drennan Papers, LC, and in Faunt LeRoy Senour, Major General WTS (Chicago, 1865), 23.

68. H. Miles Moore, Early History of Leavenworth . . . (Leavenworth, 1906), 333–34; WTS to TE, October 13, 1858, TE, LC; Ottumwa (Iowa) Courier, October, 1908, clipping in SFP, UNDA.

69. WTS, Memoirs, 1:160; WTS to ES, October 10, 12, 1858; WTS to JS, October 19, November 16, 1858, WTS, LC.

70. WTS, diary, November 11, 1858; MSF to WTS, November 5, November 15, 1858, copy, SFP, UNDA; ES to MSF, November 22, 1858, WTS, LC; ES to MBE, November 20, 26, 1858, copies, SFP, UNDA. ES discusses her disease in numerous letters. See, for example, ES to MBE, January 10, February 27, 1859, copies, March 29, 1859, TE to ES, February 8, 1859, WTS to ES, April 3, 1859, SFP, UNDA.

71. ES to MBE, December 29, February 14, 1858, copies, ES to Teresa Ewing, January 30, 1859, copy, WTS to ES, April 3, 9, 1859, SFP, UNDA; WTS to TE, January 23, 1859, TE, LC.

72. WTS, Memoirs, 1:160; WTS to ES, April 3, 1859, SFP, UNDA; WTS to F. G. Adams, November 24, 1877, Topeka Commonwealth, undated, in SFP, UNDA, and NYT, December 24, 1877.

73. WTS to ES, April 3, 7, 9, 15, 1859, WTS to F. G. Adams, November 24, 1877, in Topeka Commonwealth, undated, in SFP, UNDA.

74. WTS to ES, January 29, 1859, letterpress copy, WTS to JS, April 30, 1859, WTS to JS, November 16, 1858, January 6, 1859, JS to WTS, December 19, 1858, January 16, 18, 1859, WTS, LC.

75. WTS to JS, February 16, May 27, 1859, WTS, LC.

76. WTS to ES, June 1, 1859, ES to WTS, June 1, 1859, SFP, UNDA; WTS to

HBE, June 8, 1859, WTS, OHS; HST to WTS, June 8, 1859, WTS, LC; ES to WTS, June 3, 8, 1859, SFP, UNDA.

77. WTS to Lucas, June 18, 1859, letterpress copy, Lucas to WTS, June 23, 1859, HST to WTS, January 7, 15, 19, 1859, WTS, LC; WTS to HBE, January 11, 1859, WTS, OHS; WTS to Lucas, June 27, 1859, letterpress copy, WTS, LC.

78. WTS to D. C. Buell, June 11, 1859, letterpress copy, Buell to WTS, June 17, 1859, WTS, LC.

79. WTS to R. G. Wickliffe, July 1, 1859, letterpress copy, WTS, LC; WLF, ed., *General Sherman as a College President* (Cleveland, 1912), 28–29; WTS to TE, November 27, 1859, TE, LC; G. M. Stafford, "Autobiography of GMG," *Louisiana Historical Quarterly* 20 (January 1937): 56; GMG to WTS, July 3, 1859, WTS, LC.

80. WTS to Buell, July 1, 1859, WTS to J. G. Martin, July 1, 1859, letterpress copies, WTS, LC; HBE to WTS, June 4, 5, July 18, 25, 1859; WTS to HBE, July 5, 16, 22, 1859, HBE, journal, vol. 1, WTS, OHS; E. D. Townsend to WTS, August 4, 1859, WTS, LC; WTS, diary, August 3, 1859, SFP, UNDA.

81. R. G. Wickcliffe to WTS, August 5, 1859, WTS, LC; WTS to HBE, August 13, 1859, WTS to JS, August 20, 1859, WTS, LC.

82. WTS to GMG, August 15, 1859, WTS, VHS, copy, DFB, LSU; WTS to GMG, August 20, 1859, copy, WTS, diary, August 24–27, 1859, SFP, UNDA.

83. WTS to G. W. Cullom, September 5, 1859, G. W. Cullom Papers, USMA; WTS to TE, Jr., September 6, 1859, TE, LC.

CHAPTER 6 CONTENTED SOUTHERN SCHOOLMASTER

1. Richard Delafield to WTS, August 30, 1859, D. C. Buell to WTS, September 24, 1859, WTS, LC; George B. McClellen to WTS, October 23, 1859, in WLF, ed., *General Sherman as a College President* (Cleveland, 1912), 40–42; WTS to JS, September 1, 1859, WTS, LC; WTS to GMG, September 7, 1859, in WLF, ed. *General Sherman,* 37–39; WTS, diary, September 9, 30, 1859, SFP, UNDA; WTS to Francis H. Smith, September 25, 1859, Virginia Military Institute Archives, copy in DFB, LSU; WTS to JS, October 6, 1859, September 1, 1859, WTS, LC.

2. ES to WTS, October 5, 24, 27, November 25, 1859, WTS to ES, November 6, 1859, SFP, UNDA.

3. WTS to ES, October 29, 1859, SFP, UNDA.

4. WTS to ES, November 12, 1859, SFP, UNDA; Germaine Reed, *David French Boyd, Founder of Louisiana State University* (Baton Rouge, 1977), 16.

5. WTS to ES, November 12, 1859, SFP, UNDA; WLF, *Louisiana State University, 1860–1896* (Baton Rouge, 1936), 26; WTS to MES, November 21, 1859, SFP, UNDA; WTS to TE, November 27, 1859, WLF, ed., *General Sherman,* 63.

6. WTS to ES, November 19, 25, 1859, SFP, UNDA; Bragg to WTS, November 13, 1859, WLF, ed., *General Sherman,* 52; JS to WTS, November

18, 1859, WTS, LC; Grady McWhiney, *Braxton Bragg and Confederate Defeat* (New York, 1969), 147–49.

7. WTS to ES, December 2, 1859, SFP, UNDA; WTS to MSF, December 7, 1859, WTS, OHS.

8. WTS to ES, December 12, 16, 1859, SFP, UNDA.

9. JS to WTS, December 24, 1859, WTS, LC; WTS to ES, December 23, 1859, SFP, UNDA.

10. WTS to ES, January 12, 1860, WTS to GMG, January 13, 1860, SFP, UNDA; GMG to WTS, January 15, 1860, WLF, ed., *General Sherman*, 123; Bragg to WTS, December 16, 1859, WTS, LC; Beauregard to WTS, January 12, 1860, WTS to TE, Jr., February 17, 1860, WLF, ed., *General Sherman*, 110, 173.

11. WTS, *Memoirs*, 1:167–68; WTS to TE, Jr., December 23, 1859, WLF, ed., *General Sherman*, 89; WTS to TE, Jr., June 21, 1860, TE, LC.

12. WTS to ES, December 28, 1859, January 4, 1860, SFP, UNDA; Beauregard to WTS, January 4, 1860, WLF, ed., *General Sherman*, 100.

13. WTS to ES, January 4, 27, 1860, WTS to GMG, January 13, 1860, copy, SFP, UNDA; DFB, "William Tecumseh Sherman, First Superintendent of the Louisiana State Seminary, Now the Louisiana State University," [LSU] *Alumnus* 5 (October 1909): 5. For similar information, see DFB, "Gen. W. T. Sherman, His Early Life in the South and His Relations with Southern Men," *Confederate Veteran* 28 (September 1910): 409–14; WTS to MSF, January 22, 1860, WTS, OHS.

14. *Louisiana Democrat*, August 3, 1859, WLF, ed., *General Sherman*, 24–26; WLF, *Louisiana State University*, 31–33; Reed, *David French Boyd*, 18–19.

15. WLF, ed., *General Sherman*, 28–29, 36–37, 64–68; WTS to DFB, August 30, 1860, WLF, ed., *General Sherman*, 262; WTS to ES, June 28, 1860, SFP, UNDA.

16. WLF, *Louisiana State University*, 46, WTS to GMG, January 29, 1860, copy, WTS to ES, February 3, 1860, SFP, UNDA; WTS to GMG, May 16, June 15, 1860, copy, DFB, LSU; WTS to GMG, January 30, February 6, 1860, "P.T-R" to GMG, WLF, ed., *General Sherman*, 142–43, 147–48; WTS to GMG, February 10, 1860, copy, SFP, UNDA.

17. WTS to GMG, June 16, 1860, SFP, UNDA; GMG to "P.T-R," February 10, 1860, WLF, ed., *General Sherman*, 149; WTS to ES, February 10, 1860, SFP, UNDA; DFB, "General W. T. Sherman as a College President," *American College* 2 (April 1910): 6.

18. DFB, "WTS," 4–6.

19. Ibid., 6; DFB, "College President," 3.

20. ES to WTS, December 5, 20, 26, 1859, SFP, UNDA; TE to WTS, January 10, 14, 1859, WTS, LC.

21. WTS to ES, December 23, 1859, January 4, 27, 1860, SFP, UNDA; WTS to HBE, February 9, 1860, WTS, LC; TE, Jr., to WTS, February 2, 1860, copy, TE, LC; WTS to GMG, February 8, 1860, SFP, UNDA.

22. WTS, diary, February 11, 1860, SFP, UNDA; WTS to TE, February 12, 1860, WLF, ed., *General Sherman*, 161; WTS to JS, February 12, 1860, WTS, LC.

23. WTS to ES, February 13, 1860, SFP, UNDA.

24. WTS to JS, February 21, 1860, WTS, LC; WTS to GMG, February 21, March 1, 1860, copy, SFP, UNDA; WTS to Board of Supervisors, March 1, 1860, WLF, ed., *General Sherman*, 182–83.

25. Thomas O. Moore to GMG, February 21, 1860, Beauregard to WTS, February 23, 1860, WLF, ed., *General Sherman*, 181–82; WTS, diary, March 1, 1860; WTS to GMG, March 1, 1860, WLF, ed., *General Sherman*, 183; WTS to ES, March 3, 1860; SFP, UNDA.

26. WTS, diary, March 11, 14, 30, 1860, ES, diary, March 11, 13, 15, 20, 1860, SFP, UNDA; HBE, diary, March 14, 18, 1860, HBE, OHS; WTS to GMG, March 15, 1860, copy, SFP, UNDA; WTS to GMG, March 21, 1860, WLF, ed., *General Sherman*, 193.

27. WTS to HBE, April 15, 1860, WTS, OHS.

28. ES to WTS, March 28, June 11, 17, May 1, 1860, SFP, UNDA; WTS to GMG, March 6, 21, 1862, WLF, ed., *General Sherman*, 187–88, 192–93.

29. WTS, *Memoirs*, 1:169, 120; WTS to Boyd, August 5, 1860, WLF, ed., *General Sherman*, 250–51.

30. WTS to TE, Jr., May 11, 1860, TE, LC.

31. WTS to GMG, August 12, 30, 1860, copies, SFP, UNDA.

32. WTS, *Memoirs*, 1:168–69; WLF, "W. T. Sherman as a History Teacher," Louisiana State University *Bulletin* 11 (October 1911): 235–36.

33. WTS to DFB, August 19, 1860, copy, SFP, UNDA; DFB, "College President," 5; DFB, "WTS," 8; WTS to DFB, September 16, 1860, WLF, ed., *General Sherman*, 280; WTS to JS, May 8, 1860, WTS, LC; WTS to GMG, September 30, 1860, copy, SFP, UNDA.

34. MBE to HBE, October 1, 1860, HBE, OHS; WTS to JS, October 3, 1860, WTS, LC; ES to WTS, October 18, 1860, WTS to GMG, September 16, 1860, copy, SFP, UNDA.

35. WTS to HBE, August 30, 1860, WTS, OHS; WTS to GMG, September 16, 1860, copy, ES to WTS, November 3, 1860, WTS to GMG, September 20, 1860, copy, SFP, UNDA; Bragg to WTS, October 25, 1860, Beauregard to WTS, October 27, 1860, WLF, ed.,*General Sherman*, 298–99; WTS to ES, November 3, 1860, SFP, UNDA; WTS to DFB, October 29, 1865, WLF, NYPL.

36. WTS to E. B. St. Ange, November 4, 1860, WLF, ed., *General Sherman*, 302–3; WLF, *Louisiana State University*, 94–95; WTS, *Memoirs*, 1:170.

37. GMG to WTS, November 5, 1860, WTS to ES, November 10, 1860, SFP, UNDA.

38. WTS, *Memoirs*, 1:171–72.

39. WTS to ES, November 23, 1860, SFP, UNDA; WTS to ES, December 15[?], 1860, WLF, ed., *General Sherman*, 214.

40. WTS to PBE, December 17, 1860, copy, SFP, UNDA; WTS to JS, December 18, 23, 1860, WTS, LC; WTS to ES, December 18, 23, 1860, WTS to GMG, December 25, 1860, January 5, 1861, copies, SFP, UNDA. Robert W. Johannsen made the following comment in respect to the Mexican War: "Such was the nature of early 19th century patriotism—the identification of the individual with the republic—that advancement of self was frequent-

ly inseparable from advancement of the country." Robert W. Johannsen, *To the Halls of Montezumas* . . . (New York, 1985), 66.

41. DFB, "WTS," 9–10; DFB to PTS, December 27, 1891, copy, David Stuart Hornshell to JS, April 19, 1892, SFP, UNDA; DFB to WTS, July 17, 1875, WTS, LC. E. Martin Coulter argued that WTS believed secession meant "disintegration and servile insurrection. If it had appeared certain to Sherman that the Confederacy would have become a stable government developing in peace, he would likely have felt no great concern over secession." E. Merton Coulter, "Sherman and the South," *North Carolina Historical Review* 8 (January 1931): 45.

42. WTS to ES, December 16, 1860; WTS to Moore, January 18, 1861, WTS to JS, January 18, 1861, WTS, LC.

43. WTS, *Memoirs*, 1:173–80; Braxton Bragg to WTS, January 27, 1861, SHMB, ed., "Some War Letters," *North American Review* 143 (November 1886): 504; Kenneth T. Urquhart, "General Richard Taylor and the War in Virginia, 1801–1862" (master's thesis, Tulane University, 1958), 5. In 1885, Cump said he had been "approached by a member of the Knights of the Golden Circle" to take part in a Southern conspiracy against the Union. WTS to Secretary of War, January 6, 1885, Senate Ex. Doc. 48th Cong., 2d sess., copy in WTS, LC; T. Kilby Smith to Mrs. E. B. Smith, March 24, 1864, KS75, HL.

44. WTS to ES, January 20, 1861, ES to WTS, January 29, 1861, SFP, UNDA; HBE, diary, December 14, 1860, HBE, OHS; JS to WTS, January 30, 1861, WTS, LC.

45. WTS to JS, February 1, 1861, WTS, LC; WTS to ES, February 1, 1861, SFP, UNDA; ES to JS, undated but c. February 1, 1861, WTS, LC; WTS to ES, February 10, 1861, ES to WTS, February 6, 1861, SFP, UNDA.

46. WTS, diary, February 19, 1861, SFP, UNDA; Boyd, "WTS," 11; WLF, *Louisiana State University,* 101. Just two years later, WTS heard of Moore's capture and thought a successful trial for treason might undercut the Southern constitutional argument for secession. WTS to TE, June 14, 1863, USMHI.

47. WTS to DFB, February 23, 1861, SFP, UNDA; Powhaten Clarke to LeRoy Boyd, May 21, 1903, copy, SFP, UNDA. In 1883 WTS had a different view: "I recognized that the question at stake was whether we should be free men or slaves. If we had allowed these Southern gentlemen to dictate to us at that time we should have been white slaves." NYT, November 10, 1883.

CHAPTER 7   RELUCTANT WARRIOR UNDER ATTACK

1. WTS, *Memoirs*, 1:184–6. Confederate General E. P. Alexander, in his travels in May 1861, thought the North was taking the war more seriously than the South. Gary W. Gallagher, ed., *Fighting for the Confederacy: The Personal Recollections of General Edward Porter Alexander* (Chapel Hill, 1989), 35.

2. WTS, *Memoirs*, 1:184–86; undated clipping, microfilm roll 51, WTS, LC.

3. WTS, *Memoirs*, 1:185–86; WTS to CE, March 9, 1861, CE, LC; HBE, diary, March 10, 1861, HBE, OHS; WTS to TE, Jr., April 26, 1861, TE, LC.

4. The section on Missouri during this period is based on the excellent account in William E. Parrish, *A History of Missouri*, vol. 3: *1860–1875* (Columbia, 1973), 1–10.

5. WTS, diary, March 20, 1861, SFP, UNDA; WTS to JS, March 9, 21, 22, 1861, WTS, LC; WTS to DFB, April 4, 1861, copy, SFP, UNDA. WTS told RA that he hoped the war would not "degenerate into an unnatural one—maybe of antagonism to slavery." He would only support a war fought "to prevent our people falling into anarchy." WTS to RA, May 20, 1861, RA, LC.

6. ES to MBE, April 7, May 20, 1861, copies, ES to PBE, April 15, 1861, SFP, UNDA.

7. WTS, *Memoirs*, 1:186–87; WTS to JS, May 24, 1861, WTS, LC.

8. M. Blair to WTS, April 6, 1861, WTS to Blair, April 8, 1861, WTS, LC, and WTS, *Memoirs*, 1:188–89; S. A. Smith to WTS, April 24, 1861, WLF, ed., *General Sherman as a College President* (Cleveland, 1912), 378–80; WTS to S. Cameron, May 8, 1861, WTS, LC, and WTS, *Memoirs*, 1:189–90; WTS to William Dennison, May 8, 1861, William Dennison Papers, OHS; WTS to JS, April 18, 1861, WTS, LC.

9. JS to WTS, April 3, May 3, 1861, TE, Jr., to WTS, May 6, 8, 1861, WTS, LC; TE, Jr., to WTS, May 17, 1861, ES to MBE, May 10, 20, 1861, copy, ES to TE, May 11, 1861, SFP, UNDA.

10. Parrish, *History of Missouri*, 12–13.

11. WTS, *Memoirs*, 1:190–92; WTS to TE, Jr., May 11, 23, 1861, WTS to JS, May 11, 20, 1861, WTS, LC.

12. WTS to TE, May 31, 1861, TE, LC; WTS to JS, May 22, 24, 1861, Schuyler Hamilton to WTS, May 31, 1861, C. T. Sherman to WTS, June 2, 1861, WTS, LC; TE, Jr., to HBE, June 5, 1861, HBE, OHS; WTS, diary, June 7, 1861, ES, diary, June 6, 1861, WTS to ES, June 8, 1861, SFP, UNDA; WTS to JS, June 8, 1861, WTS, LC.

13. WTS, diary, June 11, 1861, WTS to ES, June 12, 1861, SFP, UNDA; an untitled Pittsburgh newspaper clipping, February[?], 1891, WTS, OHS; WTS to ES, June 17, 20, 1861, SFP, UNDA. Politicians S. S. Cox and Thurlow Weed apparently also recommended WTS to AL. S. S. Cox, *Three Decades of Federal Legislation* (Providence, 1885), 208; G. G. Van Deusen, *Thurlow Weed* (New York, 1967), 274. In regard to Weed's claim, WTS later wrote: "I am, of course, unable to say; but it is all news to me." WTS to J. M. Dalzell, October 5, 1881, WTS, HPC.

14. WTS, diary, June 12–17, 1861, WTS to ES, June 18, 1861, SFP, UNDA; WTS, *Memoirs*, 1:195–96; WTS to JAG, July 28, 1870, WTS, NYPL, copy in WTS, LC; JS, *Recollections* (Chicago, 1895), 1:250.

15. WTS, diary, June 21–30, 1861, WTS to ES, June 20, 23, July 3, 1861, SFP, UNDA; WTS to JS, June 20, 1861, S.O. No. 105, Hq. of the Army, June 20, 1861, WTS, *Memoirs*, 1:196; E. D. Townsend to WTS, June 28, 1861, S.O. No. 16, Hqs., N.E. Virginia, June 30, 1861, WTS, LC.

16. "Sherman Recollections," undated [1891?], *Brooklyn Eagle* in MSA, scrapbook, WTS, OHS.

17. WTS, *Memoirs,* 1:197–98; WTS to MSF, July 14, 1861, WTS, OHS; WTS to ES, July 16, 1861, SFP, UNDA.

18. GMG to WTS, May 22, 1861, WTS, LC; WTS to MSF, July 14, 1861, WTS, OHS; ES, diary, July 5, 1861, WTS to ES, July 15, 16, 1861, SFP, UNDA.

19. William C. Davis, *Battle at Bull Run* (Garden City, N.Y., 1977), 96.

20. The following description of WTS's role at the Battle of Bull Run is based on the following sources: WTS to A. Baird, July 25, 1861 (WTS official report), O.R., I, 2, 368–71; WTS to ES, July 28, 1861, SFP, UNDA; WTS, *Memoirs,* 1:198–206.

21. WTS to ES, July 28, 1861, SFP, UNDA.

22. WTS to Adjutant General, July 22, 1861, O.R., I, 2, 755; WTS, *Memoirs,* 1:206–7; Davis, *Battle at Bull Run,* 258–59.

23. William T. Lusk to "My Dear Mother," August 5, 1861, William T. Lusk Papers, HL; WTS to Adjutant General, July 23, 1861, in unnamed, undated newspaper clipping, in John P. Nicolson, memoirs, 1866 volume, John P. Nicolson Papers, HL; WTS to ES, August 17, 1861, SFP, UNDA; WTS, *Memoirs,* 1:206.

24. WTS, *Memoirs,* 1:206–8.

25. WTS, speech, *Proceedings of the 7th Annual Reunion of the Army of the Cumberland,* September 17, 18, 1873, pp. 98–99.

26. WTS, *Memoirs,* 1:208.

27. WTS to ES, August 15, 1861, SFP, UNDA.

28. WTS to TE, September 15, 1861, TE, LC; George B. McClellan, *McClellan's Own Story* (New York, 1887), 69–70; WTS to ES, August 3, 17, July 24, 1861, SFP, UNDA.

29. WTS to ES, August 3, 17, 6, 15, 1861, SFP, UNDA.

30. WTS to ES, July 24, August 17, 1861, SFP, UNDA.

31. Brigadier General Commission, August 15, 1861, SFP, UNDA; WTS, *Memoirs,* 1:210; WTS to JS, August 19, 1861, WTS, LC; unaddressed WTS letter, probably to ES, August 1861, SFP, UNDA.

32. WTS to JS, August 19, 1861, WTS, LC; unaddressed WTS letter, probably to ES, August 1861, SFP, UNDA.

33. An excellent brief summary of Kentucky in the Civil War is Lowell H. Harrison, *The Civil War in Kentucky* (Lexington, 1975). E. Merton Coulter, *The Civil War and Readjustment in Kentucky* (Chapel Hill, 1926), is still the fullest account. Unless otherwise indicated, my account of Kentucky on the eve of the war is based on these books.

34. Lowell H. Harrison, "The Civil War in Kentucky; Some Persistent Questions," *Register of the Kentucky Historical Society* 76 (January 1978): 4; O.R., III, 1, 801, IV, 1, 962, quoted in Edward C. Smith, *The Borderland* (New York, 1927), 307.

35. WTS, *Memoirs,* 1:212–14; WTS to ES, September 18, 1861, SFP, UNDA.

36. WTS to ES, September 18, 1861, SFP, UNDA; WTS, *Memoirs,* 1:214; WTS to JS, September 9, 1861, WTS, LC.

37. WTS, *Memoirs*, 1:214–15.

38. Ibid., WTS to Oliver D. Green, September 27, 1861, O.R., I, 4, 278–79.

39. WTS, *Memoirs*, 1:215–16; Joel Tyler Headley, *Grant and Sherman* (New York, 1865), 141–42; W. F. G. Shanks, *Personal Recollections* . . . (New York, 1866), 51–52; Henry Stone, "In Memoriam . . . Sherman," Massachusetts Commandary, MOLLUS, April 9, 1891, 97.

40. Lowell H. Harrison, "A Confederate View of Southern Kentucky, 1861," *Register of the Kentucky Historical Society* 70 (July 1972): 171; Allan Nevins, *War for the Union* (New York, 1959), 2:20.

41. WTS to ES, September 26, 1861, SFP, UNDA; WTS to JS, October 5, 1861, WTS, LC.

42. For an analysis of WTS's antipress attitude in Kentucky, see John F. Marszalek, *Sherman's Other War: The General and the Civil War Press* (Memphis, 1981), chap. 3; WTS to P. P. L'Hommedieu, July 7, 1862, WTS, LC.

43. WTS to ES, October 6, 1861, SFP, UNDA.

44. G.O. No. 6, Department of the Cumberland, October 8, 1861, O.R., I, 4, 297; WTS to Lorenzo Thomas, October 8, 1861, WTS, LC; Thomas to WTS, October 10, 1861, O.R., I, 4, 299–300.

45. WTS to AL, October 10, 14, 1861, O.R., I, 4, 300, 306–7; USG to Chauncey McKeever, October 16, 1861, O.R., I, 3, 536, Salmon P. Chase to WTS, October 13, 1861, WTS, LC; WTS to Chase, October 14, 1861, Salmon P. Chase Papers, HSPa; WTS to ES, October 12, 1861, SFP, UNDA; Shanks, *Personal Recollections*, 54.

46. This description of the Cameron meeting is based on WTS, *Memoirs*, 1:218–20, and Lorenzo Thomas to Simon Cameron, October 21, 1861, O.R., I, 3, 548–49, I, 4, 313–14, reprinted in newspapers all over the country.

47. WTS to ES, October 20, 23, 25, 1861, SFP, UNDA; WTS to L. Thomas, October 22, 1861, O.R., I, 4, 316; WTS to JS, October 26, 1861, WTS, LC; George D. Prentice to AL, November 5, 1861, AL, *Collected Works*, ed. Roy P. Basler (New Brunswick, N.J., 1954), 5, 15n.

48. Marszalek, *Sherman's Other War*, 59–61. When Cameron died in 1889, WTS sent a warm letter of condolences to his family making no reference to this incident. WTS to Wayne McVeigh [*sic*] June 27, 1889, Isaac W. MacVeigh Papers, HSPa.

49. WTS to ES, November 1, 1861, SFP, UNDA; WTS to RA, November 3, 1861, RA, LC; Henry Villard, *Memoirs* (Boston, 1904), 1:209–11; NYT, November 11, 1861; WTS to William Dennison, November 6, 1861, William Coffey Papers, OHS; Salmon P. Chase, *Inside Lincoln's Cabinet* . . . , ed. David Donald (New York, 1954), 51; Marszalek, *Sherman's Other War*, 61–63.

50. WTS to G. H. Thomas, November 11, 12, 1861, AdeC, PU; ES to JS, November 10, 1861, WTS, LC; Marszalek, *Sherman's Other War*, 63; ES, diary, November 8, 9, 1861, ES to MBE, November 11, 1861, copy, SFP, UNDA; ES to JS, November 10, 1861, WTS, LC; TE to ES, November 14, 1861, EFP, LC; WTS to ES, November 1, 1861, WTS to JS,

November 17, 1861, SFP, UNDA; WTS to JS, November 21, 1861, WTS, to LC.

51. S.O. No. 8, Department of Missouri, November 23, 1861, O.R., I, 8, 374; WTS, *Memoirs*, 1:233–34; HWH to WTS, November 24, 1861, WTS, LC; WTS to HWH, November 26, 1861, HWH to WTS, November 27, 1861, WTS to HWH, November 28, 1861, O.R., I, 8, 379, 381–82, 391; ES, diary, November 26, 27, 1861, SFP, UNDA; David S. Stanley, *Personal Memoirs* . . . (Cambridge, Mass., 1917), 79–80; Scuyler Hamilton to WTS, November 28, 1861, O.R., I, 52, I, 198.

52. WTS, *Memoirs*, 1:233–36; HWH to McClellan, December 2, 1861, O.R., I, 52, I, 198.

53. MBE to TE, December 9, 1861, EFP, LC; ES to JS, December 10, 1861 with undated NYT clipping, WTS, LC; *Cincinnati Commercial*, December 11, 1861.

54. Marszalek, *Sherman's Other War*, 63–66; ES to JS, December 12, 1861, WTS, LC; WTS to TE, December 12, 1861, WTS, LC.

55. WTS to HWH, December 12, 1861, O.R., I, 8, 819.

56. PBE to HWH, December 13, 1861, O.R., I, 52, I, 200.

57. Marszalek, *Sherman's Other War*, 65–66; Lyman S. Widney, "Campaigning with 'Uncle Billy,'" *Neales Monthly* 2 (August 1913): 131.

58. JS to ES, December 14, 1861, SFP, UNDA.

59. HWH to PBE, December 17, 1861, HWH to WTS, O.R., I, 8, 441–42, 445; HWH to Elizabeth Halleck, December 14, 1861, SCW, WLC.

60. ES to WTS, December 20, 22, 1861, SFP, UNDA; TE to JS, December 22, 28, 1861, WTS, LC; ES to "My Dear Brother," December 30, 1861, EFP, LC; TE to WTS, December 22, 1861, SFP, UNDA, and TE, LC.

61. WTS to ES, December 17, 1861, SFP, UNDA; S.O. No. 87, Hqs., Department of the Missouri, December 23, 1861, O.R., I, 8, 459; WTS to TE, December 24, 1861, WTS, LC; ES to WTS, December 24, 26[?], 1861, January 1, 4, 1862, SFP, UNDA.

62. ES to WTS, January 8, 1862, SFP, UNDA; Marszalek, *Sherman's Other War*, 72.

63. ES to AL, January 10, 1862, copy, ES to WTS, January 29, 1862, WTS to ES, January 16, 1862, SFP, UNDA.

64. WTS, *Memoirs*, 1:236–37; WTS to ES, January 16, 1862, ES to WTS, January 22, 23, 1862, SFP, UNDA; January 26, February 7, 1862, entries in Clark D. Reynolds, "The Civil and Indian War Diary of Eugene Marshall, Minnesota Volunteer" (master's thesis, Duke University, 1963).

65. Faunt LeRoy Senour, *Major General William T. Sherman* . . . (Chicago, 1865), 51.

66. TE to HWH, February 13, 1862, HWH, DU; ES to HWH, February 13[?], 1862, ES Papers, ISL; HWH to McClellan, July 22, 1862, G.O. No. 37, Hqs., Department of the Missouri, February 14, 1862, O.R., I, 8, 514, 555; HWH to TE, Jr., February 15, 1862, WTS, LC; ES to HWH, February 16, 1862, ES, ISL.

67. WTS to JS, February 23, 1862, WTS, LC; WTS to ES, March 3, 1861, SFP, UNDA.

CHAPTER 8   REBIRTH AT SHILOH

1. WTS, *Memoirs*, 1:245.

2. WTS to ES, March 1, 3, 1862, ES to WTS, March 7, 12, 14, 18, 21, 1862, SFP, UNDA; ES to JS, March 10, 1862, WTS, LC; ES to TE, Jr., March 22, 1862, L. M. Dayton to TE, Jr., March 25, 1862, EFP, LC.

3. WTS, *Memoirs*, 1:245–48; WTS to Commanders of Brigades, March 12, 1862, O.R., I, 10, II, 31; WTS to William McMichael, March 15, 1862, O.R., I, 10, I, 22–24; WTS to ES, March 12, 1862, SFP, UNDA.

4. WTS to JAR, March 17, 1862, O.R., I, 10, I, 27; James Lee McDonough, *Shiloh—In Hell Before Night* (Knoxville, 1977), is the best account of the battle. Unless otherwise noted, the following section of the battle follows this book. Another modern account of the battle is Wiley Sword, *Shiloh, Bloody April* (New York, 1974). For an in-depth account of the enlisted men in this battle, see Joseph Allan Frank and George A. Reaves, *"Seeing the Elephant," Raw Recruits at the Battle of Shiloh* (Westport, Conn., 1989).

5. S.O. No. 12, Hqs., First Division, March 16, 1862, WTS to William McMichael, March 17, 1862, O.R., I, 10, I, 24, 26; WTS to McMichael, March 20, 1862, O.R., I, 10, II, 53; ES to WTS, March 29, 1862, SFP, UNDA; Abstract from Record of Events in Sherman's Division for March, O.R., I, 10, I, 28; WTS to Colonel Stuart, WTS to Colonel Taylor, April 2, 1862, O.R., I, 10, II, 87; WTS to JAR, April 2, 1862, O.R., I, 10, I, 83; WTS to Colonel Buckland, April 3, 1862, O.R., I, 10, II, 90.

6. WTS to ES, April 3, 1862, SFP, UNDA; John T. Taylor, *Reminiscences of the Services of an Aide-de-Camp with General William T. Sherman*, Kansas Commandery, MOLLUS, April 6, 1892, 6.

7. USG to WTS, April 4, 1862, O.R., I, 10, II, 91; *Cincinnati Gazette*, April 18, 1862.

8. WTS to JAR, April 5, 1862, O.R., I, 10, 87; WTS to USG, two notes, April 5, 1862, O.R., I, 10, II, 93–94.

9. *Cincinnati Commercial*, April 18, 1862; McDonough, *Shiloh*, 56; Sword, *Shiloh*, 126–30. After the battle, TE also insisted that WTS keep silent only to prevent a resurrection of the insanity charge. TE to TE, Jr., April 21, 1862, EFP, LC.

10. McDonough, *Shiloh*, 86–90.

11. Ibid., 91–92.

12. Ibid., 93–131; WTS to RA, April 10, 1862, O.R., I, 10, I, 248–49; WTS to Henry Coppee, June 13, 1864, O.R., I, 52, I, 559, also printed in WTS, "The Battle of Pittsburgh Landing. A Letter from General Sherman," *United States Service Magazine* 3 (January 1865): 2–4.

13. WTS to ES, April 11, 1862, SFP, UNDA; Taylor, *Reminiscences*, 7; MBE to HBE, April 11, 1862, HBE, OHS; McDonough, *Shiloh*, 115–16; Albert D. Richardson, *The Secret Service . . .* (Hartford, 1865), 238.

14. Faunt Le Roy Senour, *Major General William T. Sherman and His Campaigns* (Chicago, 1865), 75–76; WTS to TE, May 3, 1862, in Joseph H. Ewing, ed., "Sherman Bashes the Press," *American Heritage* 38 (July–August 1987): 29.

15. McDonough, *Shiloh*, 133–50, 162–66.

16. Ibid., 152–53, 177–78.

17. Ibid., 183–95; WTS to Henry Coppee, June 13, 1864, O.R., I, 52, I, 559.

18. WTS to USG, April 8, 1862, O.R., I, 10, I, 639; WTS, "Description of the Battle of Shiloh," *Proceedings of the Society of the Army of the Tennessee,* April–May 1881, 56; "Recapitulation," O.R., I, 10, I, 108.

19. Lyman S. Widney, "Campaigning with 'Uncle Billy,'" *Neales Monthly* 2 (August 1913): 133.

20. WTS, "Description," 57; WTS to WTS, Jr., April 19, 1862, WTS, OHS.

21. WTS to ES, April 11, 1862, SFP, UNDA; W. F. G. Shanks, *Personal Recollections* . . . (New York, 1886), 52–53; WTS to MBE, April 22, 1862, SFP, UNDA.

22. WTS, "Description," 58; *St. Louis Times,* June 12, 1875, SFP, UNDA; WTS to ES, April 11, 14, 1862, SFP, UNDA; ES to JS, May 4, 1862, WTS, LC; WTS to ES, June 6, 1862, ES to WTS, June 9, 1862, SFP, UNDA.

23. HWH to EPS, April 13, 1862, USG to N. H. McLean, April 9, 1862, O.R., I, 10, I, 98, 110; WTS to ES, May 26, 1862, SFP, UNDA; S. M. Bowman, "Major-General William T. Sherman," *United States Service Magazine* 2 (August 1864): 119.

24. WTS to ES, April 11, 1862, May 3, 6, 7, 1862, SFP, UNDA.

25. WTS to JS, May 12, 26, 1862, WTS, LC.

26. *New York Tribune,* May 23, 1862.

27. WTS, *Memoirs,* 1:275–76; WTS to ES, June 6, 1862, SFP, UNDA.

28. WTS to JS, April 22, 1862, WTS, LC; WTS to T. T. Gantt, May 25, 1886, copy, SFP, UNDA.

29. *Cincinnati Gazette,* April 14, 1862; WTS to TE, April 27, 1862, EFP, LC; WTS to ES, June 6, 1862, WTS to USG, copy, June 6, 1862, SFP, UNDA; WTS to JS, May 12, 1862, WTS, LC.

30. For a detailed account of the controversy, see John F. Marszalek, "William T. Sherman and the Verbal Battle of Shiloh," *Northwest Ohio Quarterly* 42 (Fall 1970): 78–85.

31. WTS to JS, April 22, 1862, WTS, LC; WTS to ES, May 1, June 6, 1862, SFP, UNDA.

32. TE to TE, Jr., April 21, 1862, EFP, LC.

33. JS to WTS, March 20, May 10, 1862, WTS, LC; John J. Patrick, "John Sherman: The Early Years, 1823–1865" (Ph.D. diss., Kent State University, 1982), 148–49; JS to *Cincinnati Commercial,* May 5, 1862; *Cincinnati Gazette,* May 6, 1862; ES to JS, June 12, 1862, WTS, LC.

34. S.O. No. 30, Hqs., Fifth Division, Army of the Tennessee, May 31, 1862, included in WTS to JS, May 31, 1862, WTS, LC; WTS to TE, June 7, 1862, CE, LC.

35. Andrew Hickenlooper, "The Battle of Shiloh," *Sketches of War History, 1861–1865.* Ohio Commendery, MOLLUS (Cincinnati, 1903): 5, 406–7. For a discussion of an example of the postwar controversy over Shiloh, see Chapter 21.

CHAPTER 9   RESTORING ORDER IN MEMPHIS

1. James M. McPherson, *Battle Cry of Freedom* (New York, 1988), 488.
2. *Cincinnati Commercial,* July 24, 1865, in Daniel O. Drennan Papers, LC; WTS to ES, June 2, 1862, SFP, UNDA.
3. HWH to WTS, June 4, 1862, O.R., I, 10, II, 255; WTS to George E. Flynt, June 10, 1862, O.R., I, 10, I, 745–46; WTS to ES, June 22, 27, 1862, SFP, UNDA; Reports of WTS, June 19, July 14, 1862, O.R., I, 17, I, 8–9, 23; WTS to CE, July 8, 1862, CE, LC; ES to WTS, July 3, 17, 1862, WTS to ES, June 27, 1862, SFP, UNDA.
4. WTS to ES, June 10, 1862, SFP, UNDA, G.O. No. 56, Hqs., Fifth Division, Army of the Tennessee, July 21, 1862, O.R. I, 17, II, 110.
5. WTS to HWH, June 16, 1862, O.R., I, 17, II, 100–101.
6. Joseph H. Parks, "Memphis Under Military Rule, 1862–1865," East Tennessee Historical Society *Publications* (1942): 34–35.
7. WTS, *Memoirs,* 1:285–86, G.O. Nos. 56, 60, 61, 64, Hqs., Fifth Division, Army of the Tennessee, July 21, 22, 24, 25, 1862, WTS to JAR, July 25, 1862, O.R., I, 17, II, 113, 117–18, 121–23; Joseph H. Parks, "A Confederate Trade Center Under Federal Occupation: Memphis 1862–1865," *Journal of Southern History* 7 (August 1941): 295–97, WTS to Samuel Sawyer, July 24, 1862, O.R., I, 17, II, 116–17.
8. Lloyd Lewis, *Sherman Fighting Prophet* (New York, 1932), 243; WTS to John Park, July 27, 1862, WTS to Captain Fitch, August 7, 1862, O.R., I, 17, II, 127, 157.
9. NYT, July 26, 1862; WTS to JAR, July 30, 1862, O.R., I, 17, II, 140–41; WTS to ES, August 5, 1862, SFP, UNDA; WTS to Adjutant General of the Army, WTS to USG, WTS to Salmon Chase, August 11, 1862, HWH to WTS, August 14, 1862, WTS to HWH, August 18, 1862, O.R., III, 2, 350, 382, 402, 454; Gerald M. Capers, *The Biography of a River Town: Memphis — Its Heroic Age* (Chapel Hill, 1939), 157–59.
10. John T. Taylor, *Reminiscences of Services as an Aide-de-Camp with General William T. Sherman,* Kansas Commandery, MOLLUS, April 6, 1892, 8–9; WTS to ES, July 31, 1862, SFP, UNDA; G.O. No. 43, Hqs., Fifth Division, Army of the Tennessee, June 18, 1862, O.R., I, 17, II, 15.
11. G.O. No. 60, Hqs., Fifth Division, Army of the Tennessee, July 22, 1862, O.R., I, 17, II, 113; WTS to L. B. Parsons, August 30, 1862, Lewis B. Parsons Papers, ISL; WTS to ES, July 31, 1862, SFP, UNDA.
12. G.O. No. 67, Hqs., Fifth Division, Army of the Tennessee, August 8, 1862, O.R., I, 17, II, 158–60; WTS to John Catron, September 9, 1862, enclosed in B. W. Sharp to AJ, October 11, 1862, AJ, LC.
13. WTS to JS, September 3, October 1, 1862, WTS, LC.
14. WTS to J. T. Swayne, November 12, 1862, WTS to B. W. Sharpe, November 14, 1862, WTS to Joseph Tagg, November 17, 1862, O.R., I, 17, II, 863–66; 370, Parks, "Military Rule," 46; John Cimprich, *Slavery's End in Tennessee, 1861–1865* (University, Ala., 1985), 41–42.
15. Albert D. Richardson, *The Secret Service . . .* (Hartford, Conn., 1865), 269–70.

16. WTS to USG, August 26, 1862, O.R., I, 17, II, 187; Parks, "Confederate Trade Center," 298–99.

17. G.O. No. 66, Hqs., Fifth Division, Army of the Tennessee, August 7, 1862, O.R., I, 17, II, 158; WTS to USG, October 9, November 8, 1862, O.R., I, 17, II, 158, 273, 861.

18. WTS to Salmon P. Chase, August 11, 1862, O.R., III, 2, 382, original in Salmon P. Chase Papers, HSPa.

19. WTS to HWH, July 14, 1862, O.R., I, 17, 23; WTS to USG, August 17, 18, O.R., I, 17, II, 178; JS to WTS, August 8, 24, 1862, WTS, LC; ES to WTS, August 30, 1862, SFP, UNDA.

20. WTS to ES, August 20, 1862, WTS to Editors of Memphis *Bulletin* and *Appeal*, August 21, 1862, SFP, UNDA; WTS to JAR, September 26, 1862, S.O. No. 254, Hqs., Fifth Division, Army of the Tennessee, O.R., I, 17, 144–45, 240.

21. WTS to T. C. Hindman, September 28, October 17, 1862, O.R., I, 13, 682–83, 742–43; WTS to John C. Pemberton, November 18, 1862, O.R., II, 4, 723–25; WTS to P. A. Fraser, WTS to Valerie Hurlbert, October 22, November 7, 1862, O.R., I, 17, II, 287–88; WTS to Samuel R. Curtis, September 29, 1862, O.R., II, 4, 574; Parks, "Military Rule," 45.

22. G.O. No. 44, Hqs., Fifth Division, Army of the Tennessee, June 18, 1862; G.O. No. 82, Hqs., Fifth Division, Army of the Tennessee, September 15, 1862, O.R., I, 17, II, 16, 19–20; WTS to ES, September 25, 1862, SFP, UNDA; WTS to DDP, November 16, 1862, O.R., I, 17, II, 867.

23. WTS to JS, October 1, 1862, WTS, LC; WTS to P. A. Fraser, October 22, 1862, WTS to USG, October 9, 1862, O.R., I, 17, II, 288, 261.

24. John W. Brinsfield, "The Military Ethics of General William T. Sherman," *Parameters* 12 (June 1982): 39–40; WTS to JS, August 13, 1862, in Carey S. Bliss, ed., "An Unpublished Letter of General William T. Sherman," *Huntington Library Quarterly* 8 (November 1944): 105–9; excerpts in "Killed or Transported," *Confederate Veteran* 32 (1924): 156–57.

25. WTS to George D. Prentice, November 1, 1862, WTS to USG, November 8, 1862, WTS to John C. Pemberton, November 18, 1862, WTS to AJ, August 10, 1862, O.R., I, 17, II, 858–59, 861, 872–73, 161.

26. WTS to ES, October 4, 1862, SFP, UNDA; John F. Marszalek, *Sherman's Other War: The General and the Civil War Press* (Memphis, 1981), 31.

27. Marszalek, *Sherman's Other War*, 107; ES to WTS, August 6, 1862, SFP, UNDA; WTS to JS, August 26, 1862, WTS, LC; WTS to R. C. Huchison, April 30, 1879, WTS, LC.

28. WTS to Edwin Booth, April 5, 1889, The Players—New York City, Miscellaneous Collection, LC; Anna S. McAllister, *Flame in the Wilderness* . . . (Notre Dame, Ind., 1944), 194–96; WTS to Orville Babcock, April 28, 1895, WTS (Addition) Collection, DU; WTS to ES, August 10, 1862, SFP, UNDA.

29. ES to MBE, November 21, 1862, SFP, UNDA.

30. WTS to MSF, August 6, October 4, 1862, WTS, OHS.

31. Marszalek, *Sherman's Other War*, 94–116; NYT, February 20, 1891; WTS to W. H. H. Taylor, August 25, 1862, O.R., I, 52, 275.

32. WTS to JS, September 22, 1862, WTS, LC; WTS to George D. Prentice, November 1, 1862, O.R., I, 17, II, 858–59; WTS to W. K. Strong, November 1, 1862, SCW, WLC.

33. USG to WTS, November 15, 1862, WTS to JS, November 25, 1862, WTS, LC; WTS to DDP, November 16, 1862, O.R., I, 17, II, 867; Allan Nevins, *War for the Union* (New York, 1961), 2:294–95.

34. WTS to JS, December 6, 1862, WTS, LC; WTS to ES, December 6, 1862, SFP, UNDA; USG to WTS, December 8, 1862, O.R., I, 17, 601.

35. ES to WTS, November 27, 1862, SFP, UNDA; WTS to JS, December 14, 1862, James H. Otey to WTS, December 1, 1862, Resolution of Washington Union Club, Memphis, December 17, 1862, WTS to JS, December 20, 1862, WTS, LC; WTS to "My Dearest Children," December 8, 1862, WTS, OHS; ES to JS, December 11, 1862, WTS to JS, December 20, 1862, WTS, LC.

36. WTS to ES, December 14, 1862, SFP, UNDA.

37. ES to WTS, December 15, 1862, SFP, UNDA.

38. ES to JS, December 11, 1862, WTS, LC; ES to WTS, December 13, 1862, August 21, 1862, SFP, UNDA.

CHAPTER 10 BATTLING THE BAYOUS TO REACH THE VICKSBURG FORTRESS

1. WTS to Alfred Townsend, December 14, 1862, Wagstaff Collection, USMA. For an excellent analysis of the symbolism of the Mississippi River to the Midwest, see Earl J. Hess, "The Mississippi River and Secession: The Northwestern Response," *Old Northwest* 10 (Summer 1984): 187–207.

2. WTS to HWH; January 5, 1863, O.R., I, 17, I, 613–14.

3. WTS to Generals Steele, Morgan, A. J. Smith, and M. L. Smith, December 23, 1862, O.R., I, 17, I, 616–17; Herman Hattaway, "Confederate Myth Making: Top Command and the Chickasaw Bayou Campaign," *Journal of Mississippi History* 32 (November 1970): 315.

4. DDP to WTS, November 12, 24, 1862, O.R., Navy, I, 23, 479, 501; WTS, *Memoirs*, 1:285. McClernand always believed that preventing his command was the reason for the expedition's swift departure. John A. McClernand to George W. Morgan, November 30, 1875, WTS, WRHS.

5. DDP, *Incidents and Anecdotes of the Civil War* (New York, 1886), 125.

6. WTS to ES, December 14, 1862, SFP, UNDA; WTS to JS, December 20, 1862, WTS, LC; WTS to JAR, December 16, 1862, O.R., I, 17, I, 603.

7. Helpful synopses of the Chickasaw Bayou battle include: Hattaway, "Confederate Myth Making," 311–26, and D. Alexander Brown, "Battle of the Chickasaw Bluffs," *Civil War Times Illustrated* 9 (July 1970): 4–9, 44–48.

8. G.O. Nos. 7, 8, Hqs., Right Wing, Thirteenth Army Corps, December 18, 1862, O.R., I, 17, I, 618–20; "Memorandum of E. Paul Reichhelm, Sergeant Major, Third Infantry Missouri Volunteers, U.S.A., 1862," unpublished manuscript, E. Paul Reichhelm Papers, Library of Congress.

9. Reichhelm, "Memorandum."

10. Ibid.; WTS, *Memoirs*, 1:312–13.

11. WTS to Generals Steele, Morgan, A. J. Smith, and M. L. Smith, December 23, 1862, G.O. Nos. 34, 36, Hqs., Right Wing, Thirteenth Army Corps, December 25, 1862, WTS to JAR, January 3, 1863, O.R., I, 17, I, 66–67, 620–22, 605–11; WTS "Remarks" [January 1863], WTS, LC; WTS to DDP, December 28, 1862, WTS, HL; Reichhelm, "Memorandum."

12. WTS to JAR, January 3, 1863, O.R., I, 17, I, 607–8; WTS, "Remarks" [January 1863], WTS, LC; Hattaway, "Confederate Myth Making," 322–24; Reichhelm, "Memorandum." Actually, WTS blamed General George W. Morgan for not pushing his part of the attack. But as a WTS biographer put it, there was more "faith than realism" in WTS's statement; B. H. Liddell-Hart, *Sherman* (New York, 1958), 164. Morgan later published a defense of his battlefield conduct. George W. Morgan, "The Assault on Chickasaw Bluffs," *Battles and Leaders of the Civil War*, ed. Robert Underwood Johnson and Clarence C. Buel (New York, 1884), 3:462–71.

13. John F. Marszalek, *Sherman's Other War: The General and the Civil War Press* (Memphis, 1981), 125–26, 120–21.

14. Reichhelm, "Memorandum"; WTS to JAR, January 3, 1863, O.R., I, 17, I, 609–10; WTS to ES, January 4, 1863, SFP, UNDA.

15. Franc B. Wilkie, *Pen and Powder* (Boston, 1888), 212–13; William L. B. Jenney, "Personal Recollections of Vicksburg," Chicago Literary Club, December 14, 1885, unpublished manuscript, William L. B. Jenney Papers, microfilm, Art Institute of Chicago.

16. "Extract from Admiral Porter's Journal," enclosed in DDP to WTS, May 29, 1875, WTS, LC; WTS, *Memoirs*, 1:319–20.

17. Reichhelm, "Memorandum"; Levi Nelson Green, diary, January 2, 1863, Green Papers, MiHS; Carlos W. Colby, "Bullets, Hardtack, and Mud: A Soldier's View of the Vicksburg Campaign," ed. John S. Painter, *Journal of the West* 4 (April 1965): 135.

18. WTS to A. Schwartz, January 13, 1863, O.R., I, 17, I, 754–59; WTS, *Memoirs*, 1:321–23, 302; WTS to ES, February 22, 1863, SFP, UNDA.

19. L. M. Dayton to ES, January 14, 1863, WTS, LC; WTS to ES, January 12, 1863, SFP, UNDA.

20. WTS to ES, January 16, 1863, SFP, UNDA; WTS to JWD, November 24, 1867, JWD, LC, published in WTS, "Vicksburg by New Years," *Civil War Times Illustrated* 16 (January 1978): 44–48; WTS to JS, January 17, 1863, WTS, LC.

21. WTS to WW, April 17, 1863, WW, ISL; DDP to Gideon Welles, January 18, 1863, DDP to James W. Grimes, January 24, 1863, DDP to A. W. Ellet, January 29, 1863, O.R., Navy [*Official Records of the Union and Confederate Navies in the War of the Rebellion*, 30 vols., 1892–1922], I, 24, 179–80, 194–95, 209–10; ES to WTS, January 19, 30, 1863, MBE to ES, copy, January 22, 1863, SFP, UNDA; TE to PBE, January 7, 1863, TE, OHS; ES to WTS, January 23, 1863, SFP, UNDA; TE to WTS, February 8, 20, 1863, TE, LC; Irvin McDowell to WTS, January 28, 1863, Ord to WTS, February 13, 1863, Officers of . . . Fifteenth Army Corps to USG, February 10, 1863, WTS, LC; USG to AL, July 22, 1863, in SHMB, ed., "Some War Letters," *North American Review* 144 (March 1887): 395.

22. WTS to ES, January 28, 1863, SFP, UNDA; WTS to JS, January 25, 1863, WTS, LC; ES to WTS, February 10, 1863, SFP, UNDA.

23. WTS to DDP, February 4, 1863, O.R., I, 17, II, 889; WTS to ES, February 15, 1863, SFP, UNDA; WTS to TE, February 6, 1863, USMHI. One of WTS's division commanders agreed with WTS. Significantly, he said: "Our country is in an awful condition, we are verging rapidly upon anarchy." Thomas Kilby Smith to Elza B. Smith, February 4, 1863, K564, HL.

24. Wilkie, *Pen and Powder*, 23–24; Emmet Crozier, *Yankee Reporters, 1861–1865* (New York, 1956), 3, 6.

25. Thomas Knox to WTS, two letters, February 1, 1863, O.R., I, 17, II, 580–81; Knox to WTS, February 1, 1863, WTS, LC.

26. WTS to Murat Halstead, April 8, 1863, O.R., I, 17, II, 896.

27. WTS to DDP, February 1, 1863, DDP to WTS, February 3, 1863, WTS to Frank Blair, February 1, 1863, Blair to WTS, February 1, WTS to Blair, February 2, 3, 1863, O.R., I, 17, 882–83, 587–90; Blair to WTS, February 3, 1863, WTS to JS, February 4, 1863, WTS, LC; WTS to JAR, February 4, 1863, O.R., I, 17, II, 763, WTS to ES, February 4, 1863, SFP, UNDA; WTS to HBE, February 4, 1863, WTS, OHS.

28. The discussion of the court-martial, unless otherwise noted, is based on Marszalek, *Sherman's Other War*, 117–53, and Marszalek, "The Knox Court-Martial: W. T. Sherman Puts the Press on Trial (1863)," *Military Law Review* 59 (Winter 1973): 197–214. A dramatization based on the account in *Sherman's Other War* is Jim Macak, "Cats in Hell Without Claws."

29. G.O. No. 13, Hqs., Department of the Tennessee, February 19, 1863, O.R., I, 17, II, 889–92.

30. WTS to JAR, February 23, 1863, O.R., I, 17, II, 892–93; Adam Badeau, *Military History of Ulysses S. Grant* (New York, 1868), 1:61.

31. A good brief overview of these plans is found in William C. Everhart, *Vicksburg* (Washington, D.C., 1954), 10–16. A detailed account is Samuel Carter III, *The Final Fortress: The Campaign for Vicksburg, 1862–1863* (New York, 1980), 110–21, 135–49.

32. HBE, diary, HBE, OHS; DDP to Gideon Welles, January 28, 1863, O.R., Navy, I, 24, 205. A successful canal had been dug earlier to divert the Mississippi at Island No. 10. In ancient times, Cyrus diverted the Euphrates River to capture Babylon. JWD, *History of the American Civil War* (New York, 1870), 3:28.

33. WTS to ES, March 16, 1863, SFP, UNDA.

34. USG to WTS, March 16, 1863, O.R., I, 24, I, 431. This account of the Steele Bayou expedition, unless otherwise noted, is based on: WTS to JAR, March 21, 29, 1863, O.R., Navy, I, 24, 474–80; WTS, *Memoirs*, 1:326–31.

35. DDP, *Incidents*, 168.

36. WTS to ES, April 6, 1863, SFP, UNDA; WTS to JS, April 3, 1863, WTS, LC.

37. Albert D. Richardson, *Secret Service . . .* (Hartford, 1865), 318–20; J. M. Winchell, "Three Interviews with President Lincoln," *Galaxy* 16 (1873): 33–34; Lincoln to whom it may concern, March 20, 1863, USG to Knox,

Knox to WTS, April 6, 1863, WTS to Knox, April 7, 1863, O.R., I, 17, II, 894–95; WTS to USG, April 8, 1863, O.R., I, 17, II, 895–96.

38. USG to WTS, March 22, 1863, O.R., Navy, I, 24, 489.

39. DDP, *Naval History of the Civil War* (New York, 1886), 307.

40. WTS, *Memoirs*, 1:339; newspaper quotation in Carter, *Final Fortress*, 150; WTS to David Tod, March 12, 1863, O.R., III, 3, 65–66.

41. WTS to JAR, April 8, 1863, in WTS, *Memoirs*, 1:39–40; USG, *Memoirs*, 318–20; WTS to Adam Badeau, March 8, 1879, WTS, LC.

42. Adam Badeau, *Military History of General Grant* (New York, 1868), 1:182–85. For Grant's postwar discussions of these matters, see John Russell Young, *Tour Around the World with General Grant* (New York, 1879), 2:216–17.

43. "Memorandum . . . Admiral Porter," O.R., Navy, I, 23, 408–9.

44. WTS, *Memoirs*, 1:344; WTS to JAR, April 19, 1863, O.R., I, 24, III, 207–8; WTS to ES, April 23, 1863, SFP, UNDA.

45. DDP, *Incidents*, 176.

46. John L. Vance to John C. Shepherd, April 9, 1863, John L. Vance Papers, OHS.

47. "Memorandum . . . Admiral Porter," O.R., Navy, I, 23, 410–14.

48. USG to WTS, April 24, 1863, G.O. Nos. 26, Hqs., Fifteenth Army Corps, April 25, 1863, WTS to USG, April 26, 1863, WTS to J. M. Tuttle, April 26, 1863, WTS to Fred Steele, April 27, 1863, O.R., I, 24, III, 231, 233–35, 240–41; WTS to ES, April 23, 1863, SFP, UNDA; WTS to JS, April 23, 1863, WTS, LC; WTS to L. Thomas, April 24, 1863, O.R., III, 3, 164–65.

49. USG to WTS, April 27, 1863, O.R., Navy, I, 24, 591; WTS to USG, April 28, 1863, two letters, O.R., I, 24, III, 242–44.

50. Edwin C. Bearss, "Sherman's Demonstration Against Snyder's Bluff," *Journal of Mississippi History* 27 (1965): 168–86; WTS to ES, May 2, 1863, SFP, UNDA; WTS to JAR, May 24, 1863, O.R., I, 24, I, 752.

51. WTS, *Memoirs*, 1:345. For an excellent account of John C. Pemberton and the Confederate military effort around Vicksburg, see Michael B. Ballard, *Pemberton: A Biography* (Jackson, Miss., 1991).

52. WTS to Frank Blair, May 24, 1863, G.O. No. 29, Hqs., Fifteenth Army Corps, May 2, 1863, USG to WTS, May 3, 1863, WTS to J. M. Tuttle, May 5, 1863, O.R., I, 24, III, 262–64, 268–69, 271–74; *St. Louis Republic*, February 21, 1891, in WTS, OHS.

53. WTS to ES, May 9, 1863, UNDA; WTS to USG, USG to WTS, May 9, 1863, O.R., I, 24, III, 285–86. A detailed account of the Vicksburg campaign is Carter, *Final Fortress*. Brief accounts are Stephen E. Ambrose, *Struggle for Vicksburg* (Harrisburg, Penn., 1967); William C. Everhart, *Vicksburg* (Washington, D.C., 1954). Unless otherwise indicated, the following account of this campaign is based on these sources.

54. Grant, *Memoirs*, 298; WTS, *Memoirs*, 1:347–48.

55. G.O. No. 2, Hqs., Right Wing, December 6, 1862, G.O. No. 3, Hqs., Fifteenth Army Corps, January 12, 1863, O.R., I, 17, II, 390–91, 556–57; WTS to ES, May 6, 1863, SFP, UNDA.

56. WTS to Frederick Steele, March 31, 1863, O.R., I, 24, III, 158.

57. WTS to Steele, April 19, 1863, O.R., I, 24, 209; WTS to David Tod, March 12, 1863, O.R., III, 3, 65.

58. WTS, *Memoirs*, 1:348–49.

59. USG to AL, July 22, 1863, copy, SFP, UNDA; WTS to USG, May 17, 1863, O.R., I, 24, III, 322; WTS, *Memoirs*, 1:349.

60. WTS, *Memoirs*, 1:350; USG, *Memoirs*, 309. Young, *Tour*, 2:624.

61. WTS, *Memoirs*, 1:351–52; WTS to DDP, May 19, 1863, O.R., I, 24, III, 328–29; WTS to JAR, May 24, 1863, O.R., I, 24, I, 755–56.

62. WTS to ES, June 11, 1863, SFP, UNDA.

63. HBE, journal, vol. 1, May 31, 1863, HBE, OHS.

64. WTS to ES, May 19, 1863, SFP, UNDA.

65. Ibid., May 25, 1863, WTS, LC.

66. Unnamed, undated newspaper clipping, box 14, WTS, OHS. See also WTS, *Memoirs*, 1:352, and WTS to EPS, August 8, 1863, quoted in S. M. Bowman and R. B. Irwin, *Sherman and His Campaigns* (New York, 1865), 127; Fred Dent Grant, "With Grant at Vicksburg," *Outlook*, July 2, 1898, 54.

67. William S. McFeely, *Grant: A Biography* (New York, 1981), 132; WTS to ES, June 2, 1863, SFP, UNDA.

68. G.O. No. 40, Hqs., Fifteenth Army Corps, May 23, 1863, O.R., I, 24, III, 343–44; WTS to ES, June 2, 1863, SFP, UNDA; AL to John A. Dix, June 8, 1863, Roy P. Basler, ed., *The Collected Works of Abraham Lincoln* (New Brunswick, N.J., 1953), 6: 254; ES to WTS, June 21, 1863, SFP, UNDA; WTS to MSF, June 13, 1863, WTS, OHS; WTS to WTS, Jr., June 21, 1863, ES to WTS, June 23, July 1, 1863, SFP, UNDA.

69. WTS to ES, May 25, 1863, SFP, UNDA; USG to WTS, June 22, 1863, O.R., I, 24, III, 428.

70. WTS to JS, June 20, 1863, WTS, LC; WTS to JAR, June 27, 1863, O.R., I, 24, II, 247; WTS to JAR, June 17, 1863, O.R., I, 24, I, 162.

71. WTS to USG, July 1, 1863, O.R., I, 24, II, 248–49; WTS to ES, June 21, 27, 1863, SFP, UNDA; WTS, *Memoirs*, I, 329–30.

72. WTS to ES, July 5, 1863, SFP, UNDA.

73. Ibid.; WTS to USG, July 4, 1863, O.R., I, 24, III, 472; WTS to J. C. McCurdy and Company, copy, May 4, 1884, WTS, LC.

74. WTS to USG, July 4, 1863, O.R., I, 24, III, 472; Memorandum Order, Hqs., Expeditionary Army, July 14, 1863, WTS to USG, July 14, 1863, O.R., I, 24, II, 510, 524–25; WTS to DDP, July 4, 1863, WTS to Ord, July 17, 1863, WTS to Colonel Hubbard, July 19, 1863, WTS to USG, July 17, 1863, WTS to DDP, July 19, 1863, O.R., I, 24, III, 531–38; WTS to USG, July 17, 18, 1863, O.R., I, 24, II, 528–29. For one detailed account that shows that Jackson was not burned to the ground, as myth would have it, see Beverly Kennon to WTS, September 24, 1886, WTS, LC.

75. WTS to USG, July 21, 1863, WTS to C. H. Manship, July 21, 1863, O.R., I, 24, II, 530–31, 539; USG to WTS, July 21, 1863, O.R., I, 24, III, 539, WTS to USG, July 22, 1863, O.R., I, 24, II, 531–32; WTS to Jesse Reed et al., August 3, 1863, O.R., I, 24, III, 571–72.

76. WTS to USG, July 14, 1863, O.R., I, 24, II, 526; WTS to JAR, August 4, 1863, O.R., I, 24, III, 574–75.

77. WTS to JS, July 19, 1863, WTS, LC; USG to AL, July 22, 1863, O.R., I, 24, III, 540–42; HWH to WTS, August 4, 1863, SFP, UNDA; WTS to TE, August 13, 20, 1863, TE, LC; Charles A. Dana, "Reniniscences . . . ," McClure's Magazine 10 (January 1898): 255; JS to WTS, July 18, 1863, WTS, LC.

78. WTS to ES, July 15, 1863, ES to WTS, April 7, July 26, 1863, SFP, UNDA; WTS to JS, July 28, August 3, 1863, WTS, LC; WTS to General Parke, July 30, 1863, O.R., I, 24, III, 563.

79. WTS to Officers and Soldiers of Fifteenth Army Corps, July 27, 1863, O.R., I, 24, III, 556.

CHAPTER 11   PRACTICING DESTRUCTIVE WAR IN MISSISSIPPI

1. WTS, Memoirs, 1:370

2. MSF, "My Father's Letters," Cosmopolitan 12 (December 1890): 187–88; WTS to PBE, July 28, 1863, in Joseph H. Ewing, ed., "Sherman Bashes the Press," American Heritage 38 (July–August 1987): 36.

3. WTS to JS, September 9, 1863, SFP, UNDA; WTS, Memoirs, 1:370–71; ES, "A Sketch of William Tecumseh Sherman, Jr.," Soldier's Casket (September 1865), original and copy in SFP, UNDA.

4. Cedar Rapids Gazette, March 16, 1896 in MSA, scrapbook, WTS, OHS.

5. WTS, Memoirs, 1:371; ES to MBE, August 25, 30, 1863, copy, SFP, UNDA; WTS to James B. McPherson, September 4, 1863, O.R., I, 30, III, 336; WTS, "Old Shady with a Moral," North American Review 147 (August 1888): 361–68; WTS to JS, September 9, 1863, WTS, LC.

6. ES to MBE, August 28, 1863, SFP, UNDA; New York World, undated, MSF, "Album of the Heart," SFP, UNDA; JS to WTS, August 3, 29, 1863, George E. Yeatman, August 20, 1863, Frank Blair to WTS, August 24, 1863, Dennis Hart Mahan to WTS, August 28, 1863, WTS, LC; TE to WTS, August 4, 1863, EFP, LC; WTS to USG, August 15, 1863, O.R., I, 30, III, 31; WTS to HWH, August 15, 1863, copy, SFP, UNDA; WTS to TE, August 13, 20, 1863, TE, LC.

7. USG to WTS, WTS to USG, August 6, 1863, O.R., I, 24, III, 578; WTS to E. F. Winslow, August 8, 1863, O.R., I, 30, I, 7; WTS to General Dennis, August 29, 1863, O.R., I, 30, III, 211.

8. WTS to H. W. Hill, September 7, 1863, O.R., I, 30, III, 402.

9. WTS to Charles Anderson, August ?, 1863, Charles Anderson Papers, HL.

10. New York World, undated, SFP, UNDA; WTS to JS, September 9, 1863, WTS, LC.

11. HWH to WTS, August 29, 1863, WTS, LC; WTS to HWH, September 17, 1863, O.R., I, 30, III, 694–700.

12. WTS to JAR, September 17, 1863, in WTS, Memoirs, 1:368–69; WTS to

General Asboth, September 11, 1863, WTS to McPherson, September 16, 1863, O.R., I, 30, III, 527, 662.

13. WTS, *Memoirs*, 1:371–72; Theodore F. Upson, *With Sherman to the Sea* . . . (Baton Rouge, 1943), 68–69.

14. WTS to JAR, September 27, 1863, O.R., I, 20, III, 884; WTS, *Memoirs*, 1:347–38; WTS to PBE, October 6, 1863, PBE, OHS; E. O. F. Roler to ES, March 27, 1864, SFP, UNDA: J. C. Carrier to WTS, November 26, 1863, ES to WTS, November 9, 1863, SFP, UNDA.

15. WTS to HWH, October 4, 1863, O.R., I, 20, IV, 73; WTS to C. C. Smith, October 4, 1863, in WTS, *Memoirs*, 1:374–75; WTS to TS, October 4, 1863, WTS to ES, October 6, 10, 28, 1863, SFP, UNDA.

16. ES to WTS, October 10, 15, 21, November 10, 25, 30, 1863, SFP, UNDA.

17. WTS to JAR, September 22, 1863, WTS to Stephen Hurlbut, September 25, 1863, O.R., I, 30, III, 773, 844–45.

18. WTS to JAR, October 14, 1863, O.R., I, 30, II, 731–33; WTS, *Memoirs*, 1:376–78; E. O. Hurd, "The Battle of Collierville," in W. H. Chamberlain et al., *Sketches of War History, 1861–1865* (Cincinnati, 1903): 5, 249; Patrick J. Carmody, "The Battle of Collierville," Society of the Army of the Tennessee and MOLLUS, Ohio Commandery, November 3, 4, 1909, in WTS-Ewing Pamphlets, OHS. A blow-by-blow account of this incident is Edwin C. Bearss, "Sherman's Collierville Escape," *Morningside News*, Morningside Bookshop Catalogue Number 26, 1989, pp. 3–24.

19. WTS to USG, October 10, 1863, O.R., I, 30, IV, 236.

20. HWH to USG, October 16, 1863, in WTS, *Memoirs*, 1:379–80; JAR to WTS, October 19, 1863, O.R., I, 30, IV, 475–76; G.O. No. 11, Hqs., Department and Army of the Tennessee, October 24, 1863, USG to WTS, October 24, 1863, WTS to JAR, October 24, 1863, O.R., I, 31, I, 712, 713–14.

21. WTS to Hurlbut, October 24, 1863, G.O. No. 2, Hqs., Department and Army of the Tennessee, October 2, 1863, O.R., I, 31, I, 718–19, 730–32.

22. WTS, *Memoirs*, 1:385–86.

23. WTS to Hurlbut, October 26, 1863, WTS to Editors of *Memphis Bulletin*, October 27, 1863, O.R., I, 31, I, 747–48, 765.

24. WTS to J. B. Bingham, November 9, 1863, O.R., I, 31, III, 97–98.

25. WTS to ES, November 8, 1863, SFP, UNDA; S. M. Bowman, "Major General William T. Sherman," *United States Service Magazine* 2 (September 1864): 243.

26. WTS to JAR, December 19, 1863, O.R., I, 31, II, 571; USG to WTS, September 30, 1863, WTS to JAR, September 16, 1863, O.R., I, 31, III, 945, 661; OOH, "Chattanooga," *Atlantic Monthly* 38 (1876): 210–11; OOH, *The Autobiography of Oliver Otis Howard* (New York, 1907), 1:473–74.

27. OOH, "Chattanooga," 211; OOH, *Autobiography*, 1:474–76; W. B. Hazen, *Narrative of Military Service* (Boston, 1885), 164.

28. WTS, *Memoirs*, 1:387–89.

29. Unless otherwise indicated, the following account of the Battle of Chattanooga is based on WTS's battle report: WTS to JAR, December 19, 1863, O.R., I, 31, II, 568–83, and James Lee McDonough, *Chattanooga: Death*

Grip on the Confederacy (Knoxville, 1984), the most thorough monograph on the battle. Also useful is James R. Sullivan, *Chickamauga and Chattanooga Battlefields* (Washington, D.C., 1956). A good synopsis of the Union battle plan is William Farrar Smith to Editor, June 1, 1885, *Century* 9 (1885): 146–47.

30. SHMB, "Some Personal Recollections of General Sherman," *McClure's* 3 (August 1894): 212; WTS to JAR, December 19, 1863, O.R., I, 31, II, 573.

31. WTS to JAR, December 19, 1863, O.R., I, 31, II, 574.

32. W. F. G. Shanks, *Personal Recollections . . .* (New York, 1866), 27; SHMB, *With Fire and Sword* (New York, 1911), 106.

33. W. F. G. Shanks, "Gossip About Our Generals," *Harper's New Monthly Magazine* 35 (July 1867): 212; "Reminiscences of Comrades," *Chaperone* (1891): 619–20, in SFP, UNDA.

34. WTS to JAR, December 19, 1863, O.R., I, 31, II, 575–76; WTS to JAL, November 22, 1882, JAL, LC; WTS, *Memoirs*, 1:390; WTS to W. F. Smith, March 9, 1886, Military History Society Papers, Boston University Library.

35. A former colleague criticized WTS's performance at the battle, arguing that he saw no proof that the Confederates shifted troops from the middle to their right. James Harrison Wilson, *Under the Old Flag* (New York, 1912), 1:290–99.

36. WTS to USG, December 1, 1863, O.R., I, 31, III, 297.

37. WTS, *Memoirs*, 1:392–93.

38. Lyman S. Widney, "Campaigning with 'Uncle Billy,'" *Neales Monthly* 2 (August 1912): 135; WTS to HWH, December 26, 1863, WTS to JAL, WTS to USG, December 29, 1863, O.R., I, 31, III, 497–98, 459–60, 527–28.

39. Grenville M. Dodge, *Personal Recollections . . .* (Council Bluffs, Iowa, 1914), 139–42.

40. WTS to JS, December 29, 1862, WTS, LC; WTS to USG, December 29, 1863, O.R., I, 31, III, 528.

41. WTS to JS, December 30, 1863, WTS, LC; TE to HBE, January 31, 1864, HBE, OHS; ES to Mother Angela, December 16, 1863, Notre Dame Collection, UNDA; NYT, January 10, 1864; WTS to HWH, December 26, 1863, O.R., I, 31, III, 497.

42. WTS to ES, January 5, 1864, SFP, UNDA; *New York Tribune*, February 15, 1864; unmarked clipping, ES, 1864 diary, SFP, UNDA.

43. WTS, *Memoirs*, 1:417–18; WTS to USG, January 4, 1864, O.R., I, 32, II, 25; WTS to ES, January 5, 11, 1864, SFP, UNDA; John F. Marszalek, *Sherman's Other War . . .* (Memphis, 1981), 160–61.

44. WTS to A. J. Smith, January 6, 1864, O.R., I, 32, II, 36.

45. WTS to MSF, January 19, 1864, WTS, OHS.

46. WTS to HWH, January 12, 1864, WTS to Nathaniel Banks, January 16, 1864, WTS to USG, January 24, 1864, O.R., I, 32, II, 75, 113–15, 201–2.

47. S.F.O No. 11, Hqs., Department of the Tennessee, January 27, 1864, O.R., I, 32, I, 182; WTS to HWH, January 27, 1864, O.R., I, 32, II, 259–61; WTS to Banks, January 31, 1864, O.R., I, 34, II, 266–7; WTS to William

Sooy Smith, January 27, 1864, WTS to E. K. Owen, January 30, 1864, WTS to McPherson, January 10, 1864, O.R., I, 32, I, 181–85.

48. WTS to R. M. Sawyer, January 31, 1864, O.R., I, 32, II, 278–81, published in *Cincinnati Commercial*, April 26, 1864, Charles O. Drennon Papers, LC.

49. WTS to JS, January 19, 20, 1864, WTS, LC; WTS to ES, January 19, 28, 1863, SFP, UNDA.

50. WTS to JS, February 1, 1864, WTS, LC; WTS to ES, January 19, 28, 1863, SFP, UNDA; WTS to MSF, January 28, 1864, *Cosmopolitan* (December 1891): 191.

51. D. B. R. Keim, *Sherman: A Memorial* . . . (Washington, D.C., 1904), 244.

52. WTS to ES, January 28, 1864, SFP, UNDA; WTS to JS, January 20, 1864, WTS, LC; WTS to HWH, January 29, 1864, O.R., I, 32, II, 259–61; *New York Herald*, February 3, 1864; *New York Tribune*, February 15, 1864; ES to WTS, February 2, 1864, SFP, UNDA.

53. The following account of the Meridian expedition is, unless otherwise indicated, based on: WTS, *Memoirs*, 1:418–23; WTS to JAR, March 7, 1863, O.R., I, 32, I, 173–79; Richard M. McMurry, "Sherman's Meridian Campaign," *Civil War Times Illustrated* 14 (1975): 24–32. A blow-by-blow description of the campaign is Margie Riddle Bearss, *Sherman's Forgotten Campaign* . . . (Baltimore, 1987).

54. WTS to J. M. Tuttle, February 2, 1864, O.R., I, 32, II, 316; WTS to ES, February 7, 1864, SFP, UNDA.

55. JWD, *History of the American Civil War* (New York, 1870), 3:212–13; Bruce Catton, *This Hallowed Ground* (New York, 1956), 306–7.

56. WTS to Steele, March 4, 1864, O.R., I, 34, II, 496–97; WTS to ES, March 10, 12, 1864, WTS, LC; Marszalek, *Sherman's Other War*, 160–61.

57. Stephen D. Lee, "Sherman's Expedition from Vicksburg to Meridian, February 3, to March 6, 1864," *New Orleans Picayune*, July 27, 1904, in *Southern Historical Society Papers* 32 (1908): 318–19.

58. DFB to WTS, February 13, 1864, WTS, LC; WTS, *Memoirs*, 1:423–25; WTS to ES, March 10, 1864, WTS, LC; DFB to WTS, copy, March 2, 1864, WTS to DFB, March 3, 1864, WTS, LC; WTS to ES, January 25, 1864, SFP, UNDA. WTS also received a letter from a husband and wife he had been friends with during the 1840s in north Alabama asking for help. D. M. Martin to WTS, January 22, 1864, WTS, LC.

59. WTS, *Memoirs*, 1:425; WTS endorsement on Steele to Banks, February 28, 1864, O.R., I, 34, II, 449.

60. WTS, *Memoirs*, 1:425–26; F. Steele to WTS, March 7, 1864, O.R., I, 34, II, 522–23, 611.

61. WTS to JS, January 6, 1864, WTS, LC; USG to WTS, March 4, 1864, WTS to USG, March 10, 1864, O.R., I, 32, III, 18, 49.

62. WTS, *Memoirs*, 1:429–30.

63. G.O. No. 98, War Department, March 12, 1864, O.R., I, 21, III, 58; ES to WTS, February 2, 20, 29, 1864, ES, diary, February 20, 1864, SFP, UNDA; WTS, *Memoirs*, 2:463–65.

CHAPTER 12   ATLANTA FALLS

1. There is a tremendous volume of literature on the Atlanta campaign. The following sources were particularly helpful for this chapter: Richard M. McMurry, "Atlanta Campaign, Rocky Face to the Dallas Line, the Battles of May 1864," *Blue and Gray* 6 (May 1989): 11–23, 46–49, 54–62; Dennis Kelly, "Atlanta Campaign, Mountains to Pass, a River to Cross: The Battle of Kennesaw Mountain and Related Actions from June 10 to July 9, 1864," *Blue and Gray* 6 (June 1989): 10–12, 15–30, 46–50, 52–58; Stephen Davis, "Hood Fights Desperately, the Battle for Atlanta: Events from July 10 to September 2, 1864," *Blue and Gray* 6 (August 1989): 9–39, 45–62; David Evans, "The Atlanta Campaign," *Civil War Times Illustrated* 28 (Summer 1989): entire issue; WTS to HWH, September 15, 1864, O.R., I, 38, I, 61–84; WTS, *Memoirs*, 2:463–611. For Joseph E. Johnston's side, see Johnston, "Opposing Sherman's Advance to Atlanta," *Century* 12 (September 1887): 585–96. For an excellent survey of Atlanta campaign literature, see Stephen Davis and Richard M. McMurry, "A Reader's Guide to the Atlanta Campaign," *Atlanta Historical Journal* 28 (Fall 1984): 99–111. Albert Castel's forthcoming book promises to become the standard account of this campaign.

2. WTS to S. G. Burbridge, March 29, 1864, O.R., I, 32, III, 181; WTS, *Memoirs*, 2:469.

3. E. O. Townsend to WTS, March 25, 1864, EMS to WTS, April 2, 1864, WTS to R. M. Sawyer, March 28, 1864, G.O. No. 6, Hqs., Military Division of the Mississippi, April 6, 1864, G.O. No. 8 Hqs., Military Division of the Mississippi, April 19, 1864, O.R., I, 32, III, 148–49, 220, 174, 279–80, 42; WTS to Silas F. Miller, April 14, 1864, in John Mason Brown, "Sherman in the Saddle," *Saturday Review of Literature*, February 28, 1948, 26–28; N. B. Stewart, *Dan McCook's Regiment* (Alliance, Ohio, 1900), 95.

4. F. S. Kellogg, *Mother Bickerdyke* (Chicago, 1907), 64–65.

5. WTS to Governor of Minnesota, April 1, 1864, Stephen Miller, Governors' Papers, MiHS; WTS to Governor of Kansas, April 6, 1864, T. C. Stevens Papers, Kansas State Historical Society, WTS to M. D. Leggett, April 3, 1864, O.R., I, 32, III, 241; WTS to N. P. Banks, April 3, 1864, O.R., I, 34, III, 24; WTS to TE, April 18, 1864, TE, LC; WTS to USG, April 2, 1864, USG to WTS, April 4, 1864, O.R., I, 32, III, 221, 247; WTS to Joseph Holt, April 6, 1864, Holt to WTS, April 7, 1864, O.R., II, 7, 18–20; Marszalek, *Sherman's Other War,* (Memphis, 1981), 163–64.

6. M. Brayman to WTS, April 16, 1864, O.R., I, 32, II, 361; USG to WTS, April 15, 1864, WTS to Brayman, April 16, 1864, O.R., I, 32, III, 213, 381; WTS to DDP, April 3, 1864, O.R., I, 34, III, 25; WTS to JAR, April 4, 1864, O.R., I, 32, III, 247–48.

7. WTS to JS, April 5, 11, 1864, WTS, LC; WTS to C. A. Dana, April 21, 1864, in Charles A. Dana, *Recollections of the Civil War* (New York, 1964), 154; WTS to S. G. Burbridge, WTS to William S. Rosecrans, April 23, 1864, O.R., I, 32, III, 463–64.

8. USG to WTS, April 4, 1864, WTS to USG, April 10, 24, 1864, O.R., I, 32, III, 245–46, 312–14, 465–66.

9. WTS to MSF, May 1, 1864, in MSF, ed., "My Father's Letters," *Cosmopolitan* 12 (December 1891): 191; WTS to TE, April 25, 1864, WTS to Edward Sorin, May 3, 1864, WTS to ES, May 4, 1864, SFP, UNDA.

10. AL to WTS, May 4, 1864, WTS to AL, May 5, 1864, O.R., I, 38, IV, 25, 33–34.

11. Charles W. Wills, *Army Life of an Illinois Soldier . . . Letters and Diary* (Washington, D.C., 1906), May 13, 1864, 252.

12. WTS, *Memoirs*, 2:500; WW to ES, February 22, 1876, in ibid., 539. For various historical evaluations of this incident, see Freeman Cleaves, *Rock of Chickamauga: Life of General George H. Thomas* (Norman, Okla., 1949), 209–10; JMS, *Forty-six Years in the Army* (New York, 1897), 125–27; John T. Hubbell, "A Bright, Particular Star: James Birdseye McPherson," *Timeline* 5 (August–September, 1988): 41–42; Michael J. Klinger, "Botched Union Attack," *America's Civil War* 2 (September 1989): 22.

13. WTS, *Memoirs*, 2:504–6; OOH, "The Struggle for Atlanta," *Century* 12 (1887): 449.

14. WTS, *Memoirs*, 2:507–8.

15. EMS to WTS, May 20, 1864, EMS Papers, OHS; TE, Jr., to PBE, May 24, 1864, PBE, OHS; WTS to ES, May 22, 1864, SFP, UNDA.

16. David P. Conyngham, *Sherman's March Through the South . . .* (New York, 1865), 71.

17. WTS, *Memoirs*, 2:511.

18. OOH, "Struggle," 451–52; WTS "From Chattanooga to Atlanta—One Hundred Days Under Fire," *Proceedings of the Society of the Army of the Cumberland*, 4th Reunion, November 24, 25, 1870, 153.

19. WTS, *Memoirs*, 2:514–15.

20. Conyngham, *Sherman's March*, 107; S.F.O. No. 17, Hqs., Military Division of the Mississippi, June 4, 1864, O.R., I, 38, IV, 405–6.

21. WTS to ES, June 1, 1864, SFP, UNDA; WTS to USG, June 18, 1864, O.R., I, 38, IV, 507.

22. WTS, *Memoirs*, 2:516–18; WTS to HWH, June 8, 1864, O.R., I, 38, I, 61.

23. WTS, *Memoirs*, 2:523.

24. WTS to S. G. Burbridge, June 21, 1864, in NYT, December 29, 1867; WTS to EMS, June 21, 1864, O.R., I, 39, II, 31–32.

25. Marszalek, *Sherman's Other War*, 164–67; WTS to ES, June 9, 1864, SFP, UNDA.

26. Marszalek, *Sherman's Other War*, 168–69; WTS to JS, April 22, 1864, WTS, LC; WTS to ES, August 4, 1864, SFP, UNDA; WTS to "J. A. R.," September 12, 1864, in *Historical Magazine* 21 (February 1872): 113.

27. WTS to HWH, September 15, 1864, O.R., I, 38, I, 67.

28. WTS, *Memoirs*, 2:525.

29. Lyman S. Widney, "Campaigning with 'Uncle Billy,'" *Neales Monthly* 2 (August 1913): 137.

30. WTS to HWH, June 5, 13, 1864, O.R., I, 38, IV, 408, 466; WTS to ES, June 9, 1864, SFP, UNDA.

31. WTS to HWH, June 16, 1864, O.R., I, 38, IV, 492; WTS to HWH, September 15, 1864, O.R., I, 38, I, 68.

32. S.F.O. No. 28, Hqs., Military Division of the Mississippi, June 24, 1864, O.R., I, 38, IV, 588.

33. H. David Williams, "'On the Fringe of Hell': Billy Yank and Johnny Reb at the Siege of Kennesaw Mountain," *Georgia Historical Quarterly* 70 (Winter 1986): 704.

34. WTS to Anne Gilman Bowen, June 30, 1864, Misc. Manuscripts, American Antiquarian Society; WTS to ES, June 30, 1864, SFP, UNDA.

35. Cleaves, *Rock of Chicamauga,* 225; WTS, "From Chattanooga to Atlanta," 154.

36. WTS to John Shellaberger, May 13, 1881, copy, WTS, LC; WTS to HWH, July 9, 1864, WTS to USG, July 12, 1864, O.R., I, 38, V, 91, 123.

37. David S. Stanley, *Personal Memoirs of . . .* (Cambridge, Mass., 1917), 173.

38. OOH, "Struggle," 456.

39. JAC to Wife, July 12, 1864, in JAC, *Three Years in the Army of the Cumberland . . . ,* ed. Paul M. Angle (Bloomington, 1959), 234.

40. WTS to HWH, July 7, 1864, WTS to Kenner Garrard, July 7, 1864, O.R., I, 38, V, 73, 76–77; Theodore F. Upson, *With Sherman to the Sea . . . ,* ed. Oscar O. Winther (Baton Rouge, 1943), July 12, 1864, 119; "Yankees Come to Roswell," *Blue and Gray* 6 (June 1989): 57.

41. Edward Corydon Foote with Olive Deane Hormel, *With Sherman to the Sea* (New York, 1960), 189–90; WTS to HBE, July 13, 1864, WTS, OHS, Alan Bussel, "The Atlanta *Daily Intelligencer* Covers Sherman's March," *Journalism Quarterly* 51 (Autumn 1974): 405–10.

42. USG to WTS, July 16, 1864, O.R., I, 38, V, 149; Widney, "Campaigning," 137.

43. WTS, *Memoirs,* 2:543–44; WTS, "From Chattanooga to Atlanta," 154; S.F.O. No. 39, July 19, 1864, O.R., I, 38, V, 193.

44. WW, "Remarks," *Proceedings of the Society of the Army of the Tennessee,* 24th Annual Reunion, October 7, 8, 1891, 500.

45. Byron R. Abernathy, ed., *Private Elisha J. Stockwell Jr. Sees the Civil War* (Norman, Okla., 1958), 97; Gilbert D. Munson, "Battle of Atlanta," *Sketches of the War;* Ohio Commandery, MOLLUS, ed. Robert Hunter (Cincinnati, 1890), 3:229.

46. WTS to Emily Hoffman, June 9, August 5, 1864, in Walter Lord, "General Sherman and the Baltimore Belle," *American Heritage* 9 (April 1958): 102–4.

47. ES to WTS, July 25, 1864, SFP, UNDA.

48. WTS to JS, June 21, 1884, WTS, LC; OOH, "The Battles Around Atlanta," *Atlantic Monthly* 38 (October 1876): 395. A thorough discussion of the controversy is found in James P. Jones, *"Black Jack": John A. Logan and Southern Illinois in the Civil War Era* (Tallahassee, 1967), 212–22.

49. WTS to JAL, July 27, 1864, photostat, JAL, LC; WTS to R. B. Hayes, March 12, 1881, WTS, HPC; E. C. Brinkman, "They Wronged John A. Logan," *Filson Club Historical Quarterly* 41 (April 1967): 154–68; John A. Carpenter, *Sword and Olive Branch: Oliver Otis Howard* (Pittsburgh, 1964), 69–70;

James P. Jones, "The Battle of Atlanta and McPherson's Successors," *Civil War History* 7 (December 1961): 401–2; WTS to HWH, July 27, 1864, O.R., I, 38, V, 271–72; WTS to C. C. Washburn, August 3, 1864, O.R., I, 39, II, 222.

50. Widney, "Campaigning," 137; WTS to Thomas, August 10, 1864, O.R., I, 38, V, 448; James M. McPherson, *Battle Cry of Freedom* (New York, 1988), 755n.

51. WTS to HWH, August 20, 1864, O.R., I, 38, V, 609–10.

52. WTS to Stephen A. Miller, August 1, 1864, Stephen A. Miller, Governors' Papers, MiHS; WTS to Leslie Coombs, August 11, 1864, O.R., I, 39, II, 240–41.

53. WTS to Daniel M. Martin, August 10, 1864, in NYT, September 7, 1865.

54. James F. Rusling, *Men and Things I Saw in Civil War Days* (New York, 1899), 113.

55. Widney, "Campaigning," 138; "Generals in the Saddle," *Southern Historical Society Papers* 19 (1891): 169–70.

56. WTS to HWH, August 13, 1864, O.R., I, 38, V, 482.

57. WTS to OOH, August 17, 1864, O.R., I, 38, V, 557.

58. Widney, "Campaigning," 139; WTS to Thomas, August 28, 1864, O.R., I, 38, V, 688.

59. WTS to JMS, September 1, 164, WTS to OOH, September 2, 1864, WTS to HWH, September 3, 1864, O.R., I, 38, V, 754, 771, 777.

60. WTS to HWH, September 15, 1864, O.R., I, 38, I, 82–83; WTS, "From Chattanooga to Atlanta," 155. For three different evaluations of WTS's actions, see Alfred H. Burne, *Lee, USG and Sherman* (New York, 1939), 137; Errol M. Clauss, "Sherman's Failure at Atlanta," *Georgia Historical Quarterly* 53 (September 1969): 321; Davis, "Hood Fights," 62.

61. Conyngham, *Sherman's March*, 216; George W. Pepper, *Personal Recollections . . .* (Zanesville, Ohio, 1866), 171.

62. JS to WTS, July 24, 1864, WTS, LC; WTS to TE, Jr., September 7, 1864, WTS, LC; *New York Tribune*, September 3, 1864; *Louisville Journal*, September 5, 1864; NYT, September 5, 1864; EMS to WTS, September 5, 1864, O.R., I, 38, I, 86; JGB, *Twenty Years of Congress, 1861–1881* (Norwich, Conn., 1886), 531; USG to WTS, September 10, 1864, O.R., I, 39, II, 355; USG to WTS, September 12, 1864, in WTS, *Memoirs*, 2:581–82; WTS to Edward Everett, September 17, 1864, Edward Everett Papers, MaHS; TE to WTS, September 10, 1864, EFP, LC; James G. Randall and Theodore C. Pease, eds., *The Diary of Orville H. Browning* in *Collections of the Illinois State Historical Library* (Springfield, 1925), 20:680–81; Henry Adams to Charles Francis Adams, Jr., September 30, 1864, in Worthington C. Ford, ed., *A Cycle of Adams Letters, 1861–1865* (Boston, 1920), 2:199–200; Edward L. Pierce, ed., *Memoirs and Letters of Charles Summer* (Boston, 1893), 4:199; Adam Gurowski, *Diary . . . 1861 to 1865* (New York, 1968), 3:330; Uriah Arnold to "Dear Brother," October 3, 1864, Uriah and William Arnold Papers, Michigan State University.

63. WTS to TE, September 15, 1864, TE, LC.

64. S.F.O. No. 67, Hqs., Military Division of the Mississippi, September 8, 1864, WTS to HWH, September 19, 1864, O.R., I, 38, V, 837, 839.

65. James M. Calhoun et al. to WTS, September 11, 1864, WTS to James M. Calhoun et al., September 12, 1864, O.R., I, 39, II, 417–19; WTS to Tyler [Louisville Agent of the New York Associated Press], September 24, 1864, O.R., I, 39, II, 481.

66. The Sherman-Hood correspondence (September 7–14, 1864) is located in O.R., I, 39, II, 414–16, 419–22, and O.R., II, 7, 784, 791–92, 799, 808, 822. The former group concerns the debate, the latter group prisoner-of-war exchange. A brief overview of the controversy is Peggy Robbins, "Hood vs. Sherman, a Duel in Words," *Civil War Times Illustrated* 17 (July 1978): 22–29.

67. *Cincinnati Gazette,* September 20, 1864; John G. Winter to AJ, October 8, 1864, AJ, *Papers,* ed. Leroy P. Graf et al. (Knoxville, 1986), 7:233; ES to WTS, September 17, 1864, SFP, UNDA; HWH to WTS, September 28, 1864, O.R., I, 39, II, 503.

68. Henry C. Lay, "Sherman in Georgia," *Atlantic Monthly* 149 (February 1932): 166–72.

69. ES, diary, June 11, 1864, WTS to ES, June 12, 1864, SFP, UNDA; WTS to HBE, July 13, 1864, WTS, OHS; ES to WTS, July 9, 16, 20, August 16, 1864, WTS to ES, July 13, August 9, 1864; ES to JS, August 20, 1864, SFP, UNDA.

70. Albert Castel, "The Life of a Rising Son, Part III: The Conqueror," *Civil War Times Illustrated* 6 (October 1979): 16; "William Tecumseh Sherman," *Illustrated American,* March 7, 1891, 132; WTS, "Remark," *Proceedings of the Society of the Army of the Cumberland,* 1st Annual Reunion, February 6, 7, 1868, 80.

71. WTS to Duke of Cambridge, September 3, 1879, Beauchamp Walker to WTS, January 21, 1880, WTS to Walker, February 5, 1880, copies, WTS, LC; undated Atlanta campaign course itinerary, U.S. Army Infantry and Cavalry School and Staff College, WTS, USMA.

CHAPTER 13   MARCH TO THE SEA

1. WTS, *Memoirs,* 2:612; JAC to Wife, September 18, 1864, in JAC, *Three Years in the Army of the Cumberland: The Letters and Diary . . . ,* ed. Paul M. Angle (Bloomington, Ind., 1959), 260; George H. Thomas to WTS, September 30, 1864, O.R., I, 39, II, 532.

2. WTS, *Memoirs,* 2:612–13; WTS to AL, September 17, 1864, O.R., I, 39, II, 395–96; J. P. Austin, *The Blue and the Gray . . .* (Atlanta, 1899), 145–47; Joshua Hill and A. R. Wright later gave separate detailed accounts of their conversations with Sherman, Joe Brown, and others. *Atlanta Herald,* February 28, 1875; reprinted in NYT, March 7, 1875; A. R. Wright to I. W. Avery, July 6, 1879, in *Philadelphia Times,* July 6, 1879, A. R. Wright Papers, Tennessee State Archives.

3. Horace Porter, *Campaigning with Grant* (New York, 1897), 289–96; WTS to USG, September 20, 1864, O.R., I, 39, II, 413.

4. WTS, "The Grand Strategy of the War of the Rebellion," *Century* 13 (February 1888): 595; WTS, *Memoirs*, 2:615–16.

5. WTS to John Bell Hood, September 22, 29, 1864, WTS to James E. Yeatman, September 22, 27, 1864, Hood to WTS, September 27, 1864, O.R., II, 7, 857–88, 883, 885, 891; *New York Tribune*, September 6, 1864; *Chicago Tribune*, September 29, 1864; ES to WTS, September 29, 1864, SFP, UNDA.

6. WTS, *Memoirs*, 2:622–23; WTS to O. H. Peck, February 22, 1882, G. Dunlap Papers, CU; WTS to R. Rowell, copy, May 27, 1882, John M. Corse to WTS, March 11, 1885, WTS to Corse, copy, March 12, 1885, WTS, LC; WTS to James M. McClintock, January 13, 1887, McClintock Papers, LC.

7. JAC to Wife, October 15, 1864, in JAC, *Three Years*, 278; WTS, *Memoirs*, 2:626; Charles W. Wills, *Army Life of an Illinois Soldier . . .* , comp. Mary E. Kellogg (Washington, D.C., 1906), 307.

8. S.F.O. No. 86, Hqs., Military Division of the Mississippi, October 7, 1864, O.R., I, 39, I, 771–72; Charles A. Mosman, *The Rough Side of War . . .* , ed. Arnold Gates (Garden City, N.Y., 1987), October 8, 9, 1864, p. 288.

9. WTS to Corse, October 7, 1864, S.F.O. No. 95, Hqs., Military Division of the Mississippi, October 17, 1864, O.R., I, 39, IV, 135, 324–25.

10. JAC to Wife, October 17, 1864, in JAC, 279; David S. Stanley, *Personal Memoirs of . . .* (Cambridge, Mass., 1917), 190.

11. WTS to USG, November 6, 1864, O.R., I, 39, III, 658–61.

12. USG to WTS, October 11, 1864, WTS to USG, November 6, 1864, October 9, 1864, O.R., I, 39, III, 202, 658–61, 162.

13. USG to WTS, October 11, 1864, EMS to WTS, October 13, 1864, USG to WTS, November 2, 1864, O.R., I, 39, III, 202, 240, 594.

14. WTS to Thomas, October 20, 1864, O.R., I, 39, II, 378.

15. WTS to Joseph P. Thompson, October 21, 1864, William G. Thompson Papers, YL.

16. WTS, *Memoirs*, 2:643–44; Absalom H. Markland, handwritten statement [November 1864], Absalom H. Markland Papers, LC.

17. Fenwick Y. Hedley, *Marching Through Georgia: Pen Pictures . . .* (Chicago, 1890), 258–65.

18. WTS, *Memoirs*, 2:646–54; W. R. White, "Sherman to the Sea," *Quartermaster Review* 10 (May–June 1931): 53; George E. Turner, *Victory Rode the Rails . . .* (Indianapolis, 1953), 358; JWD, *History of the American Civil War* (New York, 1868), 3:323.

19. S.F.O. No. 119, Hqs., Military Division of the Mississippi, November 8, 1864, S.F.O. No. 120, November 9, 1864, O.R., I, 39, III, 701, 713–14.

20. Thomas Osborn to Abraham C. Osborn, December 26, 1864, in Richard Harwell and Philip N. Racine, eds., *The Fiery Trail* (Knoxville, 1986), 51.

21. D. J. DeLaubenfels, "Where Sherman Passed By," *Geographical Review* 47 (July 1957): 382–89; David P. Conyngham, *Sherman's March Through the South . . .* (New York 1865), 250; George W. Pepper, *Personal Recollections of Sherman's Campaigns . . .* (Zanesville, Ohio, 1866), 246–47.

22. WTS to O. M. Poe, November 7, 1864, O.R., I, 39, III, 680; HMH,

Marching with Sherman, ed. M. A. deWolfe Howe (New Haven, 1927), November 16, 1864, p. 60; E. A. Pollard quoted in Otto Eisenschiml and Ralph Newman, *The Civil War: The American Iliad* (New York, 1956), 647; E. P. Oberholtzer, *History of the United States Since the Civil War* (New York, 1917), 1:57n.

23. WTS to J. F. Burke, copy, March 10, 19, 1880, WTS, LC; WTS, *Memoirs,* 2:177; John F. Marszalek, "Was Sherman Really a Brute?" *Blue and Gray* 7 (December 1989): 46–51; *Richmond Sentinel,* n.d., in NYT, December 24, 1864; James M. Russell, *Atlanta, 1847–1890* . . . (Baton Rouge, 1988), 114–15.

24. WTS, *Memoirs,* 2:655–56.

25. CE to MSF, November 9, 1864, WTS to MSF, November 9, 1864, WTS, OHS; WTS to PBE, November 10, 1860, in Joseph H. Ewing, ed., "Sherman Bashes the Press," *American Heritage* 38 (July–August 1987): 27, 40; WTS to TS, November 10, 1864, WTS, OHS.

26. G. T. Beauregard, B. H. Hill, et al. to the People of Georgia, November 18, 19, 1864, in WTS, *Memoirs,* 2:665–66; HMH, *Marching,* December 5, 1864, 148; J. D. Hittle, ed., *Jomini and His Summary of the Art of War* (Harrisburg, Pa., 1958), 67; WTS, "Strategy," 595.

27. WTS to Charles A. Dana, November 10, 1864, O.R., I, 39, III, 727; Lucy S. Stewart, *The Reward of Patriotism* . . . (New York, 1930), chap. 19. A 1955 study of the sixty-mile area from Covington to Milledgeville found that of seventy-two houses built before Sherman's march, twenty-two were still standing in 1955; nine others had been torn down after the Civil War. On twenty-seven other sites that could be discovered, the disposition of the houses was unclear, and eleven building sites could not be found. The author's conclusion: "a great many houses, perhaps even most of them, escaped destruction" during the march to the sea. David J. DeLaubenfels, ed., "With Sherman Through Georgia: A Journal [John Rzeha]," *Georgia Historical Quarterly* 41 (September 1957): 291–92. General Manning F. Force insisted, after the war, that the Seventeenth Corps burned only four houses in Georgia. "Three of these were burned by order for cause." Force, "The Army of the Tennessee and Georgia, and Sherman's March to the Sea," *Proceedings of the Annual Meeting of the Society of the Army of the Cumberland,* November 15, 16, 1871, p. 92.

28. Hedley, *Marching Through Georgia,* 267–77; Pepper, *Personal Recollections,* 275–77; J. L. Underwood, *The Women of the Confederacy* (New York, 1906), 162; Carl Schurz, *The Reminiscences of* . . . (New York, 1908), 3:134.

29. Dolly Sumner Lunt, *A Women's Wartime Journal* . . . (Macon, Ga., 1927), November 19, 1864, pp. 34–35; Pepper, *Personal Recollections,* 261; Conyngham, *Sherman's March,* 313–14. For a hostile account of Sherman's strategy of destruction, see John B. Walters, *Merchant of Terror, General Sherman and Total War* (Indianapolis, 1973).

30. WTS, *Memoirs,* 2:658; E. Norton, "Tales at First Hand," *Blackwood* 233 (January 1933): 37–39;

31. HMH, *Marching,* November 25, 1864, *Marching,* pp. 92–93.

32. WTS to Caroline Carson, January 20, 1865, James L. Petigru Papers, LC; WTS to ES, January 5, 1865, SFP, UNDA; WTS, speech, New England Society of New York, December 22, 1886; Henry W. Grady gave his famous "New South" oration immediately after Sherman's speech.

33. Hedley, *Marching Through Georgia*, 278–94; George W. Nichols, *The Story of the Great March* . . . (New York, 1865), 48–55; Daniel Oakey, "Marching Through Georgia," *Century* 12 (October 1877): 919; Corydon E. Foote with Olive Deane Hormel, *With Sherman to the Sea* . . . (New York, 1960), 208, 230.

34. WTS, *Memoirs*, 2:662; Charles Brockman, ed., "The John Van Duzer Diary of Sherman's March . . . ," *Georgia Historical Quarterly* 53 (June 1969): November 17, 1864, 222.

35. JAC to Wife, November 23, 1864, in JAC, *Three Years*, 318–19; HMH, *Marching*, November 26, 19, December 5, November 27, 1864, pp. 198, 76, 146, 104; James C. Patten, "An Indiana Doctor Marches with Sherman," ed. Robert G. Athearn, *Indiana Magazine of History* 49 (December 1953), December 18, 1864, p. 420.

36. HMH, *Marching*, December 5, 1, 6, 13, 1864, pp. 142, 122, 150, 178.

37. David Nevin, *Sherman's March* (Alexandria, Va., 1986), 66; WTS, *Memoirs*, 2:194.

38. An excellent study of Sherman's soldiers is Joseph T. Glatthaar, *The March to the Sea and Beyond: Sherman's Troops in the Savannah and Carolinas Campaign* (New York, 1985). See also Glatthaar, "Sherman's Army and Total War: Attitudes on Destruction . . . ," *Atlanta Historical Journal* 29 (Spring 1986): 41–52.

39. JS, "An Address Commemorative of General William T. Sherman," New York Commandery, MOLLUS, April 6, 1892, 15; George Templeton Strong, *Diary of the Civil War, 1860–1865*, ed, Allan Nevins (New York, 1962), December 8, 1864, 3:526; *Cincinnati Commercial*, December 13, 1864.

40. Lyman S. Widney, "Campaigning with 'Uncle Billy,' " *Neales* 2 (August 1913): 140.

41. WTS, *Memoirs*, 2:672–74; Conyngham, *Sherman's March*, 285–86; W. B. Hazen, *Narrative of Military Service* (Boston, 1885), 332–33; HMH, *Marching*, December 13, 1864, pp. 178–80; William E. Strong "The Capture of Fort McAllister, December 13, 1864," manuscript, WTS, LC.

42. WTS, "Old Shady with a Moral," *North American Review* 147 (August 1888): 367–68; Hazen, *Narrative*, 333–34.

43. USG to WTS, December 6, 1864, O.R., I, 44, 636–37.

44. Maxwell V. Woodhull, "A Glimpse of Sherman Fifty Years Ago," *War Paper*, Commandery of the District of Columbia, MOLLUS, December 2, 1914; USG to HWH, December 15, 1864, WTS to USG, December 16, 1864, HWH to WTS, December 16, 1864, WTS to Hardee, December 17, 1864, O.R., I, 44, 715, 726–29, 737–38; Brockman, "John Van Duzer Diary," December 17, 22, 1864, 238, 240; Harwell and Racine, *Fiery Trail*, December 26, 1864, p. 73.

45. Widney, *Narrative*, 140.

46. WTS to USG, December 18, 24, 1864, O.R., I, 44, 741–43, 797–98.

47. E. A. Carmen, "General Hardee's Escape from Savannah," *War Paper*, District of Columbia Commandery, MOLLUS, May 3, 1893, p. 30.

48. Stephen E. Ambrose mentions several ways that WTS adhered to Jomini. Ambrose, *Halleck: Lincoln's Chief of Staff* (Baton Rouge, 1962), 182–83; WTS to MSF, January 19, 1864, WTS, OHS.

49. WTS to N.W., Esq., January 8, 1865, in NYT, January 19, 1865.

50. WTS to George H. Thomas, January 21, 1865, Frederick M. Dearborn Collection, HLH.

51. WTS to AL, December 22, 1864, in WTS, *Memoirs* 2:711.

52. Widney, "Campaigning," 141; untitled February 21, 1891, newspaper clipping, WTS, MoHS, and WTS, OHS; Foote, *With Sherman*, 229–30; WTS to Douglass Green, copy, March 21, copy, Meldrim Family Collection, Georgia Historical Society; WTS to Col. and Mrs. Markland, January 3, 1865, CHH, WLC; WTS to General Morgan, January 3, 1865, Historical Society of Quincy and Adams County, Illinois; HMH, *Marching*, December 24, 29, 1864, 197–204; S.F.O. No. 143, Hqs., Military Division of the Mississippi, December 26, 1864, O.R., I, 44, 812–13; John P. Dyer, "Northern Relief for Savannah During Sherman's Occupation [1864–1865]," *Journal of Southern History* 19 (November 1953): 457–72; WTS to P. J. Stanfield et al., December 28, 1864, WTS to EMS, January 2, 1865, O.R., I, 44, I, 827, II, 5–6.

53. Eleanor Kinzie Gordon, "The Maid Announced General Sherman," and Frances Thomas Howard, "Do You Wish to Be Introduced to General Sherman?" in Katherine M. Jones, ed., *When Sherman Come . . .* (Indianapolis, 1964), 97–98, 85–90.

54. "Diary of Captain Robert E. Park, Twelfth Alabama Regiment," *Southern Historical Society Papers* 2 (1876): 307; AL to WTS, December 26, 1864, USG to WTS, December 18, 1864, HWH to WTS, December 18, 1864, DDP to WTS, December 29, 1864, O.R., I, 809, 44, 740–41, 832; EMS to ES, December 26, 1864, SFP, UNDA; Congressional Resolution in G.O. No. 3, War Department, O.R., I, 44, 856; New York State Legislature Concurrent Resolution, January 5, 1865, O.R., I, 49, I, 575–76; Sherman Testimonial Papers, Cincinnati Historical Society; testimonial, Columbus, January 11, 1865, WTS, HPC; Benjamin H. Stanton to H. H. Hunter, January 16, 1865, WTS, LC; Frederick F. Low to WTS, January 2, 1865, O.R., I, 44, 17–18; Dennis Hart Mahan to WTS, December 19, 1864, WTS, LC; *Chicago Tribune*, December 26, 28, 1864; *Edinburgh Review*, undated, in James Grant Wilson, *Sketches of Illustrious Soldiers* (New York, 1874), 461; *London Times*, undated, in Joel Tyler Headley, *Grant and Sherman . . .* (New York, 1865), 198; Thomas E. Smith to Brother, January 17, 1865, Smith Papers, Cincinnati Historical Society; WTS to USG, December 24, 1865, O.R., I, 44, 797–98.

55. JS to WTS, December 18, 1864, ES to JS, December 26, 1864, WTS, LC; WTS to TE, December 31, 1864, TE, LC; WTS to ES, January 5, 1865, SFP, UNDA.

56. WTS to ES, December 16, 31, 1864, ES, diary, December 4, 7, 1864, ES to WTS, December 29, 1864, January 8, 1865, SFP, UNDA.

57. JAC to Wife, November 20, 1864, JAC, *Three Years*, 312–13; John B. Dennis to WTS, June 22, 1875, WTS, LC.

58. HMH, *Marching*, November 17, 18, December 2, 1864, 66–70, 125–28.

59. Howard C. Westwood, "Sherman Marched—and Proclaimed 'Land for the Landless,'" *South Carolina Historical Magazine* 85 (January 1984): 38–39; James P. Jones, "General Jeff. C. Davis, U.S.A., and Sherman's Georgia Campaign," *Georgia Historical Quarterly* 47 (March 1962): 242–45.

60. *Richmond Examiner*, December 3, 1864, in Paul D. Escott, *After Secession . . .* (Baton Rouge, 1977), 253–54; HWH to WTS, December 30, 1864, in WTS, *Memoirs* 2:727–29; Chase to WTS, January 2, 1865, WTS, LC; Charles T. Sherman to WTS, December 28, 1864, SFP, UNDA.

61. WTS to HWH, January 12, 1865, O.R., I, 47, II, 36–37; WTS to Chase, January 11, 1865, Chase Papers, HSPa.

62. An excellent account of blacks and the march is Benjamin Quarles, *The Negro in the Civil War* (Boston, 1953), chap. 14. Also valuable is Edmund L. Drago, "How Sherman's March Through Georgia Affected the Slaves," *Georgia Historical Quarterly* 57 (Fall 1973): 361–75. Detailed accounts of EMS's visit are found in WTS, *Memoirs*, 2:722–33, and Benjamin P. Thomas and Harold M. Hyman, *Stanton, The Life and Times . . .* (New York, 1962), 343–45.

63. WTS, *Memoirs*, 2:727; "Minutes of an Interview . . . ," January 12, 1865, O.R., I, 47, II, 37–41.

64. S.F.O. No. 15, January 16, 1865 in WTS, *Memoirs*, 2:730–32; Westwood, "Sherman Marched," 39–50; Frank A. Flowers, *Edwin McMasters Stanton . . .* (Akron, 1905), 298; AJ to WTS, February 1, 1866, WTS to AJ, February 1, 2, 1866, AJ, LC; WTS to ES, January 15, 1865, SFP, UNDA.

65. WTS to ES, January 2, 1865, SFP, UNDA.

66. John W. Daniel, "Unveiling of Valentine's Recumbent Figure of Lee," *Southern Historical Society Papers* 11 (1883): 356; Elizabeth Wysor Klingberg, "Campaigns of Lee and Sherman," *Confederate Veteran* 24 (1916): 357–59. George C. Rable, *Civil War Women and the Crisis* (Urbana, 1989), 171.

67. WTS to A. Hickenlooper, April 6, 1881, *Proceedings of the 15th Annual Meeting of the Society of the Army of the Tennessee*, April 6, 1881, 122–31; WTS to L. B. Church, copy, January 8, 1880, WTS, LC; WTS to Charles A. Morton, copy, January 9, 1880, WTS, LC.

CHAPTER 14 PUNISHING SOUTH CAROLINA AND ENSURING VICTORY

1. R. N. Arnold to WTS, January 30, 1865, O.R., I, 47, II, 166–69; John F. Marszalek, ed., *The Diary of Miss Emma Holmes* (Baton Rouge, 1979), January 23, 1865, 394; WTS to ES, January 5, 1865, SFP, UNDA.

2. USG to WTS, December 27, 1864, WTS to USG, December 24, 1864, O.R., I, 44, 797; WTS to HWH, April 4, 1865, O.R., I, 47, I, 17–18; OOH,

"The Campaign of the Carolinas," Eleventh Annual Dinner of the Commandery of Ohio, MOLLUS, May 2, 1894, 22; William H. Kent to Sidney Howard Gay, January 22, 1865, Sidney Howard Gay Papers, CU; WTS to DDP, January 21, 1865, O.R., I, 47, II, 104.

3. "Confidential Instructions from Rear Admiral Dahlgren . . . ," January 15, 1865, O.R. Navy, 16, 169; WTS to J. G. Foster, January 19, 1865, O.R., I, 47, II, 197; WTS to HWH, April 4, 1865, O.R., I, 47, I, 18; WTS to USG, January 29, 1865, O.R., I, 47, II, 154.

4. J. E. P. Doyle, "Sherman's Sixty Days in the Carolinas," *United States Service Magazine* 3 (June 1865): 512; WTS to USG, December 24, 1864, O.R., I, 44, 797; WTS to USG, January 2, 1865, O.R., I, 47, II, 6–7; Thomas Osborn to S. C. Osborn, January 25, 1865, in Richard Harwell and Philip N. Racine, eds., *The Fiery Trail . . .* (Knoxville, 1986), 83.

5. John G. Barrett, *Sherman's March Through the Carolinas* (Chapel Hill, 1956), 48–49. This book remains the most comprehensive account of this campaign.

6. Manning F. Force, "Marching Across Carolina," *Sketches of the War 1861–1865,* Ohio Commandery, MOLLUS, (Cincinnati, 1888), 1:1.

7. WTS to USG, January 29, 1865, O.R., I, 47, II, 155; Andrew Hickenlooper, "Sherman," *Proceedings of the 23rd Annual Meeting of the Society of the Army of the Tennessee,* October 7, 1891, p. 490; HMH, *Marching with Sherman,* ed. M. A. De Wolfe Howe (New York, 1927), February 4, 1865, p. 250; Barrett, *Sherman's March,* 36; Daniel Oakey, "Marching Through Georgia and the Carolinas," *Century* 12 (October 1877): 926; Lyman S. Widney, "Campaigning with 'Uncle Billy,' " *Neales* 2 (August 1913): 142.

8. SHMB, "Some Personal Recollections of General Sherman," *McClure's* 3 (August 1894): 214–16.

9. WTS to HWH, January 27, 1865, O.R., I, 47, II, 136; Joseph T. Glatthaar, *The March to the Sea and Beyond . . .* (New York, 1985); Glatthaar, "Sherman's Army and Total War . . . ," *Atlanta Historical Journal* 29 (Spring, 1986): 47–49; Joseph B. Foraker, *Notes of a Busy Life* (Cincinnati, 1916), 1:53; WTS to HWH, December 24, 1864, O.R., I, 44, 799; WTS, *Memoirs,* 2:734; HWH to Francis Lieber, February 18, 1865, LI 1723, HL.

10. Glatthaar, "Sherman's Army," 47; George W. Nichols, *The Story of the Great March from the Diary of a Staff Officer* (New York, 1865), 173.

11. Edwin S. Redkey, "They Are Invincible," *Civil War Times Illustrated* 28 (April 1989): 33.

12. Force, *Marching,* 12.

13. Samuel Mahon, "The Forager in Sherman's Last Campaign," in *War Sketches and Incidents,* Iowa Commandery, MOLLUS (Des Moines, 1898), 2:198–99; Thomas Osborn, diary, February 7, 1865, in Harwell and Racine, *Fiery Trail,* 106–7; Force, *Marching,* 15; WTS to George H. Thomas, January 21, 1865, Frederick M. Dearborn Collection, HLH; DDP, *Naval History of the Civil War* (New York, 1886), 759–60.

14. WTS, *Memoirs,* 2:753–57.

15. *New York Herald,* March 18, 1865.

16. WTS, *Memoirs*, 2:760–61; Marion B. Lucas, *Sherman and the Burning of Columbia* (College Station, Texas, 1976), 68–69. This book is a detailed and convincing analysis of the chaos in Columbia before, during, and after Sherman's visit.

17. Levi Nelson Green, diary, February 17, 1865, copy, MiHS; Theodore F. Upson, *With Sherman to the Sea . . .* , ed. Oscar O. Winther (Baton Rouge, 1943), 152; Nichols, *Story*, 161–62; Faunt Le Roy Senour, *Mayor General William T. Sherman and His Campaign* (Chicago, 1865), 393–94; WTS, *Memoirs*, 2:761–64; SHMB, "Personal Recollections," 212.

18. WTS, *Memoirs*, 2:764–66.

19. Ibid., 22:766.

20. OOH, *The Autobiography of Oliver Otis Howard* (New York, 1907), 2:122; WTS, *Memoirs*, 2:766–67; S. A. Crittenden, "This Is General Sherman," in Katherine M. Jones, ed., *When Sherman Came: Southern Women and the Great March* (Indianapolis, 1964), 200–201.

21. Lucas, *Sherman*, 12; WTS, *Memoirs*, 2:767; Thomas Osborn, diary, February 18, 1865, in Harwell and Racine, *Fiery Trail*, 134–35; George W. Pepper, *Personal Recollections of Sherman's Campaign in Georgia and the Carolinas* (Zanesville, Ohio, 1866), 315; F. Y. Hedley, *Marching Through Georgia . . .* (Chicago, 1887), 395.

22. C. P. Kingsbury to WTS, May 1, 1868, WTS, LC; WTS, diary, February 18, 1865, SFP, UNDA; WTS, *Memoirs*, 2:767, 980–88; Wade Hampton to Reverdy Johnson, April 21, 1866, *Southern Historical Society Papers* 7 (1881): 156–58. See, e.g., "Wade Hampton and W. T. Sherman," *Confederate Veteran* 16 (1908): 518–19.

23. Lucas, *Sherman*, particularly the conclusion; Bell I. Wiley, Foreword, in Lucas, 13; WTS, speech, Annual Meeting of the Society of the Army of the Potomac, NYT, June 9, 1881.

24. WTS to Hampton, February 24, 1865, Hampton to WTS, February 27, 1865, O.R., I, 47, II, 546–47, 597–98; OOH, *Autobiography*, 2:130–31.

25. WTS to Judson Kilpatrick, February 23, 1865, O.R., I, 47, II, 544; Francis B. Carpenter, *Six Months in the White House with Abraham Lincoln* (New York, 1868), 233; WTS, July 1867 notes on fly leaf of *The Laws of the United States of America*, vol. 1: *The Constitution of the United States* (Philadelphia, 1796).

26. Senour, *Major General Sherman*, 402–4.

27. SHMB, *With Fire and Sword* (New York, 1911), 182–83; W. B. Hazen, *Narrative of Military Service* (Boston, 1885), 358; WTS, *Memoirs*, 2:773–74.

28. WTS to Alfred H. Terry, March 16, 1865, O.R., I, 47, II, 867; WTS to JWD, March 15, 1870, JWD, LC; WTS, *Memoirs*, 2:774.

29. WTS to Kilpatrick, March 7, 1865, O.R., I, 47, II, 721; Glatthaar, "Sherman's Army," 50–51.

30. Oakey, "Marching," 925; Barrett, *Sherman's March*, 118; Thomas Osborn, diary, February 27, 1865, in Harwell and Racine, *Fiery Trail*, 155.

31. WTS, *Memoirs*, 2:777; WTS to USG, March 12, 1865, WTS to EMS, March 12, 1865, O.R., I, 47, II, 793–95; WTS to ES, March 12, 1865, SFP,

UNDA; WTS to TE, March 12, 1865, TE, LC; SHMB, *With Fire and Sword*, 192–93.

32. WTS to USG, March 12, 1865, WTS to Easton and Beckwith, March 12, 1865, WTS to Terry, March 12, 1865, O.R., I, 47, II, 794–95, 803.

33. SHMB, *With Fire and Sword*, 185–86; Thomas Osborn, diary, March 1, 1865, in Harwell and Racine, *Fiery Trail*, 175.

34. Sally Hawthorne, "Heralded by Columns of Smoke," in Jones, *When Sherman Came*, 280.

35. WTS to JMS, March 14, 1865, WTS to Terry, March 14, 1865, WTS to Q. A. Gilmore, March 15, 1865, USG to WTS, March 16, 1865, O.R., I, 47, II, 834–35, 856–57, 860.

36. WTS, *Memoirs*, 2:782–84; WTS to OOH, March 17, 1865, O.R., I, 47, II, 870–71.

37. WTS, *Memoirs*, 2:783–86. The most thorough account of the battle is in Jay Luvaas, "Johnston's Last Stand—Bentonville," *North Carolina Historical Review* 33 (July 1956): 332–58.

38. WTS, *Memoirs*, 2:785–89; WTS to Henry W. Slocum, March 20, 1865, WTS to USG, March 22, 1865, USG to WTS, March 22, 1865, EMS to WTS, March 22, 1865, O.R., I, 47, II, 919, 947–50; S.F.O. No. 35, Hqs., Military Division of the Mississippi, March 22, 1865, O.R., I, 47, I, 44.

39. SHMB, "Some Personal Recollections," 216; S.F.O. No. 35, Hqs., Military Division of the Mississippi, March 22, 1865, O.R., I, 47, I, 44.

40. WTS to Caroline Carson, January 20, 1865, James L. Petegru Papers, LC; WTS to T. Turner, March 25, 1865, Society Collection, HSPa.

41. WTS to Thomas, January 21, 1865, Frederick M. Dearborn Collection, HLH.

42. WTS to DDP, December 31, 1864, O.R., I, 44, 843; WTS to ES, April 15, 1859, SFP, UNDA.

CHAPTER 15   FAME TARNISHED

1. WTS to ES, March 23, 1865, SFP, UNDA.

2. Y. P. Powell to Ellen Aumach, March 25, 1865, Aumach Papers, DU; J. B. Foraker, *Memorial Address . . . Cincinnati, Ohio . . .* , February 23, 1891, p. 19, in Selected Pamphlets, OHS.

3. WTS to ES, March 23, 1865, SFP, UNDA; WTS to USG, March 24, 1865, O.R., I, 47, III, 4.

4. WTS to JS, January 19, 1865, WTS, LC; USG to WTS, February 1, 1865, O.R., I, 47, II, 194.

5. S.F.O. No. 38, Hqs., Military Division of the Mississippi, March 25, 1865, O.R., I, 47, III, 120; J. R. Hamilton to William Swinton, March 28, 1865, VHS; Horace Porter, *Campaigning with Grant* (New York, 1897), 417–18.

6. Charles C. Coffin, *Four Years of Fighting . . .* (New York, 1888), 488; Porter, *Campaigning*, 418–19; *New York Herald*, March 31, 1865.

7. WTS, *Memoirs*, 2:810.

8. Porter, *Campaigning*, 420–21.

9. DDP, *Incidents and Anecdotes of the Civil War* (New York, 1886), 313–15; WTS, *Memoirs*, 2:810–17; Porter, *Campaigning*, 423–24; WTS, speech, *Eighteenth Annual Reunion of the Society of the Army of the Potomac*, June 22, 23, 1887, 61–65; WTS to P. A. Healy, January 13, 1868, WTS, USMA.

10. WTS to EMS, March 28, 1865, O.R., I, 47, III, 42; WTS to ES, March 31, 1865, SFP, UNDA; WTS to TE, March 1, 1865, in WTS, *Home Letters . . .* , ed. M. A. DeWolfe Howe (New York, 1909), 337–38; EMS to WTS, March 28, 1865, O.R., I, 47, III, 42.

11. WTS to JS, April 5, 1865, WTS, LC; WTS to Q. A. Gillmore, April 6, 1865, WTS to OOH, April 7, 1865, WTS to USG, April 8, 1865, O.R., I, 47, III, 115–16, 119, 128–29; WTS to ES, April 10, 1865, SFP, UNDA; WTS to PBE, April 9, 1865, EFP, LC.

12. WTS to A. Baird, April 3, 1865, in WTS, *Memoirs*, 2:1051–52; WTS to Michael Hahn, April 5, 1865, O.R., I, 47, III, 101–2.

13. WTS to Messrs. Sutter et al., April 4, 1865, in *Cincinnati Commercial*, April 18, 1865, clipping in Daniel O. Drennan Papers, LC; WTS to RA, April 5, 1865, O.R., I, 47, III, 107.

14. S.F.O. No. 54, Hqs., Military Division of the Mississippi, April 12, 1865, in WTS, *Memoirs*, 2:832; WTS to USG, April 12, 1865, O.R., I, 47, III, 177; Alonzo D. Cady to Wife, April 16, 1865, Cady-Randolph Papers, MiHS; John C. Arbuckle, *Civil War Experiences of a Soldier Who Marched with Sherman* (Columbus, 1930), 146; ES to WTS, April 10, 1865, SFP, UNDA.

15. Michael B. Ballard, *A Long Shadow: Jefferson Davis and the Final Days of the Confederacy* (Jackson, 1986).

16. Zebulon Vance to WTS, April 11, 1865, copy, David L. Swain Papers, NCDH; Vance to WTS, April 12, 1865, WTS to Vance, April 12, 1865, two letters, WTS to ?, April 12, 1865, O.R., I, 47, III, 178–79; WTS to Provost Marshall, April 13, 1865, William Alexander Graham Papers, NCDH; pass, initialed by WTS, April 13, 1865, Walter Clark Papers, NCDH; HMH, *Marching with Sherman*, ed. M. A. DeWolfe Howe (New Haven, 1927), April 14, 1865, pp. 296–97; WTS to USG, April 15, 1865, WTS to Langsdon C. Easton, April 14, 1865, O.R., I, 47, III, 227, 207; WTS, *Memoirs*, 2:833.

17. Theodore F. Upson, *With Sherman to the Sea . . .* , ed. Oscar O. Winther (Baton Rouge, 1943), April 15, 1865, p. 166; Charles W. Wills, *Army Life of an Illinois Soldier* (Washington, D.C., 1906), 369; Carl Schurz to Wife, April 14, 1865, Joseph Schafer, ed. and trans., *Intimate Letters of Carl Schurz, 1841–1869* (New York, 1928), 333.

18. George Ward Nichols, *The Story of the Great March . . .* (New York, 1865), 298.

19. JEJ to WTS, April 14, 1865, WTS to JEJ, April 14, 1865, O.R., I, 47, III, 207–8; HMH, April 16, 1865, p. 302; WTS to Kilpatrick, April 14, 1865, O.R., I, 47, III, 215.

20. Oscar L. Jackson, *The Colonel's Diary* (Sharon, Pa., 1922), 206; WTS to Langsdon C. Easton, April 14, 1865, WTS to Kilpatrick, April 15, 16, 1865, O.R., I, 47, III, 207, 225, 234; WTS to Joseph D. Webster, April 17, 1865, HM 23316, HL; Wills, *Army Life*, April 15, 1865, p. 371; WTS to USG and EMS, April 15, 1865, O.R., I, 47, III, 221.

21. EMS to WTS, April 15, 1865, HWH to WTS, April 15, 1865, O.R., I, 47, III, 220–21; WTS, *Memoirs*, 2:835–38; WTS to JWD, November 6, 1868, JWD, LC.

22. George W. Pepper, *Personal Recollections* . . . (Zanesville, Ohio, 1866), 408–12; HMH, *Marching*, April 25, 1865, 310–11.

23. S.F.O. No. 56, April 17, 1865, O.R., I, 47, III, 238–39.

24. ES to MSF, April 19, 1865, WTS, OHS; Thomas Ward Osborn to Abraham C. Osborn, April 19, 1865, in Richard Harwell and Philip N. Racine, eds., *The Fiery Trail* (Knoxville, 1986), 213–14; Wills, *Army Life*, April 13, 1865, p. 371; Arbuckle, *Civil War Experiences*, 149; James P. Jones, "'Lincoln's Avengers': The Assassination and Sherman's Army," *Lincoln Herald* 64 (Winter 1962): 187–88; Roy M. Brown to Editor, *Saturday Review of Literature*, February 21, 1953, p. 25; WTS to Mary Miles, September 18, 1868, NAM, LC.

25. WTS, *Memoirs*, 2:839–40; Phillip to Uncle, March 28, 1865, CHH, WLC.

26. WTS, *Memoirs*, 2:840–45; WTS to JWD, November 6, 1868, JWD, LC. Detailed accounts of these negotiations include: John F. Marszalek, "The Stanton-Sherman Controversy," *Civil War Times Illustrated* 9 (October 1970): 4–12; Marszalek, *Sherman's Other War* . . . (Memphis, 1981), 183–209; Raoul S. Naroll, "Lincoln and the Sherman Peace Fiasco: Another Fable?" *Journal of Southern History* 20 (November 1954), 459–83; Harry W. Pfanz, "The Surrender Negotiations Between General Johnston and General Sherman," *Military Affairs* 16 (Summer 1952): 61–70; JEJ, "My Negotiations with General Sherman," *North American Review* 143 (August 1886): 183–97.

27. WTS to USG or HWH, April 18, 1865, WTS to HWH, April 18, 1865, O.R., I, 47, III, 243–45.

28. WTS to Langsdon C. Easton, April 18, 1865, S.F.O. No. 58, Hqs., Military Division of the Mississippi, April 19, 1865, O.R., I, 47, III, 246, 250; WTS to ES, April 18, 1865, SFP, UNDA; Carl Schurz to Wife, April 18, 1865, Frederick Bancroft, ed., *Speeches, Correspondence, and Political Papers of Carl Schurz* (New York, 1913), 1:253; Thomas Ward Osborn to S. C. Osborn, April 19, 1865, in Harwell and Racine, *Fiery Trail*, 211.

29. USG to EMS, April 21, 1865, O.R., I, 47, III, 263; Edgar T. Welles, ed., *The Diary of Gideon Welles* (Boston, 1911), April 21, 1865, 2:294–95.

30. USG to WTS, April 21, 1865, EMS to HWH, April 21, 1865, O.R., I, 47, III, 263–64; James G. Randall and Theodore C. Pease, eds., *The Diary of Orville H. Browning*, (Springfield, Ill., 1933); April 22, 1865, 2:24; WTS to JEJ, April 21, 1865, O.R., I, 47, III, 265–66.

31. Stephen E. Ambrose, *Halleck, Lincoln's Chief of Staff* (Baton Rouge, 1962), 199; HWH to EMS, April 22, 1865, O.R., I, 47, III, 277–78.

32. EMS to John A. Dix, April 22, 1865, O.R., I, 47, III, 285–86.

33. NYT, April 23, 1865; WTS to JEJ, April 23, 1865, O.R., I, 47, III, 286; Jefferson Davis to "Winnie," April 23, 1865, in Jefferson Davis, *Private Letters*, ed. Hudson Strode (New York, 1966), 156; WTS to JEJ and Hardee, April 23, 1865, O.R., I, 47, III, 287.

34. WTS, diary, April 24, 1865, SFP, UNDA; WTS to A. J. Flagg, November 5, 1885, copy, WTS, LC; USG to EMS, April 24, 1865, WTS to JEJ, April 24, 1865, O.R., I, 47, III, 293–94; WTS, *Memoirs*, 2:846–47; EMS to USG, April 25, 1865, O.R., I, 47, III, 301–2.

35. ES to WTS, April 26, 1865, SFP, UNDA; WTS to EMS, April 25, 1865, WTS to USG, April 25, 1865, O.R., I, 47, III, 302–3.

36. JEJ to WTS, April 25, 1865, WTS to JEJ, April 25, 1865, "Terms of a Military Convention . . . April 26, 1865 . . . ," USG to EMS, April 26, 1865, Johnston to WTS, April 28, 1865, WTS, LC.

37. WTS to JEJ, April 23, 1865, O.R., I, 47, III, 320; WTS to ES, April 28, 1865, SFP, UNDA.

38. WTS to USG, April 28, 1865, O.R., I, 47, III, 234–35.

39. *Lancaster* (Ohio) *Eagle*, May 18, 1865; Elias Smith to Sidney Howard Gay, April 20, 1865, Sidney Howard Gay Papers, CU; *New York Tribune*, April 24, 1865; *Chicago Tribune*, April 24, 1865; *Washington Star*, April 24, 1865; *New York Herald*, April 25, 1865; HMH, *Marching*, 476–77.

40. Joseph B. Foraker, *Notes of a Busy Life* (Cincinnati, 1916), 1:68; Frances P. Blair, Jr., to Montgomery Blair, April 30, 1865, in William E. Smith, *The Frances Preston Blair Family in Politics* (New York, 1933), 2:184–85; *Cincinnati Commercial*, April 27, 1865; *Louisville Journal*, April 28, 1865; WTS to MSF, April 29, 1865, WTS, OHS.

41. Frederick Bancroft and William A. Dunning, eds., *The Reminiscences of Carl Schurz* (New York, 1908), 3:116–17; WTS, *Memoirs*, 2:861–62.

42. WTS, *Memoirs*, 2:862; WTS to JAR, April 29, 1865, O.R., I, 47, III, 345–46; Salmon P. Chase to WTS, May 5, 1865, WTS, LC; Chase to William G. Deshler, April 29, 1865, in "Sherman's Truce," *United States Service Magazine* 3 (June 1865): 499.

43. WTS to JMS, May 5, 1865, O.R., I, 47, III, 406; S.F.O. No. 69, Hqs., Military Division of the Mississippi, May 6, 1865, SCW, WLC; HWH to EMS, April 26, 1865, WTS, LC; WTS to Chase, May 6, 1865, two letters, O.R., I, 47, III, 410–12; Chase to AJ, May 7, 1865, in James E. Sefton, ed., "Chief Justice Chase as an Advisor on Presidential Reconstruction," *Civil War History* 13 (September 1976): 247–48.

44. S.F.O. No. 65, Hqs., Military Division of the Mississippi, April 27, 1865, O.R., I, 47, III, 322; Wills, *Army Life*, April 29, 1865, p. 372.

45. Wills, *Army Life*, April 29, 1865, pp. 372–73; WTS to HWH, May 7, 1865, HM 23317, HL; HWH to WTS, May 9, 1865, WTS to HWH, May 9, 10, 1865, O.R., I, 47, III, 454, 446, 454–55.

46. Jackson, *Colonel's Diary*, May 11, 1865, pp. 214–15; WTS to JAL, May 12, 1865, O.R., I, 47, III, 477–78; Leslie Anders, *The Eighteenth Missouri* (Indianapolis, 1968) 330; WTS to ES, May 10, 1865, SFP, UNDA.

47. Jackson, *Colonel's Diary*, May 12, 1865, p. 215; L. M. Dayton to Colonel Sumner, May 11, 1865, O.R., I, 46, III, 1137; Alpheus S. Williams, Journal of Alpheus S. Williams, May 15, 1865, copy, Alpheus S. Williams Papers, Detroit Public Library; WTS to JAR, May 14, 1865, WTS to AJ, May 19, 1865, O.R., I, 47, III, 530–31; Henry M. Hitchcock, *Marching with*

Sherman, ed. M. A. DeWolfe Howe (New York, 1927), May 26, 1865, pp. 319–20.

48. WTS to JAR, May 9, 1865, O.R., I, 47, I, 32–33; USG to WTS, May 19, 1865, O.R., I, 47, III, 531; A. B. Anderson to WTS, May 20, 1865, WTS, LC; Welles, May 19, 1865, 2:309–10; HBE, journal, vol. 2, May 20, 1865, HBE, OHS; JS, *Recollections . . .* (Chicago, 1895), 1:356.

49. TE, Jr., to WTS, May 1, 1865, SFP, UNDA; TE, Jr., to TE, May 1, 1865, EFP, LC; JS to WTS, May 2, 1865, WTS, LC; TE to Editor, *Cincinnati Commercial,* May 8, 1865; Thurlow Weed to EMS, May 27, 1865; Breen to EMS, June 1, 1865, EMS, LC.

50. WTS to the Chairmen of the Joint Committee on the Conduct of the War, May 19, 1865, O.R., I, 47, III, 532; "Testimony of Major General William T. Sherman, Washington, May 22, 1865," *Report of the Joint Committee on the Conduct of the War,* 38th Cong. 2d sess. (Washington, D.C., 1865), vol. 3.

51. *New York Tribune,* May 22, 1865, in NYT, May 24, 1865; W. F. G. Shanks, *Personal Recollections of Distinguished Generals* (New York, 1866), 41; WTS to ES, May 8, 1865, SFP, UNDA; WTS to USG, May 10, 1865, in *Collection of W. K. Bixby of St. Louis* (privately printed, 1919), HL; WTS to ES, May 10, 1865, SFP, UNDA; WTS to JAL, May 12, 1865, O.R., I, 47, III, 478.

52. S.F.O. No. 239, Hqs. of the Army, May 18, 1865, O.R., I, 47, III, 526; James H. Wilson, *The Life of Charles A. Dana* (New York, 1907), 362–63; NYT, May 24, 1865; A detailed account is Thomas Fleming, "The Big Parade," *American Heritage* 41 (March 1990): 98–104; WTS, "Address," *Annual Meeting of the Grand Army of the Republic,* July 3, 4, 1890; OOH, *Autobiography,* 1:211–12.

53. Alonzo D. Cady to Wife, May 25, 1865, Cady-Randolph Papers, MiHS; J. W. Anderson, "The Grand Review," in Jackson, *Colonel's Diary,* 220; Pepper, *Personal Recollections,* 469; John Y. Simon, ed., *The Personal Memoirs of Julia Dent Grant* (Carbondale, 1975), 159.

54. WTS to JAL, May 20, 1865, JAL, LC; Porter, *Campaigning,* 509; *New York Herald,* May 25, 1865; Benjamin F. Fisher to Professor, May 24, 1865, Fisher Papers, DU; F. Y. Hedley, *Marching Through Georgia . . .* (Chicago, 1887), 463.

55. WTS, *Memoirs,* 2:865–66.

56. Ibid.; Noah Brooks, *Washington in Lincoln's Time* (New York, 1896), 361; J. M. Forbes, "Recollections of Sherman and Porter," *Nation,* March 5, 1891, p. 192; *Cincinnati Gazette, Missouri Republican,* May 25, 1865.

57. Harry J. Sievers, *Benjamin Harrison, Hoosier Statesman* (Indianapolis, 1952), 1:306; WTS to TE, January 8, 1866, EFP, LC; Elbridge Copp, *Reminiscences* (Nashua, N.H., 1911), 527; Lucy S. Stewart to PTS, February 6, 1937, SFP, UNDA.

58. WTS to S. M. Bowman, May 19, 1865, in NYT, May 26, 1865; Benjamin P. Thomas and Harold M. Hyman, *Stanton . . .* (New York, 1962), 417; Randall and Pease, eds., *Diary of Orville Hickson Browning,* May 29, 1865, 2:30.

59. WTS to T. S. Bowers, WTS to JMS, WTS to USG, May 28, 1865, O.R., I, 47, III, 583, 585–86, 582–83; S.F.O. No. 76, Hqs., Military Division of the Mississippi, May 30, 1865, in WTS, *Memoirs*, 2:869–71.

60. WTS to James E. Yeatman, May 21, 1865, copy, SFP, UNDA.

CHAPTER 16 NATIONAL HERO AND THE SOUTH'S FRIEND

1. There are many excellent books on Reconstruction. The definitive account is Eric Foner, *Reconstruction, America's Unfinished Revolution* (New York, 1988). Still very valuable is Kenneth Stampp, *The Era of Reconstruction, 1865–1877* (New York, 1965). A good account of the politics at the national level is Martin E. Mantell, *Johnson, Grant, and the Politics of Reconstruction* (New York, 1973). Though imbued with an anti-interventionist view, the most detailed account of the army in Reconstruction is James E. Sefton, *The United States Army and Reconstruction, 1865–1877* (Baton Rouge, 1967). See also Joseph G. Dawson III, *Army Generals and Reconstruction: Louisiana, 1862–1877* (Baton Rouge, 1982).

2. NYT, June 3, 4, 1865; WTS to TE, June 3, 1865, CHH, WLC.

3. WTS, diary, June 7, 21–23, 1865, *Michawaka* (Indiana) *Enterprise*, June 10, 17, 24, 1865, in SFP, UNDA; ES to TE, June 8, 1865, EFP, UNDA; *Cincinnati Commercial*, June 28, 1865, in *New Orleans Picayune*, June 28, 1865, reprinted in S. M. Bowman and R. B. Irwin, *Sherman and His Campaign* (New York, 1865), 464–66.

4. USG to WTS, January 5, 1868 [1869], WTS, OHS; WTS to JS, January 15, 1869, WTS, LC; USG to ES, February 2, 1869, SFP, UNDA; WTS to Benjamin H. Field, March 27, 1869, WTS, DU; WTS to DFB, August 10, 1870, WLF, NYPL; WTS to Sam Reber, February 5, 1873, WTS, LC.

5. On DFB, see Germaine M. Reed, *David French Boyd* . . . (Baton Rouge, 1977); on Warner, see *Biographical Directory of the American Congress;* on Moorman, see "Gen. George Moorman Died in Harness," *Confederate Veteran* 11 (1903): 8–9; DFB to WTS, September 22, 1865, WTS, LC; DFB to WTS, January 8, 1866, WLF, NYPL.

6. WTS, "General Sherman's Tour of Europe," *Century* n.s. 35 (April 1899): 740.

7. ESF, untitled, undated, handwritten note, box 10, SFP, UNDA; Joseph C. Audenried, "General Sherman in Europe and the East," unpublished journal dated November 1878, WTS, OHS, pp. 53–55; WTS, "Tour," 734.

8. Benjamin Moran, journal, vol. 32, August 5, 1872, July 30, 1872, Benjamin Moran Papers, LC; SHMB, *Twenty Years in Europe* . . . (Chicago, 1900), 59–60.

9. WTS to TE, June 25, 1865, TE, LC; WTS to JAR, June 25, 1865, WTS to E. D. Townsend, June 25, 1865, O.R., I, 47, III, 663.

10. G.O. No. 118, War Department, June 27, 1865, O.R. I, 46, III, 662–63, 1298–99.

11. WTS to T. S. Bowers, July 15, 1865, O.R., I, 48, II, 1083; WTS to ES, July 16, 1865, SFP, UNDA.

12. WTS to William C. Church, July 28, 1865, William C. Church Papers, LC;

Silva T. Zsoldos, "The Political Career of Thomas Ewing, Sr." (Ph.D. diss., University of Delaware, 1977), pp. 280–81.

13. WTS to JS, November 4, 29, 1865, WTS, LC; WTS to TE, December 23, 1865, TE, LC; unnamed December 11, 1865, newspaper clipping, WTS, scrapbook, WTS, OHS; WTS to JAR, December 22, 1865, WTS, HPC; WTS to William B. Hodges, December 14, 1867, Charles Colcock Jones, Jr., Papers, DU.

14. AJ to WTS, February 1, 1866, WTS to AJ, February 1, 1866, AJ Papers, LC; WTS to WW, February 11, 1866, WTS, ISL; WTS to AJ, February 11, 1866, copy, WTS, LC; WTS to JS, February 23, 1866, WTS, LC; WTS to JS, January 19, 1866, WTS, LC.

15. TE to JS, February 12, 1866, WTS, LC; Zsoldos, "Political Career," 284–85; JS to WTS, July 8, 1866, WTS, LC; ES to WTS, September 10, 1866, SFP, UNDA.

16. WTS to AJ, October 16, 1866, AJ, LC; USG to WTS, October 18, 1866, WTS, LC; WTS to USG, October 19, 1866, USG to WTS, October 22, 1866, John Y. Simon, ed., Papers of U. S. Grant (Carbondale, 1967–), 16:339–40.

17. WTS to JGB, November 8, 1885, copy, WTS, LC. For a detailed uncritical account, see Martin Hardwick Hall, "The Campbell-Sherman Diplomatic Mission in Mexico," Bulletin of the Historical and Philosophical Society of Ohio 13 (October 1955): 254–70.

18. For an insider's view of WTS and USG and Mexico, see Cyrus B. Comstock, diary, October 23, 24, 31, 1866, Cyrus B. Comstock Papers, LC; WTS to ES, October 26, 1866, SFP, UNDA; JS to WTS, October 26, 31, 1866, WTS, LC.

19. WTS to JS, November 11, 1866, WTS, LC; WTS to ES, November 18, 1866, SFP, UNDA; WTS to JGB, November 8, 1885, copy, WTS, LC; WTS to ES, November 19, 1866, SFP, UNDA; EMS to WTS, December 21, 1866, WTS to JS, December 30, 1866, January 3, 1867, WTS, LC.

20. USG to WTS, WTS to USG, January 4, 1867, USG to WTS, January 5, 1867, USG, LC; WTS to JS, January 8, 1867, WTS, LC; WTS to PBE, January 10, 1867, PBE, OHS; USG to WTS, January 13, 1867, USG, LC.

21. WTS to DFB, January 25, 1867, WLF, NYPL; WTS to WW, February 16, 1867, WTS, ISL.

22. WTS to PBE, March 8, 1867, PBE, OHS; JS to WTS, WTS to JS, March 14, 1867, JS to WTS, March 20, 1867, WTS, LC.

23. WTS to JS, April 3, 1867, WTS, LC; WTS to Gentlemen, May 25, 1867, in NYT, May 31, 1867; WTS to Ord, May 28, 1867, WTS, MoHS; WTS to JS, August 3, 1867, WTS, LC.

24. AJ to WTS, October 2, 1867, WTS, LC; WTS to AJ, AJ to WTS, October 3, 1867, AJ, LC; WTS, diary, October 7, 9, 10, 11, 1867, WTS to ES, October 7, 1867, SFP, UNDA; WTS to JS, October 28, 1867, WTS, LC; WTS, "Address," Proceedings of the Second Annual Meeting of the Army of the Tennessee, November 13, 14, 1867, pp. 97–128; USG to WTS, November 21, 1867, WTS, LC; TE to WTS, November 24, 1867, SFP, UDNA.

25. WTS to USG, January 27, 1868, copy, WTS, LC; Zsoldos, "Political Careers," 296.

26. WTS to USG, January 27, 1868, copy, WTS, LC; James G. Randall and Theodore C. Pease, eds., *The Diary of Orville H. Browning* (Springfield, Ill., 1933), January 14, 1868, 2:173–74; WTS to ES, January 15, 1868, WTS to ES, January 13, 1868, ES to WTS, January 18, 21, 1868, SFP, UNDA.

27. WTS to ES, January 23, 1868, SFP, UNDA; WTS to TE, January 25, 1866, TE, LC; WTS to AJ, January 27, 1868, WTS, LC; WTS to AJ, January 31, 1868, AJ, LC; Howard K. Beale, ed., *Diary of Edward Bates, 1859–1866,* in *Annual Report of the American Historical Association, 1930* (1933), February 5, 1868, 3:272; TE to WTS, February 18, 1868, TE, LC; WTS to JS, February 10, 1868, WTS to AJ, February 14, 1868, copy, WTS, LC; WTS to TE, February 14, 1868, TE, LC; WTS to USG, February 14, 1868, WTS, LC; Zsoldos, "Political Careers," 297; AJ to WTS, WTS to AJ, February 19, 1868, AJ, LC.

28. WTS to JS, February 28, March 14, 1868, WTS, LC.

29. George F. Brown to WTS, March 31, 1868, WTS, LC; Zsoldos, "Political Careers," 300; Randall and Pease, *Diary,* April 6, 1868, 2:190–91; WTS to JS, March 14, 1868, WTS, LC; *Trial of Andrew Johnson, President of the United States . . .* (Washington, D.C., 1868), 1:460–91, 498–531.

CHAPTER 17 INDIAN COUNTRY CHAOS

1. There is a rich literature on the relationship of the American Indian and white American society. See Francis Paul Prucha, ed., *A Bibliographical Guide to the History of Indian-White Relations in the United States* (Chicago, 1977), and *Indian-White Relations in the United States: A Bibliography of Works Published, 1975–1980* (Lincoln, Neb., 1982).

2. C. D. Townsend to WTS, July 6, 1865, O.R., I, 48, II, 1056; WTS to D. R. Garrison, August 16, 1865, WTS, LC.

3. Allan R. Millett and Peter Maslowski, *For the Common Defense: A Military History of the United States of America* (New York, 1984), 233; Russell Weigley, *History of the United States Army* (New York, 1967), 266–67; WTS, "Report of the General of the Army," November 20, 1869, U.S. Serial Set, No. 1412.

4. For examples of WTS supporting Indian rights on reservations, see *St. Louis Globe,* April 21, 1875, in NYT, April 26, August 22, 1875; WTS to Herbert A. Preston, April 17, 1873, copy, WTS, LC.

5. Charles H. Devens, Jr., and WTS, *Addresses to the Graduating Class of the U.S. Military Academy, West Point, N.Y., June 14th, 1876* (New York, 1876), 36–37.

6. Most of these individuals have had biographies published about them. For quick overviews, see Paul Andrew Hutton, ed., *Soldiers West: Biographies from the Military Frontier* (Lincoln, Neb., 1987); Howard R. Lamar, ed., *The Reader's Encyclopedia of the American West* (New York, 1977); Sherry L. Smith, *The View from Officers Row: Army Perceptions of Western Indians* (Tucson, 1990); Donna M. E. Thomas, "Army Reform in America: The

Crucial Years, 1876–1881" (Ph.D. diss., University of Florida, 1980), 51–72; Robert Wooster, *The Military and United States Indian Policy, 1865–1903* (New Haven, 1988), 48–51.

7. Edward Coffman, *The Old Army: Portrait of the American Army in Peacetime, 1784–1898* (New York, 1986), 328–99; Thomas, "Army Reform," 25–37; Arlen L. Fowler, *The Black Infantry in the West, 1869–1891* (Westport, Conn., 1971), 9–12. A good study of the postwar army is Robert M. Utley, *Frontier Regulars: The United States Army and the Indian, 1866–1891* (New York, 1974); see also Don Richey, *The Enlisted Soldier Fighting the Indian Wars* (Norman, Okla., 1963).

8. NYT, January 29, 1887; *Southern Workman* 21 (April 1892): 63.

9. There are numerous tribal histories. See, for example, Peter J. Powell, *People of the Sacred Mountain: A History of the Northern Cheyenne Chiefs and Warrior Societies, 1830–1879* (New York, 1981), and Mildred Mayhall, *The Kiowas* (Norman, Okla., 1962). For Indian-white relations, in addition to the books cited in this chapter's notes, see Philip Weeks, *Farewell, My Nation: The American Indian and the United States, 1820–1890* (Arlington Heights, Ill., 1990); Francis Paul Prucha, *American Indian Policy in Crisis: Christian Reformers and the Indian, 1865–1900* (Norman, Okla., 1976); Frederick E. Hoxie, *A Final Promise: The Campaign to Assimilate the Indians, 1880–1920* (Lincoln, Neb., 1984); Loring B. Priest, *Uncle Sam's Stepchildren: The Reformation of United States Policy, 1865–1887* (New York, 1969). A brief comment on Indian culture is found in Utley, *Frontier Regulars,* 4–7.

10. Jerry M. Cooper, *The Army and Civil Disorder . . . 1877–1900* (Westport, Conn., 1980), 181–82; Russell Weigley, *The American Way of War* (New York, 1973), 153–63; Prucha, *The Great Father,* 547–49; Coffman, *Old Army,* 254. For a brief discussion of Indian casualties, see Prucha, *The Great Father,* 594n.

11. Prucha, *The Great Father,* 544–48. See also Robert Winston Murdock, *The Reformers and the American Indian* (Columbia, S.C., 1971), and Henry E. Fritz, *The Movement for Indian Assimilation, 1860–1890* (Philadelphia, 1963).

12. Richard A. Andrews, "Years of Frustration: William T. Sherman, the Army, and Reform, 1869–1883" (Ph.D. diss., Northwestern University, 1968), 75–76; WTS to JAR, October 23, 1865, John Y. Simon, ed., *Papers of U. S. Grant* (Carbondale, Ill., 1988), 15:382.

13. William S. McFeely, *Grant: A Biography* (New York, 1981), 305–18; Donald J. D'Elia, "The Argument over Civilian or Military Indian Control, 1865–1880," *Historian* 24 (February 1962): 207–25; Thomas, "Army Reform," 214–15; Andrews, "Years of Frustration," 77–80; USG to WTS, January 16, 1878, USG, LC; WTS to PHS, November 21, 1878, PHS, LC; NYT, December 4, 1878.

14. USG to EMS, January 29, 1866, in WTS, *Memoirs,* 2:939–40.

15. G.O. No. 11, War Department, March 5, 1866, in NYT, March 10, 1869.

16. WTS to USG, March 26, 1869, copy, WTS, LC; G.O. No. 28, War Department, March 26, 1869, WTS, *Memoirs,* 2:932.

17. Manning F. Force, *General Sherman* (New York, 1899), 325–26.

18. WTS to Charlotte E. Hall, November 18, 1879, WTS, "General Sherman's Opinion of General Grant," *Century* 31 (March 1879): 821.

19. WTS, *Memoirs*, 2:933; WTS to JS, September 12, 1869, WWB to WTS, August 8, 25, 1865, WTS, LC; WTS to WWB, October 8, 1869, Frederick M. Dearborn Collection, HLH; WTS to Strong, October 23, 1869, WRHS.

20. WTS to PHS, December 10, 1869, PHS, LC; WTS to WWB, August 17, 1870, USG to WTS, August 18, 1870, WTS to USG, September 2, 1870, copy, WTS, LC; WTS to PHS, April 1, 1871, PHS, LC; USG to WTS, July 31, 1870, WTS to JS, July 8, August 9, 1871, WTS, LC; WTS to WWB, September 30, 1871, SFP, UNDA.

21. WTS to PHS, November 1, 1872, WTS to WWB, December 2, 1872, copies, WTS, LC.

22. WTS to HST, March 26, 1873, WTS, OHS; WTS, "Report of the General of the Army," November 7, 1873, U.S. Serial Set, No. 1597.

23. WTS to WWB, May 8, 1874, copy, WWB to WTS, May 11, 1874, WTS to S. A. Hurlbut, May 29, 1874, copy, WTS to William Warner, August 14, 1885, copy, WTS, LC.

24. C. B. Comstock to WTS, May 14, 1872, NAM to WTS, July 4, 1874, WTS, LC; WTS to Comstock, May 18, 1874, C. B. Comstock Papers, LC; WTS to Ord, May 22, 1874, WTS, MoHS; WTS to PHS, June 4, 1874, PHS, LC; WTS to William C. Church, July 18, 1874, William C. Church Papers, LC.

25. G.O. No. 108, September 3, 1874, WTS, *Memoirs*, 2:944; WWB to WTS, September 30, 1874, JS to WTS, March 4, 1876, WTS, LC; WTS to JWD, March 9, 1876, JWD, LC; WTS to CWM, March 9, 1876, JS to WTS, March 14, 1876, WTS to JS, March 16, 1876, WTS, LC; JS to A. Taft, March 19, 1876, SFP, UNDA; JS to WTS, March 19, 1876, WTS, LC; WTS to PHS, April 1, 1876, PHS, LC; G.O. No. 28, Adjutant General's Office, April 6, 1876, WTS, *Memoirs*, 2:945.

26. John S. Gray, *Centennial Campaign: The Sioux War of 1876* (Norman, Okla., 1976), 10–15; Robert G. Athearn, *William Tecumseh Sherman and the Settlement of the West* (Norman, Okla., 1956), 170–88; Utley, *Frontier Regulars*, 130–41.

27. WTS to JS, August 3, 1867, WTS, LC; WTS to EMS, July 23, 1867, EMS, LC; WTS to DFB, August 9, 1867, WLF, NYPL.

28. WTS to ES, September 7, 14, 1867, SFP, UNDA.

29. Henry M. Stanley, *My Early Travels and Adventures in America* (Lincoln, 1895; 1982 reprint), 208–12.

30. WTS to AJ, October 3, 1867, AJ, LC; WTS to ES, July 15, 1868, SFP, UNDA; Marvin E. Kroeker, *Great Plains Command: William B. Hazen in the Frontier West* (Norman, Okla., 1976), 72–75.

31. Samuel F. Tappan to WTS, August–September 1868, WTS to Tappan, September 6, 1868, Samuel F. Tappan Papers, Colorado Historical Society; WTS to Tappan, September 24, 1868, copy, WTS, LC.

32. For a brief discussion of WTS and post–Civil War railroads, see Robert G. Athearn, "General Sherman and the Western Railroads," *Pacific Historical Review* 24 (January 1957): 39–48; WTS to JS, May 25, 1869, WTS, LC;

Grenville Dodge, *Personal Recollections of President Abraham Lincoln, General Ulysses S. Grant and General William T. Sherman* (Council Bluffs, Iowa, 1914), 184–85; WTS to C. C. Augur, June 9, 1870, C. C. Augur Papers, ISL.

33. Jesse C. Burt, "Sherman, Railroad General," *Civil War History* 2 (March 1956): 53; WTS to JS, April 27, 1866, AJ, LC; WTS to Charles D. Carter, October 16, 1870, in NYT, November 17, 1870; WTS to ES, August 17, 1867, SFP, UNDA.

34. Dodge, *Personal Recollections,* 185–86; Dodge to WTS, May 10, 1869, WTS to Dodge, May 11, 1869, in ibid., 203.

35. WTS, "Report of the General of the Army," November 10, 1880, U.S. Serial Set No. 1952.

36. WTS to ES, May 10, 1871, SFP, UNDA; J. T. Headley, *Grant and Sherman . . .* (New York, 1865), 232; James F. Rusling, *Men and Things I Saw in Civil War Days* (New York, 1899), 137.

37. Rusling, *Men and Things,* 141; Robert G. Athearn, "The Education of Kit Carson's Son," *New Mexico Historical Review* 31 (April 1956): 133–39.

38. WTS to TS, May 29, 1871, SFP, UNDA; "Extracts from Inspector General R. B. Marcy's Journal of an Inspection Tour While Accompanying the General in Chief During the Months of April, May, and June, 1871," May 18, 27, 1871, Lawrie Tatum to Jona Richards, May 30, 1871, copy, Carl Coke Rister Papers, Texas Tech University; Rister, *Border Command: General Phil Sheridan in the West* (Norman, Okla., 1944), 173–81; Utley, *Frontier Regulars,* 209–212; Athearn, *William Tecumseh Sherman,* 289–96; Richard N. Ellis, *General Pope and U.S. Indian Policy* (Albuquerque, 1970), 151–53. PTS named his pony Satanta because he liked the sound of the name better than Satank, whom he really wanted to honor. PTS, "Reminiscences," 15–16.

39. WTS to ES, May 20, 1871, SFP, UNDA; WTS to Ranald McKenzie, May 19, 1871, WTS to John Pope, May 24, 1871, WTS to E. D. Townsend, May 24, 1871, WTS to PHS, May 29, 1871, in Rister, "Documents Relating to General W. T. Sherman's Southern Plains Indian Policy, 1871–1875," *Panhandle-Plains Historical Review* 9 (1936): 7–28, 10 (1937): 48–63; WTS to TS, May 29, 1871, SFP, UNDA, WTS to Benjamin Grierson, June 8, 1871, Benjamin Grierson Papers, Newberry Library.

40. Rister, *Border Command,* 186–91; WTS to C. Delano, April 23, 1873, copy, Edward J. Dana to WTS, February 7, 1874, WTS, LC; WTS to SHMB, April 24, 1873, SHMB, IHS; WTS to Edward J. Davis, February 16, 1874, copy, WTS, LC; WTS to PHS, July 23, 1874, PHS, LC.

41. WTS to JS, February 24, 1876, WTS, LC. On Custer and his famous battle, see John S. Gray, *Centennial Campaign: The Sioux War of 1876* (Norman, Okla., 1988), Robert M. Utley, *Cavalier in Buckskin: George Armstrong Custer and the Western Military Frontier* (Norman, Okla., 1988), Stephen Ambrose, *Crazy Horse and Custer: The Parallel Lives of Two American Warriors* (Garden City, N.Y., 1975), Frederic F. Van De Water, *Glory Hunter: A Life of General Custer* (Lincoln, Neb., 1988 reprint of 1934 edition).

42. WTS, "Remarks," Tenth Annual Reunion of the Army of the Cumberland, July 6, 7, 1876, p. 59.

43. WTS to Tappan, July 21, 1876, copy, WTS, LC; NYT, July 22, 1876.

44. WTS, "Report of the General of the Army," November 10, 1876, U.S. Serial Set, No. 1742; WTS to PHS, August 17, 1876, February 17, 1877, PHS, LC.

45. Utley, *Frontier Regulars*, 293–321, 344–413; WTS to Ord, November 2, 1876, copy, WTS, LC; WTS to PHS, July 25, 1879, PHS, LC; WTS to George Crook, April 28, 1883, copy, WTS, HPC; WTS to HST, July 25, 1879, copy, SFP, UNDA; WTS to Robert Clarke, February 29, 1880, copy made by David Magee Book Store, San Francisco, YL.

46. NYT, December 21, 1890.

CHAPTER 18   THE ANCHOR OF HOME

1. ES to MSF, January 20, 1878, January 12, 1883, WTS to HST, November 14, 1878, copy, SFP, UNDA; William B. Parker, *The Life and Public Services of Justin Smith Morrill* (Boston, 1924), 222.

2. George B. Goode, ed., *The Smithsonian Institution* . . . (Washington, D.C., 1897), 108; Dartmouth College, Doctor of Laws, July 25, 1866, WTS, LC; *St. Louis Republican,* February 21, 1891, PTS, scrapbook, WTS, OHS; University of Notre Dame Scholarship, October 20, 1867, SFP, UNDA; John F. Marszalek, "The Inventor of Total War," *Notre Dame Magazine* 18 (Summer 1989): 28–31.

3. *St. Louis Republican,* February 21, 1891, PTS, scrapbook, WTS, OHS; W. Fletcher Johnson and OOH, *The Life of General William Tecumseh Sherman* . . . (Philadelphia, 1891), 550–51.

4. SHMB, *Twenty Years in Europe* (Chicago, 1900), 288; Hiram Hitckcock in Johnson and OOH, *Life of General Sherman,* 300; WTS to Spencer Fullerton Baird, October 25, 1884, RH 3834, HL; WTS to W. G. Eliot, October 15, 1885, W. G. Eliot Papers, MoHS; WTS to J. S. Pond, November 2, 1885, WTS, MoHS; WTS to Alonzo Foster, June 15, 1884, BLY.

5. For subscription campaigns, see chapter 16; WTS to Tourtelotte, January 28, 1883, HM 29166, HL.

6. PTS, "Reminiscences of Early Days," unpublished 1940 manuscript, 38, SFP UNDA; WTS to PBE, September 26, 1873, EFP, UNDA; WTS to EST, July 10, 1884, WTS to MSF, June 30, 1885, WTS, OHS.

7. EST, unpublished, undated manuscript, ST, VU.

8. C. E. Carr, *My Day and Generation* (Chicago, 1908), 172–73.

9. EST, manuscript; ES, diary, April 1, 1866, August 7, 1865, WTS to ES, January 2, 1868, April 24, 1873, ES to MSF, December 27, 1873, SFP, UNDA; WTS to James Henry Hackett, December 29, 1865, CHH, WLC; WTS, diary, January 6, 9, 22, 1887, SFP, UNDA; PTS, "Reminiscences," 15–17.

10. PTS, "Reminiscences," 12–13, 27–28, 37–38.

11. ES to TS, July 31, 1873, ST, VU.

12. ESF, untitled, undated note, box 10, SFP, UNDA; PTS, "Reminiscences," 4–5, 14.

13. MSF, "Recollections of Ellen Ewing Sherman," WTS, OHS; Bessie Smith, typed 1914 manuscript concerning the wedding, SFP, UNDA. She was a bridesmaid.

14. *New York Herald,* October 2, 1874, and *Philadelphia City Item,* October 2, 1874, SFP, UNDA.

15. ESF, untitled, undated note, box 10, SFP, UNDA.

16. WTS to JGB, October 13, 1871, JGB, LC; WTS to JS, October 26, 1871, WTS, LC; ES to PBE, November 2, 1871, SFP, UNDA.

17. WTS, "General Sherman's Tour of Europe," *Century* n.s. 35 (April 1899): 729.

18. ES to PBE, November 2, 1871, SFP, UNDA.

19. Jack J. Detzler, "The Religion of William Tecumseh Sherman," *Ohio History* 75 (Winter 1966): 26–34, 68–70.

20. WTS to JS, August 28, 1874, WTS, LC; WTS to TS, September 24, 1874, SFP, UNDA; WTS to DFB, February 13, 1878, WLF, NYPL; WTS to TS, October 19, 1876, SFP, UNDA.

21. WTS to TS, January 21, 1878, TS to WTS, January 28, 1878, SFP, UNDA; graduation notice, May 13, 1878, WTS, LC; WTS to TS, March 15, 1878, SFP, UNDA.

22. TS to WTS, May 20, 1878, SFP, UNDA.

23. TS to MSF, May 24, 1878, SFP, UNDA; WTS to HST, May 27, 1878, WTS, OHS; WTS to SHMB, June 30, 1878, SHMB, IHS. See also WTS to JTD, July 7, 1878, WTS, CHS.

24. ES to MSF, May 30, 1878, TS to WTS, May 31, 1878, SFP, UNDA; TS to HMH, May 30, 1878, WTS to HMH, May 27, 1878, HMH, MoHS; ES to MSF, May 31, 1878, RST to ES, June 3, 1878, SFP, UNDA; WTS to EST, June 4, 1878, WTS, OHS.

25. WTS to JMS, June 5, 1878, HB, HL; WTS to John McClosky, June 3, 1878, copy, WTS, LC; WTS to EST, June 4, 1878, WTS to HST, June 5, 1878, WTS to EST, June 5, 1878, WTS, OHS.

26. WTS to PHS, June 5, 1878, PHS, LC; WTS to NAM, June 7, 1878, NAM, LC; ES to PBE, June 19, 1878, Thomas W. Fitch to WTS, June 8, 1878, SFP, UNDA; WTS to MSF, June 11, 1878, WTS, OHS; WTS to Lizzie Sherman Cameron, June 22, 1878, NAM, LC; WTS to Sam Reber, June 25, 1878, copy, WTS, LC.

27. S. M. Bowman to WTS, July 4, 1878, WTS, LC; WTS to HST, July 7, 1878, WTS, OHS; ES to WTS, July 5, 1878, WTS to HST, July 24, 1878, copy, SFP, UNDA; Adam Badeau to WTS, August 2, November 14, 1878, WTS, LC; WTS to Lizzie Sherman Cameron, August 7, 1878, NAM, LC; WTS to HST, August 10, November 29, 1878, WTS, OHS.

28. *Chicago Inter-Ocean* (newspaper), in NYT, August 22, 1878; ES to WTS, May 25, 1878, SFP, UNDA; MSF, untitled, undated manuscript, WTS, OHS; TS to WTS, May 20, 1878, SFP, UNDA; EST to ES, June 1, 1878, ST, VU; WTS to MSF, October 12, 1878, WTS, OHS; WTS to Editor of

Chicago Tribune, October 27, 1878, SFP, UNDA; NYT, November 5, 1878.

29. WTS to HST, December 10, 1878, copy, ES to WTS, December 21, 1878, WTS to ES, December 22, 1878, SFP, UNDA; WTS to MSF, December 23, 1878, WTS, OHS; WTS to HST, December 25, 1878, copy, SFP, UNDA.

30. WTS to A. E. Burnside, December 15, 1878, copy, WTS, LC; WTS to PHS, December 18, 30, 1878, PHS, LC; WTS to JMS, December 23, 29, 1878, HB, HL; JMS to WTS, December 24, 1878, PHS to WTS, January 4, 1879, WTS to Z. B. Towner, December 24, 1878, copy, WTS, LC; WTS to JMS, January 19, 1879, HB, HL; WTS to MSF, February 5, 1879, WTS, OHS; John F. Marszalek, "Celebrity in Dixie: Sherman Tours the South, 1879," *Georgia Historical Quarterly* 66 (Fall 1982): 368–83.

31. TS to ES, May 9, 1880, TS to WTS, July 14, 1880, RST postscript to WTS to ES, August 24, 1880, TS to MSF, August 25, 1880, TS to WTS, September 1, 1880, SFP, UNDA; WTS to MSF, August 25, 1880, WTS to EST, December 30, 1880, WTS, OHS; WTS to ES, March 12, 1882, SFP, UNDA; WTS to MSF, June 2, 1889, WTS, OHS.

32. Ismael to ES, December 3, 1874, translation, WTS to His Highness, khedive of Egypt, January 13, 1875, copy in WTS hand, SFP, UNDA; WTS to JS, January 8, 1874, WTS, LC.

33. WTS to MSF, February 21, 1875, SFP, UNDA.

34. MSF to WTS, March *[sic]* 1875, WTS to TS, March 18, 1875, WTS to ES, March 25, 1875, WTS to MSF, March 26, 1875, WTS to ES, May 16, 1876, ES to WTS, May 23, 25, 28, 1876, copies, SFP, UNDA; WTS to MSF, October 20, 1878, WTS, OHS.

35. ESF statement on back of a photograph of the diamonds, SFP, UNDA.

36. *New York World,* February 22, 1891, WTS, OHS; Byers, *Twenty Years,* 281.

37. Mildred McLean Hazen Dewey, unpublished memoirs, 98–105, HPC.

38. ES to WTS, May 27, 1868, SFP, UNDA.

39. WTS to PHS, May 5, 1875, PHS, LC.

40. ES to WTS, June 3, 1887, with unnamed, undated newspaper clipping attached, SFP, UNDA.

41. Charles G. Miller, *Donn Piatt . . .* (Cincinnati, 1893), 244–45.

42. WTS to VRH, April 19, 1873, May 6, 1874, February 8, 25, May 10, 1875, VRH, LC.

43. WTS to VRH, July 1, 1874, VRH, LC.

44. WTS to VRH, August 26, 1875, December 5, 1877, VRH, LC.

45. WTS to VRH, April 23, 1878, October 9, 1878, VRH, LC.

46. MOLLUS, "In Memoriam Joseph C. Audenreid, June 3, 1880," WTS, LC; G.O. No. 45, Hqs. of the Army, June 3, 1880, WTS to HST, June 8, 1880, WTS, OHS; WTS to MA, July 31, August 16, 1880, February 8, March 25, 1881, February 7, 1882, WTS, HPC.

47. WTS to MA, July 11, 1882, WTS, HPC.

48. Ibid., March 4, October 6, 1883, WTS, HPC.

49. Ibid., February 5, 6, 11, 1884, June 21, August 10, November 20, 1884, October 4, 1887, February 21, 1890, WTS, HPC.

Chapter 19   COMMANDING GENERAL VERSUS THE POLITICIANS

1. T. Harry Williams, *McClellan, Sherman and Grant* (New Brunswick, N.J., 1962), 46.

2. WTS to WW, March 26, 1872, WTS, ISL; James G. Randall and Theodore C. Pease, eds., *The Diary of Orville H. Browning* (Springfield, Ill., 1933), July 5, 1875, 2:416.

3. WTS to TS, March 29, 1877, SFP, UNDA.

4. "General Sherman's Habits," *Army and Navy Journal* 21 (October 27, 1883): 295 in Richard A. Andrews, "Years of Frustration: William T. Sherman, the Army, and Reform, 1869–1883," Ph.D. diss., Northwestern University, 1968, 36.

5. WTS to JS, March 21, 1871, WTS, LC; WTS to DFB, March 27, 1871, WLF, NYPL; NYT, April 29, 1871.

6. Undated newspaper clippings in SFP, UNDA; Henry S. Foote to WTS, May 20, 1871, WTS, LC; G. W. Moorman to WTS, June 18, 1871, WTS, LC; John F. Marszalek, "Celebrity in Dixie: Sherman Tours the South, 1879," *Georgia Historical Quarterly* 66 (Fall 1982): 368–83.

7. WTS to JS, January 7, 1875, Alfred H. Terry to WTS, June 20, 1870, WTS to Terry, June 27, July 9, 1870, copy, WTS, LC.

8. WTS to J.A. Mower, April 3, 1869, in Joseph G. Dawson III, *Army Generals and Reconstruction: Louisiana 1861–1877* (Baton Rouge, 1982), 98; WTS to Adelbert Ames, August 2, 1869, WTS, MoHS; Ames to WTS, August 17, 1869, WTS, LC; WTS to PHS, January 2, 1875, PHS, LC; WTS to TS, January 16, 1873, SFP, UNDA.

9. WTS to HST, August 11, 1876, copy, SFP, UNDA; WTS to MSF, August 18, 1876, WTS, OHS; WTS to DDP, August 29, 1876, DDP, LC; WTS to Ord, August 18, 1876, HLH; WTS to E. R. Kennedy, August 30, 1876, in NYT, September 8, 1876; WTS to TS, October 27, 1876, SFP, UNDA; WTS to JS, October 30, 1876, Mansfield-Richland (Ohio) Public Library.

10. WTS to PHS, November 8, 1876, PHS, LC; WTS to USG, two telegrams, November 10, 1876, USG, LC; Ari Hoogenboom, *The Presidency of Rutherford B. Hayes* (Lawrence, Kans., 1988), 27; WTS to MSF, November 27, 1876, WTS, OHS.

11. WTS to HST, December 5, 1876, WTS, OHS; John M. Corse et al. to WTS, December 8, 1876, in NYT, December 14, 1876; Judson Kilpatrick to WTS, December 16, 1876; Cuthbert Bullett to WTS, December 8, 1876, WTS, LC; WTS to PHS, December 11, 1876, PHS, LC.

12. W. S. Hancock to WTS, December 28, 1876, January 2, 1877, WTS, LC.

13. The two most important books on the Compromise of 1877 are C. Vann Woodward, *Reunion and Reaction . . .* (New York, 1951), and Keith I. Polakoff, *The Politics of Inertia . . .* (Baton Rouge, 1973).

14. WTS to MSF, January 18, 1877, WTS, OHS; WTS to TS, January 19, 1877, SFP, UNDA; WTS to JMS, January 19, 1877, HB, HL; WTS to PHS, January 19, 1877, PHS, LC; WTS to DFB, January 23, 1877, WLF, NYPL; WTS to C. C. Augur, January 22, 1877, C. C. Augur Papers, ISL; WTS to

PHS, January 29, 1877, copy, WTS to Hancock, January 29, 1877, WTS, LC.

15. WTS to TS, February 2, 1877, WTS to HST, January 27, 1877, February 23, 1877, copy, SFP, UNDA; WTS to DFB, March 4, 1877, WLF, NYPL; WTS to PHS, March 4, 1877, PHS, LC; WTS to H. W. Corbett, March 21, 1877, Henry W. Corbett Papers, MS 1110, Oregon Historical Society.

16. There are numerous books on the army during these years. See Robert M. Utley, *Frontier Regulars: The United States Army and the Indian, 1866–1891* (New York, 1973); Edward Coffman, *The Old Army: Portrait of the American Army in Peacetime, 1784–1898* (New York, 1986); Jack D. Foner, *The United States Soldier Between Two Wars: Army Life and Reform, 1865–1898* (New York, 1970). For Sherman and the army during these years, see Robert G. Athearn, *William Tecumseh Sherman and the Settlement of the West* (Norman, Okla., 1956); Richard A. Andrews, "Years of Frustration: William T. Sherman, the Army and Reform, 1869–1883" (Ph.D. diss., Northwestern University, 1968); Donna M. E. Thomas, "Army Reform in America: The Crucial Years, 1876–1881" (Ph.D. diss., University of Florida, 1980).

17. Thomas, "Army Reform," 231–36; WTS to PHS, January 19, 1877, PHS, LC.

18. WTS to Ambrose Burnside, May 2, 1869, Knollenberg Collection, YL; George H. Thomas to WTS, March 14, 1870, WTS to JS, March 21, 1870, WTS, LC.

19. WTS to Henry Wilson, March 22, 1870, copy, WTS, LC; Oliver Knight, *Life and Manner in the Frontier Army* (Norman, Okla., 1978), 6; WTS to Grenville Dodge, April 11, 1870, WTS, LC; WTS to Edward Sorin, May 5, 1870, Edward Sorin Collection, UNDA, and in SFP, UNDA.

20. Andrews, "Years of Frustration," 59; Mary S. C. Logan, *Reminiscences of a Soldier's Wife* (New York, 1913), 279; WTS to JS, July 27, 1870, WTS, LC; *The Statistical History of the United States . . .* (New York, 1976), 164–65; Joseph Nathan Kane, *Facts About the Presidents . . .* , 4th ed. (New York, 1981), 417.

21. WTS to HST, March 1, 1877, copy, SFP, UNDA; WTS to PHS, March 4, 1877, PHS, LC; WTS to JMS, March 13, 1877, box 28, HB, HL; WTS to MSF, March 14, 1877, WTS, OHS; Andrews, "Years of Frustration," 157–70.

22. WTS to ES, May 6, 1877, SFP, UNDA; "109th Anniversary Banquet of the Chamber of Commerce, May 1877," WTS Pamphlets, vol. 1, OHS; WTS to NAM, June 1, 1877, NAM, LC; WTS to TS, November 10, 1877, SFP, UNDA.

23. Thomas, "Army Reforms," 236–38; Andrews, "Years of Frustration," 197–98.

24. WTS to J. D. Cameron, January 31, 1878, copy, WTS to H. P. Banning, February 10, 1878, copy, WTS, LC; *Washington Post*, in NYT, March 1, 1878; WTS to Editor of *Washington Post*, March 28, 1878, WTS, OHS.

25. JAG, "The Army of the United States," *North American Review* 126 (March–April, May–June 1878): 193–216, 442–65; WTS to Emory Upton, January 9, 1879, copy, WTS, LC; WTS to JAG, February 9, March

23, 28, June 21, 30, 1878, JAG, LC; WTS, Decoration Day address, May 30, 1878, printed copy, WTS, LC; Andrews, "Years of Frustration," 189–90.

26. WTS to MSF, June 20, 1878, WTS, OHS.

27. Thomas, "Ambrose E. Burnside and Army Reform, 1850–1881," *Rhode Island History* 37 (February 1978): 3–13; Stephen E. Ambrose, *Upton and the Army* (Baton Rouge, 1964), 15; WTS to Burnside, July 15, 1878, WTS, LC, and draft in SFP, UNDA; WTS to Matthew C. Butler, July 17, 1878, copy, WTS, LC.

28. Thomas, "Burnside," 9–11.

29. WTS to Burnside, December 15, 1878, copy, WTS, LC; WTS to PHS, December 18, 30, 1878, PHS, LC; WTS to Z. B. Tower and Burnside, December 24, 1878, JMS to WTS, January 4, 1879, WTS, LC; WTS to HST, December 25, 1878, WTS to JMS, December 23, 1878, HB, HL; WTS to G. W. Childs, January 6, 1879, Dreer Collection, HSPa.

30. WTS to JMS, January 19, 1879, box 28, HB, HL.

31. Thomas, "Burnside," 11–12; Thomas, "Army Reform," 254–55; Andrews, "Years of Frustration," 217.

32. WTS to HST, April 5, May 16, 1879, copies, SFP, UNDA; WTS to MSF, April 6, May 16, 1879, WTS, OHS; WTS to W. G. Eliot, May 26, 1879, W. G. Eliot Papers, MoHS; WTS to USG, July 27, 1879, copy, WTS, LC; WTS to HST, July 13, 1879, copy, SFP, UNDA; WTS to Irvin McDowell, July 31, 1880, WTS, HPC.

33. John F. Marszalek, *Court-Martial: A Black Man in America* (New York, 1972); WTS to PHS, December 13, 1880, PHS, LC; WTS to JMS, December 16, 1880, box 28, HB, HL; WTS to R. B. Hayes, November 18, 1880, WTS, HPC; WTS to Alfred H. Terry, December 12, 1880, Terry Family Papers, YL; WTS to William Scott, December 15, 1880, copy, WTS, LC; WTS to HST, January 16, 1881, copy, SFP, UNDA; WTS to JS, January 31, 1881, WTS, HPC; WTS to JAL, February 5, 1881, copy, WTS, LC; Charles R. Williams, ed., *Diary and Letters of Rutherford B. Hayes . . .* (Columbus, Ohio, 1924), January 23, 1881, 3:640; WTS to MSF, February 9, 1881, WTS, OHS.

34. WTS to Alexander Thackara, July 1, 1881, WTS, LC; Theodore Clarke Smith, ed., *The Life and Letters of James Abram Garfield* (New Haven, 1925), 2:1184–85; Charles E. Rosenberg, *The Trial of the Assassin Guiteau* (Chicago, 1968), 3–5; WTS to Thackara, July 1, 1881, WTS, OHS. WTS, LC roll 47, contains most of this assassination correspondence; WTS to HST, July 4, 1881, WTS, OHS; WTS to ES, July 16, 1881, SFP, UNDA; JS, *John Sherman's Recollection . . .* (Chicago, 1895), 2:822–23; WTS to George F. Hoar, August 25, 26, 1881, George F. Hoar Papers, MaHS; JS to WTS, August 27, 1881, WTS to Amos Webster, August 27, 1881, copy, WTS, LC; WTS to HST, August 28, 1881, copy, SFP, UNDA.

35. On Stone, Egypt, and Statue of Liberty, see correspondence in WTS, LC, and WTS to H. Eaton Coleman, March 20, 1876, Stone to WTS, December 18, 1873, October 9, 1882, WTS to J. W. Pinchot, March 30, 1883, copy, WTS, LC; Chester L. Barrows, *William M. Evarts . . .* (Chapel Hill, 1941),

469; on *Virginius* affair, see WTS to Frederick Tracy Dent, November 25, 1873, Frederick Tracy Dent Collection, Southern Illinois University, and WTS to Nathan Bedford Forrest, November 28, 1873, in NYT, December 9, 1873; on OOH, see *The Autobiography of O. O. Howard* (New York, 1907), 2:449–52; on Fitz John Porter, see WTS to Porter, March 6, 1868, Fitz John Porter Collection, USMA, and WTS to Porter, October 22, 1878, December 30, 1881, copies, WTS, LC; on Hazen and Stanley, see Marvin E. Kroeker, *Great Plains Commander: William B. Hazen . . .* (Norman, Okla., 1976), 155–62, and WTS to Stanley, March 12, 1877, copy, WTS, LC; on Custer, see WTS to USG, Jr., May 4, 1876, copy, WTS, LC; on USG and Hancock, see David M. Jordan, *Winfield Scott Hancock . . .* (Bloomington, Ind., 1988), 213–14, and Hancock-WTS correspondence, WTS, LC; for Pope, Gibbon, and PHS, see WTS to PHS, September 12, 1874, PHS, LC, and WTS to Gibbon, May 31, 1879, copy, WTS, LC, and WTS to Gibbon, June 15, 1879, Gibbon Papers, Maryland Historical Society; on embezzling nephew, see WTS to Henry B. Reese, September 19, 1872, WTS to B. Alvord, September 19, 1972, copies, WTS, LC; on Atlanta fort, see E. Speer to WTS, February 5, 1880, WTS to Speer, February 6, 1880, copy, WTS, LC; on bigamist, see WTS to Mrs. Thomas P. Nichols, October 18, 1878, Thomas Blair to WTS, December 18, 1878, WTS to Maria Blair, December 19, 1878, copies, WTS, LC; on young girl, see Ella Fraser Welles, "Stranger Than Fiction . . . Unpublished Letters by General Sherman," *McClure's* 8 (April 1897): 546–50; on Field and history, see Field to WTS, October 28, 1873, *Overland Monthly* Collection, BL, and WTS to Field, October 31, 1873, HM 31029, HL, and November 2, 1873, *Overland Monthly* Collection, BL, and March 31, November 9, 1879, February 19, May 18, 1880, HM 31032–34, 31036, HL.

36. Undated, unnamed newspaper clipping in MSA, scrapbook, WTS, OHS; NYT, August 4, 1881.

37. PTS, "Reminiscences," 47.

38. TS to MSF, March 5, 1873, WTS, OHS.

39. James P. Jones, *John A. Logan . . .* (Tallahassee, 1982), 128–29; WTS to Heister Clymer, February 15, 1878, copy, Dennis Hart Mahan to WTS, March 21, 1866, WTS, LC; WTS, "Report of the General of the Army," November 7, 1878, U.S. Serial Set, No. 1843.

40. WTS to PHS, August 1, 1879, PHS, LC; WTS to G. W. Cullom, February 15, 1868, WTS, USMA; WTS, *Address to the Graduating Class of the U. S. Military Academy, West Point, June 15th, 1869* (New York, 1869), 9; WTS to JMS, October 24, 1877, HB, box 28, HL. For a thorough study of the Military Academy during these years, see Walter S. Dillard, "The United States Military Academy, 1865–1900: The Uncertain Years" (Ph.D. diss., University of Washington, 1972).

41. Russell F. Weigley, *History of the United States Army* (New York, 1967), 273; WTS to J. Sumner Rogers, July 30, 1878, in NYT, August 27, 1878; WTS to Upton, January 3, 1873, February 9, November 10, 1878, copies, Upton to WTS, September 23, 1874, November 6, 1879, WTS, LC; WTS to Francis V. Greene, January 13, July 28, 1878, Francis V. Greene Papers, NYPL;

Donald N. Bigelow, *William Conant Church and the Army and Navy Journal* (New York, 1952); WTS to Hancock, December 19, 1879, copy, WTS, LC; WTS, "Address to the Class of 1880, United States Artillery School, April 28th, 1880," WTS, pamphlets, vol. 7, OHS; G.O. No. 42, May 7, 1881, Hqs. of the Army, in Elvid Hurt and Walter E. Thomas, *History of Fort Leavenworth 1827–37* (Ft. Leavenworth, 1937), 133. A modern study is Timothy K. Nenninger, *The Leavenworth Schools and the Old Army . . . 1881–1918* (Westport, Conn., 1978), chap. 2.

42. WTS to PHS, July 31, 1881, PHS, LC.

43. WTS to Upton, November 18, 1878, copy, WTS, LC.

44. For Winfield Scott's ideas, see John F. Marszalek, "Where Did Winfield Scott Find His Anaconda?" Lincoln *Herald* 89 (Summer 1987): 77–81; WTS to PHS, December 28, 1881, PHS, LC.

45. WTS to John Pope, April 24, 1876, copy, WTS, LC.

Chapter 20 RETIRING FROM THE ARMY AND REFUSING THE PRESIDENCY

1. WTS to Hancock, June 13, 1881, copy, WTS, LC; WTS to GMG, July 23, 1882, VHS; WTS to Robert T. Lincoln, October 8, 1883, copy, WTS, LC; Lincoln to WTS, October 10, 1883, WTS, LC.

2. WTS to JAL, February 11, 20, 1883, JAL, LC; JAL to WTS, February 18, 1883, WTS, WTS, LC; WTS to Marcus J. Wright, October 23, 1883, Autograph File, HLH; WTS to PHS, May 20, 1883, copy, WTS, LC; NYT, June 13, 1883; WTS, "Report of the General of the Army," October 27, 1883, U.S. Serial Set, No. 2182.

3. WTS to EST, September 16, 1883, WTS, OHS; WTS to Mrs. Francis U. Farquhan, November 27, 1883, Francis Ulric Farquhan Papers, DU; WTS to OOH, January 11, 1884, copy in WTS hand, WTS, LC.

4. Chester A. Arthur Order, February 8, 1881, WTS, LC, and Chester A. Arthur, LC; WTS to Arthur, February 9, 1884, Arthur, LC.

5. WTS to JMS, November 21, 1888, copy, WTS to Lincoln, February 4, 9, 1885, copies in WTS hand, Lincoln to WTS, February 7, 1885, WTS to William C. Endicott, November 16, 1866, January 8, June 24, July 11, 1887, copies, Endicott to WTS, January 21, 1887, R. C. Drum to WTS, May 3, 1886, WTS to Montgomery Meigs, January 29, 1890, copy, WTS to John Harlan, February 14, 1890, copy, Stephen J. Field to WTS, February 26, 1890, WTS to Field, February 27, 1890, copy, WTS, LC.

6. PTS, "Reminiscences of Early Days," unpublished 1940 manuscript, pp. 10–11, SFP, UNDA.

7. WTS to SHMB, December 12, 1882, SHMB, IHS; WTS to MSF, December 14, 1882, WTS, OHS.

8. James Buchanan to William Bigler, February 15, 1868, in NYT, August 12, 1935; R. K. Williams to WTS, November 25, 1867, Charles G. Halpine to WTS, June 23, 1868, WTS, LC; undated newspaper clipping, c. May 18, 1871, SFP, UNDA; Henry S. Foote to WTS, May 20, 1871, JS to WTS, April 6, 1875, WTS, LC.

9. NYT, July 26, 1865; WTS to Charles G. Halpine, July 8, 1868, HP 161, HL; NYT, June 9, 1871; WTS to James O. Dalzell, February 2, 1876, *Chaperone* 1 (March 1891): 629.

10. C. H. Van Wyck, November 9, 1883, WTS, LC; WTS to MSF, January 7, 1883, WTS, OHS; Murat Halstead to WTS, December 14, 1882, WTS, LC; Mary R. Dearing, *Veterans in Politics: The Story of the Grand Army of the Republic* (Baton Rouge, 1952), 190–91; JS to WTS, June 10, November 24, 1883, WTS, LC; WTS to JMS, December 3, 1883, HB, HL; Sidney Herbert to WTS, January 21, 1884, J. Horace Kent to WTS, February 13, 1884, Isaac N. Arnold to WTS, February 20, 1884, WTS to CWM, November 14, 1882, WTS, LC.

11. NYT, March 6, 25, 1884; JS to WTS, May 14, 1884, C. M. Butt to WTS, May 14, 1884, WTS to Butt, May 16, 1884, copy, WTS, LC.

12. JGB to WTS, May 25, 1884, copy, WTS, LC; Murat Halstead, "The Defeat of Blaine for the Presidency," *McClure's* 6 (January 1896): 161–62. Matilda Gresham insisted that JGB was hoping to use WTS as a foil against JS. Matilda Gresham, *Life of Walter Quinton Gresham* (Chicago, 1919), 1:495; WTS to JGB, May 28, 1884, JGB, LC; WTS to William Grenville Temple, May 28, 1884, HM 39960, HL.

13. Halstead, "Defeat of Blaine," 162; CWM to WTS, June 1, 1884, J. B. Henderson to WTS, June 2, 1884, WTS to Henderson, June 2, 1884, copy in WTS hand, WTS, LC.

14. Henderson to WTS, WTS to Henderson, June 3, 1884, WTS, LC; James R. Doolittle to WTS, June 3, 1884, James R. Doolittle Papers, LC; WTS to Doolittle, June 5, 1884, HLH.

15. Halstead, "Defeat of Blaine," 162; George F. Hoar, *Autobiography of Seventy Years* (New York, 1903), 1:407–8; Vincent P. De Santis, "Catholicism and Presidential Elections, 1865–1900," *Mid-America* 42 (April 1960): 73.

16. Mary F. Henderson to WTS, June 4, 1884, Henry F. Sherman and Thomas Fitch to WTS, June 5, 1884, WTS, LC.

17. Henderson to WTS, WTS to Henderson, June 5, 1884; TS, "Conclusion," in WTS, *Memoirs*, rev. ed. (New York, 1891), 2:466; PTS, "Reminiscences," 38; NYT, June 5, 1884; *Republican National Convention, 1884, Proceedings*, microfilm, pp. 141, 147, 149–50, 162.

18. WTS to JGB, June 7, 1884, JGB, LC; WTS to P. Cortland Field, June 15, 1884, WTS, LC.

19. EST to WTS, November 11, 1880, ST, VU; WTS to EST, November 14, 1880, WTS to MSF, January 7, 1883, WTS, OHS. For a brief but perceptive discussion of WTS and the Catholic issue, see Robert G. Ingersoll, *Works* (New York, 1909), 8:106. For a sympathetic newspaper's view which shows WTS's anger over the issue, see *Wheeling* (West Virginia) *Intelligencer*, in NYT, March 6, 1884.

20. ES to WTS, May 8, 1876, SFP, UNDA.

21. WTS to JS, April 29, 1888, WTS; T. H. Reeves to WTS, January 29, 1876, WTS to Hancock, June 25, 1880, copy, WTS, LC; WTS to CWM, June 13, 1884, SFP, UNDA.

22. Carl Schurz, "Reminiscences," *McClure's* 30 (November 1907): 95–96.

23. C. H. Chamberlain to WTS, November 23, 1886, WTS to JS, April 1, 1888, WTS, LC; WTS to ES, December 15, 1887, in M. A. DeWolfe Howe, ed., *Home Letters of General Sherman* (New York, 1909), 399; *Boston Globe,* January 22, 1888, SFP, UNDA; WTS to JS, June 27, 1888, WTS, LC.

24. WTS to JS, June 7, 1883, WTS, LC.

25. WTS to MSF, June 28, 1885, SFP, UNDA; WTS to JS, January 13, 1888, WTS, LC.

26. "Memorandum of Property . . . ," June 15, 1866, SFP, UNDA; WTS to PTS, September 4, 1889, WTS, OHS; "Statement of Affairs," January 1, 1888, January 1, 1889, in WTS, ledger book, SFP, UNDA.

27. WTS to CE, January 4, 1866, CE, LC. WTS repeated a nearly identical thought in WTS to SHMB, June 29, 1885, SHMB, IHS. WTS to JS, December 18, 1872, April 20, 1886, WTS, LC; WTS to ES, October 12, 1874, SFP, UNDA; WTS to JS, April 20, 1886, WTS, LC; TE, "Memo," October 19, 1868, EFP, UNDA; TE, Jr., to HBE, March 31, 1872, HBE, OHS.

28. WTS to J. E. Tourtelotte, July 28, 1883, HM 29166, HL; WTS to Daniel Ammen, December 4, 1884, Daniel Ammen Papers, UCLA; WTS to EST, December 24, 1884, WTS, OHS; WTS to PBE, September 26, 1872, EFP, UNDA; WTS to Don Garrison, December 11, 1884, WTS, MoHS; PTS, "Reminiscences," 38; WTS to PBE, September 26, 1873, EFP, UNDA; WTS to EST, July 10, 1884, WTS to MSF, June 30, 1885, WTS, OHS.

29. WTS to ES, October 18, 1874, SFP, UNDA; WTS to JS, October 23, 1874, November 17, 1877, December 2, 1883, WTS, LC; WTS to William Scott, July 5, 1884, WTS, MoHS.

30. WTS to JS, September 30, 1884, WTS, LC; WTS to J. E. Tourtelotte, October 5, 1844, WTS, MoHS; JS to WTS, October 5, 1884, WTS, LC; WTS to Lizzie Sherman Cameron, March 12, 1885, NAM, LC; WTS to EST, March 20, 1885, WTS to MSF, June 28, 1886, January 1, 1888, WTS, OHS.

31. WTS to William C. Church, January 29, 1870, William C. Church Papers, LC; Bernard De Voto, ed., *Mark Twain in Eruption* (New York, 1922), 175; Charles L. Webster to WTS, April 17, 28, September 26, 1890, WTS to Webster, May 5, 1890, William W. Appleton to WTS, May 15, 1875, WTS, LC; Appleton to WTS, September 5, 1889, William W. Appleton Papers, CU; WTS to SHMB, June 14, 1890, SHMB, IHS.

32. PTS, undated notes, WTS, UNDA; WTS to CWM, May 16, 1886, Autograph File, HLH.

33. Robert U. Johnson to WTS, March 31, 1885, H. C. Bowen to WTS, April 1, 1885, WTS, LC; WTS to SHMB, June 29, 1886, SHMB, IHS; WTS to NAM, November 21, 1888, NAM, LC; Johnson to WTS, April 8, 1887, WTS, LC; WTS to EST, October 9, 1888, WTS, OHS; WTS to Allen Thorndike Rice, October 16, 1888, WTS, LC; WTS to JS, November 8,

1888, Tourtelotte to WTS, January 1, 1889, WTS, LC; WTS to General Woodbury, September 5, 1889, WTS Miscellany, LSU.

34. WTS to W. G. Eliot, October 15, 1885, W. G. Eliot Papers, MoHS; WTS to J. S. Pond, November 2, 1885, WTS, MoHS; WTS to Alonzo Foster, June 15, 1884, BLY.

Chapter 21 SAFEGUARDING HISTORICAL ORDER

1. On O.R., see, for example, WTS to H. B. Carrington, January 5, 1874, Carrington Family Papers, YL; WTS to R. N. Scott, September 6, 1885, WTS, LC; John Bell Hood to WTS, January 14, 1878, WTS to Randall L. Gibson, January 16, 1879, copies, WTS, LC; series of WTS letters to JWD, June 30, 1867–November 27, 1868, JWD, LC; Adam Badeau to WTS, June 19, 1880, WTS to Badeau, May 19, 1881, copy, WTS, LC; WTS to O. M. Poe, November 15, 1865, January 15, 1866, O. M. Poe Papers, LC; WTS to W. L. B. Jenney, January 17, 1866, W. L. B. Jenney Papers, Art Institute of Chicago; WTS to Emory Upton, January 3, 1877, copy, WTS, LC; WTS to G. W. Cullom, February 5, 1877, G. W. Cullom Papers, USMA; WTS to Robert Allen, December 3, 1883, WTS to Mary A. Livermore, February 26, 1886, copy, WTS, LC; WTS to Stephen J. Field, November 28, 1880, HM 31037, HL; WTS to Sherman Publishing Co., February 29, 1884, copy, WTS, LC; WTS to W. J. Landrum, December 5, 1881, in NYT, December 18, 1881.

2. WTS to JMS, March 12, 1874, HB, HL; WTS to J. S. Burrell, February 23, 1882, WTS, LC; WTS to WW, February 9, 1888, WTS, ISL.

3. WTS to JWD, August 12, 1874, JWD, LC; WTS to JS, January 23, 1875, WTS, LC; WTS to Henry L. Sheperd, October 11, 1874, WTS, DU.

4. WTS to Robert Clarke and Co., January 10, 1875, T. W. Norris Collection, BL; Clarke to WTS, January 11, 1875, WTS, LC; WTS to TS, January 16, 1875, SFP, UNDA; WTS to PBE, January 22, 1875, EFP, UNDA; WTS to JS, January 23, 1875; WTS to William Scott, January 23, 1875, WTS, MoHS; WTS to JS, February 3, 1875, WTS, LC.

5. Mark E. Neely, Jr., "Sherman: Time for a New Image?" *Lincoln Lore*, no. 1771 (September 1986).

6. The 1990 republication of the 1886 edition of the memoirs is part of the prestigious Library of America published by Literary Classics of the United States.

7. Jay Luvaas, *The Military Legacy of the Civil War* (Chicago, 1959), 128n; *Kingston* (New York) *Journal*, March 20, 1878, in WTS, LC; "Sherman's Memoirs," *Galaxy* 20 (October 1875): 463–64; *Louisiana State Register*, June 12, 1875; D. H. Maury, review of *History of the Army of the Cumberland* by Thomas B. Van Horne, in *Southern Historical Society Papers* 1 (1876): 400. A representative sampling of reviews is found in WTS, LC, microfilm reel 51.

8. Emory Upton to WTS, May 29, 1875, in WTS, *Memoirs*, 2:958; JAG to WTS,

July 5, 1875, WTS, LC; Charles P. Stone to WTS, August 30, 1875, WTS, LC.

9. Henry W. Slocum to WTS, May 20, 1875, in New York Monument Commission, *In Memoriam Henry Warren Slocum, 1826–1894* (Albany, 1904), 111; NYT, May 28, 1875; John A. McClernand to George W. Morgan, November 30, 1875, WRHS; W. E. Smith, *The Francis Preston Blair Family in Politics* (New York, 1933), 2:468–69; WTS to Montgomery Blair, May 27, 1875, Blair Family Papers, LC; WTS to Mrs. Frank Blair, July 15, 1875, WTS, LC; WTS to JAL, February 11, 1883, JAL, LC; Franc B. Wilkie to WTS, May 22, 1875, Norman B. Conney to WTS, June 7, 1875, WTS, LC; WTS to George W. Childs, July 16, 1875, HSPa; J. A. Sutter to WTS, July 26, 1875, William (Sooy) Smith to WTS, July 2, 9, 14, 20, 1875, WTS to Smith, July 11, 16, 1875, WTS to J. D. Webster, July 11, 1875, JS to WTS, May 23, 1875, WTS, LC.

10. Henry Van Ness Boynton, *Sherman's Historical Raid: The Memoirs in the Light of the Record* (Cincinnati, 1875), 8, 272–76.

11. WTS to CWM, November 1, 9, 1875, WTS, NYPL; JWD to WTS, November 25, 1875, WTS, LC; WTS to J. D. Cox, November 13, 1875, WTS, LC; Cox, "Boynton's Review of Sherman," *Nation,* November 25, December 2, 1875, pp. 342–43, 358–59; WTS to CWM, November 15, 1875, WTS, LC; WTS to CWM, December 4, 1875, WTS, NYPL; WTS to JWD, November 25, 1875, WTS, LC; WTS to Samuel M. Bowman, December 2, 1875, WTS, Northwestern University; ES to JWD, December 10, 1875, JWD, LC; NYT, December 29, 1875; Judson Kilpatrick to WTS, December 30, 1875, WTS, LC.

12. WTS to Roscoe Conkling, October 5, November 1, 1875, January 18, 1876, Roscoe Conkling Papers, LC; Conkling to WTS, October 15, 1875, WTS, LC; Harry J. Brown and Frederick D. Williams, eds., *The Diary of James A. Garfield* (East Lansing, 1973), January 16, 1876, 3:216–17; WTS to USG, January 19, 1876, WTS, MoHS; USG to WTS, January 29, 1876, WTS to USG, February 2, 1876, copy, WTS, LC.

13. H. V. Boynton to WTS, January 16, 1880, WTS to Boynton, January 16, 1880, WTS, LC.

14. WTS to Kilpatrick, January 24, 1880, copy, WTS, LC; WTS to G. W. Balloch, January 27, 1880, WTS, HPC; WTS to J. M. Glover, January 31, 1880, copy, WTS, LC; Orville Babcock to WTS, February 4, 1880, WTS, LC; NYT, January 31, February 10, 1880; WTS to R. B. Hayes, February 17, 1880, WTS, HPC; WTS to Matt H. Carpenter, February 1, 1880, WTS, OHS; WTS to OOH, February 29, 1880, OOH, BC; WTS to JTD, March 12, 1882, JTD, CHS; WTS to J. Warren Keifer, May 18, 1887, J. Warren Keifer Papers, Syracuse University.

15. WTS to CWM, April 27, May 7, 10, 13, 19, 25, 1885, copies, WTS, LC; WTS to ES, July 10, 1885, SFP, UNDA; WTS to D. Appleton and Company, June 2, 1885, copy, WTS, LC; Fred Grant to WTS, July 20, 1885, WTS, LC; WTS to William C. Church, December 6, 1885, William C. Church Papers, LC.

16. Charles Royster, "Note on the Text," in WTS, *Memoirs*, 1122–23.

17. CWM to WTS, May 12, 1886, WTS, LC; WTS to CWM, May 16, 1886, HLH; WTS to SHMB, June 11, 1886, SHMB, IHS.

18. *St. Louis Globe-Democrat*, in NYT, May 18, 1882. For another account of WTS as a presiding officer, see Joseph B. Foraker, *Notes of a Busy Life* (Cincinnati, 1916), 1:306–7.

19. Fenwick Y. Hedley, *Marching Through Georgia* . . . (Chicago, 1887), 444–45; *Proceedings of the Annual Meeting of the Army of the Tennessee,* November 12, 13, 1879, pp. 112–13.

20. Hedley, *Marching,* 445–46; *Rock Island Argus,* September 17, 1886.

21. For three versions of the same speech, which vary in length and content but not in essence, see *Proceedings,* Tennessee, September 17, 18, 1873, pp. 95–100; A. W. Whelpley Papers, Cincinnati Historical Society; and SFP, UNDA.

22. Horace Porter chapter in Thomas Clement Fletcher, ed., *Life and Reminiscences of General William T. Sherman* . . . (Baltimore, 1891), 317; Charles E. Benton, *As Seen from the Ranks* (New York, 1902), 128–30; NYT, July 10, 1866.

23. *Proceedings, Tennessee,* April 6, 7, 1871, p. 488; NYT, February 17, 1887, June 17, 1865, November 10, 1883; unnamed newspaper clipping, December 15, 1868, WTS, scrapbook, WTS, OHS; NYT, July 10, 1866, August 29, 1889.

24. *Proceedings, Tennessee:* for Shiloh, see April 6, 1881; for march to the sea, September 29, 1872; for City Point, June 20, 1887; for Grand Review, July 3, 1890; for Atlanta, November 24, 1870, and September 25, 1889; for Kentucky, June 2, 1886.

25. WTS, "The Grand Strategy of the War of the Rebellion," *Century* 13 (February 1888): 582–98; WTS, "Grant, Thomas, Lee," *North American Review* 144 (May 1887): 442; WTS to Editor, March 12, 1887, copy, WTS, LC; WTS to Alexander S. Webb, December 25, 1888, Alexander S. Webb Papers, YL.

26. WTS to EST, October 20, 1885, WTS, OHS; WTS to JS, December 22, 1885, WTS, LC; WTS to T. T. Munford, August 11, 1873, Munford-Ellis Family Papers, DU; WTS to JWD, November 11, 1868, JEJ to WTS, June 13, 1877, May 17, 1889, Braxton Bragg to WTS, June 25, 1867, James Longstreet to WTS, July 10, 1877, WTS to Longstreet, December 28, 1888, copy, WTS, LC; WTS to Ord, June 9, 1876, James S. Copley Library, La Jolla, California; Gideon Pillow to WTS, May 24, June 2, 1877, Alexander H. Stephens to WTS, May 21, 1881, WTS to Stephens, May 23, 1881, copy, WTS, LC; NYT, March 11, 1886; WTS to J. B. Gordon, April 7, 1884, copy, WTS to Mrs. P. Frazer Edmunds, February 20, 1889, copy, WTS, LC.

27. WTS to JMS, March 11, 1879, HB, HL; John F. Marszalek, "Celebrity in Dixie, Sherman Tours the South," *Georgia Historical Quarterly* 46 (Fall 1982): 368–83.

28. WTS to George A. Townsend, November 21, 1886, WTS, USMA; WTS to

DFB, June 12, July 26, 1875, WLF, NYPL; WTS to T. T. Munford, April 22, 1873, copy, WTS, LC; WTS to HST, July 24, 1878, copy, SFP, UNDA.

29. Lewis Cruger to Jeff Davis, July 30, 1878, in Dunbar Rowland, ed., *Jefferson Davis . . . His Letters . . .* (Jackson, Miss., 1923), 8:244; Davis, *The Rise and Fall of the Confederate Government* (New York, 1881), 2:627–29, 564; *Indianapolis Sentinel*, June 10, 1884, in scrapbook, WTS, LC; see also NYT, June 12, 1881.

30. WTS to HST, June 18, 1881, copy, SFP, UNDA; WTS to WW, August 3, 1881, WTS, ISL; Marszalek, "Celebrity," 382; WTS to H. J. Kimball, December 1, 1881, copy, City of Atlanta Resolution, February 19, 1883, J. B. Goodman to WTS, February 20, 1883, WTS, LC.

31. NYT, November 2, 1884; Davis to Editor of *St. Louis Republican*, November 6, 1884, in scrapbook, WTS, LC.

32. *Congressional Record*, 48th Cong., 2d sess., January 12, 1885 p. 627; January 13, 1885, pp. 649–53.

33. WTS to Secretary of War, January 6, 1885, in U.S. Senate, *Executive Documents*, 48th Cong., 2d sess., No. 36.

34. Davis to J. Thomas Scharf, September 23, 1886, *Southern Historical Society Papers* 14 (1886): 257–74.

35. WTS to DFB, February 17, 1885, WLF, NYPL; WTS to G. A. Townsend, November 21, 1886, WTS, UNDA; WTS to H. P. Cutler, October 31, 1887, WTS, HPC.

36. WTS to Fry, September 3, 1884, Fry to WTS, September 14, 22, 28, 1884, USG to WTS, September 8, 1884, WTS to Fry, September 18, 25, October 1, 1884, WTS, LC.

37. Fry, "An Acquaintance with Grant," *North American Review* 141 (December 1885): 540–52.

38. WTS to A. Thorndike Rice, December 1885, copy, Fry to Rice, December 5, 1885, copy, WTS to Rice, December 10, 1885, copy, WTS, LC.

39. WTS to R. C. Drum, December 17, 1885, Drum to WTS, December 23, 1885, WTS to Rice, January 2, 1886, copy, Fry to WTS, January 4, 1886, WTS to CWM, January 11, 1886, copy, WTS to J. D. Cox, January 14, 1886, copy, WTS to George Morrison, January 12, 1886, copy, JS to WTS, January 20, 1888, WTS to JS, January 23, 1886, Robert N. Scott to WTS, January 26, 1886, WTS to Scott, January 29, 1886, copy, WTS, LC. The letter in question is WTS to Scott, September 6, 1885, WTS, LC; WTS to Fred Grant, December 18, 1885, copy, January 2, 1886, WTS, LC; Fry to Editor, January 29, 1886, in "An Open Letter," *North American Review* 142 (March 1886): 292–94; WTS to J. E. Tourtelotte, February 3, 1886, WTS, MoHS; John M. Bacon to WTS, February 5, 1886, Stewart Van Vliet to WTS, February 6, 1886, WTS to Fred Grant, February 4, 1886, copy, WTS, LC; WTS, "An Unspoken Address to the Loyal Legion," *North American Review* 142 (March 1886): 295–308; WTS to EST, March 4, 1886, WTS, OHS.

40. (Columbus) *Ohio State Journal*, August 12, 1880; NYT, August 19, 1880;

WTS, "Campfires of the G.A.R.," *North American Review* 147 (May 1888): 497.

41. *Columbus Dispatch,* August 12, 1880; WTS to Jacob D. Cox, May 19, 1882, copy, WTS, LC; NYT, July 11, 1884; WTS to OOH, March 1, 1889, OOH, BC; NYT, May 28, 1922.

42. "Banquet . . . February 8, 1883," in WTS, Selected Pamphlets, vol 8, OHS.

CHAPTER 22   A FULL LIFE ENDS

1. Joseph Henry to WTS, February 10, 1871, SFP, UNDA; WTS to Joseph Henry, October 28, 1874, Record Unit 26, Office of the Secretary, 1863–1879, vol. 148, Smithsonian Institution Archives; NYT, March 12, 1878; WTS to O. M. Poe, January 3, 1886, O. M. Poe Papers, LC; WTS to JAG, January 18, 1871, Garfield, LC; Newton Crane to WTS, December 31, 1883, John T. Davis et al. to WTS, February 27, 1884, John T. Crittenden to WTS, April 24, 1884, WTS, LC; C. R. Williams, ed., *Diary and Letters of Rutherford B. Hayes* (Columbus, Ohio, 1926), October 7, 1885, 4:240–41; WTS to EST, November 9, 1885, WTS, OHS; David L. Westol to author, January 2, 1990; WTS to MSF, June 9, 1889, WTS, OHS; NYT, February 24, 1891.

2. WTS to JS, March 17, 1888, WTS to Albion T. Pease, March 5, 1884, copy, WTS to John McElroy, July 15, 1885, copy, W. S. McNair to WTS, July 8, 1887, WTS, LC; NYT, July 8, 1887; WTS to JS, July 23, 1887, WTS, LC.

3. WTS to Edwin Booth, April 5, 1889, The Players—New York City Collection, LC; WTS to OOH, January 24, 1887, OOH, BC; WTS, Toast, in Robert G. Ingersoll, *Robert G. Ingersoll, Gen. William T. Sherman, Chauncey Depew: Their Speeches at the Robson and Crane Banquet, New York, November 21st, 1887* (New York, 1887).

4. Garff B. Wilson, *Three Hundred Years of American Drama and Theatre . . .* (Englewood Cliffs, NJ, 1973), 241–48.

5. PTS, "Reminiscences of Early Days," unpublished 1940 manuscript, SFP, UNDA, 47; Fletcher, 78–79; WTS to Mary Anderson, October 11, 1885, copy, WTS, LC; WTS to MES, April 14, 1887, WTS, OHS; WTS to Ada Rehan, signed dinner program, March 17, October 12, 1888, February 9, 1890, Ada Rehan Papers, University of Pennsylvania; Augustin Daly to WTS, April 15, 1887, WTS, LC.

6. Donald B. Russell, *The Lives and Legends of Buffalo Bill* (Norman, Okla., 1960), 74–75; WTS, diary, January 6, 9, 22, 1887, June 15, 1888, SFP, UNDA; William F. Cody to WTS, June 15, 1882, December 27, 1886, May 5, June 24, 1887, WTS, LC; SHMB, *Twenty Years in Europe . . .* (Chicago, 1900), 280; unidentified St. Louis newspaper, September 20, 1884, scrapbook, WTS, LC.

7. PTS, "Reminiscences," 19–20; ES to PTS, November 11, 1886, January 26, 1887, SFP, UNDA; WTS to W. E. Strong, October 29, 1888, WTS, LC.

8. "A Souvenir . . . George Patrick Alexander Healy . . . Virginia Museum of

Fine Arts in Richmond, 24 January–5 March 1950," 75–76; Marie De Mare, *G. P. A Healy* . . . (New York, 1954), 238–41; WTS to Healy, January 13, 1868, WTS, USMA; WTS to Daniel Huntington, November 20, 1874, CHH, WLC; Augustus S. Gaudens to WTS, February 28, 1888, WTS, LC; WTS to Poe, October 1, 1888, Poe, LC; WTS to Mrs. RA, January 2, 1890, AdeC, PU; Albert Bierstadt to WTS, May 5, 1883, WTS, LC.

9. WTS to Newbold H. Trotter, March 18, 1879, WTS, LC; Horace Porter, in Fletcher, *Life and Reminiscences,* 318–19; WTS to James E. Taylor, June 9, 1883, copy, WTS, LC.

10. EST, manuscript, VU; WTS to HST, June 5, 1881, WTS, OHS.

11. "Memorandum of Property . . . ," April 13, 14, 15, 1869, WTS, LC; book list, June 6, 1883, November 1, 1883, O. M. Poe, LC and WTS, LC; "Memo of Books . . . Deposited in Mercantile Library of St. Louis, June 12, 1886," WTS, LC; WTS to Poe, October 19, 1883, Poe, LC.

12. PTS, "Reminiscences," 37; WTS to William S. Case, January 10, 1886, WTS, DU; TS to WTS, October 30, 1886, SFP, UNDA; WTS to MSF, December 17, 20, 1888, WTS, OHS; EST, manuscript ST, VU; WTS to S. L. M. Barlow, December 16, 1887, BW, box 180 (23), HL.

13. Thomas C. Fletcher, ed., *Life and Reminiscences of General William T. Sherman* . . . (Baltimore, 1891), 80; W. Fletcher Johnson and OOH, *The Life of General William Tecumseh Sherman* . . . (Philadelphia, 1891), 465, 468; *New York World,* February 9, 1890, and unnamed, undated newspaper clipping, in MSA, scrapbook, WTS, OHS; PTS, "Reminiscences," 28.

14. Examples of ES illnesses are noted in ES to WTS, March 8, 1879, WTS to TS, March 4, 1877, SFP, UNDA, WTS to John Jay, May 23, 1874, Jay Family Papers, CU, WTS to MSF, March 12, 1881, WTS, OHS. For WTS health problems, see WTS to Eugene Casserly, January 23, 1868, AdeC, PU; ES to WTS, January 19, 1869, WTS, OHS, WTS to E. D. Morgan, March 4, 1869, E. D. Morgan Papers, New York State Library; WTS to Corse, December 18, 1885, WTS, LC; ES, diary, March 9, 1868, SFP, UNDA.

15. ES to WTS, July 30, 1887, SFP, UNDA; WTS to EST, October 12, 1887, WTS, OHS.

16. ES to WTS, March 8, 1879, May 29, April 30, May 4, 1887, SFP, UNDA; WTS to MSF, June 27, 1887, WTS, OHS.

17. WTS to ES, May 10, July 7, 1887, SFP, UNDA; WTS to JTD, June 10, 1888, WTS, CHS; WTS to NAM, October 15, 1887, NAM, LC; WTS to MSF, October 22, 1887, WTS, OHS; WTS to JS, October 26, 1887, WTS, LC; ES to ESF, November 4, 1887, WTS, OHS; WTS to PBE, November 5, 8, 1887, ES to PBE, November 7, 1887, EFP, UNDA.

18. WTS to ES, December 15, 1887, in Mark A. DeWolfe Howe, ed., *Home Letters of General Sherman* (New York, 1909), 400; WTS to WW, February 16, 1888, WTS, ISL; WTS to MSF, April 1, 1888, WTS, OHS; ES to PBE, March 23, May 16, 1888, SFP, UNDA.

19. WTS to MSF, July 20, 1888, WTS to EST, August 3, 1888, WTS, OHS; ES to WTS, August 10, 1888, ES to WTS, September 22, 1888, SFP, UNDA.

20. *San Francisco Examiner,* in NYT, July 24, 1886; Horatio G. King in Fletcher, *Life and Reminiscences,* 256–57; Washington Irving, *The Adventures of Captain Bonneville USA in the Rocky Mountains and the Far West* (New York, 1837, rev. ed., 1868).

21. WTS to "Cousin Elizabeth," November 19, 1887, Misc. Manuscripts, "S" Collection, American Antiquarian Society; WTS to JS, September 2, 1888, WTS, LC; Edwin Tribble, "Marching Through Georgia," *Georgia Review* 21 (Winter 1967): 428; James P. Pond to WTS, April 13, 1885, WTS, LC; WTS to Pond, November 2, 1885, WTS, MoHS.

22. Thomas Ewing (III) to B. H. Liddell-Hart, March 5, 1930, TE, LC.

23. TS, "Conclusion," in WTS, *Memoirs,* rev. ed. (New York, 1891), 2:471; PTS, "Reminiscences," 46; Letters of Condolences, November–December 1888, WTS to Tourtelotte, December 6, 1888, SFP, UNDA.

24. PTS, "Reminiscences," 46.

25. *New York World,* February 22, 1891, in WTS, OHS; WTS to General McCook, January 11, 1891, McCook Family Papers, LC; WTS to Benjamin H. Field February 3, 1891, in NYT, February 17, 1891, WTS to JS, February 3, 1891, SFP, UNDA.

26. WTS to Mary Anna Palmer Draper, January 3, 1891, Henry Draper Papers, NYPL; JMS, *Forty-six Years in the Army* (New York, 1897), 542; W. Fletcher Johnson and OOH, *The Life of General William Tecumseh Sherman . . .* (Philadelphia, 1891), 479–80; Henry J. Coggeshall, Eulogy, New York State Senate, February 23, 1891, WTS, LC. Several medical prescriptions, two from 1886, are preserved in box 11, SFP, UNDA. Interpretations by several pharmacists indicate that Cump took respiratory stimulants, expectorants, laxatives, and sedatives. Chris Bonner to author, undated [July 1991].

27. WTS to General McCook, January 11, 1891, McCook Family Papers, LC; WTS, "Sherman's Last Speech" *Century* 20 (December 1890): 189–92.

28. Johnson and OOH, *Life,* 474–79; Edward Chase, *The Memorial Life of General William Tecumseh Sherman* (Chicago, 1891), 538–43; MSF, "Account of Last Illness and Death . . . ," unpublished ms., WTS, OHS; WTS, *Memoirs,* rev. ed. (New York, 1891), 473–75; MES to JS, February 9, 1891, WTS, LC; Peter Wright and Son to PTS, Vernon H. Brown to PTS, February 13, 1891, PTS to "all vessels," undated, WTS, LC; PTS, diary, February 15, 1891, SFP, UNDA.

29. Mark Twain to WTS, Benjamin Harrison to WTS, February 10, 1891, Harrison to JS, February 11, 1891, VRH to WTS, both undated, Mrs. RA to Miss Sherman, February 12, 1891, Joseph Chamberlain to WTS, February 12, 1891, Murat Halstead to Misses Sherman, February 11, 1891, WTS, LC; Alexander Mackay-Smith to PTS, February 11, 1891, SFP, UNDA; Richard Porter to WTS, February 11, 1891, WTS, LC.

30. JS to NYT, February 13, 1891, copy, SFP, UNDA. The debate over Cump's religion continued long after his death. See, e.g., George S. Boutwell, *Reminiscences of Sixty Years in Public Affairs* (New York, 1902), 2:243–44.

31. *Congressional Record,* 51st Cong., lst sess., February 14, 16, 1891, pp.

2678–81, 2764–67; announcements and resolutions on WTS death, in Appointment, Commissions, and Personal branch, Adjutant General's Office, R.G. 94, NARS; condolences, resolutions, and so forth, SFP, UNDA; S.O. No. 1, Hqs., Ransom Post No. 131, Department of Missouri, GAR, February 14, 1891, in HMH, MoHS.

32. Condolences and so forth, beginning on February 14, 1891, are found in WTS, LC; Johnson and OOH, *Life of Sherman,* 532–38; NYT, February 17, 1891; Charles H. George to Misses Sherman, February 18, 1891, WTS, LC.

33. *Literary Digest,* February 21, 1891, pp. 20–21; "Feeling the Beat of the Public Pulse," *Chaperone* 1 (March 1891): 577–80, 643; *San Francisco Examiner,* February 15, 1891, in WTS, CHS.

34. J. W. Nicholson to PTS, March 2, 1891, WTS, LC; NYT, February 18, 1891, *Congressional Record,* 51st Cong., 1st sess., February 14, 16, 1819, pp. 2680, 2767.

35. *Literary Digest,* February 21, 1819, pp. 20–21.

36. *New York World,* February 21, 1891; Thomas Clement Fletcher, ed., *Life and Reminiscences of General William T. Sherman . . .* (Baltimore, 1891), 218–21.

37. Benjamin Harrison to JS, February 14, 1891, WTS, LC; NYT, February 21, 1891; Chase, *Memorial Life,* 544–47.

38. OOH, *The Autobiography of Oliver Otis Howard* (New York, 1907), 2:553–54.

39. WTS, *Memoirs,* rev. ed., 2:477–82; NYT, February 20, 1891.

40. Alonzo Gore Oakley to PTS, December 28, 1939, box 8, SFP, UNDA.

41. NYT, February 21, 1891.

42. "Sherman's Funeral," *Harpers Weekly,* March 7, 1891, p. 171; Charles R. Williams, ed., *Diary and Letters of Rutherford B. Hayes . . .* (Columbus, Ohio, 1922–26), February 19, 1891, 4:638–39.

43. Harriet Adams Sawyer, "Burial of Sherman," *Chaparone* 1 (March 1891) : 566.

44. WTS, *Memoirs,* rev. ed., 2:482–83; Johnson and OOH, *Life of Sherman,* 491–92; OOH, *Autobiography,* 2:553; Grenville M. Dodge, *Personal Recollections of Abraham Lincoln, General Ulysses S. Grant, and General William T. Sherman* (Council Bluffs, Iowa, 1914), 231; NYT, February 23, 1891; William Hyde and Howard L. Conard, *Encyclopedia of the History of St. Louis* (New York, 1899), 1:336, in box 9, SFP, UNDA.

BIBLIOGRAPHY

MANUSCRIPTS

Albany (New York) Institute of History and Art, McKinney Library: Ten Eyck/Gansevoort Family.

American Antiquarian Society: Civil War Collection, 1861–1868; D. C. Heath: Miscellaneous Manuscripts.

Art Institute of Chicago: William L. Jenney.

Atlanta Historical Society: Ladies Memorial Association, Atlanta Records.

Bancroft Library, University of California, Berkeley: Hilgard Family; Ord, E. O. C.; *Overland Monthly;* Scott, William A.; Sheldon, Frank M.; Sherman, W. T.; Wilkinson, Waring.

Beinecke Rare Books and Manuscripts Library, Yale University: Ord, E. O. C.; Sherman, W. T.

Boston Public Library, Rare Books and Manuscripts: Sherman, W. T.

Boston University Library, Special Collections, Mugar Memorial Library: Military Historical Society Papers.

Bowdoin College Library: Abbot Autograph Collection; Howard, O. O.; Mellen, Clara Hawkins.

Brown University, Special Collections, John Hay Library: Hay, John; Lincoln Collection; Thayer, Eli.

California Historical Society, San Francisco: Effinger, Robert P.; Johnson, John Neely: Sherman, W. T.

California State Library, California Section, Sacramento: Bidwell, John; Committee of Vigilance, San Francisco Records, 1856.

Chicago Historical Society: Alphabetical File; Brayman, Mason; Grand Army Hall and Memorial Association, Civil War Papers; Grant, U. S.; Healy, George P. A.; Hoffman, Wickham; Sherman, W. T.

Chicago Public Library, Special Collections Division: Grand Army of the Republic Collection.

Chicago, University of, Joseph Regenstein Library: Lincoln (Oldroyd); Butler-Gunsaulus.

Cincinnati Historical Society: Cist, Charles E.; Hannaford, Roger; Ohio Testimonial to General Sherman (January 4–March 24, 1865); Sherman, W. T.; Smith, Thomas E.; Shelpley, A. W.

Colorado Historical Society, Denver: Tappan, Samuel F.

Columbia University, Rare Books and Manuscripts Library: Alexander, P. W.; Appleton, D. and Company; Appleton, William W.; Barnard, Frederick A. P.;

Dix, John A.; Dunlap, G.; Gay, Sidney Howard; Jay Family; Matthews, B.; Schang, Frederick C.; Sprague, William; Sherman, W. T.

Connecticut Historical Society, Hartford: Sherman, W. T.

Cornell University Library, Department of Rare Books: Bancroft, George; Sherman, W. T.

Dartmouth College Library, Special Collections: Abraham Lincoln and His Generals Collection; Sherman, W. T.

Detroit Public Library, Burton Historical Collection: Autograph Collection; Shelton, Lucy; William Alpheus S.; Zug, Robert M.

Dickinson College Library: King, Horatio C.

Duke University, Special Collections Department, William R. Perkins Library: Aumach, Ellen; Bennitt, James; Farquhan, Francis U.; Fisher, Benjamin F.; Gray, Mrs. Hiram; Halleck, Henry W.; Hayne, Paul H.; Jones, Charles C. Jr.; Lossing, Benjamin J.; McIntosh, Thomas M.; Marshall, Eugene; Munford-Elbe Family; Pierce, John H.; Quintard, Charles T.; Sherman, W. T.; Van Duzer, John C.

Eugene C. Barker Texas History Center, University of Texas: Carter, Robert G.; Civil War Miscellany.

Franklin D. Roosevelt Library, Hyde Park, New York: Sherman, W. T.

Free Library of Philadelphia: Sherman, W. T.

George Washington University, Special Collections, Gelman Library: Depew, Chauncey.

Georgetown University Library: Ewing-Sherman.

Georgia Historical Society, Savannah: Bragg, Lillian Chaplin; Gordon Family; Meldrim Family; Sherman, W. T.; Stovall, Pleasant A.

Hagley Museum and Library, Wilmington, Delaware: DuPont, Daughters of E. I.; DuPont, Henry A.; DuPont, Samuel Francis

Harry Ransom Humanities Research Center, University of Texas, Austin: Downing/Theatre Art Collection; Johnson, Robert U.; Sherman, W. T./ Theatre Art Collection; Story, William W.

Historic New Orleans Collection: Sherman, W. T.

Historical Society of Delaware, Wilmington: Sherman, W. T.

Historical Society of Pennsylvania, Philadelphia: Chase, Salmon P.; Dreer Civil War Union Generals Collection; Gratz Collections; MacVeagh, Isaac W.; Meredith, William M.; Sherman, W. T.; Society Collection; Swank, James M.; Twenty Fourth Administration Collection.

Historical Society of Quincy and Adams County, Quincy, Illinois: Thomas, George H.; Morgan, James D.

Houghton Library, Harvard University: Autograph File; Dearborn, Frederick M.; Scudder, Horace E.; Sherman, W. T.

Huntington Library, San Marino, California: Anderson, Charles; Barney, Hiram; Lusk, William T.; Nicolson, John P.; Sherman, W. T.

Illinois State Historical Library, Springfield: Augur, C. C.; Browning, Orville H.; Connolly, James A.; Farragut, David G.; Grierson, Benjamin H.; McClernand, John A.; Palmer, John M.; Parsons, Lewis B.; Ricks, Jesse E.; Sherman, Ellen Ewing; Sherman, W. T.; Strong, William E.; Wallace-Dickey Family; Warner, Willard.

Indiana State Library, Indianapolis: Sherman, W. T.

James S. Copley Library, La Jolla, California: Sherman, W. T.

Johns Hopkins University, Milton S. Eisenhower Library: Gilman, Daniel C.

Kansas State Historical Society, Topeka: Ewing, Thomas Jr.; History, Military, Eighteenth Kansas; Sherman, W. T.; Stevens, T. C.

Library of Congress: Anderson, Robert; Arthur, Chester A.; Banks, Nathaniel P.; Bayard, Thomas F.; Beard, Donald C.; Benham-McNeil Family; Bevan, Edith R.; Bickerdyke, Mary Ann; Blaine, James G.; Bradbury, William H.; Capron, Horace; Carlton, Caleb H.; Church, William C.; Comstock, Cyrus B.; Conkling, Roscoe; Cope, John; Cotton, Josiah D.; Cushman, Charlotte S.; Dewey, George; Doolittle, James R.; Draper, John W.; Drennan, Daniel O.; Evarts, William; Ewell, Richard S.; Ewing, Charles; Ewing, Thomas; Gibson-Getty-McClure Family; Goodnow, James H.; Grant, U. S.; Gresham, Walter Q.; Hardie, James A.; Hartz, Edward L.; Hitchcock, Henry; Hoxie, Vinnie Ream; Hurja, Emil; Hunt, Henry J.; Johnson, Andrew; Johnson, Reverdy; Keating, Harriette C.; Logan, John A.; McClintock, James M.; McCook Family; Meigs, Montgomery C.; Miles, Nelson A.; Moody, Dwight L.; Morrill, Justin S.; Naval Historical Miscellany; Pettigru, James L.; Pinchot, Gifford; Players, New York City; Poe, O. M.; Porter, D. D.; Reid, Whitelaw; Reichhelm, E. Paul; Schofield, John M.; Sheridan, Philip; Sherman, John; Sherman, W. T.; Spinner, Francis E.; Spofford, Ainsworth R.; Stanton, Edwin M.; Stuart, George H.; Summerall, Charles P.; Symington, Evelyn; Ticknor, Benjamin H.; VanCise, Edwin A.; Waite, Morrison R.; Washburne, Elihu B.; Wilder, Marshall P.; Young, John Russell.

Louisiana State University, Louisiana and Lower Mississippi Valley Collections, LSU Libraries: Boyd, David French; Caffrey, Donelson, and Family; Gayarre, Charles E. A.; Liddell, St. John R. Family; Robertson, Marian McKenre Winter; Sherman, W. T.; Stephen, Edwin L.; Sullivan, Petter J.; Vincent, Thomas C. Family

Mansfield-Richland County Public Library, Mansfield, Ohio: Sherman, John.

Maryland Historical Society, Baltimore: Carroll, Cradock, Jenson; Gibbon, John; McLane-Fisher Family; Vertical File.

Massachusetts Historical Society, Boston: Bancroft, George; Beale, James; Everett, Edward; Hoar, George F.; Norcross, Grenville H.; Schouler, James; Winthrop, Robert C.

Michigan State University, Archives and Historical Collections, East Lansing: Arnold, Uriah and William; Campbell Family; Civil War Papers; Taft, Jesse.

Minnesota Historical Society, St. Paul: Cady-Randolph Family; Eddy, Charles G.; Green, Levi N.; Lochren, William and Family; Miller, Stephen, Governors' Papers; Ramsey, Alexander; Rice, Henry M.; Sherman, W. T.; Sibley, Henry H.; Simpson, James H.; Swift, Henry A.; Taylor, James W.; Whipple, Henry Benjamin.

Missouri Historical Society, St. Louis: Bixby, W. K.; Civil War Papers; DeSmet, Pierre; Eads, James B.; Easton, Rufus; Eliot, William G.; Filley Family; Francis, David R.; Hamilton, Charles; Harrison Family; Hitchcock, Henry M.; Jones, Lelia; Lucas and Hunt; Lucas, James H.; Missouri Militia; Mullanphy

Family; Reaves, L. U.; Reynolds, Thomas; Sherman, W. T.; Sturgeon, Isaac H.; Wagoner, H. H.

National Archives and Record Service, Washington, D.C.: Adjutant General's Office, Record Group 94; Headquarters of the Army, Record Group 108; Military Governor and Secretary of the State of California, March 1, 1847–September 23, 1848, Microfilm 182; Tenth Military District, Record Group 98 and Microfilm 210.

Nebraska State Historical Society, Lincoln: North, Frank J.

New England Historic Genealogical Society, Boston: Old Manuscript Collection (Biography).

New York Public Library, Astor, Lenox and Tilden Foundations, Rare Books and Manuscripts Division: Billings, John; Bryant-Godwin; Carman, Ezra; Draper, Henry; Fleming, Walter L.; Goddard-Roslyn; Greene, Francis V.; Kohns, Lee; Personal Miscellaneous; Sherman, W. T.

New York State Library, Albany: Morgan, E. D.; Sherman, W. T.

Newberry Library, Special Collections, Chicago: Autographs, Individual; Babcock, Orville E.; Sherman, W. T.

North Carolina Division of Archives and History, Raleigh: Clark, Walter; Graham, William A.; Grant, Dorothy Freemont; Lavender, Alston, Miscellaneous Civil War Records; Nicholas, Thomas W.; Spencer, Cornelia Phillips; Swain, David L.; Taylor, John D.; Vance, Zebulon, B.

Northwestern University Library: Sherman, W. T.

Notre Dame, University of, Archives: Brownson, Orestes; Edwards, James F.; Ewing Family; Ewing, Thomas; Notre Dame; Sherman Family; Sorin, Edward.

Ohio Historical Society, Columbus: Coffey, William; Delano, Columbus; Dennison, William, Jr.; Ewing, Hugh B.; Ewing, Philemon B.; Ewing, Thomas; Gilmore, William E.; Lowes, William W.; McMillen, William L.; Rice, Charles E.; Robinson, James S.; Sherman, Charles R.; Sherman, John; Sherman, W. T.; Smith and Dine; Smith, William H,; Stanton, Edwin M.; Vance, John L., Jr.; Vertical File; Walter, Harvey W.

Oregon Historical Society, Portland: Corbett, Henry W.; Sherman, W. T.

Pennsylvania State University, Pattee Library: Sherman, W. T.

Pennsylvania, University of, Special Collections Department, Van Pelt Library: Rehan, Ada.

Pierpont Morgan Library, Department of Autograph Manuscripts, New York: Autograph, American Collection; Sherman, W. T.

Princeton University Library: Alexander Autograph; Caldwell, Robert G.; DeCoppet, Andre; Hyatt, Alpheus; Hyatt and Mayer; General Manuscripts, Miscellaneous; Williams, Charles R.

Rochester, University of, Library: Brown, Charles A.; Seward, William H.; Sherman, W. T.

Rosenbach Museum and Library, Philadelphia: Sherman, W. T.

Rutherford B. Hayes Presidential Center, Fremont, Ohio: Claflin, William; Crook, George; Hayes, Rutherford B.; Reynolds, John P.; Sherman, W. T.

Sherman House, Fairfield Heritage Association, Lancaster, Ohio: Sherman, W. T.

Smithsonian Institution Archives: Office of the Secretary; Sherman, W. T.

South Carolina, University of, South Caroliniana Library, Columbia: Benham, H. W.; Hampton Family; Sherman, W. T.

South Dakota State Historical Resource Center, State Historical Archives, Pierre: Kidder, Jefferson P.

Southern Historical Collection, University of North Carolina, Chapel Hill: Walter, Harvey W.; Boyd, David French.

Southern Illinois University, Special Collections, Morris Library, Carbondale: Civil War Documents; Dent, Frederick T.

Stanford University Libraries, Department of Special Collections: Harwood Family; Plumb, Edgar L.; Robinson, Elmer E.; Sherman, W. T.; Steele, Frederick.

State Historical Society of Iowa, Special Collections, Des Moines: Byers, S. H. M.; Sherman, W. T.

State Historical Society of Wisconsin, Madison: Sherman, W. T.; Vilas, William F.

Stephenson County Historical Society, Freeport, Illinois: Sherman, W. T.

Syracuse University, George Arents Research Library for Special Collections: Huntington, Collis P.; Keifer, J. Warren.

Tennessee State Library and Archives, Nashville: Civil War Collection; Ewell, Richard S.; Granger, Arthur; Jackson, William H.; Wright and Lincoln; Yeatman-Polk.

Texas Tech University, Southwest Collection: Rister, Carl.

United States Military History Institute, Carlisle Barracks, Pennsylvania: Sherman, W. T.

United States Military Academy Library, Special Collections Division: Cullom, G. W.; DeTrobriand, Phillipe; Dorst, James A.; Draper, A. A.; Edmunds, Frank H.; Frémont, John C.; Gardner, William M.; Grant, U. S.; Porter, FitzJohn; Porter, Lucia C.; Sherman, W. T.; Tidball, John C.; Wagstaff, David.

United States Naval Academy, the Museum: Rosenbach Collection.

University of California at Los Angeles, Department of Special Collections, University Research Library: Ammen, Daniel.

University of California at Santa Barbara Library: Sherman, W. T.

Vanderbilt University: Sherman, W. T.

Vermont Historical Society, Montpelier: Sherman, W. T.

Villanova University, Falvey Memorial Library: Sherman-Thackara Family.

Virginia Historical Society, Richmond: Bates, Edward; Cooke Family; Sherman, W. T.; Thornton Family; Tompkins Family; Virginia Military Institute.

Virginia Military Institute Archives, Lexington: Sherman, W. T.

Virginia State Library (Richmond): Sherman, W. T.

Virginia, University of, Special Collections Department, Alderman Library: Barrett Minor Authors Collection; Heth-Selden; Hutton, Hamilton; Lee Family; Sherman, W. T.

Washington, University of, Library: Beals, Walter B.; Hammersly, Thomas H.; Stevens, Isaac I.

Washington University, St. Louis: Eliot, William G.

Western Reserve Historical Society, Cleveland: Palmer, William P.; Sherman, W. T.

William L. Clements Library, University of Michigan, Ann Arbor: Cooke, Aaron; Diedrich, Duane; Ellet, Charles; Haskell, Clinton H.; Schoff Civil War Collection; Sherman, W. T.

Yale University Library, Manuscripts and Archives: Beecher Family; Brewer, William H. Capron, Horace; Carrington Family; Evarts Family; Flagg, S. Griswold; Goodyear, Anson C.; Knollesburg, Bernhard Logan; March, O. C.; Terry Family; Thompson, William G.; Webb, Alexander S.

MILITARY SOCIETY PUBLICATIONS

Confederate Veteran, 1893–1932.

Grand Army of the Republic. *Records* of National Encampments, 1867–1892.

Journal of the Military Service Institution of the United States, 1879–1892.

Military Order of the Loyal Legion of the United States. *War Papers* and *Personal Reminiscences*. Various Commanderies, 1866–1914.

Society of the Army of the Cumberland. *Proceedings*, 1868–1891.

Society of the Army of the Potomac. *Proceedings*, 1880–1891.

Society of the Army of the Tennessee. *Proceedings*, 1867–1893.

Southern Historical Society Papers, 1876–1920.

United States Service Magazine, 1864–1866.

United Services Magazine: A Monthly Review of Military and Naval Affairs, 1879–1892.

BOOKS (SELECTED LISTING)

Abrahamson, James L. *American Arms for a New Century* (1981).

Ambrose, Stephen E. *Crazy Horse and Custer: The Parallel Lives of Two American Warriors* (1975).

——. *Duty, Honor, Country: A History of West Point* (1966).

——. *Halleck: Lincoln's Chief of Staff* (1962).

——. *Upton and the Army* (1964).

Angle, Paul M., ed. *Three Years in the Army of the Cumberland: The Letters and Diary of Major James A. Connolly* (1959).

Athearn, Robert G. *William Tecumseh Sherman and the Settlement of the West* (1956).

Badeau, Adam. *Grant in Peace: From Appomattox to Mount McGregor: A Personal Memoir* (1887).

——. *Military History of General Grant.* 2 vols. (1868).

Bailey, John W. *Pacifying the Plains: General Alfred Terry and the Decline of the Sioux, 1866–1890* (1979).

Bailey, Ronald H. *The Battles of Atlanta* (1985).

Bancroft, Frederick, ed. *Speeches, Correspondence and Political Papers of Carl Schurz.* 6 vols. (1913).

Bancroft, Hubert Howe. *The Works of Hubert Howe Bancroft.* Vol. 22: *History of California*, vol. 5: *1846–1848* (1886).

Barrett, John G. *The Civil War in North Carolina* (1963).

——. *Sherman's March Through the Carolinas* (1956).

Basler, Roy P., ed. *The Collected Works of Abraham Lincoln.* 8 vols. (1953).

Bates, David H. *Lincoln in the Telegraph Office* (1907).

Bauer, K. Jack. *The Mexican War* (1974).

———. *Surfboats and Horse Marines: U.S. Naval Operations in the Mexican War, 1846–1848* (1969).

Beale, Howard K., ed. *Diary of Edward Bates, 1859–1866.* In *Annual Report of the American Historical Association, 1930,* vol. 4 (1933).

Bearss, Margie Riddle. *Sherman's Forgotten Campaign: The Meridian Expedition* (1987).

Benton, Charles E. *As Seen from the Ranks: A Boy in the Ranks* (1902).

Bigelow, Donald N. *William Conant Church and the Army and Navy Journal* (1952).

Blaine, James G. *Twenty Years of Congress, 1861–1881.* 2 vols. (1886).

Blassingame, Wyatt. *William Tecumseh Sherman, Defender of the Union* (1970).

Bok, Edward. *The Americanization of Edward Bok* (1926).

Bolton, Sarah K. *Famous Leaders Among Men* (1894).

Boutwell, George S. *Reminiscences of Sixty Years in Public Affairs.* 2 vols. (1902).

Bowman, S. M., and Irwin, R. B. *Sherman and His Campaigns: A Military Biography* (1865).

Boyd, James P. *The Life of General William T. Sherman* (1891).

Boynton, Henry Van Ness. *Sherman's Historical Raid: The Memoirs in the Light of the Record* (1875).

Bradford, Gamaliel. *Union Portraits* (1916).

Bradley, Erwin S. *Simon Cameron, Lincoln's Secretary of War: A Political Biography* (1966).

Bradley, George S. *The Star Corps; or Notes of an Army Chaplain, During Sherman's Famous "March to the Sea"* (1865).

Brockett, Linus P. *Our Great Captains: Grant, Sherman, Thomas, Sheridan, and Farragut* (1865).

Brown, Harry J., and Williams, Frederick D., eds. *The Diary of James A. Garfield.* 3 vols. (1967–1973).

Burne, Alfred H. *Lee, Grant and Sherman: A Study in Leadership in the 1864–1865 Campaign* (1939).

Burton, Katherine. *Three Generations: Maria Boyle Ewing (1801–1864), Ellen Ewing Sherman (1824–1888), Minnie Sherman Fitch (1851–1913)* (1947).

Byers, S. H. M. *The March to the Sea, a Poem* (1896).

———. *Twenty Years in Europe . . . with Letters from General W. T. Sherman* (1900).

———. *With Fire and Sword* (1911).

Cadwallader, Sylvanus. *Three Years with Grant* (1956).

Capers, Gerald M., Jr. *The Biography of a River Town: Memphis—Its Heroic Age* (1939).

Carpenter, John A. *Sword and Olive Branch: Oliver Otis Howard* (1964).

Carr, Clark E. *Day and Generation* (1908).

Carter, Samuel, III. *The Final Fortress: The Campaign for Vicksburg, 1861–1863* (1980).

Castel, Albert. *The Presidency of Andrew Johnson* (1979).

Cate, Wirt A. *Lucius Q. C. Lamar, Secession and Reunion* (1935).

Chase, Edward. *The Memorial Life of General William Tecumseh Sherman* (1891).

Chittenden, L. E. *Personal Reminiscences* (1893).

Clarke, Dwight L. *William Tecumseh Sherman* (1969).

Cleaves, Freeman. *Rock of Chickamauga: The Life of General George H. Thomas* (1949).

Coffman, Edward. *The Old Army: Portrait of the American Army in Peacetime, 1784–1898* (1986).

Conyngham, David P. *Sherman's March Through the South with Sketches and Incidents of the Campaign* (1865).

Copp, Eldbridge. *Reminiscences* (1911).

Cothran, William. *History of Ancient Woodbury, Connecticut* . . . 2 vols. (1872).

Coulter, E. Merton. *Civil War and Readjustment in Kentucky* (1926).

Cox, Jacob D. *Atlanta* (1882).

———. *The March to the Sea: Franklin and Nashville* (1882).

Cresap, Bernarr. *Appomattox Commander: The Story of General E. O. C. Ord* (1981).

Croffert, W. A., ed. *Fifty Years in Camp and Field: Diary of Major General Ethan Allan Hitchcock* (1909).

Cummings, Charles M. *Yankee Quaker Confederate General: The Curious Career of Bushrod Rust Johnson* (1971).

Curl, Donald. *Murat Halstead and the Cincinnati Commercial* (1980).

Daly, Maria Lyding. *A Diary of a Union Lady, 1861–1865* (1962).

Dana, Charles A. *Recollections of the Civil War*. 1964 reprint (1898).

Davis, Burke. *Sherman's March* (1980).

Davis, Jefferson. *The Rise and Fall of the Confederate Government* (1881).

Davis, Varina H. *Jefferson Davis, Ex-President of the Confederate States of America: A Memoirs by His Wife*. 2 vols. (1890).

Davis, William C. *Battle at Bull Run* (1977).

Dawley, Thomas R. *The Life of William T. Sherman* (1864).

Dawson, Joseph G., III. *Army Generals and Reconstruction: Louisiana, 1861–1877* (1982).

Deitz, Ambrose P. *For Our Boys: A Collection of Original Literary Offerings by Popular Writers at Home and Abroad* (1879).

De Mare, Maree. *G. P. A. Healy American Artist* . . . (1954).

Dodge, Grenville M. *The Battle of Atlanta and Other Campaigns* (1911).

———. *Personal Recollections of President Abraham Lincoln, General Ulysses Grant and General William T. Sherman* (1914).

Dodge, Richard I. *Our Wild Indians*. Introduction by W. T. Sherman (1884).

Draper, John W. *History of the American Civil War*. 3 vols. (1870).

Duke Brothers and Company. *A Short History of Gen. W. T. Sherman*. Histories of Civil Generals Packed in Duke's Cigarettes (1888).

Durkin, Joseph T. *General Sherman's Son* (1959).

Ellis, Edward S. *The Life of Kit Carson* (1889).

Fleming, Thomas J. *West Point: The Men and Times of the United States Military Academy* (1959).

Fletcher, Thomas C., ed. *Life and Reminiscences of General William T. Sherman by Distinguished Men of His Time* (1891).

Foner, Jack D. *The United States Soldier Between Two Wars: Army Life and Reform, 1865–1898* (1970).

Foote, Corydon Edward, with Olive Deane Hormel. *With Sherman to the Sea, A Drummer's Story of the Civil War* (1960).

Foraker, Joseph B. *Notes of a Busy Life.* 2 vols. (1916).

Forbes, Ida B. *General Wm. T. Sherman, His Life and Battles* (1886).

Force, Manning F. *General Sherman* (1899).

Ford, W. C., ed. *Letters of Henry Adams, 1858–1891.* 2 vols. (1930).

Fowler, Arlen L. *The Black Infantry in the West 1869–1891* (1971).

Fritz, Henry E. *The Movement for Indian Assimilation, 1860–1890* (1963).

Garrett, Franklin. *Atlanta and Its Environs.* 3 vols. (1954, 1969).

Gates, Arnold., ed. *The Rough Side of War: The Civil War Journalism of Charley A. Mosman* (1987).

Glatthaar, Joseph T. *The March to the Sea and Beyond: Sherman's Troops in the Savannah and Carolina Campaigns* (1985).

Glazier, Willard. *Heroes of Three Wars* (1884).

Gordon, John B. *Reminiscences of the Civil War* (1915).

Gorham, George C. *Life and Public Services of Edward M. Stanton.* 2 vols. (1899).

Graf, LeRoy P., ed. *The Papers of Andrew Johnson.* 8 vols. (1967–1989).

Graves, Charles P. *William Tecumseh Sherman, Champion of the Union* (1968).

Gresham, Matilda. *Life of Walter Quinton Gresham.* 2 vols. (1919).

Guddle, Erwin, G. *Sutter's Own Story* (1936).

Hamilton, Gail. *James G. Blaine* (1895).

Hancock, A. R. *Reminiscences of Winfield Scott Hancock, by His Wife* (1887).

———. *Correspondence Between General W. T. Sherman U.S. Army and Major General W. S. Hancock U.S. Army . . .* (1871).

Harrison, Lowell H. *The Civil War in Kentucky* (1975).

Harwell, Richard, and Racine, Philip N., eds. *The Fiery Trail* (1986).

Hattaway, Herman, and Jones, Archer. *How the North Won: A Military History of the Civil War* (1983).

Hazen W. B. *Narrative of Military Service* (1885).

Headley, Joel T. *Grant and Sherman: Their Campaigns and Generals* (1865).

Headley, Phineas C. *Life and Military Career of Major-General William Tecumseh Sherman* (1865).

———. *Facing the Enemy: The Illustrated Story Life of General W. T. Sherman* (1870).

Hedley, Fenwick Y. *Marching Through Georgia . . .* (1890).

Hein, O. L. *Memories of Long Ago, by an Old Army Officer* (1925).

Hitchcock, Henry M. *Marching with Sherman.* Edited by M. A. DeWolfe Howe (1927).

Hood, John Bell. *Advance and Retreat: Personal Experiences in the United States and Confederate States Armies* (1880).

Howard, O. O. *The Autobiography of Oliver Otis Howard.* 2 vols. (1907).

Howe, Daniel W. *Civil War Times, 1861–1865* (1902).

Howe, M. A. DeWolfe, ed. *Home Letters of General Sherman* (1909).

Hunt, Elvid, and Thomas, Walter E. *History of Fort Leavenworth, 1827–1937* (1937).

Hutton, Paul A. *Phil Sheridan and His Army* (1985).

———. ed. *Soldiers West: Biographies from the Military Frontier* (1987).

Ingersoll, Robert G. *Robert G. Ingersoll, Gen. Wm. T. Sherman, Chauncey M. Depew: Their Speeches at the Robson and Crane Banquet, New York City, Nov. 21st, 1887* (1887).

Jackson, Oscar L. *The Colonel's Diary* (1922).

Johnson, Bradley T., ed. *A Memoir of the Life and Public Service of Joseph E. Johnston* (1891).

Johnson, Robert U., and Buell, Clarence C., eds. *Battles and Leaders of the Civil War.* 4 vols. (1884–1888).

Johnson, Virginia. *The Unregimented General: A Biography of Nelson A. Miles* (1962).

Johnson, W. Fletcher, and Howard, O. O. *The Life of Gen'l Wm. Tecumseh Sherman* (1891).

Johnston, Joseph E. *Narrative of Military Operations* (1874).

Johnston, Robert M. *Leading American Soldiers* (1907).

Jones, James P. *"Black Jack": John A. Logan and Southern Illinois in the Civil War Era* (1967).

———. *John A. Logan: Stalwart Republican from Illinois* (1982).

Jones, Katherine M., ed. *When Sherman Came: Southern Women and the Great March* (1964).

Keim, De B. Randolph. *Sherman, A Memorial . . .* (1904).

Kennedy, James H. *History of the Ohio Society of New York, 1885–1905* (1906).

Kent, Zachary. *The Story of Sherman's March to the Sea* (1987).

Kerr, Laura E. *William Tecumseh Sherman: A Family Chronicle* (1984).

Kerr, Winfield S. *John Sherman, His Life and Public Services* 2 vols. (1907).

Keyes, Erasmus D. *Fifty Years Observation of Men and Events Civil and Military* (1884).

Knox, Thomas W. *Campfire and Cottonfield . . .* (1865).

Koerner, Gustave P. *Memoirs of Gustave P. Koerner.* 2 vols. (1909).

Lane, Mills ed. *"War Is Hell": William T. Sherman's Personal Narrative of His March Through Georgia* (1974).

Leckie, William H. *The Buffalo Soldiers: A Narrative of Negro Cavalry in the West* (1967).

Lewis, Lloyd. *Sherman, Fighting Prophet* (1932).

Liddell-Hart, Basil Henry. *Sherman, Soldier, Realist, American* (1929).

Linderman, Gerald F. *Embattled Courage: The Experience of Combat in the American Civil War* (1987).

Logan, Mary S. C. *Reminiscences of a Soldier's Wife* (1913).

Lucas, Marion B. *Sherman and the Burning of Columbia* (1976).

Lusk, William T. *War Letters . . .* (1911).

Luvaas, Jay. *The Military Legacy of the Civil War* (1959).

McAllister, Anna. *Ellen Ewing, Wife of General Sherman* (1936).

———. *Flame in the Wilderness: Life and Letters of Mother Angela Gillespie, C.S.C. . . .* (1944).

McClellan, George B. *McClellan's Own Story . . .* (1887).

McClure, Alexander K. *Abraham Lincoln and Men of War-Times* . . . (1892).

———. *Colonel Alexander K. McClure's Recollections of Half a Century* (1902).

McDonough, James Lee. *Chattanooga: A Death Grip on the Confederacy* (1984).

———. *Schofield: Union General in the Civil War and Reconstruction* (1972).

———. *Shiloh—In Hell Before Night* (1977).

McFeely, William S. *Grant, A Biography* (1981).

———. *Yankee Stepfather: General O. O. Howard and the Freedmen* (1968).

McKinney, Francis F. *Education in Violence: The Life of George H. Thomas and the History of the Army of the Cumberland* (1961).

McPherson, James M. *Battle Cry of Freedom: The Civil War Era* (1988).

McWhiney, Grady. *Braxton Bragg and Confederate Defeat* (1969).

Mahon, John K. *History of the Second Seminole War, 1835–1842* (1967).

Marszalek, John F., ed. *The Diary of Miss Emma Holmes* (1979).

———. *Sherman's Other War: The General and the Civil War Press* (1981).

Mayes, Edward. *Lucius Q. C. Lamar: His Life, Times, and Speeches, 1825–1893* (1896).

Merrill, James M. *William Tecumseh Sherman* (1971).

Michie, Peter S. *The Life and Letters of Emory Upton* (1885).

Michigan Legislature. *Memorial Proceedings of Gen. William T. Sherman and Admiral D. Porter* (1891).

Miers, Earl Schenck. *The General Who Marched to Hell: William Tecumseh Sherman* (1951).

Miller, Charles G. *Donn Piatt: His Work and His Ways* (1893).

Morrison, James L., Jr. *"The Best School in the World": West Point, the Pre–Civil War Years, 1833–1866* (1986).

Neider, Charles, ed. *The Autobiography of Mark Twain* (1959).

Nenniger, Timothy K. *The Leavenworth Schools and the Old Army: Education, Professionalism, and the Officer Corps of the United States Army, 1881–1918* (1978).

Nevin, David. *Sherman's March: Atlanta to the Sea* (1986).

New York Chamber of Commerce of the State of New York. *Tribute . . . to the Memory of William T. Sherman, February 17, 1891* (1891).

New York Monument Commission. *In Memoriam, Henry Warner Slocum, 1826–1894* (1904).

New York State Legislature. *Proceedings of the Senate and Assembly of the State of New York on the Life and Services of Gen. William T. Sherman* (1892).

Nichols, George W. *The Story of the Great March from the Diary of a Staff Officer* (1865).

Norris, Thomas W., ed. *A Letter of Lieut. W. T. Sherman Reporting on Conditions in California in 1848* . . . (1949).

Northrup, Henry D. *Life and Death of General Sherman* . . . (1891).

Nunis, Doyce B., ed. *The San Francisco Vigilance Committee: Three Views: William T. Coleman, William T. Sherman and James O'Meara* (1971).

Parrish, William E. *A History of Missouri. Vol. 3: 1860–1875* (1973).

Pepper, George W. *Personal Recollections of Sherman's Campaign in Georgia and the Carolinas* (1866).

Perkins, Eli. *Kings of the Platform and Pulpit* (1891).

Porter, David Dixon. *Incidents and Anecdotes of the Civil War* (1885).

———. *Naval History of the Civil War* (1885).

Porter, Horace. *Campaigning with Grant* (1897).

Post, Marie Caroline deTrobriand. *Memoirs of Count Regis deTrobriand, Major General in the Army of the United States* (1910).

Priest, Loring G. *Uncle Sam's Step-children: The Reformation of United States Indian Policy, 1865–1887* (1942).

Prucha, Francis Paul. *American Indian Policy in Crisis: Christian Reformers and the Indian, 1865–1900* (1976).

———. *The Great Father: The United States Government and the American Indians* (1986).

Quarles, Benjamin. *The Negro in the Civil War* (1953).

Rable, George C. *Civil War Women and the Crisis* (1989).

Randall, James G., and Pease, Theodore C., eds. *The Diary of Orville Hickson Browning.* 2 vols. (1925, 1933).

Reed, Germaine. *David French Boyd, Founder of Louisiana State University* (1977).

Reid, J. Whitelaw. *Ohio in the War.* 2 vols. (1893).

Reston, James, Jr. *Sherman's March and Vietnam* (1984).

Richardson, Albert D. *The Secret Service, the Field, the Dungeon and the Escape* (1865).

Richardson, Charles B. *Our Great Captains, Grant, Sherman, Thomas, Sheridan, and Farragut* (1865).

Rister, C. C. *Border Command: General Phil Sheridan in the West* (1944).

Robins, Edward. *William T. Sherman* (1905).

Ropes, John C. *Critical Sketches of Some of the Federal and Confederate Commanders* (1895).

Rowland, Dunbar, ed. *Jefferson Davis Constitutionalist: His Letters, Papers and Speeches.* 10 vols. (1923).

Royster, Charles. *The Destructive War, William Tecumseh Sherman, Stonewall Jackson, and the Americans* (1991).

Rusling, James F. *Across America . . .* (1874).

———. *Men and Things I Saw in Civil War Days* (1899).

Russell, Donald B. *The Lives and Legends of Buffalo Bill* (1960).

Schofield, John M. *Forty-six Years in the Army* (1897).

Schurz, Carl. *The Reminiscences of Carl Schurz . . .* 3 vols. (1908).

Sefton, James E. *The United States Army and Reconstruction, 1865–1877* (1967).

Senkewicz, Robert M. *Vigilantes in Gold Rush San Francisco* (1985).

Senour, Faunt LeRoy. *Major General William T. Sherman and His Campaigns* (1865).

Shanks, W. F. G. *Personal Recollections of Distinguished Generals* (1866).

Sheridan, Phil. *Personal Memoirs.* 2 vols. (1888).

Sherman, Ellen E., ed. *Memorial of Thomas Ewing of Ohio* (1873).

Sherman, John. *John Sherman's Recollections of Forty Years in the House, Senate and Cabinet: An Autobiography* (1895).

Sherman, Thomas T. *Sherman Genealogy . . .* (1920).

Sherman, William T. et al. *Addresses Given at the Third Annual Commencement of the Law Department of Georgetown University . . .* (1874).

————. *General and Field Orders, Campaigns of the Armies of the Tennessee, Ohio, and Cumberland, 1864–1865* (1865).

————. *General Sherman's Address, New York City, May 30th, 1878* (1878).

————. *General Sherman's Address to the Grand Army of the Republic, San Francisco, 1886* (1886).

————. *General Sherman's Official Accounts of His Great March Through Georgia and the Carolinas* (1865).

————. *A Letter from Sherman to Colonel Stevenson . . . From the Collections of the University of California, Los Angeles* (1960).

————. *Major General Sherman's Reports* (1865).

————. *Memoirs of General William T. Sherman.* 2 vols. Notes by Charles Royster (1990).

————. *Military Orders of General William T. Sherman 1861–'65* (1865).

———— , et al. *Travel Accounts of General William T. Sherman to Spokane Falls, Washington Territory, in the Summers of 1877 and 1883* (1984).

————. *Two Letters from General William Tecumseh Sherman . . .* (1916).

Simon, John Y., ed. *The Papers of Ulysses S. Grant.* 18 vols. (1967–1991).

————. *The Personal Memoirs of Julia Dent Grant* (1975).

Slocum, Charles E. *Life and Services of Major General Henry Warner Slocum, Officer in the United States Army* (1913).

Smith, Helen A. *One Hundred Famous Americans* (1902).

Smith, William E. *The Francis Preston Blair Family in Politics.* 2 vols. (1933).

Stanley, David S. *Personal Memoirs of Major General D. S. Stanley, U.S.A.* (1917).

Stanley, Henry M. *My Early Travels and Adventures in America* (1895).

Steiner, Paul E. *Medical-Military Portraits of Union and Confederate Generals* (1968).

Stewart, Lucy S. *The Reward of Patriotism . . .* (1930).

Stewart, N. B. *Dan McCook's Regiment, 52nd O.V.I. . . .* (1900).

Stowe, Harriet Beecher. *Men of Our Times; or Leading Patriots of the Day* (1868).

Stratton, Bertha L. *Sherman and Allied Families* (1951).

Strode, Hudson. *Jefferson Davis.* 3 vols. (1955–1964).

Sullivan, Joseph A., ed. *Recollections of California 1846–1861 by General William T. Sherman* (1945).

Supplemental Report of the Joint Committee on the Conduct of the War. 2 vols. (1866).

Sword, Wiley, *Shiloh: Bloody April* (1974).

Thomas, Benjamin P., and Hyman, Harold M. *Stanton: The Life and Times of Lincoln's Secretary of War* (1962).

Thorndike, Rachel Sherman, ed. *The Sherman Letters: Correspondence between General and Senator Sherman from 1837 to 1891* (1894).

Trefousse, Hans L. *Impeachment of a President: Andrew Johnson, the Blacks, and Reconstruction* (1975).

The Trial of Andrew Johnson, President of the United States, on Impeachment by the House of Representatives, for High Crimes and Misdemeanors. 3 vols. (1968).

Turner, George E. *Victory Rode the Rails: The Strategic Place of the Railroads in the Civil War* (1953).

Utley, Robert M. *Frontier Regulars: The United States Army and the Indians, 1866–1891* (1973).

Van Orden, W. H. *General William Tecumseh Sherman: A Story of His Life and Military Services* (1895).

Walters, John B. *Merchant of Terror: General Sherman and Total War* (1973).

War of the Rebellion . . . Official Records of the Union and Confederate Armies. 128 vols. (1880–1901).

Weigley, Russell F. *The American Way of War: A History of United States Military Strategy and Policy* (1973).

————. *History of the United States Army* (1967).

Welles, Gideon. *Diary.* Edited by Howard K. Beale. 3 vols. (1960).

West, Richard S., Jr. *The Second Admiral: A Life of David Dixon Porter, 1813–1891* (1937).

Wheeler, Richard. *Sherman's March* (1978).

Wilder, Marshall P. *The People I've Smiled With: Recollections of a Merry Little Life* (1889).

Wilkie, Franc B. *Pen and Powder* (1888).

Williams, Charles R., ed. *Diary and Letters of Rutherford B. Hayes, Nineteenth President of the United States.* 5 vols. (1922–1926).

Williams, George H., ed. *Occasional Addresses* (1895).

Williams, Mary Floyd. *History of the San Francisco Committee of Vigilance of 1851 . . .* (1921).

Williams, T. Harry. *McClellan, Sherman and Grant* (1962).

Wills, Charles W. *Army Life of an Illinois Soldier . . . Letters and Diary 48* Compiled by Mary E. Kellogg (1906).

Wilson, James Grant. *Sketches of Illustrious Soldiers* (1874).

Wilson, James H. *Under the Old Flag . . .* 2 vols. (1912).

Winther, Oscar O., ed. *With Sherman to the Sea: The Civil War Letters, Diaries and Reminiscences of Theodore F. Upson* (1943).

Wise, John S. *The End of an Era* (1899).

Wood, C. J. *Reminiscences of the War . . .* (1880).

Wooster, Robert. *The Military and United States Policy, 1865–1903* (1988).

Young, John Russell. *Tour Around the World with General Grant* (1879).

ARTICLES (SELECTED LISTING)

Ambrose, Stephen E. "Emery Upton and the Armies of Asia and Europe." *Military Affairs* 28 (1964): 27–32.

————. "William T. Sherman: A Reappraisal." *American History Illustrated* 1 (1967): 4–12.

————. , et al. "Struggle for Vicksburg: The Battle and Siege That Decided the Civil War." *Civil War Times Illustrated* 6 (July 1967): entire issue.

Athearn, Robert G. "General Sherman and the Western Railroads." *Pacific Historical Review* 24 (1957): 39–48.

————. "The Education of Kit Carson's Son." *New Mexico Historical Review* 31 (1956): 133–39.

————. "General Sherman and the Montana Frontier." *Montana Magazine of History* 3 (1953): 55–65.

Audenreid, J. C. "General Sherman in Europe and the East." *Harpers* 47 (1873): 225–42, 481–95, 652–71.

Barrett, John G. "Sherman and Total War in the Carolinas." *North Carolina Historical Review* 37 (1960): 367–81.

Bearss, Edwin C. "Sherman's Demonstration Against Snyder's Bluff." *Journal of Mississippi History* 27 (1965): 168–86.

Black, Wilfred W., ed. "Marching with Sherman Through Georgia and the Carolinas: Civil War Diary of Jesse L. Dozer." *Georgia Historical Quarterly* 52 (1968): 308–36, 451–79.

Bliss, Carey S. ed. "An Unpublished War Letter of General William T. Sherman." *Huntington Library Quarterly* 8 (1944): 105–9.

Bonner, James C. "Sherman at Milledgeville in 1864." *Journal of Southern History* 22 (1956): 273–91.

Boutwell, George S., ed. "Important Historical Letters." *North American Review* 143 (1886): 77–86.

Bowman, S. M. "Major General William T. Sherman." *United States Service Magazine* 2 (1864): 113–24, 240–55.

————. "Sherman's Atlanta Campaign." *United States Service Magazine* 3 (1865): 305–22.

————. "Sherman's Georgia Campaign—From Atlanta to the Sea." *United States Service Magazine* 3 (1865): 426–46.

Boyd, David French. "General W. T. Sherman As a College President." *American College* 2 (1910): 6–10.

————. "Gen. W. T. Sherman; His Early Life in the South and His Relations with Southern Men." *Confederate Veteran* 18 (1910): 409–14.

Boylan, Bernard L. "The Forty-fifth Congress and Army Reform." *Mid-America* 41 (1959): 173–86.

Brackett, Albert G. "General William T. Sherman." *United Services Magazine* n.s. 5 (1891): 577–82.

Bradford, Gamaliel. "Union Portraits: William T. Sherman." *Atlantic Monthly* 114 (1914): 318–29.

Brinkman, E. C. "They Wronged John A. Logan." *Filson Club Historical Quarterly* 41 (1967): 154–68.

Brinsfield, John W. "The Military Ethics of General William T. Sherman." *Parameters* 12 (1982): 36–48.

Brockman, Charles, ed. "The John Van Duser Diary of Sherman's March from Atlanta to Hilton Head." *Georgia Historical Quarterly* 53 (1969): 220–40.

Brown, D. Alexander. "Battle at Chickasaw Bluffs." *Civil War Times Illustrated* 9 (July 1970): 4–9, 44–48.

Brown, John Mason. "The Man and the Myth." *Saturday Review of Literature*, January 17, 1953, 25–28.

————. "Sherman in the Saddle." *Saturday Review of Literature*, February 28, 1948, 26–30.

Brown, R. M. "Letter to Editor: Sleepless Nights." *Saturday Review of Literature*, February 21, 1953, 25.

Brumgardt, John R. " 'Overwhelmingly for "Old Abe" ': Sherman's Soldiers and the Election of 1864." *Lincoln Herald* 78 (1976): 153–60.

Buell, Don Carlos. "Major-General W. T. Sherman and the Spring Campaign of 1862 in the West." *Historical Magazine* n.s. 8 (1870): 74–82.

———. "Shiloh Reviewed." *Century* 9 (1886): 749–81.

Burt, Jesse. "East Tennessee, Lincoln and Sherman." East Tennessee Historical Society *Publications* 34 (1961): 3–25.

———. "Sherman Railroad General." *Civil War History* 2 (1956): 45–54.

Bussel, Alan. "The Atlanta *Daily Intelligencer* Covers Sherman's March." *Journalism Quarterly* 51 (1974): 405–10.

Byers, S. H. M., ed. "Grant, Thomas, Lee." *North American Review* 144 (1887): 437–50.

———. "The March to the Sea." *North American Review* 145 (1887): 235–45.

———. "Sherman and McPherson." *North American Review* 142 (1886): 330–31.

———. "Sherman's March to the Sea." *Literary Digest* 8 (1894): 507.

———. "Some Personal Recollections of General Sherman." *McClure's* 3 (1894): 212–24.

———. "Some More War Letters." *North American Review* 144 (1887): 374–80.

———. "Some War Letters." *North American Review* 143 (1886): 498–504; 144 (1887): 291–97.

———. "Some War Letters: Admiral Porter to General Sherman (June 10, 1863)." *North American Review* 145 (1887): 553–54.

———. "Some War Letters of Sherman, Grant and Others." *North American Review* 144 (1887): 291–97, 374–80.

Castel, Albert. "The Life of a Rising Son." *Civil War Times Illustrated* 18 (July, August, October 1979): 4–7, 42–46; 12–22; 10–21.

Chesney, Charles C. "Sherman and Johnston and the Atlanta Campaign." *Fortnightly Review* 24 (1875): 611–24.

Clauss, Errol M. "Sherman's Failure at Atlanta." *Georgia Historical Quarterly* 53 (1969): 321–29.

———. "Sherman's Rail Support in the Atlanta Campaign." *Georgia Historical Quarterly* 50 (1966): 413–20.

Coleman, William T. "San Francisco's Vigilance Committees. By the Chairman of the Committees of 1851, 1856 and 1877." *Century* 43 (1891): 133–50.

Coulter, E. Merton. "Sherman and the South." *North Carolina Historical Review* 8 (January 1931): 41–54.

Cox, Jacob D. "Boynton's Review of Sherman." *Nation* 21 (1875): 342–43, 358–59.

———. "General Sherman." *Nation* 52 (1891): 153–55.

———. "General Sherman's Memoirs." *Nation* 20 (1875): 397–99, 411–12.

———. "The Sherman-Johnston Convention." *Scribner's* 28 (1900): 489–505.

Cunningham, S. A. "Major Boyd's Sketch of General Sherman." *Confederate Veteran* 18 (1910): 453–54.

Davis, Stephen. "Hood Fights Desperately: The Battles for Atlanta, Events from July 10 to September 2, 1864." *Blue and Gray* 6 (August 1989): 9–39, 45–62.

Davis, Theodore R. "With Sherman in His Army Home." *Cosmopolitan* 12 (1891): 195–205.

Deas, Alston, contributor. "A Ball in Charleston [1851]." *South Carolina Historical Magazine* 75 (1974): 49.

DeLaubenfels, D. J. "Where Sherman Passed By." *Geographical Review* 47 (1957): 381–95.

D'Elia, Donald J. "The Argument over Civilian or Military Indian Control, 1865–1880." *Historian* 24 (1962): 207–25.

Detzler, Jack J. "The Religion of William Tecumseh Sherman." *Ohio History* 75 (1966): 26–34, 68–70.

Dickinson, John N. "The Civil War Years of John Alexander Logan." Illinois State Historical Society *Journal* 56 (1963): 212–32.

Disbrow, Donald W., ed. "Vett Noble of Ypsilante: A Clerk for General Sherman." *Civil War History* 14 (1968): 15–39.

Doyle, J. E. P. "Sherman's Sixty Days in the Carolinas." *United States Service Magazine* 3 (1865): 511–14.

———. "Sherman's Winter Campaign Through Georgia." *United States Service Magazine* 3 (1865): 164–69.

Drago, Edmund L. "How Sherman's March Through Georgia Affected the Slaves." *Georgia Historical Quarterly* 57 (1973): 361–75.

Dwight, T. F. "Critical Sketches of Some of the Federal and Confederate Commanders." *Massachusetts Historical Society Papers* 10 (1895): 125–52.

Dyer, John P. "Northern Relief for Savannah During Sherman's Occupation [1864–1865]." *Journal of Southern History* 19 (1953): 457–72.

Editor. "Sherman's Truce." *United States Service Magazine* 3 (1865): 497–99.

Ellis, Edward S. "Reminiscences of General Sherman." *Chatauquan* 27 (1898): 474–76.

Evans, David. "The Atlanta Campaign." *Civil War Times Illustrated* 28 (Summer 1989): entire issue.

Ewing, Joseph H., ed. "Sherman Bashes the Press." *American Heritage* 38 (July–August 1987): 24–37, 40–41.

Ewing, Thomas. "Diary, August and September, 1841." *American Historical Review* 18 (1912): 98–112.

Fingerson, Ronald L., ed. "A William Tecumseh Sherman Letter." *Books at Iowa*, no. 3 (November 1965): 34–38.

Fitzgerald, David. "Annotations by General Sherman." *Journal of the Military Service Institution of the United States* 14 (1893): 978–79.

Fleming, Thomas. "The Big Parade." *American Heritage* 41 (March 1990): 98–104.

Fleming, Walter L. "William Tecumseh Sherman as College President." *South Atlantic Quarterly* 11 (1912): 33–54.

———. "W. T. Sherman as a History Teacher." Louisiana State University *Bulletin* 11 (1911): 235–38.

Florcken, Herbert G., ed. "The Law and Order View of the San Francisco Vigilance Committee of 1856." *California Historical Society Quarterly* 14 (1935): 350–74.

Forbes, J. M. "Recollections of Sherman and Porter." *Nation* 52 (1891): 192–93.

"From a Private to a General." *Field Artillery Journal* 25 (1935): 89–91.

Fry, James B. "An Open Letter." *North American Review* 142 (1886): 292–94.

Futrell, Robert J. "Federal Military Government in the South, 1861–1865." *Military Affairs* 15 (1951): 181–91.

Garfield, James A. "The Army of the United States." *North American Review* 126 (1878): 193–216, 442–65.

"General Sherman." *Critic* 18 (1891): 98.

"General Sherman." *Harpers Weekly* 34 (1890): 103, 109.

"General Sherman and His Memoirs." *International Review* 2 (1875): 779–817.

"General Sherman on the Power of the Pen." *Critic* 18 (1891): 116.

"General Sherman's Civil Career." *Spectator* 66 (1891): 721–22.

Gilder, Richard W. "Sherman." *Century* 20 (1891): 192.

Glatthaar, Joseph T. "Sherman's Army and Total War: Attitudes on Destruction in the Savannah and Carolinas Campaigns." *Atlanta Historical Journal* 29 (1986): 41–42.

Graham, S. "Marching Through Georgia." *Harpers* 140 (1920): 612–20, 813–23.

Grant, U. S. "The Battle of Shiloh." *Century* 29 (1885): 593–613.

Gray, Tom S. Jr. "The March to the Sea." *Georgia Historical Quarterly* 14 (1930): 111–38.

Guback, Thomas H. "General Sherman's War on the Press." *Journalism Quarterly* 36 (1959): 171–76.

Guernsey, A. H. "Sherman's Great March." *Harpers* 31 (1865): 571–89.

Hall, Martin H. "The Campbell-Sherman Diplomatic Mission to Mexico." Historical and Philosophical Society of Ohio *Bulletin* 13 (1955): 254–70.

Halstead, Murat. "The Defeat of Blaine for the Presidency." *McClure's* 6 (1896): 159–72.

———. "Recollections and Letters of General Sherman." *Independent* 51 (1899): 1610–13, 1682–85.

Harrison, Lowell H. "The Civil War in Kentucky: Some Persistent Questions." *Register of the Kentucky Historical Society* 76 (1978): 1–21.

Hattaway, Herman, "Confederate Myth Making: Top Command and the Chickasaw Bayou Campaign." *Journal of Mississippi History* 32 (1970): 311–26.

Howard, O. O. "Chattanooga." *Atlantic Monthly* 38 (1876): 203–19.

———. "The Battles About Atlanta, I, II." *Atlantic Monthly* 38 (1876): 385–99, 559–67.

———. "Sherman's Campaign of 1864." *United Services Magazine* 13 (1885): 660–73; 14 (1886): 20–26.

———. "Sherman's Personal Memoirs." *Journal of the Military Service Institution of the United States* 12 (1891): 671–75.

———. "The Struggle for Atlanta." *Century* 12 (1887): 442–63.

Howe, M. A. deWolfe. "Gen. Sherman's Letters Home." *Scribners Monthly* 45 (1909): 397–415, 532–47, 737–52.

Huffstot, Robert S. "Post of Arkansas." *Civil War Times Illustrated* 7 (1969): 10–19.

James, Josef C. "Sherman at Savannah." *Journal of Negro History* 39 (1954): 127–37.

Johnston, Joseph E. "My Negotiations with General Sherman." *North American Review* 143 (1886): 183–97.

———. "Opposing Sherman's Advance to Atlanta." *Century* 12 (1887): 585–97.

Jones, James P. "The Battle of Atlanta and McPherson's Successor." *Civil War History* 7 (1961): 393–405.

———. "'Lincoln's Avengers': The Assassination and Sherman's Army." *Lincoln Herald* 64 (1962): 185–90.

———. "General Jeff C. Davis, U.S.A. and Sherman's Georgia Campaign." *Georgia Historical Quarterly* 47 (1962): 231–42.

Julian, Allen P. "From Dalton to Atlanta—Sherman vs. Johnston." *Civil War Times Illustrated* 3 (July 1964): 4–7, 34–39.

Kelly, Dennis. "Atlanta Campaign, Mountain to Pass, a River to Cross: The Battle of Kennesaw Mountain and Related Actions from June 10 to July 9, 1864." *Blue and Gray* 6 (1989): 10–12, 15–30, 46–50, 52–58.

Kessel, John L. "General Sherman and the Navajo Treaty of 1868: A Basic and Expedient Misunderstanding." *Western Historical Quarterly* 12 (1981): 251–72.

Kime, Marlin G. "Sherman's Gordian Knot: Logistical Problems in the Atlanta Campaign (1864)." *Georgia Historical Quarterly* 70 (1986): 102–10.

King, Spencer B., Jr., ed. "Fanny Cohen's Journal of Sherman's Occupation of Savannah." *Georgia Historical Quarterly* 41 (1957): 407–16.

Kite, Elizabeth S. "Genius of the Civil War." *Commonweal* 27 (1938): 541–43.

Klinger, Michael J. "Botched Union Attack." *America's Civil War* 2 (September 1989): 21–25.

Lay, Henry C. "Sherman in Georgia." *Atlantic Monthly* 149 (1932): 166–72.

Little, W. C. "The Sherman of Early Days." *Overland Monthly* 17 (1891): 358–61.

Lord, Walter, ed. "Gen. Sherman and the Baltimore Belle." *American Heritage* 9 (1958): 102–4.

Luvaas, Jay. "An Appraisal of Joseph E. Johnston." *Civil War Times Illustrated* 4 (January 1966): 28–32.

———. "Johnston's Last Stand—Bentonville." *North Carolina Historical Review* (1956): 332–58.

McClure, Alexander C. "The Last Chance of the Confederacy." *Atlantic Monthly* 50 (1882): 389–400.

McMurry, Richard M. "The Atlanta Campaign of 1864: A New Look." *Civil War History* 22 (1976): 5–15.

———. "Atlanta Campaign, Rocky Face to the Dallas Line: The Battles of May, 1864." *Blue and Gray* 6 (1989): 11–23, 46–49, 54–62.

———. "Sherman's Meridian Campaign." *Civil War Times Illustrated* 14 (1975): 24–34.

———. "Kennesaw Mountain." *Civil War Times Illustrated* 8 (1970): 19–34.

Marszalek, John F. "Celebrity in Dixie: Sherman Tours the South, 1879." *Georgia Historical Quarterly* 66 (1982): 368–83.

————. "Censorship and the Northern Reporter." *Blue and Gray* 4 (1987): 36–41.

————. "Fighting Peacemaker: William T. Sherman." *Timeline* 5 (1988/1989): 2–13.

————. "The Inventor of Total Warfare." *Notre Dame Magazine* 18 (Summer 1989): 28–31.

————. "The Knox Court-Martial: W. T. Sherman Puts the Press on Trial (1863)." *Military Law Review* 56 (1973): 197–214.

————. "The Stanton-Sherman Controversy." *Civil War Times Illustrated* 9 (October 1970): 4–12.

————. "William T. Sherman and the Verbal Battle of Shiloh." *Northwest Ohio Quarterly* 42 (1970): 78–85.

————. ed. "William T. Sherman on West Point—A Letter." United States Military Academy *Assembly* 30 (Summer 1971): 14–15, 38; also in *Civil War Times Illustrated* 10 (January 1972): 22–23.

————. "W. T. Sherman: Was He Really a Brute?" *Blue and Gray* 7 (December 1989): 46–51.

Martzloff, Clement L., ed. "The Autobiography of Thomas Ewing." Ohio Archeological and Historical Society *Publications* 22 (1913): 126–204.

Mead, Rufus J. "With Sherman Through Georgia and the Carolinas: Letters of a Federal Soldier." Edited by James A. Padgett. *Georgia Historical Quarterly* 32 (1948): 284–322; 33 (1949): 49–81.

Miewald, Robert D. "The Army Post Schools [1865–1898]: A Report from the Bureaucratic Wars." *Military Affairs* 39 (1975): 8–11.

Morgan, George W. "The Assault on Chickasaw Bluffs." In *Battles and Leaders of the Civil War*. Edited by Robert U. Johnson and Clarence C. Buel (1884).

Morrison, James L., Jr. "Educating the Civil War Generals: West Point, 1833–1861." *Military Affairs* 38 (1974): 108–11.

Mruck, Armin. "The Role of Railroads in the Atlanta Campaign." *Civil War History* 7 (1961): 264–71.

Murray, Robert K. "General Sherman, the Negro and Slavery: The Story of an Unrecognized Rebel." *Negro History Bulletin* 22 (1959): 125–30.

Naroll, Raoul S. "Lincoln and the Sherman Peace Fiasco—Another Fable?" *Journal of Southern History* 20 (1954): 459–83.

Newcomer, Lee N., ed. " 'Think Kindly of Us of the South': A Letter to William Tecumseh Sherman." *Ohio History* 71 (1962): 148–50.

Nichols, George W. "Sherman's Great March." *Harpers* 31 (1865): 571–89.

Nichols, Roy F., ed. "William Tecumseh Sherman in 1850." *Pennsylvania Magazine of History* 75 (1952): 424–35.

Noblitt, Phil. "Heedless Frontal Assault." *America's Civil War* 2 (1990): 35–41.

Oakey, Daniel. "Marching Through Georgia and the Carolinas." *Century* 12 (1877): 917–27.

"Obituary: General William T. Sherman." *Literary Digest* 2 (1891): 468–69.

O'Connor, Richard. "Sherman: Imaginative Soldier." *American Mercury* 67 (1948): 555–64.

Osborn, George C., ed. "Sherman's March Through Georgia: Letters from

Charles Ewing to His Father Thomas Ewing." *Georgia Historical Quarterly* 42 (1958): 323–27.

Palfrey, F. W. "Memoirs of General W. T. Sherman." *North American Review* 121 (1875): 337–65.

Palfrey, John C. "General Sherman's Plans After the Fall of Atlanta." *Military History Society Papers* 8 (1910): 490–527.

Parks, Joseph H. "A Confederate Trade Center Under Federal Occupation: Memphis, 1862–1865." *Journal of Southern History* 7 (1941): 289–314.

———. "Memphis Under Military Rule, 1862–1865." East Tennessee Historical Society *Proceedings* 15 (1942): 31–58.

Peake, P. H. "Why the South Hates Sherman." *American Mercury* 42 (1937): 247–48, 505–8; 43 (1937): 123–25.

Pfanz, Harry W. "The Surrender Negotiations Between General Johnston and General Sherman." *Military Affairs* 16 (1952): 61–70.

Pickett, William D. "Why Sherman's Name Is Detested." *Confederate Veteran* 14 (1906): 295–98.

Porter, David D. "First Meeting of Admiral Porter and General Sherman." *Magazine of American History* 23 (1891): 298–99.

Porter, Horace. "General Sherman." *Harpers Weekly* 35 (1891): 134–37.

"Possible Presidents: General William Tecumseh Sherman." *North American Review* 146 (1888): 416–23.

Quillen, Martha A. "A Letter on Sherman's March Through Georgia." Edited by George W. Clower. *Georgia Historical Quarterly* 37 (1953): 160–62.

Rankin, M. "When Sherman Marched Down to the Sea." *American Magazine* 65 (1907): 136–39.

Rayburn, John C. "General Sherman Visits the Mexican Frontier, 1882." *West Texas Historical Association Yearbook* 38 (1962): 72–84.

"Recollections of Sherman and Porter." *Nation* 52 (1891): 192–93.

Redkey, Edwin S. "They Are Invincible." *Civil War Times Illustrated* 28 (1989): 32–37.

Rice, Allen Thorndike. "Sherman's Opinion of Grant." *North American Review* 142 (1886): 200–8.

Riley, Edward M. "Historic Fort Moultrie in Charleston Harbor." *South Carolina Historical Magazine* 51 (1950): 63–74.

Rister, Carl C. "Documents Relating to General W. T. Sherman's Southern Plains Indian Policy, 1871–1875." *Panhandle-Plains Historical Review* 9 (1936): 7–28; 10 (1937): 48–63.

Robbins, Peggy. "Hood vs. Sherman: A Duel in Words." *Civil War Times Illustrated* 17 (1978): 22–29.

Ropes, John C. "General Sherman." *Atlantic Monthly* 68 (1891): 191–204.

Rzeha, John. "With Sherman Through Georgia: A Journal." Edited by David J. DeLaubenfels. *Georgia Historical Quarterly* 41 (1957): 288–300.

Sanchez, N. V. "Grafting Romance on a Rose-tree: The True Story of Dona Maria Bonifacio and General Sherman of Monterey." *Sunset* 36 (April 1916): 40.

Schurz, Carl. "Reminiscences of a Long Life." *McClure's* 30 (1907): 85–98.

Schwabe, Edward Jr. "Sherman's March Through Georgia: A Reappraisal of the Right Wing." *Georgia Historical Quarterly* 69 (1985): 522–35.

Sefton, James E., ed. "Chief Justice Chase As an Advisor on Presidential Reconstruction." *Civil War History* 13 (1967): 242–64.

Shanks, W. F. G. "Chattanooga, and How We Held It." *Harpers* 36 (1868): 137–49.

——. "Gossip About Our Generals." *Harpers* 35 (1867): 210–15.

——. "Recollections of Sherman." *Harpers* 30 (1865): 640–46.

"The Sherman Letters." *Literary Digest* 9 (1894): 684–85.

Sherman, Maria Ewing. "My Father's Letters." *Cosmopolitan* 12 (1891): 64–69, 187–94.

"Sherman's Memoirs." *Galaxy* 20 (1875): 325–36, 450–64.

Sherman, Rachel E., ed. "Letters; Passages from the Correspondence of General and Senator Sherman." *Century* 45 (1892, 1893): 88–101, 425–40, 689–99, 892–903.

Sherman, William T. "The Battle of Pittsburg Landing: A Letter from General Sherman." *United States Service Magazine* 3 (1865): 1–4.

——. "Campfires of the G.A.R." *North American Review* 147 (1888): 497–502.

——. "General Sherman and the March to the Sea." *Century* 12 (1877): 464–65.

——. "General Sherman in Russia." *Century* 35 (1899): 866–75.

——. "General Sherman's Opinion of General Grant." *Century* 31 (1897): 821.

——. "General Sherman's Tour of Europe." *Century* 35 (1899): 729–40.

——. "Gen. W. T. Sherman Anecdote." *Harpers* 71 (1885): 970.

——. "Graduation Address, USMA, 1869." *Army* 16 (1966): 61–65.

——. "The Grand Strategy of the War of the Rebellion." *Century* 13 (1888): 582–98.

——. "Hon. James G. Blaine." *North American Review* 147 (1888): 616–25.

——. "The Late Major-General J. B. McPherson." *Hours at Home* 2 (1866): 485–63.

——. "Military Law." *Journal of the Military Service Institution of the United States* 1 (1880): 129–53, 320–55, 385–437.

——. "The Militia." *Journal of the Military Service Institution of the United States* 6 (1885): 1–15.

——. "Old Shady with a Moral." *North American Review* 147 (1888): 361–68.

——. "Old Times in California." *North American Review* 148 (1889): 269–79.

——. "Our Army and Militia." *North American Review* 151 (1890): 129–45.

——. "Sherman on Franco-Prussian Battle-Fields." *Century* 36 (1899): 278–87.

——. "Sherman on Grant." *North American Review* 142 (1886): 111–13.

——. "Sherman and the San Francisco Vigilantes." *North American Review* 21 (1892): 296–309.

——. "Sherman's Estimate of Grant's Character." *Century* 70 (1905): 316–18.

——. "Sherman's Last Speech." *Century* 20 (1891): 189–92.

————. "The Surrender of Gen. Johnston: Letter from General Sherman." *Historical Magazine* 18 (1869): 333–34.

————. "Tribute to Allen Thorndike Rice." *North American Review* 149 (1889): 114.

————. "True Copy of a Letter Written by General Sherman in 1864." *Historical Magazine* 21 (1872): 113.

————. "Two Immortal Letters: Letter from General Grant to Sherman and the Reply." *Magazine of American History* 25 (1891): 334–35.

————. "Unpublished Letters of General Sherman." *North American Review* 152 (1891): 371–75.

————. "An Unspoken Address to the Loyal Legion." *North American Review* 142 (1886): 295–308.

————. "Vicksburg by New Years." *Civil War Times Illustrated* 16 (January 1978): 44–48.

————. "Why General Sherman Declined the Nomination in 1884." *North American Review* 171 (1900): 243–45.

"Sherman's Funeral." *Harpers Weekly* 35 (1891): 152–54.

"Sherman's Memoirs." *Galaxy* 20 (1875): 325–36, 450–64.

Shippin, E. "General Sherman." *United Services Magazine* 5 (1891): 339–41.

Sill, L. M. "William Tecumseh Sherman." *Magazine of American History* 30 (1893): 62.

Slocum, Henry W. "Sherman's March from Savannah to Bentonville." *Century* 12 (1877): 928–39.

Smalley, Edward V. "General Sherman." *Century* 5 (1884): 450–62.

Smith, S. Winifred. "The Sherman House." *Museum Echoes* 29 (September 1956): 67–70.

Stafford, G. M., contributor. "Autobiography of Geo. Mason Graham." *Louisiana Historical Quarterly* 20 (1937): 43–57.

Thomas, Donna. "Ambrose E. Burnside and Army Reform, 1850–1881." *Rhode Island History* 37 (1978): 3–13.

Thompson, J. P. "Major-General William T. Sherman: The Great March." *Hours at Home* 1 (1865, 1866): 11–22, 314–20.

"The Vigilance Committee of 1856." *Overland Monthly* 12 (1874): 105–16.

Walters, John B. "General William T. Sherman and Total War." *Journal of Southern History* 14 (1948): 447–80.

Warren, Viola L., ed. "Dr. John S. Griffin's Mail. 1846–53." *California Historical Society Quarterly* 33 (1954): 237–48; 34 (1955): 21–39.

Welles, Ella Fraser, ed. "Stranger Than Fiction: A True Story Told Mainly in a Series of Unpublished Letters by General Sherman." *McClure's* 8 (1897): 546–50.

Westwood, Howard C. "Sherman Marched—and Proclaimed 'Land for the Landless.'" *South Carolina Historical Magazine* 85 (1984): 33–54.

"Where General Sherman Went, and What He Did." *United States Service Magazine* 1 (1864): 400–401.

White, W. R. "Sherman to the Sea." *Quartermaster Review* 10 (1931): 42–54.

Widney, Lyman S. "Campaigning with 'Uncle Billy.'" *Neales Monthly* 2 (1913): 131–43.

"William Tecumseh Sherman, General, U.S.A." *Republic Magazine* 1 (1890): 97–99.

"William T. Sherman." *Illustrated American* 6 (1891): 119.

"William T. Sherman's Funeral Train to St. Louis." *Harpers Weekly* 35 (1891): 171–73.

Williams, H. David. " 'On the Fringes of Hell': Billy Yank and Johnny Reb at the Siege of Kennesaw Mountain (Ga., June 1864)." *Georgia Historical Quarterly* 70 (1986): 703–16.

Wilson, James G., ed. "A Sheaf of Sherman's Letters." *Independent* 54 (1902): 213–15.

———. "War Horses of Famous Generals . . ." *Century* 86 (1913): 45–55.

Wilson, James H. "General Sherman and His Memoirs." *International Review* 2 (1875): 779–817.

Winchell, James M. "Three Interviews with President Lincoln." *Galaxy* 16 (1873): 33–41.

Wolseley, Viscount. "General Sherman." *Literary Digest* 3 (1891): 379–80.

Yenchas, John G. "Sherman—First Modern Soldier." *Quartermaster Review* 17 (1938): 24–28, 67–68.

"Yankees Come to Roswell." *Blue and Gray* 6 (June 1989): 57.

Young, Jared. "General Sherman's Puritan Heritage." *Eugenical News* 13 (1928): 106–9.

———. ed. "General Sherman on His Own Record; Some Unpublished Comments." *Atlantic Monthly* 108 (1911): 289–300.

DISSERTATIONS AND THESES

Andrews, Richard A. "Years of Frustration: William T. Sherman, the Army, and Reform, 1869–1883." Ph.D. diss., Northwestern University, 1968.

Clauss, Errol M. "The Atlanta Campaign, 18 July–2 September, 1864." Ph.D. diss., Emory University, 1965.

Dillard, Walter Scott. "The United States Military Academy, 1865–1900: The Uncertain Years." Ph.D. diss., University of Washington, 1972.

Firebaugh, Charles D. "General William T. Sherman's Attitude Toward the Newspaper Press, 1861–1865." M.A. thesis, Ohio State University, 1958.

McMurry, Richard M. "The Atlanta Campaign, December 23, 1863, to July 18, 1864." Ph.D. diss., Emory University, 1967.

McNeill, William J. "The Stress of War: The Confederacy and William Tecumseh Sherman During the Last Year of the Civil War." Ph.D. diss., Rice University, 1973.

Menius, Arthur C. "A Beginning to Reconstruction: The Surrender of J. E. Johnston to W. T. Sherman." M.A. thesis, University of North Carolina, Chapel Hill, 1982.

Miller, Paul I. "Thomas Ewing, Last of the Whigs." Ph.D. diss., Ohio State University, 1933.

Murray, Robert K. "Sherman, Slavery and the South." M.A. thesis, Ohio State University, 1947.

Patrick, John J. "John Sherman: The Early Years, 1823–1865." Ph.D. diss., Kent State University, 1982.

Schoonover, Thomas D. "The Military Thought of Thomas Jonathan Jackson and William Tecumseh Sherman . . ." M.A. thesis, Louisiana State University, 1961.

Skirbunt, Peter D. "Prologue to Reform: The 'Germanization' of the United States Army, 1865–1898." Ph.D. diss., Ohio State University, 1983.

Stafford, Jon M. "Sherman's Preparations for the Atlanta Campaign: The Rome and Snake Creek Gap Plans." M.A. thesis, University of Alabama, 1974.

Thomas, Donna M. E. "Army Reform in America: The Crucial Years, 1876–1881." Ph.D. diss., University of Florida, 1980.

Young, Walter A. ". . . The Conduct of Sherman's March in the Light of International Rules of War." Ph.D. diss., University of Chicago, 1912.

Zsoldos, Silvia T. "The Political Career of Thomas Ewing, Sr." Ph.D. diss., University of Delaware, 1977.

INDEX

Abdul Aziz, 363
Abolitionism, 46, 119. *See also* Slavery
Adams, Charles Francis, 363
Adams, Henry, 284
Adams, Jasper, 20–21
Alexander, Charles J., 491, 492
Alexander II, Czar, 363
Alexandria, La., 124, 138
Allatoona Pass, Ga., 291–92
Amadeus I, King, 363
American Revolution, 1, 2, 7
Ames, Adelbert, 426–27
Anderson, George W., 307
Anderson, Mary, 481
Anderson, Mrs. Robert, 353, 492
Anderson, Robert, 43, 44, 154–56, 158, 160, 339
Andersonville Prison, 279, 290, 305
Andrassy, Count Julius, 363
Angela, Mother, 197
Anthony, D. C., 239
Appler, Jesse, 177
Arkansas Post, 208, 209, 210
Army. *See* Confederate forces; Sherman, William Tecumseh; Union forces; and names of generals and battles
Arnold, Isaac N., 448–49
Arthur, Chester A., 439, 445, 446, 448
Ashlock, 34, 35
Atlanta, Battle of, 277, 280, 283–84, 287, 288
Atlanta, Ga.: importance of, 260; Sherman's order for evacuation of, 285–86; after Sherman's capture

of, 288–89; destruction of, 299–300; Sherman's postwar visit to, 472
Audenreid, Joseph C., 419
Audenreid, Mary, 418, 419–20, 485
Augur, C. C., 380, 390, 428

Badeau, Adam, 413, 461
Bancroft, George, 363
Banking: Sherman's banking job in California, 91–104; failure of Page and Beacon of St. Louis, 99–100; Sherman's handling of bank crisis, 99–102; Sherman's closing of San Francisco bank, 110–14; Sherman's opening of bank in New York, 110; closing of New York bank, 113; offer to Sherman to manage American bank in London, 121, 124, 129–31
Banks, Nathaniel P., 203, 217, 221, 249, 250, 255, 256, 262, 263, 269
Banning, Henry, 429, 432–34, 436
Barnard, Major J. G., 111
Barnum, P. T., 482
Barrett, James M., 489
Barrett, Lawrence, 491, 494
Bartlett, William H. C., 21
Battles. *See* names of specific battles
Beauregard, P. G. T.: at West Point, 23; and Sherman's superintendency of Louisiana Military Seminary, 126, 127, 131, 134; Union officers' view of, 148–49; in Tennessee during Civil War, 175; at Battle of Shiloh, 179–180; after Battle of Shiloh, 188;

VINTAGE CIVIL WAR LIBRARY

___ *The Civil War Dictionary* by Mark M. Boatner	$18.00	0-679-73392-2
___ *The Long Surrender* by Burke Davis	$12.00	0-679-72409-5
___ *Sherman's March* by Burke Davis	$11.00	0-394-75763-7
___ *Lincoln Reconsidered* by David Donald	$10.00	0-679-72310-2
___ *The Civil War* by Shelby Foote		
volume I: Fort Sumter to Perryville	$24.00	0-394-74623-6
volume II: Fredericksburg to Meridian	$24.00	0-394-74621-X
volume III: Red River to Appomattox	$24.00	0-394-74622-8
3-Volume boxed set	$72.00	0-394-74913-8
___ *Chancellorsville 1863* by Ernest B. Furgurson	$14.00	0-679-72831-7
___ *The Civil War in the American West* by Alvin M. Josephy, Jr.	$15.00	0-679-74003-1
___ *Sheridan* by Roy Morris, Jr.	$14.00	0-679-74398-7
___ *All for the Union* by Robert Hunt Rhodes	$11.00	0-679-73828-2
___ *General A. P. Hill* by James Robertson	$14.00	0-679-73888-6
___ *The Destructive War* by Charles Royster	$15.00	0-679-73878-9
___ *The Brothers' War* by Annette Tapert	$11.00	0-679-72211-4
___ *Bold Dragoon* by Emory M. Thomas	$13.00	0-394-75775-0
___ *Lincoln and His Generals* by T. Harry Williams	$9.00	0-394-70362-6

Available at your bookstore or call toll-free to order: 1-800-733-3000.
Credit cards only. Prices subject to change.